Walking in
SWITZERLAND

Clem Lindenmayer

LONELY PLANET PUBLICATIONS
Melbourne • Oakland • London • Paris

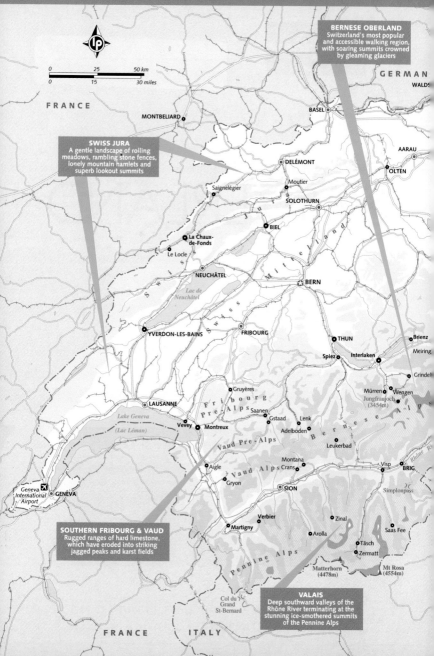

SWITZERLAND

BERNESE OBERLAND
Switzerland's most popular and accessible walking region, with soaring summits crowned by gleaming glaciers

SWISS JURA
A gentle landscape of rolling meadows, rambling stone fences, lonely mountain hamlets and superb lookout summits

SOUTHERN FRIBOURG & VAUD
Rugged ranges of hard limestone, which have eroded into striking jagged peaks and karst fields

VALAIS
Deep southward valleys of the Rhône River terminating at the stunning ice-smothered summits of the Pennine Alps

FRANCE

GERMAN

WALDS

0   25   50 km
0   15   30 miles

MONTBELIARD

BASEL

DELÉMONT

AARAU

OLTEN

Saignelégier

Moutier

SOLOTHURN

Jura

La Chaux-de-Fonds

Le Locle

BIEL

NEUCHÂTEL

Lac de Neuchâtel

Mittelland

BERN

THUN

Brienz

Meiring

YVERDON-LES-BAINS

FRIBOURG

Spiez

Interlaken

Grinde

Fribourg Pre-Alps

Gruyères

Saanen

Gstaad

Lenk

Adelboden

Mürren

Wengen

Jungfraujoch (3454m)

Bernese Alps

LAUSANNE

Lake Geneva (Lac Léman)

Vevey

Montreux

Vaud Pre-Alps

Leukerbad

Aigle

Vaud Alps

Montana

Crans

Visp

BRIG

Simplonpass

Rhône R

Gryon

SION

Geneva International Airport

GENEVA

Verbier

Martigny

Zinal

Arolla

Saas Fee

Täsch

Zermatt

Penning Alps

Matterhorn (4478m)

Mt Rosa (4554m)

Col du Grand St-Bernard

FRANCE   ITALY

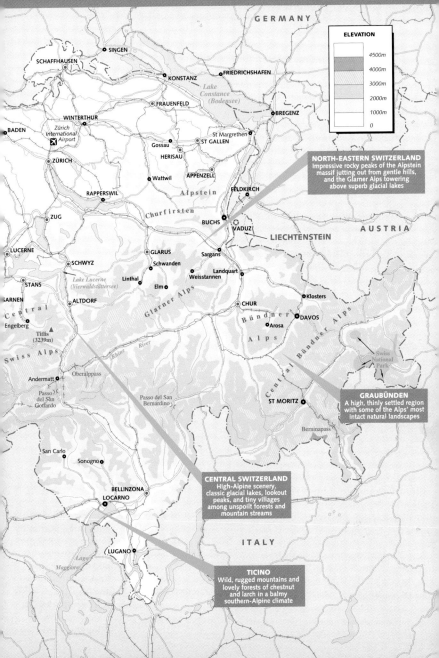

ELEVATION

4500m
4000m
3000m
2000m
1000m
0

GERMANY

SINGEN
SCHAFFHAUSEN
KONSTANZ
FRIEDRICHSHAFEN
Lake Constance (Bodensee)
FRAUENFELD
BREGENZ
WINTERTHUR
Zürich International Airport
BADEN
St Margrethen
ST GALLEN
Gossau
HERISAU
ZÜRICH
Wattwil
APPENZELL
RAPPERSWIL
Alpstein
FELDKIRCH
ZUG
Churfirsten
BUCHS
VADUZ
LUCERNE
GLARUS
Sargans
LIECHTENSTEIN
AUSTRIA
SCHWYZ
Schwanden
Landquart
Lake Lucerne (Vierwaldstättersee)
Linthal
Weisstannen
STANS
Elm
SARNEN
ALTDORF
Glarner Alps
CHUR
Klosters
Central
DAVOS
Engelberg
Titlis (3239m)
Bündner
Arosa
Swiss National Park
Swiss Alps
Rhine River
Alps
Andermatt
Oberalppass
Central Bündner Alps
Passo del San Gottardo
Passo del San Bernardino
ST MORITZ
San Carlo
Berninapass
Sonogno
BELLINZONA
LOCARNO
LUGANO
Lago Maggiore
ITALY

NORTH-EASTERN SWITZERLAND
Impressive rocky peaks of the Alpstein massif jutting out from gentle hills, and the Glarner Alps towering above superb glacial lakes

GRAUBÜNDEN
A high, thinly settled region with some of the Alps' most intact natural landscapes

CENTRAL SWITZERLAND
High-Alpine scenery, classic glacial lakes, lookout peaks, and tiny villages among unspoilt forests and mountain streams

TICINO
Wild, rugged mountains and lovely forests of chestnut and larch in a balmy southern-Alpine climate

Walking in Switzerland
2nd edition – August 2001
First published – May 1996

Published by
Lonely Planet Publications Pty Ltd ABN 36 005 607 983
90 Maribyrnong St, Footscray, Victoria 3011, Australia

Lonely Planet Offices
Australia Locked Bag 1, Footscray, Victoria 3011
USA 150 Linden St, Oakland, CA 94607
UK 10a Spring Place, London NW5 3BH
France 1 rue du Dahomey, 75011 Paris

Photographs
All of the images in this guide are available for licensing from
Lonely Planet Images.
email: lpi@lonelyplanet.com.au

Main front cover photograph
Tall larch and fir trees, Swiss National Park, Engadine valley (Martin Moos)

Small front cover photograph
Walker atop Munt La Schera, Swiss National Park (Martin Moos)

ISBN 0 86442 737 9

text © Lonely Planet 2001
photos © photographers as indicated 2001
The contoured maps in this book are reproduced by permission of the
Swiss Federal Office of Topography (BM12066)

Printed by Craft Print International Ltd, Singapore

Although the authors
and Lonely Planet try
to make the informa-
tion as accurate as
possible, we accept
no responsibility for
any loss, injury or
inconvenience sus-
tained by anyone
using this book.

Contents

The Walks	Duration	Standard	Season
Bernese Oberland			
Justistal	4–5½ hours	easy	June–Nov
Stockhorn Circuit	3¼–4½ hours	easy	June–Oct
Grosse Scheidegg	6½–9 hours	easy	June–Oct
Faulhornweg	4¾–6¼ hours	medium	June–Oct
Kleine Scheidegg	5¾–7¼ hours	easy	June–Nov
Sefinenfurgge	6–8 hours	medium	June–Oct
Hohtürli	6–8½ hours	hard	June–Oct
Bunderchrinde	5–6¾ hours	medium	June–Oct
Gemmipass & Rote Chumme	2 days	medium-hard	June–Oct
Hahnenmoospass	3½–4½ hours	easy-medium	June–Nov
Trüttlisbergpass	4½–6 hours	easy-medium	June–Nov
Chrinepass	2¼–2¾ hours	easy	May–Oct
Wildstrubel Traverse	3 days	medium-hard	June–Oct
Central Switzerland			
Napf Traverse	3½–4½ hours	easy	May–Nov
Bürgenstock Felsenweg	2–2½ hours	easy	May–Nov
Rigi Höhenweg	2¾–3¼ hours	easy	May–Nov
Klausenpass	2 days	easy-medium	June–Nov
Surenenpass	2 days	medium-hard	June–Oct
Jochpass	2 days	medium	June–Oct
Fuorcla da Cavardiras	3 days	medium-hard	June–Oct
Swiss Jura			
Weissenstein	3¾–4½ hours	easy	May–Nov
Chasseral via Combe Grède	5¼–6¾ hours	easy-medium	May–Nov
Creux du Van via Poëta-Raisse	5–6 hours	easy	May–Nov
Mont Tendre	5¼–6½ hours	easy-medium	May–Nov
Southern Fribourg & Vaud			
Vanil Noir	2 days	medium	June–Oct
Kaiseregg	4¾–7 hours	medium	June–Oct
Col de Chaude	1-2 days	easy-medium	June–Oct
Col des Andérets	2 days	easy-medium	June–Oct
Tour de Famelon	3½–4½ hours	easy-medium	June–Oct
Tour des Muverans	4 days	medium-hard	June–Oct
Valais			
Cornopass (Passo del Corno)	2¼–3 hours	easy-medium	July–Oct
Grosser Aletschgletscher	4–5¼ hours	easy-medium	June–Oct
Höhenweg Grächen-Saas Fee	6–8 hours	medium	June–Oct
Sunnegga to Riffelalp	1½–2 hours	easy	June–Nov
Höhenweg Höhbalmen	5¼–6½ hours	medium	June–Oct
Lötschental	4½–7 hours	easy-medium	June–Oct

Features	Page
A traverse around a precipice to descend through a valley trough	102
A short high-level circuit across a lookout summit	105
A classic route in the shadow of the Wetterhorn	108
A superb high-level panoramic walk	111
One of the Alps' most scenic paths, under the mighty walls of the Eiger	114
A marvellous walk across a gap in a craggy range	115
A challenging but spectacular climb over a high pass	119
A ramble over a narrow pass in a craggy ridge	122
A gentle pass contrasts with the rugged glaciated ranges of the Bernese Alps	124
A historic Alpine pass route over a green, grassy saddle	127
A low pass crossing through gentle highland pastures below craggy peaks	131
A short, gentle ramble over a low saddle with views of Les Diablerets and the Saanental	132
A fascinating route through a heavily glaciated high-Alpine landscape	133
A gentle ridge-top walk across the panoramic summit of the Napf	144
A spectacular route cut into cliffs high above Lake Lucerne	147
A scenic walk across minor lookout summits of the Rigi range	149
An ancient route from the Glarnerland into Uri Canton past the mighty Clariden	155
A wild pass crossing with dramatic mountain scenery	159
A varied route from Central Switzerland into the eastern Bernese Oberland	162
A walk up through the wild Maderanertal and down into Graubünden's Surselva region	166
A panoramic route across a lookout summit and down past a historic hermitage in a tiny gorge	177
A walk to a major Jura summit giving vistas of the main Alpine massifs	179
A route combining the interesting Poëta-Raisse gorge and the superb Creux du Van cirque	183
An ascent of the rounded Mont Tendre, the Swiss Jura's highest peak	186
A spectacular walk through a wild and rugged nature reserve	194
An energetic climb to one of the region's best lookout summits	198
A rewarding ramble through the high, rolling Alpine foothills	200
A picturesque route through a largely untouched Alpine landscape	203
A high traverse along the upper slopes of the mystical Famelon range	206
A thrilling high-level circuit with superb views of Mont Blanc and the Pennine Alps	207
A gentle walk across an Alpine pass past a meltwater lake at the snout of a glacier	220
A walk beside the Alps' largest glacier	222
An exhilarating traverse high above a sheer-sided valley	226
A scenic stroll past lovely tarns set before the Matterhorn	229
A classic route across glorious Alpine meadows opposite the Matterhorn	230
An interesting circuit at the head of a remote valley	233

The Walks *continued*	Duration	Standard	Season
Valais *continued*			
Bisse de Clavau	2–2½hours	easy	April–Dec
Col de Riedmatten/Pas de Chèvres	5½–7 hours	medium-hard	June–Oct
Prafleuri–Louvie Traverse	2–3 days	medium-hard	June–Oct
Fenêtre d'Arpette	5–6¼ hours	medium	June–Oct
Pas de Lovenex	5–7¼ hours	easy-medium	June–Nov
Ticino			
Lago Ritóm Circuit	3 days	easy-medium	June–Oct
Val di Carassino	2 days	medium	June–Oct
Campolungo Circuit	4¼–6 hours	easy-medium	June–Oct
Passo di Cristallina	2 days	medium	June–Oct
San Carlo to Bosco/Gurin	2 days	hard	June–Oct
Barone Circuit	4 days	hard	June–Oct
Cima del Trosa	3¾–5 hours	easy	June–Oct
Tamaro–Lema Traverse	3¾–4½ hours	easy-medium	May–Nov
Monte Brè to Soragno	2¾–3¼ hours	easy	May–Dec
Monte Generoso	5¼–6½ hours	easy	May–Oct
Graubünden			
Rhätikon Höhenweg	4 days	medium-hard	July–Oct
Parpaner Rothorn	5–7 hours	medium	July–Oct
Vereinatal	2 days	medium	June–Oct
Sertigpass	4–5 hours	medium	July–Oct
Lai da Tuma Circuit	3¼–4½ hours	easy-medium	July–Oct
Plaun la Greina	2 days	medium	June–Oct
Ruin' Aulta	3¼–3¾ hours	easy-medium	May–Nov
Safienberg	4½–5¼ hours	medium	June–Oct
Upper Engadine Lakes	2¾–3½ hours	easy	June–Nov
Fuorcla Funtana da S-charl	3–3½ hours	easy	June–Oct
Lais da Rims	2 days	hard	July–Oct
Lakes of Macun	6½–8½ hours	medium-hard	July–Oct
Val Cluozza	5–7 hours	medium	July–Oct
North-Eastern Switzerland			
Säntis	4¼–5½ hours	medium-hard	June–Oct
Zwinglipass	2 days	medium	June–Nov
Churfirsten	3¾–5 hours	easy-medium	May–Nov
Pizol Lakes Circuit	3–4 hours	easy-medium	June–Oct
Foopass	2 days	medium	June–Oct
Murgseefurggel	2 days	medium	June–Nov
Richetlipass	6½–8 hours	medium	June–Oct
Panixerpass	6½–8 hours	medium-hard	June–Oct

Features	Page

The Maps

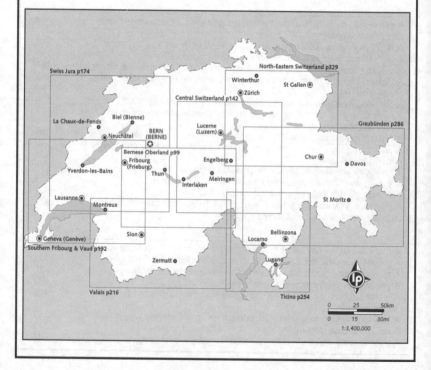

The Author

Clem Lindenmayer

Clem has lived and walked in Switzerland (on and off) for almost two decades. Although he has developed a special affection for the Swiss Alps, Clem has made extensive hiking trips to numerous other regions of the world. He researched and authored Lonely Planet's *Trekking in the Patagonian Andes* and the Rocky Mountains chapter of *Hiking in the USA*. Clem has also helped update Lonely Planet travel guidebooks to China, South-East Asia (Malaysia) and Western Europe (Germany and Sweden).

From the Author

My wife, Romi Arm, who accompanied me on many of the walks, gets a Swiss kiss for her patience and ongoing help.

The following regional tourist offices were kind enough to provide me with free walking maps for my research: Château d'Oex, Brig, Leukerbad, Bergün, Nendaz, Visp, Zernez, Grimentz, Spiez, Grindelwald and Crans-Montana. Thanks as well to the numerous tourist offices who answered my queries.

The following organisations also provided me with important information: Federal Office for Foreigner Issues; Pro Natura; Swiss Alpine Club (SAC); Swiss Friends of Nature; Swiss Hiking Federation (SAW/FSTP); Postauto Schweiz; Swiss Youth Hostels and Switzerland Tourism.

This Book

The 1st and 2nd editions of *Walking in Switzerland* were researched and written by Clem Lindenmayer.

Material from the 3rd edition of Lonely Planet's *Switzerland* guidebook, by Mark Honan, was used in this book.

From the Publisher

Walking in Switzerland was brought to you from LP's Melbourne office by: coordinating editor Janet Brunckhorst and coordinating designer Glenn van der Knijff; editorial team Andrew Bain, Anne Mulvaney and Jennifer Garrett; mapping team Andrew Smith, Chris Klep, Jacqui Saunders, Jarrad Needham and Yvonne Bischofberger; layout queens Jacqui Saunders and Yvonne Bischofberger; language gurus Quentin Frayne and Emma Koch; climate chart artiste Andrew Smith; flora & fauna guide Lindsay Brown; illustration maestro Matt King; illustrator Martin Harris; cover designer Jamieson Gross; the good folk of Lonely Planet Images; the letters ü and ö, and the number 9.

Thanks

Thanks to all the readers who wrote in with useful comments about the first edition of *Walking in Switzerland*:

Hilde & William Arnett, Kim Brown, Juerg Buehler, Margaret Clark, Bryan Dettman, Paul L Droz, P A Ground, Wesley Heiser, James L Hood, Janet M Ireland, Adrien Naylor, Ian Robertson, Wijnand Schonewille, Gary Spinks

Foreword

ABOUT LONELY PLANET GUIDEBOOKS

The story begins with a classic travel adventure: Tony and Maureen Wheeler's 1972 journey across Europe and Asia to Australia. Useful information about the overland trail did not exist at that time, so Tony and Maureen published the first Lonely Planet guidebook to meet a growing need.

From a kitchen table, then from a tiny office in Melbourne (Australia), Lonely Planet has become the largest independent travel publisher in the world, an international company with offices in Melbourne, Oakland (USA), London (UK) and Paris (France).

Today Lonely Planet guidebooks cover the globe. There is an ever-growing list of books and there's information in a variety of forms and media. Some things haven't changed. The main aim is still to help make it possible for adventurous travellers to get out there – to explore and better understand the world.

At Lonely Planet we believe travellers can make a positive contribution to the countries they visit – if they respect their host communities and spend their money wisely. Since 1986 a percentage of the income from each book has been donated to aid projects and human rights campaigns.

Updates Lonely Planet thoroughly updates each guidebook as often as possible. This usually means there are around two years between editions, although for more unusual or more stable destinations the gap can be longer. Check the imprint page (following the colour map at the beginning of the book) for publication dates.

Between editions up-to-date information is available in two free newsletters – the paper *Planet Talk* and email *Comet* (to subscribe, contact any Lonely Planet office) – and on our Web site at www.lonelyplanet.com. The *Upgrades* section of the Web site covers a number of important and volatile destinations and is regularly updated by Lonely Planet authors. *Scoop* covers news and current affairs relevant to travellers. And, lastly, the *Thorn Tree* bulletin board and *Postcards* section of the site carry unverified, but fascinating, reports from travellers.

Correspondence The process of creating new editions begins with the letters, postcards and emails received from travellers. This correspondence often includes suggestions, criticisms and comments about the current editions. Interesting excerpts are immediately passed on via newsletters and the Web site, and everything goes to our authors to be verified when they're researching on the road. We're keen to get more feedback from organisations or individuals who represent communities visited by travellers.

Lonely Planet gathers information for everyone who's curious about the planet – and especially for those who explore it first-hand. Through guidebooks, phrasebooks, activity guides, maps, literature, newsletters, image library, TV series and Web site we act as an information exchange for a worldwide community of travellers.

11

Research Authors aim to gather sufficient practical information to enable travellers to make informed choices and to make the mechanics of a journey run smoothly. They also research historical and cultural background to help enrich the travel experience and allow travellers to understand and respond appropriately to cultural and environmental issues.

Authors don't stay in every hotel because that would mean spending a couple of months in each medium-sized city and, no, they don't eat at every restaurant because that would mean stretching belts beyond capacity. They do visit hotels and restaurants to check standards and prices, but feedback based on readers' direct experiences can be very helpful.

Many of our authors work undercover, others aren't so secretive. None of them accept freebies in exchange for positive write-ups. And none of our guidebooks contain any advertising.

Production Authors submit their raw manuscripts and maps to offices in Australia, USA, UK or France. Editors and cartographers – all experienced travellers themselves – then begin the process of assembling the pieces. When the book finally hits the shops, some things are already out of date, we start getting feedback from readers and the process begins again ...

WARNING & REQUEST

Things change – prices go up, schedules change, good places go bad and bad places go bankrupt – nothing stays the same. So, if you find things better or worse, recently opened or long since closed, please tell us and help make the next edition even more accurate and useful. We genuinely value all the feedback we receive. A well travelled team reads and acknowledges every letter, postcard and email and ensures that every morsel of information finds its way to the appropriate authors, editors and cartographers for verification.

Everyone who writes to us will find their name in the next edition of the appropriate guidebook. They will also receive the latest issue of *Planet Talk*, our quarterly printed newsletter, or *Comet*, our monthly email newsletter. Subscriptions to both newsletters are free. The very best contributions will be rewarded with a free guidebook.

Excerpts from your correspondence may appear in new editions of Lonely Planet guidebooks, the Lonely Planet Web site, *Planet Talk* or *Comet*, so please let us know if you *don't* want your letter published or your name acknowledged.

Send all correspondence to the Lonely Planet office closest to you:

Australia: Locked Bag 1, Footscray, Victoria 3011
USA: 150 Linden St, Oakland, CA 94607
UK: 10A Spring Place, London NW5 3BH
France: 1 rue du Dahomey, 75011 Paris

Or email us at: talk2us@lonelyplanet.com.au

For news, views and updates see our Web site: www.lonelyplanet.com

Introduction

Switzerland is such a small country, and yet there's so much of it! Switzerland lies at the cultural and linguistic crossroads of western Europe, and it's fascinating that such a small country should have such great regional variation. Some patient person once worked out that Switzerland has around 5000 individual valleys. In fact, virtually every region in the country has its own unique style of architecture, its own traditional dress, its own local customs, even its own kind of cheese – its own special charm. Switzerland has four main national languages, but everywhere you go the local people speak a different dialect. The only thing that scarcely seems to change are the flower boxes in the windows, all full of bright red geraniums.

Although less than 15% of the Alps actually lie within Switzerland, the country has rather more than its fair share of the great Alpine scenery. With few real exceptions, the Swiss Alps have the highest peaks, the largest glaciers, the deepest valleys and the loveliest mountain lakes. Indeed, Switzerland has some of the most beautiful and spectacular mountain scenery found anywhere on earth.

One of the most appealing aspects of walking in the Swiss countryside is the mixture of cultural and natural elements, which sometimes blend smoothly together but just as often present a dramatic contrast. A quaint old farmhouse sits amongst gentle flowery meadows grazed by tinkling cows, while a high waterfall tumbles down the sheer rock walls of a nearby snowcapped peak to meet a gushing glacial torrent far below in the valley – such scenes typify the Swiss Alps.

This guidebook offers a broad selection of suggested walks in virtually every region of the country. It includes many of Switzerland's most classic hiking routes – of which there are dozens – but the selection is still far from complete. Many of the suggested routes are day walks that can be done by anybody with minimal experience. The book also details longer trips, on which walkers stay overnight in huts or mountain hotels high in the Alps.

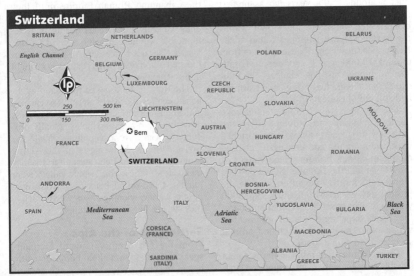

Facts about Switzerland

HISTORY
Early Inhabitants
The earliest undisputed evidence of human habitation of the Alps has been found in the Alpstein massif in north-eastern Switzerland. Here, in limestone caves (known as the Wildkirchlihöhlen) 1500m above sea level, remains of a Palaeolithic hunter-gatherer culture dating from a warmer inter-glacial period some 100,000 years ago have been found. Archaeologists surmise that the first humans may well have reached the Alpine region much earlier still, but any evidence of this has probably since been erased by intervening glaciations.

Higher areas of the Jura and Alpine foothills were the only significant snow-free areas in this ice-age landscape and were mostly covered by an open tundra-type vegetation. This higher ground nevertheless supported a surprising variety of creatures, including the so-called megafauna. These large animals – such as hairy mammoths, giant elk and cave bears – had become extinct by around 15,000 years ago, as the first Mesolithic (or middle Stone-Age) hunters began to recolonise the now slowly warming lowlands. Cave paintings found at the Kesserloch (near Schaffhausen) dating from around 10,000 years ago depict frigid-climate animals such as reindeer – an indication that the gradual postglacial warming had still only just begun.

The ice ages left behind a landscape highly favourable to human settlement, with new broadened valley floors enriched by fertile moraines and low, easily crossed mountain passes. Following the valleys of the Rhône and the Danube, Neolithic (late Stone-Age) farmers began arriving in the present-day Swiss Mittelland about 6000 years ago. These settlers cleared and burnt the forests, creating a new environment in which other migratory plant and animal species could gain a foothold.

These primitive farming cultures found suitable sites for settlement around the large lowland lakes and rivers. Remains of pile-dwellings – raised houses on stilts – have been found in submerged or buried sites around the shores of Lakes Zürich and Constance. With the arrival of the metal-working culture some 5000 years ago the Alps became an important source of copper, since ore deposits were most easily discovered and worked from the exposed-rock mountain-sides. The sensational discovery of the mummified body of a prehistoric man – the now famous 'Ötzi' – on the continental divide in the nearby Tirolean Alps proves that trans-Alpine routes were already well established at this time.

Celts & Romans
In the 1st century BC, the area of modern Switzerland was largely inhabited by Celtic tribes (the word 'Alps' is of Celtic origin). The most important of these were the Hel-vetians, in the Swiss Mittelland, and the Rhaetians, in today's Graubünden. The Celts increasingly came into conflict with the expanding Roman Empire until they were largely subdued by the Roman gen-erals Tiberius and Drusus during their re-markable Alpine campaign around 15 BC. Under Caesar's successor, Augustus, all of the area of today's Switzerland was brought under Roman control.

The Romans built paved roads and estab-lished centres like Helvetiorum (Avenches) and Augusta Rauricorum (Augst). A process of assimilation began, which gradually pro-duced a 'Gallo-Roman' culture. While the Swiss Mittelland and parts of the Alpine foothills had permanent agricultural settle-ments, few of the higher Alpine valleys were inhabited year-round, being visited only dur-ing the warmer months of summer for activ-ities such as hunting and mining.

Settlement of the Alps
From the 5th century onward German-speaking tribes with their herds of cattle began pushing southward into the area of

today's Switzerland. In the western regions these Germanic newcomers were quickly assimilated into the Latinised-Celtic population, but in the east they supplanted this culture completely. Modern Switzerland's French/German linguistic division can be traced back to that time.

The moist climate in the Alps and their foothills makes this ideal grazing country, and the German-speaking cattle-herders gradually spread out into the Alpine valleys. A typical feature in the settlement of many high valleys was that the farmers first made use of the upper reaches, where glaciers had levelled out the terrain. Such upper valleys were often accessible only by way of an Alpine pass, this being less dangerous than the gorges at the bottom of the valley.

Origins of the Swiss Confederation

In the early medieval period the Habsburg kingdom (centred in modern-day Austria)

sought to bring the profitable trade route over the Passo del San Gottardo under its control. To this end the Habsburgs forcefully subjugated the German-speaking forest communities around the shores of Lake Lucerne. These 'Inner Swiss' refused to accept domination by the Habsburgs, however, and in 1291 they formed a military pact to assert their independence. In a struggle epitomised by the legend of Wilhelm Tell, the Habsburgs were permanently expelled.

Originally consisting of Uri, Schwyz and Nidwalden, by 1383 Bern, Glarus, Lucerne, Zug and Zürich had joined this first loose Swiss Confederation. Throughout the subsequent centuries Switzerland further expanded its territory by military conquest and by the admission of other neighbouring communities or 'cantons'. Despite often bitter intercantonal rivalry, the Swiss Confederation has proven cohesive enough to withstand more than 700 years of often turbulent European history.

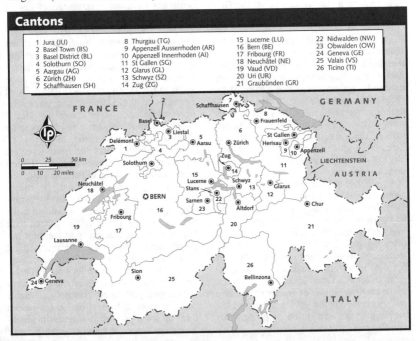

Cantons

1 Jura (JU)
2 Basel Town (BS)
3 Basel District (BL)
4 Solothurn (SO)
5 Aargau (AG)
6 Zürich (ZH)
7 Schaffhausen (SH)

8 Thurgau (TG)
9 Appenzell Ausserrhoden (AR)
10 Appenzell Innerrhoden (AI)
11 St Gallen (SG)
12 Glarus (GL)
13 Schwyz (SZ)
14 Zug (ZG)

15 Lucerne (LU)
16 Bern (BE)
17 Fribourg (FR)
18 Neuchâtel (NE)
19 Vaud (VD)
20 Uri (UR)
21 Graubünden (GR)

22 Nidwalden (NW)
23 Obwalden (OW)
24 Geneva (GE)
25 Valais (VS)
26 Ticino (TI)

Walser Migrations

The uppermost part of the Valais – the area near the source of the Rhône River known as Goms – was one of the first large Alpine valleys to be settled. From around AD 800, German-speaking farmers of the Bernese Oberland began migrating over the Grimselpass and Lötschenpass to Goms, draining highland moors and clearing mountain forests for pastures and agriculture. This was a bold and novel undertaking for these early times, and although Celtic tribes had inhabited the Rhône Valley from at least 1000 BC, it was the first serious attempt by medieval farmers to establish permanent settlements above 1500m in the Alps. The settlers developed sound methods of highland farming, such as driving their grazing stock up to the high pastures in summer so that the valleys could be cropped or mown for winter feed.

In Goms the practice of passing on the family farm to a single heir forced sons to seek out new lands, and by the end of the 12th century these Walsers (from the German *Walliser*, meaning Valaisan) had colonised all important side valleys of the Upper Valais. The Walsers now began to migrate out of the Rhône Valley basin, driving their herds south and eastward across Alpine passes and introducing the dairy-farming culture to wide areas of the central Alps. Due to their expertise in colonising hitherto unproductive highland valleys, the Walsers were favoured by feudal landholders, who offered them freedom from bondage and hereditary rights of land use (although usually not ownership) as a reward for opening up new territories.

The Walser migrations lasted for several centuries, and by the end of the Middle Ages even the highest valleys of the Swiss Alps had been penetrated by Walser settlers. The Walsers were not always welcome, however, often being regarded with suspicion by the local population. Large numbers of Walsers put down roots in Romansch-speaking regions of today's Graubünden. As a response to the continual influx of Walser colonists, a law was passed in the Val Lumnezia in 1457 prohibiting the acquisition of property by non-Romansch-speaking peoples.

Today some 150 towns and villages – widely dispersed in a 300km-long arc stretching across the central Alps as far Tirol – are known to be original Walser settlements. Numerous localities have names that betray their Walser origins: Valsesia near Monte Rosa in northern Italy, Valzeina in the Prättigau region of Graubünden, and the Grosses Walsertal in Austrian Vorarberg to name a few.

Trans-Alpine Pass Routes

There are around a dozen major north-south pass routes in the Swiss Alps, including the Bernina, Splügen, San Bernardino, Lucomagno (Lukmanier), San Gottardo (St Gotthard), Simplon and Grande St-Bernard, as well as many east-west passes such as the Col de Jaman, Furka, Susten and Klausen. These important transport and communication routes have been crossed regularly for thousands of years. The Romans laid down the first well-graded and paved routes across the Alps, which allowed the transportation of much greater quantities of cargo by teams of pack animals.

The mountains presented the road builders with numerous hindrances. Bridges were needed to span the numerous streams, narrow gorges made it necessary to make a high detour, and Alpine moors had to be filled out with rock. Particularly difficult obstacles in the Alpine terrain were slippery ice-polished slabs caused by glacial action – a problem that was overcome by chiselling grooves or steps into the rock.

In the Middle Ages the route over the Simplonpass was the shortest and lowest route between Milan and Paris, but after the 13th-century construction of the legendary Teufelsbrücke – the 'Devil's Bridge' spanning a gorge of the Reuss River known as the Schöllenen – the Passo del San Gottardo (St Gotthard Pass) developed into the most important trans-Alpine route in the central Alps. The increased availability of explosives from the middle of the 17th century made it practicable to blast a safe-transit route along even the steepest cliff faces. This not only made pass transport and travel easier, but helped open up some previously inaccessible highland areas to regular summer grazing.

The control of the most important pass routes brought considerable power and prosperity, and the privileges of this profitable trade were jealously guarded. The notorious Kaspar Jodok von Stockalper (1609–91), otherwise known as the 'King of the Simplon', was able to amass a phenomenal fortune by monopolising the pass trade in the Valais.

It may at first seem odd that more cargo was actually transported in winter than in summer. The reason for this was that most of the mule drivers (*Säumer* in German, *mulattieres* in French) were mountain farmers, who in summer were simply too busy to work on the pass routes. In winter the otherwise idle farmers had to work hard to keep the passes open. A trail was laid on the mule paths after the first snow, and this had to be stamped flat by mules, horses or oxen after every new fall. This produced a hard, icy surface over which large quantities of goods could be transported on sleds; travellers actually preferred the softer winter snows to the bumpy summer ride. The dangers of avalanches were often extreme, however, and whole mule teams were sometimes claimed by the 'white death'.

Commodities with a high value-to-weight ratio were the preferred cargo. Products exported south across the passes included hard Swiss cheeses and livestock; while wine, rice, salt, spices and leather were typical northbound goods. The expansion of road and rail routes during the 19th century finally led to the decline and eventual abandonment of the age-old muleteer profession. Today traces of the mule trails that for hundreds of years served as the sole travel and transport routes can still be seen throughout the Swiss Alps. In recent years these old routes have been rediscovered and restored as paths for recreational walking.

Exploration & Tourism in the Swiss Alps

Monks and the clergy were the first true pioneers of Alpine exploration. The earliest recorded ascent of a prominent peak in Switzerland took place in 1387, when six priests scaled the 2132m Pilatus – and were promptly thrown into jail for breaking a law specifically prohibiting climbing this mountain. Pastor Nicoline Sererhard was the first to climb Graubünden's 2964m Schesaplana in 1740. The agile Benedictine monk Placidus à Spescha (1752–1833) of Disentis-Mustèr made first ascents of more than 30 summits over 3000m in Graubünden and Central Switzerland, including the Rheinwaldhorn (3402m) and the 3327m Oberalpstock (Piz Tgietschen). A landmark summit of Central Switzerland, the 3238m Titlis, was first scaled in 1744 by two monastic brothers from Engelberg.

The Romantic period produced a wave of interest in the Alps, which for the first time came to be regarded as more than just an awesome and forbidding barrier. From the mid-1700s onward, Europe's intellectuals, including the philosopher Jean-Jacques Rousseau, his fellow-Genevan and naturalist Horace Bénédict Saussure, and Johann Wolfgang von Goethe flocked to the Swiss Alps for poetic inspiration, scientific studies – or just to have a good look. After developing a fascination for the Alps on his first visit in 1775 (aged 26), Goethe undertook a longer second journey that took him up the Rhône Valley across the Furkapass, then down the Reuss and across Lake Lucerne, where he climbed the Rigi.

English-speaking visitors also came in droves. The poet Lord Byron toured the Bernese Oberland in the early 1800s. His compatriot, the landscape artist William Turner, visited Switzerland six times between 1802 and 1844, producing thousands of drawings and sketches as well as some important watercolour and oil paintings. Charles Dickens made lengthy trips to the Swiss Alps in the 1840s. In his classic *A Tramp Abroad*, the American writer Mark Twain describes his travels in the Bernese Oberland during the 1890s, including his crossing of the Gemmipass on foot taking several arduous days.

The so-called 'heyday of mountaineering' in the Alps was dominated by the British. In 1855 Grenville and Christopher Smyth conquered the highest summit of the Swiss Alps, the Dufourspitze in the Monte Rosa massif, and several years later the journalist Sir Leslie Stephen made various first ascents in the Bernese and Valaisan (Pennine) Alps. In 1861 the acclaimed English physicist John Tyndall scaled the 4505m Weisshorn, before turning his attention to the Bündner, Bernese and Vaud Alps. The summit of the 4479m Matterhorn was first reached in 1865 by a party of seven led by Edward Whymper. On the descent tragedy struck, and four of Whymper's climbers fell to their deaths.

Promoted largely by wealthy British tourists, Switzerland led the development of Alpine tourism. Known as the *belle époque*, the period between 1880 and 1914 saw the establishment of many Alpine resorts (such as Grindelwald, St Moritz and Zermatt), which have maintained their premier status until the present day. Most of Switzerland's classic old funiculars and cog railways date from those years. A pioneering achievement of this early 'railway tourism' in the Swiss Alps was the completion of the Jungfraujoch cog railway in 1912, whose upper station is the highest in Europe at 3454m. Since WWII, mountain cable cars have proliferated rapidly, providing summer and winter access to areas otherwise reachable only on foot.

GEOGRAPHY & GEOLOGY

Switzerland's surface area totals 41,285 sq km, although by some calculations the country would be about six times as large (or the size of Great Britain) if – God forbid! – all the bumps were ironed out. Politically speaking, the Swiss landscape is divided into 26 cantons and half-cantons, which are self-governing and have considerable autonomy in domestic affairs. Their borders don't always follow natural or 'logical' divisions (such as mountain ranges or rivers), with numerous isolated enclaves and other irregularities hinting at the jealous intercantonal rivalry during Switzerland's 700-year-long history.

Switzerland can be divided into three basic geographical regions arranged from north-west to south-east in progressively broader bands: the Jura, the Mittelland and the Alps.

Swiss Jura

Taking in around 10% of the country, the Swiss Jura is a low chain of limestone mountains stretching some 150km north-eastward along the French border from near Lake Geneva as far as the city of Basel. Only the Swiss Jura's highest peaks manage to reach much more than 1500m, including La Dôle (1677m), Mont Tendre (1679m), Le Chasseron (1606) and Le Chasseral (1607m). The Jura extends west and southward well into French territory, where the highest summits in the region are found.

The Swiss Jura is younger and much less complex geologically when compared to the Alps, with high rolling plateaus of mixed meadows and forest (largely beech and red spruce) being its most typical landscapes. This is prime dairying country, and the region is known for its soft, full-flavoured cheeses. Although it has a moist climate and experiences intensely cold winters (which in some areas pushes the timberline down to 1200m), the Jura has no glaciers at all. On its south-eastern edge the mountains fall away often quite abruptly into the Mittelland, making ideal lookout peaks.

Swiss Mittelland

The Swiss Mittelland (sometimes called the Swiss Plateau or the Swiss Midlands) extends right across the country from Lake Geneva to Lake Constance, forming an undulating, roughly 80km-wide basin hemmed in between the Jura and the Swiss Alps. Taking in large parts of Fribourg, Bern, Lucerne, Vaud and Zürich cantons, the Swiss Mittelland makes up only around 30% of Switzerland's area, yet over 80% of the country's population and nearly all of its important industries are based here. Embracing both French- and German-speaking regions, the Mittelland is also Switzerland's true cultural and political heartland, with most of its major cities and significant historical sites.

This is a landscape typified by cornfields and pastures interspersed with high hills, where altitudes range from as little as 350m up to almost 1000m – in other European countries the Mittelland would even qualify as 'mountainous terrain'. The rock layers here lie almost horizontally, however, not having been subjected to the folding and uplifting that produced the Alps and the ranges of the Jura. Drained by the large tributaries of the Rhine such as the Sarine (Saane), the Aare, the Emme, the Reuss and the Limmat, the Mittelland is divided by numerous valley basins which slope gently north-eastward.

The Mittelland's sheltered location and moderate altitudes produce a mild climate, which – together with its fertile soils composed largely of ancient moraine deposits left behind by ice-age glaciers – makes this region the 'breadbasket' of the nation. Although agricultural development is intensive, large pockets of fir, spruce and beech forest lie scattered throughout the Mittelland. Roads and motorways, railways and power lines, rivers and canals crisscross this region from all directions. Largely because of its built-up nature and less interesting contours, no walks in the Swiss Mittelland have been included in this guidebook.

Swiss Alps

Separating northern and southern Europe, the Alps form a sort of crescent-shaped ridge that sweeps around from the Mediterranean Riviera in the west to near Vienna in the east. The Swiss Alps are in the rather more elevated central-western part of this great mountainous arc.

The Swiss Alps account for around 60% of Switzerland's territory. They form a geographically complex area centred at the pivotal Gotthard region (named after the Passo del San Gottardo), where Western Europe's three main watersheds converge. Four of Switzerland's largest rivers, the Rhône, the Reuss, the Rhine (especially the Vorderrhein) and the Ticino have their sources in the Gotthard region.

The Rhône-Gotthard-Vorderrhein line, which stretches along the two great longitudinal valleys of the Rhône and the Rhine Rivers, divides the Swiss Alps into northern and southern sections. On the northern side are the Vaud, the Bernese, the Central Swiss and the Glarner Alps, while to the south the mighty Valaisan (Pennine) and the Bündner Alps form the continental divide. The Rhône and Rhine Valleys themselves form a kind of intermediate zone very much hemmed in on either side by high solid-rock mountains.

The western half the Swiss Alps is especially high and rugged, with many classic peaks – such as the Eiger, the Schreckhorn and the Lauteraarhorn of the Bernese Oberland; and the Matterhorn, the Weissmies, the Dent Blanche and the Grand Combin in the Valais – rising well above 4000m. Despite steady glacial recession since the mid-1800s, the Swiss Alps remain the most intensely glaciated part of the Alpine chain.

Dramatic scenery surrounds you on the rocky trails of Val Murtarol, Graubünden.

MARTIN MOOS

Glaciers

At high altitudes most precipitation falls as snow rather than as rain. In areas where so much snow falls that it cannot melt away completely during the short summer, so-called névés and glaciers form. 'Valley' glaciers, best typified by Switzerland's mighty Grosser Aletschgletscher, are the largest kind of glacier. These 'rivers of ice' move at an extremely slow yet immensely powerful pace, grinding and shearing away at their supporting rock base and transporting large volumes of debris (or moraine) out of the mountains.

'Shelf' glaciers form elongated icy strips, or nestle within rounded cirques, which themselves are formed by this same pattern of erosion by snow and ice. The French word névé (*Firnfeld* in German) is used to describe a high-Alpine snowfield. As the older snow moves downslope, pushed by the weight of new snow farther uphill, it becomes compacted and gradually turns into a glacier. Névés often lie at the head of a glacier, constantly feeding it with new ice.

Like glaciers over the world, Switzerland's areas of perpetual ice and snow have receded markedly over the last 150 years. The country's glaciers have lost around one third of their surface area. Glaciologists calculate that if this trend continues at the present rate, many smaller glaciers will have thawed out completely by the end of the second decade of the next century. Glacial thawing is more than just an academic concern, however. Areas at the foot of high mountain ranges, such as Valais, would become parched without glacier meltwater.

Below is an explanation of some glacier terminology. For a description of landform features left behind by melted glaciers, see the boxed text 'Signs of a Glacial Past' in the Valais chapter.

ablation zone – where the annual rate of melt exceeds snowfall
accumulation zone – where the annual snowfall exceeds the rate of snowmelt
bergschrund – crevasse at the head of a glacier
blue ice – ice compacted and metamorphosed into an airtight mass
crevasse – deep crack or fissure in the ice
firn line – the line between the accumulation and ablation zones
ice fall –the frozen equivalent to a waterfall as the glacier descends over steep ground
lateral moraine – mounds of debris deposited along the flanks of a glacier
névé – masses of porous ice not yet transformed into blue (glacier) ice; also called firn
serac – pinnacle of ice among crevasses on a glacier
sinkhole – depression in the glacial surface where a stream disappears underground
terminal moraine – mound of debris at the end of a glacier

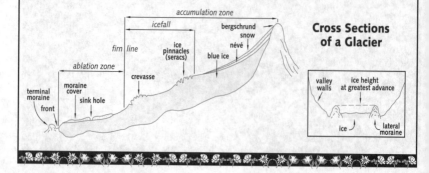

Cross Sections of a Glacier

Of the 10 largest glaciers in the Alps, eight lie entirely within Swiss territory. Glaciers cover around 1300 sq km – or slightly more than 3% – of Switzerland's surface.

On their northern and southern sides, the Swiss Alps are fringed by a wide band of lower and often heavily forested foothills, known as the pre-Alps *(Voralpen, préalpes)*. While dwarfed by the major summits of the Alps proper, these pre-Alpine ranges can reach surprising heights, sometimes approaching 2500m.

Formation of the Alps The formation of the Alps began around one hundred million years ago. At this time, Africa, under the powerful forces of plate tectonics, began to drift north toward Europe, slowly pushing its way across the ancient Tethys Ocean, the shallow predecessor of the Mediterranean Sea. The African continent advanced like a giant bulldozer, causing the intervening sea floor to buckle and uplift under the enormous stress. As this process continued, a peninsula running east to west was formed, dividing the emerging Mediterranean Sea into northern and southern branches.

New rivers – such as the once-mighty 'proto-Reuss' which must have flowed somewhere through the middle of that ancient Switzerland – cut their way along mountain fault lines, eroding vast amounts of gravel and sand onto the surrounding sea floor. On both sides of the young Alpine range, these deposits gradually accumulated to reach thousands of metres in depth, finally filling in the northern branch of the early Mediterranean Sea and creating the broad Lombardy Plain in today's northern Italy. The cement-like amalgam rocks (known in German as *Nagelfluh*) that are especially widespread in the pre-Alpine ranges consist of alluvial-marine deposits originating from that latter stage in the Alps' formation. A final phase of mountain-building pushed up the ranges of the Jura, the Alpstein and the pre-Alps.

This whole process was accompanied by a great amount of folding and sandwiching of the different rock types. Some regions were pushed far northward, while others –

Mountainslides

Ice-age glaciers sheared the sides of Alpine valleys to create structurally unstable, near-vertical rock walls, which occasionally break away suddenly and collapse into the valleys. The Alps' largest ever mountainslide (known in German as *Bergsturz*, or *éboulement* in French) was the ancient Flimser Bergsturz (see the boxed text 'The Swiss Grand Canyon' in the Graubünden chapter), but more recent mountainslides have obliterated entire villages in Switzerland.

The Val Bavona in Ticino never recovered from a catastrophic mountainslide in 1594. Even more disastrous was the 1806 Rossberg mountainslide, in which 40 million cubic metres of debris thundered down on Goldau, in Central Switzerland, wiping out the entire village. Elm, in the Glarnerland, suffered a similar fate in 1881, albeit due to irresponsible mining practices rather than a whim of nature. Another large mountainslide occurred in September 1714 above Derborence in the lower Valais, when a cliff face of the Diablerets collapsed, crushing whole forests and Alpine pastures under great masses of rubble. Obvious signs of major instability such as eerie cracking noises accompanied by occasional falling rocks were heeded by most of the local herders, so the number of human deaths was relatively low. Very often fallen debris dams a valley to create a new lake, as is the case with the Tchingelsee in the Bernese Oberland, which resulted from a relatively small landslip in 1950.

such as the central massifs of the western Alps – were scarcely moved at all. (If shifted back to its original ancient site, for example, St Moritz would be on the same latitude as the city of Bologna in Italy.) Today the fossilised remains of sea creatures can be found in ancient marine sediments throughout the northern Alps. In places molten magma spilled up from beneath the limestone crust, creating areas with granite-based rocks. Where this marine limestone occurs, underground caverns may form; the most notable are those at

Beatus on Lake Thun and the Höllach caves in the Muotatal, which form the largest cave system in Europe.

Ice Ages Beginning around one million years ago, the earth experienced a repeated cycle of ice ages, with extended cold intervals following climatically warmer periods. When the last ice age reached its peak around 25,000 years ago, the Alps were covered by a vast sheet of ice. Huge glaciers sprawled down from the mountains, smothering most of today's Switzerland under icy masses up to 1000m deep. The ice-age glaciers' slow but enormous force carved out and deepened the mountain valleys to give them their characteristic post-glacial U-shaped appearance.

Mountainsides were sheared to create bare sheer rock walls – the Matterhorn's classic pyramid form is the finest such example in the Alps. Where the glaciers melted, great quantities of rock rubble transported within the ice built up to form high walls. These glacial moraines acted as natural dams, impounding rivers to create the large bodies of water such as Lakes Geneva, Maggiore and Constance along with numerous other smaller lakes.

CLIMATE

The Alps provide Europe's most marked climatic division, largely cutting off the north of the continent from the milder conditions prevailing around the Mediterranean Sea. Conversely, the Alps shelter the Mediterranean from the periodic intrusions of cold Arctic air that produce starkly lower than average temperatures on the northern side of the range.

Several climatic regions overlap in Switzerland, and the country has rather a complex weather pattern. Summer weather is influenced by four main wind currents. Northerly airstreams bring frigid Arctic air masses into the Alps, usually producing snowfalls. The warm and moist southerlies bring rainfall, but the bad weather normally doesn't last for very long. In summer north-easterly winds are dry and warm (but cold in winter). Easterlies are generally responsible for longer periods of wet weather.

Most areas above around 1200m (or 1500m in Ticino) are covered by a thick blanket of snow at least from January to March. The midwinter snowline even drops down into the Swiss Mittelland, although during the last few decades the snow cover has rarely stayed more than a week or so at such low altitudes.

Snow and rainfall levels can vary radically over relatively short distances in the

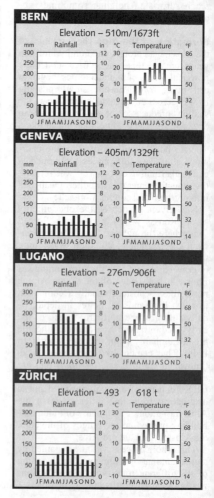

Föhn Winds

The word *Föhn* originates – via Romansch – from the Latin *ventus favonius* ('mild wind'). It's also standard German for 'hair drier' – an apt adaptation, as anyone who has experienced the full blast of this hot, dry wind will testify.

Typical Föhn conditions arise whenever a low-pressure system lies above the British Isles with a high centred over Italy or the Balkans. The broad anticlockwise circulation of winds around the low draws in air masses from the Alpine foothills of northern Italy. This air is sucked northward, cooling so rapidly that its moisture soon precipitates (as often heavy rain or snow) on the Alps' southern ranges. These now relatively dry air masses continue north across the mountains, regaining some moisture as they blow across highland lakes and snowfields, then warm up quickly as they descend toward the lower Alpine foothills.

On the northern side of the Alps, the arrival of strong Föhn winds is often an indication – although not an infallible one – of approaching bad weather. The Föhn may persist for several days, however, bringing generally warm and windy conditions to the northern Alps. An interesting effect of strong Föhn conditions is the exceptionally clear skies which make the Alps appear very close and detailed even from as far away as Zürich or Bern. Despite these apparently pleasant features, few Swiss people welcome the arrival of the Föhn, blaming it for headaches, sleeplessness and irritability. Some people, however, find Föhn conditions quite invigorating – even positively uplifting. Severe storms associated with Föhn conditions are a particular threat in April or May, and can cause catastrophic flooding or flatten whole forests.

On the northern side of the Swiss Alps are certain so-called 'Föhn valleys', most notably the Murgtal by the Walensee (Lake Walen) and the Haslital in the Bernese Oberland. These Föhn valleys' south-to-north course draws in the warm southerly airstream to produce a milder local microclimate.

Under different weather conditions a reverse effect known as the 'north Föhn' occurs. The north Föhn produces wet (or snowy) weather on the northern side of the Alps while on the southern side strong – but often quite cold – northerlies blow down from the mountains, bringing sunny conditions in Ticino.

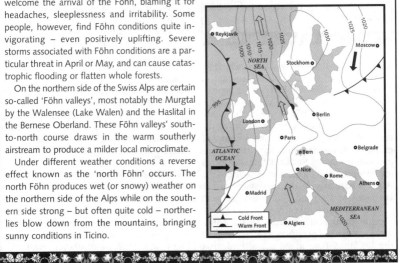

Swiss Alps. For example, the Jungfraujoch in the Bernese Oberland has an annual precipitation – most of it falling as snow – exceeding 4000mm, while the Central Valais, lying just 40km to the south-west, only receives around 500mm.

The climate chart in this section provides an overview of regional weather patterns; see also Weather Information in the Facts for the Walker chapter.

Northern Swiss Alps

The northern side of the Alps lies in the path of the oceanic westerly airstreams, which bring frequent alternations between high-pressure and low-pressure systems. These regions have moist climates with heavy winter snowfalls and appreciable summer rain. On the windward sides of the mountains where cloud build-up frequently occurs, precipitation levels are considerably

Weather Patterns

Certain seasonal weather phenomena – many with descriptive local names – occur in Switzerland with surprising regularity. The cold snap around mid-May known as the *Eisheiligen* ('ice holies') is greeted warmly by Swiss farmers as it marks the start of the frost-free season. Another welcome chilly spell, the *Schafskälte* ('sheep's cold'), comes in mid-June and actually heralds the start of summery conditions. During the *Altweibersommer* ('old wives' summer') Switzerland generally enjoys an extended run of stable weather in mid-autumn (familiar to English speakers as the Indian summer), which can bring weeks of fine, settled conditions. The 'St Martin's summer', around the first week in November, is usually the last warm-weather period before the onset of winter.

higher than on their leeward sides, which lie within the 'rain-shadow' of the mountains.

In places, warm southerly air is repeatedly ducted through 'Föhn valleys' (see the boxed text 'Föhn Winds'), which consequently enjoy temperatures well above the regional averages. Due to the amount of moisture in the air, summers can be unpleasantly humid. Summer thunderstorms are very prevalent on the northern side of the Alps, particularly in the mountains of the Bernese Oberland and Central Switzerland.

From autumn until early winter a heat inversion occurs in northern Switzerland, when colder temperatures are recorded in the lowlands than at higher altitudes. A thick layer of fog often builds up over the Swiss Mittelland, which visitors often mistake for overcast conditions. Above a maximum altitude of 1300m, however, the sun may be clothing the mountains in glistening autumn light.

Swiss Jura

The Swiss Jura is cooled by westerly winds, and as a consequence average temperatures are decidedly lower than at identical altitudes in the Alps. Annual precipitation on the Jura's upper slopes averages 1500mm, with high summer rainfall due to frequent and often heavy thunderstorms. The Swiss Jura experiences frigid winters with positively 'Siberian' temperatures, which in places drop below -40°C.

Longitudinal Valleys

The longitudinal valleys of the inner Swiss Alps comprise the Rhône Valley in the Valais, most of Graubünden's upper Rhine Valley and the Engadine. These regions have a very pronounced 'continental' type of climate, with major seasonal and daily temperature variations. Summer days are typically warm – often rising above 30°C – while night temperatures can be decidedly chilly.

Enclosed by high mountains on either side, the longitudinal valleys receive substantially less precipitation (whether rain or snow) than regions situated directly on the southern or northern side of the Alpine chain. The longitudinal valleys are also rather more sheltered from storms, and the drier conditions tend to hinder the development of the heavy summer thunderstorms. Solar radiation is very intense in the longitudinal valleys, but walkers tend to feel the summer heat much less due to the lower humidity levels.

Southern Swiss Alps

The mighty ranges of the Swiss Alps, particularly the Gotthard massif, are a very effective climatic barrier and ensure that a much milder climate prevails in southern regions – essentially thes canton of Ticino and the four south-facing valleys of Graubünden. Affectionately known as the 'sunroom of Switzerland', Ticino lies within the Mediterranean's climatic sphere of influence – a fact strongly reflected in its local vegetation. The northernmost part of Ticino around the Gotthard massif itself is a partial exception, however, and tends to hold in bad weather for longer. Summer thunderstorms are somewhat less frequent than on the northern side of the Alps, but once the rainclouds break the downpours can be incredibly heavy.

Flora & Fauna of Switzerland

D ue to Switzerland's climatic variations, the species represented differ widely from region to region. As the walks in this book are concentrated in mountain areas, this section deals specifically with plants and animals that walkers are likely to encounter on the trail.

FLORA

In the mountains, the growing season (essentially the snow-free period) becomes shorter with increasing altitude, and therefore Alpine plants take longer to recover from any setback in their growth cycle. Walkers should always consider this, and take particular care to avoid damaging the fragile flora of the Alps.

VEGETATION ZONES

Swiss botanists distinguish four rough vegetation zones: lowland, montane, sub-Alpine and Alpine. These vary considerably due to the local microclimate, exposure to the elements or even human alteration of the ecosystem. In Ticino the vegetation zones are up to 300m higher than those listed below.

The lowland zone reaches up to 600m, and is the warmest, most agriculturally productive and densely populated zone. It includes most of the Swiss Mittelland as well as larger valleys of the Jura, the Alps and Ticino. The montane zone takes in areas up to about 1200m. In the montane zone animal husbandry is already more important than agriculture, and broadleaf forests of beech, elm, maple, linden (lime), oak and birch predominate. Ticino's beautiful chestnut forests (known locally as *selva*) also lie within the montane zone.

The subalpine zone goes up to roughly 1700m, and is largely covered by coniferous forests. Lower down, the most common tree species tends to be the red (Norway) spruce *(Picea excelsa)*, which higher up gives way to larch *(Larix decidua)*, Arolla pine *(Pinus cembra)* or other highland conifers such as mountain pine *(P. montana)* and Scots (Scotch) pine *(P. sylvestris)*.

The Alpine zone begins at the timberline, although exactly where this lies is not always directly obvious. The upper line of the forest can vary considerably, with isolated stands of trees even managing to survive well above it. Fields of Alpine heathland that include

Birch trees in autumn, Ardez, Graubünden.

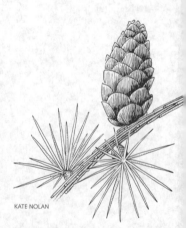

KATE NOLAN

Branch section of the European larch.

Title page: Orange larches on slope of Munt La Schera, Swiss National Park, Graubünden.
Photograph by Martin Moos.

MARTIN MOOS

small semiprostrate shrubs like dwarf mountain pine, juniper and Alpine rhododendrons (alpenroses) often extend upwards far above the last trees. The rich highland meadows (called *Alpen* or *Matten* in German, and *alpe* or *alpage* in French) form the basis of dairy farming in the Alps, and are subject to regular summer grazing. They are surprisingly rich in species, with many native grasses and well over 100 common wild flower plants. Nonflowering mosses, fungi and lichen or loose, unvegetated talus and scree slopes present the upper limit of the Alpine zone.

MOUNTAIN TREES

Some 25% of the Swiss Alps and pre-Alps are covered by forest. On mountain slopes, trees play a vital role in preventing winter avalanches. The average timberline in the Swiss Alps varies widely – from 1700m up to 2300m above sea level. Some common Alpine trees are described here.

Arolla Pine

Arolla pine (*Pinus cembra*, also called Swiss stone pine) is a high-mountain conifer with five needles on each bunch (rather than the two of other Swiss pines) that is rarely found below 1300m. This amazingly hardy tree can withstand extreme conditions well above the normal timberline – the highest specimens found are in the Valais at 2850m! Often taking on a twisted form, with a trunk up to 1.5m thick, arolla pine may live for 1000 years. Its resinous, purple-brown cones contain nuts that nourish birds, squirrels and foxes.

European Larch

Unique among the Swiss conifers, European larch (*Larix decidua*) is a deciduous tree that turns a striking golden colour before the first autumn storms strip the needles from the branches. If needles fall into a lake, an interesting phenomenon may sometimes be observed where they are rolled together to form 'larch balls'. Demanding dry, sunny conditions, larches are common in areas with a 'continental' climate such as the Valais or Graubünden. This highland species grows right up to the timberline (sometimes with Arolla pine), often in open stands with a heather understorey. Larch wood is harder and more weather resistant than any other Alpine timber, and for centuries it has been a favoured building material in mountain communities.

MARTIN MOOS

European larch

Mountain Maple

One of Switzerland's loveliest trees, the mountain maple *(Acer pseudoplatanus)* can reach an age of 500 years and a height of 40m. It prefers moist montane and Alpine sites, where its characteristic form is a broadly spread crown above a thick and gnarled old trunk, and in autumn its large leaves turn a striking red-gold colour.

Mountain Pine

Another large high-mountain conifer is the mountain pine *(Pinus montana)*. This tree can grow to 20m in height, and frequently occupies rocky ground or stabilised talus slopes where it may form pure stands. The mountain pine has oval-shaped cones with two-needle branchlets.

Mountain pine

Red Beech

Red beech *(Fagus sylvatica)* is the most abundant broadleaf tree in Switzerland. Preferring moist locations in the montane zone, beech forms almost pure stands in every region except the Engadine and Central and Upper Valais. The trees often attain a height of 45m and an age of 300 years. Beech forests are rich ecosystems, as the oily beech nuts are a major food for many birds and animals, particularly pheasants, squirrels and wild pigs. Beech has smooth, pearl-grey bark and oval-shaped leaves that in autumn turn golden brown before falling in a thick carpet on the forest floor (where they can form a dangerously slippery walking surface).

Red Spruce

Red spruce (*Picea excelsa*, also called Norway spruce) is a densely foliated conifer whose cones point downwards. Foresters and farmers have favoured this useful and fast-growing tree for centuries, and as a result the red spruce is ubiquitous throughout northern Switzerland, where it forms closed forests at altitudes of up to 1800m. Perhaps due to its (over) representation in the forests of Switzerland, in recent decades the red spruce has shown itself to be particularly susceptible to damage by acid rain and the bark beetle.

Silver Fir

Silver fir *(Abies alba)* is similar to, but has a much neater appearance than the much more common red spruce. Although it prefers moister and lower altitudes

Red spruce

Silver fir

– rarely growing above 1200m – the silver fir's range overlaps with the red spruce's and the two species are often found together. The silver fir is most easily distinguished from the latter by its cones, which protrude upwards like candles, and by a whitish tinge in its branches and trunk.

Sweet Chestnut

The sweet chestnut (*Castanea sativa*, sometimes called European chestnut) is a large, attractive tree with long serrated leaves. It develops hairy capsules that split open in autumn to release the ripe brown nuts – see the boxed text 'Ticino's Chestnut Forests' in the Ticino chapter.

ALPINE HEATHLAND PLANTS
Alpenrose or Alpine Rhododendron

Known as alpenroses in Switzerland, Alpine rhododendrons typify the high-Alpine landscape perhaps more than any other species of plant. Two species of rhododendron grow in the Swiss Alps; the rust-leaved alpenrose (*Rhododendron ferrugineum*) and the hairy alpenrose (*R. hirsutum*), often forming lovely rolling Alpine heaths up to 2500m. The most common is the rust-leaved alpenrose, which favours the acidic soils typical of Switzerland's mountain regions.

Bilberry & Blueberry

The bilberry (*Vaccinium gaultherioides*) and blueberry (*V. myrtillus*) are low shrubs found from sub-Alpine forest to well above tree line. The bilberry can be distinguished from the closely related blueberry by its slightly smaller, ovulate leaves compared to the latter's brighter and fleshier foliage, but in autumn the rusty-red hue of both species adds a melancholy charm to the highland slopes. The tangy berries, which ripen in August, tempt many a walker to stop and pick.

Dwarf Pine

KThe dwarf pine (*Pinus mugo*) grows mostly above the tree line, typically forming semiprostrate thickets on exposed Alpine slopes. It has thick, deep-green needles in tufts of two. Being well adapted to harsh conditions, this large, hardy shrub has been successfully planted in coastal land-stabilisation programs. Owing to its fragmented distribution, the dwarf pine has developed into several subspecies.

Alpenrose or Alpine rhododendron

FLORA & FAUNA OF SWITZERLAND

Dwarf Willows

Some of the most interesting plants are the half-dozen or so dwarf willows (*Salix* species) which grow in the sheltered sites of the Alpine heaths. The lesser willow *(Salix herbacea)* has pale green thinly serrated leaves about 2cm in length. It's one of the smallest trees in the world, rarely exceeding 5cm in height. The blunt-leaved willow *(S. retusa)* has small, shiny leaves and may reach 80cm or more, often growing up larger rocks, which remain warm after nightfall.

ALPINE WILD FLOWERS

The Alps have a florescent diversity and splendour equalled by few other mountain regions of the world. Amateur botanists can delight in learning to recognise the scores of different species of Alpine flora. Each species comes into bloom at a particular time (and/or at different elevations), so from spring to midsummer (from May to late July) the Alpine slopes always offer something interesting. There are numerous species of anemone, buttercups, daisies, gentians, lilies and orchids to name a just few.

Alpine Aster

The Alpine aster *(Aster alpinus)* is a small daisy-like wild flower found only in limestone regions, typically on cliffs or well-drained mountain slopes. It blooms throughout the summer months and the flowers have elongated bluish petals radiating around a striking yellow centre.

Bearded Bellflower

The bearded bellflower *(Campanula barbata)* grows up to 2600m and is common on mountain pastures. Blooming throughout the summer, its bell-shaped lilac-blue flowers and elongated leaves are covered with coarse, stiff hairs.

Glacier Buttercup

Numerous species of buttercup grow in the Swiss Alps, but the uncommon glacier buttercup (*Ranunculus glacialis*, also called the glacial crowfoot) is probably the most hardy Alpine wild flower of all. Seldom seen below 2000m, the glacier buttercup can survive at elevations of well over 4000m, establishing itself on scree slopes, moraine rubble or crevices in cliffs. The glacier buttercup has five white petals, which gradually turn pink.

Yellow gentian

White crocus

Edelweiss

Spring gentian

White Crocus

One of the mountain world's real early bloomers is the white crocus *(Crocus vernus)*, an Alpine saffron species. In spring and early summer this hardy plant pops its purplish-white flowers straight through the melting spring snows, and until other later species come into flower whole fields are dominated by white crocus – enough to fill every walker's heart with joy.

Edelweiss

Edelweiss *(Leontopodium alpinum)* prefers sunny and remote mountainsides, and blooms from July to September. The entire plant, including the delicate star-shaped flowers, is covered with a white felt-like coating that protects it against dehydration. Edelweiss is quite rare nowadays, and although walkers often still can't resist picking it, this lovely Alpine flower is strictly protected in all Swiss cantons.

Purple Gentian

A well-represented Alpine wild flower of the genus *Gentiana*, the purple gentian *(Gentiana purpurea)* has fleshy bell-shaped velvet-purple flowers clustered at the end of a single stem up to 60cm high. The attractive flower is found sporadically on mountain pastures and in Alpine heaths, and its roots contain bitter medicinal substances similar to those of the yellow gentian.

Spring Gentian

Spring gentians *(Gentia verna)* are one of the most attractive and widespread smaller Alpine wild flowers. These are those shy sparkles of violet-blue hiding among the Alpine herbfields or pastures. Spring gentians grow close to the ground in clusters and are best seen from April to early June.

Yellow Gentian

The yellow gentian *(Gentiana lutea)* has an appearance quite unlike other Alpine gentian species, which are mostly small with bluish flowers. A single plant may reach up to 70 years of age, each season producing anew a thick succulent stem up to 100cm high, which dies back again in autumn. The yellow gentian has long, leathery, cupped leaves and bunched bright yellow flowers. For centuries an astringent essence has been produced from the roots for medicinal purposes.

Globeflower

Favouring very moist or even waterlogged sites, the globeflower *(Trollius europaeus)* grows to 60cm in height and is commonly seen along meandering streams in the highland pastures. Blooming in early summer, with its cupped, yellow flowers it bears a passing resemblance to some buttercup species.

Martagon Lily

The martagon lily *(Lilium martagon)* has mauve petals curled back in a form reminiscent of a sultan's turban. Although not especially common, the martagon lily is one of the Alps' most flamboyant Alpine wild flowers, and blooms in June and July.

Yellow Alpine Pasqueflower

The yellow Alpine pasqueflower *(Pulsatilla sulphurea)*, a pretty Alpine anemone common on mountain meadows, produces a large, single six-petal flower that blooms from late spring until mid-summer. The flower matures into a white, hairy ball that looks vaguely like the head of a dandelion.

Alpine Poppy

The Alpine poppy *(Papaver alpinum*, sometimes called the Rhaetian poppy) is rare and is found only in the northern Alps at elevations above about 2000m. The flower buds hang in a 'nodding' position before opening out into attractive white blooms.

Thorny Thistle

Rather common in the Swiss Alps, the thorny thistle *(Cirsium spinosissimum)* is often the first larger plant encountered as you descend from the bare high-Alpine slopes into the vegetation line. Growing up to 50cm tall, the thorny thistle has a pale yellow crown with long spiny leaves. In autumn it dies back and starts to decay, giving off an odour distinctly reminiscent of sour socks.

Noble Wormwood

While not particularly common, noble wormwood *(Artemisia mutellina)* is found throughout the ranges of Central Switzerland. It is a small, delicate plant with numerous little yellow flower buds, which typically grows on steep, rocky mountainsides. When rubbed between the fingers the plant gives off an intense, aromatic odour. The noble wormwood has medicinal properties (an infusion made from the

Thorny thistle

CLEM LINDENMAYER

leaves is a cure for stomach upsets) and its bitter essence is the flavouring used in Vermouth.

FAUNA

As with the flora, many animals that now inhabit the Alpine region migrated there after the ice ages. Some, such as the snow hare and snow grouse, came from Arctic regions, while others, like the marmot, were originally inhabitants of Central Asia. Certain noxious animals have recently established themselves in Switzerland, most notably the enok (or 'marten dog') from eastern Asia. Other less-than-welcome newcomers are the racoon and muskrat, which were inadvertently introduced from North America.

Below is a list of native fauna of interest to walkers. It's educational to note how many species of native animal became extinct in Switzerland – many have since been reintroduced.

MAMMALS

Lynx

The largest native European cat species, the lynx (*Lynx lynx*) reaches a maximum length of 1.5m from head to tail. It has pointed ears ending in paintbrush-like tufts, a spotted ginger-brown coat and a short thick tail with a black tip. Originally found throughout the Swiss Alps, the lynx had been wiped out by the early 20th century. From 1970 onward lynx have been progressively re-released into the wild. Lynx typically prey on deer or chamois, although smaller mammals are also taken. They present absolutely no danger to humans.

KATE NOLAN

Lynx

Wolf

Like its bears, Switzerland's wolf population was persecuted to extinction in the 19th century. In recent decades there have been repeated remigrations of individual wolves into Swiss territory, but all animals have either been shot by maverick poachers or legally destroyed after they attacked sheep flocks. The Swiss Agency for the Environment, Forests and Landscape (see Internet Resources in the Facts for the Walker chapter; for information in German, French or Italian see **W** www.wolf-forum.ch) is promoting the use of sheepdogs to guard potentially endangered flocks and compensates herders for livestock killed by wolves. Wolves will probably make a comeback before bears in the Swiss Alps.

JOHN HAY

Wolf

Red Fox

The red fox *(Vulpes vulpes)* is found throughout Switzerland and is often seen by walkers. This intelligent opportunist can adapt to widely varying environments – from remote Alpine to densely populated urban – although it thrives best in areas of mixed field and forest. The fox may dig its own burrow, but prefers to enlarge an existing rabbit warren and may even co-inhabit the burrow of a badger. In spring the vixen – don't call her a bitch! – produces a litter of up to six whelps, which she takes with her on the hunt after just one month. Mice are the staple prey of foxes in Switzerland, but they will eat anything from frogs to beech nuts.

Red fox

Badger

Despite its being a member of the stoat and marten family, the badger *(Meles meles)* is more an omnivorous scavenger, as much accustomed to feeding on seeds and fruits as snails, birds or small mammals. Badgers are outstanding diggers, building surprisingly complex burrows, with several entrances and sleeping chambers. A social animal, the badger lives in family groups, visiting and overnighting in neighbouring burrows. Legendary for its cleanliness, the badger leaves no remains of its prey after feeding and – hikers take note! – carefully buries its excrement in neat funnel-shaped holes.

Badger

Marten

Cousins of weasels and stoats, several species of these small omnivorous hunters live in Switzerland. The adaptable stone marten *(Martes foina)* is brown except for a white patch on the collar, and ranges from lowland areas to well above the timberline but often also settles in urban areas. The tree marten *(M. martes)* is almost identical to the stone marten, but inhabits undisturbed montane forests. An excellent climber, the tree marten preys mainly on squirrels and mice, but also feeds on nuts, berries, insects and birds. In winter, marten are hunted or trapped in cages for their pelts.

Stoat

This smallest predator hunts rabbits, mice or birds. Living in the Swiss Alps up to an elevation of 3000m, the stoat *(Mustela erminea)* has a reddish-brown summer coat that turns snow-white for the winter season (when the animal is referred to as an ermine). The stoat kills its prey by biting deeply into the back

Tree marten

Red deer

Roe deer

Female ibex

of the head with its sharp teeth. For better observation of their surroundings, stoats often stop and sit up on their hind legs in a 'begging' position.

Wild Pigs

Wild pigs *(Sus scrofa)* mostly inhabit areas of deciduous forest, feeding largely on beech nuts and acorns, but may sometimes move up to Alpine pastures at over 2000m. During plentiful seasons the sows produce abundant litters, but a severe winter can decimate the herd. Although not often seen by walkers, wild pigs are much more common in Switzerland than is realised. Wallowing holes and turned-up ground left by foraging animals are an unmistakable indication of their presence. Wild pigs are unpopular with farmers, whose crops they sometimes raid; foresters, on the other hand, value pigs highly, since they destroy tree pests and prepare the ground for natural seeding.

Red Deer

Red deer *(Cervus elaphus)* are Switzerland's largest wild animals and range widely in forests and Alpine meadows. This is another species that was eradicated from the Swiss Alps, although natural restocking soon occurred through migrations from neighbouring Austria. Without its natural predators (the bear and wolf), red deer numbers have now increased so much that – despite continual cullings by hunters – they compete to the detriment of other native hoofed mammals. The animals have a reddish-brown summer coat, and every year the stags develop impressive antlers that are shed in spring. The stags' formidable mating roar can often be heard from as far as several kilometres away.

Roe Deer

Being active during the day, roe deer *(Capreolus capreolus)* are quite frequently seen in forested terrain right up to the tree line. Deer numbers were actually much lower in the 19th century than today, and they can be hunted legally in all parts of Switzerland. Roe deer eat shoots, buds, berries or fungi.

Ibex

A true mountain species, ibex *(Capra ibex)* have an outstanding affinity for the Alpine environment. These long-horned beasts normally stay well above the tree line, moving to the warmer south-facing mountainsides in winter. Ibex are related to domestic goats, and will occasionally breed with farm animals if unable to find a mate in the wild. Once relentlessly exploited for the (supposed) medicinal properties of the flesh and horns, by the early 1900s there were no ibex left in Switzerland. Since the animal's gradual reintroduction into the wild from a single small pure-blood population of Italian origin, numbers have increased so much that seasonal hunting of ibex is once again permitted.

Less timid and/or more curious than chamois, ibex are the most frequently sighted game animal in the Alps. Feeding on Alpine herbs, grasses and lichens, ibex are typically seen in small herds on craggy mountain ridge tops, from where they can survey the surrounding slopes. As long as walkers stay on their downhill side, ibex will generally allow you to approach within a reasonable distance.

Red squirrel

Chamois

A member of the antelope family, the chamois *(Rupicapra rupicapra)* is characteristic of the Alpine zone. Adapted to the mountain environment at least as well as the ibex, chamois are excellent climbers and jumpers, with spread hooves to avoid sinking into the snow. The animals have short crook-shaped horns and a reddish-brown summer coat with a black stripe along the spine. Their diet consists of lichen, grass, herbs or pine needles. Although generally shy, chamois are very abundant in Alpine regions and mountain walkers have an excellent chance of spotting them.

Red Squirrel

Unlike in Britain, where the red squirrel *(Sciurus vulgaris)* has become rather scarce due to competition from the larger introduced North American grey squirrel, these small arboreal rodents are quite common in the coniferous forests of Switzerland. Eluding the eyes of earthbound humans, this shy creature rarely leaves the treetops, where it largely feeds on pine or beech nuts. In autumn squirrels bury the nuts as food reserves, but the winter snows make it hard for them to locate all these storage spots. Since some seeds stay in the ground to germinate, squirrels make an important contribution to the regeneration of their forest habitat.

Alpine Marmot

Alpine marmots *(Marmota marmota)* live in large colonies of extensive burrows. With the coming of the

KATE NOLAN
Alpine marmot

LISA BORG

Brown bear

Brown Bear

Switzerland's last brown bear *(Ursus arctos)* was shot in the Engadine village of S-charl in September 1904.

Bears demand a habitat of extensive forest with steep-sided slopes (preferably cliffs) as a protective retreat and local vegetation rich in berries and roots, and an abundance of small prey (like marmots) or larger animals to supply plenty of carrion.

Having now enjoyed protection for more than half a century, Western Europe's populations of wild bears have increased considerably. With small but resilient populations of brown bears existing in the adjoining Trentino region of Italy, the expectation that individual animals will one day wander across the border to re-establish Switzerland's bear populations is not unreasonable. Whether through migration or by deliberate reintroduction, it's likely that within the coming decades bears will again live and breed in the wilds of the Swiss Alps.

first snowfalls, the burrow entrance is sealed off with grass and stones before the animals begin their long winter hibernation. During this time they survive exclusively on the fat reserves built up over the bountiful summer months.

Marmots are extremely alert and wary, and at the slightest sign of danger will let out a shrill whistling sound to warn other members of the colony, who immediately head for shelter. Marmots are most easily observed in the autumn, when they are considerably slowed by their heavy fat reserves – a pair of binoculars and a discreet, quiet manner of approach will also help.

Snow Hare

The snow hare *(Lepus timidus)* is widely distributed throughout the Alps, where it typically feeds on twigs and grasses found in Alpine heathlands. Smaller than the lowland subspecies of hare, in summer the snow hare has reddish-brown fur with white-tinged ears and tail but in winter the entire coat turns snowy white. Snow hares are solitary and nocturnal creatures, and are not often seen.

BIRDS

According to recent ornithological surveys, some 385 species of bird inhabit Switzerland for at least part of the year (although almost 100 of these species are rarely seen). See also the boxed text 'The Chough' in the Valais chapter.

Bearded Vulture

With a wingspan of up to 2.8m and a body length of more than 1m, the bearded vulture *(Gypaetus barbatus)* is Europe's largest bird of prey. The bearded vulture (also called lammergeier, from the German term meaning 'lamb vulture') was mercilessly persecuted as a supposed predator of sheep, and finally became extinct in Switzerland in 1886. Having been reintroduced into the wild only in the early 1990s, the bird still occupies a tenuous niche in the Alpine habitat.

MARTIN HARRIS

Bearded vulture

The vulture typically preys on marmots or hares, but finds plenty to eat during the Alpine winter when animals are killed by avalanches or fall to their deaths due to icy conditions. Living in strongly bonded pairs, bearded vultures generally nest on exposed cliff ledges to allow for better take off. The birds vigorously defend their territory against competitors, and territorial fights often end in the death of one of the birds.

The plumage of the bearded vulture is slate black in colour apart from a darker stripe by its eyes. Unlike other vulture species, its head is completely covered with feathers, with a tuft of bristle-like plume under the chin. Even from a relatively close distance, it is hard to distinguish from the golden eagle.

Golden Eagle

Although sometimes called the 'king of the Alps', the golden eagle *(Aquila chrysaetos)* was once rather less common in the Alpine zone, but took refuge in the mountains to escape human persecution in its original lowland habitat. With a wingspan of up to 2.5m, the bird can frequently be observed gliding around the highest peaks seeking its prey. Marmots are the bird's staple food, but it also regularly attacks larger animals trapped in snowdrifts or injured by falls. The golden eagle is now fully protected throughout Switzerland, with several hundred breeding pairs.

Alpine Jackdaw

The Alpine jackdaw *(Pyrrhocorax pyrrhocorax)* has pitch-black feathers and a yellow beak. A relative of the common crow, this hardy opportunist is a constant companion throughout the mountains. Alpine jackdaws are often seen swooping around mountain-top

Golden eagle

Snow grouse

restaurants in search of discarded food scraps, but walkers should refrain from deliberately feeding them. The birds normally feed on worms, insects or berries.

Snow Finch

The small white, black and brown snow finch (*Montifringilla nivalis*) is an exclusively Alpine bird. Never venturing below the timberline even in winter, it nests in very high sites up to 3000m – anywhere from sheltered nooks in mountain huts to crevices on the north wall of the Eiger. Normally eating insects and seeds, the snow finch (which is really a member of the sparrow family) has a tendency to scrounge for food scraps around sites frequented by humans.

Snow Grouse

Like the snow finch, the snow grouse (*Lagopus mutus*) is a true mountain species well adapted to the Alpine zone. On winter nights the bird digs itself an insulating cavity in the snow, wandering the exposed, snow-free slopes in search of food during the day. Like the stoat and the mountain hare, the snow grouse camouflages itself for the winter by turning from a sprinkled brown to a snowy-white colour. With the sprouting of the mountain vegetation in spring, the snow grouse feeds on the protein-rich new shoots, moving progressively up the mountainside as the summer awakens.

REPTILES
Snakes

All of Switzerland's eight native species of snake are endangered and protected by law. Two species of viper, *Vipera aspis* and *V. berus*, are venomous, although their bite is fatal only in extremely rare cases. Snakes are fairly uncommon in northern Switzerland and they keep very much to themselves even south of the Alps. Being cold-blooded, snakes go into a seasonal torpor during the winter months, so your best chance of seeing them is in spring when they're still in a slow and sluggish state.

Lizards

Easily mistaken for a snake is the copper-coloured slowworm (*Anguis fragilis*), a common legless lizard that prefers a moist environment close to forest clearings. The spotted brown mountain lizard (*Lacerta vivipara*) grows to a length of 15cm, and can live up to an altitude of 3000m.

MARTIN HARRIS

Slowworm

ECOLOGY & ENVIRONMENT

Switzerland's natural habitats, particularly its Alpine environment, are under assault from a myriad of sources.

Of particular concern is forest dieback. This phenomenon, often known by its German name of *Waldsterben*, is largely caused by acid rain from industrial and motor vehicle pollutants. Acid rain damages trees' foliage and stunts growth by 'souring' the soil, often many hundreds of kilometres away from the pollution source. Average concentrations of some air-borne pollutants are not much greater in cities than they are high up in the Alps.

A wide-scale survey in 2000 found that three out of 10 trees in Swiss forests – whether broadleaf or conifer – have major damage from acid rain. The main problem is sulphuric acid, an end-product of industrial and automobile combustion, which directly attacks trees' foliage and acidifies the soil, destroying root systems.

Global warming is evident in the steady recession of Switzerland's glaciers and névés. Climatologists are predicting that up to 90% of glaciers in the Alps will have melted by 2100 and that only areas above 1500m will stay snow-covered throughout the winter. Glaciers act as a giant frozen reservoir of freshwater, and since glacial meltwater accounts for a large part of the summer flow of the large rivers that drain the Swiss Alps – such as the Rhine and the Rhône – this will have undesirable consequences for everything from hydroelectricity production to river navigation to agriculture (particularly in the parched Central Valais). The lower level of permafrost in the Swiss Alps, currently at around 2400m, is gradually moving upward, causing instability and landslides on the thawing mountainsides.

For several decades now, foresters have noted a small but significant 'upward creep' of the tree line in the Swiss Alps – another effect of gradual rising average temperatures. Exotic evergreen plants originally from warmer climes appear to have gained a major foothold in the broadleaf forests of Ticino, where their presence was previously quite marginal.

Another worrying problem is the continuing plague of bark beetles in Swiss forests. These insects weaken trees by boring under the bark to feed on the sap, leaving the trunk exposed and causing fungal rot. Walkers may often notice black-plastic traps positioned in forest areas throughout Switzerland in order to control the spread of the bark beetle.

The further expansion of the already dense road system is of major concern to Swiss conservationists. New motorways are planned for the Central Valais and Goms regions, and hundreds of kilometres of new 'access' tracks are bulldozed and blasted in Alpine regions every year. Under its new bilateral treaty with the European Union (see People later), Switzerland has been forced to allow 40-tonne trucks from EU countries to use its highways – there was previously a 28-tonne limit. As part of the Neue Alpeneisenbahntransversale (NEAT) project, over the coming decades Switzerland will invest tens of billions of francs (!) in new railway tunnels through the Simplon

---

The Alpine Convention

Largely at the instigation of the International Commission for the Protection of the Alps (CIPRA; see Internet Resources in the Facts for the Walker chapter), Europe's seven Alpine countries – Austria, France, Germany, Italy, Liechtenstein, Slovenia and Switzerland – signed the Alpine Convention in 1991. The Alpine Convention aims to:

- protect and restore natural landscapes and ecosystems

- promote the sustainable use of the Alps' resources

- minimise the environmental impact of tourism and motor traffic in the Alps

- assist increasingly stressed Alpine agricultural communities to restructure along sustainable lines

- coordinate research and the scientific monitoring of the Alpine environment

- provide a forum for conflicting interests

and Gotthard massifs, allowing heavy trucks to transit the country on special 'piggy-back' shuttle trains.

Use of the Alps as a prime recreation zone often conflicts with its role as a last strong-hold for many species of animals and plants. Alpine tourism, most particularly the skiing industry, has turned many once quiet and charming mountain villages into sprawling holiday centres. New lifts with an ever-greater carrying capacity are being installed, and the sheer numbers of visitors (including walkers) contributes to the ecological degra-dation. Walkers can make a worthwhile con-tribution to conservation in the Alps by using public rather than private transport where possible; see also Responsible Walking in the Facts for the Walker chapter.

NATIONAL PARKS & RESERVES
Although its neighbours have all been active in establishing major new nature reserves and national parks in recent years, Switzer-land continues to buck the European trend. The country has just one national park (the Swiss National Park, set up almost 100 years ago in Graubünden's Engadine region) and only a handful of nature reserves of signifi-cant size (such as the Vanil Noir in the Fri-bourg pre-Alps and the Plaun la Greina in south-eastern Graubünden). There are sev-eral hundred other nature reserves, but most are quite small – sometimes just a few 'token' hectares – or are informal arrangements with no real assurance of long-term protection.

Pro Natura has proposed that around 20% of Switzerland's land area should eventu-ally be protected by nature reserves, with no less than eight large national parks and up to 100 wilderness areas or biosphere re-serves. The organisation has recently launched a campaign to establish a second national park in Switzerland, but has re-ceived only luke-warm local support from either of its preferred 'candidates' – the Maderanertal in Uri canton and the Aletsch region in Valais.

Nature reserves are often viewed locally as a hindrance to economic development, although many attract significant numbers of tourists. The conservation movement is often frustrated by the need to accommo-date all local interests in a country with relatively dense populations and intensive land use. This is particularly difficult within Switzerland's decentralised (and fraction-alised) political system.

PEOPLE
Switzerland marks the division between the western and eastern Alps, and hence the cul-tural border between Latin-based (French, Italian and Romansch) and Germanic lan-guage groups. Switzerland has a population of just over seven million (171 inhabitants per sq km), of which around 19% are for-eign citizens. German-speaking Swiss ac-count for 66%, francophone Swiss for 18%, Italian speakers for 10% and Romansch for just 1% of the population.

Despite sharing the trappings of a nation-state, Switzerland's three main ethnic group-ings don't actually mix a great deal. Many French Swiss (Suisses Romands) know Paris better than Zürich, and – in spite of their la-tent anti-German prejudices – the German Swiss (Deutschschweizer) grudgingly orient themselves toward their powerful northern neighbour. The Italian Swiss (Svizzeri Ital-iani) complain that their northern compatri-ots treat them virtually as if they *were* Italians, although most of them do seem to get around in Alfas, Fiats or Ferraris!

French and German Swiss often jokingly refer to their cultural and geographical divi-sions as the Röstigraben (the 'Rösti Trench'; *Fossé de Röschti* in French). In the last decade or so, however, fundamental differ-ences have emerged between French Swiss and German Swiss regarding their country's future within Europe. The former are over-whelmingly in favour of Switzerland joining the EU, while a resolute majority of German Swiss reject EU membership. Interregional tensions were defused – at least for the time being – when in mid-2000 the Swiss people voted decisively in favour of a bilateral treaty regulating cross-border trade, employ-ment and transport between Switzerland and the EU.

continued on page 45

Rural Architecture

A remarkable feature of the Swiss countryside is the diversity in traditional architecture. Local architectural styles reflect cultural influences as much as the local topography and the availability of certain building materials, and have developed gradually over a period lasting centuries. Traditional houses in rural regions of German-speaking Switzerland tend to be wood based, while the French, Italian and Romansch Swiss generally build in stone. Also rather different is the traditional settlement pattern, with German Swiss often living in scattered settlements of independently organised farms, while the Latin cultures show a preference for clustered villages in which farming, social and leisure activities are organised communally. One unifying thing that changes little from canton to canton, however, are the ubiquitous flower boxes filled with bright-red geraniums that adorn houses.

Appenzell-Toggenburg Style

The typical houses of the Appenzellerland and the Toggenburg are wooden constructions with a shingled exterior. Their low ceilings (which never bothered their generally small-statured Appenzeller occupants) give them a quaint 'doll's house' character. Along the front of the building between each floor is a narrow overhanging canopy running above the windows, which have built-in sliding shutters. Until fairly recently many rural households relied on additional income from weaving and embroidering, and many houses in this region have extensions with larger windows that provide more natural light. Rural scenes are frequently painted on the house facade in a traditional 'naïve' style.

A simple Bernese-style wooden farmhouse.

Bernese Style

The grandiose wooden architecture of the Bernese Oberland gradually developed between 1600 and 1850, and is a testimony to the prosperity and self-confidence of the Alpine dairy farmers, who saw no need to imitate the stone houses of the urban gentry. With their enormous overhanging roofs, the massive Bernese farmhouses are recognisable to English speakers as the much imitated 'Swiss chalet' style. Typically, ornate designs are carved and/or painted onto the wooden exterior along with biblical and folk sayings. Some of the finest examples of the Bernese Oberland style can be seen in the Simmental or the Hasliberg area of the Haslital.

The traditional houses of an Engadine village.

Engadine (Bündner) Style

The standard structural form in (formerly) Romansch-speaking regions of Graubünden, the Engadine (or Bündner) style integrates farmhouse, barn,

Rural Architecture

cowshed and granary within a single large building. The massive stone walls can be up to 1.5 metres thick, and are traditionally adorned with *sgraffito* – geometric or floral designs, which are scratched into the exterior rendering before it sets. Some of the best examples are the grand old houses of the Val Müstair or Lower Engadine, many having been originally built by local mercenaries who returned from foreign wars much the richer.

Central Swiss Style

The traditional multi-storey wooden houses of Central Switzerland typically rest on a heavy stone ground-floor foundation. They have sharply tilted gables that maximise attic storage space (and hence implied a level of prosperity). The external, heavily shingled (in modern times tiled) 'pre-roofs', which are similar to, although more pronounced than, those of Appenzell-Toggenburger houses – separate the floors.

Traditional Riegelhaus, Zürich Canton, Central Switzerland.

Fribourg Style

The most striking feature of the houses in the Fribourg pre-Alps is their disproportionately large roofs. Rows of elaborately arranged shingles protect the structure from the moist climate of the region, while the single-storey base of the farmhouse seems to hide below the wooden canopy. In many of the farmhouses and alp huts

in the Fribourg pre-Alps the chimney can be sealed off with an external wooden board that keeps out rain and snow. So-called *poyas* – colourfully painted scenes on exterior wooden panels similar to those seen on Appenzell houses – typically depict the annual driving of cattle up to the highland pastures.

Jura Style

Built for the severe Jurassian winters, the mountain farmhouses of the Jura are generally stone structures with

Chalet de Chaude, on the Col de Chaude walk, has a sweeping shingle roof typical of the Fribourg and Vaud regions.

shingled roofs, and roofed forecourts accessible via large arched gateways. It may seem surprising that stone is the almost universal building material in an area with such abundant forests. This was due to the historical dominance of Basel, which forbade the use of wood for building since it was needed to fire the city's iron-smelting works.

Rural Architecture *continued*

The idyllic summer hamlet of Compietto, in the Val di Carassino, northern Ticino.

Ticino Style

Typically, houses in Ticino are small, square dwellings with thick drystone walls and heavy slab-rock roofs. Space is arranged vertically, with a ground-floor kitchen below the living room and bedrooms, which are accessible only via an outside stairway. The sunny side of the house often has a grapevine arbour for summer shade. Hay barns and milking sheds are unattached, and usually situated in the fields well away from the village. In the northern part of Ticino a style know as the 'Gotthard house' developed, which blended the wood-based styles typical of regions north of the Alps with the local stone-based architecture.

Valaisan Style

The heavy timber houses of Valaisan farms and villages present another of Switzerland's romantic architectural styles. Traditional Valaisan-style buildings are constructed of larch, whose durable reddish timber gradually blackens after centuries of exposure to the elements, and roofed with heavy stone slabs up to 4cm thick. Typically, buildings are wooden, single-purpose structures, with separate barn, granary and living quarters. Striking features of the small, square Valaisan granaries are rounded stone plates fixed between the wooden pillars and the upper building to keep out thieving rodents. Medieval Walser immigrants from Goms in the upper Valais were responsible for introducing the heavy timber houses to many parts of Graubünden and Ticino.

The tiny village of Tanay, with its traditional timber homes, lies among craggy limestone peaks, Valais.

Alpine Herders

The annual tradition of driving cattle up to graze on the highland pastures for the summer dates back thousands of years in the Alps. Until quite recently it was usual for many mountain families to spend several months in virtual isolation up in the mountains. Feeding on nourishing Alpine herbs and grasses, the animals produce high-quality milk. Since the milk needed to be processed quickly to avoid spoiling, the technique of cheese-making was perfected early by the Alpine Swiss.

The animals are driven up into the mountains between late May and late June – this is always a festive occasion known as *Alpaufzug* in German and *inalpe* in French. Farmers often dress up in their traditional regional costumes, play music and adorn their cows with flowers and coloured ribbons; each animal is refitted with its own large cowbell suspended from a thick leather collar. The older animals, having made the same annual journey perhaps 10 times or more, know the way and guide the herd.

Once the cattle are up on the high pastures, the Alpine herders have little rest. Despite modern technical aids their days are still very hard. Work begins at around 5am and continues until 9pm, when the cowhands can finally bed down in the (often quite primitive) alp hut. Daily tasks include milking, processing the cheese or butter and tending the fragile mountain pastures. As the grass is eaten down the herds are driven from meadow to meadow, grazing only for a short period on the uppermost pastures.

Highland pastures, or 'alps', are usually the property of the valley community, which engages a herder to tend the various farmers' herds for the duration of the summer. The hard and lonely work of tending to the cows from dawn to dusk is not everyone's ideal summer pastime, and nowadays finding suitable cowhands is not always easy. For this reason an increasing number of steers are driven up to the highland pastures for fattening, as they require much less attention than dairy cattle.

In early autumn, when the Alpine vegetation is already beginning to wind down for the winter, the driving down of the cattle begins. Known as the *Alpabzug* or *desalpe*, this is also an important festive occasion.

continued from page 41

In terms of lifestyle, the real contrasts within Swiss society are urban/rural, not French/German. Most Swiss farms are only viable with massive subsidies – some mountain farmers receive almost half their income in direct payments from the government. While urban Swiss taxpayers often grumble about the enormous expense of subsidising agriculture, most are pleased to see 'traditional' farming culture preserved, especially when it also pleases the tourists! Many of the country's most celebrated folk traditions and activities – from yodelling and playing the Alphorn to competitive sports like body wrestling and flag swinging – are still widespread in rural areas.

Facts for the Walker

Highlights

- Best one-day traverse: the Faulhornweg in the Bernese Oberland

- Best multi-day traverse: the Rhätikon Höhenweg

- Most impressive cirque: Creux de Van in the Swiss Jura

- Easiest lookout summit: Monte Tamaro in Ticino

- Most challenging lookout peak: the 3243m summit of the Wildstrubel in the Bernese Oberland

- Wildest scenery: the Val Cluozza in the Swiss National Park in Graubünden

- Best wild-flower walk: the Stockhorn Circuit in the Bernese Oberland

- Most spectacular view: the rock pyramid of the Matterhorn from the Grindjisee in the Valais

SUGGESTED ITINERARIES

Your itinerary will be largely determined by how long you spend in Switzerland. As travelling between different regions will probably take at least half a day, walkers with less time would do best to concentrate on areas closer to their entry/exit points (which are likely to be Basel, Geneva and Zürich). If you have more than a few weeks, internal travelling times will not be such a consideration. Before you go, make a wish-list of the walks that particularly interest you.

One Week

If you want to do any serious walking, there will only be time to visit one or (maximum) two regions, preferably the Bernese Oberland and/or the Valais. For your first short walking trip to Switzerland consider the Grosse Scheidegg, the Faulhornweg and the Hotürli routes in eastern Bernese Oberland

or the Höhenweg Höhbalmen and Riffelalp to Sunnegga walks near Zermatt in the Valais.

Two Weeks

Consider the following walks along with those suggested above: Mont Tendre, in the Southern Swiss Jura, the Zwinglipass, in North-Eastern Switzerland, or Fuorcla da Cavardiras from Central Switzerland into Graubünden.

One Month

A really fulfilling way to spend your month – with plenty of time for rest days, bad weather and even some sightseeing – is to walk the classic Alpine Pass Route from Sargans to Montreux.

Two Months

You'll really have some fun, but still don't expect to bag all the walks on your wish-list. After you've done the more popular and/or easier walks, take advantage of your extra time to visit remoter areas, such as the Swiss National Park and Plaun la Greina in Graubünden or the Val Maggia and Val Verzasca in Ticino.

WHEN TO WALK

The walking season in Switzerland starts in mid-spring (May/June), and depending on autumn snowfalls can last until well into November.

In general, the lower the area, the longer its walking season. In the high-Alpine zone above 2500m the snow-free period can differ from season to season, with the most dramatic variations in autumn. While in warmer years newly fallen snow will melt away repeatedly until the winter starts to set in from late November, in colder years the snow may start to accumulate from early October.

Although each month has its own particular attractions and disadvantages, the recommended time for walking is from mid-August until late October, when the weather is generally cooler and more settled.

Spring

Spring officially begins in late March, but at that time skiers are still whizzing down the slopes of the Alps and the snow-free area is below 1000m. In June the sections of the path in higher areas may still be snow-bound, though not necessarily impassable. Alpine wild flowers, most notably alpenroses, are at their prime in mid to late June. In June the days reach their maximum length, with over 15 hours of sunlight.

Summer

Summer only really gets under way toward the end of June. Particularly in the Alps, thunderstorms occur frequently until about mid-August. The hot, humid weather at this time of year can make walking a sticky and uncomfortable affair. The sun can be surprisingly penetrating, but swimming in lakes and rivers is a major compensation (see the boxed text 'Swimming'). The moisture in the air makes for hazy conditions in midsummer, and while this often cuts out the fine Alpine views, the mist-shrouded peaks develop an enchanting atmosphere.

Autumn

Autumn begins in late September, and typically brings long periods of fine, settled weather. The brilliant golden and red colours of the forests and Alpine heathland give this season a special flavour. Autumn is perhaps the best time for walking in the Swiss Jura or the ranges of southern Ticino (Sottoceneri), when a carpet of thick fog covers the lowlands of the Swiss Mittelland and the Lombardy Plain of Italy, while the mountain heights bask in balmy sunshine.

Unfortunately, many postbus and mountain-transport services stop running in late October, making access to these areas difficult even though the weather conditions may still be suitable well after then. Remember also that at this time of the year any major deterioration in the weather is liable to bring snowfalls down to 1500m or lower.

November is a highly unpredictable time for walking. The daylight period is rather short (around nine hours), so late-autumn walkers should get an early start and plan their routes carefully. By the time the winter begins in late December, the only areas free of snow and ice are in lowland regions.

WHAT KIND OF WALK?

Routes described in this guidebook cover virtually every major landscape in Switzerland, from river flats and gorges, mountain moors and forested valleys, Alpine hayfields and wild flower meadows, glacial cirques and snow basins to rock ridges and craggy peaks. Many walks cross mountain passes that have been transit points for people and wildlife for thousands of years or follow historic routes along old aqueducts, stone-laid mule tracks, pilgrim trails or even ancient Roman roads. Although small areas can often be described as 'wild', true wilderness is rare in Switzerland. While certain remoter routes may not pass a village or road for days, you are never more than a long day's walk from civilisation.

Although walkers sometimes camp out in the mountains (especially in Ticino), 'wild' camping is frowned on in Switzerland. Walkers generally stay either at mountain huts and alp restaurants along the route or at hostels and hotels down in the valley. Some walkers, however, particularly those on a tight budget, carry a tent and sleeping bag, staying at organised camping grounds.

Swimming

In the sweaty weather of midsummer, cool mountain lakes and rivers can be an irresistible place for a refreshing splash. Even lowland lakes and rivers in Switzerland are exceptionally clean by European standards, and up in the hills they are of drinking-water quality. Common sense says to check the water temperature before you take the plunge – some higher Alpine lakes stay *very* chilly throughout the hottest weeks of July and August. With its southerly climes and wild waters, Ticino is unquestionably the best place for swimming. Topless bathing is now widely accepted, but skinny dipping (ie, nude bathing) is OK only in less-frequented swimming spots.

Winter Walking & Snowshoeing

Winter walking is enjoyed by a growing number of people – many of whom are fed up with the hectic pace and crowds on the ski slopes. Almost all mountain resorts snow-clear at least some of their walking trails for the benefit of winter walkers. Wild animals shelter in the snowbound mountain forests during winter, and are highly sensitive to any kind of disturbance due to their seasonally low energy reserves. For this reason winter walkers should keep to main pathways and avoid making unnecessary noise.

Also increasingly popular are more adventurous snowshoe treks on uncleared paths. The extremity of winter conditions makes 'backcountry' snowshoeing trips in the Alps a serious and often strenuous undertaking. Due to the danger of avalanches, it's not advisable to walk above the forest line without solid experience or professional guidance.

Many local outdoor tour operators and mountaineering schools organise snowshoe trips (around Sfr80/180/1000 per day/overnight/week). Several of the best are listed below.

Alpinschule Tödi
(☎ 055-283 43 82, W www.bergschule.ch) Kirchhaldenstrasse 25b, CH-8722, Kaltbrunn. Organises many guided multi-day snowshoe hikes in Uri, the Bernese Oberland and Ticino.

Höhenfieber
(☎ 032-361 18 18, W www.hoehenfieber.ch) Postfach 290, CH-2501 Biel. Offers multi-day treks (some overnighting in igloos) in all regions except the Valais.

Kaderli Tours
(☎/fax 033-855 36 81) PO Box 567, CH-3823 Wengen. Also runs trips in the Jungfrau region.

Per Pedes Bergferien
(☎ 01-461 70 00, e info@ppb.ch, W www.ppb.ch) Postfach 8728, 8036 Zürich. Has a broad range of winter walks throughout Switzerland.

Swiss Alpine Guides
(☎ 033-822 60 00, W www.swissalpineguides.ch) Interlaken. Runs day and overnight walks in the Jungfrau region.

ORGANISED WALKS

Although this book is intended primarily for 'self-guided' walkers who want to organise their walks independently, some readers may still opt for the greater comfort and convenience of a professionally guided walk. The Swiss Hiking Federation, the Swiss Friends of Nature (see Useful Organisations later) and many tourist offices organise guided walks, mostly from one to several days in length.

Local outdoor companies cater largely to Swiss walkers, but guides normally speak fluent English and foreigners are welcome. The cost of a seven-day guided walk is typically around Sfr1100, excluding travel to Switzerland. Some of the local operators are listed below – see also the boxed text 'Winter Walking & Snowshoeing'. For guided walks run by companies abroad, see Walk Operators Abroad in the Getting There & Away chapter.

Baumeler Reisen (☎ 041-418 65 65, fax 418 65 96, e info@baumeler.ch, W www.baumeler.ch) Zinggentorstrasse 1, CH-6002 Lucerne. Offers a good range of mostly seven-day treks in the Bernese Oberland, Graubünden, Säntis region and Ticino.

Grossenbacher Trekking (☎/fax 071-845 24 29) Mühlebergstrasse 7, CH-9403 Goldach. Leads treks in Graubünden, Ticino and the Swiss Jura.

RBM Eurotrek (☎ 01-434 33 66, e eurotrek @rbm.ch, W www.eurotrek.ch) Vulkanstrasse 116, 8048 Zürich. Organises numerous outdoor trips, including several guided walks in the Bernese Oberland, Ticino and the Swiss Jura.

ACCOMMODATION

In most parts of Switzerland a wide range of accommodation is available to walkers.

Tourist offices always have current lists of accommodation in all price brackets; sometimes a small booking fee and/or a deposit on the price of the room is charged. Except in the case of the most basic mattress- room accommodation (such as in mountain huts), breakfast is invariably included in the price. Lower-budget places normally give the standard 'continental' breakfast consisting of bread and jam with a pot of coffee or tea, but more upmarket hotels generally offer a breakfast buffet. In better hotels in many mountain resorts a low-, mid- and high-season rate applies with a seasonal price variation of at least 20%. Rates at budget hotels are less variable, but you may still be able to bargain them down slightly.

Web sites of local tourist offices generally offer the best online accommodation listings, but useful general sites are given in the following sections.

In Towns & Cities

Organised Camping Organised camping grounds offer the cheapest and arguably best-value places to stay. Camping grounds are often sited along a riverside or by a lake, and amenities are generally excellent; most have a pay laundry – otherwise difficult to find even in larger towns – and some offer basic cooking facilities. Tent sites cost from Sfr5 per night, with an additional charge of around Sfr7 per adult camper. Many camping grounds also have on-site caravans (trailers) costing around Sfr25 per night, and some have dorms (from around Sfr15).

Most camping grounds are affiliated with the Touring Club of Switzerland (W www .tcs.ch) or the Swiss Camping Association (W www.campingswiss.ch). The Web sites of both organisations give up-to-date listings, and each publishes an annual camping guide available in bookshops and service stations. Try W www.campingnet.ch to find camping grounds throughout Switzerland.

Youth Hostels Swiss Youth Hostels (see Useful Organisations) runs almost 60 hostels in cities, towns and villages throughout the country. Although some regions – particularly the Valais and Ticino – are poorly

covered, youth hostels often make ideal bases for walks within a region.

Youth hostels offer accommodation mainly in small dorms, but increasingly hostellers have a choice of paying a bit more for their own (double or family) room. Almost half of Switzerland's youth hostels have cooking facilities for hostellers. Some cater mainly to groups and may be booked out at various times. Reception is usually closed between 9am and 5pm. Overnight fees vary, but the average charge for members/ nonmembers is around Sfr25/30 including breakfast.

Friends of Nature Hostels The Swiss Friends of Nature (Naturfreunde Schweiz, Amis de la Nature Suisse) runs almost 90 hostels throughout the country. Each hostel (known as Naturfreundehaus in German or Maison des Amis de la Nature in French) is located in a mountain region or close to a nature reserve. Friends of Nature hostels are open to everyone, although members receive a 30% discount. Prices and conditions vary considerably depending on amenities and location, ranging from as little as around Sfr12, to Sfr35 for nonmembers. For more information on the Swiss Friends of Nature see Useful Organisations later.

Private Rooms Similar to English bed-and-breakfast establishments, places offering private rooms are most easily found through the local tourist office. They normally only have a small number of beds from around Sfr45 per person per night – comparable in price to budget hotels. The Web site W www.homestay.ch has listings of private rooms throughout Switzerland.

Hotels & Pensions In valley towns and villages, hotels and pensions are the main form of accommodation. Prices vary considerably depending on the region or time of year, but the rate for a simple room with wash basin and external shower and toilet typically starts at around Sfr35 or Sfr40. Breakfast is usually served from around 7am, but walkers keen to make that 'Alpine start' can usually arrange for an earlier sitting.

The Switzerland Tourism Web site (W www .switzerlandtourism.ch) or the Swiss Hotel Association's site (W www.swisshotels.ch) are both useful for finding places to stay in the average to mid-range anywhere in Switzerland (including discounted 'last minute' offers).

Holiday Apartments Self-contained holiday apartments can be found in and around just about every tourist resort in the country. Apartment accommodation is probably best suited to families or walking groups who need a walking base for a week or two. Tourist offices always have listings of locally available holiday apartments.

On the Walk
Wild Camping Although at times you may spy walkers making camp in some forest clearing or beside an Alpine lake, camping outside organised camping grounds – so-called 'wild' camping – is officially prohibited in Switzerland. In practice this rule is not strictly enforced provided wild campers are discreet and leave the site as they found it. Walkers who camp off limits should at least follow these basic rules:

- Exercise great circumspection when choosing a camp site; keep well away from official walking routes, farmhouses or mountain huts, and if possible ask permission first before pitching your tent
- Don't light a campfire except at established fireplaces
- To spare the fragile mountain vegetation, don't camp longer than one night at any one place
- Practise hygiene: defecate well away from lakes and streams and dispose properly of your bodily wastes
- Leave the site just as you found it – take all your rubbish with you

Alp Huts The most basic places to stay in the mountains are 'alp huts' – the simple dwellings of the Alpine herders (and their families) who spend their summers high up in the Alps. Along more popular walking routes, alp huts often have milk and cheese for sale or offer simple meals and refreshments. At some you can even sleep in the

straw for as little as Sfr5 per night. (Note, however, that most alp huts are solely farm businesses, and have nothing to offer walkers.) Conditions in alp huts can be rather spartan – the communal sleeping quarters may be the cowshed loft and the washing facilities an icy-cold spring-water fountain. Alp huts give walkers a real taste (and smell) of what life in the high mountains is all about.

Alp huts are not to be confused with mountain huts.

Mountain Huts Although there are still a few minor gaps in the national network, Switzerland has the most extensive and best maintained system of mountain huts *(Berghütten, cabanes de montagne, capanni di montagne)* anywhere in the world. Most of these huts are owned by the Swiss Alpine Club (SAC) or some other mountain club (see Useful Organisations later).

Simple dorms or 'mattress rooms' *(Massenlager, dortoirs, dormitori)* are the standard sleeping arrangement in all mountain huts, although occasionally rooms are also available. Mountain huts always supply plenty of woollen blankets, so carrying a sleeping bag is optional, although for reasons of hygiene walkers are expected to bring their own youth-hostel approved sleeping sheet. Most mountain huts in Switzerland – with the partial exception of Ticino – do not have a kitchen for the use of guests, although cooked meals are available at fairly reasonable prices. An evening meal – simple dishes like stew, cheese fondue or *rösti* are cooks' favourites – generally costs around Sfr18, and breakfast about Sfr8 per person. Few mountain huts have showers, but there are usually basic facilities for (cold-water) washing. Snack foods, soft drinks, beer and wine are on sale in virtually all huts, even when they are unstaffed.

Overnighting fees vary quite a bit depending on hut ownership, remoteness and facilities. SAC members and members of mountain clubs with reciprocal rights pay a much lower rate when staying at SAC huts. Rates range from around Sfr13 to Sfr20 for adult club members (or members of another mountain club with full reciprocal rights) to

Sfr22 to Sfr30 for nonmembers. Children usually pay half the adult rate, but the definition of 'child' varies from under 12 to 16 years of age. Additional fees are payable if you use the hut's fuel (gas or wood) for cooking or heating. Fees can be paid to the resident warden, dropped into the hut's honesty box or by post office deposit slip – see the On the Walk heading under Money.

Unfortunately, none of the mountain clubs in English-speaking countries enjoy reciprocal rights with the SAC, but those that do are as follows: the Deutscher Alpenverein, the Federation Française de la Montagne et de l'Escalade, the Club Alpino Italiano, the Federación Española de Montañismo, the Club Alpin Belgique, the Österreichischer Alpen Club and the Österreichischer Alpenverein.

Most huts are staffed only during the warmer months; when the Swiss flag and/or the local cantonal flag is flying it means the resident warden is present. Club-owned huts are always left unlocked, with access to at least the main dining room and a dorm. Even in summer it's relatively uncommon to find a hut completely full, although it certainly does happen from time to time (such as when school groups or guided mountaineering tours pass through). In such circumstances you probably won't be turned away, but if things are really tight you may have to sleep on the floor. In July, August or September, walking parties of three people or more are advised to reserve a berth.

Always observe the following basic rules when staying at mountain huts:

- Contact the hutkeeper as soon as you arrive. If no staff are present, register your name in the logbook immediately – otherwise you may be suspected of trying to avoid payment.
- Boots are not to be worn in the dorms – leave them in the vestibule by the entrance. Most huts provide slippers to wear inside.
- Be careful with fire – don't take burning candles into the dorms.
- Smoking is prohibited inside huts.
- Be very quiet in the dorms – walkers and mountain climbers often go to bed very early to ensure an early start.

The SAC publishes a trilingual mountain hut guide: *Hütten der Schweizer Alpen/Cabanes des Alpes Suisses/Capanni delle Alpi Svizzere* (Sfr38). The Web sites **W** www.bergtouris mus.ch/e/huetten.cfm and **W** www.adventure .ch also have general hut lists.

Mountain Hotels & Restaurants In popular walking areas mountain hotels and restaurants also offer accommodation for walkers. Mountain hotels and restaurants are often situated at the upper station of a cableway, funicular or cog railway, and can offer exceptionally good value in rooms and/or dorms. Hot showers – something walkers greatly appreciate after a sweaty day's hiking – are usually available, sometimes for an additional fee. The average price per person for a room (including a continental breakfast with freshly brewed coffee) is around Sfr45, and for a bed in the dorm Sfr30 (also with breakfast). As these places often cater mainly for winter tourists, getting a bed at mountain hotels and restaurants is seldom a problem. Many mountain restaurants offer dorm accommodation only to groups, but may take in individual walkers if a group is already staying there.

FOOD

Although Switzerland has some rather famous dishes, the national cuisine is sound but unspectacular. Traditional Swiss dishes tend to be simple to prepare and are therefore often standard on the menu in mountain huts and restaurants. Local salmon, trout and perch are often served in restaurants. Of course, Switzerland is famous for its chocolate (although most of the raw ingredients are imported), which is often used in desserts and cakes. Cheese and potatoes form the basis of many dishes.

Swiss Cuisine

To all Swiss, cheese *fondue* is the classic winter dish. To make fondue, Gruyères and other cheeses, like Emmentaler, are slowly melted into a mixture of white wine, *Kirsch* (cherry brandy) and garlic. Cubes of chopped bread are dipped on long forks into this aromatic, bubbling brew – truly food of the gods. Fondue is cold-weather fare, and the Swiss themselves seldom eat it between

June and September – except in the mountain huts and restaurants, that is, where fondue is a kind of Alpinists' staple.

Another very Swiss cheese dish popular for its sheer simplicity and inexpensiveness is known as *Käseschnitte* in German, or *croûtes au fromage* in French. It's a kind of pan-fried bread and cheese, served with seasoning.

Originally a typical dish of Valaisan herders who toasted their own cheeses over an open campfire, *raclette* is now second only to fondue in the (cholesterol-choked) hearts of the Swiss. Raclette's main attraction seems to be that it keeps everyone contentedly busy laying slices of well-seasoned cheese on a tiny tray, garnishing it with pickles and other spices, then sliding the whole lot under a special griller where it melts into a delicious messy mass.

Rösti is made from grated potatoes, which are pan-fried with butter, bacon or – yet again! – cheese to form a cohesive crisply browned cake. Rösti is such a symbol of German-Swiss cuisine that the language barrier which supposedly divides the German-speaking rösti-eaters from their French-speaking compatriots is known colloquially as the 'Rösti Trench'. Nonetheless, this simple and tasty dish is enjoyed by people on both sides of the country.

A dish typical for Switzerland's Italian-speaking regions, *polenta* invariably has a place on the menu in Ticino's *grotti* – small restaurants set in garden surroundings. Polenta is made from coarsely ground maize meal, which – at least according to tradition – is slowly boiled in a large cauldron over a small fire. The yellow, porridge-like mixture has to bubble away for several hours before it is ready to be served with white wine, mushrooms, garlic and parmesan cheese.

Where to Eat Even the small villages you pass through will usually have an inn or restaurant that serves simple meals. In larger towns, Migros and Coop supermarkets have cheaper self-service restaurants. Breakfast is almost always included in the price of a room or youth hostel dorm.

On the Walk

Mountain hotels generally have a cafeteria or restaurant. Especially in July and August, larger mountain huts have a resident warden/cook who prepares meals on demand, but even in midsummer don't automatically assume food will be served – ring ahead if you'll be arriving late. Many mountain huts offer a slightly lower rate for full board (*Halbpension* or *demi-pension*), which includes breakfast and dinner (sometimes also tea and/or a light snack to take with you on the day's walk; note that breakfast is *not* normally included in hut overnighting fees). Lunches can also be ordered and snack foods are available in mountain huts. Some walkers may prefer to prepare their own meals, but kitchen facilities can normally only be used by self-caterers when the hut is unstaffed.

You'll probably want to carry food for lunches and snacks along the way. Many walks lead past simple Alpine dairies that sell milk, butter and cheese. The kind and quantity of trail food will depend on your preferences, but some tried-and-true suggestions are:

fruit
A good source of glucose – carry both fresh and dried fruit
mixed nuts
An easily packed, slow-release, high-energy food
wholemeal bread
A great variety is available in supermarkets, including organic loaves
cheese
Try local Emmentaler, Gruyères and (smelly) Appenzell types
Bündnerfleisch
Called *pulpa* in Romansch, this smoked, air-dried beef is a speciality of Graubünden
Müesli
A nourishing mix of breakfast cereals, originally invented (although never quite perfected) by the Swiss
chocolate
Something to power you up the steepest inclines

Wild Food Thickets of juicy raspberries, which ripen in July, often fringe paths in many regions of Switzerland, especially on

Mushrooming

Switzerland has many edible varieties of mushrooms such as the delicious aromatic ceps *(Boletus edulis)* and chanterelles *(Cantharellus melanoxerus)*, a small yellow forest fungi. Although the regulations differ between individual cantons, mushrooming is strictly controlled throughout Switzerland. The maximum amount of wild mushrooms you may pick anywhere is 2kg per person per day, but many cantons allow no more than 1kg – which is quite enough anyway. There are many closed days, and fines are imposed for infringement of bylaws.

To protect the environment and your own health, exercise discretion when mushrooming. Avoid disturbing the ground around the stem unnecessarily, and remove any earth or plant matter immediately. Several deadly toadstool species grow in Switzerland, so never pick a mushroom you can't identify – just one poisonous mushroom is often enough to contaminate the whole lot. If in any doubt whatsoever, seek the advice of the mushroom identification service *(Pilzkontrollstelle)* offered free by local councils (ask at tourist offices).

the northern side of the Alps. In September you can pick tangy bilberries and blueberries on Alpine heaths. Mushrooms can be found in moist forest clearings (see the boxed text 'Mushrooming').

DRINKS
Nonalcoholic Drinks
Switzerland has many mineral springs, and both still and carbonated bottled water is inexpensive and widely available. In summer, Swiss consume vast amounts of ice tea, which is served in restaurants and sold in supermarkets as ready-mix powder. Also very popular is Rivella, a delicious, uniquely Swiss soft drink – Migros supermarkets sell a cheaper clone. Coffee is more popular than tea and is normally served without milk unless you specially ask for it. Hot chocolate is also popular.

Alcoholic Drinks
Swiss walkers have a weakness for *panache*, a delicious 'shandy' blend of equal parts of beer and lemonade. White wine, especially the crisp Chasselas from the Lake Geneva region, is often mixed with mineral water to produce another popular drink that German Swiss call a *Gspritzte*. Switzerland's red wines, the Dôle from the Central Valais and Merlot from Ticino, are sound if relatively unspectacular. The excellent local fruit brandies, however, especially the smooth, aromatic Kirsch (made from cherry stones), should be savoured in slow moderation.

CLOTHING & EQUIPMENT
Since mountain accommodation is abundant and the routes generally short, few walkers in Switzerland bother carrying camping gear such as tents, sleeping bags, portable stove etc. Equipment that you can't do without is listed below.

General Clothing
Continental Europeans often prefer to wear specially designed walking breeches. The legs of breeches are tapered to just below the knees, and are less restrictive than full-length pants. Long socks protect the lower legs.

Warm Weather Wear
Midsummer conditions in the Swiss Alps can be surprisingly hot, so walkers at this time of the year often prefer to wear lighter clothing such as shorts and a short-sleeved shirt – but use a UV sunscreen for exposed limbs. It's a good idea to wear a broad-brimmed hat for maximum protection from the sun. If you want to do any swimming, bring a pair of bathers.

Cold Weather Wear
Especially on longer walks or those that take you high up into the mountains, carrying plenty of warm clothing is essential. A thick woollen sweater or 'fleece' garment will keep the body warm even when wet. Walkers who intend doing overnight trips in the mountains might consider taking a down jacket. Also take gloves and a woolly hat or beanie.

Equipment Check List

This list is a general guide to the things you might take on a walk. Your list will vary depending on the kind of walking you want to do, whether you're camping or staying mainly in mountain huts, and on the terrain, weather conditions and time of year.

Equipment
- ☐ backpack with waterproof liner
- ☐ camera and spare film
- ☐ emergency, high-energy food
- ☐ gaiters
- ☐ map, compass and guidebook
- ☐ medical kit, toiletries and insect repellant*
- ☐ pocket knife (with corkscrew)
- ☐ sewing kit
- ☐ sleeping sheet
- ☐ small towel
- ☐ sunglasses and sunscreen
- ☐ survival bag or blanket
- ☐ torch (flashlight) with spare batteries and globe
- ☐ water containers
- ☐ water purification tablets, iodine or filter
- ☐ whistle (for emergencies)

Clothes
- ☐ runners (training shoes) or sandals
- ☐ socks and underwear
- ☐ shorts and trousers
- ☐ sunhat
- ☐ sweater, fleece or windproof jacket
- ☐ thermal underwear

- ☐ T-shirt and long-sleeved shirt with collar
- ☐ walking boots and spare laces
- ☐ warm hat, scarf and gloves
- ☐ waterproof jacket
- ☐ waterproof overtrousers

Camping
- ☐ cooking, eating and drinking utensils
- ☐ dishwashing items
- ☐ insulating mat
- ☐ matches or lighter and candle
- ☐ portable stove and fuel
- ☐ sleeping bag
- ☐ spare cord
- ☐ tent (check pegs and poles)
- ☐ toilet paper and toilet trowel

Optional Items
- ☐ altimeter
- ☐ binoculars
- ☐ day-pack
- ☐ emergency distress beacon
- ☐ GPS
- ☐ lightweight groundsheet
- ☐ mobile phone
- ☐ notebook and pencil
- ☐ swimming costume
- ☐ trekking stocks
- ☐ walkman/radio
- ☐ waterproof, slip-on backpack cover

* see the Medical Kit Check List in Health & Safety

Thermal underwear ('thermals') allows walkers to maintain a comfortable temperature by layering their clothing.

Note that cotton does not insulate, and wearing cotton clothing (even just briefs) underneath thermals will significantly decrease their effectiveness. Modern woollen underwear is very light and does not feel scratchy, but polypropylene ('polypro') is the most popular choice among walkers.

Polypro does not absorb sweat, and will only 'wick' moisture away from your body if you wear a second layer of (absorbent) clothing such as a wool sweater or fleece shirt. New microbials (bacteria-hating) weaves of polypro reduce its tendency to smell soon after use.

Wet Weather Wear
It is vital that walkers carry a completely windproof and waterproof rain-jacket at all times. It should be properly seam-sealed and have a hood to keep the rain and wind off your head. Nowadays, most experienced

walkers prefer garments made from Gore-Tex or a similar 'breathable' fabric. A pair of waterproof overpants is also recommended. Plastic ponchos or other cheap solutions just won't do, however, as they tear easily, catch on branches and blow around in the wind.

Trekking Stocks

First popularised by Reinhold Messner, twin lightweight trekking stocks are standard equipment for many walkers in the Alps, yet some mountain-goers find them more of a nuisance than an additional support while ascending and descending. Similar in appearance to ski stocks, trekking stocks have a fold-away 'telescopic' design, which makes them easy to strap onto even small day-packs. Outdoor stores sell stocks from around Sfr60.

Backpack

A small, light pack is the way to go. Depending on the sort of walks you intend doing, a day-pack with a 20L capacity may be large enough to suit your needs. At least one outside pocket (preferably on the top or the rear side) makes it easier to grab your camera or snacks like that bar of chocolate.

Boots

Sturdy medium-weight walking boots that give good ankle support are recommended. The Swiss company Raichle produces high-quality walking boots from around Sfr200. Using special orthopaedic insoles, such as those made by Superfeet, will lessen 'foot-stress' on rugged mountain hikes. (See also Blisters under Common Ailments in the Health & Safety chapter).

Buying Locally

Switzerland is a comparatively expensive country, so it's unlikely you'll want to buy much in the way of walking gear here. If you do forget or lose something essential – your sunglasses, your compass, your boots! – finding a replacement is rarely a problem. Virtually every town or larger village near a popular walking route will have an outlet selling equipment, although prices and range may not always be satisfactory.

Best are several smaller chains: Transa (W www.transa.ch), Eiselin Sport (W www.eiselin-sport.ch) and Bächli Bergsport (W www.baechli-bergsport.ch), whose outlets, which are concentrated in Switzerland's larger German-speaking cities, offer a broad range of travel, hiking and mountaineering gear. Together the much larger Intersport (W www.intersport.ch) and Ochsner (W www.ochsner-sport.ch) chains have outlets in just about every larger centre in Switzerland. Some locations are given under Gateways and Access Towns in the regional chapters. A short list of outlets in major cities follows:

Basel
 Eiselin Sport (☎ 061-331 45 39, e eiselin .sport.basel@active.ch) Gundeldingerstrasse 66/Falkensteinerstrasse 66
 Ochsner Sport (061-683 40 00) Rebgasse 20
 Transa (☎ 061-273 53 33, e outdoor.basel @transa.ch) Aeschengraben 13

Bern
 Bächli Bergsport (☎ 031-312 92 82) Bollwerk 31
 Eiselin Sport (☎ 031-381 76 76) Monbijou-strasse 20
 Ochsner Sport (☎ 031-329 23 23) Am Bahn-hofplatz 9
 Transa (☎ 031-312 12 35, e outdoor.bern @transa.ch) Speichergasse 39

Geneva
 Charles Sports (☎ 022-731 59 60) quai des Bergues 23
 Sporloisirs (☎ 022-7074460) rue Muzy 8
 Sport Coquoz (☎ 022-735 23 21) rue Villereuse 10

Lausanne
 Ochsner Sport (☎ 021-331 34 10) rue de Grand-Pont 1
 Passe Montagne Bourgeois (☎ 021-625 25 55) ave d'Echallens 40
 Yosemite (☎ 021-617 31 00) blvd de Grancy 12

Zürich
 Bächli Bergsport (☎ 01-312 41 03) Schwa-mendingenstrasse 41, Zürich-Oerlikon
 Bächtold Sport (☎ 01-252 09 34) Rämistrasse 3
 Eiselin Sport (☎ 01-362 48 28, e itrepazzi @bluewin.ch) Stampfenbachstrasse 138
 Exped (☎ 01-497 10 10, W www.exped.com) Hardstrasse 81

Ochsner Sport (☎ 01-212 80 40) Löwenstrasse 31
Transa Travel- & Outdoor-Laden (☎ 01-278 90 60, e outdoor.zuerich@transa.ch) Josefstrasse 59

MAPS & NAVIGATION

Surveying and cartography is something (else) the Swiss excel in; their maps are veritable works of precision, if not of art. The national mapping authority is the Federal Office of Topography (Bundesamt für Landestopographie (BL) in German, Office Fédéral de Topographie (OFT) in French; ☎ 031-963 21 11, W www.swisstopo.ch), Seftigenstrasse 264, CH-3084 Wabern.

Small-Scale Maps

Although they are unsuitable for serious navigation, small-scale maps are good for basic orientation.

The 1:301,000 *Rail-map Switzerland* (Sfr19) produced by the Swiss Federal Railways (SBB/CFF) shows rail, ferry and postbus lines as well as the numerous funiculars, cog railways and cableways.

The BL/OFT publishes a two-sheet 1:200,000 road map *Freizeitkarte Schweiz/ Carte de Loisir Suisse* (Sfr24.50). Two other good road maps of Switzerland are the 1:301,000 *Schweiz/Suisse TCS* (Sfr14.80) and the 1:250,000 *Schweiz/Suisse ACS* (Sfr14.80), both published by Kümmerly + Frey (K+F) in association with the country's two car clubs.

For general use, the BL/OFT publishes a 1:300,000 map of Switzerland, the *Generalkarte der Schweiz/Carte général de la Suisse*, which is an identical but condensed version of four 1:200,000 sheets covering the whole country.

Large-Scale Maps

The BL/OFT produces three standard topographical maps scaled at 1:25,000, 1:50,000 and 1:100,000, which are updated on a regular six- to seven-year cycle. Maps in the 1:25,000 series cost Sfr12; Sfr13.50 in the 1:50,000 series. These maps show complex geographical features with surprising accuracy and detail, combining contour lines and shading together with skilful 'artistic' representation of important features such as gorges, mountain cirques or exposed rock ridges; this gives a clear impression of the 'lie of the land'.

Walking Maps

A wide range of topographical maps specifically produced for walkers is available. These indicate features of particular interest to walkers, such as walking routes, mountain huts or inns, public cableways and even individual postbus stops more clearly than standard topographical maps. Maps referred to and/or recommended in this guidebook are invariably walking maps rather than the BL/OFT's standard topographical series.

Most comprehensive is the 1:50,000 series of walking maps published by the Swiss Hiking Federation (SAW/FSTP; see Useful Organisations later). Distinguishable by their orange (rather than green) covers and 'T' after the grid number (eg, *Jungfrau 264T*) these sheets are drawn directly from BL/OFT maps. SAW/FSTP walking maps are generally the most accurate, most durable and cheapest walking maps available. The standard retail price for these maps is Sfr22.50, but SAW/FSTP members and subscribers can mail-order them for Sfr18.50 each. SAW/FSTP maps do not include a (full) legend on the sheet itself, but free explanatory brochures *(Zeichenerklärung, légend des signes)* are available at points of sale.

The largest commercial map publisher is Kümmerly + Frey (☎ 031-915 22 11, e info @swissmaps.ch, W www.swissmaps.ch), Alpenstrasse 58, CH-3052 Zollikofen-Bern, which has the entire country covered in several dozen overlapping sheets. Most K+F maps are scaled at 1:60,000, and although they show rather less detail than most other walking maps they are accurate enough for serious navigation. K+F's 1:60,000 sheets sell for Sfr24.80.

Another important commercial publisher of walking maps is the now defunct Editions MPA Verlag, whose high-quality 1:25,000 and 1:50,000 sheets are still widely available. Other smaller commercial publishers of walking maps include Orell Füssli, Schaad & Frey and Baeschlin.

Regional tourist authorities often produce useful walking maps of areas surrounding their resorts or valley, generally scaled at between 1:25,000 and 1:50,000. Depending on their size and quality, walking maps produced by tourist authorities normally cost between Sfr12 and Sfr20.

In some cantons, associations affiliated with the SAW/FSTP also produce walking maps. The most active of these is the St-Gallische Wanderwege, which has brought out a small series of excellent 1:50,000 and 1:25,000 walking maps covering most parts of the canton of St Gallen.

Buying Maps

Maps can be ordered online from the BL/OFT and the Swiss Hiking Federation (see Useful Organisations later). Larger bookshops invariably have a wide – although not always complete – selection of Swiss topographical, walking and travel maps, but because of the painstaking and expensive work involved in their production they are not cheap. Due to the compact nature of the Swiss Alps, you will usually only need to buy one or two maps for a (longer) walk, particularly if you choose from the 1:50,000 series.

GPS

Originally developed by the US Department of Defense, the Global Positioning System (GPS) is a network of more than 20 earth-orbiting satellites that continually beam encoded signals back to earth. Small, computer-driven devices (GPS receivers) can decode these signals to give users an extremely accurate reading of their location – to within 30m, anywhere on the planet, at any time of day, in almost any weather. The theoretical accuracy of the system increased at least 10-fold in 2000 when a deliberate, in-built error, intended to fudge the readings for all but US military users, was removed. The cheapest hand-held GPS receivers now cost less than US$100 (although these may not have a built-in averaging system that minimises signal errors). Other important factors to consider when buying a GPS receiver are its weight and battery life.

It should be understood that a GPS receiver is of little use to hikers unless used with an accurate topographical map – the GPS receiver simply gives your position, which you must then locate on the local map. GPS receivers will only work properly in the open. Directly below high cliffs, near large bodies of water or in dense tree-cover, for example, the signals from a crucial satellite may be blocked (or bounce off the rock or water) and give inaccurate readings. GPS receivers are more vulnerable to breakdowns (including dead batteries) than the humble magnetic compass – a low-tech device that has served navigators faithfully for centuries – so don't rely on them entirely.

WALKS IN THIS BOOK

The walks described in this guidebook are a varied selection taken from an almost endless number of possibilities. They aim to give a representative – but never complete – coverage of Switzerland's most outstanding natural scenery. Not surprisingly, the walks are overwhelmingly in Alpine regions, and many lead through nature reserves. Apart from high-level routes that may be undertaken when snow covers paths early or late in the season, none of the walks involves the use of mountaineering skills or equipment.

With only minor exceptions, the walks go entirely via officially designated walking routes. Paths are generally very well maintained and waymarked, but from time to time floods, landslides or avalanches make them impassable or necessitate the re-routing of minor sections.

Eight chapters cover all regions of Switzerland except for the Swiss Mittelland. Note that where a walking route crosses from one region into another, it appears in the regional chapter considered most appropriate – this usually means in the region from which you set out. Route descriptions generally begin and end at a train station, postbus stop, or the upper station of a chairlift, cable car or mountain railway.

The Access Towns and Nearest Towns sections provide basic information on places

Long Walks

Long walks are usually made of many shorter legs that can be undertaken as individual day walks, but there's nevertheless something rather satisfying about doing an entire walk from start to finish. Most long walks have some kind of geographical or historical theme – an ancient trading or pilgrims' route, the circumnavigation of a major mountain massif, the traverse of a culturally interesting valley etc. Two famous European pilgrims' routes pass through Switzerland: the Roman Way, from Canterbury to Rome, and the north-eastern branch of St James' Way to Santiago de Compostela in Spain.

The Alpine Pass Route

The 340km Alpine Pass Route (Alpenpassroute in German, Itinéraire des Cols Alpestres in French) is Switzerland's classic long walk. The east-to-west route takes you right across the country, from Sargans near the Liechtenstein border to Montreux on Lake Geneva, crossing 16 mountain passes that introduce some of the Swiss Alps' highest and most spectacular scenery. The middle sections of the Alpine Pass Route – especially those in the Bernese Oberland's Jungfrau region – are the most popular. With rest days and time off for bad weather, walking the entire length of the Alpine Pass Route takes around four weeks.

This guidebook covers the Alpine Pass Route in full, with each leg described as a day walk in its respective chapter as follows:

Leg number	Walk name	Route	Page
Leg 1	Foopass	Sargans to Elm	340
Leg 2	Richetlipass	Elm to Linthal	346
Leg 3	Klausenpass	Linthal to Altdorf	155
Leg 4	Surenenpass	Altdorf to Engelberg	159
Leg 5	Jochpass	Engelberg to Meiringen	162
Leg 6	Grosse Scheidegg	Meiringen to Grindelwald	108
Leg 7	Kleine Scheidegg	Grindelwald to Lauterbrunnen	114
Leg 8	Sefinenfurgge	Lauterbrunnen to Griesalp	115
Leg 9	Hohtürli	Griesalp to Kandersteg	119
Leg 10	Bunderchrinde	Kandersteg to Adelboden	122
Leg 11	Hahnenmoospass	Adelboden to Lenk	127
Leg 12	Trüttlisbergpass	Lenk to Lauenen	131
Leg 13	Chrinepass	Lauenen to Gsteig	132
Leg 14	Col des Andérets	Gsteig to Les Mosses	203
Leg 15	Col de Chaude	Les Mosses to Montreux	200

The Haute Route

Leading from Chamonix in France through the southern Valais to Zermatt, the Haute Route leads – as suggested by its name – through some of the highest and most scenic country accessible to walkers anywhere in the Alps. The summer Haute Route walk (which takes a rather different course from that of the more famous winter ski-touring Haute Route) takes around two weeks to complete. Like the Alpine Pass Route, the Haute Route mainly involves 'pass hopping', and demands a higher level of fitness, with very long ascents and descents on just about every section. Recommended is the guidebook *Chamonix to Zermatt – the Walker's Haute Route* by Kev Reynolds (Cicerone Press).

Long Walks

The Jura High Route

The approximately 180km Jura High Route (Jurahöhenweg, Chemin des Crêtes du Jura) runs from Geneva to Basel via some of the highest ridge tops of the Swiss Jura. The route has its own special marking of yellow-red diamonds, and takes around 10 days to complete.

Cicerone Press's *The Jura High Route* covers this walk.

Tour Wildstrubel

This walk circumnavigates the Wildstrubel massif on the Bern/Valais cantonal border. The route leads from Kandersteg via Adelboden, Lenk, Crans-Montana and Leukerbad; the sections in the Bernese Oberland correspond to those of the Alpine Pass Route.

Tour Monte Rosa

This 10-day, 160km circuit of Switzerland's loftiest mountain massif, Monte Rosa, is a newly established international long walk. The route goes via Zermatt, Grächen, Saas Fee and the Italian towns of Macugnagna, Gressoney and St-Jacques. There are some quite demanding sections, and even a pass crossing where walkers inexperienced in glacier travel will require the services of a qualified mountain guide.

Kümmerly + Frey (K+F) has produced a special 1:50,000 walking map, *Tour Monte Rosa* (Sfr24.80), with multilingual notes (including English) on the reverse side. The best guidebook (in any language!) is *The Grand Tour of Monte Rosa* by CJ Wright (Cicerone Press).

Tour des Combins

This is an eight- to 10-day international circuit hike leading around the ice-encrusted 4000m peaks of the Grand Combins massif in the Lower Valais. Traditionally, the village of Verbier is the start of the walk. The route leads up through the Val de Bagnes over the Fenêtre de Durand to Barasson into the Val Pelline in Italy. From here it returns into Swiss territory via St-Rhémy and the Col du Grand St-Bernard, and follows the Val d'Entremont back to Verbier.

Tour du Mont Blanc

The Tour du Mont Blanc is an eight- to 10-day walk circumnavigating the mighty Mont Blanc massif, which boasts the highest mountains and most glaciated scenery in Europe. Most of the walking route leads through Italy and France, with only about 1½ days spent on the Swiss side of the frontier.

Trekking 700

This long route was established in 1991 to commemorate Switzerland's 700th anniversary. The Trekking 700 starts off from the village of Mesocco, in Graubünden's Italian-speaking Valle Mesolcina, and leads east-to-west across northern Ticino via the towns of Biasca, Sonogno and Fontana to terminate in the Val Formazza (Pomattal) in Italy. This week-long pass-hopping tour gives hikers some of the very best walking that the southern Swiss Alps have to offer.

Senda Sursilvana

The Senda Sursilvana runs from the Oberalppass (see the Lai da Tuma Circuit under Vorderrhein & Hinterrhein in the Graubünden chapter) down through the valley of the Vorderrhein (Rein Anteriur) as far as Chur, leading through the culturally interesting Romansch-speaking towns and villages of the Surselva. The approximately 100km-long route forms one of the less strenuous long walks in Switzerland, taking four or five days to walk the entire length. K+F's special 1:40,000 walking map, *Senda Sursilvana* (Sfr8), fully covers the route.

that may serve as convenient bases for hikes within each region. These sections complement the information given in the description of each featured walk, but are not intended as a comprehensive list covering every regional village, town or city.

Route Descriptions

Longer walks, including some that can realistically be done without overnighting en route, are divided into two or more shorter 'Day' sections. Bear in mind, however, that the individual Day sections are often just a convenient way of breaking up the walk – dawdlers may choose to stop earlier at a mountain hut or hotel along the way, while faster walkers may decide to continue on after completing a Day section. All walks and Day sections finish somewhere with accommodation and/or public transport.

Level of Difficulty

The walking standards used in this guidebook rate the overall 'seriousness' of a walk, and are based on a combination of factors such as strenuousness, path conditions, overall length and en-route shelter options. Bear in mind that both walking times and standards can vary considerably according to factors such as weather and snow conditions.

Walks are graded *easy*, *medium* or *hard* using the following criteria:

Easy These walks can be done by virtually anyone, and a minimal level of fitness is needed. They are short in distance and follow well-marked and graded paths with gentle gradients and modest climbs or descents.

Medium These walks call for appreciably more experience and better physical condition. They are best attempted after you have completed at least several easy walks.

Hard These walks are physically demanding, and generally lead through high-Alpine terrain where some experience of mountain walking is advisable. Steep ascents and/or descents on poorly formed trails are typical hindrances, while snow may lie along parts

of the route well into summer. Robust footwear and proper wet-weather clothing is utterly essential. Route markings may still be quite good, but walkers nevertheless require a basic level of navigational ability.

Times & Distances

The length of a walk is best measured in time rather than distance, although a comparison of the two is certainly helpful in gauging a route's difficulty. The walking times given in this guidebook are based on the author's own measurements, with consideration given to normal variation in walking pace – these may differ a bit from the 'official' times shown on signposts. Walking times don't include rest stops.

Maps in This Book

Considerable effort has been made to improve the maps in this 2nd edition of the book. Each walk (including side trips) is now clearly highlighted, and other important walking routes in each area have been included along with many nearby mountain huts or hotels. Scales have been largely standardised and the addition of contours enhances clarity. Even so, the maps in this book are *not* intended for serious navigation – walkers should acquire the latest available walking map covering their route.

Altitude Measurements

Unless otherwise stated, spot heights given in this guidebook are *above sea level* and based on the most detailed and/or reliable map available. Sometimes two different maps may give – hopefully only slightly – differing altitudes for a particular feature. This is usually due to rounding – a peak at 2779.6m, for example, may be shown simply as '2780m'. At other times a map may indicate a different height from that shown on a signpost at the place itself. In such cases the latter has usually been given the benefit of the doubt – that way, at least you'll know the author has been there!

Place Names & Terminology

Switzerland is a multi-ethnic country, and naturally this is reflected in its nomenclature.

Topographical maps and trail signposts always show place names in the language predominant in that area (although unofficial signs painted on rocks and trees often betray the ethnic origins of the nonlocals who wrote them). Where two linguistic regions converge, such as the Pass da Sett/Septimerpass in Graubünden, maps (and sometimes signposts) give both place names.

Walkers may sometimes notice that somewhat different versions of the same place name exist, such as Lauchbühl/Loichbiel (near Grindelwald) or Kreuzboden/ Chrizbode (in the Saastal). This is particularly common in German-speaking regions, where pronunciation of a place name in the local dialect is different from standard (High) German. Most interesting are place names consisting of two languages, as often occurs along the linguistic borders, where French/German combinations like Vieille Rossmatte or Le Steffelbletz (in eastern Fribourg Canton) frequently come up. Note also that valleys very often carry quite a different name from the stream that flows through them; for example, the Val de Travers in the western Jura is drained by a river known as L'Areuse.

RESPONSIBLE WALKING

Walking is a very casual affair, of course, but observing the simple rules of trail etiquette will keep you in good stead with other walkers.

Except on very busy routes, it's considered impolite not to greet others you pass along the trail – see the Language chapter for a few expressions. The custom on narrow paths is that ascending walkers have right of way over those going down. Always leave farm gates as you found them. In summer, low-voltage electric fences are set up to control stock on the open Alpine pastures; where an electric fence crosses a path it usually has a hook that can be easily unfastened to allow walkers to pass through without getting zapped.

The Swiss are particularly environmentally conscious, and walkers should aim to follow their example by heeding these cardinal rules of conduct in the mountains.

All refuse, including cigarette butts, sweet wrappers and tampons, should be carried out in your pack – not dumped, buried or hidden under some rock.

Don't pick the Alpine wild flowers – they really do look lovelier on the mountainsides. Animal watchers should approach wildlife with discretion. Moving too close will unnerve wild animals, distracting them from their vital summer activity of putting on fat for the long Alpine winter.

Always keep to the marked path, and don't short-cut corners. Mountain farmers will be grateful if you refrain from stepping off paths that lead across Alpine fields and meadows.

Be thoughtful regarding where and how you dispose of your bodily wastes. Use proper toilets where they are available (such as at mountain huts and restaurants), otherwise go well away from the path and bury your scat properly.

Many people take dogs with them on walks. Dogs must be kept on a leash where the path leads through forest (which provides natural shelter for wildlife during the day), past farmland with newly born lambs or calves or into nature reserves. Note that dogs are not allowed at all in the Swiss National Park and some nature reserves.

Take special care with fire – only light fires in established fireplaces. Walkers who camp out in the mountains should read the notes under Wild Camping in the On the Walk section of Accommodation earlier.

WOMEN WALKERS

Although it caught up relatively late in accepting equality for women in (almost) all areas of life, today Switzerland is one of Europe's more progressive countries as far as women's rights and independence are concerned. Apart from the natural dangers of mountain walking itself, there are no serious issues of safety for women walkers in Switzerland. Walking is extremely popular among Swiss women, who – alone, in pairs, groups or with partners – actually seem to outnumber men on some routes.

Sexual harassment is uncommon, although in Italian-speaking Ticino catcalling young women is an (occasional) sport of young men – the best advice is not to react unless such behaviour persists. It is not advisable for women to hitchhike, especially when alone.

The Web site **w** www.adventurenetwork .com/WMNTemp.html has wide-ranging information for women walkers. For information on health on the trail, see Women's Health in the Health & Safety chapter.

WALKING WITH CHILDREN

Despite its rugged topography, Switzerland's excellent mountain infrastructure makes it an ideal place for walking with children – it's quite usual to meet families even on relatively challenging overnight routes. Mountain huts generally offer much lower rates to 'child' (up to about 10 years of age) and 'youth' (up to about 16) guests. Towns and villages along the walking routes have inexpensive rooms and family-oriented hostels. The Junior Card (see the Getting Around chapter) gives free public transport travel to children.

Doing a walk with children will always take more preparation and time, as kids walk more slowly and need frequent rest stops (with plenty of snacks). Children are sensitive to extremes of environment, and hence more prone to hypothermia, heat stroke, heat exhaustion and sunburn, and acclimatise to high altitudes less quickly than adults. Particularly in hot weather, give them plenty of liquids and make sure they are protected by proper clothing and/or liberally smeared with sunscreen. Don't let children wander off the path where there are dangerous features like cliffs or gullies. Particularly after walks in lower forested areas, check them over for disease-carrying ticks. (For more information, see the Health & Safety chapter.)

Child harnesses give security on sections of path with steep dropoffs. Children often like to carry their own little pack – daypacks are suitable. Very young children can be carried in special carrier backpacks, but for newborns (who must have extra support for their heads) it is only safe to use a *front* carrier – models specifically designed for hiking are best.

With proper care and planning, most of the walks in this guidebook can be done with children, but the most suitable routes include: the Stockhorn Circuit (Bernese Oberland), the Rigi Höhenweg (Central Switzerland), the Cornopass and the Lötschental (Valais), the Campolungo Circuit and Monte Brè to Soragno (Ticino), the Vereinatal, the Ruin' Aulta, the Upper Engadine Lakes and the Fuorcla Funtana da S-charl (Graubünden), and the Churfirsten and the Pizol Lakes Circuit (North-Eastern Switzerland).

Lonely Planet's *Travel with Children* makes educational and entertaining reading.

USEFUL ORGANISATIONS
Mountain Clubs

Most mountain huts are owned and run by local sections of the Swiss Alpine Club or the Federazione Alpinistica Ticinese.

Swiss Alpine Club The Swiss Alpine Club (Schweizer Alpenclub, Club Alpin Suisse, Club Alpino Svizzero, or SAC) is Switzerland's main mountain club. Although the club is mainly oriented to mountaineering and Alpine ski-touring, most members are also keen walkers. The SAC publishes climbing guidebooks to all parts of Switzerland in German, French and Italian. Nonresident foreigners are welcome to join the SAC. Members receive large discounts on all SAC publications and pay lower fees when overnighting in SAC huts (or huts belonging to other clubs with reciprocal rights).

Contact the Schweizer Alpenclub (☎ 031-370 18 18, **w** www.sac-cas.ch), Monbijoustrasse 61, Postfach, 3000 Bern 23 for further information .

Federazione Alpinistica Ticinese (FAT)
In Ticino, a number of independent (ie, non-SAC) mountain clubs exist that together outnumber the SAC both in their local membership and number of mountain huts. The two largest clubs are the Unione Ticinese Operai Escursionisti (UTOE; ☎ 091-825 19 47, **e** utoe_faido@leventinanet.ch, **w** www.leventinanet.ch/utoe), Pedemonte 8, 6500 Bellinzona, and the Società Alpinistica

Ticinese (SAT; ☎ 091-682 84 21, e SAT _Chiasso@ticino.com, w www.ticino.edu /usr/cgianinazzi), via Vela 2, 6830 Chiasso. Along with several smaller clubs they are represented by an umbrella organisation, the Federazione Alpinistica Ticinese (FAT; ☎ 091-866 31 81, e fbeffa@tinet.ch), CH-6777 Quinto.

Despite a long history of rivalry between FAT-affiliated clubs and the SAC, reciprocal agreements now give members discounts in huts of either club.

Swiss Hiking Federation

The Swiss Hiking Federation (Schweizerische Arbeitsgemeinschaft für Wanderwege (SAW) in German, Fédération Suisse de Tourisme Pédestre (FSTP) in French, L'ente Svizzero Pro Sentieri (ESS) in Italian) is a national organisation that promotes recreational walking in Switzerland. The SAW/FSTP oversees the construction, maintenance and waymarking of all official hiking routes. Together with its affiliated associations, the SAW/FSTP organises a vast number of guided walking tours – programs are available from the federation itself or tourist offices.

The SAW/FSTP publishes the *Wander Revue Sentiers*, a bimonthly magazine about hiking in separate German and French editions; subscription costs Sfr35 (Sfr40/45 surface/airmail outside Switzerland) per year. The SAW/FSTP also produces high-quality walking maps (see Maps earlier), which *Revue* subscribers can purchase for a substantial discount.

For further information, contact Schweizer Wanderwege (☎ 061-606 93 40, fax 606 93 45, e info@swisshiking.ch, w www.swis shiking.ch), Im Hirshalm 49, CH-4125 Riehen.

Guides & Mountaineering Schools

The professional organisation for accredited mountain guides in Switzerland is the Swiss Mountain Guide Federation (Schweizerischer Bergführerverband/Association des Guides de Montagne de la Suisse), Hadlaubstrasse 49, 8006 Zürich. Its Web site

(w www.4000plus.ch) lists all mountain guides who work in Switzerland, whether individually or in association with a mountaineering school.

Switzerland's top schools of mountaineering are represented by the Swiss Association of Mountaineering Schools (Schweizer Verband der Bergsteigerschulen, Association Suisse de Écoles d'Alpinisme; ☎ 027-473 28 03, fax 473 28 55, e bburgener@dplanet.ch, w www.bergtourismus.ch). As well as running regular instruction courses in rock- and ice-climbing techniques, the schools are agencies for qualified mountain guides. They also organise guided trekking tours and glacier hikes for walkers who may not feel completely confident by themselves in the high Alps. Many mountaineering schools are listed under Access Towns and Nearest Towns in the regional chapters, while the association's Web site has a complete list.

Swiss Friends of Nature

The Swiss Friends of Nature (Naturfreunde Schweiz, Amis de la Nature Suisse) is affiliated with the Friends of Nature, a global organisation that promotes environmentally responsible tourism. Apart from organising numerous outdoor tours and courses – from mountaineering and canoeing to animal watching and botanical walks – the Swiss Friends of Nature runs almost 90 hostels (see Accommodation earlier). Annual youth/adult/family membership is Sfr25/75/ 100. For further information contact Naturfreunde Schweiz (☎ 031-306 67 67, fax 306 67 68, e info@naturfreunde.ch, w www .naturfreunde.ch), Pavillonweg 3, Postfach, Bern 3012.

Pro Natura

With a history going back to the first decade of the 1900s, Pro Natura, formerly the Swiss Society for the Protection of Nature (Schweizer Bund für Naturschutz, Ligue Suisse pour la Protection de la Nature), was the first nationally based conservation lobby in Switzerland. Since then the society has been instrumental in the establishment of many nature reserves throughout the country, including the Swiss National Park.

The society puts out a bimonthly magazine in French and German editions.

For more information contact Pro Natura (☎ 061-317 91 91, fax 317 91 66, e mailbox @pronatura.ch, W www.pronatura.ch), Wartenbergstrasse 22, 4020 Basel.

Swiss Youth Hostels

Swiss Youth Hostels (Schweizer Jugendherbergen, Auberges de Jeunesse Suisse, Alberghi Svizzeri per la Gioventù) is affiliated with Hostelling International (HI), which runs thousands of hostels worldwide. Membership is open to anyone. It's probably cheaper and more convenient to join in your own country, but the annual membership fee in Switzerland is Sfr22 for juniors (under 19 years of age) and Sfr33 for seniors.

Swiss Youth Hostels organises a whole range of summer and winter outdoor programs lasting up to a week, including walking and rafting trips or courses in scuba-diving and mountaineering.

For further information contact Schweizer Jugendherbergen (☎ 01-360 14 14, fax 360 14 60, e bookingoffice@youthhostel.ch, W www.youthhostel.ch), Schaffhauserstrasse 14, Postfach, CH-8042 Zürich.

Gay & Lesbian Organisations

Pink Cross Pink Cross is an independent national organisation representing gays and lesbians in Switzerland. For information contact Pink Cross (☎ 031-372 33 00, e office@pinkcross.ch, W www.pinkcross.ch), Zinggstrasse 16, Postfach 7512, 3001 Bern.

TOURIST OFFICES

Every city, town and village in Switzerland has some kind of tourist office; in the smallest places the post office and/or the train station gives out basic tourist information. Brochures listing accommodation in all price ranges, tourist maps and other (usually free) literature – including suggested walks in the area – are often available in English. Many local tourist authorities produce and sell special walking maps covering their own regions.

The head office of the Swiss national tourist authority, Switzerland Tourism (Schweiz Tourismus, Suisse Tourisme; ☎ 01-288 11 11) is at Tödistrasse 7, CH-8027 Zürich.

Switzerland Tourism has recently been restructured from a service-oriented to a marketing organisation, and its offices abroad are now essentially administrative. All important tourist information, including bookings, can now be accessed directly from the Web site (W www.myswitzerland.com), via the international email address (e postoffice@switzerlandtourism .ch), or on Switzerland Tourism's free 24-hour international telephone and fax numbers, ☎ 00800-100 200 30, fax 100 200 31, or from the USA and Canada ☎ 011800-100 200 30, fax 100 200 31.

VISAS & DOCUMENTS
Visas

Citizens of many Western European countries don't require a passport to enter Switzerland; a national identity card is generally sufficient. Citizens of Australia, Canada, Hong Kong, New Zealand, Singapore, South Africa and the USA do not need a visa for stays of less than three months. Switzerland is currently examining an EU proposal to abolish regular passport controls to accord with the EU's Schengen Agreement.

Entry Requirements

Travellers entering Switzerland are *not* officially required to have an onward ticket or 'sufficient means of support', but visitors – particularly those from non-EU countries – who are unable to present either or both may arouse the suspicion of border personnel.

Other Documents

Other useful documents are mentioned in the appropriate sections, eg, driving-related documents are discussed under Car & Motorcycle in the Getting There & Away chapter. Anglers should seek advice about fishing permits (see the boxed text 'Fishing').

Student & Youth Cards An International Student Identity Card (ISIC) gives reductions on admission prices, air and international

Fishing

Many of Switzerland's highland lakes and rivers are regularly restocked with rainbow, brown and lake trout. Other fish common in Swiss waters are salmon, pike, carp and grayling. The length of the fishing season, the closed season for each species, the minimum sizes and the maximum catches all vary between regions or cantons. In most parts of Switzerland anglers need a fishing permit (issued by the cantonal or local authorities), but for some waterways no permit is needed – ask at local tourist offices.

Anglers are represented by the Schweizerischer Fischereiverband/Federation Suisse de Pêches (FVB/FSP; **W** www.sfv-fsp.ch). The German-language *Petri-Heil* (**W** www.web com.ch/petri-Heil), the country's largest fishing magazine, distributes *Angeln in der Schweiz* (Sfr16), a booklet with maps, useful addresses and other information (in German) for anglers.

---

train tickets. People under 26 who are not students can apply for a Federation of International Youth Travel Organisations (FIYTO) card, which gives (fewer) reductions. Both cards are issued by student unions and youth travel agents in your home country.

Pet Passports The eradication of rabies has allowed restrictions to be eased on dogs travelling to/from Britain, Ireland and Sweden – where rabies has never been present – and other Western European countries, including Switzerland and Liechtenstein. A new, vastly simplified Pet Travel Scheme (PTS) requires dogs to be vaccinated against rabies at least one month prior to travel. In Britain and Ireland, dogs may be required to undergo an additional antibody test to check that the vaccine has taken effect, and must also be treated for ticks and other parasites. Dogs must be identifiable by either an implanted microchip or a registration tattoo. Owners should present their dog's PTS certificates – dubbed the 'pet passport' – to border personnel.

EMBASSIES & CONSULATES
Swiss Embassies

Swiss embassies abroad include:

Australia (☎ 02-6273 3977, fax 6273 3428,
  e vertretung@can.rep.admin.ch), 7 Melbourne Ave, Forrest, ACT 2603
Canada (☎ 613-235 1837, fax 563 1394,
  e vertretung@ott.rep.admin.ch) 5 Marlborough Ave, Ottawa, Ontario K1N 8E6
Ireland (☎ 01-218 63 82, fax 283 03 44,
  e vertretung@dub.rep.admin.ch), 6 Ailesbury Rd, Ballsbridge, Dublin 4
New Zealand (☎ 04-472 15 93, fax 499 63 02,
  e vertretung@wel.rep.admin.ch), 22 Panama St, Wellington
South Africa (☎ 012-430 67 07, fax 430 67 71,
  e vertretung@pre.rep.admin.ch), 818 George Ave, Arcadia 0083, 0001 Pretoria, P0 Box 2289, 0001 Pretoria
UK (☎ 020-7616 6000, fax 7724 7001,
  e vertretung@lon.rep.admin.ch), 16–18 Montagu Place, London W1H 2BQ
USA (☎ 202-745 7900, fax 387 2564,
  e vertretung@was.rep.admin.ch), 2900 Cathedral Ave NW, Washington, DC 20008-3499

Embassies & Consulates in Switzerland

Countries with diplomatic representation in Switzerland include:

Australia
  Consulate: (☎ 022-799 91 00, fax 799 91 78,
  e info@australia.ch), Chemin des Fins 2, Geneva
Canada
  Embassy: (☎ 031-357 32 00, fax 357 32 10,
  e bern.cda@pingnet.ch), Kirchenfeldstrasse 88, Bern
Ireland
  Embassy: (☎ 031-352 14 42, fax 352 14 55), Kirchenfeldstrasse 68, 3005 Bern
New Zealand
  Consulate: (☎ 022-929 93 50,
  e mission.nz@itu.ch), 2 Chemin des Fins, Geneva
South Africa
  Consulate: (☎ 022-849 54 10, fax 849 54 32) 65 rue du Rhône, Geneva
UK
  Embassy: (☎ 031-359 77 00, fax 359 77 01,
  e information@british-embassy-berne.ch), Thunstrasse 50, Bern
  Consulate: (☎ 022-918 24 00) Rue de Vermont, Geneva

UK (continued)
Consulate: (☎ 091-950 06 06) Via Motta 19, Lugano
Consulate: (☎ 01-383 65 80) Minervastrasse 117, Zürich
USA
Embassy: (031-357-70 11, fax 357 73 44), Jubiläumsstrasse 93, Bern
Consulate: (☎ 022-798 16 05, fax 798 16 30), World Trade Center, IBC-Building, 29 Route de Pre-Bois, Geneva
Consulate: (☎ 01-422 25 66, fax 383 89 14), Dufourstrasse 101, Zürich

CUSTOMS

Duty-free limits are as follows: visitors from Europe may import 200 cigarettes, 50 cigars or 250g of pipe tobacco. Visitors from non-European countries may import twice as much. The allowance for alcoholic beverages is the same for everyone: 1L for products containing more than 15% alcohol/volume and 2L below 15%. Tobacco and alcohol may only be brought in by people aged 17 or over. Gifts up to the value of Sfr100 may also be imported, and food provisions for one day.

MONEY

The Swiss franc (Sfr, sometimes also abbreviated to 'Fr' or 'CHF'), is called *Schweizer Franken* in German or *franc suisse* in French. It's likely that after its introduction from 1 January 2002, the euro (€, the single currency of most EU countries) will be widely accepted as an alternative means of payment, even though Switzerland is outside the euro-zone.

Exchange Rates

country	unit		Sfr
Australia	A$1	=	Sfr0.92
Austria	ASch10	=	Sfr1.11
Canada	C$1	=	Sfr1.15
Euro	€1	=	Sfr1.53
France	FF10	=	Sfr2.33
Germany	DM1	=	Sfr0.78
Italy	IL1000	=	Sfr0.79
New Zealand	NZ$1	=	Sfr0.75
UK	UK£1	=	Sfr2.52
USA	US$1	=	Sfr1.77

Currency

Swiss-franc banknotes come in 10, 20, 50, 100, 200 and 1000 franc denominations. There are coins for five, 10, 20 and 50 centimes (or *Rappen* in German), as well as for one, two and five francs.

Bank Accounts & ATMs

It's not advisable to rely on only one means of carrying your money. The Cirrus system, which allows direct withdrawals from your home bank account at almost any automatic teller machine (ATM) in Switzerland, will probably be the most convenient and safest way to access cash. Major travellers cheques are accepted but credit cards give greater freedom. Regular visitors to Switzerland sometimes open a Swiss Post postcheque account *(Postcheckkonto* or *compte de cheque postal)*, as post offices have longer opening hours and are found even in small towns.

On the Walk

Bring more than enough cash to cover all possible en-route expenses, including accommodation, meals or mountain transport. You may have trouble changing banknotes in denominations higher than Sfr200, so carry some smaller cash. Most larger mountain hotels and many mountain huts now accept the main credit cards, but don't rely on always being able to pay by card.

At unstaffed huts, fees, drinks and snacks can be paid for either by dropping a cash envelope directly into the hut honesty box or by deposit slip (available from the hut) payable at any post office in Switzerland. This honesty system relies on your goodwill – don't 'forget' to pay.

Security

Although the crime rate is low in Switzerland and concentrated in larger cities, minor theft occasionally occurs even in out-of-the-way places. Taking common-sense precautions should be enough to avoid robbery, or at least to minimise the loss and inconvenience it causes. Theft is not common in Swiss youth hostels or hotels and almost unheard of in mountain huts – solidarity seems to be strong among walkers in Switzerland – but don't unnecessarily tempt potential thieves by leaving money or valuable items such as cameras unattended. Always keep a separate stash with cash and photocopies of all essential documents for emergencies.

Costs

The Swiss franc (along with the euro) has fallen against the British pound and the US dollar during the last few years. Although this has made Switzerland a less expensive place than it once was, prices for most goods and services are still relatively high. Larger cities and more heavily touristed regions (such as the Bernese Oberland or the Upper Engadine) tend to be more expensive.

Accommodation is cheaper (if more rudimentary) in the mountains. Dorms, such as in mountain huts and youth hostels, are available for a fraction of the cost of a room in even a lower-budget hotel, and organised camping grounds are cheaper still. Guests staying at most mountain resorts receive a special card (known as *Kurkarte*) that gives a wide range of discounts on anything from walking maps to cable cars.

Although prices at mountain restaurants generally compare favourably with those in Swiss cities, picnicking on some Alpine meadow will always work out a less expensive and more enjoyable alternative. Buy food and other supplies for your walk at a larger supermarket rather than a small grocery store near the trailhead – supermarket prices are generally significantly cheaper.

Depending on whether you intend basing yourself somewhere or will be moving around the country, rail and other transport passes can save you money (see the Getting Around chapter). Also inquire about cheaper Wanderpass tickets that cover transport for a particular walk.

Even the most thrifty walker would be unrealistic to budget for much less than Sfr60 per day for travel in Switzerland. Sample costs for a typical day's walking in the Swiss Alps are:

10km by postbus	Sfr5.50
Cable car (one way)	Sfr17.20
Walking map	Sfr22.50
Local phone call	Sfr0.60
Budget hotel single/double	Sfr40/80
Youth hostel	Sfr27
Mountain hut	Sfr27
100g cheese	Sfr1.80
100g sausage	Sfr1.40
Loaf of bread	Sfr2.20
Cup of coffee (restaurant)	Sfr3.50
Dinner (hut)	Sfr18
Budget restaurant meal	Sfr25

Tipping & Bargaining

Restaurant and hotel bills already include a 15% service charge, but are often rounded up slightly by satisfied patrons. Bargaining for purchases is almost unheard of (except at flea markets), but tactful persuasion can sometimes knock down the price of a hotel room somewhat, especially outside the busy tourist season.

POST & COMMUNICATIONS
Post

Switzerland's national postal service, Swiss Post (W www.post.ch), is very efficient. Post offices are generally open Monday to Friday 8am to noon and 2 to 6.30pm; and Saturday 8 to 11am, but in larger cities the central post office stays open throughout the midday break. The minimum postage for a letter within Switzerland (up to 100g) is Sfr0.70, within Europe and the Mediterranean (up to 20g) Sfr1.30, and to all other countries (up to 20g) Sfr1.80.

Poste-restante mail can be sent to any post office in Switzerland, and is held for 30 days; there is no charge for this service. Swiss Post also operates the network of postbuses which leave (at least where there is no train station) from local post offices. In villages and very small towns, the post office often serves as a tourist office and gives out basic information. Hundreds of small regional post offices are to be closed over the coming years as part of a major restructuring of Swiss Post, however.

Telephone

Switzerland's telephone system is one of the best in Europe. The main telecommunications company, both for fixed-line and mobile services, is the now partially privatised Swisscom (previously Telecom PTT). Most Swisscom public telephones are equipped with an electronic keyboard and screen that allows users to send short emails, SMS (Short Message Service) messages and make free telephone directory searches in English. At **W** www.tel.search.ch you can make your own Internet directory searches.

Most public telephones take Swisscom's Sfr5, Sfr10 and Sfr20 plastic ('smart') Tax-cards, some accept only coins, and a few take both. On public phones the minimum charge to make a call is Sfr0.60, and an SMS or email costs Sfr0.90. International prepaid cards for making calls on public and private (but not mobile) phones are available at kiosks, newsstands, post offices and train stations in Sfr10, Sfr20, Sfr50 and Sfr100 denominations. Global One prepaid cards offer better value than those of Swisscom.

The country code for Switzerland is ☎ 41. To call Switzerland from abroad, drop the initial zero from the area code; eg, for Bern dial ☎ 41 31, *preceded* by the overseas access code of the country you're calling from. The overseas access code *from* Switzerland is 00. For operator-assisted national inquiries call ☎ 111; the charge is Sfr1.60 (Sfr2.50 on public phones) plus Sfr0.25 per minute (Sfr0.79 from mobile (cell) phones).

Mobile (Cell) Phones Switzerland uses the international GSM (Global System for Mobile Telephony) standard. Mobile phones are known colloquially as *natel* or *handy* in both German and French. Foreign visitors can use mobile phones from outside the national network under the international 'roaming' system. (Later-model cell phones from the US and Canada, where the TDMA/CDMA standard is used, will also function.)

Due to the convenience and the greater safety that mobiles offer, they have become standard equipment among Swiss walkers. Although the mobile network covers most of Switzerland, major gaps still exist in Alpine regions – Swisscom has the widest coverage. If you have trouble accessing the network, moving a short distance along the slope may restore reception. The new

New Telephone Numbers

From 29 March 2002 Switzerland will drop all its regional telephone codes. Currently, standard telephone numbers in Switzerland have seven digits with an additional three-digit regional prefix code (except for Zürich, which has an exclusive two-digit 01 code). These will be replaced by new nine-digit numbers, comprising the present regional prefix code, minus the initial '0', followed by the old seven-digit number. For example, the number of the Grindelwald tourist office will change from ☎ 033-854 12 12 to ☎ 33-854 12 12; you will need to dial ☎ 33 854 12 12 whether you're in Grindelwald or elsewhere.

UMTS standard, to be introduced from 2002, will improve network coverage.

The Short Message Service (SMS) is very useful to walkers and foreign travellers, although the new WAP system, which allows Internet access from mobile phones, is slow, unstable and rather limited. Personal directory listings can be checked on ☎ 1144 (Sfr0.70 per inquiry) by typing the surname, a space, the locality, a space, then the person's first name; for names and localities consisting of more than one word, replace the space with a dot. For additional SMS-based services, see also Weather Information later and Public Transport Information in the Getting Around chapter.

eKno Communication Service

Lonely Planet's eKno global communication service provides low-cost international calls – for local calls you're usually better off with a local phonecard. eKno also offers free messaging services, email, travel information and an online travel vault, where you can securely store all your important documents. You can join online at www .ekno.lonelyplanet.com, where you will find all the local-access numbers for the 24-hour customer-service centre. The eKno access number from Switzerland is ☎ 0800-897 306. Once you have joined, always check the eKno Web site for the latest access numbers for each country and updates on new features.

Fax

Some hotels may prefer to receive bookings by fax rather than by email or phone. Faxes can be sent from larger post offices, but you'll probably be able to do it more cheaply from a hotel.

Email

Email is now very widely used in Switzerland. Virtually all tourist offices, larger hotels and youth hostels can be contacted by email, and online bookings are often possible. Emails can be sent from public phones for Sfr0.90.

INTERNET RESOURCES

Travellers in Switzerland shouldn't have much trouble finding somewhere to access the Internet. Cybercafes generally charge at least Sfr12 per hour, but libraries' terminals are much cheaper (sometimes even free). Rooms in better-standard hotels often have modem plugs for laptops.

All important Swiss organisations have Web sites, most with significant English-language content, allowing travellers to access a wide range of online information. However, Web sites for individual towns or smaller businesses may have little in English. Some relevant Web sites are mentioned under Useful Organisations earlier and under the Access Towns or Nearest Towns sections in the regional chapters. Other worthwhile Web sites include:

Background Information
W www.schweiz-in-sicht.ch 'Entry level' site
W www.about.ch Well-presented outline of Swiss culture, history and geography
W www.switzerland.com Has numerous links and is good for general research
Alpinism & Walking
W www.alpineresearch.ch An excellent well-linked site of useful for anyone with broad Alpine interests
Natural History
W www.wild.unizh.ch Site of the Swiss Wildlife Information Service (SWIS), part of the University of Zürich, with numerous links and download files in English on European fauna

News & Current Affairs
W www.swissinfo.ch Site of Swiss Radio International
Web Cams
W www.topin.ch/ch Views of mountain resorts throughout Switzerland
Ecology
W www.buwal.ch/e News and interesting articles from the Swiss Agency for the Environment, Forests and Landscape
W www.cipra.org The Web site of the International Commission for the Protection of the Alps (CIPRA), with numerous links in French, Italian, German, Slovene and (occasionally) English

BOOKS
Lonely Planet

Like all Lonely Planet guides, *Switzerland* by Mark Honan is thoroughly updated regularly. It includes information on travel and has numerous accurate city and regional maps, and is probably the best all-round travel guidebook available on Switzerland.

Walking Guidebooks

A vast range of walking guidebooks – almost entirely in German and French – covering virtually every region of Switzerland are available from bookshops, tourist offices or newsstands. Relevant titles are suggested under Information in each regional chapter.

In English There are surprisingly few walking guidebooks in English available on Switzerland. *Walking Easy: Swiss & Austrian Alps* (US$14.95) by Chet, Carole & Carolee Lipton, describes mostly shorter day walks and *Walking Switzerland – The Swiss Way* (US$16.95) by Marcia & Philip Lieberman describes walks in many parts of the country that use village inns and mountain huts as bases.

Walking in the Alps by Kev Reynolds (US$22.95) offers a good varied selection of routes in the Alpine areas of Austria, France, Germany, Italy and Switzerland.

The only publisher offering a wide range of walking guidebooks on Switzerland is Cicerone Press (W www.cicerone.co.uk), 2 Police Square, Milnthorpe, Cumbria LA7 7PY, England, whose titles are given in each chapter.

In German & French Switzerland's largest publisher of walking guidebooks is K+F (see Maps earlier). K+F has dozens of regional guides that cover every part of Switzerland; all are published in German, but many also appear as French-language titles. K+F's *Wander Atlas Schweiz* (Sfr39.80; *Le Grand Atlas Suisse des Promenades* in French) outlines excursions on foot all over Switzerland.

Pro Natura's *Guide des réserves naturelles en Suisse* (Sfr48) in French and its similar German-language *Wanderführer durch 132 Naturschutzgebiete der Schweiz* (Sfr49) give an introduction for walkers to the nature reserves of Switzerland.

Swiss publisher Werdverlag (Ⓦ www .werdverlag.ch), Postfach, 8021 Zürich, has a number of worthwhile titles, including *35 Aussichtsberge der Schweiz*, *40 Passabenteuer* and *40 Wanderungen am Wasser* (Sfr34.90 each), which have suggestions for walking in many parts of Switzerland. The Ott Verlag (Ⓦ www.ott-verlag.ch) in Thun puts out thematic guidebooks in German and French detailing cultural, historical or natural walks, such as *Wanderungen zu den schönsten Naturschutzgebieten* (Sfr37.90), and *Jakobswege durch die Schweiz* or *Les Amis du Chemin de St-Jacques* in French (either Sfr39.80). The AT Verlag (Ⓦ www.at-verlag .ch) publishes the excellent *Die Schönsten Hüttenziele der Schweiz* (Sfr70) and *Die Schönsten Gipfelziele der Schweizer Alpen* (Sfr44), both by Peter Donatsch.

The Swiss Alpine Club (SAC) publishes guidebooks to all mountain areas in Switzerland. Most are mountaineering rather than walking titles, but the SAC's *Wandern Alpin*, or *Randonnées en altitude* in French (each Sfr33), describes over 80 walks in the Swiss Alps.

Other publishers of German-language guides include Bruckmann Verlag (Ⓦ www .bruckmann.de) and Bergverlag Rother (Ⓦ www.rother.de). Bruckmann's *Wandertouren in der Schweiz* and *Hochgebirgstouren in der Schweiz* (both Sfr39.95) are very good.

Travel & Exploration

The literature left behind by the pioneers of Swiss Alpine travel and exploration takes up whole bookshelves. Larger libraries are likely to stock any of the titles listed below.

Early Travellers in the Alps by Gavin R de Beer (first published in 1930) is essentially the history of Alpine exploration and travel from the early 1700s until the late 19th century. This book recounts the experiences of people such as the Genevan naturalist Horace Bénédict Saussure, who made several scientific journeys into the mountains of the Valais. Numerous woodcuts and engravings of people and scenery are featured. De Beer is also the author of half a dozen or so interesting titles dealing with travel in Switzerland, including *Escape to Switzerland* (Penguin, 1945) and *Alps and Men* (London, 1932).

Scrambles Amongst the Alps by Edward Whymper was first published in 1871. Whymper made first ascents of several important peaks in the Valaisan Alps, and a climbing party under his leadership was the first to reach the summit of the Matterhorn. Whymper's classic work provides a good introduction to the Victorian era of mountaineering in the Alps.

As president of the British Alpine Club, Leslie Stephen made countless climbing excursions to Switzerland. His book *The Playground of Europe* (first published in 1871) gives accounts of his ascents, traverses and pass-crossings in the Alps, making excellent reading.

Wandering Among the High Alps by Alfred Wills (first published in 1939) is recommended reading for anyone interested in the heyday of mountaineering.

A History of Mountaineering in the Alps by Claire Eliane Engle (first published in 1953) traces the beginnings of mountaineering, from the first scientific ascents by 17th-century naturalists through Alpinism's 'golden years' in the 1800s to its gradual popularisation after WWII.

Natural History

In English Most recommended is *Our Alpine Flora* (Sfr45) by Elias Landolt, a translation from the original German (there's also a French edition). Landolt's compact hard-cover work is a comprehensive field guide to plants of the Swiss Alps. It's full of drawings and colourplates depicting some 500 species – just about every Alpine wild flower or shrub you're likely to want to identify on your walks. It's available in larger local bookshops or can be ordered from the SAC (see Useful Organisations earlier).

The Alpine Flowers of Britain and Europe by Christopher Grey-Wilson & Marjorie Blamey is a standard field guide covering the Alpine and subalpine flora in mountain regions of Western Europe (chiefly Britain, Scandinavia, Iberia and the Alps). This title is hard to find in Switzerland, but is widely sold throughout the British Isles for around UK£15.

The Geology of Switzerland by Kenneth J Hsu (Princeton, US$77.50) is a recent publication for anyone with a serious interest in Swiss landforms.

In German & French *Fleurs et plantes des Alpes* (Sfr14) by Jean-Denis Godet, also available in a German edition titled *Alpenpflanzen* (Thalacker, Sfr24), is a good field guide covering the most common Alpine flowers with colour photos. Two other inexpensive wild flower field guides in German and French are *GU Kompass Alpenblumen* (Sfr9.80) by Wolfgang Lippert and *Fleurs des Alpes* (Miniguide Nathan, Sfr12.50). Two more detailed German-language guides are *Alpenblumen* (Kompass, Sfr29.80) by Moritz M Daffinger and *Naturführer Alpenblumen* (ADAC Verlag, Sfr27.50). *Faune et flore des alpes et du jura* (Arthaud, Sfr28) by Keith Maurin is a general field guide in French covering Alpine flora and fauna.

General

The Xenophobe's Guide to the Swiss by Paul Bilton gives an illuminating and witty introduction to the Swiss. For a good overall run-down on Switzerland there is the paperback *Switzerland – Land, People, Economy* by Aubrey Diem. Another general title giving an insight into the country is *Why Switzerland?* by Jonathan Steinberg. Mark Twain's entertaining European travelogue *A Tramp Abroad* has been a classic for

a hundred years or more; the author spent considerable time journeying through Switzerland.

Buying Books

All of Switzerland's larger cities have bookshops that stock English-language books.

In Basel, English-language books, travel guides and maps are available at Bider & Tanner (☎ 061-206 99 99), Aeschenvorstadt 2. In Geneva, the Elm Book Shop (☎ 022-736 09 45), 5 Rue Versonnex and Book Worm (☎ 022-731 87 65), 5 Rue Sismondi, sell English-language books. In Zürich, the Travel Book Shop (☎ 01-252 38 83), Rindermarkt 20, has a broad range of travel titles as well as maps. Orell Füssli has a large general bookshop at Füsslistrasse 4 and a nearby branch at Bahnhofstrasse 70, which sells exclusively English-language titles.

Swiss-published books can be ordered online from Ⓦ www.book.ch or Ⓦ www.mediantis.ch if you are unable to find them in your home country.

WEATHER INFORMATION

Switzerland has one of the planet's most complex weather patterns, and accurate forecasting is a real challenge for the national weather service, MeteoSwiss (formerly the Swiss Meteorological Institute). In fact, analysis of four-day weather forecasts indicates well under a 75% success rate by the fourth day, so take the longer-range outlook with a pinch of snow.

General Media

Weather information is usually presented in a form graphic enough to be easily understood even if you don't know the language used. Switzerland's French- and German-language television services (TSR and DRS) broadcast the excellent *Meteo* weather report following the evening news just after 7.50pm. The Zürich-based *Tages Anzeiger* (Sfr2.20) newspaper is available all over Switzerland; it also has a good daily weather report.

Telephone

The best telephone weather report (updated five times daily) is in German, French or

Italian and available on ☎ 162 (Sfr0.50 plus Sfr0.50 per minute). For nonrecorded advice in English on weather in any part of Switzerland call ☎ 157 52 62 0 (first minute Sfr3, then Sfr1 per minute) or 0900-57 64 50 (Sfr3.13 per minute).

To receive short Alpine weather reports in English by SMS (mobile phones only, Sfr0.50 per message) dial ☎ 322 with the appropriate keyword for any of the following regions: MTWEST for Western Switzerland and the Valais; MTBEJU for the Bernese Oberland and Jura; MTCENT for Central Switzerland; MTEAST for the Alpstein (Säntis) and Northern and Central Bundner Alps; and MTSOUT for Southern Graubünden and Ticino.

Internet

The best English-language site is Ⓦ www .meteoschweiz.ch/en – it includes daily and five-day forecasts as well as an isobaric chart, and is updated frequently. For information in German visit Ⓦ www.sfdrs .ch/sendungen/meteo/karten/wetter_ch_heu te.html, or try Ⓦ www.tsr.ch/TSR/TSR meteo.html for information in French.

PHOTOGRAPHY

The Swiss countryside is so utterly photogenic that you may find yourself taking more shots than you planned (or budgeted) for. Using a UV filter protects the camera lens from scratching, and for outdoor shots invariably gives somewhat better results. For the much harsher light conditions typically encountered in snow or on large bodies of water, a polarising filter may give better results.

Approximate prices per 36-exposure roll are as follows: Agfa CTX Sfr13, Fuji Sensia Sfr20 (includes developing), Kodakchrome Sfr18 (includes developing), Kodak Gold Sfr8 and Konica VX Sfr6.

Switzerland's Inter Discount (Ⓦ www.in terdiscount.ch) chain sells film in multiplepacks at quite competitive rates. It's advisable to have undeveloped film hand-checked rather than allowing it to go through airport x-ray machines, which gradually degrades film quality.

For a thorough grounding in the tips and techniques particular to photography on the road, read Lonely Planet's *Travel Photography* by Richard I'Anson, a full-colour guide for happy-snappers and professional photographers alike.

TIME

Switzerland is one hour ahead of GMT/UTC (although the watchmaking city of Biel now claims – not altogether seriously – to be the absolute centre of a new chronometrical standard called World Time). The daylight-saving period ('summer time') is now the same all over Western Europe, and begins at midnight on the last Saturday in March (put clocks forward one hour), and ends on the last Saturday in October. A 24-hour clock is used where times are written, as on program schedules or timetables.

ELECTRICITY

Absurdly, three different power plug variants are used in Switzerland, with two or (more commonly) three round pins. The standard continental European type plug is compatible with most – but not all – Swiss electrical sockets. Where the socket is connected to an electrical cord, sawing off the socket rim is sometimes a simple way of solving the problem – it's not as dangerous as it sounds, but using an adapter plug is a less radical method.

The electric current in Switzerland is 220V, 50Hz. Most appliances designed for 240V will handle 220V quite well, but travellers from North America will need a stepdown transformer – this may be integrated in your appliance, so read the instructions.

WEIGHTS & MEASURES

Switzerland has used the vastly superior metric system for generations. Unpackaged 'delicatessen' foods like cheese or sausage are often sold per 100g. Beverages are generally measured by decilitre (0.1L) – rather than in millilitres; eg, a standard beer glass holds three decilitres (0.3L). Commas (rather than decimal points) are used for numbers of four digits or more.

BUSINESS HOURS

Shops are generally open from 8am to 6.30pm Monday to Friday, and to 4 or 5pm on Saturday. In larger cities many shops (particularly supermarkets and department stores) stay open over the midday break, but otherwise shops close for 1½ to two hours from around noon. In country areas, shops are often closed on Wednesday (or just Wednesday afternoon). Banks are almost always open Monday to Friday from 8.30am until 4.30pm.

PUBLIC HOLIDAYS & SPECIAL EVENTS

Public holidays fall on New Year's Day, 1 January; Good Friday; Easter Sunday and Monday; Ascension Day (May – 40th day after Easter); National Day, 1 August; Whit Sunday and Monday (May/June – seventh Sunday after Easter); Christmas Day, 25 December; and Boxing Day, 26 December. Some cantons observe their own holidays and religious days, for example, 2 January, 1 May (Labour Day) and Corpus Christi.

Health & Safety

On the whole, Switzerland is a very healthy and safe country for visitors. Although the risks are not to be overstated, walkers should understand that a variety of potential dangers exist, which can be minimised but not completely eliminated.

Remember that it's easy to underestimate the strenuousness of mountain walking. Routes in the Swiss Alps commonly involve ascents of 1000m or more, so a good level of physical fitness is essential. The best way to prepare yourself for your walking holiday is to undertake some regular (vigorous) exercise shortly before you arrive. Otherwise, take things slowly during the first week or so.

PREDEPARTURE PLANNING
Medical Cover
Health costs are expensive in Switzerland, and since nonresidents on holiday there do *not* have free medical coverage it is vital that visitors have some kind of travel insurance. Travel agents can advise you on the most appropriate travel-insurance package, but be sure that you will be covered for all outdoor pursuits you undertake during your trip. Some policies specifically exclude 'dangerous activities' such as paragliding or roped mountaineering, but sometimes even hiking may not be covered. Also check whether the policy covers ambulances or an emergency flight home.

Health Insurance
Make sure that you have adequate health insurance. There is no state health service in Switzerland and all treatment must be paid for. No reciprocal agreements exist for free treatment with any other country. Medication and consultations are expensive – a brief consultation costs around Sfr130. The local tourist office can tell you where to get treatment.

Physical Preparation
While the human body can often adjust remarkably quickly to the rigours of mountain walking, it's a bit late to start thinking of getting fit as you step out of the train in Grindelwald. Some kind of vigorous exercise, such as walking uphill (stairs are a fair simulation), light jogging or swimming – starting at least four weeks before arrival – should give your body enough time to adjust for the Alpine onslaught.

Immunisations
No vaccinations are required to enter Switzerland, but travellers arriving from an area where cholera and yellow fever are prevalent, such as Africa or South America, will need an International Health Certificate.

Some routine vaccinations are recommended, however, including polio, tetanus and diphtheria. It's particularly important that your tetanus is up to date – the initial course of three injections, usually given in childhood, is followed by boosters every 10 years. If you expect to spend much time in lower forest areas, also consider being vaccinated against tick-borne encephalitis – see Insect-Borne Diseases later.

First Aid
Walkers should know what to do in the event of a serious accident or illness. Consider taking a basic first aid course before you go – some points are listed later under Traumatic Injuries. Prevention of accidents and illness is as important – refer to Safety

---

Gly-Coramin

Gly-Coramin is a kind of chewy sweet sold without prescription in pharmacies (for around Sfr7.50 for a pack of 20) that Swiss walkers often eat on long or strenuous hikes. Apart from glucose, Gly-Coramin contains Nicethamid, a mild stimulant that promotes breathing and increases the body's uptake of oxygen. The Bolivians have their coca leaves, the Swiss have their Gly-Coramin.

Medical Kit Check List

Following is a list of items you should consider including in your medical kit – consult you pharmacist for brands available in your country.

First Aid Supplies
- ☐ adhesive tape
- ☐ blister plasters
- ☐ crepe bandages
- ☐ elasticised support bandage for knees, ankles etc
- ☐ gauze swabs
- ☐ nonadhesive dressings
- ☐ small pair of scissors
- ☐ sterile alcohol wipes
- ☐ paper stitches
- ☐ sticking plasters
- ☐ thermometer (note that mercury thermometers are prohibited by airlines)
- ☐ triangular bandages and safety pins
- ☐ tweezers

Medications
- ☐ anti-diarrhoea and anti-nausea drugs
- ☐ antifungal cream or powder – for fungal skin infections and thrush
- ☐ antihistamines – for allergies, eg, hay fever; to ease the itch from insect bites or stings; and to prevent motion sickness
- ☐ antiseptic (such as povidone-iodine) – for cuts and grazes
- ☐ calamine lotion, sting relief spray or aloe vera – to ease irritation from sunburn and insect bites or stings
- ☐ cold and flu tablets, throat lozenges and nasal decongestant
- ☐ multivitamins – consider for long trips, when dietary vitamin intake may be inadequate
- ☐ painkillers eg, aspirin or paracetamol (acetaminophen in the USA) – for pain and fever
- ☐ rehydration mixture – to prevent dehydration, eg, due to severe diarrhoea; particularly important when travelling with children

Miscellaneous
- ☐ eye drops
- ☐ insect repellent
- ☐ sunscreen and lip balm
- ☐ water purification tablets or iodine

on the Walk for more advice. You should also know how to summon help in case a major accident or illness occurs – see Emergency Communications under Rescue & Evacuation later.

Travel Health Guides
Serious walkers and trekkers might be interested in the following detailed health guides.

Travellers' Health, Dr Richard Dawood, Oxford University Press, 1995. Comprehensive, easy to read, authoritative and highly recommended.

Mountaineering Medicine, Fred Darvill, Wilderness Press, 1998. A technical pocket guide specifically for trekkers and mountaineers.

Medicine for Mountaineering & Other Wilderness Activities, James A Wilkerson, The Mountaineers, 1993. An excellent reference for the lay person on a remote walk or trek.

Online Resources
The Swiss Federal Office of Public Health's Web site (W www.admin.ch/bag) is a good resource. Lonely Planet's Web site (W www.lonelyplanet.com/weblinks/wlheal.htm) has links to the World Health Organization, the US Centers for Disease Control & Prevention and other useful sites.

STAYING HEALTHY
Food
Although travellers in Switzerland are highly unlikely to be served up bacterially contaminated food, from time to time unsanitary preparation (especially repeated reheating) or improper storage result in serious cases of food poisoning. Since a salmonella outbreak in the late 1980s, dairy products must be pasteurised. (Much to the chagrin of Swiss gourmands, this includes the smelly vacherin cheese from the Jura, previously made with raw milk.)

BSE (Mad Cow Disease) Bovine spongiform encephalopathy (BSE, or 'mad cow disease') attacks the central nervous system of cattle, eventually killing the animals. (The BSE epidemic may have its origins in animal waste – mainly from abattoirs – that was reprocessed and fed to cattle.) Human consumption of BSE-contaminated beef has been linked to Creutzfeldt-Jakob disease (CJD) and several other fatal diseases for which no satisfactory treatment exists. Although the real risk to humans who eat beef from BSE-affected cattle appears to be extremely low, public concern about BSE has led to a drastic drop in beef consumption in Switzerland and many other European countries. Rigorous control measures, above all the mandatory slaughter and proper destruction of all potentially BSE-affected animals, have now largely eradicated BSE from Swiss cattle, but the country will not attain 'BSE-free' status until 2003 at the earliest.

Water

Water oozes, bubbles or gushes forth at mountain springs throughout the Swiss Alps, and finding safe drinking water somewhere along the route is seldom a problem. BSE notwithstanding, livestock and wildlife in Switzerland do not carry any particularly nasty diseases (such as the dreaded giardiasis), but drinking faecally contaminated water anywhere is likely to give you a bout of the 'runs' (see Diarrhoea under Infectious Diseases later).

Throughout the mountains, drinking fountains are the most reliable source of potable water. Generally troughs hewn out of a log or rock slab and filled by piped spring water, drinking fountains can be found along most well-transited paths and walkways. Mountain huts below 2500m (or so) usually have a drinking trough for guests and passing walkers, but this is not always the case at higher elevations where running water is often in scarce supply. Towns and village squares often have fountains of running water. If the water is not of drinking quality, this will usually be indicated by *Kein Trinkwasser* or *eau non potable* signs.

When deciding whether to trust the water from a particular stream, remember that water flowing through a heavily visited area should always be treated with suspicion – avoid drinking from streams near mountain huts or downstream from any dwelling. It's advisable to carry a water bottle on longer walks to fill up at obviously reliable

sources. Throughout Switzerland, bottled mineral water is cheaply available in still and carbonated forms.

Water Purification It's unlikely you'll have to drink water from a suspect source, but the simplest way of purifying water is to boil it vigorously for five minutes. Remember that water boils at a progressively lower temperature the higher up you go, so noxious bacteria are less likely to be killed. Simple filtering will not remove all dangerous organisms, so if you cannot boil water it should be treated chemically. Chlorine tablets (Puritabs, Steritabs or other brand names) will kill many but not all pathogens, including giardia and amoebic cysts. Iodine is very effective in purifying water and is available in tablet form (such as Potable Aqua), but follow the directions carefully and remember that too much iodine can be harmful.

Common Ailments

Blisters Don't let blisters turn your holiday into a trek of torture. Although blisters may sometimes occur even with properly worn-in boots, they can usually be avoided if you treat your feet with fitting respect. Your boots should feel comfortably snug – but not tight – when you're wearing a pair of padded (preferably bright red) hiking socks. Wear in new boots well in advance of your walking holiday, and start off doing easy day walks that allow your feet time to adjust to the bump-and-rub of mountain paths. Protect those tender toes and heels with sticking tape (such as Elastoplast) well before the skin starts to get sore. Swiss druggists and pharmacies sell 'second skin' type sticking plasters that both prevent and treat blisters; one such locally made brand is Compeed.

Fatigue Walking accidents tend to occur in the latter part of the day. After many hours' hard hiking, walkers are often impatient to reach their destination and may fail to notice – or even admit to – a steady decline in their concentration and balance. This not only detracts from the appreciation of the walk but in bad weather or in dangerous terrain it becomes life-threatening. If you're still on the trail by mid-afternoon, make a deliberate effort to slow down and take regular rest stops. Keep up your blood-sugar level by snacking frequently on high-energy foods such as nuts, dried fruit or chocolate.

Knee Pain Long, steep descents put a heavy strain on the knees. As the leg bends sharply to compensate for the lower step, weight is transferred onto the bent knee, pulling the kneecap backward against the joint.

Walkers can reduce knee pain by developing a proper technique of descent. Take short, controlled steps with the legs in a slightly bent position, placing your heels on the ground before the rest of the foot. Mountain paths usually negotiate very steep slopes in numerous switchback curves to avoid a much steeper direct descent. Trekking stocks (see Clothing & Equipment in the Facts for the Walker chapter) distribute much of the load off the legs and knees (albeit at the expense of the arms), but their long-term use tends to reduce a walker's surefootedness. Many walking routes in Switzerland give you the option of making your descent by some mechanical means, such as a cable car or funicular railway.

MEDICAL PROBLEMS & TREATMENT
Environmental Hazards
Altitude Few walks described in this guidebook take you above 3000m. Although some walkers – more often older people or those with high blood pressure – may well feel the altitude after ascending, the 'altitude risk' for Alpine walkers is minimal in Switzerland.

Acute Mountain Sickness The potentially fatal condition known as Acute Mountain Sickness (AMS) is caused by the lack of oxygen and the lower atmospheric pressure at high altitudes. This prevents the lungs from passing enough oxygen into the blood.

There is no hard and fast rule about when 'true' cases of AMS can occur: although serious cases of AMS at altitudes as low 2500m have been documented, it more typically occurs above 3500m.

Mild altitude problems will generally abate after a day or so but if the symptoms persist or become worse the only treatment is to descend – even 500m can help. Breathlessness; a dry, irritating cough (which may progress to the production of pink, frothy sputum); severe headache; loss of appetite; insomnia; dizziness; nausea, and sometimes vomiting are all danger signs. Increasing tiredness, confusion, and lack of coordination and balance are more advanced symptoms. Any of these symptoms individually, even just a persistent headache, can be a warning.

If you have reason to believe you may be susceptible to AMS take the following precautions:

• Ascend slowly with frequent rests
• Drink extra fluids – in the mountains moisture is more easily lost as you breathe; certain symptoms of body dehydration are easily mistaken for AMS
• Eat light, high-carbohydrate meals for more energy
• Avoid alcohol as it may increase the risk of dehydration
• Avoid taking sedatives

Sun A large number of walks described in this guidebook take you well above 2000m. At such altitudes the summer sun can beat down with surprising intensity.

Sunburn occurs more rapidly at higher elevations, even in overcast weather. As well as being painful and unpleasant, sunburn permanently damages your skin and increases your risk of later developing skin cancer. Sunburn is a particular problem in early summer (June), since the sun's intensity is then greatest and large snowdrifts remain to reflect the UV radiation back up at you.

Snowblindness, a painful form of sunburn on the surface of the eye (cornea), occurs when the eyes are exposed to reflected snow glare for several hours. Cold cloths on closed eyelids should relieve the pain, and the eyes recover within a few days. A robust pair of sunglasses with UV lenses will prevent snowblindness (as well as drastically improve your vision in snowy terrain).

Protect your skin by wearing a broad-brimmed hat and keeping your limbs and face either covered up or well smeared with a sunblock – superior brands use the Australian numbering scale that best indicates relative anti-UV effectiveness. Calamine lotion is a good treatment for mild sunburn.

Heat Midsummer weather in Switzerland can be surprisingly hot. In July it is not unusual for the whole country to swelter for weeks in daytime temperatures of around 30°C. At lower elevations, hot weather brings sticky, humid conditions that make you wonder whether the climate is turning tropical! Humidity is less of a problem higher up on the Alpine slopes, but it can still be very hot. For walkers there is the possibility of heat exhaustion.

Dehydration or salt deficiency can cause heat exhaustion, so ensure that your body gets sufficient liquids. Salt deficiency is characterised by fatigue, lethargy, headaches, giddiness and muscle cramps, and in this case salt tablets may help. One way walkers can avoid the heat is by getting an early start, then taking it easy during the hottest part of the day.

Cold Cold conditions are the norm rather than the exception in the Alps, despite the illusion of a balmy paradise created by warm weather and luxuriant summer vegetation. The arrival of a front or a sudden thunderstorm that drenches ill-prepared walkers in freezing rain is not just unpleasant but dangerous. A slip into the frigid waters of a high-Alpine lake or river could be fatal.

Hypothermia (also known as exposure) is a real and ever-present threat to mountain walkers anywhere. Hypothermia occurs when the body begins to lose heat faster than it can produce it, causing the core temperature to fall.

It is surprisingly easy to progress from very cold to dangerously cold due to a combination of wind, wet clothing, fatigue and hunger, even if the air temperature is above freezing. Signs of hypothermia include exhaustion, lethargy, slurred speech, numbness (particularly toes and fingers), stumbling, shivering, irrational or violent behaviour, dizzy spells, muscle cramps and violent bursts of energy. Irrationality may take the form of a sufferer claiming they are warm and trying to take off their clothes.

To treat hypothermia, first get the person out of the wind and/or rain, remove their clothing if it's wet and replace it with dry, warm garments. Give them hot liquids – not alcohol – and some simple sugary food. Do not rub the victim but place them near a fire or in a warm (not hot) bath. This should be enough for the early stages of hypothermia, but if it has gone further it may be necessary to place the victim in a warm bed or sleeping bag and get in with them.

Watch for signs of impending bad weather and descend or seek shelter if things start to look dicey. Walkers should always carry a totally waterproof rainjacket (and preferably overpants) no matter how good the weather appears when they set out. Also carry basic supplies, including food containing simple sugars to generate heat quickly and lots of fluid to drink.

Infectious Diseases

Diarrhoea While a change of water, food or climate may give travellers a case of the runs, Switzerland's high standard of hygiene means that serious diarrhoea – which is caused by contaminated food or water – is fairly uncommon. If diarrhoea does hit you, however, fluid replacement is the mainstay of management. Weak black tea with a little sugar, soda water, or soft drinks allowed to go flat and diluted 50% with water are all good. With severe diarrhoea a rehydrating solution is necessary to replace minerals and salts. Commercially available oral rehydration salts (ORS) are very useful. You should stick to a bland diet as you recover.

Gut-paralysing drugs such as diphenoxylate or loperamide can be used to bring relief from the symptoms, although they do not actually cure the problem.

Fungal Infections The high humidity that typically accompanies hot summer weather in Switzerland creates ideal breeding conditions for fungi. Fungal infections most commonly affect walkers between the toes (athlete's foot). Another common walkers' complaint is 'crotch rot', a painful rash in the groin-to-buttocks area caused by the combination of rubbing and sweating as you walk; simple solutions include wearing comfortable, nonabrasive clothing and keeping clean. Ringworm (which is a fungal infection, not a worm) is picked up from infected animals or by walking on damp areas like shower floors.

Fungal infections can be treated by exposing the infected area to air or sunlight and/or applying an antifungal cream or powder like tolnaftate.

Hepatitis Hepatitis is a general term for inflammation of the liver. It is a common disease worldwide. There are several different viruses that cause hepatitis, and they differ in the way that they are transmitted. The symptoms are similar in all forms of the illness, and include fever, chills, headache, fatigue, feelings of weakness and aches and pains, followed by loss of appetite, nausea, vomiting, abdominal pain, dark urine, light-coloured faeces, jaundiced (yellow) skin and yellowing of the whites of the eyes. People who have had hepatitis should avoid alcohol for some time after the illness, as the liver needs time to recover.

Hepatitis A is transmitted by contaminated food and drinking water. You should seek medical advice, but there is not much you can do apart from resting, drinking lots of fluids, eating lightly and avoiding fatty foods. **Hepatitis E** is transmitted in the same way as hepatitis A; it can be particularly serious in pregnant women.

There are almost 300 million chronic carriers of **hepatitis B** in the world. It is spread through contact with infected blood, blood products or body fluids, for example through sexual contact, unsterilised needles and blood transfusions, or contact with blood via small breaks in the skin. Other risk situations include having a shave, tattoo or body piercing with contaminated equipment. The symptoms of hepatitis B may be more severe than type A and the disease can lead to long-term problems such as chronic liver damage, liver cancer or a long-term carrier state. **Hepatitis C** and **D** are spread in the same way as hepatitis B and can also lead to long-term complications.

There are vaccines against hepatitis A and B, but there are currently no vaccines against the other types of hepatitis. Following the basic rules about food and water (hepatitis A and E) and avoiding risk situations (hepatitis B, C and D) are important preventative measures.

HIV & AIDS Infection with the human immunodeficiency virus (HIV) may lead to acquired immune deficiency syndrome (AIDS), which is a fatal disease. Any exposure to blood, blood products or body fluids may put the individual at risk. The disease is often transmitted through sexual contact or dirty needles – vaccinations, acupuncture, tattooing and body piercing can be potentially as dangerous as intravenous drug use. HIV/AIDS can also be spread through infected blood transfusions, although all bllod used in European hospitals is screened for HIV and should be safe.

Rabies Although Switzerland was officially declared rabies-free in 1999, isolated cases of the disease continue to occur.

Rabies is caused by abrasive contact with an infected animal, so any bite, scratch or even lick from a warm-blooded, furry animal should be cleaned immediately and thoroughly. Scrub with soap and running water, and then clean with an alcohol solution. If there is any possibility that the animal is infected, medical help should be sought immediately. Even if the animal is not rabid, all bites should be treated seriously as they can become infected or can result in tetanus. A rabies vaccination should be considered if you are in a high-risk category – eg, if you work with animals.

Tetanus Tetanus is caused by a bacterium that lives in soil and in the faeces of horses and other animals. It enters the body via breaks in the skin. The first symptom may be discomfort in swallowing, or stiffening of the jaw and neck; this is followed by painful convulsions of the jaw and whole body. The disease can be fatal. It can be prevented by vaccination, so make sure you are up to date with this vaccination before you leave.

Insect-Borne Diseases

Tick-Borne Diseases In Switzerland, ticks carry two potentially very serious diseases: tick-borne encephalitis and Lyme disease. Walkers should take precautions to avoid infection – read the Bites & Stings section later for instructions on what to do about tick bites.

The epicentre of tick-borne encephalitis is in North-Eastern Switzerland, but the disease is found in the entire German-speaking area of Switzerland (with the exception of central and southern Graubünden), where it is known as Fruhsommer Meningo-Enzephalitis (FSME). Tick-borne encephalitis normally develops 10 to 30 days after the tick has bitten. Initial symptoms include headaches, confusion and paralysis, but these may progress to meningitis. Most patients make a quick and full recovery, but some have lasting health problems and in about 1% of cases the disease is fatal. A vaccination, when given well before exposure, provides virtually total protection. An antiserum treatment also exists for tick-borne encephalitis, but is only effective in preventing an outbreak in 70% of cases when given within 72 hours after infection.

Lyme disease is also passed on to humans by ticks, but is the result of infection by a bacterium *(Borrefia burgdorferi)*. Lyme disease is not concentrated in any region, but is broadly distributed throughout Switzerland. The early symptoms are similar to flu – headaches, tiredness and painful swelling of the joints – and may take months to develop. In latter stages the nervous system and heart may also be effected, but fatalities are rare. A safe vaccination is not yet available, but Lyme disease responds well to antibiotics.

Traumatic Injuries

Sprains Walkers often suffer ankle and knee sprains, particularly in rugged terrain. Ankle sprains can be avoided by wearing

sturdy boots with adequate support. If you do suffer a sprain, immobilise the joint with a firm bandage, and relieve pain and swelling by keeping the joint elevated and applying an ice pack to the swollen joint. If the sprain is mild, you may continue your walk after a few days. For more severe sprains, seek medical attention.

Major Accident Head injuries or fractures caused during a serious fall or by rockfall (see Safety on the Walk later) are a small but significant danger to walkers. Detailed first aid instruction is outside the scope of this guidebook, but some basic advice on what to do in the event of an accident such as a serious fall follows (see also First Aid under Predeparture Planning earlier).

* Make sure you and other people with you are not in danger
* Assess the injured person's condition
* Stabilise any injuries, such as bleeding wounds or broken bones
* Seek medical attention – see Rescue & Evacuation under Safety on the Walk later for more details

If the person is unconscious, check whether they are breathing – clear their airway if it is blocked – and check whether they have a pulse by feeling the side of the neck rather than the wrist. If they are not breathing but have a pulse, you should start mouth-to-mouth resuscitation immediately. In these circumstances it is best to move the person as little as possible in case their neck or back is broken. Keep the person warm by covering them with a blanket or other dry clothing; insulate them from the ground if possible.

Check for wounds and broken bones – ask the person where they have pain if they are conscious, otherwise gently inspect them all over (including their back and the back of the head), moving them as little as possible. Control any bleeding by applying firm pressure to the wound with a clean dressing. Bleeding from the nose or ear may indicate a fractured skull. Don't give the person anything by mouth, especially if they are unconscious.

Indications of a fracture (broken bone) are pain, swelling and discolouration, loss of function or deformity of a limb. Unless you know what you are doing, you shouldn't try to straighten an obviously displaced broken bone. To protect from further injury, immobilise a nondisplaced fracture by splinting it; for fractures of the thigh bone, try to straighten the leg gently, then tie it to the good leg to hold it in place. Fractures associated with open wounds (compound fractures) require more urgent treatment than simple fractures as there is a risk of infection. Dislocations, where the bone has come out of the joint, are very painful, and should be set as soon as possible by a medical professional.

Broken ribs are painful but usually heal by themselves and do not need splinting. If breathing difficulties occur, or the person coughs up blood, medical attention should be sought urgently, as it may indicate a punctured lung.

Internal injuries are more difficult to detect, and cannot usually be treated in the field. Watch for shock, which is a specific medical condition associated with a failure to maintain circulating blood volume. Signs include a rapid pulse and cold, clammy extremities. A person in shock requires urgent medical attention.

Some general points to bear in mind are as follows:

• Simple fractures take several weeks to heal, so they don't need fixing straight away, but they should be immobilised to protect them from further injury. Compound fractures need much more urgent treatment.
• If you do have to splint a broken bone, remember to check regularly that the splint is not cutting off the circulation to the hand or foot.
• Most cases of brief unconsciousness are not associated with any serious internal injury to the brain, but as a general rule of thumb in these circumstances, any person who has been knocked unconscious should be watched for deterioration. If they do deteriorate, seek medical attention straight away.

Cuts & Scratches

Even small cuts and grazes should be washed and treated with an antiseptic such as povidone-iodine. Infection in a wound is indicated by the skin margins becoming red, painful and swollen. More serious infection can cause swelling of the whole limb and of the lymph glands. The patient may develop a fever, and will need medical attention.

Bites & Stings

Bees & Wasps On lower-elevation walks in spring and summer you'll often pass beehives. Local breeds of bees and wasps tend to be mild-mannered, and rarely sting unless provoked. Bee and wasp stings are usually painful rather than dangerous, and can be treated with calamine lotion or ice packs to reduce the pain and swelling. However, in people who are allergic to them severe breathing difficulties may occur and urgent medical care is required. Be particularly careful when drinking directly from outside taps (or spring water pipes), where thirsty insects often go in search of moisture in hot weather.

Flies & Mosquitoes In summer flies can be somewhat bothersome, especially anywhere with plenty of manure lying about (like around alp huts). Blood-sucking horse flies (march flies) are worst close to streams in hot weather from early June to mid-July, but rarely become a serious pest – except to poor, defenceless cows – and are easy to swat due to their dim-wittedness. Mosquitoes are uncommon above elevations of 700m and do not carry any known diseases.

Snakes Switzerland has two species of venomous snake (see Reptiles in the Flora & Fauna of Switzerland section), which can deliver a painful rather than a fatal bite. To minimise your chances of being bitten always wear boots, socks and long trousers when walking through undergrowth where snakes may be present. Don't put your hands into holes and crevices, and be careful when collecting firewood.

In the unlikely event of someone being bitten, keep the victim calm and still, wrap the bitten limb tightly, as you would for a sprained ankle, and then attach a splint to immobilise it. Then seek medical help.

Don't attempt to catch the snake – the species can be identified later if necessary by traces of its venom on skin or clothing. A sticking plaster placed over the bite site can absorb venom traces for identification. Tourniquets and sucking out the poison are now comprehensively discredited.

Ticks Ticks are found throughout Switzerland up to an altitude of 1200m, and live in underbrush at the forest edge or beside walking tracks. The tick will crawl onto a passing animal or person, embedding its head in the host's skin in order to suck its blood.

Swiss ticks are often carriers of encephalitis diseases (see Tick-Borne Diseases earlier). Check your body carefully after walking through a potentially tick-infested area, and remove the parasites as soon as possible. While a good insect repellent will often stop ticks from biting, medical authorities now strongly discourage using oil, alcohol or the heat of a flame to persuade ticks to let go, as this may actually release pathogens into the bloodstream.

The recommended removal method is to grab the insect's head with a pair of tweezers – or better still with a specially designed tick-removal instrument sold cheaply in local pharmacies – then pull the tick out slowly without 'levering' or twisting the hand.

Women's Health
Gynaecological Problems Antibiotic use, synthetic underwear, sweating and contraceptive pills can lead to fungal vaginal infections, especially when travelling in hot climates. Fungal infections are characterised by a rash, itch and discharge and are usually treated by nystatin, miconazole or clotrimazole pessaries or vaginal cream. If these are not available, a vinegar or lemon-juice douche, or yoghurt can also help. Maintaining good personal hygiene and wearing loose-fitting clothes and cotton underwear may help prevent these infections.

Sexually transmitted diseases are another cause of vaginal problems. See the Infectious Diseases section earlier for more details. Remember that sexual partners must also be treated.

Urinary Tract Infection Cystitis, or inflammation of the bladder, is a common condition in women. Symptoms include burning when urinating and having to urinate frequently and urgently. Blood can sometimes be passed in the urine. Sexual activity with a new partner or with an old partner who has been away for a while can trigger an infection.

The initial treatment is to drink plenty of fluids, which may resolve the problem. Single dose (nonantibiotic) treatments may be effective in the early stages of mild cystitis. If symptoms persist, you need to seek medical attention because a simple infection can spread to the kidneys, causing a more severe illness.

Pregnancy If you are pregnant, see your doctor before you travel. Even normal pregnancies can make a woman feel nauseated and tired for the first three months, and have food cravings that can't be satisfied by the diet available on the trail. During the second trimester, the general feelings often improve, but fatigue can still be a constant factor. In the third trimester, the size of the baby can make walking difficult or uncomfortable.

Altitude Although little is known about the possible adverse effects of altitude on a developing foetus, almost all authorities recommend not travelling above 3500m while pregnant. There is a theoretical risk that side effects of oral contraceptives, like blood clots in the legs or lungs, may be more likely if spending extended periods at high altitude. However, there are no conclusive examples to support this theory. Women already taking oral contraceptives could face other problems, such as irregular bleeding or pregnancy, if they stop taking the pill while on the trail.

SAFETY ON THE WALK
First a sobering statistic: in some summers, the fatalities involving walkers account for almost 50% of all deaths resulting from 'mountain recreation accidents'. The remainder lose their lives pursuing more obviously dangerous activities – mainly roped

Walk Safety – Basic Rules

- Allow yourself more than enough time to complete each leg of the walk before nightfall, especially late in the season when days are shorter.
- Always be prepared to turn back if you don't feel confident about continuing.
- Avoid walking alone – two is the minimum number for safe walking in the mountains.
- Inform a responsible person – a family member, hut warden, hotel receptionist etc – of your walking route, and try to stick to your plans.
- Carry an accurate topographical map, compass (or GPS receiver) and whistle.
- Check the latest weather forecast before setting off – while you walk, keep a careful watch on the weather.
- Never leave the marked trails in foggy conditions. With care, most paths can be followed even in thick fog – otherwise, wait until visibility improves.

mountaineering, rock climbing and paragliding. Unlike other mountain sports, however, where the objective risks are far higher, most walker deaths are directly attributable to tiredness, carelessness and inadequate clothing or footwear. Falls resulting from a slide on grass, autumn leaves, scree or iced-over paths are one of the most common hazards.

Army Shooting Ranges

Among Alpinists, there's an old saying: 'it's never quiet in the mountains'. Quite often the rumbling and booming you hear resonating around the ranges isn't thunder or chunks of ice falling off glaciers at all, but the Swiss Army carrying out shooting exercises. In fact, some of the nicest Alpine valleys are periodically used as artillery or shooting ranges.

Military shooting exercises may last a couple of days or several weeks, and sentries ensure that unauthorised people keep well outside of the danger zone. Firing is generally interrupted at intervals to allow walkers to pass through (especially where no nearby alternative route exists), but in some cases access may not be permitted at all. In practice, exercises seldom seriously interfere with walkers' plans, although it's still advisable to note shooting dates.

If you happen to come across a (possibly) unexploded shell, the obvious advice is not to touch it; inform the military (☎ 033-223 57 27).

Information sheets with maps *(Schiessanzeigen, avis de tir)* showing the shooting ranges are displayed in local post offices and at all entry points to the area. Telephone numbers of regional Swiss Army offices are given for walks that pass through shooting ranges. From mid-2001, this information will be available in English on the Swiss Army's Web site (W www.vbs.admin.ch /internet/Heer/e/index.htm).

Avalanches

Snow avalanches are largely a winter phenomenon, but occasionally there may still be some risk of avalanche on Alpine routes early in the walking season or even after a heavy summer snowfall. Even experienced mountaineers often have trouble assessing avalanche danger, so walkers are advised to consult the local tourist office, mountain hut or school of mountaineering for advice. Routes that cross potential avalanche paths are normally closed until summer snow melt renders them safe.

The Federal Institute for Snow and Avalanche Research (Eidgenossisches Institut fur Schnee- und Lawinenforschung; W www.slf.ch) in Davos posts a national avalanche report on its Web site.

Black Ice

Particularly in autumn, water trickling across the path can quickly freeze to form a thin sheet known as black ice. Often looking more like damp earth or an innocuous puddle, black ice can be extremely treacherous and tricky to cross. Where the problem is very severe, wearing ice-spurs – 'mini-crampons' that fit simply onto your walking boots – is recommended. Ice-spurs are available from outdoor equipment stores from around Sfr85.

Crossing Rivers

Officially designated walking routes in Switzerland have sturdy bridges over all streams that might otherwise require a serious crossing. However, smaller footbridges that are at risk from winter avalanches are often dismantled in autumn (from around mid-October) and put back in spring (from around mid-May). As stream levels are normally at their annual low in autumn anyway, this does not affect many walks. Self-respecting walkers should nevertheless be practised in river-crossing techniques.

The safest place to ford a river is usually just downstream from a long pool. Note that it can be hard to gauge the depth of glacial streams due to the fine sediment they carry. Streams of glacial origin reach their highest level in late afternoon. Heavy rain quickly makes rivers impassable, but mountain streams fall almost as fast as they rise.

Undo the waist buckle and loosen the shoulder straps of your pack so that you can easily slip it off if you stumble or are swept off your feet. Groups should make serious crossings by linking arms and moving together in a line right-angles to the current. Lone walkers should use a sturdy pole (or an improvised tree branch) for support, leaning sideways into the current.

Glaciers

With their unstable ice and deep crevasses, glaciers make extremely dangerous obstacles. Inexperienced walkers should never venture onto the ice unless guided by someone with a sound knowledge of glacier travel. (Normally, this means all members of the party are tied onto a rope to prevent falling into hidden crevasses.)

Some walking routes lead across harmless sections of a glacier without crevasses.

Such routes are marked – usually with stakes and/or the orange or red cones used by road maintenance crews. Two simple and obvious rules apply here: *don't leave the marked route*, and *if you lose your way, turn back immediately.*

Hunting Accidents

Recreational game hunting is popular in all of Switzerland's mountain cantons, especially Graubünden. Depending on local by-laws, the open season on chamois, ibex and deer is for a limited – usually four-week – period between September and October. Although the danger need not be overstated, shooting accidents have occasionally occurred after walkers – but more often other hunters! – strayed into the line of fire. It's a good idea to keep your wits about you on autumn walks, particularly if you leave the marked trails.

Lightning & Thunderstorms

Intense electrical storms are very common in Switzerland in summer. Rapid cloud build-up from around midday produces (often quite localised) thunderstorms that can drench walkers in sudden, cold downpours – see Cold under Environmental Hazards in the Medical Problems & Treatment section earlier. Especially in high, exposed places the danger of being struck by lightning often becomes extreme.

To minimise the risk of being struck, however, walkers should note the basic safeguards outlined below:

- In open areas where there is no shelter, find a depression in the ground and take up a crouched-squatting position with your feet together.
- Do *not* lie flat on the ground – if lightning strikes close by the voltage difference between your head and feet can reach several thousand volts.
- Avoid contact with metallic objects such as ice-axes and crampons – do not use an umbrella!
- Never seek shelter under objects that are isolated or higher than their surroundings (such as trees or transmission-line poles), as these are far more likely to get zapped. Isolated buildings and trees at the edge of a forest are other key targets for lightning bolts.
- If you find yourself in a forest of regularly high trees, you are relatively safe as long as you keep

a fair distance from each tree and away from any overhanging branches.

- If a thunderstorm catches you on an exposed ridge or summit, look for a concave rock formation to shelter in – but avoid touching the rock itself.
- If you happen to be swimming or standing in a lake or river when a thunderstorm approaches, get out of the water at 'lightning' speed. Anglers should quickly pack away their fishing rods.
- Swiss mountain huts are always fitted with lightning rods and therefore offer safe shelter during thunderstorms – but don't touch externally connected objects like the telephone or water taps.
- Should anyone actually be struck by lightning, immediately begin first-aid measures such as mouth-to-mouth resuscitation and treatment of burns. Get the patient to a doctor as quickly as possible.

Rockfall

Frost action causes rocks to dislodge continually from cliff faces and steep slopes in the mountains, and even small rocks can cause serious injury or death to unwary walkers. The danger of rockfall is most acute in the Alpine zone.

Sections of path most obviously exposed to rockfall lead through steep and eroding mountainsides, or below cliffs fringed by heavy fields of talus. Don't hang around in such places any longer than necessary and keep a watchful eye for 'movements' above as you pass. If you accidentally send a loose chunk of rock into motion, shout out a loud warning to any walkers who may be below you. Chamois or ibex sometimes dislodge rocks, so animal watchers should take special care to keep well clear of the fall-path. In Switzerland, especially dangerous sections of path (or road) have warning signs – *Steinschlag* in German or *chute de pierres* in French – posted along the way.

Rescue & Evacuation

Even the most safety conscious walkers may be involved in a serious mountain accident requiring urgent medical attention. If someone in your group is injured or falls seriously ill, leave somebody with them while others seek help. If there are only two of you, leave the injured person with as much

warm clothing, food and water as it's sensible to spare, plus the whistle and torch. Mark the position with something conspicuous – an orange bivvy bag, or perhaps a large stone cross on the ground.

Emergency Communications Emergency communications in the Swiss Alps are generally very good. SAC huts and other huts for walkers are equipped at least with a radio-telephone for emergency use, as are all mountain hotels and restaurants. The emergency number is ☎ 112.

Nowadays, many walkers also carry a mobile (cell) telephone with them into the mountains (see Telephone under Post & Communications in the Facts for the Walker chapter). While mobile telephone has been a boon to mountain rescue, network coverage is decidedly patchy in remoter areas such as mountain passes or deep Alpine valleys – ie, just the places where accidents are most likely to happen. Fortunately, the emergency number, ☎ 112, can often be reached even when the standard mobile network is out of range.

Remember that when reporting an emergency on ☎ 112 you will have to give your exact position – only possible if you carry a good topographical map (and/or a GPS receiver).

Where no other emergency communication is available, use the international Alpine distress signal. This is six whistles, six calls, six smoke puffs – ie, six of any recognisable sign you can make – followed by a pause (equalling the length of time taken to make the six signs) before you repeat the signal.

If your distress call is heard/seen (and understood), you should receive a reply consisting of three signals, each separated by a long pause.

Search & Rescue Organisations The Swiss air search-and-rescue organisation, REGA, is a division of the Swiss Red Cross. REGA helicopters can reach almost every part of Switzerland within 15 minutes, and each year they carry out hundreds of emergency flights for mountaineers, skiers and walkers in distress. For REGA sponsors (annual rate Sfr30/70 per person/family) all costs of search and/or emergency evacuation are waived, but people without appropriate insurance cover may be required to pay rescue costs. Note that REGA sponsorship in no way replaces standard travel and health insurance. For more information contact REGA (☎ 01-385 85 85, ⓦ www.rega.ch), Mainaustrasse 21, CH-8008 Zürich.

REGA's 24-hour emergency telephone number is ☎ 1414.

Helicopter Rescue & Evacuation When the rescue helicopter arrives, it is important to be familiar with several conventions. Standing face on to the chopper:

- Arms up in the shape of a letter 'V' means 'I/We need help'
- Arms in a straight diagonal line (like one line of a letter X) means 'All OK'

In order for the helicopter to land, there must be a cleared space of 25m x 25m, with a flat landing pad area of 6m x 6m. The helicopter will fly into the wind when landing. In cases of extreme emergency, where no landing area is available, a person or harness might be lowered. Take extreme care to avoid the rotors when approaching a landed helicopter.

Getting There & Away

AIR

Particularly for long-distance air travellers en route to Switzerland, it may well work out cheaper and/or more convenient to fly into a major European city like Frankfurt or Milan, then take a connecting flight or a train.

Switzerland's two main international airports are in Zürich and Geneva. Bern and Lugano airports also take a small number of international flights. The nearby French city of Mulhouse serves as the international airport for the Basel region.

So many cut-price or discount deals are available that few travellers pay the full fare on their air ticket. Official cut-price (off-peak, advance-purchase or Apex) tickets can be purchased directly from the airline or its agent; airlines offer various other discounts to passengers who qualify for a youth, student or senior citizen reduction. Unofficial cut-price air tickets can be bought from a travel agent (which orders

---

Warning

The information in this chapter is particularly vulnerable to change: Prices for international travel are volatile, routes are introduced and cancelled, schedules change, special deals come and go, and rules and visa requirements are amended. Airlines and governments seem to take a perverse pleasure in making price structures and regulations as complicated as possible. You should check directly with the airline or a travel agent to make sure you understand how a fare (and ticket you may buy) works. In addition, the travel industry is highly competitive and there are many lurks and perks.

The upshot of this is that you should get opinions, quotes and advice from as many airlines and travel agents as possible before you part with your hard-earned cash. The details given in this chapter should be regarded as pointers and are not a substitute for your own careful, up-to-date research.

---

tickets in bulk and can therefore offer heavy discounts with a lower profit margin).

Return tickets usually work out substantially cheaper than two one-ways. So-called 'open jaw' returns, by which you can travel into one city and out of another, save you having to backtrack to your point of entry. Round-the-World (RTW) tickets may sometimes work out cheaper than an ordinary return ticket.

The UK

London is one of the world's major centres for discounted fares. You should have little trouble finding a flight that beats the equivalent fare by rail.

Trailfinders (☎ 020-7937 1234, W www .trailfinders.co.uk), 194 Kensington High St, London, W8 7RG, has quite competitive air fares to Switzerland. For Trailfinders' other UK offices visit the Web site. Also good is USIT Campus (☎ 0870-240 1010, W www.usitcampus.co.uk), 52 Grosvenor Gardens, London SWI, which caters largely to students and travellers under 26; its Web site lists its other branches. STA Travel (London: ☎ 08701-600 599, northern: ☎ 0161-8304713, W www.statravel.co.uk) has 40 branches in the UK. Also look for ads in *Time Out*, the *Evening Standard* and *Exchange & Mart*, or free magazines and newspapers like *TNT* and *Southern Cross*.

Depending on when you travel, you should be able to pick up a cut-price return air ticket to Switzerland for £80. Charters won't be much cheaper and flights are sporadic, but you can try the Charter Flight Centre (☎ 020-7565 6744, W www.charterflights.co.uk).

Easily the cheapest scheduled flights are with the 'no frills' airline Easyjet (☎ 0870-6000 000, W www.easyjet.com), whose lowest return fares from London (if booked online) work out at £70 to Geneva and as little as £45 to Zürich.

Swissair (W www.swissair.com) and British Airways (W www.britishairways .com) have frequent flights from London

(Heathrow and/or Gatwick) to Geneva and Zürich; cheapest are Swissair's flights to Zürich (from £97 return).

KLM alps/Air Engiadina (☎ 0845-766 6777, W www.klmalps.ch) flies from London City to Bern (the best arrival point for the Bernese Oberland) from £119 return.

Continental Europe

Depending on where you are coming from, it may work out cheaper and more convenient to take a train to Switzerland.

Athens is a good centre for cheap fares – shop around the travel agents in the backstreets between Syntagma and Omonia squares. A reliable agent is USIT ETOS (☎ 01-41 32 950, W www.usitetos.gr), 31 Ethinikis Antistaseos in Pireaus.

Amsterdam is another recognised centre for cheap tickets: try Malibu Travel (☎ 020-626 32 30) or the student agency, NBBS (☎ 0900-235 62 27, W www.nbbs.nl).

There are also good outlets in other major European cities. In Paris, try Voyages Wasteels (☎ 08-03 88 70 04, W www.voyages-wasteels.fr), 11 rue Dupuytren. Return air fares from Paris to Zürich start at around FF1500 (€ 230). From Berlin, the cheapest flights are with KLM to Geneva (from around DM540, €275 return) – try Air Travel Service (☎ 30-864 90 50, W www.ats.de), Hohenzollerndamm 193. In Rome, try Passaggi (☎ 06-474 0923), Stazione Termini FS, Gelleria Di Tesla.

The USA

Numerous airlines have trans-Atlantic flights. Some of the larger outlets selling cut-price tickets are STA (☎ 800-781-4040, W www.statravel.com) and Council Travel (☎ 1800-2268 6245, W www.counciltravel.com). The *New York Times*, the *LA Times*, the *Chicago Tribune* and the *San Francisco Chronicle Examiner* have travel sections advertising cheap flights. On Web sites such as W www.travelocity.com and W www.expedia.com you can check fares and make online bookings.

The lowest summer return (round-trip) air fares to Geneva and Zürich from Miami, Chicago and New York start at around US$650, and from Los Angeles at around US$750; the main carriers are Air France, Continental, Lufthansa, Swissair and United. Air Courier Association (☎ 1800-282 1202, W www.aircourier.org) offers cheap stand-by flights from major US cities to European cities, including Paris or Milan (from US$275 return) and to Frankfurt (from US$378 return).

Canada

One of the large outlets is Travel Cuts (☎ 800-667-2887, W www.travelcuts.com), which has offices in all major cities. Scan the budget travel agents' ads in the *Toronto Globe & Mail*, the *Toronto Star* and the *Vancouver Province*.

Fares are slightly higher than from the USA. There are frequent flights from Toronto, Montreal and Vancouver to Geneva and Zürich. Summer return fares start at around C$800 from Montreal or Toronto and from around C$1000 from Vancouver. The main carriers are Air Canada, Air France, British Airways and Swissair.

Australia & New Zealand

There are no direct flights from Australia or New Zealand to Switzerland, but various route combinations of partnered airlines allow for a relatively straightforward one-stop trip. Travel sections of the weekend newspapers in the capital cities have advertisements for cheap fares.

In Australia, Flight Centre (☎ 1300-362 665, W www.flightcentre.com.au) is the largest outlet for cheap air fares. Also try STA (☎ 1300-360 960, W www.statravel.com.au). A return ticket from Sydney to Zürich (eg, Qantas/Aeroflot via Singapore or Bangkok) costs from around A$1500/1800 low/high season. Flights from Perth are A$200 or so cheaper.

In New Zealand, try STA (☎ 0800-874 773 W www.statravel.co.nz). The Downtown Flight Centre (☎ 09-358 0074), Downtown Shopping Centre, Queen St, Auckland, is one of many Flight Centre outlets in New Zealand. Tickets to Switzerland go either via Asia or North America, and start at NZ$2400/2800 low/high season.

Asia

The cheapest tickets are generally routed via another European city such as Amsterdam, Frankfurt, London or Paris.

From Singapore and Bangkok, return fares (eg, with Finnair or Korean Air) start at around US$755/1100 high/low season.

Mumbai (Bombay) has the cheapest flights out of India. One-way/return fares to Zürich start at around Rs 15,750/28,250 with Emirates Airlines. Stic Travels (☎ 022-2180603, Ⓦ www.stictravel.com), 6th Maker Arcade, Cuffe Parade, Mumbai 4000 05, offers cheap tickets.

From Hong Kong, some of the cheapest return tickets to Zürich or Geneva are with Lufthansa (HK$8180) and Korean Air (HK$7955). A reliable operator is Tiglion Travel (☎ 852-2511 7189, Ⓦ www.tiglion .com), Room 902, Yue Xiu Building, 160–174 Lockhart Rd, Wanchai.

South Africa

The cheapest return fares to Switzerland in the high season (which includes the northern summer) start at around R3700 with Alitalia to Geneva or at round R3900 with South African Airways to Zürich.

LAND
Border Crossings

Border controls have now been abolished between all European Union (EU) countries except for Britain and Ireland. Switzerland is outside the EU, however, and regular identity and customs checks are made on incoming people and traffic.

Travellers arriving from cities in northern Europe will probably arrive at Basel or near Geneva, and from the south at Chiasso, in southern Ticino.

Many walking routes lead over the border into Switzerland – typically via an uncontrolled mountain pass from Austria, France or Italy. Non-resident foreigners may legally enter Switzerland at uncontrolled border crossings but are required to present their papers at the nearest police office or border post.

See also Visas & Documents in the Facts for the Walker chapter.

Bus

Buses are slower and less comfortable than trains, although somewhat cheaper. Eurolines (☎ www.eurolines.com) runs Europe's largest network of international buses. Eurolines' advance purchase return tickets from London to Basel, Geneva or Zürich cost UK£74. In summer there are several weekly services to each city. From Geneva there are international connections to Rome, southern France and Spain.

Eurolines' bus passes give unlimited travel on its whole European network from UK£195/245 for adult/youth for 30 days in the high season (1 June to 31 August). Budget travellers who want to explore several countries by bus should also compare Busabout (☎ 020-7950 1661, Ⓦ www.busabout .com). Busabout passes cost from UK£169/ 149 for adults/students and allow unlimited travel during validity.

Train

Given the time taken up in getting to and from an airport (not to mention customs and baggage delays), the *real* travel time by (fast) train often turns out to be little longer than by plane. Unfortunately, rail has struggled to remain competitive against air travel in recent years – the standard adult return fare from London to Zürich is around £130.

All major Swiss cities can be reached by very frequent direct ultra-rapid trains from Amsterdam, Hamburg, Milan, Munich, Paris, Rome and Vienna. French TGV trains run from Paris (via Charles de Gaulle airport) to Geneva, Lausanne and Bern. Italian Cisalpino tilt-trains run from Florence, Milan, Rome and Venice to Zürich, Geneva (via Lausanne) and Basel (via Bern). German ICE trains connect Berlin and Hamburg with Zürich (via Basel). Express 'hotel trains' run nightly in either direction between Zürich and Hamburg. From the UK, the fastest way to Switzerland is on Eurostar to Paris, from where connecting trains go to Basel and Geneva (both 14 hours). Supplements can apply on fast trains and international services. It's often advisable (at times compulsory) to reserve a seat (in Switzerland a reservation charge of Sfr5 to Sfr30 applies). Overnight trips usually offer a choice of couchette (around US$30) or a more expensive sleeper.

Discounts & European Rail Passes

Travellers under 26 can buy Billet International de Jeunesse (BIJ) tickets, which give discounts of up to 50% on international train tickets. A return BIJ ticket to Zürich costs around UK£110. Rail Europe (☎ 08705-848 848), 179 Piccadilly, London W1, sells BIJ tickets and rail passes.

Eurail Passes (Ⓦ www.eurail.com) can only be bought by residents of non-European countries, and are valid for unlimited rail travel on national (and certain private) railways in all Western European countries *except* Britain. Inter-Rail (Ⓦ www.interrail .com) passes are limited to travellers under 26 years, and allow unlimited travel similar to Eurail passes but also cover most central European countries.

For people primarily interested in walking in Switzerland, however, European rail passes are unlikely to work out cheaper than buying a standard train ticket to Switzerland then using a national rail pass (see the Getting Around chapter).

Car & Motorcycle

Switzerland is connected to its European neighbours by modern motorways. An important tunnel if approaching from the south is the Grand St-Bernard between Aosta (Italy) and Bourg St-Pierre.

The minor roads are more interesting scenically but special care is needed when negotiating winding mountain roads. Some, such as the N5 (E21) route from Champagnole (in France) to Geneva, are not recommended if you have not had previous experience of driving in the mountains.

All vehicles driving on motorways in Switzerland must display a special windscreen sticker, known as a *vignette*, which costs Sfr40 per calendar year. Drivers caught on a motorway without one pay a Sfr100 fine plus the vignette cost.

Vehicles registered abroad can be driven within Switzerland for up to 12 months. Foreign driving licences are also valid for a

period of one year, but you may find it useful to obtain an International Driving Permit (IDP). The IDP is written in 10 languages, including French, German and Italian, and is issued by your motoring organisation for a small fee. The Green Card, the international third-party insurance certificate, is not compulsory in Switzerland as long as you already have third-party insurance. If you intend driving across Europe to Switzerland it's a good idea to get a Green Card (issued by your vehicle insurer) before leaving.

Hitching

Seasoned hitchers will usually confirm that pairs of either two women or a man and woman make the safest and most successful combination for getting lifts. A woman hitching on her own is taking a risk. Organised hitching agencies, such as Allostop-Provoya in France and Germany's Mitfahrzentrale, can usually arrange a ride with someone going your way – but they charge a fee, including your share of the driver's petrol (gasoline) costs.

Don't waste time hitching out of urban areas: take public transport to the main city exit route. In all countries it's illegal to hitchhike on motorways or their entry/exit roads, but service stations can be very good places to pick up a ride. Look presentable and cheerful, and make a cardboard sign indicating your intended destination in the local language. Never hitch where drivers can't stop in good time or without causing an obstruction.

Although many travellers hitchhike, it's not a totally safe way of getting around. How and where to hitchhike is discussed in this book but it isn't necessarily recommended.

WALK OPERATORS ABROAD

Numerous outdoor tour companies run one-to two-week guided walking trips of varying difficulty. Prices usually include all major expenses, including air/rail fares to Switzerland, accommodation and meals. It's best to finalise arrangements before you arrive in Switzerland. For a list of Swiss companies running organised walks, see Organised Walks in the Facts for the Walker chapter.

Canada

Randonnee Tours (☎ 204-475 6939 or 1-800-465-6488, W www.randonneetours.com) 249 Bell Ave, Winnipeg, Manitoba R3L 0J2, Canada. Runs eight-day walking tours in Ticino and the Bernese Oberland.

UK

UK-based companies offer one-/two-week guided walking trips in Switzerland from around UK£630/920 (including air fares).

Headwater Holidays (☎ 01606-813333, W www .headwater-holidays.co.uk) 46 London Rd, Northwich, Cheshire CW9 5HH. Guided walks in the Bernese Oberland and Valais.

International School of Mountaineering (☎ 01766-890441, W www.ds.dial.pipex.com /ism) Hafod Tan-y-Graig, Nant Gwynant, Caernarfon LL55 4NW. Organises mostly week-long treks.

Keycamp Holidays (☎ 0870-7000 123, W www .keycamp.co.uk) 92–96 Lind Rd, Sutton, Surrey SM1 4PL. Runs one guided walk in the Bernese Oberland.

New Experience Holidays (☎ 01922-410 909, W www.newex.co.uk) 62 Hut Hill Lane, Great Wyrley, Staffs WS6 6PB. Offers various one- and two-week Alpine treks, including the Alpine Pass Route, Haute Route and Wildstrubel Circuit.

USA

US-based companies (some with offices in Europe) offer one-/two-week guided walking tours in Switzerland from around $US1500/2000 (including air fares).

Adventure Sport Holidays (☎ 800-628 9655 or 413-568-2855, W www.advonskis.com) 815 North Rd, Westfield, MA 01085. Specialises in 'luggage-free' hikes.

Andiamos Aventours
US: (☎ 800-549 2363, W www.andiamoadventours.com) 930 Corcoron Drive, Santa Cruz, CA 95062
Switzerland: (☎ 052-624 9336) Lagernstrasse 5, CH-8200 Schaffhausen. Walks in the Bernese Oberland, Ticino and Graubünden.

Backroads (☎ 800-GO-ACTIVE (462-2848) or 510-527-1555, W www.backroads.com) 801 Cedar St, Berkeley, CA 94710-1800. Offers one- and two-week guided trips in the Bernese Oberland.

Distant Journeys (☎ 888-845 5781 or 207-236 9788, W www.distantjourneys.com) PO Box 1211, Camden, Maine 04843-1211. One-week trips in the Bernese Oberland and Valais, including the Tour du Mont Blanc and the Haute Route.

European Walking Tours (☎ 217-398 0058, W www.walkingtours.com) 1401 Regency Drive East, Savoy, IL 61874.

Euro-Bike & Walking Tours
US: (☎ 800-321 6060) PO Box 990, DeKalb, IL 60115
Switzerland: (☎ 041-637 4258, W www.eurowalk.com) PO Box 528, CH-6391 Engelberg. Offers one eight-day walking tour (run twice each season) in the Bernese Oberland.

Ryder Walker Alpine Adventures (☎ 888-586-8365 or 970-728-6481, W www.ryderwalker .com) PO Box 947, 5 Lake Fork Junction, Telluride, Colorado 81435. Does seven- to 14-day walking tours in the eastern Bernese Oberland.

Wanderweg Holidays (☎ 800-270-ALPS or 856-321-1040, W www.wanderwegholidays .com) 519 Kings Croft, Cherry Hill, NJ 08034. Specialises in hikes in the Swiss and Austrian Alps.

The Wayfarers (☎ 800-249 4620 or 401-849 5087, W www.thewayfarers.com) 172 Bellevue Ave, Newport, RI 02840. Offered a walk from Chateau d'Oex to Gstaad in summer 2000.

Getting Around

Switzerland has a difficult topography for road and railway construction. Mountain routes invariably take a long winding course with repeated sections of tunnel, so travel times are often much longer than they look on the map – eg, a train trip from the Lower Engadine to the Lower Valais takes all day.

With no real exceptions, walks included in this book are accessible by public transport, which is the most environmentally friendly way of getting around. Standard rail and bus fares are rather expensive in Switzerland, but numerous special tickets and passes are available which reduce public transport costs dramatically.

Note that all train, bus, ferry and mountain cableway routes are numerically coded, and appear in that numerical order in public transport timetables. Switzerland has an extremely efficient and well-integrated public transport system.

TICKETS & TRAVEL PASSES
From autumn 2001, rail passengers will be able to purchase and present tickets electronically on their mobile phones. The new 'electronic ticket', consisting of an SMS with a seven-digit code that can be verified by the conductor, will make it unnecessary to have a conventional ticket.

Rail tickets purchased at train stations can include postbuses and sometimes mountain transport as well.

Children between six and 16 years of age travel at half-price when accompanied by an adult; with a Junior Card (available free with Swiss passes and travel cards, otherwise Sfr20) all children under 16 years accompanied by at least one parent travel free. All train tickets allow you to break your journey, but advise the conductor before your ticket is punched.

Where stations are unstaffed, tickets can be purchased from a vending machine or from the train conductor. Many regional lines, however, especially those of smaller,

privately owned railways, operate on a 'self-control' basis without a regular conductor. Whenever this system applies, passengers must have a valid ticket *before* boarding the train, or risk paying a fine of Sfr60. On self-control train services a yellow 'eye' pictogram is displayed prominently inside and/or outside each carriage.

Walkers may want to send their luggage ahead to the town or village at the end of the walk. If you have a rail pass or a valid ticket from the place you are sending your luggage you will usually only be charged a flat rate of Sfr10 for this service.

Half Fare Card
The Half Fare Card costs Sfr90 for one month or Sfr150/222 for one/two years. It allows you to purchase half-price tickets for all trains, postbuses, ferries, suburban trams and buses as well as many forms of mountain transport.

Single Tickets & Return Tickets
Single tickets for distances under 48km are valid only for the day of issue, but all tickets for overall distances between 49km and 80km are valid for two days. All return tickets give a discount of 20% (compared to the price of two singles) and are valid for one month for distances over 81km.

A 2nd-class return ticket from Zürich airport to Interlaken (via Bern) costs Sfr108 (or Sfr54 with the Half Fare Card).

Circuit Tickets
A circuit ticket (*Rundfahrt-Billet* or *billet circulaire*) also brings a 20% discount. Circuit tickets allow you to travel via a circuitous route, stopping at numerous places before returning to your starting point, so walkers may find them a cheaper alternative to rail passes. Postbuses, ferries and most forms of mountain transport can be included on your ticket. As long as you complete the journey within one month, your itinerary can be as long or as complicated as you like.

Public Transport Information

Most public transport information walkers are likely to need, including (often) fares, passes and special offers, can be found in English on the Swiss Federal Railways (SBB/CFF) Web site (**w** www.rail.ch). The site software calculates your best connections by train, postbus, ferry and (sometimes) mountain cableway. For information on fares to/from anywhere in Switzerland call ☎ 0900-3003 00 (Sfr1.19 per minute) or email **e** RailinfoP3@ssb.ch.

Swiss Post's information service (☎ 031-386 65 65, **w** www.post.ch/e/bus/bus) can also help with inquiries on postbus schedules and fares.

Mobile (cell) phone owners can find out their best connections using the SMS (Short Message Service) on ☎ 222 (Sfr0.60 per inquiry); type the name of your starting point, a space, then the destination.

Bear in mind that more than one public-transport route to and from your walk may be viable. Especially where several train and/or bus connections are involved, travelling via a longer route may actually work out faster, although probably more expensive if you don't have a pass. Station staff – who usually speak at least some English – can give you a print-out showing departure and arrival times.

Swiss Card

The Swiss Card is valid for one month and allows you to travel to and from the Swiss border (or airport); during your stay it serves as a Half Fare Card (see earlier). It costs Sfr144 (2nd class) or Sfr175 (1st class).

General Passes

General passes are especially worthwhile if you intend travelling around the country a fair bit rather than basing yourself somewhere during your walking holiday. Note that on some important private railways – most notably the Furka–Oberalp–Bahn (FOB) between Brig and Disentis or the Brig–Visp–Zermatt (BVZ) railway in the Valais – Swiss Federal Railways (SBB/CFF) and European rail passes are not valid, although they will get you a 50% fare reduction.

Day Pass Standard day passes cost Sfr52 (Sfr86 in 1st class) but are worthwhile only if you intend travelling virtually to one end of the country and back again within a single day (which leaves little opportunity for walking). From time to time, however, the SBB/CFF offers special day-ticket deals, typically in the months of May and November or on summer Sundays. Examples include a Sfr15 day pass giving unlimited travel on slower regional trains, and a Sfr20 day ticket valid for all trains (apart from a few private lines) after 9 am.

Swiss Pass The Swiss Pass gives unlimited travel by rail, postbus and ferry within a period of up to one month. It is valid on public buses and trams in 36 towns and cities, and also gets you major reductions on many forms of mountain transport. A one-month 2nd-class Swiss Card costs Sfr500/425 per person for one/two adults and Sfr250 for children.

Swiss Flexi Pass The Swiss Flexi Pass offers the same reductions as the Swiss Pass, but only gives up to nine days of unlimited travel within a one-month period. A nine-day 2nd-class Swiss Flexi Pass costs Sfr430/366 for one/two adults and Sfr215 for children.

Regional Passes

A large number of regional passes are available, and are often a cost-saving alternative for walkers who prefer to base themselves in one region. They can be purchased in major cities and the respective regional train stations or post offices.

Most regional passes are valid for a one-month, 15-day or seven-day period. They generally give a number of days of unlimited travel, plus other days of travel at half-price within the period and region of validity. Holders of the Swiss Card, Swiss Pass or Half Fare Card can buy the regional passes for a considerable reduction. Most regional passes are available only during the summer season (from the start of May until the end of October).

Regional passes generally cover most postbuses and trains, but on other mountain transport – cable cars, chairlifts, funiculars and cog railways – they often only get you a 50% or a 25% reduction. Synoptic maps clearly indicate the services that allow unlimited travel and those that only offer a fare reduction. Regional passes can be purchased at train stations and/or post offices, and sometimes at tourist offices.

Regional passes of particular use to walkers are given under the Getting Around sections of each chapter.

AIR

Due to the country's compact nature and excellent ground transport, internal air transport is of little interest to most visitors to Switzerland. Swissair, or its subsidiary, Crossair, have numerous daily flights between Zürich or Basel and Geneva. The full one-way fare between Zürich and Geneva is Sfr225, but the return fare can be as little as Sfr190. In Alpine resorts, expensive scenic flights are available.

TRAIN

The SBB/CFF forms the backbone of the national transport system. Switzerland also has dozens of privately owned railways – more than any other country in Europe – which are well integrated into the national network. Virtually all Swiss trains have separate 2nd- and 1st-class sections and most have smoking and nonsmoking compartments.

Switzerland's two busiest and most important rail lines are the Zürich–Lugano line – the so-called 'Gotthard' railway – and the Geneva–St Gallen line crossing the Swiss Mittelland via Fribourg, Bern and Zürich. On both lines, fast, direct Intercity trains run in either direction at hourly intervals. Other major rail lines include the Bern–Brig–Domodossola – the so-called 'Lötschberg/Simplon' railway – and the Lausanne–Brig and the Zürich–Chur lines. The flagship of Switzerland's tourist trains is the famous *Glacier Express*, which takes 7½ hours to run the scenic route between St Moritz and

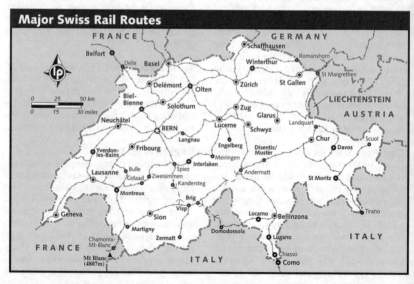

Major Swiss Rail Routes

Zermatt, giving a continually changing Alpine panorama.

POSTBUS

With their melodic bugle horns, yellow postbuses are one of the characteristic sights and sounds of the Swiss countryside. Operated by Swiss Post, postbuses run some 700 different routes with a combined length of more than 8500km – almost double that of the national rail network. Since virtually every mountain valley with road access can be reached by scheduled postbus, they are an indispensable means of public transport for walkers – a postbus ride is often the last part of the trip to the start of a walk.

Postbuses leave from train stations or (where there's no railway) the local post office, and schedules are synchronised with trains. Regional timetables are available free at post offices, train stations or tourist offices; postbus routes are numbered, and are listed according to their numerical code.

On some Alpine postbus routes holders of travel passes must buy a supplementary ticket for between Sfr1.50 and Sfr9, dependent on the journey's distance. The Swiss Pass and regional passes (see Tickets & Travel Passes earlier) are good for travel on all postbus routes apart from some minor summer-only services, where they give only a discount or are not valid at all. Prior reservation is necessary on some postbus routes – indicated by an 'R' symbol at the top of the timetable column. Seats can be reserved by telephone or in person through the local train station or post office.

For a flat rate of Sfr12, unaccompanied luggage can be sent to any post office on the same postbus route – but this service no longer includes transfer of luggage between postbuses. For all bicycles transported by postbus a surcharge of Sfr12 is payable.

The Half Fare Card and other (Swiss) general and most regional passes (see Tickets & Travel Passes) get you the full 50% reduction. Regional postbus passes, which give unlimited travel for up to seven days on all postbus lines within areas such as the Lower Engadine or Schwyz Canton, can also be quite good value.

MOUNTAIN TRANSPORT

The Swiss Alps probably have a higher concentration of mountain lifts than anywhere else in the world. Almost 300 mountain cableways, funiculars and cog railways provide access to Alpine resorts or panoramic peaks. (This figure does not include winter-only ski tows or the countless small, private utility cableways used to transport goods to and from isolated alp huts and pastures.)

While 'purist' walkers may find such mountain transport unsightly or superfluous, on a hot day your attitude tends to be more approving as you (and that weighty pack) are hauled up from the sweaty depths of the valley to the cool upper slopes at the start of your hike.

Most of the mountain lifts are privately owned, and this makes fares expensive with limited concessions. A one-way cable-car trip of 1000m vertical can cost up to Sfr18. Frequently, private lifts will give you some sort of reduction for your Swiss Pass or Half Fare Card, but less often for Inter-Rail and almost never for Eurail passes. Many mountain communities rely almost solely on a funicular or cable car for basic access, however, and in such cases the service is heavily subsidised and fares are only a fraction of what similar privately run services charge.

For lowlanders unfamiliar with the various 'artificial means of ascent', here is a brief explanation. A cog railway or rack-railway *(Zahnradbahn, chemin de fer à crémaillère)* is a steeper-gradient narrow-gauge railway with a rack between the tracks into which a cogwheel grips as the train climbs or descends. The term 'cableway' can apply to several kinds of mountain lift. A funicular railway *(Standseilbahn, funiculaire, funivia)* is an inclined track on which a pair of counter-balancing cars are drawn by cables. A cable car *(Luftseilbahn, téléphérique, funivia)* is a carriage taking up to 70 passengers suspended from a – hopefully! – extremely robust cable, also with a counter-balancing twin that goes down when it goes up. A gondola lift *(Gondelbahn, télécabine)* is a continuously running cable onto which four-or six-person compartments are hitched.

A chairlift *(Sesselbahn, télésiège, seggiovia)* is similar, but passengers ride on an unenclosed 'chair' secured only by a safety bar.

CAR & MOTORCYCLE

The use of a private vehicle to get to the start of any walk is unnecessary in Switzerland. Actually, it's not particularly environmentally considerate either, since cars are the main cause of the high levels of ozone, nitrous oxide and other pollutants regularly recorded in Alpine regions (see Ecology & Environment in the Facts about Switzerland chapter) and any increase in motor traffic will worsen the problem. In any case, cars are a less practical option for getting to and from walks given the excellent standard of public transport. Apart from circuit routes, motorists will always be inconvenienced by having to return to their parked car. Walkers who do use a car in Switzerland are advised to leave it at the hostel, hotel or local train station.

Die-hard drivers should note that many smaller back roads in the Alps are strictly closed to all but authorised (forestry and agricultural) traffic, and anyone caught driving on them without a special permit is likely to be fined. To drive on motorways in Switzerland your car must have a motorway sticker, or *vignette* (see Car & Motorcycle under Land in the Getting There & Away chapter); rental cars registered in Switzerland have vignettes.

BICYCLE

Cycling is the next-best thing to walking, and Switzerland is one place where it's not at all difficult to combine the two activities. Although somewhat outside the scope of this guidebook, plenty of walking routes can actually be done by mountain bike (MTB). As there is sometimes friction between walkers (who find MTBs intrusive and intimidating) and mountain bikers (who complain of deliberately obstructive walkers), a

Distance Chart (km)

	Basel (Bâle)	Bellinzona	Bern (Berne)	Biel (Bienne)	Brig	Chur	Fribourg	Geneva (Genève)	Interlaken	Lausanne	Lugano	Lucerne (Luzern)	Neuchâtel	St Gallen	St Moritz	Schaffhausen	Sion	Zürich
Basel (Bâle)	---																	
Bellinzona	241	---																
Bern (Berne)	97	253	---															
Biel (Bienne)	93	247	41	---														
Brig	190	161	91	129	---													
Chur	228	115	242	237	174	---												
Fribourg	132	285	34	71	179	274	---											
Geneva (Genève)	267	420	171	209	214	409	138	---										
Interlaken	153	195	57	92	73	209	92	230	---									
Lausanne	203	359	107	146	151	346	72	62	167	---								
Lugano	267	28	279	273	187	141	331	446	221	383	---							
Lucerne (Luzern)	103	140	115	107	149	140	147	280	71	218	166	---						
Neuchâtel	141	294	46	31	141	283	43	123	104	73	320	156	---					
St Gallen	191	217	204	197	288	102	236	371	225	307	243	138	244	---				
St Moritz	313	150	327	321	241	85	359	494	294	430	176	225	368	178	---			
Schaffhausen	161	246	173	167	259	182	205	340	228	276	272	108	214	80	266	---		
Sion	252	214	160	195	53	399	128	161	86	98	240	271	166	356	294	329	---	
Zürich	113	195	125	119	208	118	157	292	177	229	221	57	166	81	203	51	281	---

bit of give-and-take is called for. Special cycling maps (*Velokarten* or *cartes cyclistes*) indicating road and MTB routes are available (from Kümmerly & Frey among other publishers) for most parts of Switzerland. Tourist offices often produce brochures detailing local MTB routes.

Larger train stations also have touring and MTB bikes for hire (for around Sfr27 per day before discounts), which can be returned to other larger stations. Bikes can be transported on many trains for a flat rate of Sfr15 (Sfr10 with Half Fare Card). Cyclists are permitted to personally load their own precious two-wheeler onto the train.

HITCHING

Hitching is never entirely safe in any country in the world, and we don't recommend it. Travellers who decide to hitch should understand that they are taking a small but potentially serious risk. People who do choose to hitch will be safer if they travel in pairs and let someone know where they are planning to go.

Given the relatively high cost of public transport (along with most other things!) in Switzerland, some travellers may decide to thumb their way around. These days hitch-hiking is a relatively uncommon means of travel in Switzerland – with the notable exception of Ticino – but the universal rules of hitching seem to apply here. If possible choose a spot where vehicles can easily pull over, such as a roadside lay-by. Rides are much easier to get on less transited back roads, and especially in bad weather, drivers will often stop to offer walkers a lift. Hitch-hiking is not permitted on motorways.

BOAT

Ferries operate on all of Switzerland's larger water bodies, such as Lakes Constance, Geneva, Lucerne, Lugano, Maggiore, and Neuchâtel and Zürich. Most ferries cater to tourists, and services are most frequent during the busy summer season from around May to late September, but a few run during the winter months. Rail passes are generally also good for travel by boat.

Bernese Oberland

Forming a 100km-long strip extending westward from the Col du Pillon as far as the summit of the Titlis, the German-speaking region of the Bernese Oberland (Berner Oberland) takes in almost half of the mountains along the northern edge of the Swiss Alps. Moving west to east, these southern 'uplands' of Bern Canton become progressively higher, peaking (both in altitude and scenery) at the 4000m giants of the Jungfrau region. Known as the Bernese Alps (Berner Alpen in German), this is the highest range within the great Alpine chain that does not form part of the main continental divide.

The Bernese Alps separate Bern Canton from the Valais, and apart from a small area fringing the Fribourg and Vaud Alps they are drained by direct tributaries of the Aare River. Long side valleys such as the Simmental, the Kandertal, the Lötschental and the Haslital reach southward deep into the highest mountains. The range presents a formidable geographical and cultural barrier, with only half a dozen or so high-Alpine passes serving as crossing points between the two cantons. Although these passes have been used since prehistoric times, their altitude and steepness render them unviable for modern roadways, yet routes from the Bernese Oberland into the Valais make ideal walking tours.

With its soaring summits crowned with gleaming-white glaciers, thundering waterfalls that spill into sheer-sided glaciated valleys and white-water rivers rushing through wild gorges, the Bernese Oberland offers a 'full-spectrum Alpine experience'. The region also has plenty of rural mountain charm, with large wooden Bernese-style farmhouses and barns embellished by ornate designs or proverbs on their facades. Walkers stroll across the rich dairying pastures to the tinkling of cowbells, greeting highland farmers who still mow their mountainside meadows using traditional hand-held scythes.

Serviced by a well-developed network of trains, postbuses, ferries, cableways, cog

Highlights

CLEM LINDENMAYER

The north wall of the Wetterhorn, viewed from the First region above Grindelwald.

- Viewing the massive north walls of Schreckhorn and Wetterhorn from the shore of the Bachsee on the Faulhornweg walk
- Descending past the dramatic Blüemlisalpgletscher icefall to the delightful Oschinensee on the Hohtürli walk
- Experiencing the raw, glaciated landscape of the tiny Tierberg valley on the Wildstrubel Traverse
- Tucking into a pot of steaming cheese fondue at the historic Berghotel Schwarenbach on the Gemmipass walk

railways and funiculars, probably no mountain region in the world is so easily accessible as the Bernese Oberland. With thousands of kilometres of well-marked walking routes crisscrossing the mountains, the network of pathways is even thicker – the hiking is as splendid as it is varied.

Bernese Oberland

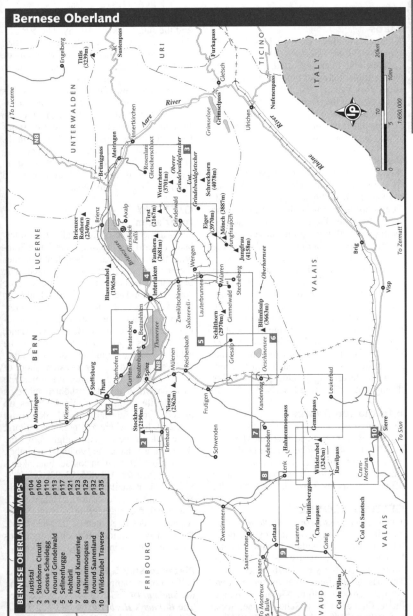

INFORMATION
Maps

Kümmerly + Frey's (K+F) 1:120,000 *Holiday Map Berner Oberland* (Sfr24.80) gives an excellent overview of the region and shows trails, huts and other important features for walkers. BL/OFT's 1:200,000 Sheet No 3 of the (four-sheet) series covers the entire Bernese Oberland except for the Gadmental-Haslital area east of Meiringen, which is on sheet No 4.

Books

Swiss Bernese Oberland: A Summer Guide by Philip and Loretta Alspach (Sfr28), sold at regional Swiss bookshops and tourist offices, outlines simple walks and excursions in the Bernese Oberland. Perhaps the best available walking guide covering the Bernese Oberland in English is *The Bernese Alps* by Kev Reynolds (Cicerone Press).

Numerous regional titles are available in German. Franz and Brigitte Auf der Maur's *20 Bergwanderungen Region Berner Oberland* (Sfr29.90, Werdverlag) contains 20 easy to medium standard mountain walks, many of which take advantage of mountain transport. K+F's *Rundwanderungen Berner Oberland* (Sfr22.80) has a regional walking guide in separate French and German editions describing circuit (loop) walks throughout the Bernese Oberland.

Information Sources

The tourist office which covers the entire region is Berner Oberland Tourismus (☎ 033-823 03 03, e info@berneroberland.com, w www.berneroberland.com), Jungfraustrasse 38, CH-3800, Interlaken. For other offices, see Nearest Towns under each walk.

GETTING AROUND

The *Regionalpass Berner Oberland* covers all rail lines, lake ferries, almost all postbuses and most mountain transport in the Bernese Oberland. It costs Sfr180/220 for seven/15 days (or Sfr144/176 concession). The pass gives free travel on the Niederhorn, Brienzer Rothorn, Niesen, Schynige Platte, First and Grosse Scheidegg services, but only a 25% reduction on Stockhorn

cable car, the Hahnenmoospass chair lifts and the Jungfraujoch railway. The 50% reduction also applies on certain connecting postbus and rail lines that run well outside the Bernese Oberland (including services to Bern, Montreux and Brig).

The one-month *Sunnecharte* pass covers the Jungfrau region in eastern Bernese Oberland, and costs Sfr158 (Sfr261 in 1st class) for unlimited travel on postbuses and trains (but not on the expensive Jungfraubahn!). Similar is the *Carte Bleue* pass, which covers the western Bernese Oberland from Zweisimmen as far as the Col du Pillon, and costs Sfr126 (Sfr95 to age 25).

GATEWAY
Interlaken

As its name suggests, the small city of Interlaken (570m) lies 'between lakes' on a 3km-wide alluvial plain called Bödeli that divides the Brienzersee from the Thunersee. The original town is on the northern bank of the Aare River, and has interesting old buildings including the 15th-century town hall. Interlaken's central location has made it the leading tourist centre of the Bernese Oberland, and it makes a good base for walks in the area – if you don't mind a bit of commuting. The walk around the north-eastern shore of the Thunersee to the extensive limestone cave system of the Beatushöhlen makes a worthwhile outing. A funicular goes up directly from Interlaken to Harder Kulm (1322m), from where a panoramic walking route follows the ridgetops high above the Brienzersee as far as the 1965m Blasenhubel.

For more information contact Interlaken's tourist office (☎ 033-826 53 00, fax 033-823 56 75, e mail@InterlakenTourism.ch, w www.interlakentourism.ch), Höheweg 37. The local mountaineering school, Swiss Alpine Guides Interlaken (☎ 033-822 6000, w www.swissalpineguides.ch), organises walks and climbs in the Jungfrau region.

Places to Stay & Eat Interlaken has over half a dozen camping grounds, including the *Sackgut* (☎ 033-822 44 34) by the river. The *Balmer's Herberge* (☎ 033-822 19 61, e balmers@tcnet.ch, Hauptstrasse 23) has dorm beds from Sfr19 and singles/doubles for Sfr40/68. An official *youth hostel* (☎ 033-822 43 53, ⓔ boenigen@youthhostel.ch) is at nearby Bönigen on the Brienzersee. While the *Hotel Sonne* (☎ 033-822 88 35, Bahnhofstrasse 9) has rooms from Sfr44/84.

Both the *Migros* supermarket opposite Interlaken West, and the *Coop* supermarkets at Bahnhofstrasse 33 and opposite Interlaken Ost have self-service restaurants.

Anker Restaurant (Marktgasse 57) has a varied menu with meals from Sfr12 to Sfr38. *Gasthof Hirschen*, on the corner of Hauptstrasse and Parkstrasse, is a good place for traditional fare.

Getting There & Away There are two train stations, Interlaken West and Interlaken Ost. Trains run hourly between Lucerne and Interlaken Ost (via the Brünigpass), and there are more frequent connections from Bern via Spiez. Interlaken is the changing point for the private BOB trains to Lauterbrunnen and Grindelwald.

Around the Brienzersee & Thunersee

The region surrounding the Brienzersee and Thunersee (Lake Brienz and Lake Thun) offers a wonderful variety of walking possibilities. This lovely landscape of idyllic mountain hamlets, historic castles, rich dairying country and panoramic mountain tops gives magnificent watery views from almost every vantage point. The slopes on the southern side of the Thunersee are gentle and fertile, with orchards and vineyards thriving in the mild microclimate of the lakeshore. The Brienzersee, on the other hand, has a steeper shoreline fringed by high sunny terraces and rugged ranges.

Surrounded by mountains reaching well over 2000m, the Brienzersee and Thunersee mark a transition point between the much lower ranges of the Bernese Pre-Alps and the stupendously high summits of Bernese Oberland. These deep-water lakes were formed by the ancient Aaregletscher (Aare Glacier), the ices of which gouged out a deep trough within the mountainous landscape. The height of both lakes differs only slightly – being little more than 550m above sea level – and immediately after the last ice age (some 9000 years ago) they were connected by a narrow strait. Over the following millennia, however, a broad alluvial plain gradually formed (where the city of Interlaken now stands) as enormous volumes of mountain rubble were deposited by the Lütschine River.

The region has a great deal of tourist infrastructure, with excellent rail connections and a dozen or so ferries that ply the lakes in summer. Mountain railways and funiculars provide effortless access to a number of popular lookout summits.

ACCESS TOWNS
Brienz
Brienz is the centre of the Swiss woodcarving industry and the main town on the Brienzersee. The Brienz tourist office (☎ 033-952 80 80, ⓔ info@alpenregion.ch, ⓦ www.alpenregion.ch), Hauptstrasse 143, is in the centre of town.

The *Camping Aaregg* (☎ 033-951 18 43, ⓦ www.aaregg.ch) has sites from Sfr6, plus Sfr6.60 per person. The *youth hostel* (☎ 033-951 11 52, ⓔ brienz@youthhostel.ch), in a traditional wooden Bernese Oberland house on Strandweg, has dorm beds for Sfr25.50. Two lower-budget hotels are *Hotel Sternen* (☎ 033-951 35 45) and *Hotel Schützen* (☎ 033-951 16 91, ⓔ schuetzen@rooms.ch), both on Hauptstrasse, which charge around Sfr60/100.

Restaurants are along Hauptstrasse; many have seating overlooking the lake. Try *Tea Room Hotel Walz* (☎ 033-951 14 59, Hauptstrasse 102), which has a two-course Tagesmenu for Sfr14.50. There is also the *Helvetia Pub (Hauptstrasse 59)*, which serves pizzas and fast food.

Brienz is on the Interlaken–Lucerne rail line, with hourly trains in either direction. There are postbuses to Axalp and the historic steam-driven trains run from Brienz up to the Brienzer Rothorn (see Other Walks at the end of the chapter).

Spiez

This attractive town lies about midway along the south-western shore of the Thunersee almost opposite the Justistal. Two lower budget places are the *Hotel Krone* (☎ *033-654 41 31*) near the train station, with singles/doubles from Sfr45/90, and the nearby *Hotel Bellevue* (☎ *033-654 84 64*), which has better rooms for Sfr65/120.

The *Migros* supermarket by the train station has a self-service restaurant, and by the lake are a couple of pizzerias.

Spiez is an important rail junction for trains of the Montreux-Oberalp-Bahn (MOB) line. Spiez is the transit point for train travellers to/from Bern, Interlaken, Brig (in the Valais), and the Fribourg and Vaud Alps in western Switzerland (via Zweisimmen). Spiez can also be reached by the Thunersee lake ferries from Interlaken or Thun.

Thun

The small historic city of Thun is at the northern end of the Thunersee, where the Aare River flows out of the lake. The city has an attractive old quarter dominated by the medieval castle on a prominent outcrop. The Thun tourist office (☎ 033-222 23 40, fax 033-222 83 23, [e] thun@thunersee.ch, [w] www.thuntourismus.ch) is located in the train station.

The *Herberge Zur Schadau* (☎ 033-222 52 22, [e] *info@herberge.ch*), which is an eight minute walk from the train station, offers beds in small dorms for Sfr35. The *Hotel Metzgern* (☎ *033-222 21 41*) on Rathausplatz has singles/doubles from Sfr55/100.

Migros supermarket is on the island by Kuhbrücke, and the *Coop* supermarket is across the river. Both have the usual, inexpensive self-service restaurants. *Restaurant Zum Tell* (*Obere Hauptgasse 28*) and the *Walliser Kanne* (*Marktgasse 3*) both have affordable Swiss food.

In summer, ferries run regularly around the lake, stopping at Spiez, Beatenbucht and Interlaken.

Justistal

Duration	4–5½ hours
Distance	16km
Standard	easy
Start	Niederhorn upper chairlift station
Finish	Beatenberg
Nearest Towns	Interlaken, Spiez

Summary This rewarding semi-circuit from the lookout summit of the Niederhorn leads around the precipitous ridgeline forming the Justistal's eastern rim before descending via the narrow trough of the valley floor.

Rail passengers travelling around the southern shore of the Thunersee are often struck by the interesting geological form of the Justistal. Like a miniature Alpine valley with perfect 'textbook' proportions, the Justistal descends from a remarkable, horseshoe-shaped pass between two parallel ranges that reach up to 2000m. The steep-sided mountains surrounding the Justistal nurture small colonies of ibex and chamois, while the grassy valley basin is given over to dairy farming.

Maps

Walkers have a choice of either the SAW/FSTP 1:50,000 *Interlaken* map No 254T (Sfr22.50) or Schaad & Frey's 1:50,000 map *Wanderkarte Thuner- und Brienzersee*. K+F's 1:33,000 *Thunersee* (Sfr24.80) also covers the Justistal.

NEAREST TOWN
Beatenberg

The scattered village of Beatenberg sits at around 1200m on a terrace high above the Thunersee. Beatenberg's official Web site [w] www.beatenberg.ch has information.

The *Friends of Nature hostel* (☎ *033-233 12 30*, [e] *annew@bluewin.ch*) has dorm beds for Sfr15. *Pension Riedboden* (☎ *033-841 11 64*), near the upper funicular station, and *Hotel Jungfrāublick* (☎ *033-841 15 81*, [e] *jungfraublick-beatenberg@bluewin.ch*) in Spirenwald have singles/doubles from around Sfr40/80.

For details on transport to Beatenberg see Getting to/from the Walk.

GETTING TO/FROM THE WALK

This walk uses a funicular and chairlift to avoid an exhausting climb. The start is the upper station of the Beatenberg–Niederhorn chairlift (1932m), which operates daily at least until around 5pm from the end of May to the end of October.

The lower chairlift station at Beatenberg can be reached directly by hourly postbus from Interlaken West train station. You can also catch one of the Thunersee ferries or the frequent postbuses, which run along the northern shore of the lake (between Interlaken and Thun) to Beatenbucht. From Beatenbucht the old funicular railway, built in 1889, travels up to Schmocken/Beatenberg at approximately half-hourly intervals between the end of May and mid-November (with a reduced service operating until mid-December). From the upper funicular station it's a 15 to 20 minute walk to the lower chairlift station. Postbuses run all year round and are synchronised with the funicular service. Boats on the Thunersee only operate from the end of May until the last Sunday in October. Integrated tickets that include the postbus, boat, funicular and chairlift are available. The one-way fare from Beatenbucht to the Niederhorn is Sfr27.20 (Sfr21 from Beatenberg); standard concessions apply.

The walk finishes either at the upper funicular station or the lower chairlift station, from where the same postbus/cable car/ferry options apply. The last bus to Interlaken West leaves Beatenberg some time before 8pm.

THE WALK

The chairlift carries you to the upper station (1932m) below an enormous telecommunications tower on the slopes of the 1949m **Niederhorn**. *Berghaus Niederhorn (☎ 033-841 11 10)*, open from early June to mid-October, has singles/doubles for Sfr45/90 and dorm beds for Sfr30.

Here you get the first spectacular views across Interlaken and the Thunersee to the icy giants of the Bernese Oberland. Note that there is no running water on the Güggisgrat ridge on the first part of the walk, so in hot weather carry some liquid refreshment.

From the upper chairlift station take the wide path leading north-eastward along the grassy mountainsides (one of the most popular paragliding take-off points). The white-red-white marked route follows the undulating ridge top of the Güggisgrat past weathered dwarf pines. On your left the land falls 600m down to the meandering stream in the Justistal, and the classic U-shaped pass of Sichle (1679m) forms the end of the valley ahead. Continue over the 2063m **Burgfeldstand** (whose shape supposedly resembles a ruined castle), skirting around occasional rock outcrops to reach **Gemmenalphorn** at 2061m, 1¼ to 1½ hours from the Niederhorn. This lookout point makes a scenic – though sometimes all too popular – spot for a rest.

Drop down steeply leftward on a stepped pathway to avoid cliffs on the Gemmenalphorn's northern side, then resume the northward traverse along the main ridge.

The Chästeilet

The Chästeilet ('cheese distribution') festival has been held in Spicherberg in the Justistal for centuries. Each September the cheese of the several hundred cows that graze in the valley over the summer is ceremonially divided among the members of the valley dairy cooperative. The round 'loaves' are stacked into piles and apportioned according to the number of cows each sharefarmer owns. The Chästeilet includes traditional activities like folk dancing, flag swinging and alphorn playing, and attracts hundreds of visitors. Of course, there is also the opportunity to sample the season's produce. Marking the end of the Alpine grazing season, the Chästeilet ends in the local *Alpabfahrt*, when the cows are driven down to the lowlands for the winter.

The Web site Ⓦ www.thunersee.ch has information on dates (which vary somewhat each year).

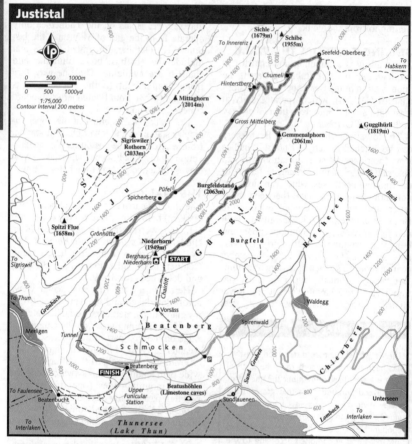

Justistal

The route makes its way on through light forest and scattered clumps of Alpine rhododendrons toward the sloping karst rock slabs of the Sieben Hengste to meet a signposted junction at the hollow of **Seefeld-Oberberg** (1752m). Descend south-west below a few alp huts into a gradually broadening gully, passing the barnyard of **Chumeli** before you come to another old barn. Here cut leftward into the trees and follow a winding foot track quickly down to reach *Hinterstberg*, 1¼ to 1¾ hours on. This farmhouse/restaurant lies at 1369m at the uppermost part of the Justistal and offers light refreshments.

Walk on gently down the narrow road through the green pastures past the farmlets of **Gross Mittelberg** and **Püfel** (1254m). From down here you can appreciate the enclosed nature of the Justistal, which is bordered on either side by high craggy ranges. After crossing the gurgling Grönbach the route begins a somewhat steeper descent through pockets of damp spruce forest, passing by the old hamlet of **Spicherberg** (1237m; see the boxed text 'The Chästeilet' earlier) to arrive at a road intersection near the **Grönhütte** (1124m) after 50 minutes to one hour.

Turn left here and follow the sealed road out of the Justistal. The road contours around the steep-sided and heavily wooded slopes and then passes through a 300m-long tunnel, before coming back out onto the long terrace of **Beatenberg**. Continue past the scattered holiday houses and farms high above the Thunersee to reach the upper funicular station (1121m) after 50 minutes to one hour. The car park at the chairlift is a further 15 to 20 minute walk up the road.

Stockhorn Circuit

Duration	3¼–4½ hours
Distance	9km
Standard	easy
Start/Finish	Chrindi cable-car station
Nearest Towns	Erlenbach, Spiez, Boltigen

Summary This short walk around a compact but varying range culminates in the 2190m Stockhorn summit, a natural lookout offering superb Alpine vistas on the threshold between the Bernese Oberland and the Swiss Mittelland.

Forming a unique botanical and geographical region, the Stockhorn lies within a small nature reserve that boasts the richest Alpine flora in the Bernese Oberland. Several of the species of wild flower found here are seen in few other parts of the region and various botanical trails wind around its upper slopes.

Underground streams drain much of this small limestone massif, and in certain places water seeping through the porous rock has formed extensive caverns. Filling the natural funnel-like sinkwells on the Stockhorn's southern slopes are the Oberstockensee and Hinterstockensee, two small lakes with subterraneous outlets, whose deep, trout-stocked waters attract anglers; (one-day fishing permits for the Erlenbach–Stockhorn cable-car ticket office).

The walk involves a steep climb of around 550m on the initial section from Chrindi to the Stockhorn summit.

Maps

Recommended is the SAW/FSTP 1:50,000 *Gantrisch* map No 253T (Sfr22.50). Two other walking maps that cover the route are Schaad & Frey's 1:50,000 *Wanderkarte Gantrisch* and Editions MPA Verlag's 1:50,000 *Berner Oberland Ost* (Sfr27.90)

NEAREST TOWN
Erlenbach (im Simmental)

This village at the foot of the Stockhorn has some wonderful examples of massive-roofed Bernese wooden architecture and a striking medieval church with lovely frescoes originating from the 14th and 15th centuries.

The *Hotel Stöckli* (☎ *033-681 21 26*) has singles/doubles for around Sfr55/110. There is a *Friends of Nature hostel* (☎ *033-654 83 16*) 3km south-west of Erlenbach at Feldmöser (1342m).

Erlenbach can be reached by hourly trains from Spiez (see Access Towns earlier); rail routes from western Switzerland run via Zweisimmen. Note that express trains do not stop at Erlenbach.

GETTING TO/FROM THE WALK

The Stockhorn Circuit begins and ends at Chrindi (1640m), the intermediate station on the Erlenbach–Stockhorn cable car (Stockhornbahn). The lower station of the Stockhornbahn can be reached on foot in 15 minutes from Erlenbach train station by walking up a winding laneway before turning left along the main road through the village. Private vehicles can be left free of charge at the car park immediately below the lower Stockhornbahn cable-car station in Erlenbach.

The Stockhornbahn (☎ 033-681 21 81, W www.stockhorn.ch) operates half-hourly from late May to early November. The return fare to Chrindi is Sfr12/24 for children/adults (concessions apply). The last downward cable car leaves Chrindi shortly after 5.30pm. Taking the cable car from Chrindi up to the upper station at the Restaurant Stockhorn (an additional Sfr8/4 children/adults) shortens the walk by around 1½ hours.

BERNESE OBERLAND

THE WALK

The cable car from Erlenbach heaves you up over 900m of ascent to the intermediate station of **Chrindi** (1640m) just above the **Hinterstockensee**. This lovely turquoise lake lies within an enclosed basin completely surrounded by high peaks, and often remains icebound into early summer. Walk a short way down past an interesting karst rock formation, then follow an alp track off to the right. This ascends the steep grassy slopes past the alp huts of **Oberbärgli** to a ridgetop saddle below the Chummli, before traversing westward around the mountainside high above the lake to reach a signposted intersection directly under the cableway.

Continue up steeply again past a jumping ramp for paragliders to the ***Restaurant Stockhorn*** (☎ *033-81 21 81*) at the upper cable-car station. This restaurant (open late May to early November) has a small dorm with beds for Sfr15 (breakfast extra). A final climb via a stepped path leads quickly up to the (often crowded) 2190m summit of the Stockhorn, 1¼ to 1¾ hours from Chrindi. Up here you get a spectacular full-spectrum Alpine panorama that includes some 200 peaks, which stretch all the way from the Titlis to Mont Blanc. The Thunersee (Lake Thun) is visible far below to the east, while the land drops steeply away to the north of the Stockhorn, directly into the Bernese Mittelland.

Drop back down to the junction below the cableway, taking the right-hand (west) branch, which descends steadily in occasional twists to reach the ***Berggasthaus Oberstockenalp*** (☎ *033-681 14 88*), at 1776m, after 35 to 45 minutes. This alp hut (open mid-June to mid-October) serves meals and refreshments and charges Sfr15 (breakfast extra) per person in the large cosy dorm.

Head on across the little grassy shelf along a partially stone-laid foot track, ignoring trails diverging to the left and right. The route brings you gently down through scattered coniferous forest to the **Oberstockensee**, another small lake occupying a trough with no apparent outlet. The

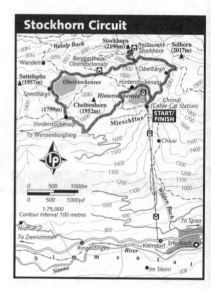

Oberstockensee is fed only by two tiny inlet streams and the lake's given water level of 1665m actually varies quite a bit depending on rainfall.

Make your way around to the western side of the Oberstockensee, rising briefly to the cottage of **Speetbärgli**. The path sidles on around the slopes, before climbing away to a grassy saddle at 1799m, 35 to 45 minutes from Oberstockenalp. Cut down over green pastures to a route intersection at the first alp huts of **Vorderstockenalp**. Here take the path that branches gently away leftward (not the way going off more sharply to the left), and contour around north-eastward over herbal meadows before coming to a small gap in the ridge between the Cheibenhorn and the Mieschflue.

The route now heads back down via a small spur toward a tiny forested peninsula in the Hinterstocksee to meet the broad walkway running around the lake. Turn left here and continue around past the farmlet of **Hinterstockenalp** (1616m), arriving back at the Chrindi cable-car station after a final 40 to 50 minutes. Keen downhill walkers can make the descent back to Erlenbach on foot in around two hours.

Jungfrau Region & Haslital

Stretching east from the 2970m Schilthorn to meet Central Switzerland at the Jochpass, the Jungfrau region and Haslital form the eastern Bernese Oberland. Dominated by the staggeringly sheer rock faces of the Eiger, Mönch and Jungfrau – arguably the Alpine world's most famously scenic threesome – and the almost equally impressive 'horned' summits of the Schreckhorn, Lauteraarhorn and Wetterhorn, this is a region of true superlatives. Presenting a seemingly ubiquitous backdrop, these awesome mountains are identifiable in the distance from places far outside the Bernese Oberland. The heart of the eastern Bernese Alps is an icebound wilderness only properly accessible to experienced mountaineers (or at least fit, professionally guided walkers). The lower surrounding ranges, however, have some classic routes that can be undertaken by just about anybody.

The Jungfrau region is drained by the glacial-grey Lütschine River, which divides into the two branches of the Weisse Lütschine of the Lauterbrunnental and Schwarze Lütschine of the Lütschental. In these twin upper valleys are Lauterbrunnen (with two nearby mountain villages of Wengen and Mürren perched on high terraces either side of it) and the large centre of Grindelwald. Not surprisingly, the Jungfrau region is the most heavily touristed part of the Swiss Alps, and after savouring the magnificent views for a while some walkers may register the urge to head for wilder places.

The area to the east of the 1962m Grosse Scheidegg lies within the valley basin of the Haslital, and forms the easternmost corner of the Bernese Oberland. At the uppermost reaches of the Aare River, the Haslital is unlike any other valley in the Bernese Oberland, penetrating deeply into the mountains as far as the 2165m Grimselpass. This pass was the first (or final) stage of the historically important trans-Alpine routes going over the Nufenen (Novena) and Simplon passes.

ACCESS TOWNS

Meiringen

Situated at 595m in the lower Haslital, since early medieval times Meiringen was favoured as a transit point for the travel and trade routes across the Susten, Grimsel, Grosse Scheidegg and Joch passes. Two popular short day walks from Meiringen go to the nearby Reichenbach Falls (famous as the place where the fictional character Sherlock Holmes fell to his death) and the Aareschlucht, a spectacular gorge (entry Sfr4/6 adults/concession).

The Meiringen regional tourist office (☎ 033-972 50 50, e info@alpenregion.ch, w www.alpenregion.ch), Bahnhofstrasse 22, is near the station. A mountaineering school, Castor Bergsteigerschule Haslital (☎ 033-971 43 18, e pollux.sport@swissonline.ch), in the Pollux Sport store, organises Alpine walks and climbs.

Meiringen's **Camping Balmweid** (☎ 033-971 51 15), 2km west of town across the Aare River, has tent sites from Sfr6 plus Sfr6.50 per person. **Simons Herberge** (☎ 033-971 17 15, fax 033-971 39 19, Alpbachstrasse 17), 10 minutes' walk upvalley by the railway line, offers dorm beds for Sfr28. The **Hotel Landgasthof Hirschen** (☎ 033-971 18 12, fax 033-971 47 12) has rooms for Sfr40/80 single/double. The newer **Hotel Tourist** (☎ 033-971 10 44, fax 033-971 64 17), across the river in Willigen, charges Sfr50/90.

A 50m walk from the train station is a **Migros** supermarket and restaurant. **Brunner** (Bahnhofstrasse 8) is a bakery and cafe, and also offers accommodation.

Meiringen is midway on the Lucerne–Interlaken Ost rail line, with approximately hourly trains in either direction via the Brünigpass. Important postbus connections go to Andermatt and Grindelwald (via the Grosse Scheidegg).

Grindelwald

Nestled below the peaks of the Eiger, Mönch and Jungfrau, Grindelwald (1034m) is perhaps the most scenic (and touristy) town in the Swiss Alps. World-famous is the cog railway tunnelled through the Eiger's north face to the 3454m saddle of the Jungfraujoch, where there is an observatory and weather station (known as the Sphinx). There are many wonderful walks in the mountains surrounding Grindelwald, including routes over the Kleine Scheidegg, Grosse Scheidegg and the Faulhornweg (all featured in this guidebook), and to the impressive glaciers known as the Unterer Grindelwaldgletscher and Oberer Grindelwaldgletscher.

Grindelwald's tourism office (☎ 033-854 12 12, e touristcenter@grindelwald.ch, w www.grindelwald.ch), is in the Sportzentrum. The mountaineering school, Bergsteigerzentrum Grindelwald (☎ 033-853 12 00, e bergsteigerzentrum@grindelwald.ch, w www.grindelwald.ch/bergsteigerzentrum) organises guided walks and is a good source of advice. The school also sells maps and guidebooks.

There are four local camping grounds, including the *Aspen* (☎ 033-853 11 24) and the *Gletscherdorf* (☎ 033-853 14 29). The Grindelwald *youth hostel* (☎ 033-853 10 09, e grindelwald@youthhostel.ch) on Terrasenweg has dorm beds for Sfr28/25.50 high/low season. *Friends of Nature hostel* (☎ 033-853 13 33, fax 033-853 43 33), also on Terrasenweg, has better dorm accommodation for Sfr29/35 members/non-members. The *Mountain Hostel* (☎ 033-853 39 00, e mhostel@grindelwald.ch) offers dorm beds from Sfr32 and double rooms from Sfr84 (prices include breakfast).

Opposite Grindelwald's tourist office is a *Coop* supermarket. *Uncle Tom's Hütte*, on the east side of the village, is a cheap eating option, with small pizzas from Sfr8.50. *Hotel Derby* by the station has meals from Sfr13.

Grindelwald is reached from Interlaken by regular trains of the Berner-Oberland-Bahn (BOB) running via Zweilütschinen.

Lauterbrunnen

Lauterbrunnen lies at 797m in the deep glacial trough of the upper Lauterbrunnental. From the village, an easy two-hour walk leads past numerous waterfalls plummeting over the cliffs to the road terminus at Stechelberg (910m) in the head of the valley. The walk passes the Trümmelbach Falls,

where a tunnel-path is cut into a spectacular glacial gorge with amazing churning waterfalls (entry Sfr10/4 adults/concessions).

Lauterbrunnen's tourist office (☎ 033-856 85 68, e info@lauterbrunnen-tourismus.ch, w www.lauterbrunnen-tourismus.ch) is near the train station.

The village has two camping grounds, which also provide dorm accommodation. The first is the *Schützenbach* (☎ 033-855 12 68, e info@schuetzenbach.ch) and the second is the *Jungfrau* (☎ 033-856 20 10, e info@camping-jungfrau.ch). Another option is *Hotel Horner* (☎ 033-855 16 73, e mail@hornerpub.ch) with beds in small rooms for Sfr32 and doubles from Sfr96.

Metzg-hus meat store, between the *Coop* supermarket and the tourist office, serves hot sausages and roast chicken. *Hotel Crystal* (☎ 033-856 90 90) serves Swiss meals from Sfr12.

Lauterbrunnen is accessible by at least hourly trains from Interlaken Ost. The cog railway via Wengen and Kleine Scheidegg connects Lauterbrunnen with Grindelwald.

Grosse Scheidegg

Duration	6½–9 hours
Distance	21km
Standard	easy
Start	Meiringen
Finish	Grindelwald
Nearest Towns	Brienz, Interlaken

Summary This extremely popular walk over the gentle 1962m Grosse Scheidegg ('great watershed') offers ever-changing scenery, which builds up to its highlight around the pass itself. It forms the sixth leg of the Alpine Pass Route.

The route leads up through the Reichenbachtal below the limestone needles of the Engelhörner, a side valley of the Haslital. It continues past the Rosenlauigletscher, whose roaring meltwaters have carved out an amazing gorge, to the head of the Reichenbachtal. Here stands the 3701m Wetterhorn, with massive and overpowering grey-rock walls that will bring a shiver of awe even to well-seasoned Alpine walkers.

The walk involves a lengthy but mostly gentle rise of around 1350m to the Grosse Scheidegg pass, then a rather steeper descent of 950m to Grindelwald. It can normally be done at least from late May to mid-October. Going the whole way in one day makes a very long and tiring walk, so – with such lovely scenery to savour – it's recommended that walkers stop off for the night at one of the en-route guest houses or hotels.

Maps

One of the best walking maps available is the local tourist authority's excellent small 1:50,000 sheet *Wanderkarte Oberhasli*. Editions MPA Verlag's 1:50,000 *Berner Oberland Ost* (Sfr27.90) covers a larger area and is useful for many other walks in the region; K+F's 1:60,000 sheet *Jungfrau-Region Oberhasli* (Sfr24.80) is similar. Alternatively, you can use two SAW/FSTP 1:50,000 sheets: *Sustenpass* No 255T and *Interlaken* No 254T (Sfr22.50 each).

GETTING TO/FROM THE WALK

The walk sets out from Meiringen and ends in Grindelwald; see Access Towns earlier for information on transport to both towns. From the end of May until early October post-buses run along the road between Meiringen and Grindelwald. There are bus stops at many places along the way, so if you get tired or lazy opting out is a simple matter. The last bus leaves Grosse Scheidegg for Grindelwald shortly after 5.30pm.

THE WALK

From the Meiringen railway station, signposts point along the main road and quickly guide you south-east across the swift, milky waters of the Aare to the village of **Willigen**. Here, 50m above the Hotel Tourist, turn right onto a sealed lane. This goes up beside restored old Bernese houses and continues as a grassy path bordered by stone walls and raspberry bushes to meet a road. Follow the road a short way uphill, then leave off to the right along a partially stone-laid path.

The route leads up steeply through forest and pasture, recrossing the road a number of times before coming to the *Hotel Schwendi*

(☎ 033-971 28 25), which has simple singles/doubles for Sfr35/70. Head on up via Tannenhubel (where a trail to the Reichenbach Falls diverges) to reach the *Gasthaus Zwirgi* (☎ 033-971 14 22), approximately 1¼ to 1½ hours from Meiringen. You can sleep in the dorm and eat a hearty breakfast here for around Sfr30.

Find the path at the left of the road. Often within earshot of the rushing Rychenbach stream, it goes through forest and clearings from where you get the first views of the high snowcapped peaks ahead, then crosses the road once more at two sharp curves. From here the road itself provides the main walkway until you reach the *Restaurant Kaltenbrunnen* (☎ 033-971 63 71), which has singles/doubles for around Sfr40/80, after 30 to 40 minutes. Not far up from the restaurant (near where a signposted trail branches off to the Engelhornhütte) follow a foot track leading off right into the forest.

Taking a course close to the Rychenbach, the path again crosses the road several times while the valley broadens and flattens out. Don't cross at the first road-bridge, but continue five minutes along the grassy flats beside the stream, where another bridge leads across to **Gschwantenmad**, 30 to 40 minutes after leaving Kaltenbrunnen. A nice spot for a rest-stop, Gschwantenmad (1303m) is just a scattering of old barns and farmhouses. From here there are superb views of the adjacent jagged peaks of the Engelhörner range and the Rosenlauigletscher plus the Wellhorn and Wetterhorn farther upvalley.

From Gschwantenmad, a new walking route continues 15 to 20 minutes along the opposite (true right) bank of the stream through pleasant forest, returning to the road on a bridge a short way before you reach the *Hotel Rosenlaui* (☎ 033-971 29 12). This grand old mountain hotel at 1328m is open from mid-May to mid-October and offers singles/doubles for Sfr69/118 and dorm beds for Sfr38. Well worth visiting here is the **Rosenlaui Gletscherschlucht** (entry Sfr6), a few minutes up from the hotel. This deep and narrow glacial gorge is accessible only via an amazing walkway that leads past thundering waterfalls and churning whirlpools.

Grosse Scheidegg

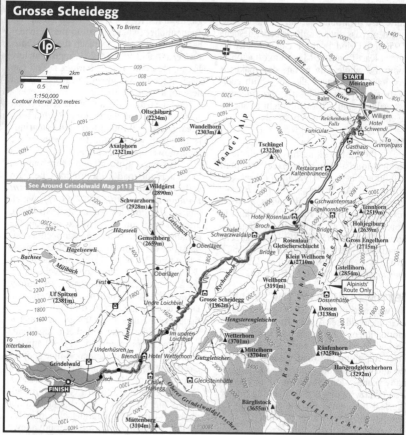

Near the entrance to Gletscherschlucht, pick up the path immediately above the road. This gravelled walking track takes you past **Broch** (where the road crosses to the other side of the Rychenbach), and continues along the southern side of the stream past a footbridge leading over to the *Chalet Schwarzwaldalp* (☎ 033-971 35 15) at 1454m after 30 to 40 minutes. The chalet is open from March to early November, and has accommodation in dorms from Sfr33 (shower available) and singles/doubles for Sfr53/106. This is the end of the road for all but authorised local traffic and postbuses.

The route doesn't cross the footbridge at Schwarzwaldalp, but follows the trail away from the stream through patches of forest until it comes out onto fields of wild flowers after 20 to 25 minutes. Clinging to the walls of the Wetterhorn directly above you are the hanging glaciers of the Hengsterengletscher, from which large chunks of ice continually break off and crash down onto the cliffs. Make your way around to the right, crossing a small wooden bridge over the milky stream coming down from these glaciers, then head up a vehicular track to meet the road once again a further five to 10 minutes on.

From now on the path climbs up steadily beside the road, cutting off numerous bends; white-red-white markings on the bitumen, trees or fence posts indicate these short cuts. Well-spaced benches along the way provide plenty of excuses to sit and admire the magnificent views of the 3701m Wetterhorn, whose striking north face appears breathtakingly near. After 1½ to two hours you reach **Grosse Scheidegg** at 1962m, where the *Berghotel Grosse Scheidegg (☎ 033-853 67 16)*, open early June to around 20 October, offers singles/doubles for Sfr45/90 and dorm beds for Sfr38 with breakfast; due to a shortage of water, washing facilities are basic. Views and altitude reach a high point here, with splendid vistas across Grindelwald to the Kleine Scheidegg.

The initial descent from the Grosse Scheidegg is rapid and often steep. Follow the road a few paces on from the Berghotel, then continue down through mixed pasture and Alpine heathland. As before, the well-graded path short-cuts the many sharp curves in the road, dropping through **Undre Loichbiel** (1455m, shown on some maps and signposts as Unterlauchbühl) and then descending beside the road to reach the *Hotel Wetterhorn (☎ 033-853 12 18)* after one to 1½ hours. The hotel, which has been recently renovated and has both mid-range rooms and dorm accommodation, looks out toward the impressive form of the Oberer Grindelwaldgletscher.

A short way below the hotel, follow a signposted vehicle track off left through the forest. Head down past **Im Brendli**, then continue westward along a marked walking trail which crosses several streams as it contours the hillside via **Underhüsren** (also called Unterhäusern), **Im Stutz** and **Isch**. At Isch walk down to a small lane which leads around right to rejoin the main Grindelwald-Grosse Scheidegg road at the village church after 30 to 40 minutes. From here **Grindelwald** train station is 10 to 15 minutes' stroll through town.

For the following (seventh) leg of the Alpine Pass Route see the Kleine Scheidegg (Grindelwald to Lauterbrunnen) walk later in this chapter.

Faulhornweg

Duration	4¾–6¼ hours
Distance	15km
Standard	medium
Start	Schynige Platte
Finish	First
Nearest Towns	Interlaken, Grindelwald

Summary The high-level panoramic route from the Schynige Platte via the 2680m Faulhorn to First deserves its reputation as one of the Bernese Oberland's classic walks.

The Faulhornweg leads through the geologically interesting range separating the Jungfrau region from the Brienzersee, with fine examples of twisted and overlayed rock strata and karst fields as well as some of the most dramatic ridge formations you're likely to find anywhere in the Swiss Alps. Constant companions are the towering north faces of four of Europe's most famous peaks; Wetterhorn, Eiger, Mönch and Jungfrau.

The Faulhornweg can be broken into two leisurely days by overnighting en route. The walk uses mountain transport to avoid any really heavy climbing, but still involves a (gradual) rise totalling around 600m and makes a rather tiring day.

The final section of this trail between the Berghotel Faulhorn and First is a popular winter walking route and is snow-cleared.

Warning

The Faulhornweg is entirely above the tree line at elevations mostly over 2000m – watch for signs of approaching bad weather. There is little running water on this ridgetop walk, so unless you carry your own water the only sources of liquid refreshment are several restaurants along the way.

Maps

Recommended is the SAW/FSTP 1:50,000 *Interlaken* No 254T (Sfr22.50). Other good options are Editions MPA Verlag's 1:50,000 *Berner Oberland Ost* (Sfr27.90), or K+F's

1:60,000 map *Jungfrau-Region Oberhasli* (Sfr24.80). Schaad & Frey's *Wanderkarte Grindelwald* is not recommended.

GETTING TO/FROM THE WALK

The start of the hike is Schynige Platte (1987m), which is accessible by the historic narrow-gauge cog railway from Wilderswil on the Interlaken to Grindelwald line of the Berner-Oberland-Bahn (BOB). Trains run up to Schynige Platte at approximately 40-minute intervals until around 5pm from about early June until the middle of October, although the period of operation varies somewhat from year to year depending on weather and snow conditions. The one-way fare is Sfr32. For more information call ☎ 033-828 71 11.

The walk ends at First (2167m), from where the over 5km-long First-Bahn (Europe's longest gondola lift) takes you down to Grindelwald (see Access Towns earlier). The First-Bahn runs daily from late May to around 22 October; the one-way fare is Sfr28 and the last ride is at around 5.30pm.

Slightly cheaper combined tickets for walkers, which include the Schynige Platte and First-Bahn as well as the BOB trains from Grindelwald back to Interlaken, are available with various concessions.

THE WALK

See the Around Grindelwald map, p113
The old cog railway hauls walkers up some 1400m to the Schynige Platte station (1987m) in around 40 minutes. From this superb natural lookout you get the first of the day's breathtaking views across to the great white summits of the Jungfrau region. Here *Restaurant Schynige Platte Kulm* (☎ 033-822 34 31, e hotel@schynigeplatte.ch), open from late May to late October, offers singles/doubles for Sfr60/120 and dorm beds for Sfr33 with breakfast.

Before setting off for the day's walk it is well worth visiting the Schynige Platte's Alpengarten (entry Sfr3, open from mid to late June until mid-September), which shows typical Alpine flora in simulated landscapes such as moors, rock cliffs and scree slides.

Walk north-east along an alp track over rolling pastures past the alp hut of **Oberberg**, heading gently upward above the green basin of Inner Iselten to reach **Louchera** (shown on some signposts as Laucheren) at 2020m. (Not far on from the Schynige Platte station the **Panoramaweg**, a somewhat longer alternative route diverges left and leads via the 2069m **Oberberghorn** to Louchera, giving outstanding views down to Interlaken and the Brienzersee).

Head around scree slopes on the western side of the **Loucherhorn** (2230m) to cross over a low grassy crest. The way dips and rises as it sidles on through two gaps in rocky spurs on the mountain's southern flank before coming to **Egg**, a wide grassy pass at 2067m strewn with boulders and Alpine herbs, 1¼ to 1½ hours from Schynige Platte.

Egg opens out north-eastward into the Sägistal, a tiny valley completely enclosed by ridges and without an above-ground outlet. Filling the lowest point within the basin, the waters of the small Sägistalsee (1935m) seep away subterraneously. Skirt up the Sägistal's southern side below the precipitous Indri Sägissa before swinging around southwest above the raw, talus-choked gully of Bonera (or Hühnertal). The route picks its way on up through an interesting landscape of rough karst slabs to arrive at the *Weberhütte* (☎ 033-853 44 64) on the little saddle of **Männdlenen** (2344m), one to 1½ hours on. This private restaurant/mountain hut is open from July to the end of September and has a small dorm for walkers.

Make a rising traverse along a broad ledge between stratified cliffs to gain the ridge of Winteregg, following white-red-white markings and metal posts north-eastward. A short distance past a minor turn-off at 2546m, take a signposted foot track leading up left along the main range to arrive at the top of the 2680m **Faulhorn**, one to 1¼ hours from Männdlenen. Just below the summit stands the historic *Berghotel Faulhorn* (☎ 033-853 27 13).

This hotel, which first opened for business in 1832, is the oldest and highest mountain hotel in the Alps, and offers singles/doubles for Sfr66/132 and dorm beds for Sfr36. The

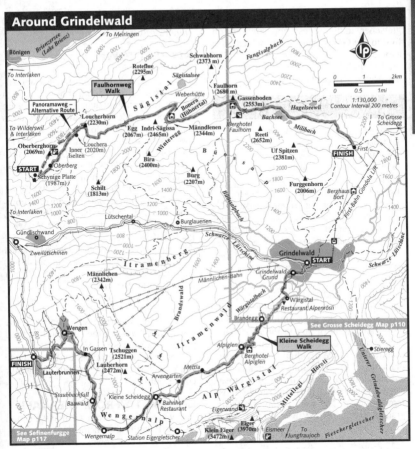

Around Grindelwald

Berghotel is open from around 20 June to 20 October (and also in winter, when it is a popular destination for snow walks from First). These lofty heights enjoy a stunning Alpine panorama dominated by the grand trio of the Eiger, Mönch and Jungfrau.

Descend the rounded, sparsely vegetated ridge to the little col of **Gassenboden** (2553m), then drop down eastward past an emergency shelter into the tiny grassy basin of the **Bachsee** (2265m). The tranquil waters of this picturesque lake contrast starkly with the imposing, ice-shrouded peaks of (from left to right) the Wetterhorn (3701m), the Schreckhorn (4078m) and the Finsteraarhorn (4274m), which rise directly behind it – yet another of the Swiss Alps' marvellous views!

Head on around the northern shore of the Bachsee, climbing gently past a smaller and slightly lower lake. A wide and well-trodden path now sidles gradually down through Alpine pastures high above the marshy Milibach streamlet to the distant tinkling of cowbells, reaching the upper gondola-lift station at **First** (2167m) 1½ to two hours after leaving the Hotel Faulhorn. First looks straight across to the narrow, snaking icefall of the Oberer Grindelwaldgletscher, and – unless you continue on foot to the Grosse Scheidegg, which adds another 1½ hours or so to the walk – this is the last high-level viewing point for what has been a particularly scenic walk.

Kleine Scheidegg

Duration	5¾–7¼ hours
Distance	18km
Standard	easy
Start	Grindelwald
Finish	Lauterbrunnen
Nearest Towns	Interlaken, Wengen

Summary Although the Bernese Oberland offers wilder walks, the Kleine Scheidegg is unquestionably one of the most scenic in the Swiss Alps – well worth the day's walk despite the hordes of international tourists. It forms the seventh leg of the Alpine Pass Route.

The Kleine Scheidegg lies in the shadow of the Eiger, whose stunning 1800m north face is at once the most notorious and the most captivating of any in the Alps. This broad saddle of the comparatively low Männlichen range dividing the two upper branches of the Lütschine River makes a natural lookout, with incredible close-range views taking in Switzerland's most famous peaks. The walk involves a fairly gradual ascent of just over 1000m and a 1200m descent).

Excursions to the Kleine Scheidegg have long been popular, and Goethe and Byron hiked over the pass on visits to the Jungfrau region in the early 1800s. Today the Kleine Scheidegg is accessible from both sides by way of a busy mountain railway running between Grindelwald and Lauterbrunnen, with a large station on the pass height itself from where trains continue up to the 3454m Jungfraujoch.

Maps

The best maps for this walk are either the SAW/FSTP's 1:50,000 *Interlaken* map No 254T (Sfr22.50) or Editions MPA Verlag's 1:50,000 *Berner Oberland Ost* (Sfr27.90). A reasonable alternative is K+F's 1:60,000 *Jungfrau-Region Oberhasli* (Sfr24.80).

NEAREST TOWN

Wengen

The walk passes through this pleasant village perched almost 500m above the trough of the Lauterbrunnental. Like Mürren on the opposite side of the valley, Wengen is one of Switzerland's dozen or more car-free mountain resorts. The tourist office (☎ 033-855 14 14, fax 033-855 30 60, ⓔ info@wengen.com, Ⓦ www.wengen.com) is around the corner from the train station.

The ***Hot Chili Peppers*** *(☎ 033-855 50 20, ⓔ chilis@wengen.com)* has dorm accommodation from Sfr24 (without breakfast) and singles/doubles for Sfr45/80. At Wengen's ***YMCA Alpenblick*** *(☎ 033-855 27 55, ⓔ jungfraublick@wengen.ch)* there is a small dorm (Sfr22 per person without breakfast) and more upmarket rooms from Sfr86 per person. ***Hotel Hirschen*** *(☎ 033-855 15 44, ⓔ hirschen @wengen.com)* has rooms from around Sfr60/115.

The ***Coop*** supermarket is opposite the station. ***Da Sina***, by the cinema, has good pizza/pasta from Sfr13.50.

Wengen can be reached by cog railway from Lauterbrunnen (Sfr5.60/2.80 adult/concession).

GETTING TO/FROM THE WALK

The walk sets off from Grindelwald and ends at Lauterbrunnen; for transport information see Access Towns earlier in this section. Since the walk largely traces the line of the Wengeneralp-Bahn (WAB) narrow-gauge cog railway, hikers can cop out by boarding the train at any of the well-spaced train stations passed en route.

THE WALK

See the Around Grindelwald map, p113

From the main Grindelwald railway station, follow a signposted laneway leading down beside the Hotel Regina then past the Hotel Glacier to reach the Grindelwald-Grund railway station after 15 to 20 minutes. Most trains to the Kleine Scheidegg and the Jungfraujoch leave from here.

Cross the road bridge and walk 50m to the right. After taking a sealed pedestrian laneway up left, ascend steeply past holiday cottages to meet a broad road, then continue on to cross the WAB rail lines via an underpass. Signposts direct you on across a smaller road to the *Restaurant Alpenrösli*, from where a path leads up beside the Sandbach stream. Take this often steep foot track up through the forest, recrossing the road briefly about halfway before you pass under a tiny arched-stone rail bridge. The route now climbs up close to the train lines, again dipping under a small rail tunnel just before reaching the *Berghotel Alpiglen* (☎ *033-853 11 30*), two to 2½ hours from Grindelwald-Grund. The Berghotel stands at 1616m under the north face of the Eiger a short way down from the Alpiglen train station, and has singles/doubles for Sfr50/100 and dorm beds (shower available) for Sfr33.

The path recrosses the rail lines a short way above the hotel, climbing more gently now past clusters of weather-beaten mountain pines and the farmhouses in the hollow of **Mettla** (1809m). Make your way on up to the ski lifts of **Arvengarten**, where you meet the 'Weg 2000' (a path contouring the mountainsides at roughly 2000m) before sidling up around the slopes below the rail line to arrive at the **Kleine Scheidegg** (2061m) after 1¼ to 1¾ hours. The *Bahnhof Restaurant* (☎ *033-955 11 51*, e info@bahnhof-scheidegg.ch), right beside the station platform, has singles/doubles for Sfr58/116 and dorm beds for Sfr43 (both with breakfast).

This minor pass provides a tremendous close-range vantage point of the savage ice and rock walls of the Eiger, Mönch and Jungfrau that soar almost 2000m above you. From the bustling Kleine Scheidegg train station walkers can opt to make the return trip by cog railway up to the Jungfraujoch – but don't expect the ticket price to be much cheaper than the extremely expensive fare charged from Grindelwald itself!

Head smoothly down along the broad path to the left of the train line, dipping under the tracks shortly before you come to the station of **Wengernalp** at 1874m. There are more wonderful vistas ahead that include the

Gspaltenhorn and Schilthorn beyond where the land plunges away into the deep glacial trough of the Lauterbrunnental. An alp track leads on northward through pockets of Alpine forest to cross the railway yet again, whereafter a well-formed roadway winds around the slopes via **In Gassen** (1402m) to reach the car-free mountain resort of **Wengen** (1275m) after 1½ to two hours.

From Wengen train station, follow the signposted walking track back under the rail lines onto a narrow road. The route soon begins a steep descent in short spirals through tall forests of spruce and maple, twice crossing the railway in quick succession. There are occasional glimpses through the foliage up-valley toward the 3785m Lauterbrunner Breithorn and the long spectacular Staubbachfall cascade. Drop on down through open slopes to cross the raging torrent of the Weisse Lütschine on a footbridge just before coming out at the main street in **Lauterbrunnen** (797m) after a final 40 to 50 minutes.

For the following (eighth) leg of the Alpine Pass Route see the Sefinenfurgge walk (Lauterbrunnen to Griesalp) following.

Sefinenfurgge

Duration	6–8 hours
Distance	21km
Standard	medium
Start	Grütschalp
Finish	Griesalp
Nearest Towns	Lauterbrunnen, Mürren
Summary	As the lowest point in the high craggy ridge extending from the Gspaltenhorn to the Schilthorn, the 2612m pass known as the Sefinenfurgge leads out of the Jungfrau region into the Frutigland. The walk forms the eighth leg of the Alpine Pass Route.

Walkers crossing the Sefinenfurgge (shown on some signposts and maps as 'Sefinenfurke') will savour more of the eastern Bernese Oberland's best scenery, without having to share it with (quite) as many people as on other routes.

Despite the use of mountain transport, this is a long day walk that can be broken by overnighting en route. The (roughly 1200m) climb and descent is mostly steady and gradual, but there are some steeper loose-rock sections.

Maps

The SAW/FSTP 1:50,000 sheet *Jungfrau (264T)* is recommended, although it omits the first short section of the walk, which is on the adjoining 1:50,000 *Interlaken* map No 254T (Sfr22.50 each). The local tourist authorities' 1:40,000 *Wanderkarte Lauterbrunnental* and K+F's 1:60,000 *Jungfrau-Region Oberhasli* walking map (Sfr24.80) both show the whole route on a single sheet but are less detailed.

NEAREST TOWN
Mürren

The walk passes through Mürren (1638m), a car-free resort catering mainly to the well-to-do winter sports set. Situated high up on the western side of the Lauterbrunnental, the village looks directly out across the valley toward the sheer rock walls of the Eiger, Mönch and Jungfrau. A popular day excursion goes up to the Schilthorn, a 2970m lookout peak accessible either via a steep foot track or by the Mürren-Schilthorn cable car.

Mürren's tourist office (☎ 033-856 86 86, fax 033-856 86 96, e info@muerren.ch, w www.muerren.ch) is located in the Alpine sports centre.

Pension Sonnenberg (☎ 033-855 11 27) has dorm beds for Sfr55 and double rooms for Sfr106, while *Hotel Regina (☎ 033-855 42 42, e regina.muerren@swissonline.ch)* has singles/doubles from Sfr65/114 (all prices include full board).

There is a *Coop* supermarket, and a few paces away *Stägerstübli* has filling meals for Sfr12.50.

Mürren is accessible by the Bergbahn BLM (a funicular and mountain train combination) from Lauterbrunnen, or by cable car from Stechelberg at the head of the Lauterbrunnental.

GETTING TO/FROM THE WALK

Although some people may prefer to set out from Lauterbrunnen itself (see Access

Towns earlier), the recommended place to start the walk is the upper station of the Lauterbrunnen-Grütschalp funicular railway. The funicular runs at least half-hourly and the one-way adult fare is Sfr7.40; various concessions apply.

For transport details from the end of the walk at Griesalp see Access Towns in the Frutigland section later in this chapter.

THE WALK

The Lauterbrunnen-Grütschalp funicular hauls you from around 800m straight up to the glacial shelf high above the valley at 1489m in just seven minutes. (For directions on walking from Lauterbrunnen, see the Alternative Start at the end of this route description.) The way from Grütschalp to Mürren is easy and very scenic, so don't even consider taking the railway.

From the upper station at **Grütschalp**, cross over the train tracks and walk along the broad path running just above the rail lines. The gradient is fairly smooth, causing no distraction from the glorious panorama, which takes in all the great summits of the Jungfrau region, including the Jungfrau itself, the Mönch and the Eiger to your left. After passing **Winteregg** station (1578m) and the *restaurant*, the route swings southeastward, with a clear view of the Breithorn in front of you at the head of the Lauterbrunnental, and continues on to reach the terminal station at the edge of **Mürren** after 50 minutes to one hour.

Follow the main street up right through the village to about 500m past the Schilthorn cable-car (Schilthornbahn) station. Here a right-hand trail leaves the road, skirting up across sunny hay-making meadows dotted with quaint old wooden barns as it brings you around into a small grassy basin. Cross the Schiltbach and walk a few paces over to reach the *Restaurant-Pension Spielbodenalp (☎ 033-855 14 75)* at 1790m, 40 minutes from Mürren train station. This private mountain hut is open from early June to mid-October, with singles/doubles for Sfr45/90 and dorm beds for Sfr31 with breakfast.

Head over to the foot of a steep ridge, and begin climbing this in (often exposed)

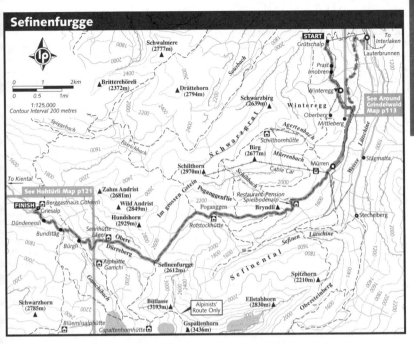

switchbacks leading up to a signposted trail junction at **Bryndli** (2020m). Sitting benches along this stretch offer a welcome respite and the chance to take in more of the wonderful vistas. Taking the right branch, sidle around the flower-covered mountainsides high above the Sefinental, a wild Alpine valley beneath the striking form of the 3436m Gspaltenhorn, to reach **Poganggen** after 1¼ to 1¾ hours. At 2039m in this rocky basin lies the *Rotstockhütte* (☎ 033-855 24 64), open from early June to mid-October. The local Skiclub Stechelberg owns this cosy (if somewhat basic) hut, and charges just Sfr18 for dorm beds.

Make your way upvalley over terrain strewn with debris washed down by a mountain torrent, passing numerous piles of stones laboriously collected to keep these rough pastures open. The path rises steadily through grassed-over moraine mounds, then zigzags up more steeply through eroding shale. These slopes are often snow-bound

well into summer, but walkers generally arrive at the 2612m **Sefinenfurgge** one to 1½ hours after leaving the Rotstockhütte. Although just a crack in the saw-blade ridge between the Hundshorn and the Bütlasse, this pass gives a fine view south-west toward the Blüemlisalp massif. Looking back you'll see the 2970m Schilthorn and its lower, castle-like neighbour, the Birg (2677m), both with cable-car stations on their summits.

Drop directly down the steep, loose-rock sides below the pass, where fixed cables, railings and steel ladderways give added confidence. The descent continues over bare talus slopes above a streamlet, following this down through the gradually thickening vegetation of **Obere Dürreberg** to reach the *Sennhütte Läger* (☎ 033-676 26 09) at 1995m after 50 minutes to 1¼ hours. At this hut (open from mid-June to mid-September) walkers can sleep on straw in the loft for around Sfr8, but be prepared for plenty of rustic 'atmosphere'.

The route now crosses the stream, winding its way down grassy fields that look over to the perpetual snows of the Blüemlisalp, before coming onto a dirt road at the neat farmhouse of **Bürgli** (1620m). Walk on right across the Dürreberg stream, then take a marked path running down left through the trees past Bundstäg to an attractive riverside clearing by the Gamchibach. Here cross the bridge to pick up a wide track leading on through more light forest via **Dündenessli**, passing by some interesting 'glacier pots' – enormous rock cavities formed by pressurised, silt-laden water flowing beneath ice-age glaciers. A few paces down is the tiny village of Griesalp (1408m), 1¼ to 1¾ hours from Obere Dürreberg.

For the following (ninth) leg of the Alpine Pass Route see the Hohtürli walk (Griesalp to Kandersteg) in the Frutigland section of this chapter.

Alternative Start: Lauterbrunnen

2–2½ hours, 4km, 692m ascent

Walkers who decide to hike up from Lauterbrunnen should take the well-marked walkway that leaves off right, 250m uphill from the lower funicular station. This route rises briefly beside the channelled Gryfenbach stream, then swings left to ascend diagonally through occasional clearings in the tall mixed forest. You pass by the picnic tables at Staubbach, which is about halfway before meeting the Grütschalp-Mürren railway at Mittelberg (1620m), a short way before you get to Mürren.

Frutigland

Lying between the Wildstrubel and the Schilthorn, the Frutigland region forms the central part of the Bernese Oberland. This compact area comprises the Kandertal and its large side valleys, the Engstligental and the Kiental, and is enclosed by long, high ranges that branch northward from the main chain of the Berner Alps. Although the average elevations are somewhat lower than in the neighbouring Jungfrau region, the Frutigland has at least as much of the

classic mountain scenery that 'sums up' the Swiss Alps.

Routes resounding with the cheerful clang of cowbells lead up to Alpine meadows dotted with brilliant blue lakes before a backdrop of high snow-capped ranges. One of the true jewels of the Frutigland is the Oeschinensee, a large high-Alpine lake in the Blüemlisalp massif. Situated right on the Lötschberg rail corridor, the Frutigland is easily accessible both from northern Switzerland and from the Valais, so there are no acceptable excuses for leaving this region out!

ACCESS TOWNS
Griesalp

This tiny village lying at 1408m in the upper Kiental consists of a cluster of less than a dozen houses and hotels at the end of the transitable road through the valley. Griesalp is a walking base for the Sefinenfurgge route in the Jungfrau Region & Haslital section earlier and the Höhtürli walk covered later in this section. Another excellent walk from Griesalp goes up to the 1965m Abendberg, from where the descent can be made into the valley of Spiggengrund. A short way from the village are some interesting 'glacier pots' formed by pressurised water flowing beneath ancient ice-age glaciers.

A regional tourist office (☎ 033-676 10 10, e ferien@kiental.ch, w www.kiental.ch) is in the village of Kiental, 6km down the Kiental valley.

Griesalp has four places to stay, all offering well-priced rooms and dorms: most recommended are the *Berghaus Griesalp* (☎ *033-676 12 31*) and *Berggasthaus Golderli* (☎ *033-676 21 92,* w *www.golderli.ch)*, just north of the village, which have dorm beds for Sfr35 and singles/doubles from around Sfr70/130. There is also a (rather basic) *Friends of Nature hostel* (☎ *033-654 59 64)* at nearby Gorneren (1570m) with dorm beds from Sfr18.

There are postbus connections to Griesalp from Reichenbach (on the Spiez–Kandersteg rail line) via Kiental up to six times daily between early June and mid-October. Outside this period the postbus only runs as far as Kiental. Reservations for the postbus are strongly advised (☎ 033-828 88 28). This is the steepest postbus route in Europe!

Kandersteg

Little more than a cluster of hamlets before the construction of the Lötschberg railway, Kandersteg (1176m) lies in the upper Kandertal. Although it has little in the way of historical interest, this scenic little village makes an ideal base for walks in the central Bernese Oberland, including the Hohtürli (Oeschinensee), Bunderchrinde and Gemmipass & Rote Chumme walks featured in this guidebook. A popular and simple day walk from Kandersteg leads down along the banks of the Kander to the Blausee, a beautiful crystal-clear lake in a riverside nature reserve (entry Sfr4.50).

The local tourist office (☎ 033-675 80 80, fax 033-675 80 81, Ⓔ info@kandersteg.ch, Ⓦ www.kandersteg.ch) is in the village centre. The mountaineering school is Bergsteigerschule Kandersteg (☎ 033-75 22 10).

Camping Rendez-vous (☎ *033-675 15 34,* Ⓔ *rendez-vous.camping@bluewin.ch)* at the lower Kandersteg-Oeschinen chairlift station has dorm beds for Sfr20 (no breakfast) and tent sites from Sfr6 plus Sfr5.80 per person. The *Hotel Zur Post* (☎ *033-675 12 58,* Ⓔ *hotel-zur-post@datacomm.ch)* offers singles/doubles from Sfr46/92. *Pension Spycher* (☎ *033-675 13 13, fax 033-675 13 16)* and *Pension Edelweiss* (☎ *033-675 11 94)* are only slightly more expensive.

The *Banhof* has a restaurant, and between here and the main street is a *Coop* supermarket.

Kandersteg is situated just north of the Lötschberg tunnel on the Bern-Valais rail corridor, through which car-carrying trains continue south to Brig. Train connections are regular, and all but a few international expresses stop here.

Adelboden

Adelboden lies at 1348m in the upper Engstligental, and although a bit touristy it is a pleasant enough place with all the modern conveniences. The town's central St Anton church dates from the 15th century. A popular walk is the Engstligentaler Höhenweg,

a panoramic route, which leads along the eastern slopes of the valley to (or from) the town of Frutigen.

For information contact the tourist office (☎ 033-673 80 80, Ⓔ info@adelboden.ch, Ⓦ www.adelboden.ch, www.adelboden-a.ch) Dorfstrasse 23.

There are two camping options: the *Albo* (☎ *033-673 12 09,* Ⓔ *albo@bluewin.ch)* and there is the *Bergblick* (☎ *033-673 14 54,* Ⓔ *bergblick@bluewin.ch). Jugendhotel Schönegg* (☎ *033-673 16 61, fax 033-673 16 01, Landstrasse 13)* has dorm beds for Sfr25 and rooms from Sfr40 per person. *Pension Bodehüttli* (☎ *033-673 37 00)* and *Pension Schermtanne* (☎ *033-673 10 51,* Ⓔ *schermtanne@bluewin.ch, Stiegelschwandstrasse 66)* both have somewhat more expensive rooms.

Buses run hourly in either direction between Adelboden and Frutigen, on the Lötschberg rail line (with hourly train connections to Bern and Brig). The last bus leaves Adelboden at around 10.15pm and returns to Frutigen at around 11.15pm.

Hohtürli

Duration	6–8½ hours
Distance	15km
Standard	hard
Start	Griesalp
Finish	Kandersteg
Nearest Town	Spiez

Summary The walk over the 2778m Hohtürli, the 'high doorway' pass linking the upper valley of the Kiental with Kandersteg, forms the ninth leg of the Alpine Pass Route.

The Hohtürli looks out onto the mighty Blüemlisalp, whose icy névés feed half a dozen smaller but spectacular glaciers. Directly under this massif lies the Oeschinensee, often regarded as Switzerland's most beautiful Alpine lake. Formed thousands of years ago when unstable mountainsides below the Dolderhorn collapsed across the Öschibach stream, the Oeschinensee lake has no visible outlet, but drains away subterraneously before re-emerging as a natural stream about halfway down to Kandersteg.

With an altitude gain of around 1370m (including an extremely steep final ascent to the Hohtürli itself), the walk requires very good fitness. Given a reasonably early start the Hohtürli can be done in a long day, but to better enjoy the magnificent surroundings consider overnighting at one of the half-dozen en-route places to stay.

Maps

You can use either of two K+F 1:60,000 walking maps: *Jungfrau-Region Oberhasli* or *Saanenland-Simmental-Kandersteg* (both Sfr24.80). Another option is Editions MPA Verlag's 1:50,000 map *Berner Oberland West* (Sfr27.90), though the route is a bit close to the edge of this map for comfort. Otherwise, two of SAW/FSTP's 1:50,000 maps are required for the walk: *Jungfrau* map No 264T, and *Wildstrubel* map No 263T (Sfr22.50 each).

GETTING TO/FROM THE WALK

For information on transport to Griesalp and Kandersteg, see Access Towns at the start of the section.

THE WALK

From the Berghaus in Griesalp, make your way upvalley through field and forest (re-tracing your last steps if you walked over the Sefinenfurgge to Griesalp). When you get to the bridge over the Gamchibach, follow the right-hand path (which is signposted 'Blüemlisalphütte') winding up through the trees beside a cascading stream to meet a surfaced road. Short-cut steeply on over the high Alpine pastures of **Bundalp** past the *Bergstübli Bundalp* (☎ 033-676 12 64), open late June to late September, a typical Bernese Alpine dairy, where you can look in on the daily cheese-making. A short way on at **Oberi Bund** (1840m), one to 1¼ hours from Griesalp, is the *Berggasthof Enzian* (☎ 033-676 11 92). This cosy restaurant is open from early June to mid-October, and offers singles/doubles for Sfr36/72 and dorm beds for Sfr23 (with breakfast and hot showers). There is little reliable water

after Bundalp, so make sure you take enough for the sweaty climb ahead.

Head 500m up the (now dirt) road, then turn off right onto a marked foot track. This quickly cuts across the grassed slopes, then begins climbing very steeply up a badly eroding ridge of old moraines, eventually connecting with a larger rocky spur. The strenuous ascent continues along the left side of this ridge – in many places ladders or stairways with fixed cables provide the only way up – finally arriving at the tiny 2778m platform of the **Höhtürli**, 2¼ to 3½ hours from Oberi Bund.

The *Blüemlisalphütte* (☎ 033-676 14 37) stands just 60m farther up the ridge at 2834m. This SAC hut (staffed from late June until mid-October, but always open) provides stunning, close-up views of the Blüemlisalp peaks and the crevassed icy mass of the Blüemlisalpgletscher. If the altitude doesn't bother you, this is the most scenic en-route place to spend a night (dorm beds for non-members cost Sfr13/27 for children /adults).

Descend in spirals around to the right through loose talus, before following a narrow shelf past icefalls at the lower tip of the adjacent Blüemlisalpgletscher. The path leads on along the crest of a high lateral moraine ridge left by the receding glacier, with a murky meltwater lakelet visible below. Drop on down rightward through the first wild flowers to reach the *Restaurant Oberbärgli* (☎ 033-671 11 87) at 1980m after 1¼ to 1¾ hours. This basic alp hut is open from mid-July to late August, and beds in the small dorm cost Sfr12 (without breakfast); the only washing facility is a cold spring trough.

Walk down a short way to the edge of a precipice, where the magnificent emerald-coloured Oeschinensee comes into sight, then climb down via stepways, which are safeguarded by cables, to the *Berghaus Unterbärgli* (☎ 033-671 11 87) at 1767m. This slightly larger alp hut (open from mid-June to mid-July, and from late August to mid-September) is under the same management as Restaurant Oberbärgli, and offers very similar accommodation.

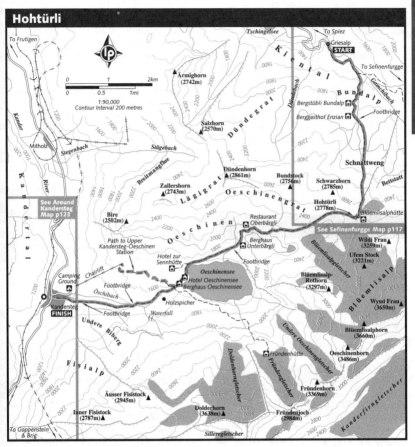

Hohtürli

To Frutigen

Tschingelsee

To Spiez

Griesalp
START

To Sefinenfurgge

0 ___ 1 ___ 2km
0 ___ 0.5 ___ 1mi
1:90,000
Contour Interval 200 metres

Ärmighorn (2742m)

K i e n t a l

Dündibach

Gamchibach

Bergstübli Bundalp

B u n d a l p

Berggasthof Enzian

Footbridge

Salzhorn (2570m)

D ü n d e g r a t

Stägebach

Schnättweng

Mitholz

Stegenbach

Breitmangflue

Dündenhorn (2861m)

Bundstock (2756m)

Schwarzhorn (2785m)

Bettstatt

Zallershorn (2743m)

L ä g i g r a t

O e s c h i n e n g r a t

Hohtürli (2778m)

Blüemlisalphütte

K a n d e r

River

See Around Kandersteg Map p123

Bire (2502m)

O e s c h i n e n

Restaurant Oberbärgli

See Sefinenfurgge Map p117

Wildi Frau (3259m)

Blüemlisalpgletscher

Ufem Stock (3221m)

Path to Upper Kandersteg-Oeschinen Station

Hotel zur Sennhütte

Berghaus Unterbärgli

Footbridge

Blüemlisalp-Rothorn (3297m)

B l ü e m l i s a l p

Camping Ground

Chairlift

Oeschinensee

Hotel Oeschinensee
Berghaus Oeschinensee

Wyssi Frau (3650m)

Footbridge

Öschibach

Kandersteg
FINISH

Footbridge

Holzspicher

Waterfall

U n d e r e B i b e r g

Undere Oeschinengletscher

Blüemlisalphorn (3660m)

Fründenhütte

Fründengletscher

Oeschinenhorn (3486m)

F i s i a l p

Doldenhorngletscher

Fründenhorn (3369m)

Fründenfirngletscher

To Goppenstein & Brig

Äusser Fisistock (2945m)

Inner Fisistock (2787m)

Dolderhorn (3638m)

Fründenjoch (2984m)

Silleregletscher

Kanderfirngletscher

Continue on down, bearing right to cross a footbridge, after which a well-cut trail begins a traverse of the lake's steep northern sides. Across the **Oeschinensee**, waterfalls drop over sheer cliffs directly into the lake from the towering glacier-clad peaks. There are frequent resting benches along this stretch, which are ideal for contemplating the outstanding natural scenery.

The way leads down to a tiny cove with a pebble beach, where – in hot weather only – walkers may be tempted to go in for a dip. Head a short distance around through lovely, tall stands of spruce to reach the hotels at the lake's western shore, 50 minutes to one hour from Oberbärgli. *Hotel Oeschinensee* (☎ 033-675 11 19, @ info@oeschinensee.ch) has rooms for Sfr65/130 singles/doubles and provides dorm beds for Sfr35, while the *Berghaus Oeschinensee* (☎ 033-675 11 66) offers better rooms for around Sfr80/130 and dorm beds for Sfr36. Prices include breakfast and both hotels open from late May to late October.

Otherwise, a somewhat shorter route alternative (20 to 25 minutes) goes to the upper Kandersteg-Oeschinen chairlift station, which brings you the rest of the way down to Kandersteg (Sfr13/6.50 one-way adult concession).

Make your way down left along the dirt service track, picking up a foot trail off right just as you pass a high waterfall coming down from the Dolderhorn. This leads along forested slopes above the Öschibach, before coming onto a sealed road just below the lower chairlift station. Follow the sealed road a short way around left to arrive in Kandersteg after 50 minutes to one hour. The train station, at 1176m, is a short walk down across the river.

For the next (10th) leg of the Alpine Pass Route see the Bunderchrinde walk (Kandersteg to Adelboden) following.

Bunderchrinde

Duration	5–6¾ hours
Distance	16km
Standard	medium
Start	Kandersteg
Finish	Adelboden

Summary This walk (the 10th leg of the Alpine Pass Route) is a perfect day-long ramble over a 2385m-high rocky gap.

Although it's relatively short in distance as the crow flies, this surprisingly high and craggy ridge completely separates Kandersteg and Adelboden. On its eastern flank the range has a classic tiered form, with a broad intermediate terrace between high cliffs fringed by scree slides. These precipitous crags are popular with local rock climbers, though walkers on the Bunderchrinde route are far more numerous.

With an ascent of 1200m, the going can be rather strenuous and there are many sections of loose rock or scree. Overnighting options en route allow the walk to be broken into two shorter days.

Maps

Best for this route are the special 1:25,000 walking map *Wanderkarte Kandersteg* (although it just cuts out Adelboden) and the SAW/FSTP 1:50,000 sheet *Wildstrubel* No 263T (Sfr22.50). Two other walking

maps, Editions MPA Verlag's 1:50,000 *Berner Oberland West* (Sfr27.90) and K+F's 1:60,000 *Saanenland-Simmental-Kandersteg* (Sfr24.80), make quite good alternatives.

GETTING TO/FROM THE WALK

For in formation on getting to/from Kandersteg and Adelboden, see Access Towns at the start of the section.

THE WALK

See the Around Kandersteg map, p123

From the Kandersteg train station, walk below the rail underpass then continue southward along a sealed lane. This briefly runs beside the rail lines, before leading off rightward past the landing ground of the Kandersteg paragliding school. A broad path leads on along the banks of the Kander River, passing the Pfadfinder Zentrum (☎ 033-675 11 39, ⓦ www.kisc.ch) a few paces before you come to a road bridge, 20 to 25 minutes from Kandersteg. This international scouting centre offers camping from Sfr8 and dorm beds Sfr15 (non-scouts are welcome).

A signpost here directs you off right along a foot track that goes over the riverside meadows for five to 10 minutes, before branching right to begin a long and steep ascent up the partially forested valley sides. The route soon meets a surfaced road and follows this for short sections, cutting out the numerous switchback curves as it climbs on beside the Alpbach stream to reach **Usser Üschene** at 1595m after a further one to 1¼ hours. Here the pretty Üschene valley opens out below the spectacular terraced cliffs of the Grosser Lohner.

Make your way left for 10 minutes across the green pastures to the road, and proceed to a signpost a few paces farther upvalley. The route first zigzags up beside a gravel-filled stream, then moves left to climb steeply through the cliffs past a small waterfall. Rising to a high shelf, the trail turns right then traverses undulating slopes before coming to the farmstead of **Alpschele** at 2094m, one to 1½ hours farther on. Alpschele looks across to the white-topped

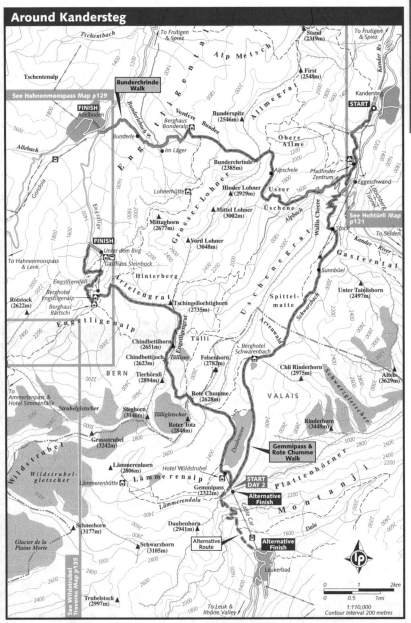

Around Kandersteg

Tschentbach

To Frutigen
& Spiez

Stand
(2319m)

To Frutigen
& Spiez

First
(2548m)

Kandersteg

Tschentenalp

**Bunderchrinde
Walk**

See Hahnenmoospass Map p129

FINISH
Adelboden

Vordere
Bunder

Berghaus
Bonderalp

Bunderspitz
(2546m)

Obere
Allme

Bunderle

START

Allebach

Im Läger

Bunderchrinde
(2385m)

Alpschele

Pfadfinder
Zentrum

Eggeschwand

Gondola

Lohnerhütte

Hinder Lohner
(2929m)

Usser
Üschene

Alpbach

Wallis Cheere

Lötschberg
Tunnel

See Hohtürli Map
p121

Mittaghorn
(2677m)

Mittel Lohner
(3002m)

Stock

To Selden

Kander
River

Gasterntal

To Hahnenmoospass
& Lenk

FINISH
Unter dem Birg

Vord Lohner
(3048m)

Sunnbüel

Unter Tatelishorn
(2497m)

Gasthaus Steinbock

Hinterberg

Spittel-
matte

Engstligenfall

Rötstock
(2622m)

Berghotel
Engstligenalp

Berghaus
Bärtschi

Tschingellochtighorn
(2735m)

Schwarzbach

Altels
(3629m)

Engstligenalp

Chindbettihorn
(2651m)

Tälli

Berghotel
Schwarenbach

Chindbettijoch
(2623m)

Tällisee

Felsenhorn
(2782m)

Chli Rinderhorn
(2975m)

Arvenwald

To Ammertenpass &
Hotel Simmenfälle

Tierhörnli
(2894m)

BERN

Strubelgletscher

Steghorn
(3146m)

Tälligletscher

Rote Chumme
(2628m)

VALAIS

Roter Totz
(2848m)

Grossstrubel
(3242m)

Rinderhorn
(3448m)

Wildstrubel-
gletscher

Lämmerenhorn
(2806m)

Lämmerenalp

Daubensee

**Gemmpass &
Rote Chumme Walk**

Lämmerenhütte

Hotel Wildstrubel

Gemmipass
(2322m)

Plattenhörner

Montanji

**START
DAY 2**

**Alternative
Finish**

Schneehorn
(3177m)

Lämmerendalu

Daubenhorn
(2941m)

Dola

Glacier de la
Plaine Morte

Schwarzhorn
(3105m)

**Alternative
Route**

**Alternative
Finish**

Leukerbad

See Wildstrubel Traverse Map p135

Trubelstock
(2997m)

To Leuk &
Rhône Valley

0   1   2km

0   0.5   1mi

1:110,000
Contour Interval 200 metres

Hanging Valleys

Walkers in the Swiss Alps will often note that a higher, gently sloping side valley drops away precipitously or flows through a tight gorge where it meets the main valley. The Gasterntal is one of the Alps' best examples of such a hanging valley and owes its interesting form to the ice-age glaciers that gouged out and deepened the main (Kandertal) valley, leaving the mouth of the Gasterntal 'hanging' high above the new valley floor. Immediately after the ice-age glaciers receded, the streams of many side valleys would have met the main valley as a high waterfall, but in most Alpine hanging valleys the stream has gradually eroded out a narrow gorge. Other examples of hanging valleys in Switzerland are the Safiental in Graubünden's Surselva region or the lateral valleys of the Rhône Valley.

summits of the Balmhorn and Altels towering above the sheer-walled Gasterntal, one of the Bernese Oberland's most classic glacial valleys. Basic refreshments are for sale here.

Continue up toward an obvious grassy saddle on the Alpschengrat, doubling back left when you get to the track turn-off to Obere Allme on your right. The well-trodden path now cuts up across talus slopes to arrive at the **Bunderchrinde** after 40 to 50 minutes. This narrow, 2385m pass is merely a gap in the ridge between some interesting layered-rock crags. There are views of all the previously mentioned sights, and the Oeschinensee is now clearly identifiable slightly downvalley behind Kandersteg. To the west is the Albristhorn, with the village of Adelboden immediately below.

Descend in spirals through a scree-filled gully, before easing steadily over to the right to avoid more broken-up terrain. The route turns right at a dirt road and briefly follows this to the *Berghaus Bonderalp* (☎ 033-673 17 16) at **Vordere Bunder**, 45 minutes to one hour from the pass. This alp dairy at 1755m is open from mid-June to

mid-September and has basic dorm accommodation for around Sfr20 with breakfast; house-made cheese is for sale.

From below the Berghaus, take the sign-posted foot track which cuts across the grassy slopes to the left. Drop down through forest, crossing minor roads a number of times before coming out onto a broader road just before a bridge over the Bunderlebach after 30 to 40 minutes. The road leads on another 20 to 30 minutes past the scattering of holiday chalets and restaurants at **Bunderle** to cross the Engstlige stream just before intersecting with the Unter dem Birg turn-off.

Turn right and walk over a second road bridge (crossing the Allebach) to the main Adelboden–Frutigen road. From here a steep pedestrian laneway leads up beside houses for 15 to 20 minutes to the centre of Adelboden.

For the following (11th) leg of the Alpine Pass Route, refer to the Hahnenmoospass walk (from Adelboden to Lenk) later in this chapter.

Gemmipass & Rote Chumme

Duration	2 days
Distance	28km
Standard	medium-hard
Start	Kandersteg
Finish	Unter dem Birg
Nearest Town	Adelboden

Summary This wide-ranging route climbs to the lovely Daubensee on the Gemmipass, one of the Bernese Alps' classic crossing points, then climbs over rugged glaciated ranges down through the summer pastures of Engstligenalp and past the spectacular Engstligen Falls.

For centuries the 2322m Gemmipass was the most transited summer crossing route between the Bernese Oberland and the Valais. After the widening of the amazing winding mule path cut into cliffs high above Leukerbad in the early 1700s, the Gemmi became the only significant pass for travel and transport between the two cantons. While some walkers may prefer to continue down into the Valais, the described route continues over the 2628m gap of the Rote Chumme through an impressive glaciated landscape to the broad green bowl of Engstligenalp, one of the largest expanses of high-Alpine pastures in the Bernese Oberland.

The walk has some heavy climbs and steep descents, and requires weather conditions to be fine and stable – watch out for midsummer thunderstorms!

Maps

The recommended map for this walk is the SAW/FSTP 1:50,000 sheet *Wildstrubel* No 263T (Sfr22.50). Reasonable alternative maps are Editions MPA Verlag's 1:50,000 *Berner Oberland West* (Sfr27.90) or K+F's 1:60,000 *Saanenland-Simmental-Kandertal* (Sfr24.80)

NEAREST TOWN
Leukerbad

An alternative route option ends at Leukerbad (1401m), a thermal-bath resort in the Central Valais. This small mountain municipality was literally bankrupted by its over-investment in an enormous new tourist complex built in the late 1990s.

For information contact the tourist office (☎ 027-472 71 71, ⓔ info@leukerbad.ch, ⓦ www.leukerbad.ch).

Camping Sportarena (☎ 027-470 10 37) has tent sites for Sfr5 plus Sfr8.20 per person. *Touristenheim Bergfreude (☎ 027-470 17 61, ⓔ touristenheim@rhone.ch)* offers dorm beds for Sfr38. The *Hotel Garni Chamois (☎ 027-472 76 00)* charges Sfr41/82 for singles/doubles.

There are at least hourly postbuses to Leuk, on the main Rhône Valley rail line, until around 7.45pm.

GETTING TO/FROM THE WALK

For information on transport to/from Kandersteg, see Access Towns earlier. Day 1 can be shortened by around three hours by taking a postbus/cable-car combination from Kandersteg train station. There are 10 or so daily postbuses to Eggeschwand, from where the cable car up to Sunnbüel runs

half-hourly; the last upward car leaves at about 5.20pm from around 1 June to early July, and from mid-September to around 22 October, and at around 5.50pm from early July to mid-September. The one-way fare is Sfr18.60/9.30 adult/concession.

The walk ends at Unter dem Birg, from where postbuses run half-hourly to Adelboden until around 6pm (otherwise another pleasant hour's walk away). Less recommended is the Unter dem Birg-Engstligenalp cable car (which runs half-hourly at least until 5.15pm between early June and mid-October), as you will miss the very spectacular final hour of the walk. The one-way fare is Sfr11/8.25 adult/concession.

THE WALK
See the Around Kandersteg map, p123
Day 1: Kandersteg to Gemmipass
4¼–5½ hours, 15km, 1146m ascent
The route begins as for the Bunderchrinde walk. From the Kandersteg train station, walk below the rail underpass then continue southward along a sealed lane. This briefly runs beside the rail lines, before leading off rightward. A broad path leads on along the banks of the Kander River, passing the Pfadfinder Zentrum (☎ 033-675 11 39, ⓦ www.kisc.ch) a few paces before you come to a road bridge, 20 to 25 minutes from Kandersteg. Here, cross the Alpbach on a footbridge to meet the main Kandersteg–Gasterntal road not far up from the cable-car station at Eggeschwand, 30 to 40 minutes from Kandersteg.

Go 300m uphill to a tight curve in the road, where a signpost directs you straight ahead into the forest. A broad track now takes you on a long spiralling ascent up the steep slopes below the interesting tilted sediments of the Wallis Cheere. As you gain altitude, the occasional avalanche clearing brings good views down to the upper Kandertal, and after 1½ to two hours the path passes above the middle cable-car station at **Stock** (1834m).

As the gradient evens out the trail sidles around the side of an abrupt precipice, and through the trees to your left the land falls away directly into the flat-bottomed Gasterntal, a classically formed glacial trough-valley. The local wild flowers in this area are particularly varied, and many of the Alpine plants growing beside the way are helpfully identified with individual nameplates. Continue on past the roaring Schwarzbach, and then begin rising gently into the Alpine pastures of **Spittelmatte**. These rolling slopes were the site of a tragedy in the early morning of September 1895, when the lower section of the Altelsgletscher (a glacier on the 3629m Altels just to the south-east) suddenly collapsed. A massive ice avalanche swept over Spittelmatte and Winteregg, crushing six herders and their cattle under millions of tonnes of ice that took five years to melt.

Not far on, the walking route merges with a wider alp track coming from the upper cable-car station at Sunnbüel (1930m), and follows this past a dairy farm fringed by the trees of the Arvenwald. Continue up across the cantonal border into the Valais, climbing around to the right over stabilised moraines to reach *Berghotel Schwarenbach* (☎ 033-75 12 72, ✉ info@schwarenbach.ch), which is 1¼ to 1¾ hours from Stock. The Berghotel (2061m) is open from March to late October and has a few singles/doubles for Sfr60/116 and dorm beds from Sfr30 (which includes breakfast and hot showers).

Bearing left past a turn-off just beyond the hotel, make your way up the steady incline

Berghotel Schwarenbach

One of the oldest mountain hotels in Switzerland, the Berghotel Schwarenbach was originally constructed in 1742 as a customs house on the old Valais-Bern frontier that once separated the Duchy of Savoy from the Swiss Confederation. Despite various major renovations, the old fire walls are still visible. Over the centuries the Berghotel has hosted a good number of eminent guests, including Horace-Bénédict de Saussure, Albrecht von Haller, Alexandre Dumas, Mark Twain and even Pablo Picasso.

The Gemmipass Schäferfest

Each year in late July the Gemmipass Schäferfest takes place around the shores of the Daubensee – once the site of bloody battles between the warring Bernese and Valaisans. In the early 1950s, shepherds from both cantons began organising annual meetings to exchange breeding stock, and today flocks of people and sheep from all over Switzerland turn up to eat raclette (and grass) on the lakeside meadows.

to reach a little bay at the northern end of the **Daubensee** after 30 to 40 minutes. Filling a long, undrained basin at 2206m, the Daubensee is the highest of the Bernese Oberland's larger natural lakes. High-tension power lines, which run along the western shore of the Daubensee, are an unfortunate intrusion into the otherwise splendid Alpine scenery.

Stroll on easily for a further 30 to 40 minutes around the lake's pleasant and grassy eastern shores to the cable-car station at the **Gemmipass** (2322m). Accommodation is available at the modern *Hotel Wildstrubel* (☎ 027-470 12 01, ✉ gemmi@rhone.ch), which offers luxurious singles/ doubles for Sfr75/138 and dorm beds from Sfr37; it's open all year. The view extends southward to the majestic mountains of the Matterhorn region, while mighty cliffs sweep down from the pass to Leukerbad, a modern resort at 1401m accessible from Gemmipass (see the Alternative Finish: Gemmipass to Leukerbad following).

Alternative Finish: Gemmipass to Leukerbad

1½–2 hours, 3km

This easy option makes your walk a real Alpine crossing. The route makes a spectacular winding descent on an excellent broad path (hacked and blasted through the massive limestone precipice fronting the Rhône Valley during the early 1740s), then cuts directly south-east down the steep slopes to Leukerbad.

Day 2: Gemmipass to Unter dem Birg

5½–7½ hours, 13km, 306m ascent

Backtrack a short way, then take a trail down to cross the Lämmerendalu stream on a wooden footbridge near where it enters the Daubensee. Head on around the western shore, climbing high over scree slopes before swinging left away from the lake. Paint markings guide you on up through a long rocky, grassy gully that ends with a steep ascent of switchbacks to arrive at the **Rote Chumme** (2628m) after 1½ to two hours. This barren gap near a striking monument-like rock column marks your return into Bernese territory. Before you lies the heavily glaciated upper valley of Tälli, whose most interesting features are the receding ices of the Tälligletscher and a small lake known as the Tällisee. Small herds of ibex may sometimes be spied loitering around this seemingly inhospitable area.

Drop down to the left over loose moraines and snowdrifts, which often linger well into July, to cross the freezing stream, then cut back rightward up the well-trodden scree slopes above the Tällisee to another pass crossing, the 2623m **Chindbettijoch**, just 30 to 40 minutes on. At the signposted junction a few paces down from here you get a nice view of the Engstligenalp.

Continue around to the right below the Chindbettihorn to begin a surprisingly easy and spectacular high traverse along the **Engstligengrat**. Following this bare ridge, the route steers past the odd rock outcrop as it rises over a broad hump before cutting left across talus under the 2735m Tschingellochtighorn. Head down along the sharper and grassier spur of the **Ärtelengrat** to where it peters out above sheer cliffs falling straight into the upper Engstligental. A short and milder descent left over hillside meadows brings you down to an alp track near the upper cable-car station at **Engstligenalp** (1964m) after 1¼ to 1¾ hours.

Here, the large *Berghotel Engstligenalp* (☎ 033-673 22 91) offers dorm beds for Sfr32 and singles/doubles from Sfr54/108. The *Berghaus Bärtschi* (☎ 033-673 13 73, e *berghaus@bluewin.ch*), a short way

south, is cosier and slightly cheaper. Both places have showers and are open from early June to around 22 October.

Engstligenalp is a wide, grassy bowl enclosed on almost every side by the domineering form of the Wildstrubel and high craggy ridges running off that massif. In ancient times Engstligenalp was covered by a lake, which was gradually filled in by rubble washed down from the surrounding mountains.

Take the alp track a short way south of the Berghotel directly across a footbridge over the Engstlige. A well trodden path soon cuts away rightward down over grassy ridges, before dropping steeply through mist-sprayed slopes underneath the thundering **Oberer Wasserfall**. Here the stream spills over a high precipice and smashes onto the rocks below. Recross the Engstlige and sidle down through larches, cutting under the cableway before you come to a signposted trail off left.

Follow down through spruce forest to recross a final time below the **Engstligenfall**, which is at least as spectacular as the upper waterfall. A broad path continues gently down to intersect with a road, one to 1½ hours from Engstligenalp. The lower cable-car station and local bus stop are a few minutes right along the sealed road at **Unter dem Birg** (1400m), where the *Gasthaus Steinbock* (☎ 033-673 16 26) has rooms at average prices.

Hahnenmoospass ✪

Duration	3½–4½ hours
Distance	13km
Standard	easy-medium
Start	Adelboden
Finish	Lenk
Nearest Town	Frutigen

Summary This walk (the 11th leg of the Alpine Pass Route) leads up out of the Engstligental over the gentle 1956m Hahnenmoospass into the Simmental.

In medieval times the broad grassy Hahnenmoospass was the common meeting place of the local Alpine herders from both valleys, and a wrestling competition, or *Schwingfest*, was held there each year. More recently, the upper Engstligental has seen modest ski development, but the gentle nature of this area has not been lost.

This day walk can be stretched out or shortened at will by staying overnight en route, or by taking one of the transport options along the way. The Hahnenmoospass involves a relatively unstrenuous climb of around 1000m ascent and a descent of some 800m.

Maps

The recommended walking maps are the local tourist authority's 1:25,000 *Wanderkarte Lenk*, or the SAW/FSTP 1:50,000 *Wildstrubel* map No 263T (Sfr22.50). K+F's 1:60,000 *Saanenland-Simmental-Kandertal* (Sfr24.80) also shows the route.

GETTING TO/FROM THE WALK

The walk leaves from Adelboden and finishes at Lenk; for transport details to/from Adelboden, see Access Towns earlier. For transport options from Lenk, see Access Towns under The Saanenland & Upper Simmental section later.

The walk can be shortened by taking any of the following forms of public or mountain transport. There are seven daily postbuses from Adelboden via Bergläger to Geilsbüel; you can also take the gondola lift from Adelboden-Oey to Bergläger (Sfr8/6 adult/concession), which in summer operates daily until around 5pm. From Geilsbüel a gondola lift (Sfr7.50/4.50) runs up to the Hahnenmoospass until around 5.30pm. Finally, in summer there are up to seven daily postbuses from Büelberg to Lenk.

THE WALK

From the church clock tower, walk gently uphill along the main road out of town, heading left at a fork near the Pension Schermtanne. Immediately after crossing the Allebach stream, take a path going left under the concrete road bridge to cross the Gilsbach, 25 to 30 minutes from Adelboden. The route continues up the eastern side of the stream, crossing a farm track before

it climbs away left under a gondola lift to meet a sealed road. Here turn right and cross the river to reach **Bergläger** gondola station (1486m) after a further 30 to 40 minutes.

Follow the gravelled road 700m upvalley, then take a trail leading off left. This crosses the stream on a small footbridge and makes its way up through pockets of damp, mossy forest before coming out at another surfaced road, 30 to 40 minutes on from Bergläger. Just over the rise at 1707m is **Geilsbüel**, from where a cable car runs up to the Hahnenmoospass. Here also is the *Restaurant Geilsbrüggli* (☎ 033-673 21 71), which has dorm beds for around Sfr28 with breakfast.

The climb to the pass is easy and straightforward, and goes along a narrow sealed road from just above the cable-car station. The route winds up through the grassy rolling basin, with a few short cuts to avoid curves in the road, and arrives at the 1956m **Hahnenmoospass** after 40 to 50 minutes. Here *Berghotel Hahnenmoospass* (☎ 033-673 21 41, ⓔ spori@hahnenmoos.ch), opens mid-June to mid-October, has simple rooms for Sfr49/98 per single/double and dorm beds (with shower) for Sfr35. The pass offers great views south-eastward to the Wildstrubel massif.

Dropping to the right, follow an alp track down the attractive open slopes giving more views across the upper valley of the Simmental to the Weisshorn and glaciers that drain the Plaine Morte. The gravelled lane crosses under a winter ski-tow about halfway before reaching a sealed road at **Büelberg** (1661m), 30 to 40 minutes from the pass.

Continue rightward, crossing and briefly following the roadway as it descends through flowery Alpine meadows to **Brandegg** (1536m). Here a signposted old mule trail leads on steeply down to the right alongside a forested gully, twice recrossing the road before coming out at a bridge over the Innere Sitebach stream, 45 minutes to one hour on. Lenk train station is now just 10 minutes' walk down to the left.

For the following (12th) leg of the Alpine Pass, refer to the Trüttlisbergpass (Lenk to Lauenen) walk in the Saanenland & Upper Simmental section following.

Top: The Oberer Grindelwaldgletscher carves its way toward Grindelwald, Bernese Oberland.
Middle Left: Dawn light on mountainside cottages perched above Grindelwald.
Centre: Trümmelbach Falls, Lauterbrunnen. **Right:** The Faulhorn towers above the Bachsee.
Bottom Left: A walker climbs above the Tällisee on the Gemmipass & Rote Chumme walk.

Top Left: The yellow tormentilla is common in Alpine pastures. **Top Right:** The Flueseeli lies in a glacial hollow in the upper Simmental, Wildstrubel Traverse. **Middle:** The dramatic Blüemlisalpgletscher icefall sprawls over cliffs below the Höhtürli. **Bottom Left:** Thunderclouds over peaks in the Jungfrau region. **Bottom Right:** A herd of male ibex grazes a high ridge top near the Brienzer Rothorn.

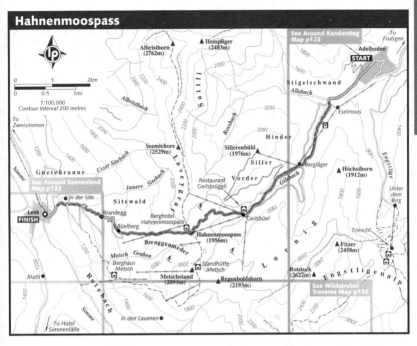

Hahnenmoospass

Saanenland & Upper Simmental

West of the Wildstrubel massif the Bernese Alps have decidedly less impressive heights than their neighbours in the eastern Bernese Oberland, with only a few of the higher summits – such as the Oldenhorn and the Wildhorn – breaching the 3000m mark. The region is typified by high glaciated plateaus of up to 2800m that fall away abruptly northward, and lovely upper valleys that always seem to begin at a large spectacular waterfall: the Simmenfälle, Engstligenfall, Geltenschuss and Iffigfall.

The Saanenland, in the Bernese Oberland's westernmost corner, is drained by the Saane River (Sarine in French), which flows westward through Fribourg and Vaud cantons before entering the Aare River near Biel/Bienne. Divided from the rest of Bern

Canton only by the low and indistinct Saanenmöser watershed, the Saanenland is the only German-speaking area in the upper valley. The Simmental, on the other hand, is a long valley that meets the Aare River at the Thunersee.

Although the Saanenland and upper Simmental are rather less popular than the central and eastern Bernese Oberland, the lower average height of the mountains in this region allows (unroped) walkers to venture high up among the loftiest summits on foot. There are some excellent trans-Alpine routes leading over the main range into the Valais.

ACCESS TOWNS
Lenk

Lenk lies at 1054m in the upper Simmental and has long been known for its sulphurous thermal baths, which were first developed in 1688. A fire in 1878 destroyed most of the original village and today Lenk is a pleasant though modern tourist resort.

The village's tourist office (☎ 033-733 31 27, ⓔ info@lenk.ch, ⓦ www.lenk.ch) is just across the bridge from the train station.

Campers can go to **Camping Hasenweide** near the Hotel Simmenfälle – see Simmenfälle under the Wilstrubel Traverse walk later. **Kurs- und Sportzentrum** (☎ 033-733 28 23), known as KUSPO, offers dorm beds with full board for Sfr42.50 (kids Sfr33.50) The **Hotel Alpenruh** (☎ 033-733 10 64) and **Hotel Alpina** (☎ 033-733 10 57) both have singles/doubles for around Sfr50/100.

Lenk is accessible by train via a branch line of the private Montreux-Oberland-Bahn (MOB) from Zweisimmen. From the southern Jura and the Lake Geneva region, you can take the MOB via Saanen-Gstaad, although from the lower Valais a rail/postbus combination via either the Col du Pillon or the Col des Mosses may be quicker. Zweisimmen is best reached from German-speaking Switzerland, Ticino or the northern Jura via Spiez (on the Brig-Bern line).

Gstaad

This an upmarket resort (1050m) is in the western Bernese Oberland. A short walk follows the Yehudi Menuhin Philosophenweg ('philosophy path') along the banks of the Saane River to the nearby village of Saanen.

For details on Gstaad, Lauenen and Gsteig, try the regional tourist office (☎ 033-748 81 81, fax 033-748 81 83, ⓔ gst @gstaad.ch, ⓦ www.gstaad.ch). The local mountaineering school is Alpinzentrum Gstaad (☎ 033-744 60 01, ⓦ www.alpinzentrum.ch).

Riverside camping is available at **Camping Bellerive** (☎ 033-744 63 30). Dorm beds are provided at the **youth hostel** (☎ 033-744 13 43, ⓔ saanen@youthhostel.ch) in Saanen for Sfr25.60/23.10 in high/low season. The **Hotel Boo** (☎ 033-748 88 33, ⓔ boofamily@ bluewin.ch) has rooms from Sfr83/126 for singles /doubles.

The **Coop** supermarket and restaurant in Gstaad is on Hauptstrasse to the left of the train station.

Gstaad is a major stop on the MOB railway line between Spiez and Montreux. Postbuses run to Lauenen (described next) and via Gsteig to Les Diablerets.

Lauenen

This pleasant and unspoilt village at 1241m has many fine examples of the wooden architecture typical of the Bernese Oberland, such as the early 16th-century St Petrus church with its quaint shingled steeple.

Lauenen has a small supermarket and a tourist office (☎ 033-765 91 81, fax 033-765 91 89).

The **Hotel Geltenhorn** (☎ 033-765 30 22, fax 033-765 32 31) has singles/doubles from Sfr55/110; the **Hotel Wildhorn** (☎ 033-765 30 12, fax 033-765 34 32) is slightly more expensive.

From late June to mid-October there are around 10 daily buses between Lauenen and Gstaad. The last bus from Lauenen leaves at around 6pm.

Gsteig

Gsteig (1189m) is a quaint old village in this forgotten south-west corner of the Bernese Oberland. Like nearby Lauenen, it has been mostly overlooked by tourist developers and also has some good examples of local architectural styles. Of particular interest is Gsteig's late-medieval Joderkirche (church) built in 1453.

Gsteig tourist office (☎ 033-755 81 81, fax 033-755 81 89, ⓔ gsteig@gstaad.ch) can organise dorm accommodation from around Sfr16.

About 1.5km upvalley toward the Col du Pillon, **Camping Heiti** (☎ 033-755 11 97, fax 033-755 12 91) has tent sites from Sfr6 plus Sfr4.30 per person. The 18th-century **Hotel Bären** (☎ 033-755 19 37) has singles/ doubles for around Sfr50/100 or there is the slightly more upmarket **Hotel Sanetsch** (☎ 033-755 11 77, fax 033-755 19 15).

A general store is the only place in town for supplies.

From late June to late September postbus connections between Les Diablerets and Gstaad (via the Col du Pillon) meet at Gsteig, where you often have to change. There are about a dozen daily postbuses between Gstaad and Gsteig. The last postbus from Gsteig to Gstaad departs around 8pm; the last bus to Les Diablerets leaves around 5pm.

Trüttlisbergpass

Duration	4½–6 hours
Distance	15km
Standard	easy-medium
Start	Lenk
Finish	Lauenen
Nearest Towns	Gstaad

Summary This relatively low pass crossing (12th leg of the Alpine Pass) leads through a gentle landscape of highland pastures at the foot of the rugged peaks of the western Bernese Oberland.

The 2038m Trüttlisbergpass leads out of the Simmental into the Saanenland in the south-western corner of the Bernese Oberland. Unspoilt highland meadows interrupted by limestone protrusions surround the quiet pass heights on both sides. The walk gives excellent views of the upper Lauenental, making this a very pleasant outing indeed.

The ascent to the pass and the descent to Lauenen are long, but fairly mild. Walkers doing the Alpine Pass Route often combine the Trüttlisbergpass with the much shorter Chrinepass walk (described next).

Maps

A good walking map is the local tourist authority's 1:25,000 *Wanderkarte Lenk*. Also recommended is the SAW/FSTP 1:50,000 *Wildstrubel* map No 263T (Sfr22.50). The Editions MPA Verlag 1:50,000 walking map *Berner Oberland West* (Sfr27.90) shows the route accurately, but cuts off much of the western Bernese Alps to the south.

GETTING TO/FROM THE WALK

For information on getting to/from Lenk and Lauenen, see Access Towns at the start of this section.

THE WALK

See the Around Saanenland map, p132
From Lenk railway station walk west across the Simme River, then up beside the small park to where a signpost points you off right. Follow this road out of the village, turning left onto a smaller road just before the bridge, then continue up beside the Wallbach stream.

Just past the lower station of the Betelberg chairlift a wide track branches off right into the cool, damp forest and leads alongside the stream, which it soon crosses on a footbridge.

Walk a short way on to the **Wallbach-schlucht**, climbing steel ladders and stone stairways through this gorge past mossy cascades and small ponds, then recross and ascend steeply away from the stream. The path comes out of the forest to meet the chairlift just above the ***Restaurant Wallegg***, 45 minutes to one hour from Lenk. Head 100m directly up then dip back into the forest along an old vehicle track that rises gradually against the contour to cross the Wallbach once more after another 40 to 50 minutes.

Make your way up to a dirt road and follow this a short way upvalley to where a signposted path departs off right. The path cuts up across the open slopes, passing several old barnyards to reach **Obere Lochberg** at 1910m after 50 minutes to one hour. Continue on over the lovely rolling pastures dotted with patches of Alpine heath, from where interesting karst (limestone) formations on the opposite side of the valley come into view. You'll arrive at the broad **Trüttlisbergpass** at 2038m after a further 45 minutes to one hour. From here the Hahnenmoospass is visible back toward the north-east, and to the south-east lie the peaks of the Wildstrubel.

Walk around left to a trail junction (where the path to Stübleni diverges), then descend right along a broad grassy spur, coming to **Vordere Trütlisberg** (1818m), a farmhouse at the end of a rough alp track. Apart from the odd marked short cut, the route follows this road down to reach a sealed road at **Flueweid** after 45 minutes to one hour.

Head gently down through **Flue**, an open shelf at 1480m from where the Tungelschuss and Geltenschuss waterfalls can be seen at the head of the Lauenental, before turning left off the main road at **Zwischenbächen** (shown on some maps as 'Zwüschbäche') onto a gravelled lane. This crosses several streams as it makes its way over to the right through field and forest to meet another surfaced road at **Bode**, 30 to 40 minutes on.

Continue left a short way, then take the first dirt track leading off left. Follow this

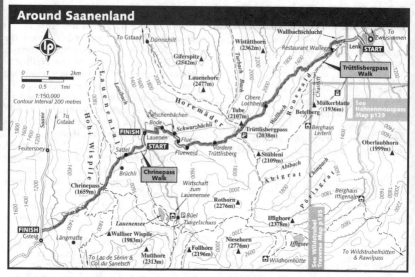

Around Saanenland

back down to the **Mülibach**, from where well-marked trails and lanes fringed with wild raspberry bushes bring you down beside the stream to reach the main valley road near the **Lauenen** post office after a further 20 to 30 minutes.

For the following (13th) leg of the Alpine Pass see the Chrinepass walk (Lauenen to Gsteig) following.

Chrinepass

Duration	2¼–2¾ hours
Distance	7km
Standard	easy
Start	Lauenen
Finish	Gsteig

Summary This walk (the 13th leg of the Alpine Pass) is a short, gentle ramble over a low pass.

The Chrinepass (shown on some signposts as 'Krinnenpass') is a mere low point in a small ridge dividing the Lauenental and upper valley of the Saane River. While it lacks some of the majestic scenery of other routes in the region, the Chrinepass makes a gentle day walk. This short walk involves only minor

ascents and descents and is often done with the previous Trüttlisbergpass route.

Maps

The SAW/FSTP 1:50,000 sheet *Wildstrubel* map No 263T (Sfr22.50) and the Editions MPA Verlag 1:50,000 *Berner Oberland West* walking map (Sfr27.90) both cover the route.

GETTING TO/FROM THE WALK

For information on transport to/from Lauenen and Gsteig, see Access Towns at the start of the section.

THE WALK

See the Around Saanenland map
Walk 500m south along the road out of the village, enjoying magnificent views of the tiny upper valley of the Geltenbach and glaciated peaks behind, then take a signposted path down across a small wooden bridge over the turgid glacial waters of the Louibach. Make your way up beside a tiny sidestream to a gravelled road and continue right past several houses to where a foot trail goes up left. The route ascends gently over open slopes scattered with graceful, old maples to reach a farm track at **Sattel**

(1400m) near the end of a ski lift, 40 to 50 minutes from Lauenen.

Follow the road across a stream, then (first ignoring a side track up right to Höhi Wispile) leave off right across vegetated old moraine mounds. The path sidles above **Brüchli**, an attractive farmlet cradled in a small grassy basin enclosed by forested hills, before climbing on through the spruce trees to arrive at the 1659m **Chrinepass** after a further 40 to 50 minutes. Although little more than an indistinct dip in this low ridge, the pass offers nice views down to Gsteig in the upper Saanental and across the Col du Pillon toward the Les Diablerets massif.

Drop down 200m to meet a dirt track at a farmhouse, and follow this on through the tiny open valley, crossing the stream before coming onto a broader sealed road. The route leads down this road, leaving the sharper curves at paint-marked short cuts, to reach a turn-off on the left (signposted 'Gsteig/Post'), 30 to 40 minutes from the pass. From here descend left alongside a small stream until the path brings you back onto the sealed road. Continue on down past occasional chalets to the main Gstaad-Col du Pillon road, then walk left a short way to the **Gsteig** post office after a further 20 to 30 minutes.

For the following (14th) leg of the Alpine Pass Route refer to the Col des Andérets walk (Gsteig to Les Mosses) in the Southern Fribourg & Vaud Alps chapter.

Wildstrubel Traverse

Duration	3 days
Distance	24km
Standard	medium-hard
Start	Simmenfälle
Finish	Crans-Montana
Nearest Towns	Lenk, Sierre

Summary This superb multi-day walk leads through fascinating, heavily glaciated high-Alpine landscape around the massif of the 3243m Wildstrubel, a landmark dividing the central and western Bernese Oberland.

Combining some of the best features of high-Alpine landscapes, this long and varied hike leads across the Bernese Alps into the Valais. At the western foot of the Wildstrubel lies the Plaine Morte, a 'dead plain' that forms a large expanse of permanent snow filling a rocky depression. The meltwaters of the Plaine Morte flow into the Rhône and the snowfield once belonged to the Valais, although – much to the exasperation of the thirsty southern canton – the area has been part of Bern Canton for more than a century. The final section of the walk follows a breathtakingly spectacular path alongside the old Bisse du Ro, a 3km long aqueduct built to transport water to the central Valais resort of Crans-Montana.

The walk requires a high level of fitness and perhaps some experience of mountain walking. There is loose rock in many places and some areas above 2500m are likely to remain snow-covered well into July. It's unlikely that conditions will be suitable for walking in these mountains before mid-June or after mid-October. The walk is not suited to walkers who suffer from vertigo.

Maps

Two SAW/FSTP 1:50,000 maps cover the route: Wildstrubel No 263T and Montana No 273 (both Sfr22.50). A fair single-sheet alternative is K+F's 1:60,000 *Saanenland-Simmental-Frutigland* (Sfr24.80), although it omits the village of Crans-Montana by a hair's breadth.

NEAREST TOWNS & FACILITIES
Crans-Montana

This large winter sports resort sprawls along the slopes above Sierre (Siders) in central Valais. The Colombire Alpine Museum, in a working alp hut, deals with the history of mountain dairying. The Crans-Montana tourist office (☎ 027-485 08 00, fax 027-485 08 01, **e** information@crans-montana.ch, **w** www.crans-montana.ch) organises short, guided walks in the region costing Sfr5/10 for children/adults.

Camping La Moubra (☎ *027-481 28 51, fax 027-481 05 51*) has lakeside sites from Sfr6.50 plus Sfr6 per person, and dorm beds for Sfr22. The *Pension Centrale*

(☎/fax 027-481 37 67) has singles/doubles from Sfr40/80.

The *Coop* supermarket is in Montana centre. *La Raccard (Route du Rawyl)* has affordable dishes and good lunch menus.

There are regular public buses connecting Crans-Montana with Sierre, but taking the funicular is a nicer way of getting down.

Simmenfälle

The *Hotel Simmenfälle (☎ 033-733 10 89, fax 033-733 21 97)*, has singles/doubles for Sfr53/106; the hotel also offers dorm beds (primarily for groups) for Sfr28. Nearby is the TCS *Camping Hasenweide (☎ 033-733 26 47)*, where tent sites cost from Sfr4.50 plus Sfr5.60.

GETTING TO/FROM THE WALK

The walk begins at Simmenfälle (Oberried) near the head of the Simmental, 5km south-east of Lenk. Lenker Verkehrsbetriebe (LVB) buses run from Lenk to Simmenfälle roughly hourly until around 6pm (until around 5pm after mid-September). For transport information on Crans-Montana at the end of the walk, see Nearest Towns & Facilities.

THE WALK
Day 1: Hotel Simmenfälle to Flueseelihütte

2½–3 hours, 4km, 942m ascent

From just above the hotel a signposted path turns off right to the **Simmenfälle**, where the Simme splashes down in a delightful waterfall. The path climbs up beside the stream, which in places is ducted down a natural spillway, to rejoin the road after 15 minutes. At the time of research, the upper section of this path had become dangerous and was closed, but once reopened it will be the preferred route.

Otherwise, follow the rough vehicle track upvalley through the forest (past where the Simmenfälle path intersects) to reach the *Gasthaus Rezliberg (☎ 033-733 12 86)* at 1405m after 50 minutes to one hour. This alp restaurant offers basic dorm accommodation for around Sfr25 per person. At the nearby **Sibe Brünne** a spring bubbles forth from the cliffs in many – the name supposes

seven – streamlets, which form the source of the Simme.

Turn left at the junction 50m beyond the Gasthaus and cut directly across the paddock to where the route commences a steep ascent. Damage from the Rezliberg avalanche, which in February 2000 swept away two – luckily unoccupied – alp huts nearby, is still evident. Although the slopes above appear impassable due to several rows of sheer buttresses, a well-cut foot track (with occasional fixed chains to hold onto) picks its way up through gaps in the rock. After 1½ to two hours of steady climbing, you finally rise out of the cliffs to reach the **Flueseeli** at 2045m. This lovely emerald-green lake dips into a terrace under the Wildstrubel's north-western flank. On the far side fields of raw scree come right down to the water, while lush pastures fringe the Flueseeli's outer shore. The small *Flueseelihütte (☎ 033-733 21 08)*, a few minutes away across the outlet, belongs to a dedicated local club (Verein Flueseelihütte) and offers dorm beds for Sfr20 (pay by postal deposit slip). It is a a basic self-catering style hut with no resident hutkeeper and sleeping space for just 14 people.

Day 2: Flueseelihütte to Wildstrubelhütten

3¼–4½ hours, 7km, 748m ascent

Walk back over the lake outlet and on over grassy meadows past a boggy tarn to the top of the small ridge running off right to the **Flueseehöri** (2133m). This point grants a stark view of the grey glaciated landscape ahead, with a heavy meltwater cascade splattering down from the Rezligletscher. Continue left up this rocky spur to a poorly indicated fork at around 2250m (see the Wildstrubel Summit Side Trip at the end of this day's walk description).

Take the right branch leading some way up to reach the **Rezligletschersee** at 2261m, 50 minutes to one hour from the Flueseelihütte; the snout of the glacier that formed this turgid lake overhangs the barren rock just above it. Crossing the wild glacial streams on sturdy footbridges, you follow the path around the Rezligletschersee over

Wildstrubel Traverse

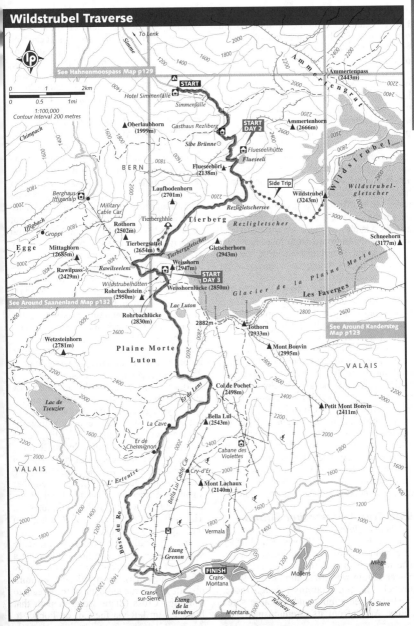

See Hahnenmoospass Map p129

START

Hotel Simmenfälle

Simmenfälle

To Lenk

Simme

▲ Oberlaubhorn
(1999m)

Gasthaus Rezliberg

Sibe Brünne

**START
DAY 2**

Ammertengrat

**Ammertenpass
(2443m)**

▲ **Ammertenhorn
(2666m)**

Flueseelihütte

Flueseeli

Flueseehöri ▲
(2138m)

BERN

▲ Laufbodenhorn
(2701m)

Berghaus
Iffigenalp

Military
Cable Car

Iffigbach

Groppi

Tierberghhle

Rezligletschersee

Side Trip

**Wildstrubel
(3243m)**

Wildstrubel-
gletscher

Wildstrubel

Rezligletscher

TIERBERG

Tierberg

Chimpach

▲ Rothorn
(2502m)

▲ Tierbergsattel
(2654m)

Tierberggletscher

▲ Gletscherhorn
(2943m)

Schneehorn
(3177m) ▲

EGGE

▲ Mittaghorn
(2685m)

Rawilpass
(2429m)

Rawilseeleni

Wildstrubelhütten
▲ Rohrbachstein
(2950m)

Weisshorn
(2947m)

**START
DAY 3**

Weisshornlücke (2850m)

Lac Luton

Glacier de la Plaine Morte

Les Faverges

See Around Saanenland Map p132

Rohrbachlücke
(2830m)

▲ Wetzsteinhorn
(2781m)

Plaine Morte
Luton

2882m

▲ Tothorn
(2933m)

See Around Kandersteg
Map p123

▲ Mont Bonvin
(2995m)

VALAIS

Lac de
Tseuzier

Er de Lens

Col de Pochet
(2498m)

▲ Petit Mont Bonvin
(2411m)

L' Ertentse

La Cave

Er de
Chermignon

Bella Lui
▲ (2543m)

Cabane des
Violettes

Cry-d'Er

▲ Mont Lachaux
(2140m)

Bella Lui Cable Car

VALAIS

Bisse du Ro

Vermala

Étang
Grenon

FINISH
Crans-
Montana

Miège

Mollens

Crans-
sur-Sierre

Étang
de la
Moubra

Montana

Funicular
Railway

To Sierre

N

0   1   2km
0   0.5   1mi
1:100,000
Contour Interval 200 metres

debris-strewn slabs looking down toward Lenk. Stone cairns and the familiar red and white paint splashes guide you on over a gravelly stream bed into the tiny upper valley of Tierberg.

After rising some distance along the lightly vegetated northern slopes, dip down left and make your way up through the moraine-filled gully below the long icy ledge of the Tierberggletscher. Zigzags lead up over a persistent snowdrift to **Tierbergsattel** at 2654m, 1¼ to 1¾ hours from the Rezligletschersee. Directly below you lie several sparkling little lakes called the Rawilseeleni, and farther behind the Rawilpass, an historic trans-Alpine route. The fit and agile can make the worthwhile side trip to the **Tierberghöhle**, a cave that once sheltered prehistoric visitors to these mountains. Head around north-eastward from just below the Tierbergsattel, climbing over loose scree to reach the rock opening on a grassy ledge below the craggy ridge.

From Tierbergsattel, drop down to the right to the **Rawilseeleni**, where you meet a more prominent path (coming up from Iffigenalp) near the middle station of a military cable car (not shown on topographical maps). Head up left between the lakes and begin a steep spiralling climb up the western flank of the Weisshorn below the line of cables to arrive at the SAC *Wildstrubelhütten* (☎ 033-744 33 39) after one to 1¼ hours. These two SAC-run huts – a newer main building and the original stone hut erected in 1927 – stand at 2793m on a levelled-out terrace not far below the summit of the Weisshorn. The Wildstrubelhütten are staffed from late June to mid-October by a resident cook/hutkeeper and dorm beds cost (non-members) Sfr13/27 children/adults.

Side Trip: Wildstrubel Summit
4–5 hours return, 9km, 1198m ascent
This excellent side trip leaves from the fork (at around 2250m) above the Flueseelihütte. The left branch is a rough trail up to the higher 3243m western summit of the Wildstrubel. The route climbs through loose, frost-shattered rubble and unstable scree slides. Apart from its strenuousness, the

route presents few difficulties given fine weather and normal summer snow conditions, but there are some sections of exposed dropoffs around the summit. The stunning summit panorama is particularly fine looking south and south-west across the Glacier de la Plaine Morte toward the Valais Alps or the strikingly close Wildhorn (3247m).

Day 3: Wildstrubelhütten to Crans-Montana
3¾–5 hours, 13km, 57m ascent
From the main hut, head up around to the right across patches of old snow to the **Weisshornlücke**, the obvious low point in the bare rock ridge at approximately 2850m, where the broad snow basin of the Glacier de la Plaine Morte comes into view. Except for its northern edge, the Plaine Morte has no dangerous crevasses and draws cross-country skiers even in midsummer.

Make your way south-east (in the direction of the Rohrbachstein, the square-shaped peak with a large cross mounted on its summit) to a narrow gap at around 2830m, which mountaineers know as the **Rohrbachlücke**. Continue across the cantonal border into the Valais, descending easily over firm scree slopes to reach **Lac Luton**, a lake set in barren surroundings at 2575m, after 50 minutes to one hour.

Make your way down through the rocky slopes of the **Plaine Morte Luton**, which is sparsely vegetated with hardy species of buttercups, past two tunnels in low moraine mounds evidently built to drain tiny lakes. When you come to a fork almost 2km on, take the route that goes eastward. The cut path sidles above cliffs, passing interesting rock columns before sinking to another signposted intersection at the head of the tiny **L'Ertentse** valley, 40 to 50 minutes on. The Bella Lui cable car is visible high on the ridges over to the left.

Take the trail signposted down the steep slopes daubed with wild flowers to meet a dirt road on the **Er de Lens** on the valley floor. Yellow markings now lead a few minutes along the true left bank of the stream to a bridge. Cross (disregarding a path that branches up left via the Col de Pochet to

BERNESE OBERLAND

Crans-Montana) and descend along an alp track, passing the dilapidated old slate-roof cottage at **La Cave**, a short way before you get to the Alpine pastures of the **Er de Chermignon** after 40 to 50 minutes. There is an emergency shelter here for wayward winter skiers.

Follow the dirt road down across the stream and continue five minutes to pick up an unmarked but obvious foot track leading off left up into the forest. The path climbs slightly below loose cliffs – keep moving here as there is some risk of rockfall – then begins a long contouring traverse around the moutainside beside the **Bisse du Ro**, an historic aqueduct that brings water to Crans-Montana. This route has been cut into the cliff face, with some exhilarating sections on wooden walkways secured by fixed cables and safety rails mounted onto sheer rock, and finally comes out onto a rough roadway after one to 1½ hours.

The well-signposted last part of the walk leads eastward around the slopes past villas and holiday chalets, crossing or following roads and tiny aqueducts before arriving at the artificial lake Étang Grenon after 25 to 30 minutes. The upper funicular station is a further 10 to 15 minutes' walk on through the centre of **Montana** township. Although more oriented to winter tourism, this modern resort is quite lively during the summer months.

Other Walks

Brienzer Rothorn

Marking the meeting point of the cantons of Lucerne, Obwalden and Bern, the Brienzer Rothorn rises up abruptly from the town of Brienz at the north-eastern end of the Brienzersee. The mountain's 2349m summit presents visitors with an almost unsurpassed Alpine panorama that embraces the long chain of peaks stretching eastward from Les Diablerets as far west as the Säntis. The Brienzer Rothorn is directly accessible from Brienz on the Brienz-Rothornbahn (**W** www.brienz-rothorn-bahn.ch), another of Switzerland's classic cog railways, whose old steam-driven locomotives puff their way up inclines of up to 25%.

A spectacular walk leads quickly from the upper train station (2244m) to the Brienzer

MARK HONAN

A typical sight for walkers in the Brienz region – the town is famous for its wood-carvings.

Rothorn. Two equally popular route alternatives exist: either make a long sidling descent around the northern side of the range via Chäseren and Schäri to the Brünigpass (1002m), or continue eastward along the ridgetop to Schönbüel (2012m), from where two cable cars carry you down via Turren to Obsee (752m) near Lungern. Both the Brünigpass and Lungern are on the Interlaken-Lucerne rail line.

The average walking time to the Brünigpass is 4½ hours, or around three hours to Schönbüel. Walkers can also reach the heights of the Brienzer Rothorn by cable car from Sörenberg (itself accessible by postbuses running between Lungern and Schüpfheim) on the other side of the range.

The *Hotel Rothorn Kulm* (☎ *033-915 12 51*) near the summit of the Brienzer Rothorn has rooms and a dorm. The only available walking map that (fully) shows the route(s) on a single sheet is K+F's 1:40,000 *Flühli Sörenberg*. The SAW/FSTP's 1:50,000 *Escholzmatt* No 244T and *Interlaken* No 254T (Sfr22.50 each) also cover the walk, but are less convenient as the route meanders along the edge of these sheets.

Niesen

The 2362m Niesen forms a final triangular outcrop at the northern end of the sharp and narrow range separating the valleys of the Kandertal and the Emmental, whose rivers meet at the foot of the mountain just before entering the Thunersee. Occupying this unique position, the Niesen is one of the region's prime lookout points, and – inevitably – has long been accessible by the Niesenbahn (**W** www.niesen.ch), a two-stage funicular railway from the village of Mülenen in the Kandertal. The summit gives grand views across the valleys of the Central Bernese Oberland to the main ranges of the

Alps. A very enjoyable four-hour downhill route leads from the Niesen over broad spurs along the east side of the range via Oberniesen (1813m), Hubelweid (1513m) and Eggweid (1371m) to the town of Frutigen (780m) in the Kandertal.

The *Hotel-Restaurant Niesen-Kulm* (☎ 033-676 11 13) at 2343m by the upper funicular station has rooms and dorms. Both Mülenen and Frutigen are on the main Spiez-Kandersteg rail line. The best walking map covering the route is the 1:25,000 *Frutigen*, published by the local tourist authorities.

Urbachtal

The Urbachtal, a side valley of the Haslital, is one of the most wild and interesting areas of the region. Extensive glaciers and 3000m peaks surrounding the upper valley present a formidable barrier that only experienced climbers can breach. For this reason the Urbachtal is probably more often visited by mountaineers than by walkers, who are obliged to backtrack via the access route.

From Innertkirchen (625m), 5km from Meiringen, a road leads up to lovely open plains along the Urbachtal's middle reaches. From there a well-marked path climbs steadily on up through the valley to reach the *Gaulihütte* (☎ 033-971 31 66), an SAC-run hut at 2205m, after five to seven hours. The ascent totals 1600m and requires good physical fitness. Recommended 1:50,000 walking maps are the locally produced *Wanderkarte Oberhasli*, Editions MPA Verlag's *Berner Oberland Ost* (Sfr27.90) or the SAW/FSTP *Sustenpass* map No 265T (Sfr22.50).

Upper Haslital & Grimselpass

The 2165m Grimselpass was an established trade route for centuries, although nowadays tourists vastly outnumber the mule trains. This moderate walk starts at the village of Guttannen (1049m) and leads through the upper Haslital between craggy giants to reach the Grimselpass after four or five hours. Although the landscape of the upper valley has been altered for hydroelectricity production, it has kept its wild and intensely glaciated feel.

The route mostly avoids the pass road, following the still-transitable romantic old mule trail in places. Note, however, that before August there is a (slight) danger of avalanches. The *Hotel Handeck* and *Grimsel Hospiz* (☎ 033-982 66 11, e grimselhotels@kwo.ch), and *Grimsel Blick* (☎ 027-973 11 77, e grimselblick@rhone.ch) have dorms and rooms. Several daily postbuses run between Andermatt and Meiringen from 1 July to 1 October (reservation obligatory ☎ 033-

828 88 28, 041-887 13 22). Use the 1:50,000 walking maps *Wanderkarte Oberhasli*, Editions MPA Verlag's *Berner Oberland Ost* (Sfr27.90), or both of the SAW/FSTP sheets *Sustenpass* map No 255T and *Nufenenpass* map No 265T (Sfr22.50 each).

Grindelwald Glaciers

Virtually in Grindelwald's backyard, the two glaciers known as the Oberer (upper) Grindelwaldgletscher and the Unterer (lower) Grindelwaldgletscher tumble down from a vast system of icefalls and perpetual snowfields clothing the great summits high above the town. Almost nowhere else (only near Chamonix in France) do glaciers in the Alps descend so far into the valley as at Grindelwald. Today, the snout of the Oberer Grindelwaldgletscher reaches down to around 1250m, although just 200 years ago it approached the 1000m level.

A suggested walk leads up from the Hotel Wetterhorn to the Oberer Grindelwaldgletscher, stopping for a look at the ice grottoes. From here the route climbs up to Halsegg, before contouring via Breitlouwina to Pfingstegg at 1391m (where a cable car runs down to Grindelwald). From Pfingstegg you can continue directly down past the *Berghaus Marmorbruch* (☎ 033-853 13 18), which has dorm beds for around Sfr30, to the gorge below the Unterer Grindelwaldgletscher. Recommended to sure-footed walkers is the spectacular side trip along a path cut into ledges high above the Unterer Grindelwaldgletscher to the *Berghotel Stieregg* (☎ 033-853 17 66, 079-656 53 18) at 1702m, which also offers dorm accommodation. Walkers can go farther still to the SAC's *Schreckhornhütte* (☎ 033-855 10 25) at 2529m.

The average walking time from the Hotel Wetterhorn to the Berghaus Marmorbruch is three hours; the return walk to the Berghotel Stieregg takes an extra three hours. There are regular postbuses from Grindelwald to the Oberer Grindelwaldgletscher (most of them continuing up to the Grosse Scheidegg). Use either the SAW/FSTP 1:50,000 *Interlaken* map No 254T (Sfr22.50) or Editions MPA Verlag's 1:50,000 *Berner Oberland Ost* (Sfr27.90).

Sulsseewli

The Sulsseewli is an Alpine tarn lying at 1920m high above the junction of the Lauterbrunnental and the Lütschental. From the upper funicular station at Grütschalp (1496m) the route gently rises around through the forest to Sousläger, there crossing the Sousbach stream and climbing up to a contouring path that brings you over the Sulsbach to the Sulsseewli. The SAC-run

Lobhornhütte (☎ 077-56 53 20, 033-855 27 12) nearby offers a splendid lookout point for the enormous white summits of the eastern Bernese Oberland.

The descent can be made by dropping down to the scattered hamlet of Sulwald (1081m), from where a private cableway runs down to the Isenfluh, or by continuing over the Tschingel ridge to the tiny village of Saxeten (1003m). The average walking time from Grütschalp to the Sulsseewli is two hours; the descent to Sulwald takes no more than two hours, or around three hours to Saxeten. From Isenfluh there are postbuses every one or two hours to Lauterbrunnen until around 5.30pm. Postbuses run from Saxeten to Widerswil three times daily, the last leaving shortly before 5pm; reservations are advisable (☎ 033-828 88 28). The 1:50,000 SAW/FSTP *Interlaken* map No 254T (Sfr22.50) best covers the walk.

Upper Lauterbrunnental

The upper Lauterbrunnental is enclosed on three sides by massive summits presided over by the 3785m Lauterbrunner Breithorn. The sides of this upper valley are hung with glaciers and icefalls, and this unique area forms a nature reserve. From the end of the road at Stechelberg (910m) a rewarding five to six-hour circuit can be made via Obersteinberg to the little Alpine lake of Oberhornsee (2065m). From here you can continue up to the *Schmadrihütte* (☎ 033-855 23 65) at 2262m, before descending via Schwand to Schürboden (1379m). The last leg back to Stechelberg leads along the river past Trachsellauenen (1201m).

Postbuses run hourly year-round between Lauterbrunnen (see Access Towns under The Jungfrau Region & Haslital) and Stechelberg. The last bus returns to Lauterbrunnen around 5.30pm. The SAW/FSTP 1:50,000 *Jungfrau* map No 264T (Sfr22.50) and the 1:40,000 *Wanderkarte Lauterbrunnental* both cover the upper Lauterbrunnental.

Gasterntal & Lötschenpass

The Gasterntal above Kandersteg is one of the Alps' classic glacial hanging valleys. Having been sheared by the Kanderfirn glacier, the rock walls enclosing the Gasterntal rise almost vertically to culminate in summits over 3500m high. The broad, flat floor of the Gasterntal was filled in and flattened out by the accumulation of some 200m of glacial and alluvial debris, and the valley's gradient varies only slightly over its 8km length.

From Kandersteg, an easy 2½-hour walk leads up via the Chluse gorge to the hamlet of Selden

(1537m), where the *Hotel Steinbock* (☎ 033-675 11 62), *Hotel Gasterntal-Selden* (☎ 033-675 11 63) and the *Berghaus Heimritz* (☎ 033-675 14 34) 1km upvalley all have singles/doubles from around Sfr50/100 and dorm beds for around Sfr30. Regular minibuses run from Kandersteg to Selden; reservations are essential (☎ 033-671 11 72).

From Selden, a challenging long day (or better overnight) walk leads over the classic 2690m Lötschenpass, an Alpine crossing used since prehistoric times. The route, which often follows old mule paths, climbs steeply southward via Gfällalp, skirting a small névé to reach the pass, then descends either via Kummenalp to Felden or via Laucheralp to Wiler into the remote valley of the Lötschental in the Upper Valais.

En route places to stay with dorms are the *Berghaus Gfällalp* (☎ 033-675 11 61), one hour above Selden, the *Lötschenpasshütte* (☎ 027-939 19 81), on the pass height, the *Berghaus Lauchern* (☎ 027-939 12 50) and the *Gasthaus Kummenalp* (☎ 027-939 12 80), both on the Valais side.

Use either the 1:25,000 *Wanderkarte Kandersteg* or the SAW/FSTP 1:50,000 *Jungfrau* map No 264T (Sfr22.50).

Rawilpass

The 2429m Rawilpass is another classic route crossing the Bernese Alps into the Valais. The route leaves from Iffigenalp (1584m), where the *Berghaus Iffigenalp* (☎ 033-733 13 33), open June to mid-October, offers singles/doubles from Sfr42/74 and dorm beds for Sfr25. A good path spirals up through massive precipices on the southern sides of the Iffigental, then climbs gently over the Rawilpass into the rolling meadows of the Alpage de Rawil and on down around the Lac de Tseuzier reservoir to the dam wall (known as Barrage du Rawil).

Between early June and early to mid-October there are up to eight daily postbuses to Iffigenalp from Lenk until around 5.15pm. Outside these times the buses run only on demand (minimum five passengers or equivalent fare paid; call ☎ 033-733 14 12).

Postbuses leave Barrage du Rawil (via Botrye) to Sion at around 11am and 5pm daily from late June to around 22 August, then on Saturday and Sunday only until the last week in September. The route is covered by two SAW/FSTP 1:50,000 sheets: *Wildstrubel* map No 263T and *Montana* map No 273T (both Sfr22.50).

Iffigsee

Embedded in an undrained sink at the base of the 3247m Wildhorn, this delightful lake makes an excellent destination for a longer day (or overnight) walk. The waters of the Iffigsee (2065m) ooze out subterraneously before gushing forth in springs that form the Iffigbach, a large sidestream of the Simme River. The way to the Iffigsee starts at Iffigenalp, and leads smoothly up to the alp huts of Groppi (1741m) before beginning the steeper climb along the ridge of Egge to reach the lake. A worthwhile continuation goes west over the Stigele ridge to Lauenen in the upper Lauenental.

The **Wildhornhütte** (☎ 033-675 23 82), a SAC-run mountain hut, is 45 minutes' climb up from Iffigsee. Use the SAW/FSTP 1:50,000 walking map *Wildstrubel* No 263T (Sfr22.50).

Upper Lauenental

This long return day walk from Lauenen explores the valley area above the village. Once destined for hydroelectric development, today the wild upper Lauenental is a nature reserve. The ascent route goes via the Lauenensee, a forest-fringed moor lake on a terrace above the valley, to the **Geltenhütte** (☎ 033-765 32 20), an SAC-run hut at 2003m. The return can be made via the Rohr swamp. There is a road as far as the Lauenensee, which is accessible by postbus and private car (parking fees apply), making a shorter version of this walk possible. The best

walking map is the SAW/FSTP 1:50,000 sheet *Wildstrubel* No 263T (Sfr22.50).

Col du Sanetsch

Together with the Grimselpass, the Gemmipass and the Rawilpass, the 2242m Col du Sanetsch (also called Col de Sénin) is one of four Alpine crossings from the Bernese Oberland into the Valais which is snow-free in summer. Although the area has been developed for hydroelectricity, the Col du Sanetsch remains a scenic and popular walking route. From Gsteig the 5½-hour route climbs very steeply to the Bern/Valais cantonal border then rises gently to meet a road at the Barrage du Sanetsch (the dam wall of the Lac de Sénin reservoir), where the **Auberge du Sanetsch** (☎ 033-755 12 32) has dorm beds and rooms. After continuing on or near the road to the Col du Sanetsch, the route descends via Tsanfleuron and Glarey to the hamlet of Grand Zour (1437m). From Barrage du Sanetsch there is one postbus to Sion at around 4.50pm daily between late June and around 20 August, then on Saturday and Sunday only until the last week in September; it passes Grand Zour at about 5.30pm.

Two SAW/FSTP 1:50,000 walking maps cover the route: *Wildstrubel* No 263T and *Montana* No 273T (Sfr22.50 each).

Central Switzerland

Together the cantons of Lucerne, Uri, Schwyz, Unterwalden and Zug form Central Switzerland, the country's geographical and cultural heartland. Clustered around beautiful Lake Lucerne, this region is of special significance to all Swiss people, who trace their national origins back to 1271, when the original three cantons of Uri, Schwyz and Nidwalden signed a pact on a lakeside meadow, the famous Rütli. Central Switzerland also has a special place in Swiss legend, since the folk hero Wilhelm Tell supposedly hailed from the southern shores of Lake Lucerne.

With the exception of Lucerne, these are small, lightly settled cantons whose economic mainstays – alongside tourism – are agriculture and animal husbandry. The 'Inner Swiss' *(Innerschweizer)*, as the German-speaking people of this region are known, are generally rather conservative with a strong sense of independence. Here the upholding of traditions often takes precedence over modern needs.

Although sometimes likened to neighbouring Bern Canton (or even the Glarnerland), Central Switzerland has a physical character rather different from either. The northern section of this region (chiefly in Lucerne Canton) lies outside the basin of the Reuss River, and takes in a good part of the undulating landscape of the Swiss Mittelland, which includes the Napf District. Of greater interest to walkers is the southern half of Central Switzerland, a geographically more complicated area that embraces the lower (but nonetheless quite impressive) ranges of the Alpine foothills around Lake Lucerne as well as the much taller peaks of the Central Swiss Alps.

Although many parts of Central Switzerland are relatively unprosperous by Swiss standards, scenically speaking the region is a veritable treasure house. Here and there quaint rustic alp huts rest among fastidiously tended pastures before a grandiose backdrop of high snowcapped peaks. In early summer sweeping fields of wild flowers

CLEM LINDENMAYER

An old sign post below Rigi-Kulm indicates 'steep' (left) and 'comfortable' (right) paths.

Highlights

- Marvelling at the sheer walls of the Glarner Alps from near Braunwald on the Klausenpass walk
- Strolling along the undulating crest of the Rigi range toward the icy peaks of the Central Swiss Alps
- Following the Bürgenstock Felsenweg, cut through precipitous cliffs 500m above Lake Lucerne
- Looking out across the sparkling Seewen tarns to the majestic summit of the Titlis from the Surenenpass

carpet the mountainsides, and walkers can enjoy arguably the most splendid flora found anywhere in the Swiss Alps.

INFORMATION
Maps

Central Switzerland is covered by No 2 of the BL/OFT's 1:200,000 (four-sheet) series.

Central Switzerland

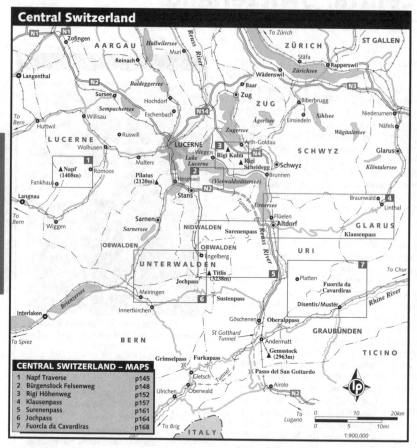

CENTRAL SWITZERLAND – MAPS

Books

The only English-language regional walking guide is *Central Switzerland* by Kev Reynolds (Cicerone Press), which is hard to find locally but available in Britain for UK£10.99.

The SAC's German-language *Alpinwandern Zentalschweiz – Glarus Alpstein* (Sfr46) by Remo Kundert & Marco Volken details dozens of mountain walks in Central and North-Eastern Switzerland. Kümmerly + Frey's (K+F) *Zentralschweiz* (Sfr22.80) is a German regional walking guide detailing circuit (loop) walks in Central Switzerland.

Information Sources

The tourist office covering Central Switzerland is Zentralschweiz-Tourismus (☎ 041-418 40 80, **e** info@centralswitzerland.ch, **w** www.centralswitzerland.ch) Alpenstrasse 1, CH-6002 Luzern.

For details on Lake Lucerne region contact Vierwaldstattersee Tourismus (☎ 041-666 50 50, **e** owtourismus@bluewin.ch, **w** www.lakeluzern.ch) Hofstrasse 2, Sarnen.

GETTING AROUND

The *Tell Pass* costs Sfr179 (Sfr144 concession) for 15 days or Sfr131 (Sfr105) for seven days. It gives unlimited travel for five/two days, plus 10/five days of travel at half-price on the Lake Lucerne ferries and many train services around the shore. The *Tell Pass* is valid for the Jochpass lifts as well as the Pilatus and both Rigi cog railways. Other postbus and rail services in a broader area of southern Central Switzerland cost half-price.

The *Passepartout* regional pass gives unlimited travel on city buses, postbuses, trains and ferries in the cantons of Lucerne, Nidwalden and Obwalden (but not Uri). The one-month pass for all zones costs Sfr184, but cheaper variations are possible.

GATEWAY
Lucerne

Lucerne's beautiful old town and scenic location on a northern arm of Lake Lucerne ensures it a place on most tourist itineraries. Unlike other large centres in Switzerland, Lucerne (Luzern in German) is a true 'Alpine city'. Lying so close to the high mountains, there are majestic views stretching southward to the Pilatus, the city's chief landmark, and the 3238m Titlis. Lucerne's Gletschergarten (Sfr8/6 adults/concessions, W www.gletschergarten.ch) is a fascinating introduction to Switzerland's glacial past, and its museum has very good relief models of the Alpstein (Säntis), Bernina and other Swiss mountain massifs. An easy and short walk directly out of Lucerne goes up from Grütsch over the Sonnenberg ridge to the Chrüzhöchi (775m), then down via the interesting gorge at Ränggloch to Obernau, from where there are buses back to Lucerne.

For information contact the Lucern tourist office (☎ 041-227 17 17, fax 041-227 17 18 e luzern@luzern.org, W www.luzern.org), Zentralstrasse 5. For walking gear see the range at Transa (☎ 041 240 38 38, fax 041-240 38 39, e outdoor.luzern@transa.ch), Pfistergasse 23; Eiselin Sport (☎ 041-240 12 12, e eiselin@eiselin-sport.ch), Obergrundstrasse 70; and Ochsner Sport (☎ 041-220 21 21), Pilatusstrasse 8.

Places to Stay & Eat Tent sites are available at *Camping Lido (☎ 041-370 21 46,*

e *info@camping.ch)* from Sfr4 plus Sfr7 per person, and dorm beds are Sfr13 (without breakfast). The nicer *Camping Steinibachried (☎ 041-340 35 58)* at the little bay of Horw has sites from Sfr5/7 plus Sfr4.50/7 per person in low/high season.

The large *youth hostel (☎ 041-420 88 00,* e *luzern@youthhostel.ch, Sedelstrasse 12)* has dorm beds for Sfr28/31.50 in low/high season. The independent *Backpackers Lucerne (☎ 041-360 04 20, Alpenquai 42),* 10 minutes' walk south-east of the station, has dorm beds from Sfr21.50 (without breakfast or sheets).

The unusual *Hotel Löwengraben (☎ 041-417 12 12,* e *hotel@loewengraben.ch, Löwengraben 18),* in an ex-prison, has single/double 'cells' from Sfr75/111 and dorm beds from Sfr20 (without breakfast).

The *Hotel Linde (☎ 041-410 31 93, Metzgerrainle 3),* off Weinmarkt, has basic singles/doubles for Sfr40/80 without breakfast. The *Tourist Hotel (☎ 041-410 24 74,* e *info@touristhotel.ch, St Karli Quai 12)* has dorm beds from Sfr28 and singles/doubles from Sfr54/88. The central *Hotel Schlüssel (☎ 041-210 10 61, Franziskanerplatz 12)* has rooms from Sfr75/100.

The *Migros* and *Coop* supermarkets on Hertensteinstrasse have budget restaurants. The *Bistro du Theatre (Theaterstrasse 5)* has dishes from around Sfr16. The small *Goldener Löwen (Eisengasse 1)* serves Swiss food from around Sfr18.

Getting There & Away There are at least hourly trains from Lucerne to Interlaken, Bern, Zürich and Geneva (via Interlaken or Langnau). Ferries (W www.lakelucerne.ch) run to numerous towns and villages around the shore of Lake Lucerne.

Napf District

Centred on the Napf itself, an isolated 1408m peak nearly 30km south-west of Lucerne, is the geologically interesting area known as Napf District (Napfgebiet in German). Numerous streams radiating out from this low summit give it a kind of 'conical symmetry', and a casual map reader might even – were this not Switzerland – mistake it for some ancient extinct volcano. On closer inspection, however, a definite ridgeline can be made out running north-southward right through the centre of the Napf District to form both a political and cultural division between (Protestant) Bern and (Catholic) Lucerne Cantons.

As its German name implies, the Napf resembles an enormous upturned bowl. Ice-age glaciers never covered the Napf but left it as a 'nunatak' island within the icy masses, and this accounts for the district's much gentler topography. This natural lookout peak is sometimes called the 'Rigi of the Emmental', and is composed of the same coarse, ancient marine sediments (known in German as *Nagelfluh*) typical for much of the Alpine foothills. The ranges of the Napf District also contain traces of gold, which has been extracted for centuries from alluvial stream deposits. From the grassy upper ridge tops a dozen or so small, thinly settled valleys open out in all directions through the low hills of dense spruce and beech forest. The scattering of villages here are accessible only via minor cul-de-sac roads that keep (motorised) traffic to an absolute minimum.

Napf Traverse

Duration	3½–4½ hours
Distance	14km
Standard	easy
Start	Romoos
Finish	Fankhaus
Nearest Towns	Langnau

Summary This is a gentle ridge-top walk across the open summit of the Napf, which grants a fantastic panorama stretching north across the Mittelland as far as the Jura and south to the icy giants in the Jungfrau region.

This short day walk is arguably the nicest way to the top of the Napf. There are no real difficulties, and there is a hotel on the summit itself. Due to its relatively low elevation, the Napf can be walked early and late in the season. The Napf is a high point at the edge of the Mittelland and therefore tends to catch passing rain clouds, making it one of the wettest parts of the country – don't forget your waterproofs.

Maps

K+F's 1:60,000 *Emmental-Oberaargau* (Sfr24.80) covers the route on a single sheet. Otherwise you'll need two SAW/FSTP 1:50,000 maps: *Escholzmatt* No 244T and *Willisau* No 234T (Sfr22.50 each).

NEAREST TOWNS
Romoos

This quaint village (791m) is the start of the walk. The *Hotel Kreuz* (☎ 041-480 13 51) is a lovely old shingled building with rooms from around Sfr50/100.

There are up to nine daily postbuses to Romoos from Wolhusen, on the railway junction of the main Bern–Langnau–Lucerne and the small Langenthal–Wolhusen lines; the last bus to Romoos leaves at around 7pm.

Langnau

Lying at the south-western edge of the Napf District in Bern Canton, Langnau is the regional centre of the Emmental – the valley from where the genuine bubbly 'Swiss' cheese originates. Langnau is also known for its traditional pottery, and has a pleasant old town. In all seasons, walks along the Emme River are an attractive proposition.

The regional tourist office, Pro Emmental (☎ 034-402 42 52, e info@emmental.ch), Schlossstrasse 3, is helpful.

The Langnau *youth hostel* (☎ 034-402 45 26, e langnau@youthhostel.ch, Mooseggstrasse 32) has dorm beds for Sfr12/14 in low/high season; it closes from the last week of September to mid-October. *Hotel Bahnhof* (☎ 034-402 14 95, Bahnhofstrasse 5) has singles/doubles for around Sfr40/70 and has a pizzeria downstairs. The *Restaurant zum Goldenen Löwen* (☎ 034-402 65 55, Guterstrass 9) has rooms at similar prices and serves fish specialities.

Langnau is about halfway along the Bern–Lucerne rail line, with alternating express and regional trains running at half-hourly intervals in both directions.

GETTING TO/FROM THE WALK

For information on travel to/from Romoos, see Nearest Towns earlier. From late May to mid-October walkers have the option of taking one of the several postbuses that continue on from Romoos to Holzwegen (Holzwage), thus shortening the walk by just over one hour.

The end of the walk is the tiny village of Fankhaus, from where there are a dozen or so daily postbuses to Langnau. The last bus leaves Fankhaus at roughly 7.40pm.

THE WALK

Walk along the street past the Hotel Kreuz, turning right at a fork near the edge of Romoos. Bear right again at a sawmill and follow the road over a small bridge, before climbing around to a farmhouse on the ridge top. Here the pre-Alpine ranges of the Schrattenfluh and Hohgant come into sight beyond the green rolling hills. Walk on westward along the crest of the grassy ridge to

Charcoal Making

The Napf District is the only part of Switzerland where the traditional method of making charcoal (*Holzkohlerei* in German) is still practised. The logs are meticulously stacked into a high rounded mound and covered with green branches; a small chimney opening in the otherwise airtight 'kiln' ensures only a gradual smouldering occurs. This humble industry (supplying fuel for Swiss barbecues) is based in the Napf villages of Romoos and Bramboden, and in autumn smoky haze hangs lazily over the surrounding valleys.

Holzwegen (also called Holzwage) after one to 1½ hours. Here the ***Restaurant Holzwegen*** (1079m) has simple meals and refreshments.

Cross a broad road here and continue along another well-graded vehicle track past the restaurant. Head up right on a signposted

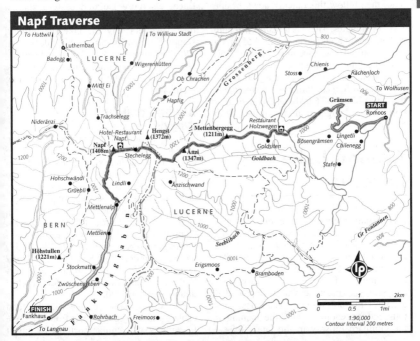

Napf Traverse

To Huttwil
To Willisau Stadt
Luthernbad
Badegg
LUCERNE
Wigerenhütten
Ob Chrachen
Grossenberg
800
Chienis
Rächenloch
Stoss
To Wolhusen
Mittl Ei
Haplig
Trachselegg
Grämsen
START
Romoos
Nideränzi
Hotel-Restaurant
Napf
Hengst
(1372m)
Mettenbergegg
(1211m)
Restaurant
Holzwegen
Lingetli
Chilenegg
Napf
(1408m)
Stechelegg
Anzi
(1347m)
Goldsiten
Bösengrämsen
Goldbach
Hohschwändi
Lindli
Anzischwand
Stafel
Grüebli
1200
Mettlenalp
LUCERNE
1000
Gr Fontannen
BERN
Mettlen
Seeblibach
800
Höhstullen
(1221m)
Stockmatt
Erigsmoos
Zwüschengraben
Bramboden
FINISH
Fankhaus
Rohrbach
Freimoos
To Langnau

0   1   2km
0   0.5   1mi
1:90,000
Contour Interval 200 metres

path soon after you pass a gravel quarry, and ascend steeply through the forest back to the top of the ridge. The route rejoins the road a short way on, rising and dipping as it follows the grassy heights above deeply eroded gorges to pass by the farmlets of **Änzi** (1347m) and **Stechelegg** (1315m).

A last climb through pockets of spruce forest brings you up to the summit of the **Napf** (1408m), 1¼ to 1¾ hours on from the Restaurant Holzwegen. Here the ***Hotel-Restaurant Napf*** (☎ 034-495 54 08) offers singles/doubles for Sfr55/110 and dorm beds for Sfr32. In clear conditions the little grassy summit plateau offers tremendous views in all directions. To the north across the Mittelland lie the ranges of the Jura, while before you to the south stand the great snowcapped peaks of Central Switzerland and the Bernese Oberland.

Take the signposted foot track that drops in steep spirals down the Napf's heavily wooded southern slopes to meet a forestry road, then follow this quickly down beside the stream to reach **Mettlenalp** (1051m) after 30 to 40 minutes. There is a *restaurant* here and one bus to Langnau at around 4.55pm on Sunday only. The last section of the walk follows the bitumen down through the quiet upper valley area of the Fankhusgraben past sporadic old Bernese farmhouses to arrive at the tiny village of **Fankhaus** (with regular postbuses to Langnau) after a further 40 to 50 minutes.

Around Lake Lucerne

The beautiful 114-sq-km Lake Lucerne is Switzerland's classic large glacial lake, with fjord-like arms branching off in all directions. As indicated by its German name (Vierwaldstättersee, or 'lake of the four forest cantons'), Lake Lucerne is fronted by the cantons of Lucerne, Uri, Unterwalden and Schwyz. This large waterway provided a natural transport route between these cantons, and for centuries – until the opening of the Gotthard railway in the late 1800s –

cargo on the Gotthard route was shipped across the lake rather than carted overland.

Lake Lucerne lies at 434m above sea level and is ringed by numerous lookout peaks of the Alpine foothills, many of them rising up directly from the irregular shoreline. The lake was formed during the last ice age by the massive Reuss Glacier, which once protruded far out into the Swiss Mittelland, gouging a deep trough into the landscape. Lake Lucerne is now gradually filling up again as its many inlet rivers continuously wash in large volumes of rock and sand. Due to its size, the lake acts as a reservoir of warmth, and enjoys a mild climate – an effect enhanced by the warm southerly Föhn winds, which frequently blow down from the Alps (see the boxed text 'Föhn Winds' in the Facts about Switzerland chapter).

Although there are some heavily settled areas scattered around the lakeshore, in most places nature reserves front the waterline. The nicest places to stay are on Lake Lucerne's more isolated eastern shores. More than 20 ferries (including five old historic steamers) ply the lake in summer, stopping off at all larger lakeside towns. The Waldstätterweg walking route leads the whole way around Lake Lucerne, and there are some excellent hikes in the surrounding mountains.

ACCESS TOWNS
Weggis

The small resort town of Weggis lies within an enclave of Lucerne Canton stretching along the great lake's eastern shore to include Vitznau. Famous for its mild, sunny climate, Weggis is a horticultural paradise and was long a major supplier of garden produce to the city of Lucerne. For information, contact the tourist office (☎ 041-390 11 55, ⓔ info@weggis.ch, ⓦ www.weggis.ch).

Budget Hotel Weggis (☎ 041-390 11 31) has double rooms from Sfr64.50. The ***Hotel Garni Victoria*** (☎ 041-390 11 28), overlooking the lake promenade, offers singles/doubles for Sfr45/90.

The valley station of the Rigi Kaltbad cable car is in Weggis. Apart from the Lake Lucerne boats, regular postbuses connect

Weggis with Küssnacht am Rigi (from where there are trains on to Lucerne and Zürich) and Schwyz (via Gersau).

Gersau

Gersau was a self-governing independent republic for over 500 years, but today this tiny town on the lakeshore belongs to Schwyz Canton. In a tradition that goes back to republican times, Switzerland's Sinti and Roma (otherwise known as Gypsies) meet each year in Gersau for the Feckerchilbi, a festival lasting several days.

For information, contact the tourist office (☎ 041-828 12 20, e tourismus@gersau.ch, w www.gersau.ch).

In nearby Rotschuo, the *youth hostel* (☎ *041-828 12 77*) has dorm accommodation for Sfr21/22.50 in low/high season. The *Gasthaus Krone* (☎ *041-828 15 35*, e *mf_krone@gersau.ch*) has singles/doubles for Sfr55/85. The *Hotel Ilge* (☎ *041-828 11 55*, e *mf_ilge@gersau.ch*) offers rooms from Sfr65/130.

Ferries run across the lake to Lucerne, and there are postbuses to Schwyz.

Bürgenstock Felsenweg

Duration	2–2½ hours
Distance	7.5km
Standard	easy
Start	Bürgenstock
Finish	Ennetbürgen

Summary This short walk with mild ascents and drops follows a spectacular route cut into sheer cliffs 500m above Lake Lucerne.

Sometimes called the 'little brother of the Rigi', the Bürgenstock is a high limestone ridge forming an impressive peninsula that reaches across Lake Lucerne almost as far as the adjacent shore. Some thousands of years ago, the Bürgenstock was an island, but alluvial debris constantly washed out of the surrounding mountains gradually created a broad, fertile plain connecting the Bürgenstock to the 'mainland'. Although its upper heights reach a relatively modest 1127m at the summit of Hammetschwand,

Bürgenstock arguably shows Lake Lucerne from the most beautiful angle, with superb views across the lake to the Pilatus, Lucerne and the Rigi itself.

Today, the Bürgenstock has regained its island status in quite a different sense. Atop the ridge is a privately owned and self-contained luxury resort – also called Bürgenstock – with palatial hotels, boutiques, magnificent gardens and a golf course. The famous entrepreneur Franz Josef Bucher-Durrer began building Bürgenstock village in 1870. To impress his well-to-do guests, Bucher-Durrer then constructed the so-called Felsenweg, a panoramic 'precipice walkway' cut into the cliff face.

The Felsenweg, along with an impressive lift mounted onto the side of the sheer rock walls to take walkers up to the Hammetschwand, was completed in 1905. Over the following decades, however, the route gradually deteriorated, eventually becoming unsafe and impassable. After its thorough restoration in 1971, the Felsenweg now forms part of the long Waldstätterweg, a walking route which circumnavigates Lake Lucerne.

Although some walkers prone to vertigo may find the Felsenweg slightly unnerving, the route is quite safe.

Maps

The best available walking map is Nidwalder Wanderwege's 1:25,000 *Nidwalder Wanderkarte* (around Sfr20). Either K+F's 1:60,000 *Luzern* or 1:60,000 *Schwyz-Zug-Vierwaldstättersee* (both Sfr24.80) also cover the walk; the latter includes Lake Lucerne and much of the Central Swiss Alps. Two SAW/FSTP 1:50,000 maps, *Rotkreuz* No 235T and *Stans* No 245T (Sfr22.50 each) are otherwise required, but using these is inconvenient as the sheets intersect right along the route.

NEAREST TOWN & FACILITIES
Bürgenstock

The walk begins at this ritzy resort (874m), high above Lake Lucerne. Several plush hotels (w www.buergenstock-hotels.ch) offer rooms from Sfr280.

CENTRAL SWITZERLAND

Ennetbürgen

This is a small village on a quiet sheltered bay of Lake Lucerne. The *Hotel Kreuz* (☎ *041-620 13 17*) offers singles/doubles for around Sfr45/90.

GETTING TO/FROM THE WALK

The easiest (and most romantic) way to reach Bürgenstock is to take a lake ferry to Kehrsiten-Bürgenstock (462m). From the end of May until late September there are about a dozen boats daily from Lucerne or Flüelen to Kehrsiten-Bürgenstock. Ferries run less frequently outside this period, and cease from the last Sunday in October to after the first week of April. From the Kehrsiten-Bürgenstock landing jetty, the Bürgenstock-bahn (**W** www.buergenstock-bahn.ch) funicular runs up to Bürgenstock from early April until late October; the one-way funicular fare is Sfr12/6 adults/children (Half Fare Card valid).

Once the ferries and funicular stop running, the best access is by postbus (maximum of four daily) from Stansstad (on the Lucerne–Engelberg rail line) to the village of Kehrsiten, from where the steep walk up to Bürgenstock takes a good 40 minutes.

The village of Ennetbürgen, at the end of the walk, is also serviced by the Lake Lucerne ferries. Postbuses (many coming from Seelisberg, near the start of the Weg der Schweiz walk – see Other Walks at the end of the chapter) run from Ennetbürgen to Stans (on the Lucerne–Engelberg rail line) roughly every 40 minutes.

The best place to leave private vehicles is the train station in Stansstad.

THE WALK

From the upper funicular station at Bürgenstock walk east along the road lined with German luxury cars past the Palace Hotel, then turn left onto a broad gravelled walkway. The path mainly contours along the side of the ridge above heavily forested cliffs that drop over 400m straight down to the lake. Frequent breaks in the trees offer lovely views across Lake Lucerne to the Pilatus behind you, the tilted form of the Rigi ahead and northward as far as the Zugersee (Lake Zug) behind Lucerne.

After 30 to 35 minutes you come to the **Hammetschwand-Lift**. Resembling a building crane, this 160m structure has been fixed onto the cliff face and is the highest

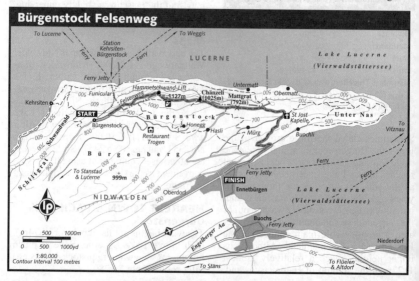

Bürgenstock Felsenweg

Forestry in Switzerland

Forest covers roughly a quarter of Switzerland's area (over 70% is publicly or community owned, with tiny privately held parcels accounting for the remainder). For countless centuries timber and firewood have been harvested from the forests, and in many regions forestry remains an important industry (but relies heavily on federal subsidies).

Swiss foresters are meticulous in their management – saplings are thinned out, dead wood is cleared and stacked, tree pests and diseases are checked and controlled – which gives the forests an orderly (yet attractive) 'park' appearance. Although there is almost no unmodified forest anywhere in Switzerland, the forests are vital biosphere reserves. Unauthorised vehicle access is strictly controlled, although walking routes often follow forest backroads.

free-standing lift in Europe. Before you go on, it's worth riding up to the lookout on the **Hammetschwand** (1127m) for a full panorama stretching around from the Mittelland to the main peaks of the Central Swiss Alps in the south; the fare is Sfr8/4.60 adults/children (Half Fare Card valid). The Hammetschwand is within a tiny enclave belonging to the municipality of Lucerne, making it the highest point in the 'city'.

Head on through a series of short tunnels blasted into the vertical rock walls, with sturdy steel railings and frequent bench seats for the giddy. The Felsenweg passes under a final tunnel-gate just before terminating at a junction, after which the white-red-white marked path (which is signposted 'Waldstätterweg') continues east along the wooded crest of the ridge via **Chänzeli** (1025m) to reach **Mattgrat**, 25 to 30 minutes on. The several houses here at the end of a gravelled road look down over open slopes toward the village of Ennetbürgen in a cove of Lake Lucerne.

Make your way gently up past a small private cableway (which services the isolated farmlet of Untermatt on the lakeshore), bearing left at a fork not far before you get to the historic **St Jost Kapelle** after 20 to 25 minutes. Situated at 690m on a grassy pasture high above the blue waters of the lake, this tiny whitewashed chapel was erected in 1733 as the final resting place of a medieval hermit who lived beneath a nearby granite boulder. During its renovation some years ago, original frescoes were discovered under the interior plaster.

Cut diagonally down over the green fields past an enormous barnyard to some scattered farmhouses, then take a signposted path that doubles back briefly left alongside an overgrown fence. After crossing a minor road the route steers right again and sidles along the lightly forested lakeside to meet a sealed street at the edge of **Ennetbürgen**. Follow this straight down past the ferry dock to arrive at the village centre, 40 to 50 minutes from St Jost.

Rigi Höhenweg

Duration	2¾–3¼ hours
Distance	10km
Standard	easy
Start	Rigi-Kulm
Finish	Rigi-Scheidegg
Nearest Towns	Arth-Goldau, Vitznau, Rigi-Kaltbad

Summary This gentle walk from the main summit of the Rigi follows the short range over minor peaks providing superb lookout points in all directions.

Marking a natural division between the lower and flatter Swiss Mittelland and the high snow-daubed summits of the Alps proper, the Rigi is perhaps the most classic panorama mountain in Switzerland. The Rigi's tilted 'beret' form rises up between Lake Lucerne and the Zugersee (Lake Zug), and is a familiar landmark to the countless rail and road travellers who whiz past the mountain every day.

Although the walk is fairly short, consider spending a night up on the mountain at one of the many reasonably priced hotels.

CENTRAL SWITZERLAND

Making use of the Rigi's various 'mechanical means of ascent' to reach the upper slopes of the mountain, the walk has no steep climbs or descents, although at times the views themselves may have you gasping for breath. The mountain's relatively low height (averaging 1500m) and sunny aspect make this an almost year-round route. Apart from the short Felsenweg section (which becomes dangerously icy and is therefore closed), the Rigi Höhenweg can be done as a winter walk since snow is regularly cleared from the path.

The Rigi is not for those seeking that solitary Alpine challenge, however, and walkers can expect gentle gradients and plenty of company. The Rigi is nonetheless an outstanding area for walking, and should not be disregarded simply because of its thoroughly developed tourist infrastructure. At the time of research, the section of path between Rigi-Staffel and Rigi-Kulm was due to be rerouted and upgraded in summer 2001.

Rigi Railways

The Rigi has been an extremely popular destination for day excursionists since the very beginnings of Alpine tourism. By the early 19th century hundreds of sightseers were making the pilgrimage up to the Rigi each day – many hauled up by sedan-chairs or on horseback.

In 1871 the world's first mountain railway, the Vitznau-Bahn, was built from Lake Lucerne up to the main Rigi summit. Soon after, a second private Rigi railway was constructed from Arth-Goldau on the other side of the mountain. Yet another section of railway, the Rigi-Scheidegg-Bahn, was then built along the Rigi's panoramic ridge top, linking Rigi-Scheidegg with Rigi-Kaltbad, but it never turned a profit and was finally closed in 1931. The Rigi Höhenweg largely follows the embankment of this long-defunct rail line.

After more than 120 years of jealous rivalry, the two private mountain railways finally merged in the mid-1990s to form Rigi Bahnen (Ⓦ www.rigi.ch).

Maps

The recommended walking map is the local tourist authority's 1:25,000 *Wanderkarte Rigi* (around Sfr16). Other good options are the SAW/FSTP 1:50,000 map *Rotkreuz* No 235T (Sfr22.50) and Orell Füssli's 1:50,000 *Kanton Schwyz* (Sfr25). K+F's 1:60,000 *Schwyz-Zug-Vierwaldstättersee* (Sfr24.80) takes in the whole of Lake Lucerne (and is also useful for the nearby Bürgenstock Felsenweg walk described earlier in this chapter).

NEAREST TOWNS & FACILITIES
Arth-Goldau

Arth-Goldau probably provides the easiest access to the Rigi. The Bergsturzmuseum dealing with the 1806 Rossberg landslide is worth a visit.

In Arth, *Hotel Rössli* (☎ *041-855 11 10*) has rooms for Sfr50/100. Its near-namesake in Goldau, *Hotel Restaurant Rössli* (☎ *041-855 13 19*, Ⓔ *roessligoldau@arth-online.ch, Gotthardstrasse 29*), has rooms available for Sfr60/100.

Arth-Goldau is on the main rail line between Ticino and Basel/Zürich.

Vitznau

The affection-inspiring old holiday resort of Vitznau lies on the isolated central-eastern banks of Lake Lucerne at the foot of the Rigi. Vitznau is the starting point of the historic Vitznau-Rigi-Bahn, built in 1871 as Europe's first cog railway.

For more information you can contact the Vitznau tourist office (☎ 041-398 00 35, Ⓔ info@vitznau.ch, Ⓦ www.vitznau.ch).

Terrassen-Camping Vitznau (☎ *041-397 12 80*, Ⓔ *zanetti@datacomm.ch*) has tent sites for Sfr14/16 plus Sfr8/9.50 per person in low/high season. *Hotel Schiff* (☎ *041-397 13 57*, Ⓔ *schiff.vitznau@bluewin.ch*) has singles/doubles for Sfr39/78 and the *Hotel Terrasse am See* (☎ *041-397 10 33*, Ⓔ *info@terrassen.ch*) offers rooms of a better standard from Sfr70 /110.

Rigi-Kaltbad

The walk passes through this scattered car-free resort on the cog railway from Vitznau.

The Rigi tourist office (☎ 041-397 11 28) is here. Rigi-Kaltbad has several better-standard hotels, including the *Hotel Alpina* *(☎ 041-397 11 52,* e *info@alpina-rigi.ch)* with rooms from Sfr60 per person and the *Hostellerie Rigi (☎ 041-397 16 16)*, which charges from Sfr78. The *Hotel Bergsonne* *(☎ 041-399 80 10,* e *info@bergsonne.ch)* has singles/doubles from Sfr90/160.

GETTING TO/FROM THE WALK

The walk begins at the Rigi-Kulm station, just below the mountain's main summit. Two historic cog railways run up to Rigi-Kulm: the Vitznau-Bahn from Vitznau and the Rigi-Bahn from Arth-Goldau (see Nearest Towns & Facilities). On both cog railways, the one-way fare is Sfr32/58 return (or through-ticket); holders of the Half Fare Card and Swiss Card receive a 50% discount, and other concessions apply. The service from Arth-Goldau stops for two weeks in late May but trains from Vitznau run all year round.

The walk finishes at Rigi-Scheidegg, a lower summit on the Rigi range (about 4km directly south-east of Rigi-Kulm). From here there are two mechanical descent options. Best is the cable car down to the Chräbel (Krabel) station on the Rigi-Bahn line to Arth-Goldau; the one-way fare is Sfr28/14 adults/children (standard concessions and special family fares apply).

Less advantageous is the Gschwänd-Burggeist chairlift down to Gschwänd (also spelled Gschwend); the downward fare is Sfr15/8. Between 1 June and 31 October a once-daily minibus runs from Gschwänd to Gersau (Sfr5/3) at around 3.45pm; making reservations is recommended – call ☎ 041-828 29 29. If you don't mind going the extra distance on foot (roughly 1½ hours) it's a pleasant walk from Gschwänd down to Gersau.

There are various combined ticket options available that integrate the several local mountain cableways with Lake Lucerne ferries. If you want to visit the Rigi as a return day trip from one of the larger cities, the SBB/CFF also offers several special package deals.

THE WALK

Both the Vitznau and Arth-Goldau cog railways terminate at **Rigi-Kulm** train station (1752m), from where the 1797m summit is only a few minutes' walk uphill. The panorama from this highest of the Rigi's various summits is quite stunning. With views stretching westward over Lake Lucerne to the city of Lucerne and northward across the Zugersee (Lake Zug) down into the Mittelland, from here the Rigi seems surrounded by water. Here the *Rigi-Kulm Hotel (☎ 041-855 03 03)* offers dorm beds for Sfr30 (with breakfast) as well as simple singles/doubles for Sfr35/70 and better rooms for up to Sfr95/190.

Walk back to the Rigi-Kulm station and take the broad, sealed footpath down beside the terraced precipice at the Rigi's northern edge, crossing over the train tracks at the station of **Rigi-Staffel** (1603m). The route follows the rail lines past the *Berggasthaus Staffel-Stubli (☎ 041-855 02 05)*, with dorm beds for Sfr35 and singles/doubles for Sfr45/90, to **Rigi-Staffelhöhe** (1550m), where the *Hotel Edelweiss Rigi (☎ 041-399 88 00)* has similar rooms. Continue ahead south-west along the ridge path (signposted 'Gratweg') to reach **Chänzeli** (1464m) after 50 minutes to one hour. This dramatic outcrop is arguably the most scenic lookout point of the Rigi range. From where you stand the land drops more than 1000m into Lake Lucerne, which appears as a watery landscape of long fjord-like arms and peninsulas.

Descend very gently south-east past the romantic St Michael's Chapel and an old spring fountain to the train station of **Rigi-Kaltbad**. A pedestrian road brings you on through the scattered chalets of this resort, sidling up the lightly forested slopes to the saddle of **First** (1453m), 30 to 40 minutes on. Here, the *Hotel Rigi-First (☎ 041-859 03 10,* e *info@rigi-first.ch)* has better-standard rooms for Sfr81/142 per single/double. Proceed right onto the **Felsenweg**, a path cut into cliffs, which quickly traverses the mountainsides below the 1454m Schild. The Felsenweg gives more wonderful views across the lake toward Lucerne and the Bürgenstock.

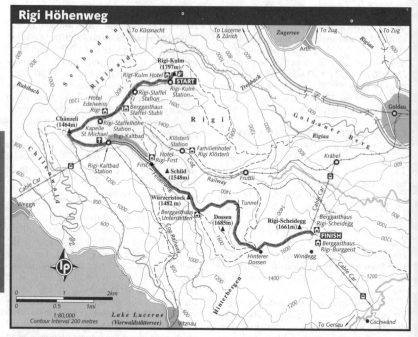

Rigi Höhenweg

Where you come to another dip on the main Rigi range, head on along the broad winding path that contours around the hill tops. This ideal walkway is actually the old Scheidegg-Bahn route (see the boxed text 'Rigi Railways' earlier). Continue across the old rail bridge past the *Berggasthaus*

Nagelfluh

Like most of the Alpine foothills around Central Switzerland, the Rigi is composed of marine sediments filled with coarse rounded stones that were laid down by the so-called proto-Reuss River some 80 million years ago. Known as *Nagelfluh* in German, this cement-like amalgam rock – particularly evident along the Felsenweg – is brittle and unstable. This factor led to the catastrophic Rossberg landslide of 1806, which wiped out the village of Goldau at the eastern foot of the Rigi.

Unterstetten (☎ *041-855 01 27*), which offers rooms from just Sfr35 per person and cheaper dorm beds. Climb almost imperceptibly on through a short tunnel and around above a little Alpine valley to reach a signpost at **Hinterer Dossen**, 50 minutes to one hour from First.

Go off to the left up over herb fields to an escarpment, following the foot track along the edge of the cliffs before easing right to reach the tiny plateau of **Rigi-Scheidegg** at 1658m after 20 to 25 minutes. Here is *Berggasthaus Rigi-Scheidegg* (☎ *041-828 14 75*, ✉ *berggasthaus@rigi-scheidegg.ch*), which provides dorm accommodation for Sfr29 and rooms for Sfr48 per person with breakfast. These open tops mark the end of the main Rigi range, and give yet another classic vista southward to Central Switzerland's highest ice-capped Alpine summits around the Titlis and south-east toward the Glarner Alps. From here it's only a few minutes' walk on along the road to the upper station of the Kräbel–Scheidegg cable car, or alternatively 10 to 15 minutes' walk directly down the slopes to the upper Geschwänd–Burggeist cable-car station, where the ***Berggasthaus Rigi-Burggeist*** *(☎ 041-828 16 86)* has dorm beds for around Sfr30.

Central Swiss Alps

South of Lake Lucerne the lower ranges of the Alpine foothills rise up gradually as they merge with the Alps proper. These are the Central Swiss Alps, which stretch eastward from the high peaks around the 3238m Titlis to the snowy crowns of the Clariden (3267m) and Tödi, and southward as far as the continental divide. Most of the interesting high-Alpine scenery lies within the 'Gotthard canton' of Uri, whose borders more or less correspond to the rugged catchment area of the upper Reuss River. Jutting deep into the Alps along the valley of the Reuss, half of Uri consists of glacial rock and ice. Large side valleys, most notably the Schächental, Maderanertal, Meiental and Göschener Tal, intersect with the Reuss on either side.

The southern half of Uri forms the so-called Urner Oberland in the pivotal Gotthard region. Apart from being the north-south watershed, the Gotthard massif marks a geographical division between the eastern and western Alps. The historic route over the Passo del San Gottardo leads up alongside the Reuss through the Schöllenen, a perilous gorge below Andermatt. From the Middle Ages until the opening of the Gotthard railway, this was the most important trans-Alpine crossing in the central Alps. Four other key passes provide well-transited road links from Uri into adjacent cantons: the 1948m Klausenpass into the Glarnerland, the 2224m Sustenpass into the Bernese Oberland's Haslital, the 2044m Oberalppass into Graubünden's Surselva region, and finally the Furkapass into Goms in the upper Valais.

Also of interest to walkers is the valley of the Engelberger Aa in Unterwalden (the collective term for the two half-cantons of Nidwalden and Obwalden). The 35km-long river descends from the glaciers of the Titlis, flowing through a wild gorge in its central section.

ACCESS TOWNS
Altdorf
Altdorf (447m) is the capital of Uri Canton. Although much of the town was reconstructed after a disastrous Föhn-storm fire in 1799, a few buildings of real historical interest remain, including St Karl monastery. According to folklore, the Tell memorial in the town square marks the spot where Wilhelm shot the arrow through an apple sitting on his son's head. Altdorf is a stop on the Alpine Pass Route, and a number of excellent walking routes lead north-east across the mountains overlooking Lake Lucerne into the interesting valley of Muotatal in Schwyz Canton (see Chinzig Chulm under Other Walks at the end of the chapter).

For more information contact the tourist office (☎ 041-872 04 50, fax 041-872 04 51, ⓦ www.altdorf.ch), Schutzengasse 11.

Remo-Camp Moosbad *(☎ 041-870 85 41)* between Flüelen and Altdorf has tent sites from Sfr4 plus Sfr6 per person, but traffic noise is excessive. In Flüelen ***Camping Windsurfing Urnersee*** *(☎ 041-870 92 22,* ⓔ *info@windsurfing-urnersee.ch)* has much nicer (and more expensive) lakeside sites. ***Hotel Bahnhof*** *(☎ 041-870 10 32, Bahnhofplatz 2)*, near the train station, has rooms from around Sfr60 a person. ***Hotel Restaurant Goldener Schlüssel*** *(☎ 041-871 20 02,* ⓔ *hotel.schluessel.altdorf@bluewin.ch, Schutzengasse 9)* charges from Sfr80.

Although Altdorf is located on the busy Gotthard rail corridor, only occasional regional trains from Arth-Goldau stop here, so it's necessary to disembark at nearby Flüelen and take one of the regular public buses from there.

Engelberg
Engelberg (1004m) is a large but surprisingly pleasant mountain resort that lies directly below the 3238m Titlis, Central Switzerland's most inspiring Alpine peak.

Engelberg has been the region's most important monastic centre since medieval times, and its main historical feature is the large Benedictine monastery (entry free). The main building dates from the 18th century, and can be visited on regular daily tours (Sfr6). A short and pleasant day walk from Engelberg leads down past waterfalls in the gorges of the Engelberger Aa to the small train station at Obermatt. A somewhat longer hiking route goes up to the Lütersee, a picturesque tarn at 1700m. Engelberg is also the starting/finishing point for the Surenenpass and Jochpass walks featured later in this chapter.

Contact Engelberg Tourist Center (☎ 041-639 77 77, e tourist.center@engelberg.ch, w www.engelberg.ch), Klosterstrasse 3, for information. *Bergführerbüro* (☎ 041-639 54 57, e info@bergfuehrer-engelberg.ch, w www.bergfuehrer-engelberg.ch) organises guided walks in the area, climbs and mountaineering courses.

Camping Eienwäldli (☎ 041-637 19 49, e eienwaeldli.engelberg@bluewin.ch) has tent sites from Sfr8.50 plus Sfr7 per person and the Engelberg *youth hostel* (☎ 041-637 12 92, e engelberg@youthhostel.ch, Dorfstrasse 80), 10 minutes' walk from the train station, has dorm beds for Sfr26/29.50 in low/high season; the hostel is closed from late October to mid-November.

The *Hotel Bellevue* (☎ 041-637 12 13, e bellevue.engelberg@telalpin.ch) on Bahnhofplatz offers singles/doubles from around Sfr30/60. The *Stop* (☎ 041-637 16 74), on

The Alp of Surenen

At one time Engelberg controlled the whole of the rich highland pastures known as Surenen as far as the pass height itself. Over the centuries, however, the more aggressive neighbouring Urner herders were able to assert their claim to these 'outer Alps' against Engelberg's weaker monastic administrators – not unlike what happened in the Urner Boden area. Today the forest line below Surenen marks the Obwalden/Uri cantonal border.

Klosterstrasse, has rooms for Sfr55 per person and its restaurant serves simple Swiss-style food. *Heimat* (☎ 041-637 13 32), on Schweizerhausstrasse, 10 minutes' walk east of the centre, has a few beds for Sfr60 per person and a restaurant.

Engelberg is most easily reached on the approximately hourly trains from Lucerne via Stans; the trip takes a little more than one hour. The best way of travelling between Engelberg and the Bernese Oberland by train is the cog railway to/from Interlaken via Meiringen and the scenic Brünigpass with a change at Hergiswil.

Andermatt

Andermatt (1436m) lies immediately north of the Gotthard massif in the Urner Oberland. Although it has a fascinating historical past as an important post servicing the trans-Alpine trade and transport routes, today Andermatt is a modern mountain resort with little in the way of interesting places to visit. The town does make a very convenient and central walking base, however, with hiking routes leading literally in all directions. Along with the Urschner Höhenweg (see Other Walks at the end of the chapter), popular walks from Andermatt go over the 2108m Passo del San Gottardo via the original old muleteers' trail and up to the Oberalppass (see the Lai da Tuma Circuit under Vorderrhein & Hinterrhein in the Graubünden chapter).

For information contact the tourist office (☎ 041-887 14 54, e info@andermatt.ch, w www.andermatt.ch), Gotthardstrasse 2. Two leading schools of mountaineering are located in Andermatt, the Alpine Sportschule Gotthard-Andermatt (☎ 041-883 17 28, w www.urionline.ch/asga), and the Bergsteigerschule Uri Mountain Reality (☎ 041-872 09 00, w www.bergschule-uri.ch).

Situated in the nearby village of Hospental, the *youth hostel* (☎ 041-887 04 01, e hospental@youthhostel.ch) has dorm beds for Sfr18/19 in low/high season. Or you could try the *Hotel Alpina* (☎ 041-887 17 56, e hotelalpina@bluewin.ch), which offers singles/doubles from Sfr50/85. There is also *Hotel Bergidyll* (☎ 041-887 14 55, e *andermatt.hotel.bergidyll@bluewin.ch),* which charges from Sfr55 per person.

On Gotthardstrasse, there is the *Coop* supermarket and the *Badus* provides meals from Sfr13.

Andermatt is a minor transport hub for the Gotthard region. Trains of the private Furka-Oberalp-Bahn (FOB) railway running between Disentis in Graubünden and Brig in the Valais pass through Andermatt almost hourly; the *Glacier Express* also passes Andermatt. From Zürich or other places in northern Switzerland, access is via Göschenen. Trains run at least hourly between Göschenen and Andermatt. From late June until late September postbuses run between Andermatt and Meiringen (via Göschenen and the Sustenpass, twice daily), Oberwald in the Valais (via the Furkapass, twice daily), and Airolo (via the Passo del San Gottardo, three times daily). A surcharge applies and reservations are strongly advised (☎ 041-828 88 28).

Göschenen

This village lies at 1106m on the upper Reuss where the lovely Göschener Tal meets the main valley. A classic 1½-hour walk from Göschenen leads up to Andermatt via the legendary Teufelsbrücke, a bridge over the gorge of Schöllenen.

For more information contact the small tourist office (☎ 041-885 18 34).

The *Herberge Tresch* (☎ 041-885 11 69) has dorm beds for around Sfr25. The *Hotel*

Switzerland's excellent postbus network is an indispensable means of transport for walkers.

Gotthard (☎ 041-885 12 63) has singles/ doubles from Sfr40/80.

Both the Gotthard railway and motorway disappear into long tunnels at Göschenen, so it's the last stop north of the Alps before passengers emerge in Ticino. Faster trains don't stop here, but there are hourly connections from Lucerne and Zürich with a change at Arth-Goldau.

Klausenpass

Duration	2 days
Distance	40km
Standard	easy-medium
Start	Linthal
Finish	Altdorf
Nearest Towns	Braunwald, Urnerboden, Bürglen

Summary The 1948m Klausenpass, at the northern foot of the mighty ice-crowned peak of the Clariden, connects the Glarnerland with Uri Canton and has been in active use as a crossing point since ancient times. The walk forms the third leg of the Alpine Pass Route.

The way over the Klausenpass leads through Urner Boden, the largest single expanse of Alpine pastures in Switzerland. Although it lies east of the watershed, Urner Boden fell into the hands of the Urner graziers long ago, and has remained a part of the Uri Canton ever since. These rich, green meadows, which spread out along the valley, are now the property of Switzerland's biggest sharefarming cooperative.

Towering more than 1000m above the Urner Boden is the craggy Jegerstöck range, whose tiered slopes have rows of classically formed Alpine terraces that run along the range almost as far as the pass itself. The really great views open out on the western side of the Klausenpass, however, where the walk follows balconies high above the Schächental. The Klausenpass was the first in the Central Swiss Alps to be upgraded for motorised traffic, and the pass road was opened to through-traffic in 1899. In most places the walking route manages to keep a respectable distance from the well-transited road, leaving

CENTRAL SWITZERLAND

MARTIN MOOS

you to view the magnificent scenery along the way with surprisingly little disturbance.

Maps

The SAW/FSTP 1:50,000 map *Klausenpass* No 246T (Sfr22.50) covers the route well. An acceptable alternative is K+F's 1:60,000 *Kanton Uri* (Sfr24.80), although it leaves off the area between Linthal and the Glarus–Uri cantonal border.

NEAREST TOWNS
Braunwald

The walk passes through (or starts from) this scattered car-free mountain resort sitting on a terrace high above the Linthtal. For information, contact the tourist office (☎ 055-653 65 85, ℮ tourismusinfo@braunwald.ch, ⓦ www.braunwald.ch).

The *youth hostel* (☎ 055-643 13 56, ℮ braunwald@youthhostel.ch) has dorm accommodation for Sfr22/24.50 in low/high season. The *Hotel Ahorn* (☎ 055-643 15 37, ℮ ahorn@surfeu.ch) offers dorm beds for Sfr35 (with breakfast) and doubles from Sfr120. Renovated *Hotel Panorama* (☎ 055-643 36 86, ℮ info@panorama-hotel.ch), just below the village, has better-standard rooms from Sfr95 per person.

The Braunwald-Bahn (☎ 055-653 65 65) funicular runs half-hourly up to Braunwald from Linthal (see Access Towns under Sarganserland & Glarner Alps in the North-Eastern Switzerland chapter) until 6.55pm, then several times until 10.55pm or 11.55pm. The one-way fare is Sfr6.80 (rail passes and standard concessions apply).

Urnerboden

Day 1 of the walk ends at Urnerboden (1372m) in the upper Linthtal. This small village sits on a partially forested hillock of ancient glacial moraines – the slightly elevated position gives nice views over the rich, green valley. The *Gasthof Urnerboden* (☎ 055-643 14 16) has rooms for around Sfr45 per person.

Bürglen

The latter part of Day 2 passes through the historic village of Bürglen. The birthplace of Switzerland's legendary folk hero Wilhelm Tell, Bürglen's historic buildings include the 13th-century Meierturm and the Wattigerturm, housing the Tell-Museum.

The *Hotel Tell* (☎ 041-870 22 04), the *Restaurant Adler* (☎ 041-870 11 33) and *Hotel Waldhof* (041-870 31 31) have rooms from around Sfr45 per person.

GETTING TO/FROM THE WALK

For information on transport to/from Linthal at the start of the walk, see Access Towns under Sarganserland & Glarner Alps in the North-Eastern Switzerland chapter.

From Linthal you can take the Braunwald-Bahn funicular up to Braunwald, thus shortening the walk by at least one hour. This avoids almost 600m steep ascent and is recommended.

Since the walking route touches the road repeatedly, you can shorten the walk (or opt out completely) at your pleasure by catching a postbus. From late June to late September there are four postbus connections between Linthal and Altdorf-Flüelen via the Klausenpass.

Reservations are strongly advised (☎ 041-870 21 36), and a fare surcharge applies on the stretch between Urnerboden and Urigen. All other postbus services to/from Flüelen and to/from Linthal go only as far as Urigen or Balm and Urnerboden respectively.

THE WALK
Day 1: Linthal to Urnerboden
4¼–5½ hours, 13km, 710m ascent

Pick up the trail above the car park near the lower funicular station. The path ducks under the funicular tracks and heads on for 10 to 15 minutes through the forest of beech trees and maples to merge with a right-hand trail coming up from Rüti. Make your way up over steeply sloping clearings to cross back under the funicular tracks, then continue ascending in sharp switchbacks past a romantic old church just before you come onto a broad walkway after a further 40 to 50 minutes.

Turn right and quickly follow the wide path around to the left above the Hotel Panorama. On the right is the turn-off to

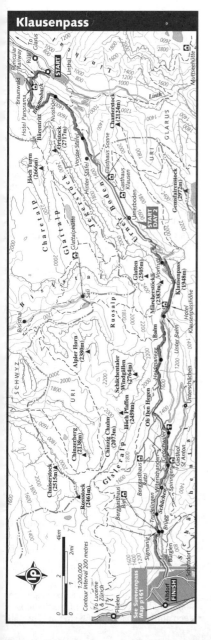

Klausenpass

See Surenenpass Map p161

Braunwald. (If you arrive on the Braunwald-Bahn, take the road below the lower station of a gondola cableway and make a right turn at the intersection above the hotel.)

The route leads on westward over undulating pastures browsed by jingling cows, with the 2717m Ortstock providing an impressive mountain backdrop. Keeping to the main track, head on across two cascading streams of the Brummbach, then swing around to the left and contour through patches of forest before coming out onto a high grassy shelf. Bear right (ignoring a walking trail from Linthal to Rietberg that crosses the track here) and continue a short way on to reach **Nussbüel**, one to 1¼ hours from Braunwald. This hamlet lies at 1248m and has a restaurant overlooking the Linthtal.

The track narrows after Nussbüel, sidling for 10 to 15 minutes across long clearings to an intersection. Take the right-hand branch, which now begins a rough rising traverse along the steep wooded slopes, leading across a small avalanche gully then over open meadows to meet a gravelled road near a holiday cottage after a further 30 to 45 minutes. This spot lies directly below the looming crags of the Ortstock, and offers the first clear views across Urner Boden to the Klausenpass.

Turn left and follow the road down to the stone farmhouse of Vorder Stafel (1399m). Here, leave off to the right along an alp track, contouring the mountainside to where a paint-marked trail goes down left a short way before Hinter Stafel. The path cuts down diagonally across pastures to reach the Klausenpass road after 35 to 45 minutes. Here, near the borderstone marking the Glarus–Uri cantonal boundary, is a local postbus stop.

The remainder of Day 1 runs on or close to the main road, which at times can get quite busy. Nevertheless, the broad open river plain of the Urner Boden makes for easy walking, with outstanding scenery including the Jegerstöck range on your right and the snow-fields of the Clariden toward the head of the valley. The route passes by the *Gasthaus Sonne* (☎ 055-643 15 12), which has double rooms for around Sfr70 and dorm beds for

CENTRAL SWITZERLAND

Sfr25, and the *Gasthaus Klausen (☎ 055-643 14 13)*, which has singles/doubles from Sfr40/80 and dorm beds for Sfr30 (all prices with breakfast). A gentle climb brings you on to the small village of **Urnerboden**, one to 1¼ hours from the cantonal boundary.

Day 2: Urnerboden to Altdorf
6–8 hours, 27km, 576m ascent

Stay on the sealed road for 2km, gradually rising up to a scattered stand of spruce trees, where the road begins its steep ascent to the pass at a sharp bend. From here, a walking trail marked white-red-white leads directly up the slopes, following the road for two brief stretches as it short-cuts the numerous switchback curves to return to the road above **Vorfrutt** (1779m), 1¼ to 1¾ hours from Urnerboden. Turn around here for a last look back across Urner Boden.

Follow the road briefly left (downhill) over the now tiny Fatschbach, then climb away right and sidle up along grassy slopes to arrive at the **Klausenpass** after a further 25 to 30 minutes. The pass lies at 1948m below the impressive square pinnacle of the Märcherstöckli, and has a restaurant/kiosk beside a spacious car park.

Walk down a few paces to a yellow signpost just below the tiny chapel, and take the path that drops down between the main road and the meandering brook (not the more obvious broad vehicle track that contours around the left side of the valley). Make your way on past an idyllic farmlet set in front of a small waterfall, then cross hillsides strewn with Alpine rhododendron bushes below the *Hotel Klausenpasshöhe (☎ 041-879 11 64, ⓔ info@klausenpasshoehe.ch)*. This historic hotel – which, despite its name, is 20 to 25 minutes from the pass – offers singles/doubles for Sfr45/90 and dorm beds for Sfr35 (prices include breakfast).

Continue gently down to meet the main road again at **Unter Balm** (1798m), 30 to 40 minutes from the pass. To your left the land falls away dramatically into the deep glacial trough of the Schächental.

Follow the Klausenpass road a short way uphill (ignoring a lower variant that leads down via Unterschächen), before heading left along a gravelled farm track. The route soon bears right at a fork and rises slightly against the contour past quaint wooden alp huts and barns before it reaches the hamlet of **Heidmanegg** (1862m), 30 to 40 minutes from Unter Balm. As you look directly over to the magnificent glacier-clad peaks of the Chammliberg and Schärhorn, these high south-facing terraces are ablaze with wild flowers until midsummer.

The now somewhat rougher alp track makes a sidling descent across the open slopes to end at the tight bend of a sealed road. Visible below is the village of Unterschächen, while toward the mouth of the valley stands the prominent rump of the Grosser Windgällen and still farther off the Uri-Rotstock. Turn left and walk down the sealed road to **Ob Den Hegen** (1530m), there taking a marked trail, which short-cuts steeply down (left) beside a streamlet. Continue downhill to pick up a signposted foot track that brings you to **Getschwiler**, one to 1¼ hours from Heidmanegg. Of interest, Getschwiler's small, 16th-century church has an altarpiece painted by the Flemish artist Denys Calvaert.

A broad stock-driving lane now serves as an easy walkway, dropping steadily down the hillside for 25 to 30 minutes to come out at the small village of **Spiringen** (923m) on the Klausenpass road, where the small *Gasthof St Anton (☎ 041-879 11 41)* offers singles/doubles for Sfr40. Since the route ahead mainly follows the road, many walkers might now prefer to take a postbus directly on to Altdorf or Flüelen.

Go 200m down the road to Spiringen's large old wooden Schulhaus, where a well-graded trail leads gently down through areas of light forest to meet the main road again at **Witerschanden** after 25 to 30 minutes. Follow the road down 2km past **Trudelingen** to where a signposted path leaves off to the right. The route climbs a short way to **Sigmanig**, then continues quickly down left along a concrete road to reach **Brügg** (648m), 30 to 40 minutes from Witerschanden.

Walk right 200m past the Kinzig cable-car station and pick up a track along the mostly steep northern banks of the stream. The path constantly rises and dips as it passes through forest patches and occasional farmyard gardens, crossing over the Schächen on a footbridge just before it reaches the village of Bürglen (523m) after 30 to 45 minutes.

The final part of the walk leads down beside the village church then along the main road past the historical museum and the St Karlin monastery to arrive at the centre of **Altdorf** after 25 to 30 minutes. The train station is a further 15- to 20-minute walk left (south-west) down Bahnhofstrasse, but most trains stop only in nearby Flüelen.

For the next (fourth) leg of the Alpine Pass Route (Altdorf to Engelberg), see the Surenenpass walk following.

Surenenpass

Duration	2 days
Distance	28km
Standard	medium-hard
Start	Altdorf
Finish	Engelberg
Nearest Town	Attinghausen

Summary This wild and spectacular walk (the fourth leg of the Alpine Pass Route) offers more dramatic mountain scenery than any other pass crossing in the Central Swiss Alps.

Linking Altdorf in Uri Canton with the Obwalden enclave of Engelberg, the Surenenpass has been a significant crossing route since the 13th century. Despite its long history of use, the Surenenpass was never developed for motorised traffic, and offers a marvellous undisturbed mountain landscape relatively rare for the region.

The walk involves an ascent of 1800m if you don't take the cable car up from Attinghausen. The descent of around 1200m is very drawn out. Although the Surenenpass is sometimes done in one very long and tiring day, almost all walkers take advantage of the excellent overnighting options en route.

Maps

You can use either Nidwaldner Wanderwege's 1:50,000 *Wanderkarte Nidwalden*

Warnings

- Intense electrical storms are very common in these mountains in summer, so carry appropriate wet-weather clothing and keep a watch for signs of bad weather.
- Infrequent military shooting exercises are carried out in the area in summer, and occasionally walkers may have a brief wait before being able to continue. For information call Swiss Army's regional office in Andermatt (☎ 041-888 86 94 90).

und Engelberg or the SAW/FSTP 1:50,000 map *Stans* No 245T (Sfr22.50). This latter sheet just cuts off Altdorf – which is on SAW/FSTP's adjoining *Klausenpass* No 246T (Sfr22.50) – but includes all of Day 2 from Brüsti.

NEAREST TOWNS & FACILITIES
Attinghausen

Attinghausen (W www.attinghausen.ch) is passed on the first section of Day 1. The village lies in the valley close to Altdorf (see Access Towns at the start of the Central Swiss Alps section). *Hotel Krone (☎ 041-870 10 55)* has rooms from Sfr44/78 for singles/doubles and dorm beds for Sfr25 with breakfast.

Buses run regularly to Attinghausen from the centre of Altdorf. Walkers can use the two-section cable car (☎ 041-870 14 61) up to Brüsti (over 1000m ascent in two sections), which runs half-hourly from around 7am. The one-way fare is Sfr4.50/9 children/adults (no concessions). Before embarking at the unstaffed lower station, push the yellow button and listen to the intercom for the intermediate-station operator's answer; once inside the cable car, press another yellow button for confirmation.

Brüsti

This is the hamlet at the upper cable-car station above Attinghausen. The *Berggasthaus Brüsti (☎ 041-870 10 77)* has dorm beds for around Sfr30 and a few rooms for around Sfr40/80 a single/double (prices include breakfast, no shower).

GETTING TO/FROM THE WALK

For information on transport to/from Altdorf and Engelberg, see Access Towns at the start of the Central Swiss Alps section. Day 1 can be avoided completely by taking the bus from the centre of Altdorf to Attinghausen, then riding the cable car up to Brüsti (1525m).

A more minor route variant involves turning off right at Stalden (on Day 2) and taking the cable car from Fürenalp down to Herrenrütiboden (1080m). In summer the Fürenalp cable car (Ⓦ www.fuerenalp.ch) operates until 5pm (6pm on weekends, closed early November to late December). The one-way fare is Sfr9 (Sfr5/7.50 children/Half Fare Card holders). A combined ticket for one-way rides on the Brüsti and Fürenalp cable cars costs Sfr14.

THE WALK
Day 1: Altdorf to Brüsti
2¾–3½ hours, 6km, 1078m ascent

For those determined to walk every step of the Alpine Pass Route, the walk description begins from Altdorf train station. From the station, follow the walking route (signposted 'Brüsti Seilbahn') south-east, turning right at the Gasthaus Walter Fürst through underpasses below the railway and motorway. Make your way over the fast-flowing **Reuss** to the village of **Attinghausen**. Continue up past the supermarket to reach the Brüsti cable car, 30 to 40 minutes from Altdorf.

The path up to Brüsti leaves from near the lower cable-car station, leading up to the right of a stream, which it crosses to reach the intermediate cable-car station after 20 to 30 minutes. Here, a wide track ascends the steep slopes in switchback curves through mixed pasture and forest before reaching **Höchiberg** (1420m) after 1½ to two hours. **Brüsti** is another 20 to 30 minutes from here.

Day 2: Brüsti to Engelberg
5½–7 hours, 22km, 766m ascent

From the upper cable-car station at 1525m, take the broad foot track leading right past Brüsti's scattering of houses. Follow a prominent ridge which soon leads out of the trees over grassy slopes dotted with Alpine

rhododendrons to **Grat**. The path continues along this increasingly sharp ridge, giving wonderful views of the Urnersee (Lake Uri) down to the right, the tiny upper valley of Waldnacht far below on the left, and the impressive craggy walls of the Brunnistock in front of you. Climb on over the open tops of the **Angistock** before descending slightly to reach **Langschnee** (2004m), after 1½ to two hours.

The final ascent to the pass is straightforward, if rather strenuous. Various well-trodden routes cut across the coarse talus slopes from Langschnee (which as its name suggests is snow-covered well into summer) before ascending in zigzags through steep and loose rock to arrive at the **Surenenpass** (2291m), 45 minutes to an hour on. The view south-west from the pass is dominated by the majestic hump of the Titlis (3238m), believed in medieval times to be the highest of the Helvetian summits. Immediately below are the sparkling Seewen tarns.

Drop down leftward more gently past a small emergency shelter, sidling on over wild-flower meadows of the **Surenen**, which have been terraced by centuries of cattle grazing, to reach **Alphütte Blackenalp** (☎ 041-637 12 30) at 1773m after 50 minutes to one hour. This rustic alp hut is open mid-June to late September and serves simple refreshments (including alp-made cheese). Dorm beds in the hay loft cost

---

Bitter Roots

The yellow gentian *(Gentia lutea)* grows abundantly on the slopes of the upper Brunnital. In late summer you may see locals digging out the roots, which contain medicinal compounds that have long been valued as a treatment for stomach complaints. The roots are also processed into an astringent extract used to make *Enzler* (from *Enzian*, the German word for the gentian), a 'digestive' liqueur with a mouth-puckering aftertaste. Due to past over-exploitation of the yellow gentian, its commercial use is now banned in Switzerland.

CLEM LINDENMAYER

PAUL PIAIA

Top: Walkers descend from the Surenenpass, dwarfed by the 3238m peak of Titlis.
Bottom: A typical floral display brightens a row of traditional Swiss houses.

Top: Cut into high cliffs, the Rigi Felsenweg makes a spectacular walkway.
Middle Left: The Mythen's two distinct peaks form the backdrop to the coastline of Lake Lucerne.
Middle Right: The Windgällen range looms behind a walker climbing to the Fuorcla da Cavardiras.
Bottom: The Hinterbalmhütte looks over the Maderanertal toward the summits of the Titlis massif.

CLEM LINDENMAYER

MARTIN MOOS

CLEM LINDENMAYER

CLEM LINDENMAYER

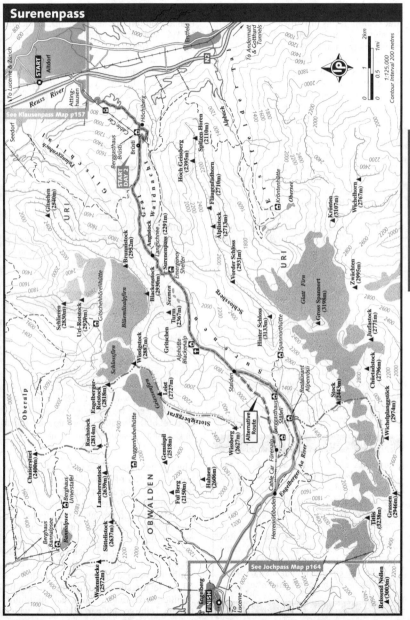

Sfr18; breakfast costs around Sfr7 extra. Blackenalp looks up toward the 2887m Wissigstock and 2930m Blackenstock, whose craggy sides fall away into a superb, perfectly rounded amphitheatre with 250m-high walls in the tiny side valley of Gritschen. Make your way on along an alp track past Blackenalp's romantic little chapel standing among the rolling green pastures to cross the Stierenbach on a narrow stone bridge. The way leads above the left bank of the stream for 1.5km, before re-crossing to reach a signposted junction at **Stalden** (1630m), another 25 to 30 minutes on (see the Alternative Route at the end of this day's walk description).

Continue left quickly down beside a gushing waterfall then alongside the stream to **Stäfeli** (see the boxed text 'Stafel, Staffel, Stäfeli' later). Here, the *Berggasthaus Stäfeli* (☎ 041-637 45 11) at 1393m (open mid-May to late October) offers dorm beds for Sfr25 with breakfast in nice six-person dorms. With small waterfalls spilling down from hanging glaciers on the 3198m Gross Spannort up to the left, walk on smoothly down into the mixed forest marking the Uri–Obwalden cantonal border past the *Restaurant Alpenrösli* at 1258m, which serves simple meals and refreshments.

Head on down directly beneath the graceful outline of the Titlis, whose ice-crowned summit towers more than 2000m above you. As the valley begins to open out, follow a path off left over moist river flats to rejoin the

road not far up from the lower cable-car station at **Herrenrütiboden** (1080m), about one to 1¼ hours from Stäfeli. Continue 500m along the sealed road, before turning right onto a narrow laneway. This takes you through pleasant farmland and scattered holiday chalets, leading you past the historic monastery to reach the centre of **Engelberg** (1004m) after a further one to 1¼ hours.

For the next (fifth) leg of the Alpine Pass Route see the Jochpass walk (Engelberg to Meiringen) following.

Alternative Route: Fürenalp Cable Car

From Stalden, a route variant goes off right across balconies above the valley to Fürenalp (1840m), where there is a cafeteria-style *restaurant*. From here a cable car runs down to Herrenrütiboden. *Alphütte Fürenalp* (☎ 041-637 39 49) is a few minutes' walk to the north-west; it offers cosy dorm beds for Sfr52/30 adults/children with full board.

Jochpass

Duration	2 days
Distance	29km
Standard	medium
Start	Engelberg
Finish	Meiringen
Nearest Town	Reuti

Summary The walk over the 2207m Jochpass (the fifth leg of the Alpine Pass Route) brings you out of Central Switzerland into the Haslital region of the eastern Bernese Oberland.

The northern side of the pass (belonging to the half-canton of Nidwalden) has been intensively developed for skiing and tourism, and some walkers may find the proliferation of cableways and mountain restaurants here a bit off-putting. With the Titlis reflecting its majestic 3238m form on the still, blue waters of the Trüebsee, the Engelberg side of the Jochpass is not without its charms, however, while just beyond the pass another gorgeous lake, the Engstlensee, dips into beautiful Alpine herb fields. The real highlight, though, is the second part of the walk, which

---

Stafel, Staffel, Stäfeli

Numerous places in the Swiss Alps have names derived from the German word *Stafel* – some typical variants are Stäfeli, Staffel, Oberstafel, Stafelbach and Staffelberg. Probably of Walser origin, in Swiss dialects *Stafel* means a 'stage' or 'level', and refers to the pastures of differing altitudes that were used by Alpine herders as they moved their cattle up and down the slopes during the summer months. The equivalent term in Switzerland's French-speaking regions is *remointse*.

Warning

Due to the area's popularity and the large amount of tourist infrastructure, water from even the smallest streams along the first part of the walk from Engelberg to the Jochpass should be treated as suspect. Carry drinking water or buy some liquid refreshments at the various restaurants along the way.

follows a high-level panoramic route far above the Gental, a glacial U-shaped side valley of the Haslital.

Depending on seasonal snow conditions, the Jochpass can normally be crossed from at least early to mid-June until late October. Going the whole way up on foot (rather than using one or more of the mountain lifts) makes a very long and exhausting day, and breaking the walk up into two shorter days with a night spent en route is a much better option.

Maps

The only walking map that seems to cover the Jochpass route on one sheet is the Engelberg tourist authority's 1:50,000 *Wanderwege Engelberg* (Sfr16). Two SAW/FSTP 1:50,000 maps cover the route: *Stans* No 263T and *Sustenpass* No 255T (Sfr22.50 each). Otherwise, you can combine the tourist authorities' 1:50,000 *Obwaldner Wanderkarte* and 1:50,000 *Wanderkarte Oberhasli* walking maps (both around Sfr18).

NEAREST TOWN
Reuti

The walk passes through this village, whose fine old wooden houses are built in a typical Bernese Oberland style. The Hasliberger Dorfweg, a marked walking route from Reuti to Hohfluh, offers a fuller introduction to local architecture.

The *Hotel Reuti* (☎ 033-971 18 32), which is located by the cable-car station, has dorm beds for Sfr30 and rooms for Sfr39. *Gasthof Weber* (☎ 033-971 19 15, e gasthof.weber@freesurf.ch) has singles/doubles available from around Sfr50/100. The *Hotel Viktoria* (☎ 033-971 11 21,

e *hasliberg@viktoria.ch)* has a better standard of room from Sfr105/180.

GETTING TO/FROM THE WALK

For information on transport to/from Engelberg and Meiringen, see Access Towns at the start of the Central Swiss Alps section and under the Jungfrau Region & Haslital in the Bernese Oberland chapter respectively.

Mountain cableways run from Engelberg right up to the Jochpass. Riding the gondola lift up to Trüebsee (Sfr17/8.50 adults/children and concession) shortens the walk by around two hours, but taking the Trüebsee–Jochpass chairlift (Sfr6/3) up to the pass rather defeats the idea of walking. The lower station of the Engelberg–Trüebsee gondola lift is a pleasant 10-minute walk from the train station downstream along the left bank of the river. The lifts operate until around 6pm from May until mid-November.

A good alternative for walkers based in Meiringen is to catch a postbus to Engstlenalp, then simply walk Day 2 from Engstlenalp back to Meiringen. Postbuses run between Engstlenalp and Meiringen up to five times daily between mid-June and late October.

The walk can be further shortened by taking the cable car from Reuti down to Meiringen (Sfr4/2 adults/children and concession). In addition, there are also a dozen or so daily postbuses from Reuti to Brünig-Hasliberg (with regular rail connections to Lucerne and Interlaken).

THE WALK
Day 1: Engelberg to Engstlenalp
4–5 hours, 10km, 1203m ascent

From the train station walk 20m around to the right, where a pedestrian laneway goes off left between rows of trees to cross to a small road bridge spanning the Engelberger Aa. Climb up past the *Hotel Bänklialp* (☎ 041-637 34 34) into the trees, bearing right at a fork before you come out of the forest. The route continues along a gravelled alp track through the rolling grassy fields of **Vorder Stafel** to reach the *Restaurant Gerschnialp* (☎ 041-637 22 12) at 1257m after 40 to 50 minutes.

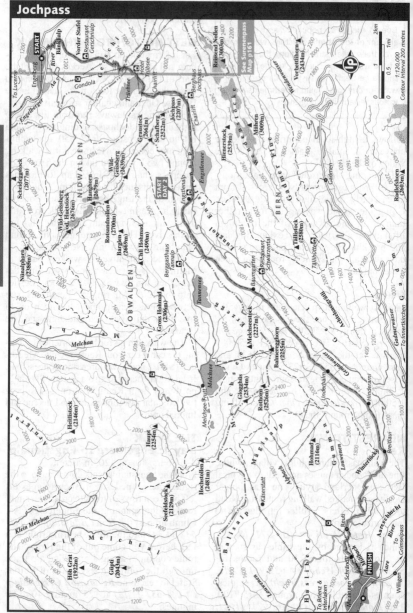

Take the signposted foot track up left-ward along a slight ridge past winter ski tows on the open pastures of **Gerschi**. As you near the lightly wooded higher slopes, commence a steep ascent in tight zigzags underneath the Engelberg–Trüebsee gon-dola lift. Continue following the path to reach the upper station and restaurant at 1796m on a high terrace overlooking the Engelbergertal, 1¼ to 1½ hours on.

The nearby *Hotel Trübsee* (☎ 041-637 13 71), open from late April to mid-October, has singles/doubles from Sfr91/146 (prices include full board).

A wide, graded walkway now leads gen-tly down around the southern shore of the Trüebsee, a delightful lake embedded in a broad basin at the foot of the Titlis (3238m), to the Trüebsee–Jochpass chairlift (1771m). Just before the lower station, begin a wind-ing climb below the cableway to the right of a grassy spur to arrive at **Jochpass** (2207m) after 1¼ to 1½ hours. The pass itself is rel-atively unspectacular, and somewhat over-developed. Here, the *Berghaus Jochpass* (☎ 041-637 11 87, e info@joch pass.ch) is open from June until late September and has dorm beds from Sfr79 and rooms from Sfr100 per person (prices include full board and showers).

Continue south-west, initially along the line of yet another chairlift. The path leads through grassy meadows to meet a dirt road beside the **Engstlensee**, an attractive Alpine lake popular with anglers. Peaks of the Wendenstöcke rise spectacularly above the Engstlensee from its opposite shore. Fol-low an alp track as it leads away from the lake to reach the tiny, scattered hamlet of **Engstlenalp** (1834m), approximately 50 minutes to one hour from Jochpass. Here, the *Hotel Engstlenalp* (☎ 033-975 11 61, e engstlenalp@oberland .ch), open early May to late October, has medium-range rooms. Dairy products, including goats' cheese, are on sale here.

Day 2: Engstlenalp to Meiringen
4¼–5¼ hours, 19km
From below the hotel, take the path sign-posted 'Melchsee/Hasliberg' (*not* the one

labeled 'Schwarzental/ Meiringen'), which leads off right along a dirt road. Make your way past old wooden barns (whose distinc-tive style indicates that you are now in Bern Canton) and signposted trails going off right to Tannenalp and Melchsee. The route now begins its long but generally easy tra-verse high above the Gental, a beautiful Alpine valley with a typically U-shaped post-glacial form, passing through **Baum-garten**, one to 1¼ hours on. This tiny ham-let sits perched at 1702m on a prominent terrace, where it is sheltered from winter avalanches.

Leave Baumgarten via the access road coming up from Schwarzental, picking up the path again at the first bend in the road. The way then gently rises and dips across flowery mountain pastures for 50 minutes to one hour, finally reaching the lone alp hut of **Underbalm** (1551m).

With the mighty snow-clad summits of the Schreckhorn, the Finsteraarhorn and the Wetterhorn group ahead in the distance, make your way along to meet a dirt road at **Hinderarni** (1459m). This sidles on smoothly down the slopes overlooking the village of Innertkirchen, at the junction of three mountain valleys, before intersecting with a much broader, sealed roadway at the village of **Breitlaui** (1370m) after another 50 minutes to one hour.

Climbing slightly, the route follows the road to **Winterlücke**, from where you get a glimpse of the Brienzersee (Lake Brienz) far beyond Meiringen. From here the route mainly follows the road, with a few sign-posted short cuts leading down through the forest, to reach **Reuti** at 1061m after 30 to 40 minutes.

The way down to Meiringen leaves off left just after the road bridge, a short dis-tance before Reuti. A steep foot track then spirals down through the oak and linden forests, in places below the cable car, and comes out onto a road at the upper part of **Meiringen** after 45 minutes to one hour. From here continue rightward through a stone gateway, following yellow route markings for 10 or 15 minutes to the train station.

Fuorcla da Cavardiras

Duration	3 days
Distance	31km
Standard	medium-hard
Start	Platten
Finish	Disentis/Mustér
Nearest Towns	Amsteg, Bristen

Summary The roughly 2650m-high pass known by its Romansch name of Fuorcla da Cavardiras connects Canton Uri's Maderanertal with the Surselva region along the Rein Anteriur (Vorderrhein) in Graubünden.

The Fuorcla da Cavardiras gives breathtaking views across the broad icy névé of the Brunnifirn toward the 3328m Oberalpstock (familiar to the Romansch-speaking dwellers on the other side as Piz Tgietschen). The way up to the Fuorcla leads up through the Brunnital, a charming Alpine valley well known for its rock crystals. This is relatively remote country by the standards of the Swiss Alps and Switzerland's main conservation organisation, Pro Natura, has proposed the Maderanertal as a potential site for a (second) national park – an idea that locals view with mixed feelings.

Maps

Two SAW/FSTP 1:50,000 maps cover the route: *Klausenpass* No 246T and *Disentis* No 256T (both Sfr22.50). Either K+F's 1:60,000 *Surselva* or its 1:60,000 *Kanton Uri* (both Sfr24.80) can be also used.

NEAREST TOWNS
Amsteg

This village is a minor transit point at the junction of the Reusstal and Maderanertal. The ***Hotel Stern und Post*** (☎ *041-883 14 40*, e *info@sternpost.ch)* has singles/doubles from Sfr43/70.

Bristen

Bristen is in the lower Maderanertal. The ***Gasthaus Wehrebrücke*** (☎ *041-883 11 19)* has dorm accommodation for Sfr25 and rooms for Sfr40 (prices are per person and include breakfast). The ***Gasthaus Alpenblick***

(☎ *041-883 12 40)* offers better-standard singles/doubles from Sfr60.

GETTING TO/FROM THE WALK

The walk starts from the lower station of the Golzern cable car at Platten, 2km upvalley from the village of Bristen. From Erstfeld (on the main Gotthard rail line), there are around six daily postbus connections (via Amsteg and Bristen) to the lower cable-car station ('Golzern Talstation Seilbahn' on timetables); the last postbus leaves Erstfeld at around 5.30pm. Johann Fedier (☎ 041-883 17 20) in Bristen operates a taxi-shuttle service into the Maderanertal for walkers.

For information on transport to/from Disentis/Mustér, see Access Towns in the Vorderrhein & Hinterrhein section of the Graubünden chapter. The final section can be shortened by taking a postbus from Punt Gronda to Disentis/Mustér. There are four buses daily, the last leaving Punt Russein at around 3.30pm.

THE WALK
Day 1: Platten to Hinterbalmhütte

3¼–4 hours, 8.5km, 985m ascent

From the lower cable-car station at Platten (832m), follow the sealed road 600m upvalley, then turn left along a dirt road. This soon takes you down over the milky-white glacial waters of the Chärstelenbach and on to the ***Berggasthaus Legni*** (☎ *041-883 11 43)*, open mid-May to late October, which has dorm beds for Sfr10 (without breakfast); washing facilities are basic. Recross the stream and head through pockets of fir trees along the gentle floor of the Maderanertal, before coming to the locality

Warning

The walk follows a generally very good and well-marked path, although on the approach to the Fuorcla da Cavardiras there is some minor scrambling and the final section to the Camona da Cavardiras leads briefly over an icy corner of the Brunnifirn – keep to the markings here.

Crystal Searching

Crystal searchers *(Strahler* or *cristalliers)* can often be spotted digging – sometimes blasting! – into fissures in cliffs around the Fuorcla da Cavardiras in search of rock crystals.

Rock crystals were formed 18 to 20 million years ago as hot, pressurised water seeped into sub-terranean cracks, first dissolving quartz then gradually re-depositing it in beautiful crystal formations back onto the rock. The Swiss Alps are especially famous for their fine smoky quartz and amethyst crystals. The most perfect crystal 'plates' are worth tens of thousands of francs, and are displayed in local museums and shop windows.

To prospect for rock crystals you must have a licence issued by the local authorities in the canton concerned.

Uniting Switzerland's many rockhounds is the Swiss Association of Crystal Searchers, Collectors of Minerals and Fossils (Schweizerische Vereinigung der Stahler und Mineraliensammler (SVSMF), Association Suisse des Cristalliers et Collectionneurs de Minéraux (ASCM; ⓦ www.svsmf.ch).

of the **Balmenschachen** at 1185m after around 1½ hours.

Don't cross the stream here, but go right a few steps to pick up a short-cut trail. This leads quickly alongside the river and returns to the road not far before you get to the farmlet of **Guferen** (1275m). There are some nice views into the head of the valley, where small glaciers cling to the 3234m Schärhorn. Walk across the footbridge, passing a broad track on the left. This goes up 10 to 15 minutes to **Balmenegg** (1349m), where the ***Berghotel Maderanertal*** (☎ 041-883 11 22), a grand old Victorian-era building, has charming rooms for Sfr45 and dorm beds for Sfr28 with breakfast (open from mid-June to mid-October). Continue along the true right bank of the Chärstelenbach through occasional grassy meadows to reach a signposted intersection, 50 minutes to one hour from Balmenschachen.

Recross the Chärstelenbach for the last time, doubling back right in a sometimes steep climb to meet the Brunnibach at a small ravine. Secured in places by steel fences, the path skirts the stream for a way before cutting up left over slopes of Alpine heath to arrive at the ***Hinterbalmhütte*** (☎ 041-883 19 39) at 1817m after one to 1¼ hours. This privately run, wooden-shingled building occupies a scenic spot gazing out west over the Maderanertal toward the ice-capped summits of the Titlis massif. It offers dorm beds for Sfr20/15 adults/children

(without breakfast), and has self-catering fa-cilities. The friendly hutkeeper is present from around early June to mid-October, but the hut is otherwise left open.

Day 2: Hinterbalmhütte to Camona da Cavardiras

2½–3½ hours, 5.5km, 832m ascent

The path makes its way along the grassy slopes into the **Brunnital**, which starts to re-veal itself as an attractive and interesting Alpine valley. Cross the Brunnibach on an arched stone footbridge at a tiny gorge, climbing gently past a thundering waterfall onto flat and open highland meadows after 40 to 50 minutes. At the termination of the valley, hanging glaciers spill down from the Brunnifirn over barren rock walls.

Recross the stream and continue above its eastern banks for about 1km, gradually rising away to the left. The white-red-white marked path leads on up through increasingly steep and rocky terrain (with the odd fixed chain to hold on to) to reach a natural lookout on a green ridge top after one to 1½ hours. There are good views of the upper valley from here.

Sidle a short way around the loose slopes, then climb as before through broken rock and slabs to a large square cairn beside the **Brunnifirn**, 30 to 40 minutes on. The glac-ier's glassy, in places heavily crevassed sur-face sweeps around to cover much of the 3328m Oberalpstock (Piz Tgietschen). A difficult alternative route to Disentis used by

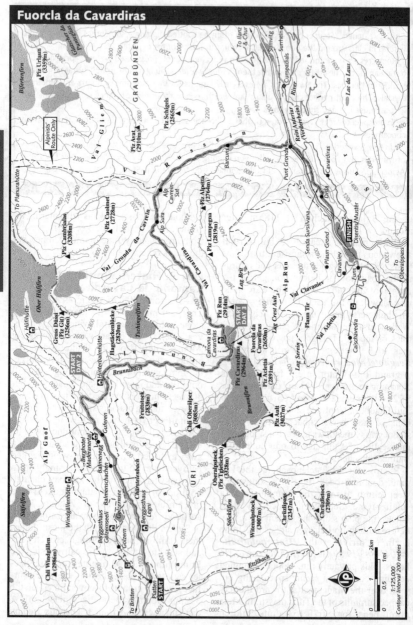

Fuorcla da Cavardiras

mountaineers leads up across the Brunnifirn via an obvious gap between Piz Ault (3027m) and Piz Cavardiras (2964m).

An arrow points you down onto the harmless uncrevassed edge of the ice, from where the hut comes into sight. Head left (roughly eastward) across the **Fuorcla da Cavardiras** marking the Uri–Graubünden cantonal border, then over snowy gullies and moraine mounds to arrive at *Camona da Cavardiras* (☎ *081-947 57 47,* ⓔ *info@cavardiras.ch)* after just 15- to 20-minutes. This SAC hut at 2649m is staffed from early July to early September (but otherwise open) and has dorm beds for Sfr29/15 adults/children (without breakfast). Looking directly out across the Brunnifirn as well as north-east toward the Tödi massif, the camona offers some of the nicest high-Alpine scenery you'll see from any mountain hut. You can also see the Oberalpstock, the area's highest peak, on the far side of the Brunnifirn.

Day 3: Camona da Cavardiras to Disentis

4–5 hours, 17km

Follow route markings down quickly via a rocky ridge to cross a small permanent snowfield, then descend on left over eroding slopes into the grassy basin at the uppermost end of the **Val Cavardiras**. From here a graded foot track continues down along the northern side of the rubble-choked stream past a lonely alp hut, and rises on through a high grassy gully before dropping down steeply again to reach **Alp Sura** (1814m) after 1¾ to 2¼ hours. Here, where the Val Cavardiras and the Val Gronda da Cavrein merge, stands an alp hut in the shelter of rock blocks.

Wander over the moist herb fields and pick up an old mule trail shortly after crossing the Cavardiras stream just above the confluence. The route winds its way down over slopes of bilberries and alpenroses, crossing and recrossing the stream on stone footbridges before meeting a good farm track at **Alp Cavrein-Sut** (1540m) after 25 to 30 minutes, where you enter the main **Val Russein**.

Head over the bridge, turning right onto the valley road running down beside river flats past the very small hydroelectric reservoir at **Barcuns** (1368m). The white tops of the Medels massif can be made out in the distance ahead. The road leads more steeply on through light forest before coming out at **Punt Gronda** (1032m) on the main Trun–Disentis road, one to 1¼ hours from Alp Cavrein-Sut. From here go 300m right (west), crossing the Russein stream via the roofed wooden pedestrian bridge (the original road bridge built in the 1860s) to the postbus stop.

Walkers continuing on foot to Disentis/Mustér can take the signposted **Senda Sursilvana** running down under the rail lines. Stroll down along the narrow road to a hairpin curve, then follow a right-hand path marked with yellow diamonds. The way rises and dips through hay fields and patches of forest, passing the tiny settlement of Cavardiras with its quaint church perched high on the adjacent side of the valley before coming to the hamlet of **Disla** (1039m). Here, leave the main Senda route and make your way up along a country lane beside the lovely old Romansch farmhouses and chapel, crossing back over the rail lines below the Pension Schuoler. Walk on left down the main road to arrive in **Disentis**, 50 minutes to one hour from Punt Gronda.

Other Walks

Grosser & Kleiner Mythen

Rising up like two rock noses directly to the east of the small city of Schwyz, the 1899m Grosser Mythen and the 1811m Kleiner Mythen are key landmarks of this minor cantonal capital. While climbing the Kleiner (small) Mythen makes a challenging hike, the way to the top of the Grosser Mythen is a simple and scenic route. The summit offers quite outstanding vistas of Lake Lucerne and the Urner Alps.

The five-hour walk is best done from the upper station of the Rickenbach–Rotenfluh cable-car station (1529m) and requires sure-footedness, but is quite safe in good conditions. From Rotenfluh a mild descent leads down to Holzegg (1405m), from where a very steep zig-zagging path cut into the cliffs (with fixed cables in places) goes up to the Grosser Mythen. After returning to Holzegg, you can either take the cable car down to Brunni (1089m; postbus to Einsiedeln), walk back to Rotenfluh, or – the recommended alternative – continue on foot around the northern side of the mountain to the impressive gap of Zwüschet Mythen (1438m), before descending steeply back to Schwyz.

Throughout summer both the Rickenbach-Rotenfluh and the Brunni-Holzegg cable cars (W www.holzegg.ch) run half-hourly until 6.30pm. The *Berggasthaus Holzegg* (☎ 041-811 12 34) at the upper gondola-lift station has rooms and a dorm.

Use either Orell Füssli's 1:50,000 *Kanton Schwyz* (Sfr25) or the SAW/FSTP 1:50,000 map *Lachen* No 236T (Sfr22.50).

Pilatus

Another of Central Switzerland's classic panoramic lookouts, the six-peak Pilatus juts up abruptly from the south-eastern shore of Lake Lucerne, dominating the views looking southward from the city of Lucerne. Although the mountain was probably sacred to the early lakeside Celtic settlers, it owes its biblical name to a medieval saga in which Pontius Pilate found his last resting place on the summit.

Dragons, witches and demons were thought to inhabit the raw upper slopes of the Pilatus. For centuries, climbing the mountain was strictly forbidden because it was believed this would bring ruin upon the surrounding populace. A group of six monks were prosecuted for climbing it in 1387. Today the Pilatus has completely lost its former mystery, with numerous walking routes, a cog railway and a gondola lift going up to hotels on the summit, but it still makes a tremendously scenic place for walking.

The most popular ascent to the Pilatus on foot follows the 2½-hour so-called Bandweg route from Fränkmünt (1416m), which is accessible by the gondola lift from the town of Kriens. The Bandweg ascends steeply to the lower summits of Oberhaupt (2106m) and Esel (2120m). From here the historic cog railway built in 1889 goes down to Alpnachstad on Lake Lucerne – it runs at a gradient of up to 48%, the steepest of any railway in the world. The main 2128m Pilatus summit is a short climb on, and gives a stupendous panorama down to the great lake.

A worthwhile five-hour continuation of the walk (requiring some sure-footedness) follows a high-level path south-west along the top of the craggy range. The descent leads on to the little village of Eigenthal (1017m), from where there are at least four daily buses to Lucerne (until about 5.30pm).

On the Pilatus' summit are *Hotel Bellevue* and *Hotel Pilatus Kulm* with singles/doubles from Sfr65/130; shared reception (☎ 041-670 12 55, e hotel.pilatus.kulm-bellevue@bluewin.ch). The recommended walking map is the 1:25,000 *Wanderkarte Pilatus* (Sfr9), available from ticket offices of the mountain transport companies.

Stanserhorn

Only slightly less popular than the other great lookout peaks around Lake Lucerne, the 1897m Stanserhorn stands just to the south of the Bürgenstock. Falling away abruptly on its eastern and western flanks, the Stanserhorn grants more of the fine watery views for which the Lake Lucerne region is famous. The Stanserhorn's standard walk is a three-hour climb from the small ski resort of Wirzweli (1220m).

The descent can be made on foot or by the Stanserhorn-Bahn (W www.stanserhorn.ch), a cable-car/funicular combination, to the town of Stans. (Originally a three-stage funicular dating from 1893 ran the whole way up, but when the engine-room and the hotel at the upper station were destroyed by fire in 1970 the two higher sections were replaced by the cable car.)

The Wirzweli resort is accessible by cable car (W www.wirzweli.ch) from near Dallenwil, which like Stans is on the Lucerne–Engelberg rail line. Use either the local tourist authority's 1:50,000 *Wanderkarte Nidwalden und Engelberg* (around Sfr18) or SAW/FSTP's 1:50,000 map *Stans* No 245T (Sfr22.50).

Weg der Schweiz

Forming part of the Waldstätterweg walking route, which was opened in 1991 for Switzerland's 700th anniversary, the 35km Weg der Schweiz (or 'Swiss Path') leads around the Urnersee (Lake Uri) from Rütli to Brunnen. The route has 26 sections, each representing one of Switzerland's cantons; these are arranged according to when the canton joined the Swiss Confederation and their length is based on the canton's population.

This easy route follows a well-marked and contoured walkway taking in some really lovely scenery. With a total walking time of 12 hours, the Weg der Schweiz is best done in two days, although you can start or finish the walk at various places (accessible by ferry, postbus or train) along the way. A special 1:25,000 walking map, *Weg der Schweiz* (Sfr9.50), has descriptions in English, French, German and Italian.

Chinzig Chulm

The 2073m Chinzig Chulm (also called 'Kinzigpass') is a pass leading out of the Schächental over into the heavily forested

Muotatal, one of the nicest larger valleys of Schwyz Canton. The Chinzig Chulm gives fine views of the nearby horned Rosstock and Kaiserstock peaks as well as southward to the Urner Alps. From the upper cable-car station at Biel-Kinzig (1627m), the three- to four-hour route climbs up along a steep spur before sidling around eastward below the main ridge to the pass. The descent takes you down through the lovely Hürlital via Lipplisbüöl (1194m) to the hamlet of Hinterthal (623m) on the main road through the valley of the Muotatal. An alternative route from just below the Chinzig Chulm departs up left (north-west) and leads via the Seenalper Seeli (1719m), an attractive tarn in a tiny side valley. The Hölloch, Europe's largest limestone cave system, is just 1.5km from Hinterthal.

The cable car to Biel-Kinzig operates half-hourly until 7.30pm between late May and the end of September. The lower cable-car station at Brügg can be reached by frequent public-bus connections from Flüelen via Altdorf. From Hinterthal there are roughly hourly postbuses to Schwyz (with train connections to Lucerne and Zürich) at least until 7pm. Use either SAW/FSTP's 1:50,000 *Klausenpass* No 246T (Sfr22.50), Orell Füssli's 1:50,000 *Kanton Schwyz* (Sfr25) or K+F's 1:60,000 *Kanton Uri* (Sfr24.80).

Golzernsee

The Golzernsee is a natural lake set among meadows and light Alpine forest on the northern slopes of the Maderanertal. A rewarding day or overnight circuit can be done from Bristen, where the cable car connects to a high route running past the Golzernsee to the SAC's *Windgällenhütte* (☎ 041-885 10 88) at 2032m. A side trip to a lookout at the Stäfelfirn, a snowfield above the hut, is also worthwhile. The descent/return to Bristen is made via Balmenegg then along an easy path down beside the river.

The recommended walking map is K+F's 1:60,000 *Kanton Uri* (Sfr24.80).

Göschener Tal

The Göschener Tal is an impressive enclosed side valley of the Reuss River that meets the main valley at the village of Göschenen. The head of the Göschener Tal is blocked by the icy giants of the Winteregg massif, including the Sustenhorn (3503m), the Dammastock (3630m) and the Galenstock (3583m). Apart from mountaineering tours, only one (difficult) walking route leads out of this 'dead end' valley, so circuit or return walks are offered. A large part of the upper-valley area is covered by the Stausee

Göscheneralp hydroelectricity reservoir, but this detracts little from the area's scenic beauty.

A particularly interesting feature of the Göschener Tal is the Sandbalmhöhle, the largest rock-crystal cave in Switzerland, which has quartzite, calcite and chlorite formations. The Sandbalmhöhle can be reached by first following the path toward Voralphütte then turning off left (the return time from the path turn-off is 2½ hours). Another thoroughly scenic five-hour return hike from the Stausee Göscheneralp leads up through the tiny Chelenalptal to the **Kehlenalphütte** (☎ *041-885 19 30)*, an SAC-run mountain hut at 2350m. Excellent day or overnight walks can also be made to three other SAC huts in the Göschener Tal area; the *Salbithütte* (☎ *041-885 14 31*, W *www.salbit.ch)*, the *Voralphütte* (☎ *041-887 04 20)* and the third SAC hut is the *Bergseehütte* (☎ *041-885 14 35*, W *www.bergsee.ch)*.

At Gwüest in the valley, the *Gasthaus Pension Mattli* (☎ *041-885 18 15)* has dorm accommodation and the *Campingplatz Gwüest* (☎ *041-885 00 85)* offers organised camping. Near the dam wall, the *Berggasthaus Dammagletscher* (☎ *041-885 16 76)* has rooms and a dorm.

From 1 July to 1 October there are hourly postbuses each day from Göschenen to Göscheneralp until 7pm; supplementary tickets apply and seat reservation is compulsory (☎ 041-885 11 80). The Göschener Tal is covered by K+F's 1:60,000 *Kanton Uri* (24.80) or SAW/FSTP's *Sustenpass* No 236T (Sfr22.50).

Urschner Höhenweg

The broad highland valley of the Ursental descends from the 2431m Furkapass to Andermatt. Largely following sunny terraces high above the Ursental at around 2000m, the Urschner Höhenweg is a five- to six-hour high-level route of easy-medium standard that affords constant views southward to the mountains of the Gotthard region. It leads eastward from the small village of Tiefenbach (2106m) via the hamlets of Tätsch, Ochsenalp, Lochbergbach, Lipferstein and the Lütersee, a crystal-clear Alpine lake at 1976m, before descending to Andermatt.

From 1 July to 1 October postbuses running between Oberwald in the upper Valais and Andermatt (via the Furkapass road) pass by Tiefenbach twice daily in both directions. The last bus leaves Andermatt at around 2.30pm and reservation before 5pm the previous day is highly advisable (☎ 041-828 88 28).

Use SAW/FSTP's 1:50,000 *Sustenpass* No 236T (Sfr22.50) or K+F's 1:60,000 *Kanton Uri* (Sfr24.80).

Benediktusweg

The Benediktusweg is an easy and very popular 3½-hour walk leading along the eastern slopes of the Walenstöcke. The route begins at the upper station (1605m) of the Brunni cable car (W www.brunni.ch) above Engelberg and leads to Walenalp (1665m). Here you can opt for the somewhat harder (but recommended) way to the Bannalpsee going over the ridge of Walegg (1943m), or follow the main route around to the lake via the hamlet of Firnhütt (1406m). A cable car (☎ 041-628 16 33) from the Bannalpsee takes you down to Fell near Oberrickenbach, from where there are four or five daily postbuses to Wolfenschiessen (on the Lucerne–Engelberg rail line).

The *Berghaus Bannalpsee* (☎ *041-628 15 56*) near the dam wall and the *Berghaus Urnerstaffel* (☎ *041-628 15 75*) some 1.5km away at Bannalp each offer rooms and dorms. Use either the SAW/FSTP 1:50,000 *Stans* No 245T (Sfr22.50) or the *Wanderkarte Nidwalden und Engelberg* (around Sfr18).

Melchsee & Tannensee

In the geographical heart of Switzerland, the Melchsee and Tannensee are two attractive lakes embedded in a lovely grassy basin. The area offers easy, laid-back walking and is extremely popular with families. From Melchsee-Frutt (W www.melchsee-frutt.ch), a small, scattered resort at 1936m, a suggested easy three- to four-hour return route leads south around the shores of the Melchsee, then up (on foot or by chairlift) to the minor lookout peak of the Balmeregghorn (2255m). From here you can continue down along the Erzegg range past the Tannensee, from where the walk back to Melchsee-Frutt can be made via Tannen and the Bonistock (2168m), or you can go directly around the lake's northern side and through the grassy basin.

An extended version (known as the 4-Seen Wanderung – 'Four-Lakes Hike') continues up eastward via Engstlenalp (see the Jochpass walk) to Engelberg. Another alternative is to head up west past the tarn of Blausee to the 2480m Hochstöllen, then down to Hohsträss (2119m), from where a cable car descends to Wasserwendi (with hourly postbuses going to Brünigpass train station).

Sporthotel Kurhaus Frutt (☎ 041-669 12 12, e *sporthotel@kurhaus-frutt.ch*) at Melchsee-Frutt has singles/doubles from Sfr51/92 and dorm beds from Sfr33. The *Berggasthaus Tannalp* (☎ *041-669 12 41*, W *www.tannalp.ch*) offers doubles from Sfr70 and dorm beds for Sfr60 with full board.

Melchsee-Frutt is accessible by cable car from Stöckalp (1081m) at the head of the Melchtal. From mid-June until the last week of October postbuses run up to nine times daily to Stöckalp from Sarnen on the Lucerne–Interlaken rail line; the last bus leaves Sarnen around 4pm (5pm on weekends and holidays). Use either the local tourist authority's 1:50,000 *Obwaldner Wanderkarte* (around Sfr18) or Orell Füssli's 1:50,000 *Kanton Schwyz* (Sfr25).

Swiss Jura

The chain of low mountains known as the Jura extends some 150km north-east along the Swiss–French border. From its highest summits near Lake Geneva, the Swiss Jura gradually drops in height before petering out at Basel. Spanning six cantons – Vaud, Neuchâtel, Bern, Jura, Solothurn and Basel – the region takes in approximately 10% of Switzerland's area. The Swiss Jura is overwhelmingly French-speaking, with a relatively small German-speaking area at its most north-easterly end between Solothurn and Basel.

The Jura is a limestone range with much lower elevations as well as a simpler and more recent geological formation than the Alps. Throughout the region, water seeping through the porous and soluble calcium-based rock has formed subterranean streams, limestone caverns, karst fields and rugged gorges (which, for walkers in the Jura, often means little water of drinking quality is available).

Separated from the Alps by only the 80km-wide basin of the Swiss Mittelland, the gentle summits of the Jura make outstanding natural lookout points. (According to local legend, God, having just finished the painstaking task of building the magnificent Alps, created the Jura as an afterthought, so that the splendour of His/Her work could be surveyed from a suitable distance.)

The word Jura originates from an ancient Celtic term meaning 'mountains of forest', which still aptly describes this region, whose higher slopes are clothed in firs and spruces and the valleys in dense beech forest. Walkers accustomed to the grandiose high-mountain scenery of the Alps may find the rolling tree-covered ranges of the Swiss Jura monotonous and relatively unspectacular. To be sure, you won't find any glaciers here and there are not many peaks that rise very far above the tree line, yet the Swiss Jura often surprises in its variety of landscapes.

Highlights

Shrouded in mist and history – monks lived and worshiped in this cottage and tiny stone church in Einsiedelei, an early 17th-century hermitage near Solothurn.

- Gazing over the Swiss Mittelland to the snowcapped Alps from the Weissenstein
- Climbing through the tiny gorge of the Poëta-Raisse
- Skirting the precipitous rim of the magnificent Creux de Van cirque
- Tracing ancient dry-stone fences on the slopes of Mont Tendre

INFORMATION
Maps

Three regional maps cover the areas described in this chapter. Editions MPA Verlag's 1:120,000 *Vaud/Waadt* (Sfr14.80) gives a good overview of the southern Jura and shows the walking routes. Sheets No 1 and No 2 of the BL/OFT's 1:200,000 (four-map) series cover the northern and the southern Jura respectively.

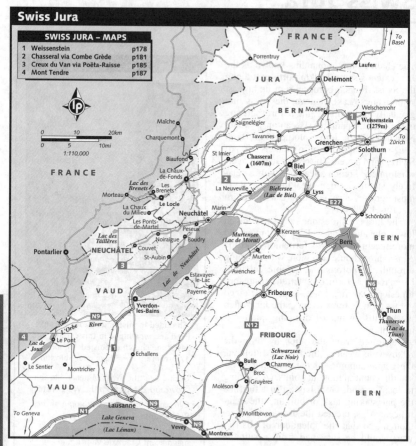

Swiss Jura

SWISS JURA – MAPS	
1 Weissenstein	p178
2 Chasseral via Combe Grède	p181
3 Creux du Van via Poëta-Raisse	p185
4 Mont Tendre	p187

Books

The Jura: High Route and Winter Ski Traverse (UK£8.99) by Kev Reynolds & R Brian Evans (Cicerone Press) covers high-level walks in the Swiss Jura.

Kümmerly + Frey's (K+F) *Jura* (Sfr22.80) is a general regional walking guide published in separate French and German editions. K+F's French-language *Jura vaudois* (Sfr22.80) covers the (southern) Vaud Jura.

Information Sources

The Swiss Jura Association (Association du Jura Suisse/Schweizer Juraverein) manages

the 640km Jura High Route. The Web site (W www.jura-hoehenwege.ch/juraverein /juraverein.html) can be viewed in French and German only.

For more information relating to the Jura Canton, you should contact Jura Tourisme (☎ 032-952 19 52, e info@juratourism.ch, W www.juratourisme.ch) Rue de la Gruère 1.

For information on Solothurn Canton, contact Kanton Solothurn Tourismus (☎ 032-626 46 56, e tourism@solnet.ch, W www .solothurn.ch/tourism) Hauptgasse 69.

The Web sites W www.jurabernois.ch and W www.ne.ch/tourism are useful for information on the Bernese Jura and the Neuchâtel Jura respectively.

For other regional tourist offices and Web sites, see the appropriate Gateways, Access Towns and Nearest Towns listings.

GETTING AROUND

Fast InterRegio trains run along the southern foot of the Jura between Lausanne and St Gallen via Yverdon-les-Bains, Neuchâtel, Biel/Bienne, Solothurn and Zürich – a somewhat slower alternative to the Inter-City trains that go through the Mittelland via Bern.

The *Arc Jurassien* day pass costs Sfr25 and covers certain bus and train routes in the northern Swiss Jura (within the cantons of Neuchâtel, Jura and Bern). A 'Plus' version (Sfr39 or Sfr44) extends the area of validity. The one-week *Onde Verte* pass costs Sfr70 and covers only Neuchâtel Canton. The *Zig Zag* pass, also for one week, costs Sfr69 and gives free travel on all buses, trains and cableways in the Bernese Jura and Seeland centred on Biel/Bienne.

The seven-day *Regional Pass Leman* costs Sfr150 (Sfr120 concession and Sfr75 for children) and covers all of Vaud Canton as well as most of the southern Jura. It gives three days of free travel and four days at half-price.

GATEWAYS
Biel/Bienne

Lying at the foot of the Chasseral range at the northern end of the Bielersee (Lake Biel), the German/French bilingual city of Biel/Bienne is the centre of Switzerland's watchmaking industry. It has an attractive old town, which is clustered around the Ring, a charming square with a 16th-century fountain. The Omega Museum (Stämpflistrasse 996) gives a (free) look at the company's watchmaking process.

For information contact the tourist office (☎ 032-322 75 75, fax 032-323 77 57, e tbs@bielstar.ch), or visit either the city Web site (W www.biel-bienne.ch) or the regional site (W www.biel-seeland.net). Eiselin Sport (☎ 032-323 56 60), Ring 5, has a good range of outdoor gear.

Places to Stay & Eat The nearby *Camping Sutz-Lattrigen (☎ 032-397 13 45)* has tent sites for Sfr5.50 plus Sfr8 per person. The central *Hotel-Bistrot Lindenegg Villa (☎ 032-322 94 66, Lindenegg 5)* offers pleasant singles/doubles from Sfr50/100 in a garden setting. The *Hotel de la Poste (☎ 032-322 25 44, Guterstrasse 3)* offers simple rooms for Sfr60/100.

Biel/Bienne's *Coop* supermarket is located on Salzhausstrasse and has a cheap cafeteria-restaurant. *Al Fonte (Zentralstrasse 57)* has excellent pizza on offer and the *Restaurant Au Vieux Valais (Untergässli 9)* serves Swiss food.

Getting There & Away In summer the Bielersee Schiffahrts Gesellschaft (☎ 032-329 88 11, W www.bielersee.ch) operates ferries around the lake, including to St Peterinsel (see Other Walks at the end of the chapter). Biel/Bienne is the rail interchange for trains via the Vallon de St-Imier and La Chaux-de-Fonds to Le Locle. Rapid Inter-Regio trains running between Lausanne and

---

Expo.02

Originally titled Expo.01, Switzerland's national exhibition was actually scheduled for 2001, but was postponed (with profound embarrassment) after it became clear that the deadline could not be met. Co-hosted by Biel/Bienne, Neuchâtel, Murten and Yverdon-les-Bains – the four main cities of the bilingual Three Lakes Region, where the cantons of Bern, Fribourg, Neuchâtel and Vaud all meet – the Expo.02 was rescheduled to be held between 15 May and 20 October 2002.

Most of the exhibition space will be on five enormous platforms (or 'arteplages') floating on the Bielersee, Lac de Neuchâtel and the Murtensee (Lac de Morat). Some 4000 different events are planned, including theatre, dance, classical and popular music, film screenings, multimedia, circus acts and street theatre.

The official Web site (W www.expo.02.ch) has more information.

St Gallen (via Zürich) pass through Biel/Bienne hourly in either direction.

Neuchâtel

The capital of its own canton, the city of Neuchâtel (Neuenburg in German) lies on the north-western shore of Lac de Neuchâtel. The Museum of Art and History (entry Sfr7), Quai Léopold Robert 2, is excellent.

For information contact the tourist office (☎ 032-889 68 90, e tourisme.neuchatelois @ne.ch, w www.neuchatel.ch) at Rue Hôtel des Postes.

Places to Stay & Eat In nearby Colombier, *Camping Paradis Plage* (☎ 032-841 24 46) has lakeside tent sites from around Sfr7 plus Sfr7 per person. *Hôtel du Marché* (☎ 032-723 23 33, Place des Halles 4) has singles/doubles from Sfr70/100. The *Hôtel des Beaux-Arts* (☎ 032-724 01 51, Pourtalès 5) offers rooms from Sfr70/125 and has a restaurant, which serves Italian and vegetarian cuisine.

The *Epa* department store (Rue des Epancheurs 3) has an inexpensive restaurant. Also cheap is *La Crêperie* (Rue de l'Hôpital 7), which serves (only) crepes. The *Café du Cerf/Le Lotus* (Rue Ancien-Hôtel-de-Ville 4) offers Thai dishes from around Sfr25.

Getting There & Away Trains run hourly to Buttes in the upper Val de Travers via Môtiers and Fleurier, from where there are connections to Pontarlier in the French Jura.

Rapid InterRegio trains running between Lausanne and St Gallen (via Zürich) pass through Neuchâtel hourly in either direction.

Lausanne

Situated almost midway along the northern shore of Lake Geneva, the city of Lausanne is the major gateway to the southern Jura. Lausanne's charming medieval old town includes a Gothic cathedral, the St François church and monastery and the Château St Marie (castle). Worth seeing are the weird and eccentric works in the Musée de l'Art Brut (entry Sfr4/6 student/adult) on Ave des Bergières and the Palais de Rumine (entry Sfr4/6) on Place de la Riponne, which houses fine-arts and natural-history collections. Also of interest is the Olympic Museum (entry Sfr9/14 concession/adult) in the Parc Olympique at 1 Quai d'Ouchy.

Lausanne's tourist office (☎ 021-613 73 21, e information@lausanne-tourisme.ch, w www.lausanne-tourisme.ch), Ave de Rhodanie 2, can help with information.

Places to Stay & Eat Lakeside tent sites are available at *Camping de Vidy* (☎ 021-622 50 00, Chemin du Camping 3) from Sfr7 plus Sfr7.70 per person. The *youth hostel* (☎ 021-626 02 22, e lausanne@youthhostel.ch) has dorm beds for Sfr25. The central *Pension Bon-Sejour* (☎ 021-323 59 52, Rue Caroline 10) offers singles/doubles for Sfr45/70. The *Pension Ada-Lodgements* (☎ 021-625 71 34, Ave de Tivoli 60) charges Sfr50/75.

The *Pension Old Inn* (☎ 021-323 62 21, Ave de la Gare 11) has rooms for Sfr60/95. The *Hôtel de la Foret* (☎ 021-647 92 11, Route du Pavement 75) has better rooms for Sfr95/180.

The *Migros* supermarket on Rue Neuve and the *Manora* (17 Place St François) have inexpensive restaurants. *Cafe de l'Everche* (4 Rue Louis Curtat) offers meals from around Sfr15.

Getting There & Away Fast InterCity trains running between Geneva and St Gallen (via Bern and Zürich) stop at Lausanne hourly from either direction. Rapid Inter-Regio trains also run hourly to St Gallen (via Yverdon-les-Bains, Neuchâtel, Biel/Bienne and Zürich). Ultra-rapid TGV trains run up to five times daily to/from Paris. From late May to late September, frequent ferries run to all the important towns around the shore of Lake Geneva.

Northern Swiss Jura

The Northern Swiss Jura stretches from the Vue des Alpes pass (between Neuchâtel and La Chaux-de-Fonds) north-eastward as far as Basel. Although generally lower in height and rather narrower than farther to the south, here the Jura range rises up rather more abruptly out of the Swiss Mittelland. The countryside to the north of the range is a beautiful landscape of woodlands and rolling meadows renowned for horse breeding. Despite the region's very moist climate, large parts of the Northern Swiss Jura – particularly in the Franches Montagnes district – are completely without above-ground rivers and streams, as the water disappears immediately into the limestone ground.

ACCESS TOWN
La Chaux-de-Fonds

The birthplace of the famous architect Le Corbusier, La Chaux-de-Fonds is another of the Jura's watchmaking centres.

Contact the local tourist office (☎ 032-919 68 95, e tourisme.montagnes@ne.ch, w www.chaux-de-fonds.ch) for information.

Camping Bois du Couvent (☎ *079-240 50 39*) has tent sites from Sfr6/7 plus Sfr3.50/4.50 per person in low/high season. The *youth hostel* (☎ *032-968 43 15*) has dorm beds for Sfr24. The *Hôtel de la Croix d'Or* (☎ *032-968 43 53, Rue de la Balance 15*) has basic singles/doubles from around Sfr35/70. The *Motel du Jura* (☎ *032-968 28 22, Rue Hôtel de Ville 50*) has rooms from Sfr40/80. The *Hôtel du Moulin* (☎ *032-926 42 26, Rue de la Serre 130*) has rooms from Sfr55/90.

There are hourly trains from Neuchâtel (30 minutes) and Biel/Bienne (via St-Imier, 40 minutes). Trains run twice daily from La-Chaux-de-Fonds to Besançon in France.

Cows laze among wild flowers on the rolling pastures of the Jura.

Weissenstein

Duration	3¾–4½ hours
Distance	12km
Standard	easy
Start	Oberbalmberg
Finish	Solothurn

Summary This delightful day walk (with moderate ascents but few steep downhill sections) leads along the rounded ridges of the Weissenstein range to the panoramic 1397m summit of the Röti, before winding down via the Einsiedelei, a historic hermitage below limestone cliffs in a tiny gorge.

Standing, so to speak, in Solothurn's backyard, the Weissenstein is one of the Swiss Jura's most popular walks. The views are particularly dramatic in autumn, when a thick layer of high-level fog often hangs over the Swiss Mittelland. The Weissenstein – whose name means 'white stone' in German – consists of a durable marble, which provided an ideal building material for many of Solothurn's grand old Baroque edifices.

Maps

Recommended is the local tourist authority's 1:50,000 *Solothurn und Umgebung* (Sfr18). You can also use any of four Kümmerly + Frey (K+F) 1:60,000 walking maps: *Kanton Solothurn*; *Delsberg Pruntrut Biel Solothurn*; *Emmental Oberaargau*; or *Berner Jura Laufental Seeland* (Sfr24.80 each). Otherwise, two SAW/FSTP 1:50,000 maps are required: *Delemont* No 223T and *Solothurn* No 233T (Sfr22.50 each).

NEAREST TOWN & FACILITIES
Oberbalmberg

In this tiny mountain resort, the large *Kurhaus Balmberg* (☎ *032-637 37 37*) has dorm beds for Sfr30 and singles/doubles for Sfr60/80.

Solothurn

The capital of Solothurn Canton, this city is situated at 432m at the southern foot of the main Jura range. Solothurn is Switzerland's most Baroque city, boasting quite a number

SWISS JURA

of superb 18th-century buildings built in local marble, including the St Ursus cathedral, the Baseltor and the Jesuit church. Solothurn has many fine museums, including the Jurassisches Museum dealing with the Swiss Jura. Solothurn makes a charming and practical base for walks into the nearby Weissenstein hills.

Contact the Solothurn tourist office (☎ 032-626 46 46, ℮ info@solothurn-city.ch, ☒ www.solothurn-city.ch or www.solothurn .ch/cityguide), Hauptgasse 69, for details on the city and region.

The local *youth hostel* (☎ 032-623 17 06, ℮ *solothurn@youthhostel.ch*), closed from early November to mid-December, is excellent and central, and has dorm beds for Sfr24/25.50 in low/high season. *Hotel Kreuz* (☎ 032-622 20 20, ℮ *kreuz@solnet.ch, Kreuzgasse 4*) offers singles/doubles from Sfr42/70. The *Hotel Schlüssel* (☎ 032-622 22 82, Kreuzgasse 3) has rooms from around Sfr55 per person. The *Hotel Baseltor* (☎ 032-622 34 22, ℮ *baseltor@solnet.ch, Hauptgasse 79*) charges from Sfr90/155 for singles/doubles.

The private RBS railway links Solothurn with Bern (note that the 'self-control' system applies on these trains – see Tickets & Travel Passes in the Getting Around chapter). Rapid InterRegio trains running between Lausanne and St Gallen (via Yverdon-les-Bains, Neuchâtel, Biel/Bienne and Zürich) stop at Solothurn hourly in either direction. In summer tourist boats run along the Aare River between Biel/Bienne and Solothurn.

GETTING TO/FROM THE WALK
Between 1 May and 1 November postbuses run from Solothurn to Oberbalmberg roughly every two hours until around 6pm.

THE WALK
A signpost near the postbus stop at **Oberbalmberg** (1078m) points you past the Kurhaus Balmberg. Head past winter ski tows and climb quickly over a low crest onto steep forested hillsides looking out towards the village of Günsberg. This 'geological path' sidles slightly upward around the slopes past fossils of ancient marine

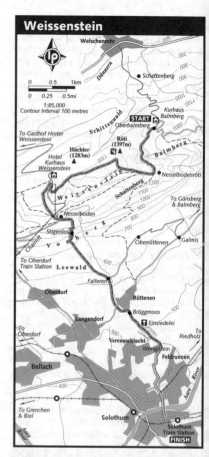

fauna, then climbs more steeply up through the forest to **Nesselbodenröti** (1290m).

Here, leave the yellow-marked route for a less prominent track going up right along the ridge. This comes out of the trees onto open pastures, leading quickly on up to the wooden cross and surveying triangle on the **Röti** at 1397m, one to 1¼ hours from Oberbalmberg. This green, rounded summit makes a superb natural lookout, and on clear days there are truly uplifting views south to the giant peaks of the Bernese Oberland, as well as north towards the lower ripples of the Black Forest in Germany.

Make your way down south-westward along the broad grassy tops and cross over a low rib in the ridge. The route descends gently along a dirt track to a minor saddle, then follows a gravelled walkway up to the **Hotel Kurhaus Weissenstein** (☎ *032-628 61 61,* ⓔ *kurhaus@hotel-weissenstein.ch)* at 1287m. This historic hotel (dating from 1828) has singles/doubles from Sfr64/128, or you can sleep in the bunkhouse for Sfr50/30 adults/children; the restaurant has a scenic terrace. The adjacent **Juragarten** (free entry) has 150 local native plant species.

Drop down to the road, taking a sign-posted path right just below **Bergrestaurant Sennhaus**, which serves meals and refreshments. This brings you down through the forest to cross under the chairlift (going from the hotel to the train station at Oberdorf) shortly before you reach **Nesselboden** (1057m), 40 to 50 minutes from Röti.

Go left across the road and continue along a broad foot track, which gradually steepens to begin a sharp descent in stepped switch-back curves down the south-facing slopes of mixed conifers. The route leads down via **Stigenlos** (805m) to meet a gravelled forest track and follows this south-east to intersect with a larger road at **Falleren** (555m). Walk along the road, past fields and houses, bearing left at a Y-junction after another 300m.

A signpost soon directs you right onto a farm track running along the edge of a clearing to pass a large restaurant, 1¼ to 1¾ hours on from Nesselboden. A few paces on at the upper end of the little gorge known as the **Verenaschlucht** is the interesting **Einsiedelei** (493m). The quaint hermit's cottage and tiny stone church built against the cliffs date from the early 17th century, and were once the abode of reclusive monks.

Follow the broad well-cut path alongside the tiny stream through beech and oak forest, crossing small footbridges before coming onto a road at **Wengistein** (455m). Yellow diamonds and signposts guide you along residential streets to a busy Y-intersection. Here, cut right across the park, past the round corner tower of the original city walls, dipping under an arched gateway into the old town and continuing down cobblestone laneways to the Baroque cathedral at the centre of **Solothurn** after 30 to 40 minutes. The train station is a further 10- to 15-minute walk down the cobblestone laneway of Kroneng, across the pedestrian bridge spanning the Aare River, then left along Hauptbahnhofstrasse.

Chasseral via Combe Grède

Duration	5¼–6¾ hours
Distance	24km
Standard	easy-medium
Start	St-Imier
Finish	Orvin

Summary A familiar walking area to lovers of the Bernese Jura, the Chasseral gives splendid vistas of the main Alpine massifs, at the centre of which the Eiger, Mönch and Jungfrau can be easily identified.

Rising up from the vineyards around the Bielersee (Lake Biel), the main Jura range forms a long hump of beautiful subalpine meadows culminating in the 1607m summit of Chasseral. On the northern side of the Chasseral is the Combe Grède, a wild limestone gorge that has cut its way into the stratified sedimentary rock, leaving imposing, almost vertical, cliffs that rise 300m or more above the tiny stream. The luxuriant forests surrounding the gorge were once exploited for charcoal production, but today the area is protected by the Parc Jurassien de la Combe Grède. This true 'Jurassic Park' may lack dinosaurs, but reintroduced populations of chamois and marmots now thrive on the slopes around the Chasseral. The Combe Grède itself provides an important habitat for endangered species of ground-dwelling birds, including the capercaillie.

The often steep climb up to the Chasseral totals more than 800m, which includes a section of stairways and steel ladders. The railings along the path are dismantled in late autumn (mid-November), but the path remains quite passable as long as you take some care. Note that there is no drinking water en-route between the Hôtel Chasseral and Orvin. This full-day walk can be stretched out to two leisurely days by staying at the Hôtel Chasseral, or shortened by ending at the hotel (see Getting To/From the Walk later).

Maps

The most suitable walk map is SAW/FSTP's 1:50,000 *Vallon de St-Imier* No 232T (Sfr22.50). A reasonable alternative is K+F's 1:60,000 *Chasseral Neuchâtel Val de Travers Ste-Croix* (Sfr24.80), although it cuts off just north of St-Imier.

NEAREST TOWNS
St-Imier

St-Imier lies at 793m in the Vallon de St-Imier of the Bernese Jura. Although the town traces its origins back to an early medieval hermit who first took up residence here, St-Imier was largely destroyed by fires in the 19th century. One of the few buildings to escape the flames was the old St-Martin church built of hewn-stone blocks. St-Imier has long been a centre of the Jurassian watchmaking industry, and the internationally renowned Longines firm is based here.

Contact St-Imier's tourist office (☎ 032-941 26 63, Ⓦ www.st-imier.ch), Rue du Marché 6, for more information on the town and the region.

Hôtel de la Fontaine (☎ 032-941 29 56) and *Hotel Erguel* (☎ 032-941 22 64), both on Rue Dr-Schwab, have singles/doubles from around Sfr55/110.

Express trains from Biel/Bienne to Le Locle (via La Chaux-de-Fonds) stop at St-Imier every two hours, and there are slower train connections (often with a change at Sonceboz) at least hourly.

Orvin

The walk ends in this small village. *Hôtel de la Crosse-de-Bâle* (☎ 032-358 12 15) has rooms at standard rates. There is a *Friends of Nature hostel* (☎ 033-331 04 72, Ⓔ nfbiel@swissonline.ch), back up the road near the Pres d'Orvin postbus terminus; the charge for a dorm bed is Sfr16.

GETTING TO/FROM THE WALK

The start of the walk proper is the village of Villeret, but since only slower trains from Biel/Bienne to La Chaux-de-Fonds stop at Villeret it may be more convenient to take an express to nearby St-Imier, about 30 minutes' walk from Villeret. The walk finishes at the village of Orvin (669m), from where there are around a dozen direct postbuses to Biel/Bienne each day. The last bus leaves Orvin at about 7pm on weekdays and Sundays, and around 6pm on Saturdays.

The walk can be turned into a much shorter semi-circuit by taking a bus from the Hôtel Chasseral back down to St-Imier. Between late June and the beginning of October there are three daily buses from the hotel, but there is otherwise at least one bus each day. From the Hôtel Chasseral you can also descend on foot or by direct chairlift to the village of Nods (885m), from where there are more frequent and regular postbuses to La Neuveville on the Biel/Bienne–Neuchâtel rail line.

Private vehicles can be left free of charge at the small car park just up from Villeret below the Combe Grède.

THE WALK

From St-Imier train station follow the 'tourisme pédestre' signs eastward out of town along Rue Tivoli and Rue Neuve, then take a short stairway down right to reach the **Villeret** train station (760m) after 25 to 30 minutes. Walk down through the village, turning left and continuing briefly along the main road to where a laneway leads up right. Take this past quaint old houses and barns onto open fields to a car park by the stream at the foot of the Jura range, 15 to 20 minutes from Villeret train station.

A short way on, a signposted track leaves off right across a footbridge and continues through the forest to the start of the **Combe Grède**. Following the bed of the stream (which in places flows subterraneously) where there is no formed path, make your way on up into the gorge proper to begin the steeper ascent via cut-rock stairways and several steel ladders. The route goes up past tumbling cascades and under high

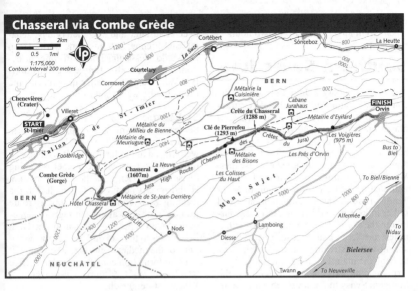

Chasseral via Combe Grède

overhanging limestone cliffs before coming out onto a gently sloping shelf at a spring-water pipe spilling into a wooden trough. Head up quickly through a small wild-flower meadow to reach a signposted track junction at 1277m, 1¼ to 1½ hours from the car park.

Ignoring side tracks running off to the left and right, climb on south-west through clearings before you leave the forest for open herb fields grazed by herds of jingling cows. The path now cuts to the left between the tight bend of a sealed road, making a steeply rising traverse up the grassy slopes above the Métairie de St-Jean-Derrière to arrive at the *Hôtel Chasseral* (☎ 032 751 24 51) after 40 to 50 minutes. The hotel, at 1548m, has singles/doubles from around Sfr45/90 and a budget dorm (showers available). From here, on top of the main Jura range, you get a sweeping view across the waters of Lac de Neuchâtel, the Bielersee and Lac de Morat in the Swiss Mittelland to the great mountain chain of the Alps, which rise up like a glistening white wall extending from the Säntis in the east to Mont Blanc in the west.

Walk 15 to 20 minutes along the road to the rather hideous telecommunications tower on the 1607m summit of the **Chasseral**. Follow red-yellow diamonds and 'Chemin des Crêtes' signs, which both indicate you are now on the Jura High Route, north-eastward over the treeless tops of the range, with cultivated fields down on your right and the high rolling tableland of the Swiss Jura over to the left. The path makes a smooth traversing descent along the ridge to reach the old barn of **Les Colisses du Haut** at 1325m after one to 1¼ hours.

Continue easily along the broad grassy ridge top past **Clé du Pierrefeu** to a car park at **Crête du Chasseral** (1288m), where a well-transited road crosses the range. Leave the Jura High Route at a signpost 200m on, cutting down rightward through pastures to join a narrow farm track coming from the *Métairie d'Evilard* (☎ 032-322 0028), an alp restaurant at 1256m that has a few rooms and a dormitory for walkers. The route proceeds down this steadily improving roadway past the occasional holiday chalets of **Les Prés d'Orvin**, before turning off left at a sharp bend. Make your way through **Les Voigières** (975m) along an old mule path lined with ageing oaks to cross the (now sealed) road. The foot track leads on through

SWISS JURA

the forest, before dropping to the right to reach **Orvin** after a final 1½ to two hours.

Southern Swiss Jura

The Southern Swiss Jura lies within the cantons of Vaud and Neuchâtel. Characterised by extensive areas of highland plateau and small upland valleys with rambling stone fences and lonely mountain hamlets, this region has some of the most typical and romantic Jurassian landscapes. With average altitudes of around 1000m culminating in the 1679m summit of Mont Tendre, the Jura range is much broader and rather more elevated here than in areas farther to the north. The two major Aare tributaries, the Orbe and Areuse, rise as large spring-water streams, cutting their way through the main Jura range in deep gorges. Experiencing extremely cold winters, the Southern Swiss Jura is a veritable mecca for cross-country skiers.

ACCESS TOWNS
Yverdon-les-Bains
First established by the Romans as a thermal bathing resort, Yverdon (**ee**-vair-doh) lies at the southern end of Lac de Neuchâtel. The 13th-century castle houses the town museum (entry Sfr6). The Centre Thermal (☎ 024-423 02 32), off Ave des Bains east of the centre, offers thermal bathing.

Contact the tourist office (☎ 024-423 62 90, e tourisme.info@yverdon-les-bains.ch, w www.yverdon-les-bains.ch/tourisme) at Place Pestalozzi for more information.

Camping des Iris (☎ 024-425 10 89) has tent sites from Sfr4 plus Sfr4.50 per person. *Hôtel de l'Ange* (☎ 024-425 25 85, Clendy 25) offers singles/doubles from Sfr40/70 and has a restaurant. The more central *Hotel l'Ecusson Vaudois* (024-425 40 15, Rue de la Plaine 29) offers rooms from Sfr65/100 and has a cafe.

The *Placette* supermarket on Rue du Lac and *Manora* (Rue de l'Ancienne Poste) have affordable restaurants. *Don Camillo* (Rue du Prè 10) has pizzas from Sfr13.

The rapid InterRegio trains running between Lausanne and St Gallen (via Neuchâtel, Biel/Bienne, Solothurn and Zürich) stop in Yverdon-les-Bains hourly in either direction. There are also frequent connections (via Vallorbe) to the Vallée de Joux (for the Mont Tendre walk) and to Ste-Croix.

St-Cergue
St-Cergue (1044m) sits below the 1677m Dôle at the end of the broad plateau-like western end of the Jura range. It is a pleasant little town typical of the French-speaking Swiss Jura. St-Cergue is the start of the Jura High Route (Chemin des Crêtes du Jura), a walking (and cross-country skiing) route leading north-east along the highest ranges of the Swiss Jura. The first part of the High Route goes to the Col du Marchairuz via the ruins of the medieval cloisters at d'Oujon.

For information contact the tourist office (☎ 022-360 13 14, e tourism@st-cergue.ch, w www.st-cergue.ch).

The *Camping Les Cheseaux* (☎ 022-360 18 98) has tent sites for Sfr4 plus Sfr6 per person. *Auberge Communale Les Cheseaux* (☎ 022-360 12 88) has singles/doubles from around Sfr40/80. The *Hôtel de la Poste* (☎ 022-360 12 05) charges from Sfr66/117.

St-Cergue can be reached on the narrow-gauge Nyon–La Cure mountain railway. Trains leave (from outside Nyon station) hourly until just after 11pm (or around 12.30am on weekends). As the train winds its way steeply up into the Jura there are nice views across Lake Geneva.

Ste-Croix
Ste-Croix (1088m) is an old, typically Jurassian town in the north of the Vaud Canton. Ste-Croix has long been famous for its mechanical music boxes, whose fascinating history is dealt with in the local CIMA museum. The town is a stop along the Jura High Route long-distance walk, which continues north-eastward via the 1607m summit of the Chasseron. A short walk near Ste-Croix goes down through the Gorges de Covatannaz to the little village of Vuiteboeuf (from where there are postbuses to Yverdon-les-Bains).

The local tourist office (☎ 024-454 27 02, e ot@ste-croix.ch, w www.ste-croix.ch), Rue Neuve 6, has more information.

Ste-Croix has a *youth hostel* (☎ *024-454 18 10, Rue Central 18*) with dorm accommodation for Sfr27. There is also *Café Beau-Séjour* (☎ *024-454 21 50, Chemin de Beau-Séjour 2*), which has rooms for around Sfr45 per person. *Hôtel de France* (☎ *024-454 38 21, Rue Centrale 25*) charges from around Sfr60/120 single/double.

Ste-Croix can be reached in 40 minutes from Yverdon-les-Bains on another of the Swiss Jura's romantic old mountain railways. Postbuses also run roughly every two hours to the village of Buttes at the terminus of the Val de Travers rail line, from where there are at least hourly trains to Neuchâtel.

Creux du Van via Poëta-Raisse

Duration	5–6 hours
Distance	21km
Standard	easy
Start	Môtiers
Finish	Noiraigue

Summary This day (or leisurely overnight) walk combines two of the most interesting features of the Val de Travers: the gorge known as the Poëta-Raisse and the Creux du Van, a remarkable cirque.

The Poëta-Raisse was formed over thousands of years, as water flowing down from the Jura tablelands cut its way into the limestone rock. Belying its name, which means 'terrible ravine' in the local Jurassian dialect, Poëta-Raisse is a romantically wild gorge of small waterfalls and gentle mossy pools, accessible by way of an intriguing stepped path.

One of Switzerland's most impressive geological landscapes, the Creux du Van is a limestone cirque with sheer, 200m-high cliffs. The area around this amazing semicircular amphitheatre formed Switzerland's first nature reserve, which was established in 1870. Having enjoyed strict legal protection for over 100 years, the animals in the reserve lack the timidity of wildlife elsewhere. The local fauna includes chamois, ibex and even lynx, which have all been reintroduced after they were hunted out in previous centuries. The Creux du Van's French name roughly translates as 'wind funnel', and the grassy meadows above the precipice are windswept and treeless. The existence of permafrost under the talus debris at the base of the rock walls (at just 1200m above sea level) clearly indicates the severity of winters in the Jura. Only low, stunted firs, some 200 years old, and plant species otherwise found above the tree line grow here.

Maps

SAW/FSTP's 1:50,000 *Val de Travers* No 241T (Sfr22.50) is the recommended map. Another option is K+F's 1:60,000 *Chasseral Neuchâtel Val de Travers Ste-Croix* (Sfr24.80).

NEAREST TOWNS
Môtiers

Môtiers lies at 737m at the foot of Jura range in the Val de Travers, and is a charming little town with fine 18th-century buildings. The French philosopher Jean-Jacques Rousseau lived in political exile here between 1762 and 1765, where he wrote his book *Promenades Solitaires* (Reveries of the Solitary Walker). His stay is commemorated by Môtiers' Rousseau-Museum. Worth visiting are the Vieux Château on a hill above Môtiers and the old asphalt mines nearby.

Môtiers has several small stores, but no supermarket or bank. For information visit the village Web site (w www.motiers.ch), which is in French only.

The *Hôtel des Six Comunes* (☎ *032-261 20 00*) has rooms from around Sfr50 per person. *Château de Môtiers* (☎ *032-861 17 30, e lechateau.demotiers@bluewin.ch*) has doubles from Sfr98. In nearby Fleurier, *Camping Belle Roche* (☎ *032-861 42 62*), open from May to the end of September, has tent sites for Sfr3/5 plus Sfr2/2.50 in low/high season.

Môtiers is on the Val de Travers rail line, with hourly trains from Neuchâtel.

Valley of Absinth

The notoriously potent drink known as absinth is made from wormwood (*Artemisia absinthium*), which grows especially well in the hills of the Val de Travers. The intensely bitter essential oils – which affect the same receptors in the brain as the THC in cannabis – are extracted by steeping the plant's leaves in concentrated alcohol. After Henri-Louis Pernod built the world's first absinth distillery at Couvet in 1797, the production of absinth rapidly became the valley's main industry. Concern about the social effects of absinth consumption, however, led in 1908 to a complete ban on its importation and sale. This effectively shut down the absinth industry in the Val de Travers, although the clandestine production of the *fée verte* (or 'green fairy'), as it is locally called, continues. In fact, the valley benefits from modest but steady 'absinth tourism'.

Noiraigue

Noiraigue (729m) lies in the flat floor of the steep-sided Val de Travers at the upper end of Gorges de l'Areuse. Its name means 'black waters', a reference to the river's dark, peat-stained waters. *Auberge de Noiraigue* (☎ 032-863 34 43) and *Auberge La Ferme-Robert* (☎ 032-863 31 40) both have rooms from around Sfr40/80 per single/double.

GETTING TO/FROM THE WALK

Both Môtiers and Noiraigue are on the Val de Travers rail line, and are easily accessible from the city of Neuchâtel.

From the end of May until mid-September postbuses also run between Couvet (in the Val de Travers) and Yverdon-les-Bains (on Lake Neuchâtel), and stop at the Chalet La Combaz. Some walkers might prefer to set out from La Combaz, leaving out the first section of the walk.

THE WALK

From Môtiers' train station, walk along the main road past the Hôtel des Six Comunes, then proceed straight along a street leading quickly out of town. At a fork near the edge

of the forest bear right onto a forest road running up beside the Poëta-Raisse, which flows underground in places. The route crosses the stream a number of times and continues as a well-cut foot track to an open cavern. Here, the **Gorges de la Poëta-Raisse** begins, as a series of cut-stone stairways and boarded walkways brings you up steeply beside tiny waterfalls – it's remarkable that this mere trickle of a stream has been able to carve such an impressive gorge. There is a signposted intersection at the upper end of the gorge, one to 1½ hours from Môtiers.

Head left over a footbridge, making your way up through a little gully and past an old barn to meet a sealed road. Turn left and climb gently 500m to where the Jura High Route crosses the road at the crest of the range. Take the left-hand track into the forest, before dropping down a short way across open paddocks to arrive at the *Chalet La Combaz* (☎ 024-436 11 53), at 1223m, on the Couvet–Yverdon-les-Bains road, after 40 to 50 minutes. Beds in the chalet's small mattress room (showers available) cost around Sfr18 (breakfast extra).

Follow the road 500m around to the left to the next postbus stop. Here, leave off right along a gravelled track and continue past a farmhouse with a traditional high, wooden-shingle roof, keeping to the dirt lane until this ends at another house, the **Croix de la Pey**. Here, jump over a stile and cut down right across a small flowery meadow to meet a rough road, making your way through mixed Jurassian forest to connect with another road. Turn right and walk a short distance downhill to reach the *Café-Restaurant Les Rochat* (☎ 024-434 11 61) at 1164m, 40 to 50 minutes from La Combaz. This restaurant is open all year and offers mattress-room accommodation for around Sfr30 per person (including breakfast and showers).

Pick up the marked path just down from Les Rochat. The route rises and dips through stands of broad-leaf trees and wide clearings before coming out at a sealed road. Follow a foot track up left beside the road for 2km to a signposted track turn-off and ascend gently to reach a little saddle

SWISS JURA

Creux du Van via Poëta-Raisse

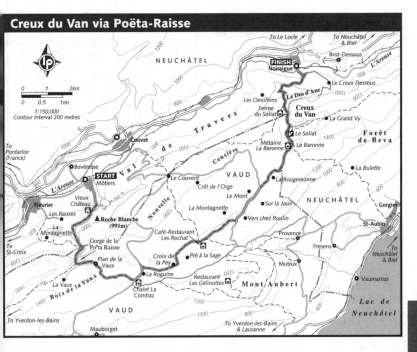

between low hills after 45 minutes to one hour. From here there is a nice view towards the rounded summit of Le Soliat slightly east of north.

Head quickly around right through two gates, then branch off left and sidle the slopes above the rolling grassy basin to the **Métairie La Baronne** (☎ *032-863 31 34*) at 1376m. This country restaurant offers dorm beds in a rustic loft at quite low rates. An old vehicle track climbs 500m around left to where a line of rock markings guides you straight up right to the 1463m top of **Le Soliat** after 30 to 40 minutes. In fine weather the panorama from Le Soliat reaches as far as the Savoy Alps in Italy.

Just a few paces on is the **Creux du Van**, the highlight of the walk. A path runs around the precipitous rim beside a drystone fence built to keep livestock (and people) a healthy distance from the cliff. A tiny enclosed valley forms a forest wilderness stretching away immediately below

the impressive 200m walls. To get the best angle on the Creux du Van head up around to the right (east), before doubling back to the cirque's lower side at the edge of the woods. From here a path cuts 350m left across the pastures to the **Ferme du Soliat** (☎ *032-863 31 36*) at 1386m. This charming restaurant (open mid-May to late October) offers beds in dorm accommodation from around Sfr45 with full board.

Follow the well-graded foot track known as the 'Sentier des Contours', which descends steeply through the forest in increasingly broad switchback curves into the clearing of **Les Oeuillons** (1014m). A narrow dirt road begins just below the restaurant here, and sidles rightward down the slope to intersect with a sealed road near a row of defensive tank obstacles. Make your way on easily down past the hamlet of **Vers chex Joly** and cross the Areuse River on a bridge to arrive at **Noiraigue** after one to 1¼ hours.

Mont Tendre

Duration	5¼–6½ hours
Distance	25km
Standard	easy-medium
Start	Le Pont
Finish	Le Sentier

Summary This full-day walk from the shore of Lac de Joux makes a steady (almost 700m) ascent over the rounded, 1679m summit of Mont Tendre, the highest point in the Swiss Jura.

Despite its relative height, Mont Tendre has a mildly contoured topography of gently rolling, lightly forested hills. Its slopes are crisscrossed by old dry-stone fences, many of which were built centuries ago and once served as lines of demarcation between farms or local communities.

Mont Tendre stands above the fjord-like Lac de Joux, the largest lake within the Jura range, and its smaller companion Lac Brenet. Lying at around 1000m, both lakes owe their existence to thick deposits of glacial silt, which formed an almost watertight seal in the otherwise porous Jurassian limestone.

With no above-ground outlet, the lake water drains away into subterraneous channels, which flow to the surface at the Grotte de l'Orbe. This powerful spring forms the source of the Orbe River. Once the most polluted lake in Switzerland, the water quality in the Lac de Joux has improved dramatically over the last few decades and the lake has now, thankfully, regained its natural crystal-clear state.

Maps

Recommended is the local tourist authorities' 1:50,000 skiing and walking map *La Vallée de Joux* (Sfr22). K+F's 1:60,000 *Lausanne La Côte St-Cergue Vallée de Joux* (Sfr24.80) also fully covers the route. Two SAW/FSTP 1:50,000 maps are otherwise needed: *La Sarraz* No 251T, and the latest (2000) edition of *St-Cergue* No 260T, which includes the adjoining map, *Vallée de Joux* No 250T (Swiss territory only) on the reverse side.

Vallée de Joux Watchmakers

It comes as a surprise to learn that the isolated Vallée de Joux – itself seemingly left behind by time – is the cradle of *haute horlogerie*, or high-precision watchmaking. Many internationally famous companies, including Breguet, Audemars-Piguet, Auguste Reymond, Berney-Blondeau and Jaeger-LeCoultre have workshops here. The world's oldest watchmaker, Blancpain, which was established in 1735 by Hugenots (Protestants of French origin), is also based in the Vallée de Joux.

The best and most expensive watches are entirely handcrafted from up to 1000 tiny parts that are accurate to within hundredths of a millimetre. A single 'work' typically costs tens – perhaps hundreds – of thousands of francs.

NEAREST TOWNS
Le Pont

The small village of Le Pont lies between Lac de Joux and Lac Brenet. The *Hôtel de la Truite* (☎ *021-841 17 71*) has rooms at standard rates.

Le Sentier

Le Sentier is near the southern tip of Lac de Joux. Regional Vallée de Joux tourist office (☎ 021-845 17 77, e otvj@valleedejoux.ch, w www.valleedejoux.ch) is in Centre Sportif.

There are lakeside tent sites at *Camping Le Rocheray* (☎ *021-845 51 74*) from Sfr4 plus Sfr6.50 per person. *Hôtel de Ville* (☎ *021-845 52 33*) offers singles/doubles from around Sfr40/80, while *Hôtel du Lion d'Or* (☎ *021-845 55 35*) and *Hôtel Bellevue* (☎ *021-845 57 20*) are slightly up-market.

GETTING TO/FROM THE WALK

The walk begins at Le Pont and ends at Le Sentier. Le Pont is best accessed by train on the Le Day–Le Brassus rail line, which runs along the Vallée de Joux. Le Sentier is on the same rail line. Le Day itself is on the Lausanne–Yverdon–Vallorbe rail line, and from Lausanne there are hourly connections to Le Pont until at least 7.40pm.

THE WALK

From the Le Pont train station, walk along the lakeside promenade and take the path leading around the reedy shoreline of **Lac de Joux** past holiday houses to reach the village of **L'Abbaye** after 35 to 40 minutes. Here the **Hôtel de Ville** (☎ *021-841 13 93)* has rooms for around Sfr50/100 per single/double. At the local bus stop a signpost directs you up a laneway to a lumberyard, then briefly left to a foot track that climbs away rightward. Carefully follow yellow markings along tracks in the forest, before cutting on up through attractive hillside meadows to meet a dirt road. Turn left here and make your way quickly on to **Les Croisettes** (1304m), where you meet the Chemin des Crêtes du Jura (Jura High Route) at a sealed road, after a further one to 1¼ hours.

Cross the cattle grid and immediately break away left onto a farm track; when you come to a fork, continue between its two branches. The route goes through lovely rolling herb fields to intersect with another sealed road at the **Pré de l'Haut** (1284m). After following this south-west until the sealed road ends just before a farmhouse, head off right along an alp track that leads through typical lightly forested Jurassian countryside. The yellow poisonous aconite, a rare member of the buttercup family, is found here. A signposted track departs left just before you reach Le Mazel (1416m) and sidles gently up the slope via a long grassy clearing to the lone barnyard of **Chalet de Pierre** at 1551m, 1¼ to 1½ hours from Les Croisettes.

Another vehicle track brings you up over the crest of the broad treeless range to the **Alpage et Buvette du Mont Tendre** (☎ *079-622 60 27)* at 1646m. This alp restaurant serves refreshments and simple meals, and walkers can sleep in the hay for a few francs. In May, the Buvette is based down at the Chalet Neuf du Mont Tendre (1513m), 1km away. From the Alpage, a white-red-white

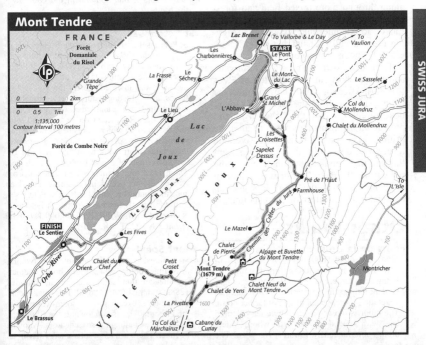

marked path guides you along the open rocky ridge to reach the top of **Mont Tendre** after 30 to 40 minutes. The 1679m summit is crowned by a prominent surveying triangle and in clear conditions gives nice views of the surrounding Jura as well as classic vistas across Lake Geneva towards the mightiest snowcapped peaks in the western Alps.

Descend gently south-west along the right-hand side of the range over snowdrifts persisting well into summer to the **Chalet de Yens** at 1589m. Make your way gently down to a signposted path junction beside an ancient stone fence and turnstile at **La Pivette** (1540m). From here, the Jura High Route continues south-west past the *Cabane du Cunay (☎ 021-907 76 150)*, which has dormitory accommodation.

Drop down northward past a track going off right to Les Bioux, following yellow diamond markings down through small pockets of trees to join a graded lane at the farmhouse of **Petit Croset** (1373m). The route rolls along through more mixed field and forest for a way, edging downward again as the Lac de Joux comes into view before reaching a sealed road at **Chalet du Chef** (1235m), 1¼ to 1½ hours from Mont Tendre.

Turn right down the road to a farm gate, and take a short-cut track left to **Les Fives** (1108m). After continuing down to meet the main road 1km from the village of Orient, head directly across the Orbe River and pick up an inconspicuous path just after the bridge. This leads left across a riverside meadow to a sawmill, then on to the right through the woods to terminate below the railway at 1013m **Le Sentier** after a final 40 to 50 minutes. Here the Rue de la Sagne can be quickly followed to the train station.

Other Walks

Etang de la Gruère

Lying at around 1000m in the Franches Montagnes district of southern Jura Canton, the Etang de la Gruère is one of the loveliest highland peat bogs in Switzerland. This area has vegetation more typical of climes farther north. The moor is mostly covered by a tea-coloured lake with several tiny armlets, whose waters drain subterraneously towards Tramelan. The original, smaller pond was enlarged by monks during the 17th century in order to provide water power for a nearby sawmill. Throughout the first half of the 20th century, conservationists fought a long battle to save this unique moor from destruction by peat cutting, and today the Etang de la Gruère is protected within a small nature reserve.

This very short and easy day walk leads from the small town of Saignelégier (where the famous Marché-Concours horse market takes place in early August) via the hamlet of Les Cerlatez to the Etang de la Gruère. While in the reserve, don't leave the paths as the peaty ground is easily damaged. The walk can be continued via Le Cernil to Tramelan. A *youth hostel (☎ 032-951 17 07,* e *bemont@youthhostel.ch)* is located at Le Bémont close to Saignelégier. Saignelégier can be reached by train either from Neuchâtel via La Chaux-de-Fonds, or from Basel and Biel/Bienne via Delémont. There are train connections from Tramelan to Biel/Bienne and Basel via Tavannes.

Both SAW/FSTP's 1:50,000 *Clos du Doubs* No 222T (Sfr22.50) and K+F's 1:60,000 *Delsberg Pruntrut Biel Solothurn* (Sfr24.80) cover the route.

St Peterinsel

St Peterinsel is an 'island' in the Bielersee connected to the shore by a narrow 3km-long spit. Once completely surrounded by water, St Peterinsel became a peninsula only after the level of the lake was lowered. Today the whole area forms an interesting nature reserve protecting the aquatic bird life and fauna. The philosopher Jean-Jacques Rousseau lived here in the 1760s, and the house in which he resided is now a museum. St Peterinsel can be visited as a very easy three-hour return walk from the village of Erlach, or as part of a boat trip on the Bielersee. The nearest train station is Le Landeron, from where there are occasional postbuses to Erlach and (in summer) regular boats to St Peterinsel. You don't really need a map, but St Peterinsel is covered by SAW/FSTP's 1:50,000 *Vallon de St-Imier* No 232T (Sfr22.50).

Mont Soleil

Steep forested slopes rise up immediately north of St-Imier before easing into a broad undulating plateau that culminates in the rounded 1288m summit of Mont Soleil. This small mountain top gives excellent views south-westward to the Fribourg Alps, south towards the Chasseral, as well as east along the stretched-out Vallon de St-Imier. There is a large solar-energy 'farm' on

Mont Soleil. Less than 1km to the east is Les Chenevières, a 400m-wide crater, which geologists believe was formed by the impact of a very large meteorite some 10,000 years ago.

From St-Imier, a 2½- to three-hour circuit walk can be made via Mont Soleil to the hamlet of Le Sergent (1182m), then down past Les Chenevières back to St-Imier.

A funicular railway goes up 350m to the scattered village of Mont Soleil, which cuts around one hour off the walking time. SAW/FSTP's 1:50,000 *Vallon de St-Imier* No 232T (Sfr22.50) covers the route in one map. (Although it does not clearly show Les Chenevières, the crater is an unmistakable feature on the map.)

Montagne de Moutier

This is an easy four-hour walk through a typically Jurassian landscape of rolling grassy plateaus dotted with old farmhouses and stone fences. The route leaves from the small industrial town of Choindez in Jura Canton and climbs south-west via the village of Vellerat, following paths to a country inn near the saddle of La Combe (1043m). From here farm tracks continue up through the gently undulating highland pastures of the Montagne de Moutier to the hamlet of Les Clos (1105m). The descent leads south-east through the Basse Montagne to Moutier (529m), the 'capital' of the Bernese Jura.

Trains running between Basel and Biel/Bienne stop at Choindez. From Moutier there are direct hourly trains to both Solothurn and Basel. K+F's 1:60,000 *Delsberg Pruntrut Biel Solothurn* (Sfr24.80) covers the walk on one map.

Dôle

The second-highest and most south-westerly summit in the Swiss Jura, the 1677m Dôle rises up surprisingly steeply between Lake Geneva and the French border. The open tops offer a full Alpine panorama sweeping across the great lake to the Mont Blanc, Dents du Midi and Les Diablerets massifs. The Dôle has long been a popular lookout point; its earliest and most distinguished visitors included the philosopher Jean-Jacques Rousseau and the young Goethe. Today, there is a television tower on the mountain, an aerial-navigation and weather station on its main peak, and the northern slopes have been developed for winter sports, yet the Dôle is worthy of the energetic climb required to reach its summit.

The Dôle can be ascended in a relatively easy four-hour semi-circuit from La Givrine (1290m), a small station on the Nyon–La Cure rail line. From La Givrine the route heads southwest across green rolling hills to the chairlift at Couvaloup de Crans, then climbs past the alp hut of Reculet Dessus (1479m) to meet a path sidling the main ridge running south-west to the summit. The descent route goes back along the main ridge to the Col de Porte (1559m), before traversing gently south-east down to another small saddle. Continue through a tiny valley past the farmlet of Le Vuarne (1319m), dropping through narrow clearings to reach a road leading down to St-Cergue.

Either SAW/FSTP's 1:50,000 *St-Cergue* No 260T (Sfr22.50) or K+F's 1:60,000 *Lausanne-La Côte-St-Cergue–Vallée de Joux* (Sfr24.80) can be used.

Chasseron

Rising up sharply from the Val de Travers, the 1606m Chasseron is the third-highest peak in the Swiss Jura. The mountain's eastern sides are an attractive, gently sloping plateau of highland pastures overlooking the Lac de Neuchâtel. The Chasseron is best reached from the town of Ste-Croix, from where a section of the long-distance Jura High Route leads along the grassy ridges to the summit. From here walkers can continue down to Môtiers via the Poëta-Raisse or ahead to the road at La Combaz.

The *Hôtel du Chasseron* (☎ 024 454 23 88), just below the summit of the Chasseron, offers panoramic rooms and dorm beds. Use either the local tourist authority's 1:25,000 *Carte d'Excursions Ste-Croix Les Rasses* (around Sfr18), SAW/FSTP's 1:50,000 *Val de Travers* No 241T or K+F's 1:60,000 *Chasseral Neuchâtel Val de Travers Ste-Croix* (Sfr24.80).

Gorges de l'Areuse

One of the nicest routes in the Neuchâtel Jura is the easy three-hour walk from Boudry (on the Yverdon-les-Bains–Neuchâtel rail line) up through the fascinating, wild Gorges de l'Areuse to Noiraigue, where the small Areuse River snakes its way through the mysterious and surprisingly narrow chasm. Following close to the rail lines past the station at the old milling hamlet of Champ de Moulin Dessous, the path leads up along stone stairways, over little stone bridges and past tumbling waterfalls in the damp, dark depths below the limestone cliffs.

In Boudry, the *Hôtel de l'Areuse* (☎ 032-842 11 40) has singles/doubles for Sfr40/80, while the *Hôtel du Lion d'Or* (☎ 032-842 10 16) has rooms for slightly more.

K+F's 1:60,000 *Chasseral Neuchâtel Val de Travers Ste-Croix* (Sfr24.80) covers the route on one map. Two 1:50,000 SAW/FSTP maps are otherwise needed: *Val de Travers* No 241T and *Avenches* No 242T (Sfr22.50 each).

SWISS JURA

Les Ponts-de-Martel to la Brévine

This is a 4½-hour walk in the Neuchâtel Jura. The route leads from the highland moors in the upper valley of the Grand Bied to the village of La Brévine near the French border in the remote Vallée de la Brévine. Although it lies only slightly above 1000m – much lower than many mountain valleys of the Alps – winter temperatures in the Vallée de la Brévine regularly fall below minus 30°C. Known as the 'Swiss Siberia', La Brévine is the coldest place in the country – but only in winter, with average summer temperatures as mild as elsewhere in the Jura. This region has Nordic-type vegetation typified by heathland and forests of birch.

The walk sets off southward from the village of Les Ponts-de-Martel (1009m) to Brot-Dessous across the marshy bed of an ancient lake, whose peaty ground is partly exploited and partly protected within a small nature reserve. The route continues westward high above the Val de Travers and across the crest of the Crête de Sapel before descending through scattered woodlands to La Brévine (1043m), where the *Hôtel de Ville* (☎ 032-935 13 44) has standard rooms.

Les Pont-de-Martel is the terminus of a small private railway from La Chaux-de-Fonds, which can be reached by frequent trains from Neuchâtel and Biel/Bienne. From La Brévine there are some five daily postbuses (until around 5.30pm) to Fleurier, from where there are hourly train connections to Neuchâtel.

Two SAW/FSTP 1:50,000 maps cover the route: *Le Locle* No 231T and *Val de Travers* No 241T (Sfr22.50).

Saut & Côtes du Doubs

Rising in France, the Doubs River drains virtually all of the northern Jura before flowing on into larger rivers of the Rhône basin. The Doubs forms a lengthy part of the Franco–Swiss border, and even flows briefly through Switzerland before re-entering the French Jura at the village of Brémoncourt. As is typical in the limestone areas of the Jura, the Doubs' water level rises and falls fairly dramatically depending on recent rainfall. In many places the river has cut out gorges. An easy four- to five-hour route follows the southern (ie, Swiss) side of the Doubs between the Lac des Brenets and the small riverside hamlet of Maison Monsieur, a wild stretch of the river that lies in Neuchâtel Canton.

To reach the start of the walk take one of the tourist boats that leave from the village of Les Brenets every 45 minutes from May until late October. The 20-minute boat trip takes you through the attractive gorges of the Lac des Brenets to the Saut du Doubs, where the waters of the lake plummet 27m into the artificial reservoir of Lac de Moron. The route leaves from the landing jetty, passing by the falls before it sidles high around the steep-sided Lac de Moron. After a short, steep descent at the dam wall, the way leads on for hours through the little mossy gorges, quiet riverside flats and anglers' cottages of the Côtes du Doubs to tranquil Maison Monsieur.

Les Brenets can be reached via private narrow-gauge railway from Le Locle, which is itself accessible by a 50-minute train ride from Biel/Bienne. Some three daily postbuses run from Biaufond via Maison Monsieur to the regional centre of La Chaux-de-Fonds, from where there are train connections to Neuchâtel and Biel/Bienne.

Several places in Les Brenets have rooms at slightly above-average rates: *Hôtel du Lac* (☎ 032-932 12 66), *Hôtel de la Couronne* (☎ 032-932 11 37) and *Hôtel-Restaurant du Doubs* (☎ 032-932 10 91). There are two en-route places to stay: *Hôtel du Saut-du-Doubs* (☎ 032-932 10 70), near Saut du Doubs landing jetty, has a few rooms, and the attractive *Hôtel de la Maison-Monsieur* (☎ 032-968 60 60), at Maison Monsieur, has dorm beds.

When waters are low the Doubs can be easily crossed, so it may be a good idea to carry a passport or identity card in case of border control. K+F's *Chasseral Neuchâtel Val de Travers Ste-Croix* (Sfr24.80) covers the route on one map. Two SAW/FSTP 1:50,000 maps are otherwise needed: *Le Locle* No 231T and *Vallon de St-Imier* No 232T (Sfr22.50 each).

Southern Fribourg & Vaud

The southern part of Fribourg (Freiburg) Canton, including the Haute Gruyères and Schwarzsee (Lac Noir) districts, is an extensive area of Alpine foothills that drains northward via the Saline River into the Rhine basin. Fribourg's higher summits push up well beyond the tree line, often surpassing the 2000m level.

The southernmost part of Vaud Canton is a mountainous region sandwiched – almost as an enclave – between the Bernese Oberland to the east, the Valais to the south and Fribourg to the north. It includes the Pays d'Enhaut and Ormond-Dessus districts as well as the mighty Muverans and Les Diablerets massif in the southern Vaud Alps.

Except for German-speaking communities living along Fribourg's cantonal border with Bern, this is a francophone region. Together the compact ranges of southern Fribourg and Vaud form an unexpectedly interesting and varied region for walking. Six routes are featured in this chapter.

INFORMATION
Maps
Editions MPA Verlag's 1:120,000 *Vaud/Waadt* (Sfr14.80), a tourist map showing walking routes and other features, gives a good overview of the Vaud Alps and parts of the Fribourg Pre-Alps.

Sheet No 3 of the BL/OFT's 1:200,000 (four-sheet) series covers the entire region.

Books
The only regional titles are in French and German. Kümmerly + Frey's (K+F) *Pays de Fribourg* and *Freiburgerland* (Sfr22.80 each), is a regional walking guide published in separate French and German editions. K+F's German-language *Rundwanderungen Westschweiz* describes walks throughout francophone Switzerland.

Information Sources
For information on the Fribourg Pre-Alps, contact Info Pays de Fribourg (☎ 026-915

Highlights

Balloons above the mountain village of Chateau d'Oex, Vaud Pre-Alps.

- Looking into the Rhône Valley almost 2000m below on the Tour des Muverans walk
- Admiring Fribourg-style shingled-roof alp huts on the Col de Chaude walk
- Gazing up to the Vanil Noir from the superb mountain cirque of Les Morteys
- Traversing below striking limestone peaks on the Tour de Famelon walk

92 92, fax 026-915 92 99, ⓔ info.tourisme @pays-de-fribourg.ch, Ⓦ www.pays-de-fribourg.ch). For information on the Vaud Alps contact the Association Touristique des Alpes vaudoises (ⓔ info@alpes.ch, Ⓦ www.alpes.ch). Some information on the Vaud Alps is also available from the Lake Geneva regional tourist office (☎ 021-613 26 26, fax 021-613 26 00, ⓔ lake .geneva.reg@fastnet.ch, Ⓦ www.lakegeneva-region .ch) .

MARK HONAN

Southern Fribourg & Vaud

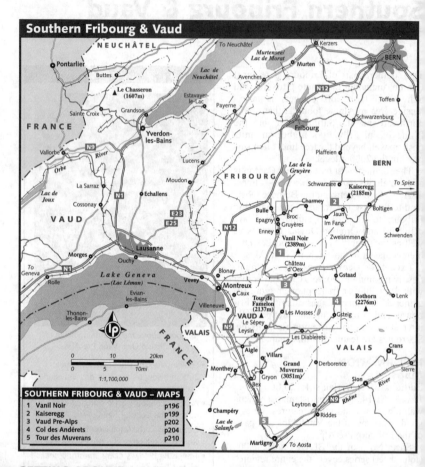

SOUTHERN FRIBOURG & VAUD – MAPS	
1 Vanil Noir	p196
2 Kaiseregg	p199
3 Vaud Pre-Alps	p202
4 Col des Andérets	p204
5 Tour des Muverans	p210

GETTING AROUND

The one-day *Fri-Pass* costs Sfr26 (or Sfr13 for holders of a Half Fare Card) and gives unlimited travel on Fribourg Canton's regional (GFM) rail and bus network. It also includes connecting bus services to Boltigen (Bernese Oberland) and to Vevey (on Lake Geneva).

The seven-day *Regional Pass Leman* costs Sfr150 (Sfr120 concession, Sfr75 children) and covers the entire Swiss shore of Lake Geneva, including all of Vaud canton. It allows three days of unlimited travel and four days at 50% reduction. Fares on postbus

services to Les Plans-sur-Bex, Les Mosses, Château d'Oex and Gstaad are also half-price; the Berneuse gondola lift and several other cableways have a 25% reduction.

GATEWAY
Montreux

Montreux is situated on the eastern Lake Geneva shoreline – an area known as the 'Swiss Riviera' that enjoys marvellous vistas across the water toward the Mont Blanc massif. Popular with well-to-do foreign (especially British) tourists since the mid-1850s, the city boasts many grand old

CLEM LINDENMAYER

MARTIN MOOS

CLEM LINDENMAYER

Top: A mountain hut stands in a cirque of sheer cliffs below the 2389m summit of the Vanil Noir, Fribourg Pre-Alps. **Bottom Left:** The postbus stop sign is a familiar sight to walkers.
Bottom Right: The imposing ridge lines of the Rochers de Naye, a lookout summit in the Vaud Pre-Alps accessible from Montreux and the Col de Jaman.

Left: The classic 'tooth' form of the Matterhorn dominates the town of Zermatt.
Top Right: A walker strides toward the Grosser Aletschgletscher, visible in the distance.
Middle Right: The small restaurant at Chalbermatten in the Zmuttal, above Zermatt.
Bottom: The Alps' longest glacier, the Grosser Aletschgletscher, descends from the Jungfraujoch.

CHRIS MELLOR

DALE BUCKTON

CLEM LINDENMAYER

CLEM LINDENMAYER

hotels and villas. The Château de Chillon, a famously picturesque medieval castle (entry Sfr7.50), stands on the lake shore several kilometres to the south.

For information, contact Montreux tourist office (☎ 021-962 84 84, fax 021-963 78 95, ⓔ tourism@montreuxtourism.ch, ⓦ www .montreux.ch), Ave du Theâtre 5.

The Rochers de Naye, a classic 2042m lookout peak, is directly accessible from Montreux by a cog railway. A scenic three- to four-hour high-level traverse route leads from the Rochers de Naye summit via the Col de Jaman and Le Molard (1703m) to the upper station of the cog railway at Les Pléiades (1360m). Montreux is also the ter-mination of the long Alpine Pass Route.

Places to Stay & Eat In Montreux-Territet are the local *youth hostel (☎ 021-963 49 34, ⓔ montreux@youthhostel.ch, 8 Passage de l'Auberge)*, with dorm beds for Sfr29, and the *Hôtel Villa Germaine (☎ 021-963 15 28, 3 Ave de Collonge)*, which offers singles/ doubles from Sfr50/100. The *Hôtel du Pont (☎ 021-963 22 49, ⓔ hoteldupont@hotmail .com, Rue du Pont 12)* has rooms from Sfr60/120.

There is a budget restaurant in the *Migros* supermarket *(49 Ave du Casino)*. At *Chez Steph (37 Ave des Alpes)* you can eat from around Sfr12 on a terrace overlooking the lake. Nearby is *Paradise (58 Grand-Rue)*, with a salad buffet (Sfr2.60 per 100 grams).

Getting There & Away Montreux is on the main Lausanne–Brig rail line with hourly express trains; slower regional trains pass through Montreux approximately half-hourly. Running through numerous tight curves and tunnels, the private Montreux-Oberland-Bahn (MOB) connects Montreux with Spiez via the towns of Château d'Oex, Saanen, Gstaad and Zweisimmen in the Vaud and Bernese Pre-Alps.

From the end of May until late Septem-ber numerous ferries link Montreux with re-sorts around Lake Geneva, including villages and towns on the lake's French (southern) shoreline. Outside the summer tourist season boats run far less frequently.

Fribourg & Vaud Pre-Alps

The pre-Alpine ranges of cantons Fribourg and Vaud (called the Préalpes romandes in French, or the Freiburger und Waadtländer Voralpen in German) form an often rugged band of mountains sweeping south-west from the Fribourg Mittelland across the dis-tricts of Gruyères and Pays d'Enhaut as far as Lake Geneva. Unlike most other areas of the Alpine foothills, these mountains are composed of hard limestone that frequently erodes into jagged peaks and interesting karst fields (see the boxed text 'Karst' in the Valais chapter). With their sheer rock faces and craggy peaks, the Fribourg/Vaud Pre-Alps excite the attentions of many a moun-tain rock climber. Despite their modest height when compared with the 'true' Alpine summits to the south, the ranges of this area offer some splendidly scenic walks.

The moist climate prevailing in southern Fribourg and Vaud makes this some of the choicest dairying country in Switzerland. Beginning in the 14th century, steadily ris-ing demand for hard, durable cheeses gave rise to an important dairy industry centred in these Alpine foothills. Local cheeses, particularly Sbrinz and Gruyères types, were exported to many parts of western Eu-rope. Cheese-making brought widespread prosperity to the local farmers, and the 'Fri-bourg' style of rural architecture (which is also common in the southern Vaud) gradu-ally developed. These graceful houses with their high roofs of wooden shingles are a typical feature of the countryside.

ACCESS TOWNS
Les Mosses
This modest winter-sport resort lies imme-diately south of the broad grassy Col des Mosses (1445m), a low pass marking the continental watershed between the Rhine basin (on its northern side) and the catch-ment area of the Rhône (to the south). A popular easy day walk goes up to Lac Lio-son, where the *Restaurant du Lac Lioson*

(☎ *024-491 14 66, fax 491 10 44)* offers dormitory accommodation.

Les Mosses has a tourist office (☎ 024-491 10 24, e otm@lesmosses.ch, w www.lesmosses.ch) and one general store.

The *Hotel Les Fontaines (☎ 024-491 12 12, fax 024-491 20 48)* has dorm beds for Sfr18 and singles/doubles from Sfr45/90 (room prices do not include breakfast). The *Hotel Chaussy (☎ 024-491 11 47)* offers rooms from Sfr40/80.

Postbuses running between Château d'Oex and Le Sépey (a station on the Aigle–Les Diablerets rail line) pass through Les Mosses up to seven times daily in either direction; the last buses to both Château d'Oex and Le Sépey leave Les Mosses just after 6.15pm.

Bulle

Bulle is the centre of the Pays de Gruyère. Its major landmark is the 13th-century castle, now administrative offices.

The town tourist office (☎ 026-919 85 00, fax 026-919 85 01, e info@la-gruyere.ch, w www.la-gruyere.ch) is on Grand Rue.

The *Hôtel le Tonnelier (☎ 026-912 77 45, fax 026-912 39 86, Grand Rue 31)* has singles/doubles from Sfr55/108. The *Cafe Fribourgeois* serves budget local cuisine from Sfr18 per meal.

There are direct hourly GFM buses from Fribourg to Bulle (30 minutes) as well as slower services via Le Bry (one hour), but train connections to Lausanne and Geneva can go via Romont, Palezieux or Montbovon.

Château d'Oex

This small town (968m) is the centre of the Pays d'Enhaut district, and has been developed into a resort for both summer and winter outdoor sports. There are some excellent day and overnight hikes in the nearby mountains, particularly around the Vanil Noir (2389m) to the north and the Gummfluh (2458m) to the south, as well as easy day walks along the Sarine River.

Château d'Oex has a helpful tourist office (☎ 026-924 25 25, fax 026-924 25 26, e chateau-doex@bluewin.ch, w www.chateau-doex.ch).

The *Au Berceau (☎ 026-924 62 34)* has riverside tent sites for Sfr4.50 plus Sfr5 per person. The *youth hostel (☎ 026-924 64 04)* has dorm beds for Sfr24. The *Buffet de la Gare (☎ 026-924 77 17)* has singles/doubles from Sfr45/80 and the *Hôtel La Printanière (☎ 026-924 61 13)* charges from Sfr45/80.

There is a restaurant in the *Coop* supermarket below the train station. *Le Relais* (closed Tuesday evening and Wednesday) serves decent pizza from Sfr12.

Château d'Oex is on the Montreux-Oberland-Bahn (MOB) rail line that links Lake Geneva with Spiez (via Zweisimmen) in the Bernese Oberland; departures are at least hourly. If you are travelling to or from Fribourg a rail/bus combination via Montbovon and Bulle is necessary. Postbuses also run frequently between Le Sépey and Château d'Oex via Les Mosses.

Vanil Noir

Duration	2 days
Distance	20km
Standard	medium
Start	Praz-Jean
Finish	Grandvillard
Nearest Towns	Jaun, Im Fang, Grandvillard, Château d'Oex

Summary A spectacular walk into the wildest part of the Fribourg Pre-Alps.

Forming a marked natural division between the Gruyères district in Fribourg and the Pays d'Enhaut of the Vaud, at 2389m the imposing Vanil Noir is one of the loftier summits of Switzerland's pre-Alps. The massif has all the feel of the Alps proper, with precipitous, rocky buttresses on both sides, which have spared it from the often excessive skiing development seen in other pre-Alpine areas.

Having been severely overgrazed by sheep in the past, today the Vanil Noir is protected in one of the wildest nature reserves in the region (see the boxed text 'The Vanil Noir Nature Reserve' following).

SOUTHERN FRIBOURG & VAUD

The Vanil Noir Nature Reserve

This topographically and biologically interesting area receives heavy winter snowfalls and has unusually varied Alpine flora. In 1964, the Swiss Society for the Protection of Nature (now Pro Natura) began a campaign to protect the Vanil Noir area, which culminated in 1972 with its first major land purchase around the massif. Today Pro Natura administers a reserve of some 15 sq km, inhabited by large numbers of free-roaming ibex and chamois.

Maps

The only walking map that fully covers the walk is the SAW/FSTP's 1:50,000 sheet *Rochers de Naye* No 262T (Sfr22.50).

Regulations

The area surrounding the Vanil Noir is a nature reserve. Here, it is strictly prohibited to bring dogs (even if on a leash), camp or light fires. Walkers should not leave the designated paths.

NEAREST TOWNS
Jaun & Im Fang

Jaun (1030m) lies at the foot of both the Jaunpass (to the east) and the Euschelpass (to the north). Jaun and Im Fang (922m), 3km downvalley on the language border, are the only German-speaking villages of the upper Saline basin. Jaun is known for its spectacular if unnatural waterfall, which spurts out of a hydroelectric tunnel, and the Cantorama/Haus des Gesangs, a wooden Fribourg-style building (entry Sfr4).

Contact Jaun tourist office (☎ 026-929 81 81, Ⓦ www.jaun.ch/tourismus) for more information. *Hotel Hochmatt* (☎/fax 026-929 82 07) in Im Fang and Jaun's *Hotel zum Wasserfall* (☎ 026-929 82 06, fax 026-929 86 03) have rooms from around Sfr45/90 single/double.

Regional GFM buses run between Bulle (see Access Towns earlier in the chapter) and Jaun via Im Fang up to 10 times daily; the last bus leaves Bulle just after 6.30pm; it's a pleasant 30-minute trip. If coming from the Bernese Oberland, there are five postbuses from Boltigen (see the Kaiseregg walk) to Jaun.

Grandvillard

Grandvillard is the largest village in the Haut Gruyères district. The *Hotel du Vanil Noir* (☎ 026-928 12 65) has rooms for around Sfr45/90. From Grandvillard there are four daily regional GFM buses to Bulle (25 minutes); the last bus leaves Grandvillard around 7pm. The buses run via Grandvillard train station, 2km west of the village, from where there are connections to Montbovon (on the MOB line) and to Bulle/Fribourg.

There are hourly trains on the MOB's Montreux–Zweisimmen–Spiez rail line, running north to Bulle and south to Montbovon.

GETTING TO/FROM THE WALK

GFM buses running between Bulle and Jaun pass Praz-Jean (also spelled Pra Jean) up to 10 times daily – there is a bus stop at the route turnoff. Walkers arriving from Boltigen via the Jaunpass will have to change buses in Jaun (or walk 1½ hours downvalley to Praz-Jean). Make sure the driver knows where you want to get off.

For information on transport from the end of the walk, see Grandvillard under Nearest Towns earlier.

THE WALK
Day 1: Praz-Jean to Cabane des Marrindes

2¾–4 hours, 11km, 978m ascent

From the GFM bus stop at Praz-Jean (890m), walk south along a narrow road past an alp hut selling cheese and butter on your right. The road gradually steepens, passing a (right) turnoff to the Vallée de Motélon as it climbs beside the cascading Riusseau du Gros Mont through clearings in the spruce forest. On both sides of the valley, swathes of forest destroyed by the storm 'Lothar' are visible (see the boxed text 'Lothar, Storm of the Century' later). The road winds on up to end in a car park at the edge of the lovely **Gros Mont** after 1¼ to 1¾ hours. From here you get spectacular views directly across

Vanil Noir

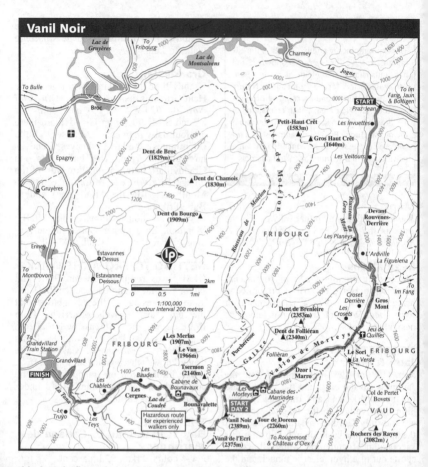

this broad, flat subalpine pasture to the 2236m Dent de Ruth and the white limestone crags of the Hochmatt jutting up behind grassy ridges to the north-east.

Follow an alp track south through a gate marking the boundary of the Vanil Noir nature reserve. The route rises almost imperceptibly across a watershed at 1404m (on the Fribourg–Vaud cantonal border) to reach a junction near a beautiful chalet with the classic Fribourg-style wooden-shingle roof and *Rauchfang* chimney. Here, take a path south-west up into the tiny **Vallon de Morteys**. Note how the valley's mostly bare

northern side (which is exposed to the sun and therefore more prone to avalanches) contrasts with its southern slopes (where the winter snow is firmer and remains much longer), which are forested with spruce and arolla pine.

The route climbs on beside the tiny splashing stream, finally switchbacking up through broken karst rock to arrive at the ***Cabane des Marrindes*** (☎ 026-436 57 47), 1½ to 2¼ hours from Gros Mont. This Pro Natura-owned hut, which has dorm beds for Sfr17, is another typical Fribourg-style construction. It stands at 1868m in a classic

Lothar, Storm of the Century

On 26 December 1999, Lothar, a massive low-pressure system with winds exceeding 200km/h, swept over southern Germany, south-eastern France and Switzerland. This storm – by far the worst since reliable records began – killed more than 20 people and caused billions of Swiss francs damage.

Lothar flattened some 200 sq km of forest in Switzerland, mostly in mountain areas. Foresters worked feverishly to clear the dead wood from the forests, often using helicopters to get the logs out of difficult sites. There is continuing concern, however, about the further spread of the bark beetle (which breed in dead wood) and the dramatic increase in deer numbers (due to additional natural fodder in newly opened clearings). Most worryingly, the storm destroyed avalanche-hindering Alpine forests (known in German as *Bannwälder*).

sheer-sided cirque under the Vanil Noir looking out north-east toward the jagged ridges of the Hochmatt and Dent de Ruth.

Day 2: Cabane des Marrindes to Grandvillard

2¾–4½ hours, 9km, 322m ascent
From a junction by the stream below the hut, follow the (left) branch on gently up-valley (south-west) over the Alpine pastures of **Les Morteys**, where chamois and ibex often browse. This broad foot track cuts up left around a bluff, then climbs around the right side of a snow basin below the valley headwall (the crack of a geological fault is visible just up to the left). These slopes are scattered with low shrubs of common mezereon (Alpine daphne), a hardy perennial that produces tiny pink flowers. Make a final steep ascent through broken karst to reach a route junction at a gap on the ridge (roughly 2190m), 50 minutes to 1¼ hours from the hut. (From this point, more experienced Alpine walkers can opt for the loop via the summit of Vanil Noir – see the Alternative Route at the end of the walk description.)

Traverse down rightward over slab ledges on the raw, steep slopes, where tiny purple pennycress grows in the shelter of the rocks, before descending north-west via a steep rocky spur to a col (1996m). From here, there is a good view north-east down to a picturesque alp hut in the upper valley of Porcheresse below the heavily slanted grassy slopes of Galère. Drop down steeply south-west directly into the glacial basin of **Bounavalette** (1773m), where a rustic alp hut stands near a small tarn right under the Vanil Noir, 30 to 40 minutes from the ridge-top junction. Sidle on down another 10 to 15 minutes over Alpine meadows dotted with yellow gentians to reach the *Cabane de Bounavaux* (☎ 079-634 20 76). This hut at 1620m is also run by Pro Natura, and is open mid-June to mid-October (otherwise locked); dorm beds cost around Sfr30 with breakfast.

Continue on down through pockets of forest above the **Lac de Coudré** to an alp hut at the end of a dirt road, then follow this over pastures to meet a sealed road. Take an unsignposted turn-off a few paces down left, and follow the stream through forest clearings before crossing on a bridge just below a small weir. A broad track leads on down the left bank of the stream (a more direct route than that shown on most walking maps) to meet another road. Here, go right directly across the stream, following the sealed road down in several curves before you turn off right again onto a gravel road reaching to the first houses of **Grandvillard**, 1½ to two hours from the Cabane de Bounavaux. The postbus stop is near the church and village square, 10 minutes along to the right.

Alternative Route via Vanil Noir Summit

2–2½ hours, 3km, 200m ascent
This is a difficult route suited only to walkers with sound Alpine experience.

From the ridge top at around 2190m, a rough unmarked foot track traverses just below the eastern side of the ridge, with fixed cables. If this first part of the route is snowed over early or later in the season, a well-used but more difficult route rock-hops along the ridgetop itself. There are fixed cables to hold onto in exposed sections. A final climb rightward over a tiny high meadow dotted with white crocus brings you to the 2389m summit of the **Vanil Noir** after 50 minutes to 1¼ hours. From up here you get a really great panorama north across the Mittelland to the Jura, south-east to the Eiger, Mönch and Jungfrau in the eastern Bernese Oberland, south to Les Diablerets and south-west to the Dents du Midi and Mont Blanc massifs. You'll find the summit logbook in a steel cylinder by the metal cross.

Descend south-west along the ridge, then cut down to the right (west) over very steep slopes (where fixed chains again add some security). The route spirals on down through gravel and broken rock before skirting around a tarn to meet the main path near the alp hut at Bounavalette, one to 1¼ hours from the summit.

Kaiseregg

Duration	4¾–7 hours
Distance	14km
Standard	medium
Start	Schwarzsee/Gypsera
Finish	Boltigen

Summary This is an energetic climb over one of the Fribourg Pre-Alps' finest lookout peaks, then down into the Simmental, a valley renowned for its Bernese-style wooden architecture.

Towering above the dark waters of the Schwarzsee, the 2185m Kaiseregg stands slightly to the west of the Fribourg–Bern cantonal border. The summit makes an excellent lookout point, with a panorama that includes the Swiss Mittelland, the surrounding jagged ranges of the Alpine foothills and the more spectacular major summits of the Alps to the south. The 1100m ascent requires some heavy legwork, while the 1200m descent is often steep and rocky. The route is generally in condition from at least early June until late October.

Warning

The Swiss Army holds shooting exercises in a number of areas around the Kaiseregg for short periods in the summer and autumn. At such times walkers may have a short wait before the sentries give the all clear to pass through. To check on the current situation, call the regional army information office in Fribourg (☎ 026-350 82 09).

Maps

The best walking map is the 1:25,000 *Schwarzseegebiet Plasselb und Jaun* (Sfr17), produced by K+F and the local tourist authorities. Also very good is the SAW/FSTP 1:50,000 *Gantrisch* map 253T (Sfr22.50).

NEAREST TOWNS
Schwarzsee

The name of both the lake and the holiday locality scattered around the reedy shoreline, Schwarzsee (called Lac Noir by francophone Swiss) lies at 1046m in the north-eastern Fribourg Pre-Alps. The Schwarzsee's dark waters are set before a backdrop of high limestone peaks with remarkable jagged summits that rise up dramatically from more softly contoured grassy hills. The local people here speak an earthy dialect similar to neighbouring regions of Bern Canton, although the Schwarzsee is on the linguistic border and walkers are likely to hear as much French spoken as German.

For information contact the Scwarzsee tourist office (☎ 026-412 13 13, fax 026-412 13 39, e info@schwarzsee-tourismus.ch, w www.schwarzsee-tourismus.ch).

Camping Seeweid (☎ 026-493 41 58) has tent sites for Sfr7 plus Sfr6 per person. The Friends of Nature's *Naturfreundehaus Aurore* (☎/fax 026-412 11 23) has dorm beds for just Sfr12. The *Hotel Gypsera* (☎ 026-412 11 12) has singles/doubles from around Sfr40/80.

Schwarzsee is accessible from Fribourg (on the main Geneva–Bern–Zürich–St Gallen rail line) by direct GFM public buses via Plaffeien around 10 times per day. The last bus leaves Fribourg train station at roughly 6.45pm; it's a pleasant one-hour trip through green rolling hills.

Boltigen

The walk ends in the village of Boltigen, which has some fine examples of grandiose Bernese-style wooden architecture. The *Hotel Bären* (☎ 033-773 73 70) and *Hotel Des Alpes* (☎ 033-773 60 42) have singles/doubles from around Sfr45/90.

Boltigen is on the MOB's Montreux–Zweisimmen–Spiez rail line. Postbuses from Boltigen run across the Jaunpass to Jaun (see the Vanil Noir walk).

GETTING TO/FROM THE WALK

Walkers can set off either directly from the Gypsera postbus stop at Schwarzsee, or take the chairlift from Gypsera up to Riggisalp (1493m). The chairlift runs from mid-June until the end of October and takes some of the grunt and wheeze out of the long climb up to the Kaiseregg; the one-way fare is Sfr8/5 adults/children.

Walkers who climb the Kaiseregg as a day trip from Fribourg may find the Fri-Pass

an economical public transport option (see Getting Around at the start of the chapter).

THE WALK

Walkers starting out directly from Schwarzsee (see also the Alternative Route from Riggisalp at the end of the walk description) can take the signposted foot track 200m east of **Gypsera** (1047m), which leads up beside the Riggisalpbach. The path soon crosses to the stream's true right (ie, eastern) bank, ascending steadily over rich Alpine pastures to the jingling of cowbells. Climb on past the alp hut of **Hürlisboden** (1440m) to arrive at the *Alpwirtschaft Salzmatt* after 1½ to two hours. This Alpine dairy at 1637m on a broad col looking down into the pleasant green upper valley of Geissalp serves simple refreshments.

Continue southward up a spur coming down from the Kaiseregg, breaking away to the right not long after you pass the upper end of the ski tow. The path makes a rising traverse along the mountainside herb fields through occasional wooden stiles, before snaking up steeply in switchbacks through broken rock to come out onto the saddle of the **Kaisereggpass** (2072m) after

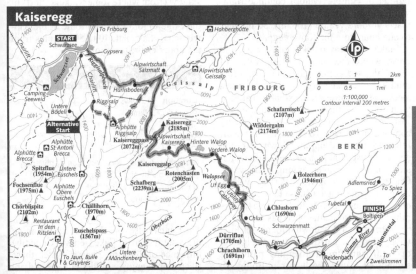

one to 1½ hours. These green lawns offer a nice place for a short rest before making the final ascent.

The 20- to 30-minute return walk to the 2185m **Kaieregg** skirts north-east along the rocky southern side of the ridge over stony slopes covered with stinging nettles. The summit panorama includes the Schwarzsee and the surrounding jagged ranges of the Fribourg/Vaud Pre-Alps, while to the north the land plummets away into the Swiss Mittelland, where the cities of Bern and Fribourg can be made out. Standing out in the distant south are the snow-topped mountains between the Wildstrubel and Les Diablerets massifs. After signing your name in the summit logbook, backtrack to the Kaiereggpass.

Descend south-east on a white-red-white marked path, which winds down to the right through raw karst rock into **Kaiereggalp**, a basin of grassed-over moraines enclosed by the craggy peaks. The route meets a vehicle track at *Alpwirtschaft Kaieregg* (1799m), a mountain dairy that sells drinks (and fresh milk) in July and August. Follow this rough road on down through a stone fence marking the Fribourg–Bern cantonal border, then immediately (ie, just before you get to the farmlet of **Hintere Walop**) continue rightward around past a small, shallow lake to reach **Vordere Walop** (1665m), 50 minutes to one hour from the Kaiereggpass.

Make your way quickly on over a slight crest, when the emerald-green waters of the **Walopsee** come into sight. The often muddy route leads high around the lake's steep eastern side along slopes scattered with dotted gentians to a small square barn just before the upper station of a utility cableway at **Uf Egg** (1664m). Here leave off left and begin dropping down into the spruce forest in numerous steep spirals beside impressive overhanging rock walls. One to 1¼ hours on from Vordere Walop, the path comes out at **Chlus** (1140m, shown on some signposts as 'Klus'), where the terrain softens into gentle open pastures.

Proceed smoothly down through this little valley along the narrow road via the hamlet of **Farni** (ignoring a diverging path here signposted 'Tubetal/Adlemsried/Boltigen')

to **Schwarzenmatt** (935m). Turn off left along a sealed laneway leading quickly out of the village, following sporadic yellow diamonds gradually down past a milking shed among meadows fringing the Simmental to meet a road. About 150m down from here take a foot track going off left down beside a stream to arrive at the main road in **Boltigen** after a final 30 to 40 minutes. The train station (818m) is a further five minutes along to the right past the tourist office.

Alternative Route from Riggisalp
40–50 minutes, 3km, 144m ascent

From the upper chairlift station at Riggisalp (1493m), walk a short way south along a rough gravelled track, then take a left-hand turn-off leading down into the grassy bowl to the *Alphütte Riggisalp* (☎ 026-412 11 07). This large alp hut with a high, Fribourg-style shingled roof is open early June to late September, and offers fresh milk, cheese and basic refreshments as well as dorm beds for around Sfr25. Follow a yellow-marked trail up to the barn past a tiny tarn nestling in a rounded crater-like trough, before sidling up along steep slopes above the Riggisalp. The route passes under a winter ski tow (from where some walkers short cut directly up the slope to rejoin the path on the ridge to join the main route at the Alpwirtschaft Salzmatt, 40 to 50 minutes from the upper chairlift station.

Col de Chaude

Duration	1–2 days
Distance	27km
Standard	easy-medium
Start	Les Mosses
Finish	Montreux
Summary	This is a long but thoroughly enjoyable ramble through the high rolling hills of the Vaud Pre-Alps. It is the 15th (final) leg of the Alpine Pass Route.

The route crosses the abrupt ranges fronting the eastern shore of Lake Geneva. Under the influence of this large body of water, these steep slopes enjoy a milder climate and are covered by luxuriant, mixed broadleaf forests.

Following a sunny and relatively low course, the walk can generally be undertaken from early May to late November. The route is a bit too long to be done comfortably in a single day (8–11 hours), but unfortunately the few better en-route accommodation options are near the start and finish of the walk.

Maps

Either the Editions MPA Verlag's 1:50,000 walking map *Alpes Vaudoises* (Sfr27.90) or the SAW/FSTP 1:50,000 *Rochers de Naye* No 262T (Sfr22.50) can be used for this hike.

GETTING TO/FROM THE WALK

For information on transport to/from Les Mosses and Montreux, see Gateways and Access Towns earlier in the chapter.

THE WALK

See the Vaud Pre-Alps map, p202

From Les Mosses post office briefly follow the main road north over the Col des Mosses pass height, then take a left sealed turnoff leading under the transmission lines. The route continues right via a short side road up a grassy slope to join a vehicle track, which itself rises slightly to meet a larger gravel road at a bend. Here go right along the edge of the forest, gently descending beside a barn to a main road and continuing right past military barracks to reach **La Lécherette** (1379m) after 40 to 50 minutes. The *Hôtel-Restaurant La Lécherette* (☎ 026-924 62 59) is one of several places in this tiny resort village with singles/doubles from around Sfr40/80.

Pick up the route at the small road behind the La Lécherette post office (signposted 'La Sia/Les Moutins'). Head up past a small chapel then along a path past houses to meet another sealed road. Turn left and continue onto slopes high above the Lac de L'Hongrin reservoir with unusual double-curved dam walls. Painted route markings lead on past the restaurant at **Col Sonlomont** (1503m) to a car park at the end of the road, from where a short foot track cuts up the grassy slope to reach the **Linderrey** farmhouse at 1669m

after two to three hours. There are clear views westward from here to the adjacent Rochers de Naye.

Drop down in zigzags through steep pastures to meet the L'Hongrin valley road and follow this right across the bridge to the farmhouse at **La Vuichoude d'en Bas**. From here an old mule track leads left up grassy slopes to a farmlet then through light forest into the head of this tiny valley past the **Chalet de Chaude** (1475m), a traditional stone homestead with a graceful wooden-shingle roof. From above the barnyard continue along the sealed road to reach the **Col de Chaude** at 1621m, 1½ to 2 hours from La Vuichoude. The village of Villeneuve on Lake Geneva is visible from here. A steep signposted path heads right up the Rochers de Naye, from where there are fine views of the lake.

Descend along the road from the col, cutting off a section of curves on a steep foot track, to reach a narrow grassed-over road leading off right after one to 1½ hours. This climbs slightly through the forest for 30 to 40 minutes to meet another surfaced road at the *Auberge de Sonchaux* (☎ 021-963 44 67), open May to October, at 1261m. The Auberge offers dorm beds for around Sfr25 with breakfast (showers available). The Dents du Midi and the mountains of the Savoy range are visible behind Lake Geneva.

Head northward along the road, which passes directly below the Auberge for 15 minutes, then take a steep path down through the trees to a gravelled vehicle track. Turn right and continue in a long gradual descent through tall broadleaf forest to a sealed road and follow this down left into the village of **Glion** (708m), 1¼ to 1½ hours from Sonchaux. From Glion station walkers can opt to take the cog railway directly down to Montreux or the funicular railway down to Montreux-Territet (look out for the 'Gare/Poste' sign).

Walk down the road through the village, then turn right onto a stepped path descending steeply through the trees to Rue de Temple in the upper part of **Montreux**. From here continue right across the bridge over the Baye de Montreux, following the Rue de

SOUTHERN FRIBOURG & VAUD

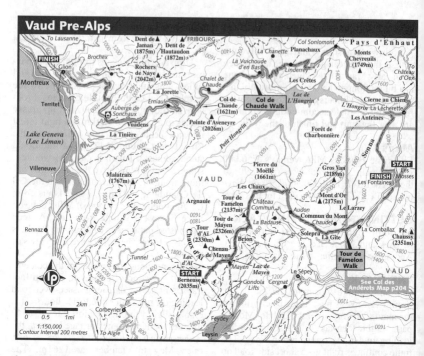

la Gare on down to reach the main train station (396m) after a final 40 to 50 minutes.

If you've just finished walking the entire Alpine Pass Route, your arrival in Montreux is something to celebrate!

Vaud Alps

South of the Col des Mosses, the lower Alpine foothills give way to the Vaud Alps (Alpes Vaudoises in French). Although they make up only a tiny part of the Swiss Alps, these ranges are full of topographical and scenic surprises. Cornered by the deep trough of the lower Swiss Rhône on their western and southern sides, the Vaud Alps drop away into the Rhône Valley with an often staggering abruptness. The region is primarily geared toward the skiing industry (which easily tops dairying as the mainstay of the local economy), with half a dozen well-known mountain resorts.

The only especially high mountains in the Vaud Alps are the Muverans and Les Diablerets, which run along the cantonal border with the Valais. These two massifs form an interesting range – essentially a south-western continuation of the Bernese Alps – which boasts several landmark 3000m summits and some quite outstanding Alpine landscapes.

ACCESS TOWN
Villars

The ski resort of Villars (1253m) lies at the northern foot of the Muveran massif and has superb views toward the Dents de Midi, Mont Blanc and the Glacier du Trient. The tourist office (☎ 024-495 32 32, 📧 information@villars.ch, 🌐 www.villars.ch) is on Rue Centrale. To hire mountain guides contact Villars Experience (☎ 024-495 41 38, 📧 villars.experience@smile.ch).

The *Hôtel Suisse* (☎ 024-495 24 25, 📧 *el gringo@vtx.ch*) and the *Hôtel Les Papillons*

(☎ 024-495 34 84, ⓔ *info.papillons@blu ewin.ch*) have single/double rooms from Sfr45/90.

Villars is best reached by hourly train on the private (BVB) mountain railway from Bex, a town on the main Rhône Valley rail line. There are also postbuses from Aigle at least every two hours. Between early July and mid-September, postbuses run three times daily between Villars and Les Diablerets (via the 1778m Col de la Croix).

Col des Andérets

Duration	2 days
Distance	23km
Standard	easy-medium
Start	Gsteig
Finish	Les Mosses
Nearest Town	Les Diablerets

Summary This lovely walk takes you through a picturesque landscape of gentle mountain pastures, high moors, Alpine heathland and isolated little hamlets perched high above the valley opposite the 3000m peaks of the Diablerets massif. It is the 14th (penultimate) leg of the Alpine Pass Route.

The 2034m Col des Andérets is a slight pass in the ranges above the Col du Pillon watershed, where the Rhine and Rhône river systems converge. Leading from the village of Gsteig in the German-speaking Bernese Oberland through the francophone Ormont-Dessus district to the Col des Mosses, the way over the Col des Andérets transcends Switzerland's linguistic division. This is frontier country from yet another aspect, since here the higher peaks of the Bernese and Vaud Alps go over into the – still quite rugged – Alpine foothills to the north.

The walk is best done in two relatively short days.

Maps

The only walking map with single-sheet coverage is K+F's 1:50,000 *Grand-St Bernard-Dents du Midi-Les Diablerets* (Sfr24.80). The SAW/FSTP's 1:50,000 *Rochers de Naye (262T)* and *Wildstrubel*

(*263T*) also cover the route, but omit the interesting mountainous area immediately to the south (on the SAW/FSTP adjoining *St-Maurice* No 272T). Each SAW/FSTP sheet costs Sfr22.50. Editions MPA Verlag's 1:50,000 *Alpes Vaudoises* (Sfr27.90) also covers the route.

NEAREST TOWN
Les Diablerets

This village lies at 1151m at the foot of the Diablerets massif just to the west of the Col du Pillon in the Ormond-Dessus district. A popular short walk from the village leads up to Lac Retaud (1685m), and a gondola lift goes up directly from Les Diablerets to La Marnèche.

The local tourist office (☎ 024-492 33 58, fax 024-492 23 48, ⓔ info@diablerets.ch, ⓦ www.diablerets.ch) has information.

The *Hôtel Mon Abri* (☎ *024-492 34 81*) has singles/doubles for Sfr40/80. *Auberge de la Poste* (☎ *024-492 31 24*, ⓔ *auberge_tfp@bluewin.ch*) has rooms for Sfr44/88 (breakfast Sfr12 extra).

Les Diablerets is best reached from Aigle on the hourly trains (via Le Sépey), or by postbus from Gstaad in the western Bernese Oberland (via the Col du Pillon).

GETTING TO/FROM THE WALK

For information on transport access, see Gsteig under Access Towns in the Saanenland & Upper Simmental section of the Bernese Oberland chapter and Les Mosses under Access Towns in the earlier Fribourg & Vaud Pre-Alps section.

THE WALK
Day 1: Gsteig to La Marnèche

3–4 hours, 11km, 845m ascent

From Gsteig post office (1189m), walk down to the upper side of the Hotel Viktoria, where a road turns off left. Follow this up around to the right, crossing a stream before heading left on a foot track along the steep ridge through mixed forest and clearings to reach **Schopfi**, a farmhouse and barn at 1502m, after 45 minutes to one hour.

Climb left up the grassy slopes, where red-white-red marker stakes lead the way to

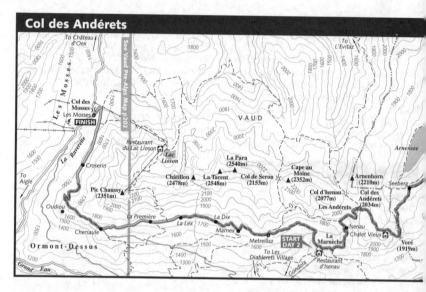

Vordere Walig at 1716m, a further 20 to 30 minutes on. An alp track runs just above this small cluster of farms, which sits high above the valley looking out toward graceful peaks to the south-east. Follow this road left for 20 to 30 minutes as it rises briefly then curves around above a very small side valley to the isolated dairy farmlet of **Topfelsberg** at 1814m.

The road peters out a short way on, and the route continues as a neatly trodden foot track. This path quickly sidles along the hillside before making a short, steep ascent rightward to reach the 1909m **Blattipass** after another 10 to 15 minutes. From the grassy tops of this small pass you get fine panoramas stretching from the Diablerets and the Spitzhorn in the south to the Wittenberghorn in the north.

Cut down toward the west through sporadic stands of spruce trees, orienting yourself by paint markings wherever the way becomes indistinct, soon meeting a trail coming up from the right. This leads 20 to 30 minutes down to the *Huus am Arnensee* (☎ 033-755 14 36), a mountain restaurant with dorm accommodation. Turn left and contour high above the Arnensee across

rolling slopes strewn with rhododendron bushes, passing the alp huts of **Ober Stuedeli** before dropping down to the isolated farmstead of **Seeberg** (1712m), 25 to 30 minutes from the Blattipass.

Follow the path quickly up left over mountain heathland to a saddle in a small side ridge. Head on across the green pastures of the tiny upper valley, then climb gently past a shallow tarn to reach the small col of **Voré** (1919m) after 30 to 40 minutes. The stone fence at Voré marks the border between the francophone canton of Vaud and German-speaking Bern. The col itself gives a tremendous view southward across the Col du Pillon to the adjacent Sex Rouge and Oldenhorn peaks of Les Diablerets.

Walk five minutes diagonally up the open hillside to your right to the *Chalet Vieux* (☎ 026-924 68 79) at the end of a dirt road. The chalet stands at 1950m, overlooking the Arnensee, and offers dorm beds from Sfr55 with full board; milk and cheese are also on sale. The route now continues along the road, rising steadily to cross the slight crest of the **Col des Andérets** (2034m), from where the Dents du Midi as well as the far-off peaks of the

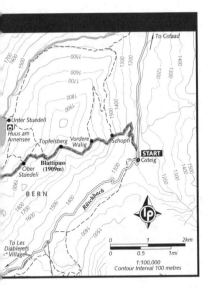

Savoy Alps move into view ahead. The Col des Andérets lies on the Rhine/Rhône watershed where two of western Europe's major river systems converge.

Head down past winter ski-lifts and begin dropping leftward into the open basin on short-cut trails that lead off the road to the farmyard of **Isenau**. The road heads on down around the slopes to the left to reach the upper station of the gondola lift at **La Marnèche** (1802m), 45 minutes to one hour from Voré. Here the *Restaurant d'Isenau* (☎ 024-492 32 93), open from early June to late September, offers dorm beds for Sfr23 and rooms for Sfr36 per person; showers are available. The gondola lift connects La Marnèche with the skiing resort of Les Diablerets in the valley below, and generally runs from early June to early October.

Day 2: La Marnèche to Les Mosses
3–4 hours, 12km
The route from La Marnèche to Les Mosses mostly leads along gently undulating terraces high above the valley, offering easy and very scenic walking.

Proceed 50m along the road, then take a yellow-marked foot track off right down through meadows to a rustic farmhouse. The path continues across a small stream before beginning a diagonal traverse up slopes below the Cape au Moine to reach **Metreillaz** (also called Meitreile) after 30 to 40 minutes. This small hamlet sits at 1803m on a ridgetop looking out across the valley. There are more great views to your left of the Muveran, Diablerets and Dents du Midi massifs.

Pick up paint markings (avoiding a more obvious walking track that departs down left) and make your way across the flowery hillsides ahead, gradually descending to meet an alp road at the farmlet of **Marnex** (1738m). The route now contours along a rough vehicular track through the small cluster of wooden alp buildings at **La Dix**, before continuing as a foot path that rises and dips slightly to reach a sealed road not far on from **Le Lex** (1802m, shown on most maps as Le Lé), 50 minutes to one hour from Metreillaz.

Continue westward along the road fringed by raspberry bushes and thickets of stinging nettles, soon passing the locality of **La Première**. After you come to another small group of dwellings at **Chersaule** (1657m) the road makes a sharp bend and begins its descent into the valley. Here, follow a farm track (signposted 'Les Mosses') leading around through pleasant spruce forest to a clearing on the low ridge just above the farmhouse of **Oudiou** (1702m), 50 minutes to one hour on. The Col des Mosses is now clearly visible ahead at the end of the upper valley of the La Raverette stream.

Pass through a farm gate, then dip leftward back into the trees and descend quickly to a road. This road winds through the forest, passing the alp hut of **Croserin**, then beginning a steady drop over open slopes to arrive at the mountain resort of **Les Mosses** (1445m) after a final 50 minutes to one hour.

For the next (and final) leg of the Alpine Pass Route, refer to the Col de Chaude walk in the Fribourg & Vaud Pre-Alps section earlier in this chapter.

Tour de Famelon

Duration 3½–4½ hours
Distance 13km
Standard easy-medium
Start Leysin/Berneuse
Finish Les Mosses
Summary This is an excellent high traverse along the Vaud Pre-Alps' most impressive range.

The grey limestone mountains immediately south-west of the Col des Mosses form a compact and geologically fascinating range culminating in the 2137m Tour de Famelon. In this area natural weathering has left deeply fluted formations and jagged outcrops in the karst rock, while glacial action has produced several impressive mountain cirques.

Using a gondola lift to gain most of the height, the walk involves little climbing and the descents are undemanding.

Maps

The most detailed walking map covering the route is Editions MPA Verlag's 1:25,000 *Leysin–Les Mosses* (Sfr26). Excellent alternatives are the SAW/FSTP's 1:50,000 *Rochers de Naye* No 262T (Sfr22.50) or Editions MPA Verlag's 1:50,000 *Alpes Vaudoises* (Sfr27.90). K+F's 1:60,000 walking map *Grand St-Bernard-Dents du Midi-Les Diablerets* (Sfr24.80) is another reasonable larger-scale alternative.

NEAREST TOWN
Leysin

Perched on sub-Alpine slopes below the Tour d'Aï, Leysin (1315m) looks out southward to the Muveran, the Dents du Midi and Mont Blanc massifs. Leysin hosts a rock festival in early July.

For information contact the tourist office (☎ 024-494 22 44, fax 024-494 16 16, [e] info @leysin.ch, [w] www.leysin.ch). The École d'Alpinisme Leysin (☎ 024-494 18 46) organises guided climbs, mountaineering courses and walks.

Camping Sémiramis (☎ 024-494 39 39) offers tent sites for Sfr4 plus Sfr3.25 per person. *Hiking Sheep Guest House (☎ 024-494 35 35)* has dorm beds for Sfr26 and rooms for Sfr36 per person (prices without breakfast). The *Hôtel Le Bel-Air (☎ 024-494 13 39)* offers singles/doubles for Sfr46/92.

For budget eating try the *New Sporting Centre*, *L'Horizon* and *Prafandaz*. The *Restaurant Le Leysin* has dishes using home-made cheese.

Leysin is accessible by roughly hourly trains on the mountain railway from Aigle, a small town south of Montreux on the main Lausanne–Brig rail line.

GETTING TO/FROM THE WALK

The walk begins from the upper gondola-lift station of Berneuse, at 2035m, above the mountain resort of Leysin. The gondola lift operates from the start of June until the last week in October; the one-way fare is Sfr14. Otherwise it's a 1½-hour walk up to Berneuse.

For information on transport to/from Les Mosses, see Access Towns in the earlier Fribourg & Vaud Pre-Alps section.

THE WALK

See the Vaud Pre-Alps map, page 202
In the gondola lift you sail up from Leysin (1315m) to the minor peak of **Berneuse**

Mystic Mountains

Perhaps due to their striking craggy forms, local peoples have long venerated the Tour d'Aï, Tour de Mayen and Tour de Famelon. Archaeologists recently discovered that the pre-Christian Celtic tribes who inhabited the south-eastern shores of Lake Geneva some 2500 years ago used these limestone peaks and their twin cirques as an enormous open-air temple. Medieval herders believed a dark hole visible high on the north wall of the Tour d'Aï to be the abode of elves. Sacrilegiously, the northern side of the range is now used by the Swiss Army as a shooting range, although the southern side of the Tour de Famelon lies within a nature reserve.

(2035m) in just over five minutes. This natural lookout grants superb views to the west across Lake Geneva as well as the Dents du Midi and Les Diablerets massifs to the south. The futuristic-looking revolving Kuklos restaurant here overlooks a small winter skifield; in summer the rich Alpine pastures contrast starkly with the raw rock walls of a precipitous spur descending from the Tour d'Aï (2330m).

Take the signposted foot track leading north-east along the left side of the ridge, before dropping diagonally down to meet an alp road at the eastern shore of **Lac d'Aï**. At 1892m near this shallow reedy tarn is a cluster of rustic barns with wooden-shingled roofs. The route traces the winding road gently down the grassy mountainsides hopping with marmots, bearing right at a fork to reach the dairy farmlet and upper gondola-lift station at **Mayen** (1842m) after 25 to 30 minutes.

Drop down a few steps to the **Lac de Mayen**, a small lake at the termination of a rocky gully coming down from the 2326m Tour de Mayen, then ascend leftward along a low ridge onto slopes scattered with yellow gentians to a signpost on a rounded grassy spur. Follow white-red-white markings right (north), traversing slanting terraces below a craggy cirque before climbing over a crest. The path now sidles through rock rubble along the base of an impressive 200m-high precipice under the 2137m Tour de Famelon, then descends into a basin of semi-forested karst fields.

Skirt past these interesting formations eroded into the rugged grey rock, before rising out onto a broad grassy ridge. A rough alp track leads eastward past several red-roofed wooden barns in the direction of the 2175m Mont d'Or, the northern sides of which are covered with large screeslides. Where the alp track swings away left, continue down a foot track to reach a road at **Pierre du Moëllé** (1661m), 1½ to two hours from the Lac de Mayen. There is a restaurant on this low pass beside an enormous three-storey rock block into which tunnels have been built to create a military bunker.

Walk south down the sealed road to the first hairpin bend, then turn off left along a forestry track. Contour along slopes of spruce and maples, bearing right at a minor fork before dropping down to meet another road. The walking route continues off to the right at a neat wooden farmlet a few paces uphill, sidling on down north-eastward through moist pastures and mixed forest. There are some rather muddy cow-trodden sections, and the yellow-diamond markers are a bit vague in places. After coming onto a sealed lane, make your way down past holiday houses to reach the main Le Sépey–Château d'Oex road (at the 1368m point) after one to 1¼ hours. There is a postbus stop here.

Take a signposted laneway off right from the main road and make your way up through the narrow upper valley below the 2351m Pic Chaussy. Not far on the lane briefly meets the road, before turning away again to reach a large holiday chalet. Here cut directly ahead over the grassy lawns on a well-worn walking pad, soon coming onto another narrow sealed lane that brings you back onto the road at the small mountain resort of **Les Mosses** (1445m) after a final 30 to 40 minutes.

Tour des Muverans

Duration	4 days
Distance	52km
Standard	medium-hard
Start/Finish	Les Plans-sur-Bex (or Derborence)
Nearest Town	Derborence
Summary	This high-level, multi-day circuit through an interesting karst massif gives breathtaking vistas across the deep Rhône Valley to the gleaming-white Mont Blanc and Pennine Alps.

The Muverans massif stands immediately west of the Diablerets massif, and is the last range before the Rhône River finally breaks northward out of its enclosed valley at the so-called Coude du Rhône. Its highest summit is the 3051m Grand Muveran, a spectacular dolomite peak that regularly attracts

Alpine rock climbers. On the Muverans' southern and western sides, where the range fringes the Valais, the land plummets a stupefying 2500m into the Rhône Valley. The Muverans lie in a transitional zone between the drier climate of the Valais and the moister oceanic climate of the Vaud Alps.

This is one of the wilder parts of Switzerland, with healthy populations of snow grouse, marmots, stoats, chamois, and ibex protected by nature reserves around Derborence and in the Vallon de Nant.

The route is rather up-and-down (its lowest and highest points are 1100m and 2600m) with several sustained (although not strenuous) climbs and descents. There are plenty of en-route places to stay, so walkers can move at their own pace. Meals, refreshments and snacks are available from restaurants and many mountain huts en route. Some huts only offer self-catering facilities, however, so walkers who intend staying at these should bring some food to cook – there are shops at Les Plans-sur-Bex and Derborence.

PLANNING
Maps

The most detailed walking map is Editions MPA Verlag's 1:25,000 *Coude du Rhône* (Sfr27), but it can be difficult to find. This map actually features the Tour des Muverans, and although otherwise excellent it only includes the route between Anzeindaz and the Pas de Cheville (literally) by a hair's breadth, cutting out all of the Diablerets massif. The SAW/FSTP's 1:50,000 *St-Maurice* No 272T (Sfr22.50) covers the entire route (with plenty of space around it). K+F's 1:60,000 sheet *Grand St-Bernard-Dents du Midi-Les Diablerets* (Sfr24.80) is another reasonable alternative.

When to Walk

The best time to undertake the Tour des Muverans is from late July until late September, but the route is often in condition a month either side of that period.

GETTING TO/FROM THE WALK

The route description assumes hikers will start/finish at Les Plans-sur-Bex (1095m)

on the Vaud side of the Muveran massif, although there are several other access possibilities, which also makes it easy if you decide to opt out along the way.

Les Plans-sur-Bex can be reached by a 25-minute postbus ride from the town of Bex. There are up to six postbuses in either direction daily. The last leaves Bex train station at around 6.40pm, returning from Les Plans-sur-Bex shortly after 7pm. Bex is on the Lausanne–Brig line; most trains stop there.

Alternative Starting Points Between early June and mid-September, the BVB railway runs minibuses from Villars (see Access Towns in the earlier Vaud Alps section) to Solalex daily at 10.45am and 3.15pm. Solalex (1462m) is 3km (or 1¼ hours' walk) from Anzeindaz on Day 1.

Some people set out from Derborence (1449m), which is accessible by postbus connections from Sion (see Access Towns under Central Valais in the Valais chapter) via the village of Aven. Between late June and late September there are two (on Sunday just one) daily postbus connections leaving Sion at around 9.30am and 2.15pm, and returning from Derborence at around 10am and 2.45pm. Outside this period there is no service.

Bougnone (1944m, see Day 3) above the village of Ovronnaz (1332m) also provides access to the Tour des Muverans. There are up to eight daily postbus connections from Sion via Leytron to Ovronnaz all year round. The last bus leaves Sion at around 6.50pm and returns from Ovronnaz at around 7.50pm. From Ovronnaz a chairlift runs up to Bougnone (Jorasse) between early July and mid-October until 4.30pm daily (Sfr6 one-way).

Private vehicles can be parked at Pont de Nant, Derborence or Ovronnaz.

THE WALK
Day 1: Les Plans-sur-Bex to Derborence

4¾–5½ hours, 15km, 943m ascent

From the post office take the minor road leading south-east past chalets among the pastureland to cross the Avançon de Nant stream on a small bridge just after entering the forest. A foot track follows the southern bank of the river, before crossing again and climbing over a small side stream to reach the hamlet of **Pont de Nant** (1253m) after 25 to 30 minutes. Here the *Auberge Communale* (☎ *024-498 14 95)*, open from June to late October, has dorm beds for Sfr27 (including breakfast and showers) and singles/doubles for Sfr42/84. Pont de Nant has an Alpine garden established by the University of Lausanne. This fascinating Alpine garden (entry free, open daily from May to late October) has the most extensive collection of Alpine plants in Switzerland, with some 2500 species from mountain regions all over the world.

The route leads north-eastward along a rough vehicle track into a little side valley. Make your way on above the southern side of a stream through mixed meadows and patches of forest (past a side path going up to the SAC's Cabane de Plan Névé) to the alp hut of **Le Richard** (1535m). Continue eastward, climbing up beside the now-tiny stream away from the last scatterings of low trees. The route eases into gentle meadows just before reaching *Buvette La Vare* (☎ *079-623 02 57)* at 1756m, 1¼ to 1¾ hours from Pont de Nant. This mountain restaurant looks south-west toward the 3051m Grand Muveran, and has a small mattress room for walkers.

Follow the white-red-white markings on smoothly up through a strip of grassy pastures within a narrow elongated basin hemmed in between the main Muveran massif and the craggy ridge of L'Argentine.

The path picks an easy way on up through white cliffs to arrive at the **Col des Essets** at 2029m after one to 1¼ hours. This pass height looks across to the craggy peaks on the adjacent Les Diablerets massif.

Descend gently northward for 20 to 25 minutes, passing the **Cabane Barraud** (a private locked hut at 1956m) to reach **Anzeindaz**, a scattered hamlet in a broad grassy bowl at 1876m. Here, two large mountain hotels offer accommodation (with showers) and serve meals from early May to the end of October. The *Refuge Giacomini* (☎ *024-498 22 95)* charges Sfr44 for dorm beds and Sfr56 for rooms (prices per person with full board). The *Refuge de la Tour* (☎ *024-498 11 47)* is only slightly more expensive.

Just up from the latter, take a signposted alp track. This leads directly across to the northern side of the burbling streamlet and rises up gently through the lovely highland valley to arrive at the **Pas de Cheville** (2038m) after 35 to 40 minutes. This gentle pass lies on the Vaud–Valais cantonal border at the foot of Les Diablerets' main 3209m summit, and affords a wonderful panorama stretching eastward as far as the Pennine Alps.

Various coloured markings lead quickly past a lonely stone shelter, then steeply down southward through the bluffs in tight zigzags to the alp hut of **Le Grenier**, at 1744m in the Vallon de Cheville. Cross the stream on a wooden footbridge a few paces below, making your way down past the holiday chalets of **Les Penés** (1660m). The path descends into beautiful forests of larch with understorey fields of white alpine pasqueflowers *(Pulsatilla alpina)*, winding its way on down to reach the tiny summer-only village of **Derborence** at 1449m, 50 minutes to one hour from the Pas de Cheville.

Here, the *Refuge de Lac* (☎ *027-346 14 28)* and the *Auberge du Godet* (☎ *027-346 15 97)* charge Sfr26 for dorm beds (including breakfast). Both have showers and are open at least from late May to mid-October.

SideTrips Around Derborence

Above Derborence is one of the Swiss Alps' classic mountain cirques, a 2km-wide rock

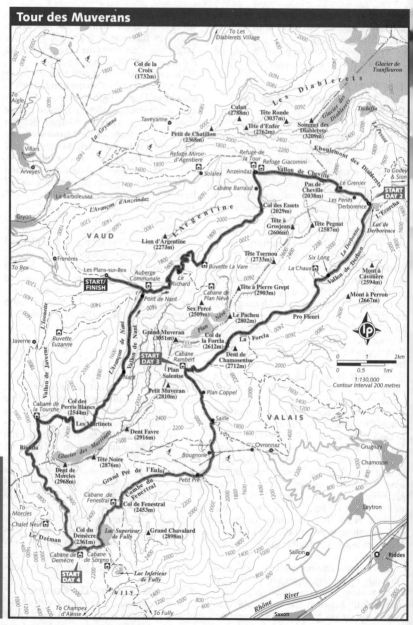

Tour des Muverans

The Derborence Mountainslides

Derborence was the site of two great landslides in 1714 and 1749 (known as the Eboulements des Diablerets), when rock faces on the southern flank of Les Diablerets – the 'devil's mountain' – crashed catastrophically into the valley. Isolated and largely abandoned since then, today the Derborence area harbours ancient, almost pristine forests found nowhere else in Switzerland.

amphitheatre in which the tiny Tschiffa glacier nestles. The **Lac de Derborence**, the shallow lake beside the village, was formed by the 18th-century landslides (see the boxed text 'The Derborence Mountainslides'), which dammed the Derbonne stream. The lake is gradually being filled in again by rubble washed from the slopes above after heavy downpours. A three-hour circuit walk leads through the regenerating rock debris to the small hydroelectricity reservoir at Godey.

The inaccessible forests on the slopes of L'Encorcha immediately south of Derborence have remained virtually unexploited over the past few centuries. Today many of most ancient red spruce and silver fir trees – some of which were already established at the time of the last great mountain landslide – have trunks up to 1.5m in diameter. This area forms a unique nature reserve, which enjoys total protection.

Day 2: Derborence to Cabane Rambert

4¾–5¾ hours, 12km, 1135m ascent

Take the signposted alp track leading southwest from the lakeshore up through slopes of low, regenerating forest, which grant good views back across Derborence. The route moves over to meet the Derbonne, before beginning its long gradual climb through the Vallon de Derbon, a small glacial valley whose U-shaped floor is divided into several levels. Crossing the stream repeatedly, head up through attractive open meadows to pass the alp huts of **Six Long** after 1¼ to 1¾ hours.

The path ascends onto another level of the valley to **Pro Fleuri**, the uppermost pastures in the Vallon de Derbon. In summer this area of high grassland is alive with inquisitive, docile cows and nervously active marmots. After recrossing to the northern bank of the stream, make your way up a small ridge toward the pyramid form of Tita Naire. Following white-red-white markings and cairns, sidle leftward over talus fields and frequent snowdrifts before coming to a small lake in the raw moraine basin of **La Forcla** between the 2712m Dent de Chamosentse and Le Pacheu (2802m), 1¾ to 2¼ hours from Six Long.

From this point a path goes off left down to the village of Chamoson in the Rhône Valley, whose wine-growers built this tiny reservoir as a water supply for their thirsty vineyards. The lake generally remains icebound well into the summer months. The Tour des Muverans route continues around the northern side of the lake, then skirts up easily over the **Glacier de la Forcla** (which is really just a broad snowfield) to the **Col de la Forcla** at 2612m after 25 to 30 minutes.

Drop down steeply through loose rock below the col to an obvious painted arrow on a large rock slab, then traverse southwest along the scree-slopes past a minor signposted turn-off to reach a small pass. The route sidles on quickly around into another small saddle (2504m), then makes a final short, steep climb to arrive at the *Cabane Rambert* (☎ 027-207 11 22), one to 1¼ hours from the Col de la Forcla.

This SAC hut sits at 2580m on a ledge beside the Plan Salentse, an arena-like cirque between the Petit Muveran (2810m) and the Grand Muveran, whose 3051m summit is only safely accessible to roped Alpine rock climbers. The Alpine panorama from the Cabane Rambert is something to behold, with a stunning line-up of glistening snow-capped massifs stretching across from Mont Blanc over to the south-west, the Grand Combin and Pigne d'Arolla toward the south, and the Matterhorn and Weissmies to the east. Immediately below the hut, the land falls away directly into the Rhône Valley.

Day 3: Cabane Rambert to Cabane de Demècre

4½–5½ hours, 11km, 671m ascent

From the saddle below the hut drop down in tight zigzags through scree-slopes into the **Plan Salentse**. Accumulated winter snow-drifts lie long here, and the young streamlet divides into several branches, as in a delta. Descend below a line of precipitous bluffs with interesting wave-like folded-rock strata, following the stream down past **Plan Coppel** at 2125m, an alp hut in a semi-ruined state. After crossing to the right (western) bank on a steel footbridge, take a last look back through this tiny 'picture book' upper-Alpine valley toward the Grand Muveran.

The route now spirals on down beside a small ravine, recrossing the stream some distance before coming to another ruined alp hut at **Saille** (1782m). Here cross the stream a final time and sidle southward high above the Rhône Valley along mountain-sides scattered with yellow gentians. After passing a large alp barn you reach the restaurant and upper chairlift station at **Bougnone** (Jorasse; 1944m), 1½ to two hours from the Cabane Rambert. (Walkers can opt to begin or end the hike here.)

Continue south-west past winter ski tows through a minor saddle (giving excellent views of the 2898m Grand Chavalard and other surrounding summits) to reach a dis-used military camp at **Petit Pré** (1995m). The well-trodden path rises steadily upward through old moraines into the broad, flat hollow of the **Grand Pré de l'Euloi**. Formed when a vast funnel-like underground cavern (known as a doline) collapsed into itself, this attractive grassy-green basin drains subterraneously into the Rhône Valley. Euloi is surrounded by the Dent Favre (2916m), Tête Noire (2876m) and other interesting peaks.

Skirt the southern side of the basin to the melodic chiming of cowbells and the shrill whistle of marmots, then head south-west up the slopes of the **Combe du Fenestral** over patches of old winter snows. A last, slightly steeper, section cuts up diagonally leftward over screes to arrive at the **Col de Fenestral** (2453m), two to 2½ hours from Bougnone (Jorasse). A few paces around to the right is the *Cabane de Fenestral* (☎ 026-746 35 59), a 45-bed hut belonging to the local Ski-Club de Fully, with dorm beds for Sfr15. It is mainly equipped for self-caterers, but the warden/cook is resident from early July to late August and on weekends. At other times the hut is left open. From up here you get a picturesque view down to the turquoise lake in the basin of Fully.

Traverse to the far end of a screeslide, then drop down into lovely meadows dotted with purple goblet-shaped Koch's gentians at the head of **Lac Superieur de Fully**. This natural lake is another doline formation, although the water level has been raised by about 4m for producing hydroelectricity. Make your way around the western shore of the lake almost to the low dam wall, then climb away gently leftward to meet a more prominent path. From this point the 50-bed *Cabane de Sorgno* (☎ 027-946 24 26), another Ski-Club de Fully hut, is 10 minutes' walk downhill at 2064m. The Cabane de Sorgno (sometimes spelled 'Sorniot') has dorm beds for Sfr15.

The route continues up to the right (ie, westward) past several small tarns to reach the *Cabane de Demècre* (☎ 024-486 99 68) on the **Col du Demècre** (2361m), one to 1½ hours from the Col de Fenestral. This converted ex-military hut serves refreshments in summer (otherwise open) and has a kitchen for self-caterers; dorm beds cost Sfr15.

Day 4: Cabane de Demècre to Pont de Nant

4½–5½ hours, 14km, 486m ascent

Drop down west as far as a line of cliffs, then double back rightward to circle around steep talus slopes. After 20 to 25 minutes you come to a signposted junction at the Alpine pastures of **Le Dzéman**, from where a left path goes 700m down to the *Chalet Neuf* (☎ 026-767 13 10), open mid-June to early October, a restaurant with dorm beds for just Sfr10. Bear right here and sidle on upward along the mountainside, climbing briefly beside a small stream before beginning a scenic high-level traverse north-westward along a series of broad grassy terraces between sheer precipices.

There are exhilarating vistas to your left, where the land falls away dramatically into the deep glacial trough of the Rhône Valley. The mighty snow-capped 'teeth' of the Dents du Midi rise up directly on the adjacent side of the valley, while the Dolent – on whose 3820m summit Switzerland, Italy and France meet – can be made out to the south-west. The path rises over a steep spur (marking the Valais–Vaud cantonal border), before descending gently to the army barracks at **Rionda** (2156m), 1¼ to 1¾ hours from Le Dzéman.

Continue quickly along a dirt road past Rionda's several military buildings, soon after which a more uplifting view opens out toward Lake Geneva in the north-west. A short way on take a foot track leading quickly up to reach the 60-bed *Cabane de la Tourche* (☎ 024-486 97 51) after 15 to 20 minutes. This SAC hut at 2198m has dorm beds for Sfr13, and offers more of the panoramas typical of this walk. It serves as a base for Alpine rock climbers tackling the crags of the 2968m Dent de Morcles visible to the south of La Tourche.

The path leads along the right side of the ridge up in zigzags as far as the line of cliffs, then crosses over leftward and contours around the coarse talus slopes of the **Vire aux Boeufs**. Follow the now familiar white-red-white route markings and rock cairns up through another field of scree, passing a (difficult) white-blue-white marked route going up the Dent de Morcles just before you get to the **Col des Perris Blancs** at 2544m after 40 to 50 minutes. This saddle overlooks the moraine-filled basin of Les Martinets, which was formed by the receding Glacier des Martinets. At this point the Petit and Grand Muveran also reappear, although from quite a different aspect to previous sections of the walk.

Drop down in steep spirals into the upper **Vallon de Nant**, then move rightward through boulder-strewn terrain into a gully often filled by winter snow accumulations. This small enclosed valley is being filled in

by constant rockfall from the surrounding slopes. The Vallon de Nant forms a wild nature reserve with surprisingly diverse Alpine flora and inhabited by large herds of chamois. The route descends on via a gap in the cliffs, winding its way down over slopes with stunted larches to intersect with an alp track (at point 1664m). Head along this dirt road across the milky-white **Torrent des Martinets** to reach the romantic little alp hut of **Nant** at 1500m after 1¼ to 1¾ hours.

The final section of the Tour des Muverans leads on down the valley through pockets of fir and spruce forest on the eastern bank of the Avançon de Nant. The route passes the **Jardin Alpin** just before arriving back at Pont de Nant after a final 30 to 40 minutes. From Pont de Nant, retrace the start of Day 1 to Les Plans-sur-Bex.

Other Walks

Gummfluh

Standing opposite the Vanil Noir in the Pays d'Enhaut district is the Gummfluh. The craggy 2458m main summit itself is difficult to get to on foot and is best left to the Alpine rock climbers, but the area has many good walking routes. A popular walk from Château d'Oex leads upstream along the forested southern banks of the Sarine to Gérignoz, before heading up into the tiny valley of the La Gérine to the lookout on La Videmanette (2130m), where the *hôtel* (☎ 026-924 64 65) has dorm beds. Shorter route variants involve taking a cable-car/chairlift combination from Château d'Oex up to La Montagnette (1625m) and/or the Rougemont–La Videmanette gondola lift. The walk continues southward around the eastern flank of the Gummfluh to the Col de Jable (1884m), and then sidles down westward to the postbus stop at L'Etivaz on the Château d'Oex-Les Mosses road. The best walking map is K+F's 1:25,000 *Pays d'Enhaut* (Sfr24.80).

Col de Jaman

Situated just north of the Rochers de Naye, the 1512m Col de Jaman connects the Gruyères and Pays d'Enhaut districts with Lake Geneva. For centuries this low pass was an important transport route for muleteers, whose pack animals carried Gruyères cheeses westward and wines from the Lake Geneva region eastward. Known as the Route du Fromage, this mule trail lost all economic importance after the opening of the (MOB) railway tunnel (which passes almost directly below the Col de Jaman) at the beginning of the 20th century.

Walking east to west, the old route runs from the MOB train station at Montbovon (797m) through the Vallée des Allières, then snakes its way up steeply to the pass. The descent leads via Les Avants (968m), from where various paths continue down to Montreux. The *Restaurant Le Manoïre (☎ 021-964 63 30)* on the Col de Jaman offers dorm beds. The local tourist authority's 1:50,000 walking map *Hauts de Montreux* and the SAW/FSTP 1:50,000 sheet *Rochers de Naye* No 262T (Sfr22.50) both cover the walk.

Moléson Circuit

Only just managing to break the 2000m barrier, Le Moléson is not spectacularly high. Cableways and a ski village dominate the mountain's northern slopes, so it's hardly wilderness country either. As a final north-western ripple in the Fribourg Pre-Alps, however, Le Moléson does give wonderful panoramas taking in Lake Geneva, the Swiss Mittelland as far as the Jura and the western Alps.

A pleasant and simple three-hour circuit starts at Plan-Francey (1520m), accessible by cable car from the resort of Moléson-Village. The route first contours along a 'botanical path' (with nameplates identifying numerous local wild flowers) to Gros Moléson at 1529m, before sidling westward and ascending to the cable-car station and observatory on the Moléson's 2002m summit. A nice descent route follows the ridgeline southward, then drops off rightward via Tremetta (1689m) and Gros Plané (1476m) back to Plan-Francey.

Moléson-Village has a *Friends of Nature hostel (☎ 0878-880 100)*, with dorm beds for Sfr19. The *Hôtel-Restaurant Plan-Francey (☎ 026-921 10 42)* has dorm beds for Sfr27 and singles/doubles from Sfr44/78. Use either Editions MPA Verlag's 1:25,000 *Moléson-Rochers de Naye* (Sfr24) or the SAW/FSTP 1:50,000 sheet *Rochers de Naye* No 262T (Sfr22.50).

From Bulle there are direct GFM buses to Moléson-Village (also train/GFM bus connections via Gruyères) up to eight times a day.

Valais

Hemmed in on its northern side by the Bernese Alps and by the Pennine Alps to the south, the canton of Valais (Wallis in German) forms Switzerland's most distinct geographical region. The Valais is the quintessential long, deep glacial valley – in fact its name originates from the Latin word *vallis*, meaning simply 'valley'. The region corresponds almost exactly to the broad and fertile basin of the (Swiss) Rhône River along with its numerous lateral valleys. The Valais was shaped during the progressive glaciations by the Rhonegletscher, whose icy bulk once stretched down through the Rhône Valley as far as Lake Geneva.

Encircled by the highest mountains of the Alps, the Valais' geographical isolation is reflected in its history and culture. Once an independent state, the Valais only joined the Swiss Confederation as a separate canton in the early 1800s. Today the Valaisans remain a proud and individualistic people whose suspicion of outsiders – including other Swiss – has gradually softened as the region opened up to the outside world during the last 150 years.

Most Valaisans live along the densely populated Rhône Valley. The lower half of the Valais – stretching up the Rhône Valley as far as the city of Sierre – is French-speaking, and francophone Valaisans make up around two-thirds of the canton's population. In the upper Valais live the Oberwalliser, a hardy German-speaking people.

Forming an almost unbroken wall of great ice-smothered summits stretching eastward along the Swiss–Italian frontier from the Mont Blanc massif as far as the border with Uri Canton, the Pennine Alps have most of Switzerland's 4000m peaks, including the Grand Combin (4314m), the Dent d'Hérens (4171m), the Weissmies (4023m) and the classic 4477m Matterhorn. Half a dozen major side valleys splay out southward deep into the Pennine Alps, while in contrast the northern side valleys of the Valais tend generally to be short and steep.

Highlights

CLEM LINDENMAYER

The Lac de Tanay in the Chablais region is surrounded by spectacular limestone crags.

- Marvelling at the mighty rock walls of the Matterhorn from the high Alpine meadows of the Höhbalmen above Zermatt

- Picnicking by the historic Alpine dairy at the Lac de Louvie on the Prafleuri–Louvie Traverse

- Looking along the vast icy mass of the Grosser Aletschgletscher from the tiny Märjelensee

- Walking along the Bisse de Clavau canal among vineyards above the Rhône River

Being enclosed by the high mountains on all sides, the Valais has a decidedly continental type of climate with low precipitation levels due to a marked 'rain shadow' effect. The Valais' long periods of hot summer weather are legendary (but walkers should beware of getting too much sun). Of course the loftier summits receive considerably

VALAIS

Valais

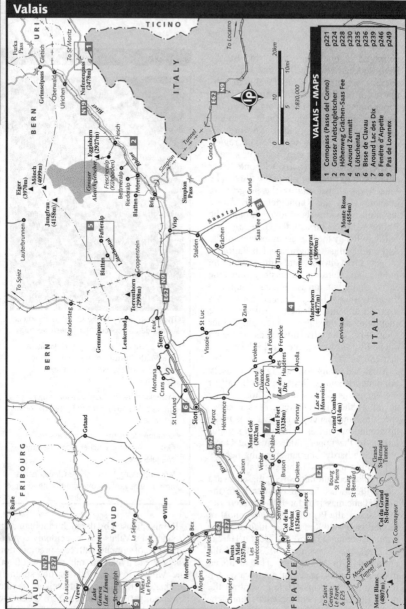

higher levels of precipitation – most of it falling as snow – and this nourishes the canton's astonishingly extensive areas of névés and glaciers. At last count the Valais boasted some 670 smaller and larger glaciers with a combined surface area of almost 700 sq km – representing around 15% of the Valais' area and over half of the area covered by glaciers in Switzerland.

With most of Switzerland's peaks above 4000m, the Valais is a mountaineer's dream. You don't have to scale the peaks to enjoy them, however. With thousands of kilometres of paths and walkways, the Valais is also prime walking country offering the most consistently spectacular scenery anywhere in the Swiss Alps.

INFORMATION
Maps
Kümmerly + Frey's (K+F) 1:120,000 *Holiday Map Wallis/Valais* (Sfr24.80) and Editions MPA Verlag's 1:180,000 *Valais, Wallis, Grands Tours* give a good overview of walking possibilities in the region, and show trails, huts and other important features. Sheet No 3 of the BL/OFT's 1:200,000 (four-sheet) series also covers all of the Valais except for upper Goms, which is on sheet No 4.

Books
Cicerone Press produces a number of useful guides. *The Valais, Switzerland: A Walking Guide* by Kev Reynolds (UK£11.99) is the best available English-language guide to the region. Reynolds' *Chamonix to Zermatt, The Walker's Haute Route* (UK£8.99) covers that classic long walk through the Pennine Alps. *The Grand Tour of Mont Rosa* by CJ Wright, a set of two volumes (£UK14.99 each), covers this popular long circuit walk through the Valais and northern Italy.

Randonnées circulaires Valais and *Rundwanderungen Wallis* (Sfr22.80), published by K+F in separate French and German editions, describes circuit (loop) walks throughout the Valais. *20 Bergwanderungen Region Wallis* (Sfr29.90) by Luc Hagmann & Franz und Brigitte Auf der Maur (Werdverlag) contains a selection of 20 regional walks.

Alpinwandern Wallis (Sfr46) by Bernhard Rudolf Banzhaf (SAC) details dozens of mountain walks in the region.

Information Sources
The helpful cantonal tourist office, Valais Tourism (☎ 027-327 35 71, fax 027-327 35 71, e info@vailaistourism.ch, w www .valaistourism.ch or www.valaisinfo.ch), Rue Pré-Fleuri 6, CH-1951, Sion, has further information.

Goms

From its source at the Rhonegletscher near the Furkapass, the Rhône (known locally as the Rotten) descends through this open highland valley before dropping down through a series of gorges to Brig. This uppermost part of the Valais is known as Goms, a region lying mostly well above 1000m with a distinctly Alpine character rather different from the rest of the Rhône Valley. Goms was the homeland of the Walsers, medieval German-speaking settlers who migrated to many previously uninhabited Alpine valleys far outside the Valais. The extreme isolation of Goms was considerably reduced by the opening in 1982 of the Furka-Oberalp railway, which provides a reliable all-seasons link between Goms and Central Switzerland's Urner Oberland as well as the Surselva region of Graubünden.

GETTING AROUND
The seven-day *Regionalpass Oberwallis* covers a large area stretching from Sierre to Göschenen (in Uri Canton), north to Spiez (Bernese Oberland) and south to Zermatt, Saas Fee and Domodossola (Italy). It costs Sfr160 (Sfr128 with Half Fare Card, children Sfr80), and gives three days of travel (2nd class only) on trains and buses plus a 50% reduction for the other four days, and 25% off mountain cableways.

The *Ferienkarte Oberwallis* only covers the area between Brig and Visp, but includes the Lötschental, Saastal and the Simplonpass road as far as Iselle in Italy. It

Signs of a Glacial Past

Many of the world's finest walks are through landscapes which have been – or are being – substantially shaped by glaciers. As a glacier flows downhill under its weight of ice and snow it creates a distinctive collection of landforms, many of which are preserved once the ice has retreated (as it is doing in most of the world's ranges today) or vanished.

The most obvious is the *U-shaped valley* (1), gouged out by the glacier as it moves downhill, often with one or more bowl-shaped *cirques* (2) at its head. Cirques are found along high mountain ridges or at mountain passes or *cols* (3). Where an alpine glacier – which flows off the upper slopes and ridges of a mountain range – has joined a deeper, more substantial valley glacier, a dramatic *hanging valley* (4) is often the result. Hanging valleys and cirques commonly shelter hidden alpine lakes or *tarns* (5), such as those featured in so many of the walks in this book. The thin ridge which separates adjacent glacial valleys is known as an *arête* (6).

As a glacier grinds its way forward it usually leaves long, *lateral moraine* (7) ridges along its course – mounds of debris either deposited along the flanks of the glacier or left by sub-ice streams within its heart (the latter, strictly, an *esker*). At the end – or snout – of a glacier is the *terminal moraine* (8), the point where the giant conveyor belt of ice drops its load of rocks and grit. Both high up in the hanging valleys and in the surrounding valleys and plains, *moraine lakes* (9) may form behind a dam of glacial rubble.

The plains which surround a glaciated range may feature a confusing variety of moraine ridges, mounds and outwash fans – material left by rivers flowing from the glaciers. Perched here and there may be an *erratic* (10), a rock carried far from its origin by the moving ice and left stranded when it melted.

View of area before glacier's retreat

gives three days free travel by postbus only within a seven-day period, and costs Sfr39 (Sfr29 children/Half Fare Card).

Together the *Martigny et Région* and *Sion et Sion Région* postbus passes cover much of the Central Valais and all of the Lower Valais. Each gives three days within a seven-day period and costs Sfr48 (Sfr38 concessions). The Sion pass also gives discounts on certain cableways and the Martigny pass includes Mont Blanc Express/St Bernard Express trains.

The one-day *Léman-Chablais Passport* covers the 'Chablais' region of the Lower Valais and Southern Vaud. It costs Sfr29 (Sfr14.50 concession/Half Fare Card) and is good for travel on Lake Geneva ferries as well as local postbuses and trains.

The seven-day *Regional Pass Léman* costs Sfr150 (Sfr120/75 concession/child) and covers the entire Swiss shore of Lake Geneva, including part of Lower Valais. It allows three days of unlimited travel and four days at 50% reduction.

ACCESS TOWNS
Oberwald
This small tourist resort sits below the Furkapass in the uppermost part of Goms.

For information contact the Oberwald tourist office (☎ 027-973 22 03, e gem einde.oberwald@freesurf.ch) in town or the regional tourist office (☎ 027-973 32 32, fax 027-973 32 33, e info@obergoms.ch, w www.obergoms.ch) in the train station.

The *Sporthotel* (☎ 027-974 25 25, fax 027-974 25 24), *Hotel Ahorni* (☎ 027-973 20 10, fax 027-973 20 32) and the *Hotel Tannenhof* (☎ 027-973 16 51, fax 027-973 27 51) have singles/doubles from around Sfr50/100.

Oberwald is the last station on the Furka-Oberalp-Bahn (FOB) rail line from Brig via Andermatt to Disentis before it enters the Furka tunnel. Car-carrying shuttle trains run between Oberwald and Realp. From early July until late September there are four daily postbus connections to Andermatt (via the Furkapass), Meiringen (via the Grimselpass) and two services (via the Nufenenpass) to Airolo in Ticino (see the Cornopass

walk in this chapter). On all services, holders of travel passes pay a surcharge.

Brig
This small city at 684m is the regional capital of the German-speaking Upper Valais. Worth visiting is the onion-domed Stockalper Schloss (entry Sfr5), an ostentatious castle built by the notorious Kaspar Jodok von Stockalper (1609–91), who amassed a considerable fortune by controlling the Simplonpass trade.

The tourist office (☎ 027-921 60 30, fax 027-921 60 31, e info@brig-tourismus.ch, w www.brig.ch) is in the train station.

Nearby *Camping Brigerbad* (☎ 027-946 46 88, fax 027-946 24 35) has sites at a thermal pool for Sfr10 plus Sfr7.40 per person. The *Sporthotel Olympica* (☎ 027-924 35 50, e olympica@rhone.ch, Im Biel) has dorm beds for Sfr28. *Restaurant Matza* (☎ 027-923 15 95, Simplonstrasse 18) has singles/doubles for Sfr45/80 and serves pizzas and Valaisan dishes. *Café la Poste* (☎ 027- 924 45 54, fax 027-924 45 53, Furkastrasse 23) offers rooms for Sfr50/100.

The *Migros* supermarket and restaurant is opposite and to the left of the station. *Channa Molino Ristorante* (Furkastrasse 5) has Italian food, while *Restaurant zum Eidgenossen* (Schulhaustrasse 2), off Bahnhofstrasse, serves Valaisan fare.

Getting There & Away Brig is an important rail and road hub, with at least hourly trains via the tunnels of Lötschberg (to Bern), the Furka (to Central Switzerland) and the Simplon (to Domodossola in Italy, from where there are regular connections to Locarno in Ticino via the Centovalli. Through-tickets are available for this rail route and rail passes valid only for Switzerland are still accepted). The private Brig–Visp–Zermatt (BVZ) line runs trains hourly via Visp to Zermatt. Hourly postbuses leave for Saas Fee calling at Visp and Stalden en route. Postbuses also run the winding and scenic route over the 2005m Simplonpass as far as the village of Iselle in Italy, from where there are bus or train connections on to Domodossola.

VALAIS

The most direct route for motorists to/from the Valais and northern Switzerland is via the car-carrying shuttle trains running between Kandersteg and Goppenstein via the Lötschberg tunnel. (There is no road tunnel.) The train does not carry cars through the Simplon tunnel to Italy.

Cornopass (Passo del Corno)

Duration	2¼–3 hours
Distance	9km
Standard	easy-medium
Start	Abzweigung Griessee
Finish	Alpe Cruina
Nearest Towns	Oberwald, Airolo

Summary This straightforward and popular walk across a gentle Alpine pass offers dramatic views of the Arctic-like Griessee, a meltwater lake at the snout of a glacier.

The Cornopass (Passo del Corno in Italian) lies on the European continental divide and forms the cantonal border between the Valais and Ticino – local nomenclature also indicates the meeting of German- and Italian-speaking regions. The highlight of the walk is undoubtedly the Griessee, an artificial lake fed by the Griesgletscher. When the reservoir is full, the snout of this 5km-long glacier almost touches the water, although several decades ago it protruded well out into the lake. Setting off from an already high altitude, the Cornopass walk entails an ascent of only 223m.

Maps

The SAW/FSTP 1:50,000 *Nufenenpass* No 265T (Sfr22.50) best covers the walk. K+F's

Warning

The Swiss military holds shooting exercises in the lower Val Corno during a number of days in summer. Safe through-access for walkers is guaranteed, though there may be a wait. See Military Shooting Ranges in the Health & Safety chapter earlier.

1:60,000 *Aletsch-Goms-Brig* (Sfr24.80) is a reasonable alternative.

GETTING TO/FROM THE WALK

Abzweigung Griessee (the Griessee turn-off) is on the road across the 2478m Nufenenpass (Passo della Novena). From late May to late September, there are two postbuses daily in either direction across the Nufenenpass, running between Oberwald and Airolo (see Access Towns under Northern Ticino in the Ticino chapter) via Alpe Cruina, at the end of the walk. From Oberwald one earlier postbus runs only as far as the Nufenenpass – it's the last stop before the pass. Travel passes are valid, but a surcharge (from Oberwald, Sfr6) is levied.

There is free but limited parking at the Griessee turn-off.

THE WALK

Follow the small sealed road (closed to unauthorised traffic) gently uphill above the snaking Nufenenpass road. Dominating the horizon to the north-west is the majestic 4274m Finsteraarhorn, one of the remotest summits in the Swiss Alps. At a turn-off on the first sharp bend, it's worth making the 10-minute return side trip off right to the **Griessee**. From the dam wall you get a first dramatic view across to the Griesgletscher, which creeps down from the 3373m Blinnenhorn (Corno Cieco) into the icy waters of the reservoir.

The road winds on up past installations belonging to the hydroelectricity company and turns gradually into a foot track before reaching a junction at roughly 2440m. Here continue right and traverse southward high above the brilliant turquoise lake over steep meadows of thorny thistles and yellow arnicas to another signposted junction (at around 2465m), 45 minutes to one hour from the pass road.

Take the left path – the right-hand branch goes to the Griespass, see the Griespass Side Trip at the end of the walk description – and head 10 minutes up through a broad gully of small but deeply eroded stream channels to reach the **Cornopass (Passo del Corno)**, at 2485m. The pass overlooks **Lago Corno**, an

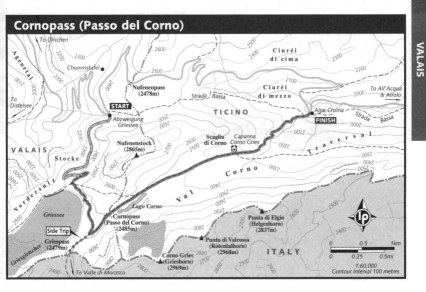

Cornopass (Passo del Corno)

To Ulrichen
Chummstafel
Arenerial
To Distelsee
Nufenenpass (2478m)
Strada Bassa
Ciuréi di cima
Ciuréi di mezzo
To All'Acqua & Airolo
START
Abzweigung Griessee
TICINO
Alpe Cruina
FINISH
Traversal
Strada Bassa
Nufenenstock (2865m)
Scaglia di Corno
Capanna Corno Gries
VALAIS
Stocke
Corno
Val
Vordersulz
Griessee
Lago Corno
Cornopass (Passo del Corno) (2485m)
Punta di Elgio (Helgenhorn) (2837m)
Side Trip
Griespass (2479m)
Griesgletscher
Punta di Valrossa (Rotentalhorn) (2968m)
ITALY
Corno Gries (Grieshorn) (2969m)
To Valle di Morasco

0   0.5   1km
0   0.25   0.5mi
1:60,000
Contour Interval 100 metres

elongated tarn in a raw glacial basin that stays ice-bound until midsummer.

Sidle on slightly upward along grassy slopes sprinkled with tiny blue Bavarian gentians opposite the 2969m Corno Gries (Grieshorn), whose north face is adorned by a small icefall. The path descends into the tiny Val Corno along an old moraine ridge, then skirts the valley's grassy fringe to avoid scree and moraine over to the right to reach the SAC's ***Capanna Corno Gries*** (☎ 091-869 11 29) at 2338m, 40 to 50 minutes from the Cornopass. This stone hut stands under the 2865m Nufenenstock looking north-east along the Val Bedretto to the peaks of the Gotthard region.

Drop down along a rolling ridge through the middle of the valley beside a small power/telephone line serving the hut. The path cuts down more steeply leftward across the Strada Bassa (walking route) to rejoin the Nufenenpass road by a hairpin curve at **Alpe Cruina** (2003m), 30 to 40 minutes from Capanna Corno Gries. The postbus stop is five minutes left up the road at **Ciuréi di mezzo** at 2035m.

Alternatively, it's 1½ hours' walk on downvalley to the tiny village of **All'Acqua**,

from where there are postbuses to Airolo until around 6.30pm all year. ***Caffè All'Acqua*** (☎ 091-869 11 85) has rooms.

Side Trip: Griespass
20–30 minutes return, 1.5km return, 14m ascent
From the junction at 2465m, it's well worth sidling gently up south-west to the Griespass at 2479m on the Swiss–Italian frontier. The pass gives good views of the 3235m Ofenhorn (Punta d'Arbola) and the 3182m

An isolated stone alp hut at La Cave in the upper Val L'Ertentse, Valais, Swiss Alps.

CLEM LINDENMAYER

VALAIS

Hohsandshorn (Punta del Sabbione) rising out of the large expanse of névés that feed the Hohsandgletscher (Ghiacciaio del Sabbione). This route continues down into Italy's Valle di Morasco, first settled by German-speaking Walsers from Goms in the 13th century, to Ponte-Valdo (from where there are buses to Domodossola).

Grosser Aletschgletscher

Duration	4–5¼ hours
Distance	17km
Standard	easy-medium
Start	Fiesch/Fiescheralp (Kühboden)
Finish	Bettmeralp/Betten
Nearest Town	Brig
Summary	This walk alongside the enormous Grosser Aletschgletscher (or 'Great Aletsch Glacier') gives a high-Alpine experience without too much effort.

The 22km-long Grosser Aletschgletscher is the longest and most voluminous glacier in the Alps. From its source at the Jungfraujoch, this massive stream of ice is fed by a number of other major glaciers, which assures it of its enormous size. At Konkordiaplatz (around 3000m above sea level) the Grosser Aletschgletscher has a maximum width of some 1800m and a depth of around 800m.

In the 1600s, during Europe's 'little ice age', the icy snout of the glacier advanced menacingly down the valley, bulldozing its way through Alpine pastures and forest as it moved. For the last 150 years or so, however, the ice has been steadily retreating at an annual rate of around 20m, and its depth – the thickness of the ice body itself – has also diminished considerably.

On its east side the Grosser Aletschgletscher runs at right-angles to a small side valley, the Märjelental. Here the ice has dammed the small stream to create a tiny lakelet, the interesting Märjelensee.

Maps

Recommended is either the SAW/FSTP 1:50,000 *Jungfrau* No 264T (Sfr22.50), or

the local tourist authority's 1:25,000 *Wanderkarte Aletschgebiet und Untergoms* (Sfr20). K+F's 1:60,000 *Aletsch-Goms-Brig* (Sfr24.80) is a fair alternative.

NEAREST TOWNS
Fiesch

Fiesch (1049m) is on the FOB rail line running from Brig via Andermatt to Disentis in Graubünden.

There is a helpful tourist office (☎ 027-970 60 70, fax 027-970 60 71, ℮ info@fiesch .ch, W www.fiesch.ch) and the Bergsteigerzentrum Aletsch (☎ 027-971 17 76, fax 027-971 41 20, W www.bergsteigerzentrum.ch) organises mountain courses and tours.

The *Hôtel du Glacier* (☎ 027-971 13 01, ℮ glacier@rhone.ch) has singles/doubles from Sfr40/80. The *Hotel Kristall* (☎ 027-971 17 17, ℮ hotel-kristall@rhone.ch) offers dorm beds for Sfr35 with breakfast and rooms from Sfr70/150.

Fiescheralp (Kühboden)

This tiny resort sits above Fiesch at 2212m. *Hotel-Restaurant Eggishorn* (☎ 027-971 14 44, ℮ hotel-eggishorn@fiesch.ch) has dorm beds for Sfr32 and rooms from Sfr45 per person (with breakfast). *Restaurant-Pension Kühboden* (☎ 027-970 12 20, ℮ info@kue hboden.ch) and *Hotel Jungfrau* ☎ 027-971 19 88, ℮ hotel-jungfrau@rhone.ch) offer similar dorm accommodation and rooms for around Sfr60/110.

Fiescheralp is at the intermediate station of the Fiesch–Eggishorn cable car; the service is half-hourly and the one-way adult fare Sfr17.20 (Half Fare Card valid). Vehicles can be left for a fee at the lower cable-car station.

Bettmeralp

The small vehicle-free mountain resort of Bettmeralp (2006m) sits on a sunny terrace far above Betten.

There is a tourist office (☎ 027-928 60 60, fax 027-928 60 61, e info@bettmeralp ch, w www.bettmeralp.ch) and the Bergsteigerzentrum (☎ 027-927 24 82) organises guided trips into the mountains.

The *Touristenhaus Seilbahn* (☎ *027-927 16 62)* has dorm beds for around Sfr25. There is a *Friends of Nature hostel* (☎ *027-927 11 65)* in nearby Riederalp with dorm beds for Sfr23. *Hotel Garni Sporting* (☎ *027-927 22 52,* e *sporting@bettmeralp.ch)* has singles/doubles from Sfr55/110.

The Betten–Bettmeralp cable car runs at least half-hourly (Sfr8/4 adults/children). Vehicles can be left at the car park (Sfr7 per day) near the station.

Betten

This village, at 814m, is also on the FOB rail line. The *Pension Bahnhof* (☎ *027-927 11 84)* near the train station has singles/ doubles from around Sfr40/80.

GETTING TO/FROM THE WALK

Cable cars take the sweat out of this walk. For information on transport to/from Fiescheralp and Bettmeralp, see Nearest Towns earlier.

THE WALK

From the Fiescheralp (Kühboden) cable-car station walk north-east along the dirt road that contours the open mountainsides, bearing right past the path going up to the Eggishorn and the turn-off to Märjela via the small Tälli tunnel. The route can be shortened by an hour by walking through the tunnel – a decidedly unscenic alternative that requires a torch (flashlight) with plenty of battery power. The route soon goes over into a broad well-graded foot track, and winds its way around the slopes high above the Fieschertal up through the grassy gully of **Unners Tälli**. Begin a steeper climb in several switchbacks leading past a small wooden cross erected on a rock platform. This makes a natural viewing

point granting a fine view up along the Fieschergletscher, which snakes down between the 3905m Gross Wannenhorn and the 4273m Finsteraarhorn.

Follow white-red-white markings around westward across rocky ledges into the tiny valley of the **Märjela**, where a signpost marks the junction of trails coming from the Fiechertal and the Tälligrat. The path continues quickly down beside the attractive Vordersee to reach the *Restaurant Gletscherstube* (☎ *027-971 14 83 or 027-971 14 88)*, 1½ to two hours from Fiescheralp. This two-storey wooden hut (also known as the Märjelenhütte) sits at 2363m below the Eggishorn on an Alpine pasture grazed by sheep. It's open early June to mid-October and offers dorm beds for Sfr20; breakfast/dinner costs Sfr8/18.

Head down past several little tarns, crossing the small stream at a large cairn before making your way down through regenerating moraine slopes to the **Märjelensee** (2300m) after 30 to 35 minutes. Bordered by the icy edge of the **Grosser Aletschgletscher**, this tiny lake presents a dramatic picture. In the past the Märjelensee was higher and larger than its present form. At times the lake would rise and suddenly break through the ice wall, causing flooding downvalley, but the glacier's steady retreat has solved that problem. From the polished-rock slabs above the Märjelensee you get a tremendous view northward across this amazingly broad, elongated expanse of glacial ice stretching

The Aletschwald

The slopes fringing the lower part of the Grosser Aletschgletscher are covered by the Aletschwald, a small nature reserve harbouring some superb specimens of larch and ancient arolla pines – many over 1000 years old. Proposals for a national park centred around the Aletschwald are under consideration. The Swiss parliament has approved the listing of the 470-sq-km Aletsch-Jungfrau region, stretching from near Grindelwald to just north of Brig, as a Unesco World Heritage area.

VALAIS

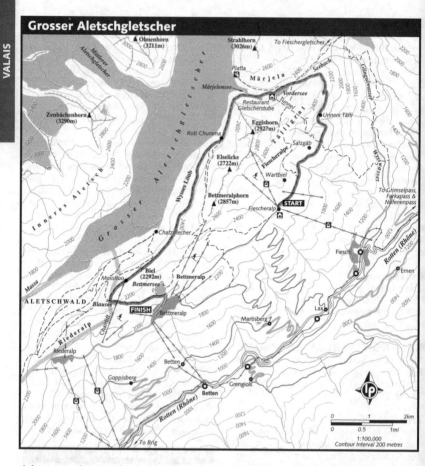

Grosser Aletschgletscher

right up to the Jungfraujoch, where the weather station/observatory stands out on the white ridge top.

Climb southward around a rocky ridge and sidle up to a signposted path fork at **Roti Chumma** (2369m). Here, take the lower right-hand way, partly following an old aqueduct along a spectacular route high above the crevassed ice. The rock shelves give spectacular views across to the great peaks dominated by the 4195m Aletschhorn. There are occasional fixed cables to hold onto. After coming to **Biel**, a saddle on the Greichergrat at 2292m, where a path turns

down right to the Aletschwald (see the boxed text later), make your way south-west along the ridge to reach the restaurant and upper chairlift station at **Mossfluo** (2333m), 1¼ to 1¾ hours from the Märjelensee. From here the striking summit of the Matterhorn can be readily identified among the icy crags far away to the south-west.

The route continues along the ridge on a short section of marked foot track (not highlighted on some walking maps), cutting down leftward to the tarn of **Blausee** (2204m). Here duck under the chairlift and drop down eastward over grassy pastures to

Top: Autumn larch forest in the upper Lötschental, which was shaped by the distant Langgletscher.
Middle Left: The silver thistle is a ground-hugging plant found on sunny slopes.
Middle Right: Walkers on the Fenêtre d'Arpette prepare to descend into the Val Trient, Valais.
Bottom: A walker traverses high above the Saastal, enjoying the unfolding panorama.

CLEM LINDENMAYER

CLEM LINDENMAYER

CLEM LINDENMAYER

CLEM LINDENMAYER

CLEM LINDENMAYER

Top Left: The Combin de Corbassière looms behind the Lac de Louvie, Valais.
Top Right: The unusual Alpine houseleek, which flowers between July and September, stores moisture in its fleshy leaves. **Middle Right:** The 3869m Mont Blanc de Cheilon rises up at the head of the Lac des Dix reservoir. **Bottom:** An old Valaisan barn clings to the hillside.

the attractive **Bettmersee**, from where a dirt road leads on across the low dam wall to the upper houses of **Bettmeralp** (2006m), 40 to 50 minutes from Mossfluo. The upper station of the Betten–Bettmeralp cable car is 10 minutes' walk down through the village.

Mattertal & Saastal

At Stalden, just 5km south of the town of Visp, the Vispatal divides into the nonidentical twins of the Mattertal (western branch) and the Saastal (eastern branch) – the longest and most spectacular side-valley system in the Valais. The two 'Vispa valleys' are walled in and separated from each other by three mighty lateral ranges extending northward from the main continental divide of the Pennine Alps. The Mattertal and Saastal have a staggering concentration of classic Alpine peaks, with some 27 of Switzerland's 34 summits over 4000m.

These mountains culminate – both in height and scenic splendour – in a continuous arc of heavily glaciated peaks fronting the Italian border, including the 4165m Breithorn, the 4634m Dufourspitze (part of the Monte Rosa massif, Switzerland's highest peak) and the amazing 4477m rock nose of the Matterhorn. The Matterhorn so dominates the scenery of the Mattertal that the valley is often promoted simply as the 'Matterhorn region'.

The Mattertal runs along a fault line caused by massive uplifting as the African continental plate pushed hard against the European plate, and the mountains on its western side (including the Matterhorn, Dent Blanche, Obergabelhorn, Zinalrothorn and Weisshorn) are composed of rock types of quite different origin from the mountains (such as the Breithorn, Pollux, Monte Rosa, Strahlhorn and the Rimpfischhorn) on the eastern side of the valley.

ACCESS TOWNS
Saas Fee
The car-free mountain resort of Saas Fee (1792m) sprawls along a high terrace above the upper Saastal. The challenging hike over the Zwischenbergpass (see Other Walks at the end of the chapter) and the Gsponer Höhenweg along the eastern side of the Saastal start/end at the village of Saas Almagell, down in the valley.

The Saas Fee tourist office (☎ 027-958 18 58, fax 027-958 18 60, e to@saas -fee.ch, w www.saastal.ch) has further information. Mountain Life Bergführerbüro (☎ 027-957 44 64, w www.rhone.ch/moun tainlife) organises mountaineering courses and numerous climbing and walking tours.

There are several camping grounds down in Saas Grund, the best of which is *Am Kapellenweg (☎ 027-957 40 40)*. *Hotel Garni Imseng (☎ 027-958 12 58, fax 027-958 12 55)* offers dorm beds for Sfr35 with breakfast. The *Gästehaus Albana (☎ 027-957 27 24, e gaestehaus.albana@freesurf .ch)* has singles/doubles from Sfr35/65. The *Hotel Feehof (☎ 027-957 23 08, e fee hof@freesurf.ch)* has rooms for around Sfr50/100.

Supermarkets are on the main street. The cheapest places to eat are Metzgerei (butcher shops) such as *Dorf Metzg* near the tourist office, serving chicken, chips and sausages. Near the ski lifts, *Boccalino* serves pizza from Sfr13, or for Swiss fare try *La Ferme*, near the tourist office.

Postbuses run at least hourly from Brig to Saas Fee via Visp and Saas Grund; reservations are essential on services to Brig (☎ 027-958 11 45).

Zermatt
Situated in the upper Mattertal below the towering form of the Matterhorn – for many *the* classic mountain – Zermatt (1620m) is the unrivalled centre of the Pennine Alps. The town has an excellent tourist infrastructure, including all classes of hotel, boutiques and outdoor equipment shops. Little remains of the original village of Zermatt, although traditional old wooden barns can still be seen in some places behind the shops and hotels along the main street. The Alpine Museum (entry Sfr5/1 adults/children) has an interesting collection that deals with the history of local mountaineering.

The mountains surrounding Zermatt attract tens of thousands of walkers, mountaineers and skiers each year. The Zermatt environs have countless superb walking routes. Since high peaks, large glaciers and sheer cliffs cut off the upper Mattertal on three sides, most walks are circuits that return to Zermatt. The Gornerschlucht, a small gorge of cascades just above the town, makes an easy and worthwhile short outing from Zermatt.

Zermatt has an excellent tourist office (☎ 027-967 01 81, ℮ zermatt@wallis.ch, ⓦ www.zermatt.ch) and one of Switzerland's leading schools of mountaineering, the Alpin Center Zermatt Bergführerbüro (☎ 027-966 24 60, ⓦ www.zermatt.ch/alpinc enter) on Bahnhofstrasse.

Spartan *Camping Matterhorn* (☎ 027-967 39 21), open June to September, near the train station, charges Sfr9 per person. The *Matterhorn Hostel* (☎ 027-968 19 19, ℮ info@matterhornhostel.com) has dorm accommodation from Sfr29, while the *youth hostel* (☎ 027-967 23 20, ℮ zermatt @youthhostel.ch) charges Sfr41.50 per bed. *Hotel Bahnhof* (☎ 027-967 24 06, ℮ hotel _bahnhof@hotelmail.ch) has rooms from Sfr45/71. The *Naturfreunde-Hotel* (☎ 027-967 27 88, ℮ naturfreunde.zermatt@spectra web.ch), which is run by the Swiss Friends of Nature, has singles/doubles from Sfr53/98.

The *Coop* supermarket is in Viktoria Shopping Centre, opposite the train station.

The idyllic, car-free town of Zermatt clusters in the Mattertal.

Past the church on the main street are *Café du Pont* and *Restaurant Weisshorn*, with Swiss dishes.

Getting There & Away Zermatt can only be reached by the private BVZ railway from Brig or Visp in the Rhône Valley. Trains run at least hourly and the one-way/return fare is Sfr38/63 (most rail passes don't cover this privately run service, but standard concessions apply). The *Glacier Express* tourist train runs between Zermatt and St Moritz. Zermatt is entirely car-free, and vehicles must be left at the large car park at the village of Täsch, some 6km down the Mattertal.

Höhenweg Grächen-Saas Fee

Duration	6–8 hours
Distance	15km
Standard	medium
Start	Grächen
Finish	Saas Fee
Nearest Town	Grächen

Summary This exhilarating and spectacular high-level route along the precipitous western side of the Saastal forms a leg of the 10-day Monte Rosa Circuit.

The 15km Höhenweg Grächen-Saas Fee follows a foot track cut into the steep – in places sheer – western side of the Saastal at around 2000m. The walk is largely above the tree line and gives some glorious vistas of the Weissmies massif and other nearby ranges. Too precipitous to allow extensive Alpine grazing, these rugged slopes have a profusion of wild flowers and are home to herds of ibex and chamois.

Ascents total 700m and in places minor rock-hopping is required.

Maps

The *Wanderkarte Saastal*, available in separate 1:25,000 and 1:40,000 versions (both Sfr16), is recommended. K+F's 1:50,000 *Tour Monte Rosa* (Sfr24.80), which covers a larger area, is a lso very good. Otherwise,

Warning

Although cables (and sometimes railings) adequately secure the way, in places the path is cut into cliffs with sheer drop-offs, and is only suited to sure-footed walkers not prone to vertigo. The route is likely to be dangerously icy after mid-October, but in summer carry water for the initial climb. Due to the danger of falling ice from the Bidergletscher, the final section of the Höhenweg has been rerouted via a lower path.

you will need two SAW/FSTP 1:50,000 maps: *Visp* No 274T and *Mischabell* No 284T (Sfr22.50 each).

NEAREST TOWN
Grächen

Grächen (1615m) sits on a ledge above the Mattertal, just south of where it joins the Saastal. From this Alpine resort you get a wonderful view upvalley to the glaciated pyramid of the Weisshorn.

For information contact the tourist office (☎ 027-956 27 27, fax 027-956 11 10, **e** info @graechen.ch, **w** www.graechen.ch).

Camping Grächbiel (☎ 027-956 32 02), 2km below Grächen at 1500m, has tent sites. *Hotel Bellevue (☎ 027-956 33 30, fax 027-956 33 11)* and the *Hotel Stutz (☎ 027-956 36 57, **e** hotel.stutz@smile.ch)* offer singles/doubles from Sfr53/90.

Grächen is reached by bus from the town of St Niklaus in the Mattertal on the BVZ rail line to Zermatt (see Access Towns earlier). The BVZ also runs bus service from St Niklaus (passes get 50% discount only).

GETTING TO/FROM THE WALK

For information on travel to/from Saas Fee, see Access Towns at the start of the section. The route can be shortened by roughly an hour by taking the Grächen– Hannigalp gondola lift (Sfr14.60, concessions available), which runs on weekends, Tuesday and Thursday from early June to early July, then daily until mid-October.

The *Kombi-Billett Höhenweg* covering the gondola lift and all buses is available from local tourist authorities for Sfr33 (Sfr16.50 children, or with Half Fare Card).

THE WALK

From the bus terminus, walk 75m up to the lower station of the Hannigalp gondola lift (see Getting to/from the Walk), then turn right and continue to the Seetalhorn lift station. A broad foot track heads up past a horse-riding centre, then sidles up north-east to reach the small lake at **Z'Seew** after 20 to 25 minutes. Here, the *Restaurant-Hotel Zum See (☎ 027-956 24 24)* offers nice rooms for Sfr52 per person.

The route begins a steady but comfortable ascent through attractive forest, passing a picnic area (a spring fountain here has the only drinking water on the climb) to reach **Hannigalp** (2121m) after 50 minutes to 1¼ hours. *Bergrestaurant Hannigalp (☎ 027-955 60 20)*, a large cafeteria by the upper gondola-lift station, has an outside terrace that looks up the Mattertal as far as the Matterhorn. It has dorm accommodation mainly for groups (Sfr47 with full board).

Cut up quickly under winter ski lifts past a modern chapel, then turn south-eastward through beautiful stands of larches and arolla pines into the Saastal. The Höhenweg traverses low herb fields of mountain houseleeks and trailing azaleas mixed with less common species like branched gentians and Alpine asters, passing turn-offs (left) to Eisten and (right) to the Seetalhorn. Secured by occasional railings and cables the path rises and dips onward high above the valley. Opposite is the 3993m Fletschhorn, while the pointed summits of the Bietschhorn (3934m) and the Lötschentaler Breithorn (3785m) rise up behind you across the Rhône Valley – the Grosser Aletschgletscher is also briefly visible.

The route drops gently down the open slopes of **Färich**, where you get a nice view up the tiny side valley of the Schweibbach to hanging glaciers on the 3796m Balfrin. Ibex and chamois favour these inaccessible slopes. Cross the fast-flowing stream on a footbridge in the forest, two to 2¾ hours from Hannigalp, and sidle back upward over broken boulders high above Tirbja and

VALAIS

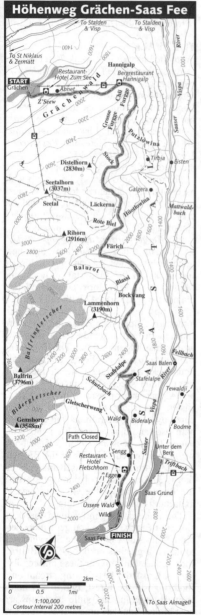

Höhenweg Grächen-Saas Fee

To Stalden & Visp
To Stalden & Visp
To St Niklaus & Zermatt
Hannigalp
Restaurant-Hotel Zum See
Bergrestaurant Hannigalp
START Grächen
Abnet
Z'Seew
Grächenwald
Chili Furgge
Grosse Furgge
Putzlöwina
Distelhorn (2830m)
Stock
Tirbia
Eisten
Seetalhorn (3037m)
Galgera
Mattwald-bach
Seetal
Läckerna
Hüotlovina
Rote Biel
▲ Rihorn (2916m)
Färich
Balurot
Blassi
Bockwang
Lammenhorn (3190m)
Balfringletscher
Stafelalpe
Saas Balen
Fellbach
Stafelalpe River
Balfrin (3796m)
Schutzbach
Tewaldji
Gletscherweng
Bidergletscher
Wald
Bideralp
Bodme
Gemshorn ▲ (3548m)
Path Closed
Unter dem Berg
Senggi
Restaurant-Hotel Fletschhorn
Triftbach
Eggen
Üssere Wald
Saas Grund
Wildi
Saas Fee **FINISH**

0   1   2km
0   0.5   1mi
1:100,000
Contour Interval 200 metres
To Saas Almagell

CHRIS MELLOR

The majestic summit of the Matterhorn lures mountaineers to the Valais.

Galgera, two idyllic hamlets sitting on isolated shelves over the Saastal.

The path skirts on around a raw talus gully under the sheer cliffs of the 3190m Lammenhorn – don't linger here as there is some danger of rockfall – before following a ledge past an overhanging outcrop that serves as a resting spot for thrill-seeking walkers. There are stunning views across the valley to the Lagginhorn and the hovering ice-dome summit of the Weissmies (4023m), whose hanging glaciers nourish cascading streams. Continue slightly downward over Alpine pastures to a path junction at 2142m, almost directly under the icefall of the **Bidergletscher**.

The way ahead is now closed due to the danger of falling ice – easy to imagine as you look up at the seracs splurging over the cliff face. Ice avalanches have in any case destroyed the old bridge, making a crossing of the Biderbach torrent hazardous. Instead, cut diagonally left down through light larch forest to reach **Stafelalpe** (2084m), an alp hut with a massive slab-rock roof, 1¾ to 2¼ hours from Färich.

The route sidles on upvalley across the Schutzbach past the alp huts of **Bideralp** (1915m) to cross the larger Biderbach on a footbridge, where the Bidergletscher again looms ominously (but at a now safer distance) above you. Continue past derelict alp huts and pockets of forest carpeted with alpenroses and bearberry shrubs to reach the hamlet of **Sengg** (1794m), 40 to 50 minutes from Stafelalpe. This cluster of traditional Valaisan houses and barns stands among hayfields opposite the Triftgletscher on the Weissmies. Here, a signposted path branches off down to Saas Grund.

The path heads a short way on through the forest to reach the ***Restaurant-Hotel Fletschhorn*** (☎ *027-957 21 31,* e *info @fletschhorn.ch)*, which offers singles/doubles for Sfr80/145 and has a terrace restaurant well known for its fine cooking. Contour along the narrow hotel access track to **Üssere Wald** (1810m), from where a sealed road continues past the first modern chalets of **Wildi** (1820m). As you walk on into Saas Fee you get a marvellous view of the Feegletscher, which smothers the slopes above the resort in a vast sheet of ice. To get to the postbus station, turn down left at the village square, 40 to 50 minutes from Sengg.

Sunnegga to Riffelalp

Duration	1½–2 hours
Distance	7.5km
Standard	easy
Start/Finish	Zermatt

Summary Taking advantage of mountain transport to gain height, this very short panoramic route has minimal altitude differences. The walk makes an easier alternative to the Höhenweg Höhbalmen described later.

This delightful short day walk from Zermatt shows the Matterhorn from some of its classic 'chocolate-box' angles. The route passes by three of the loveliest lakes in the mountains around Zermatt, from where the Matterhorn's amazing wedge-shaped ridge known as the Hörnligrat seems to point directly toward you regardless of where you're standing.

Maps

The local tourist authority's 1:25,000 *Wanderkarte Zermatt* (Sfr24.90) shows all of the Zermatt area. Editions MPA Verlag's special

1:50,000 *Zermatt/Saas Fee 5006* (Sfr27.90) covers the whole Mattertal-Saastal basin. Another reasonable alternative is K+F's 1:60,000 *Visp-Zermatt-Saas Fee-Grächen* (Sfr24.80).

GETTING TO/FROM THE WALK

The walk begins at the upper station of the Sunnegga-Bahn (☎ 027-966 29 29), Europe's first underground funicular railway. The lower funicular station is 10 minutes on foot from Zermatt train station (walk first alongside the Gornergrat-Bahn rail lines then left after you cross the river). In summer the funicular runs every 15 to 20 minutes until around 5.30pm (Sfr13.60 adults, Sfr6.80 children/Half Fare Card, Sfr10.70 with Swiss Pass).

The walk ends at the Riffelalp station of the Gornergrat-Bahn, a scenic cog railway that goes up from Zermatt (see Access Towns) to the 3090m station on a lookout ridge called the Gornergrat. Between the end of May and late October trains run approximately half-hourly. The last train down leaves Riffelalp at around 7.30pm; the one-way fare is Sfr17.20 adults, Sfr8.60 children/Half Fare Card and Sfr13 with Swiss Pass.

THE WALK

See the Around Zermatt map, p230

The funicular takes you straight to Sunnegga, on a sunny ridge above the tree line at 2288m. From here a signposted foot track drops down several minutes to the **Leisee**, a shallow and elongated tarn whose tranquil waters mirror the Matterhorn's majestic 4477m form. Head on around the lakeshore, turning left where you come onto a broad, well-graded walkway coming up from the hamlets of Findeln and Eggen.

Follow this path eastward as it makes a gentle uphill traverse along the steep grassy slopes of the Findelalp high above the milky waters of the Mosjesee. After bearing right where a trail diverges to the Stellisee, continue down through stands of larches to reach the **Grindjisee** (2334m). This pretty little lake is another irresistible occasion to pack out the camera for that classic shot of the Matterhorn.

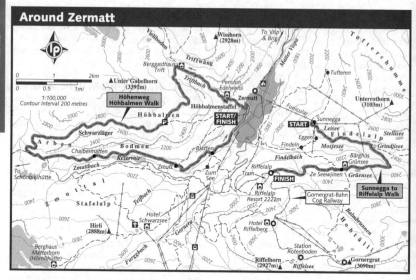

Around Zermatt

For the nicest views, walk around the Grindjisee's northern bank, and cross the tiny inlet to meet a dirt road just beyond a low lateral moraine. Here go right, tracing the roadway as it descends through a raw landscape of recent glacial deposits left by the receding Findelgletscher (up to your left), and pick up a foot track off left a short way after you cross the Findelbach bridge. The route leads up the regenerating hillsides, where there is a short section of easy boulder-hopping, to arrive at the **Grüensee** (2300m). This lake lies nestled into high meadows, with the tip of the Matterhorn poking up in the background. Make your way west across a road and down to the **Bärghüs Grünsee** (☎ 027-967 25 53), which has dorm beds for Sfr29 and singles/doubles from Sfr49/98.

A left turn a few paces on from the Bärghüs leads along a broad pathway through coarse glacial rubble, before you dip down into beautiful forests of graceful old larch and mountain pine. Contour on around slopes of Alpine heath, with airy views ahead toward the towering summits of the Ober Gabelhorn and the Zinalrothorn, to reach the train station at **Riffelalp** (2211m). The nearby

Hotel Riffelberg (☎ 027-966 65 00, ⓔ riffelberg@zermatt.ch) has singles/doubles from Sfr125/220. A newly reopened tram runs from the station to the renovated **Riffelalp Resort** (☎ 027-966 46 46, fax 027-966 05 50, ⓔ riffelalp@zermatt.ch, ⓦ www.riffelalp.com), at 2222m, which offers luxury rooms from Sfr260/480.

Höhenweg Höhbalmen

Duration	5¼–6½ hours
Distance	18km
Standard	medium
Start/Finish	Zermatt

Summary One of the longest circuit day hikes in the Zermatt area, this classic route leads directly from Zermatt up to the expanse of high-Alpine pastures known as Höhbalmen.

Lying at over 2600m, the rolling terraces of Höhbalmen provide one of the finest natural lookout points in Switzerland. The looming outline of the 4477m Matterhorn fixes the attention of walkers for much of the way, although the stunning vistas include almost two dozen other 'four-thousander' peaks.

Depending on the usual snow and weather conditions, this route can normally be done from June at least until late October. As there are some very worthwhile side trip options, the walk can be turned into an overnight outing by staying somewhere (preferably at the Berggasthaus Trift) en route.

Maps

Recommended maps are as for the Sunnegga to Riffelalp walk described earlier.

GETTING TO/FROM THE WALK

For information on transport to/from Zermatt, see Access Towns at the start of the section.

THE WALK

See the Around Zermatt map, p230

From Zermatt train station walk along the main street (Bahnhofstrasse) to an inconspicuous signpost at the Hotel Post, 200m before the village church. From here a cobbled footpath leads off to the right beside quaint old wooden barns, winding its way on more steeply up past holiday chalets and over hillside pastures. After crossing the Triftbach on a small wooden footbridge, climb on through the larch forest to reach the small *Pension Edelweiss* (☎ 027-967 22 36), open June to late September, after 40 to 50 minutes. This pension sits at 1961m on a balcony overlooking Zermatt and the upper Mattertal, and has a restaurant and singles/doubles from Sfr42/84.

The path rises gently to recross the stream near a hydroelectricity diversion tunnel, then continues up in several broad switchbacks above the Triftbach gorge to reach the *Berggasthaus Trift* (☎ 079-408 70 20) at 2337m, 50 minutes to one hour on. This cosy old three-storey mountain hotel (open July to late September) stands near a tiny chapel at the edge of a small grassy basin under the heavily crevassed Triftgletscher, and has dorm beds for Sfr54 and double rooms for Sfr64 per person (prices include full board). From here strenuous and lengthy side trips can be made up to the 3406m Mettelhorn or the SAC *Rothornhütte* (☎ 027-967 20 48), at

3198m on the rugged spur descending from the Zinalrothorn.

Cross the Triftbach a final time, quickly cutting southward across the tiny Alpine meadow, and begin a diagonal, spiralling ascent up the grassy slopes. Behind you the spectacular 4221m Zinalrothorn comes into sight, and as you move up onto the high balcony of the **Höhbalmenstaffel** an incredible panorama unfolds. The views sweep around from the Täschhorn to the Allalinhorn, the Rimpfischhorn, the Dufourspitze – at 4634m Switzerland's highest peak – the Breithorn and the Klein Matterhorn, with great highways of ice creeping down from their glacier-encrusted summits. Directly ahead stands the colossal tooth-like shape of the Matterhorn. The trail contours on through the rolling wild-flower fields known as the **Höhbalmen**, where the extremely rare purple-yellow Haller's pasque-flower grows, to reach a signpost at 2665m, 40 to 50 minutes from the Berggasthaus Trift.

Disregarding the left-hand path that goes back down into the upper Mattertal, make your way on westward into the Zmuttal. The route makes a high traverse around narrowing ledges opposite the awe-inspiring north face of the Matterhorn, reaching the highest point of the walk at **Schwarzläger** (2741m) after 40 to 50 minutes. There are excellent views of the moraine-covered Zmuttgletscher, and more ice-bound peaks rising up at the glacier's head around the 4171m Dent d'Hérens.

Make a steady, sidling descent over the sparse mountainsides of **Arben** below small hanging glaciers that spill over the high craggy cliffs on your right. The path snakes down to meet a more prominent walking track, which leads down from the easily reached SAC *Schönbielhütte* (☎ 027-967 13 54), alongside the high lateral moraine wall left by the receding Zmuttgletscher. Follow this down left in zigzags through the loose glacial rubble, before continuing along the gentler terraces above the Zmuttbach toward mighty horned peaks to pass the restaurant at **Chalbermatten** (2105m), which is one to 1¼ hours from Schwarzläger. Throughout the summer months, these grassy slopes are grazed by Valaisan black-nosed sheep.

Head on smoothly down above a small turgid-blue reservoir (whose water is diverted via long tunnels into the Lac des Dix in the adjacent Val d'Hérens), bearing right at a junction by the dam wall. This soon brings you down to the hamlet of **Zmutt** (1936m) with its St Katharina chapel built in 1797 and traditional old wooden buildings, from where an alp track descends on through hayfields dotted with neat farmhouses to intersect with a gravelled lane coming from Blatten and Zum See. Amble leisurely on past the Schwarzsee cable-car station, then take the next left turn-off leading up back into the thriving heart of Zermatt, 1¼ to 1½ hours from Chalbermatten.

Central Valais

The Central Valais stretches along the Rhône Valley from Sion to Visp, bridging the French/German language border. The region includes the Lötschental, the Turtmantal, the Val Anniviers and the Val d'Hérens – larger northern and southern lateral valleys of the Rhône.

Given its relatively small area, there are some striking climatic differences within the Central Valais. The central Rhône Valley around Sion is the driest part of Switzerland, receiving scarcely more than 500mm of rain annually. Directly south in the upper Val d'Arolla, however, precipitation levels reach 4000mm.

Although the Central Valais accounts for a large proportion of Switzerland's wine produce, agriculture here would be severely limited without the region's intricate system of small aqueducts. Called *bisses* in French or *Suonen* in the local German dialect, these little canals divert water from mountain streams to irrigate the orchards and vineyards. In places the tiny wooden aqueducts are constructed along escarpments or fixed onto high precipices. Maintenance paths leading alongside the aqueducts serve as convenient walkways, since they have very slight inclines and usually offer excellent views. Two such routes, the Bisse de Ro near Crans-Montana and the Bisse de Clavau above Sion, are featured in this guidebook.

The Rhône Valley

Until the 19th century the Rhône Valley was a landscape of wetlands, moors and impenetrable forest thickets along the river banks, and life in the valley was made difficult by repeated floods, insect plagues and swamp disease. From the 1860s, successive projects drained the waterlogged areas to create farmland and straightened the river's once wildly meandering course. Today, the Rhône is largely tamed, and in many places the river flows well above ground level between levies. The Valais cantonal government recently approved a final 'correction' plan for the Rhône aimed at protecting the valley from even the worst once-in-a-millennium flood.

ACCESS TOWNS

Sion

The capital of Valais Canton, the small city of Sion (Sitten in German) lies at 491m beside the striking outcrops of Tourbillon and Valère. Historic fortifications top each of these rock hillocks, and prehistoric inhabitants of the area built the first dwellings in the sheltered saddle between them. Sion's Notre Dame cathedral is a 12th-century construction, and the town hall dates from 1657. Other buildings of historical interest are the 'sorcerers' tower' (in a remaining section of the original city walls) and the church of St-Théodule.

For more information contact the tourist office (☎ 027-322 85 86, fax 027-322 18 82, ⓔ info@siontourism.ch, Ⓦ www.siontourism.ch), Place de la Planta. A good range of outdoor and mountain equipment is available from Ochsner Sport (☎ 027-323 84 84), Rue de la Dixence 6.

There are tent sites by the Rhône at ***Camping Les Iles*** *(☎ 027-346 43 47, fax 027-346 68 47)*. Sion's ***youth hostel*** *(☎ 027-323 74 70, ⓔ sion@youthhostel.ch, Rue de l'Industrie 2)* has dorm beds for Sfr31 (with breakfast). The *Café-Restaurant Relais du Simplon* (☎ 027-346 20 30) has singles/doubles for Sfr35/68. The *Auberge des Collines* (☎ 027-346 20 80) charges Sfr40/80.

Five minutes from the station on Ave de France is a *Migros* shopping complex; the *Coop* is on Ave du Midi. For traditional fare, explore the central pedestrian district. *Taverne Sedunoise* (Rue de Rhône 25) is typical and inexpensive.

Sion is on the main Lausanne–Brig rail route, and all trains stop here. Numerous postbus services operate out of Sion and the city even has its own airport.

Sierre

Situated among vineyards near where the Val d'Anniviers meets the Rhône, Sierre (540m) is the uppermost French-speaking centre within the main valley. Its old historic heart and dry, sunny climate give Sierre a distinctly Mediterranean character. The Sentier Viticole/Rebweg route leads from Sierre through lovely terraced vineyards to the nearby German-speaking village of Salgesch in two hours, and introduces walkers to the local viticulture.

There is a tourist office (☎ 027-455 85 35, fax 027-455 86 35, [e] sierre-salgesch@vs info.ch, [w] www.sierre-salgesch.ch) in the train station.

Tent sites at *Camping Bois de Finges/Pfynwald* (☎ 027-455 02 84, fax 027-455 33 51) are around Sfr7 plus Sfr5 per person. The *Auberge des Collines* (☎ 027-455 12 48, fax 027-456 42 60), on Chemin du Grand-Lac, has simple singles/doubles for Sfr45/75. *Hôtel La Poste* (☎ 027-455 10 03, fax 027-455 10 03, 22 Rue du Bourg) offers better-standard rooms for Sfr65/110.

Five minutes to the left of the station on Ave General Guisan is a *Migros* supermarket. A *Manora* buffet-style restaurant is in the Centre Commercial to the west, open shopping hours; take bus No 1 from the station.

Sierre is on the main Rhône Valley rail line, and is a major stop for trains between Lausanne and Brig. Postbuses from here run south into the Val d'Anniviers and up to Crans-Montana, an Alpine resort to the

north-west of Sierre (see Nearest Towns & Facilities under the Wildstrubel Traverse in the Bernese Oberland chapter).

Lötschental

Duration	4½–7 hours
Distance	17km
Standard	easy-medium
Start/Finish	Blatten

Summary This walk explores the uppermost part of the Lötschental, an interesting intensely glaciated area shaped by repeated advances and recessions of the beautiful Langgletscher.

Enclosed on both sides by craggy glacier-hung ranges on the southern edge of Bernese Alps, the Lötschental is the longest and most important northern side valley of the Valais.

The Lötschental is more isolated than any other settled Alpine valley in Switzerland. Its only access is via a once-arduous route via the Quertalschlucht, an avalanche-prone gorge, and for centuries, regular contact with the outside world remained minimal. In winter the Lötschental would remain totally cut off for months at a time. Despite its inaccessibility, as early as 800 BC Celtic visitors ventured into the Lötschental to mine its lead deposits, and the name of both the valley and its river, the Lonza, are believed to come from *loudio*, the Celtic word for lead. The opening of the Lötschberg railway tunnel linking the Bernese Oberland with the Valais in 1913 finally broke the valley's isolation, but old customs and traditions have been upheld longer here than elsewhere.

During the Fasnacht festival (Carnival or Shrovetide – 2 February to Ash Wednesday) the young men don hideous carved wooden masks, called *Scheggeten*, in a custom that may date back to pre-Christian times.

Maps

The best walking map of the Lötschental is the local tourist authority's *Wander- und Skitourenkarte Lötschental*, available in 1:25,000 and 1:50,000 versions (which cost Sfr12 and Sfr22.50). Almost as good is the

SAW/FSTP 1:50,000 *Jungfrau* No 264T (Sfr22.50).

NEAREST TOWN
Blatten

Blatten (1540m) is the uppermost village in the Lötschental.

For information contact the Lötschental tourist office (☎ 027-938 88 88, fax 027-938 88 80, e info@loetschental, w www.loetschental.ch).

The *Hotel Breithorn* (☎ 027-939 14 66, fax 027-939 22 20) offers singles/doubles for Sfr55/110. The *Hotel Edelweiss* (☎ 027-939 13 63, fax 027-939 10 53) has rooms from Sfr95/160.

From early June until mid-October, most buses continue upvalley from Blatten via Gletscherstafel to the Hotel Fafleralp. Goppenstein is at the southern end of the Lötschberg railway tunnel on the Bern–Brig line. Trains from either direction stop at Goppenstein at least hourly; rail passengers coming from Bern will probably have to change in Spiez.

Private vehicles are best left at the large car park in Gletscherstafel, 4.5km farther upvalley from Blatten.

GETTING TO/FROM THE WALK

This is a circuit walk that begins and ends in Blatten. From the train station at Goppenstein there are around 20 daily buses to Blatten. This cuts at least two hours off the average walking time.

THE WALK

From the Blatten post office, walk up across the bridge to the modern church, following the sealed road upvalley past typical old wooden Valaisan houses to the hamlet of **Eisten**. Here an old mule trail heads off left through pastureland dotted with occasional garden plots above the stream to reach the 18th-century church of **Kühmad** at 1625m, after 30 to 40 minutes.

Continue along the path beside the main road and cross the side stream flowing down from hanging glaciers at the head of the Uisters Tal. The route climbs up directly over grassy slopes between sharp bends in

the road then through light larch forest before coming to **Fafleralp** at 1787m, 50 minutes to one hour from Kühmad. Here the *Hotel Fafleralp* and the affiliated *Hotel Langgletscher* nearby (☎ 027-949 14 51 for both) are open mid-May to mid-October and offer singles/doubles from Sfr47/94 or dorm beds for Sfr32 (prices with breakfast).

Go on a few paces down the sealed road to where the road forks, then cut left over a flat lawn. After crossing another side stream on a stone footbridge, make a steeper, winding ascent to **Guggistafel** at 1933m. These dozen-odd alp huts (most now converted into holiday cottages) sit perched on a gently sloping shelf with breathtaking views southward across the upper valley toward the sheer 700m wall of the (Lötschentaler) Breithorn. Make your way up beside a little brook that flows along the base of an ancient lateral moraine, gently rising above the trees onto lovely open Alpine slopes scattered with bilberry and rhododendron bushes to reach the tiny lake known as the **Guggisee** (2007m), 50 minutes to one hour on.

Follow the white-red-white markings on through the rolling pastures and heathland of the **Gugginalp** toward the Langgletscher. The glacier's crevassed ice sprawls down from the narrow gap of the Lötschenlücke (3178m), which is also the source of the Grosser Aletschgletscher. Many other smaller hanging glaciers cling to the precipitous mountains on both sides of the enclosed upper valley. After passing through loose rockslides ease around leftward into the tiny valley of Jegital to cross a churning little gorge on a footbridge (2108m). From this point a worthwhile roughly 1½-hour return side trip can be made up to the Anensee, an Alpine tarn at around 2350m. From immediately after the bridge, the circuit climbs over Alpine meadows to pass the *Anenhütte* (☎ 027-939 17 64) at 2358m just before the lake. The hut has dorm beds for Sfr52 with full board.

Head on down first alongside the stream, then move leftward through regenerated moraine slopes to cross another bridge over the milky Lonza not far below where it emerges from the Langgletscher, 40 to 50

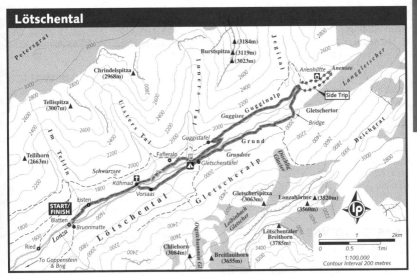

Lötschental

minutes from the Guggisee. The snout of the glacier, known as the **Gletschertor**, can be quickly reached by following rough but well-trodden trails through the rubble along the southern side of the river. Meltwaters produce interesting caves and arched forms in the debris-covered ice. The Langgletscher protruded much farther into the valley until recently, and has only receded to its present position over the last 150 years.

Proceed downstream across the rocky landscape left in the wake of the glacier's recession. The farther on you go the more advanced is the state of regrowth. The route leads on through stands of larch trees and attractive grassy terraces strewn with fallen boulders before crossing the outlet of the picturesque **Grundsee** (1842m) after 30 to 40 minutes. This shallow lake lies just off the main path, its clear, greenish waters reflecting the surrounding peaks. A broad mule trail now winds its way gently down after a further 15 to 20 minutes to recross the Lonza at the hamlet of **Gletscherstafel** at 1771m.

The foot track climbs up across pleasant forested slopes high above the grassy southern banks of the Lonza, before dropping down via the alp huts of **Vorsaas**

(1674m) to arrive back at **Kühmad** on the main road. From here retrace your steps as described at the start of the walk, to reach **Blatten** (1705m), one to 1¼ hours from Gletscherstafel.

Bisse de Clavau

Duration	2–2½ hours
Distance	7km
Standard	easy
Start	Sion
Finish	St-Léonard

Summary This half-day walk takes you into an intensively cultivated landscape along a beautiful section of the Chemin Vignoble, a long-distance trail leading through the Central Valais' sun-drenched wine-growing district.

The Bisse de Clavau is a 500-year-old aqueduct that carries water 6km to the thirsty vineyards of the Rhône Valley. These steep, south-facing slopes are devoted almost entirely to the production of the fine red and white Valaisan wines known as Dôle and Fendant. Here the vines are planted on narrow terraces supported by dry-stone retaining walls that defy the steep gradient.

The going on these sun-exposed slopes can get very hot, however, so in summer wear a hat and carry liquid refreshment. Apart from the coldest days of winter, the walk can be done in virtually all seasons, although autumn is the most recommended time.

Maps

The best walking map covering the route is SAW/FSTP's 1:50,000 *Montana* No 237T (Sfr22.50). Editions MPA Verlag's 1:25,000 *Sion-Thyon* only just includes the Bisse de Clavau. Another good alternative is K+F's 1:60,000 walking map *Val d'Anniviers-Val d'Hérens-Montana* (Sfr24.80).

NEAREST TOWNS
St-Léonard

The walk ends at this tiny village surrounded by vineyards. Nearby is the fascinating Lac Souterrain, a 200m-long underground lake. St-Léonard has a small tourist office (☎ 027-203 22 31, W www.st -leonard.vsnet.ch).

The *Café de la Place* (☎ 027-203 22 88) has singles/doubles for Sfr40/70. *Auberge*

du Pont (☎ 027-203 22 31, e auberge_ du_pont@span.ch) serves Italian and Valaisan specialities and offers double rooms from Sfr85.

GETTING TO/FROM THE WALK

For information on transport to/from Sion, see Access Towns earlier. Postbuses running at approximately half-hourly intervals between Sion and Sierre call in at St-Léonard.

THE WALK

From Sion train station, walk 200m straight ahead then turn right onto the Rue des Creusets. Follow various small pedestrian laneways on up through Sion's old town, proceeding north along the Rue de Portes Nueves and Rue du Grand-Pont just past the old **Walliser Brauerei** building. Here a signpost points you off right on a pathway leading up between stone walls through the first hillside vineyards to a hairpin bend at the start of the **Bisse de Clavau** after 40 to 50 minutes.

The route (signposted 'Chemin Vignoble') now begins an easy contouring traverse eastward beside the tiny aqueduct among steeply terraced vineyards. The grape vines

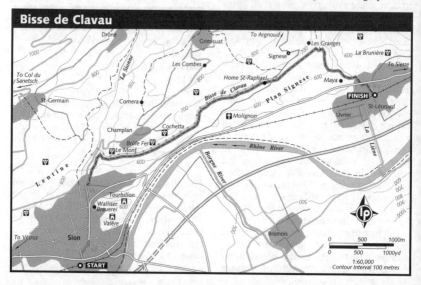

have been planted in closely spaced rows in order to maximise the yield of this valuable crop. Over to your right are the Tourbillon and Valère, two rounded outcrops crowned by historic fortresses. These high rock hills rise abruptly out of the built-up floor of the Rhône Valley. It seems remarkable that they survived the intense shearing action of the Rhône Glacier during past ice ages.

Continue on above a sweeping curve of the Rhône River, enjoying views of the high mountains right along the valley. The route crosses several small roads, passing below the tiny village of Signese and the scattering of houses at Les Granges before turning down to the right away from the Bisse de Clavau. Make your way via a gravelled farm track along the edge of the vineyards above the gorge of the Liène (the waters of which are diverted subterraneously farther upstream to feed the irrigation channels), short-cutting a few curves in the road.

Yellow arrows guide you quickly down past **Maya** to a cobblestone laneway leading across the fast-flowing stream to reach the village of **St-Léonard** (508m), 1¼ to 1½ hours from where you first met the Bisse de Clavau. The local postbus stop is 400m east along the main road.

Col de Riedmatten/ Pas de Chèvres

Duration	5½–7 hours
Distance	21km
Standard	medium-hard
Start	Arolla
Finish	Lac des Dix/Le Chargeur

Summary This exhilarating walk (the 7th leg of the two-week Haute Route) leads over either of two high, narrow passes among the heavily glaciated terrain typical of the Pennine Alps.

The Col de Riedmatten and the Pas de Chèvres, situated no more than 200m apart, are the only crossing points between the Val des Dixence and the upper Val d'Hérens. Crowned by the classic 'north face' peak of Mont Blanc de Cheilon, this dual pass is surrounded by mighty summits

The Hérens Cow

The special Hérens breed of cow, a descendent of the almost extinct European auerochs, originates from the Val d'Hérens. Once favoured by the Alpine herders for their hardiness in the mountains, today Hérens cows are most prized as fighting beasts for the (harmless) cow-fighting contests (or *combat de reines*) held in the French-speaking regions of the Valais throughout the summer.

that rise up boldly between large valley glaciers.

The walk leads to the massive Lac des Dix dam wall, an impressive feat of engineering. The area around the reservoir is a nature reserve – no dogs, mountain bikes or camping – with a surprising variety of wild flowers. This route can be combined with the following Col de Louvie walk to make an excellent three-day tour.

Maps

The local tourist authorities' 1:25,000 *Val d'Hérens* (Sfr18) is recommended, but the SAW/FSTP 1:50,000 *Arolla* No 283T (Sfr22.50), which covers a much larger area, is an excellent alternative. K+F's large-format 1:60,000 *Val d'Anniviers-Val d'Hérens-Montana* (Sfr24.80) is also good.

NEAREST TOWNS
Arolla

This tiny Alpine ski village sits at 2006m on a small shelf near the head of the Val d'Arolla, below the spired-rock ridges of the Aiguilles Rouges and the Aiguille de la Tsa. As its name suggests, attractive forests of arolla pine fringe the village. For information contact the tourist office (☎ 027-283 10 83, fax 027-283 22 70, [e] arolla @span.ch, [w] www.arolla.ch).

Camping Petit Praz (☎ 027-283 22 95, fax 027-283 22 95) down in the valley has tent sites for Sfr6 plus Sfr4.90 per person. *Chalet Edelweiss (☎ 027-283 12 18, [e] hotel .glacier@bluewin.ch)* and ***Dortoir Le Sporting (☎ 027-398 19 09)*** have dorm beds for around Sfr25. **Hôtel du Glacier** (☎ 027-283 12 18, **e** hotel@glacier@blue win.ch) on the village square has singles/ doubles from Sfr57/94. The older-style **Hôtel Mont-Collon** (☎ 027-283 12 18) charges slightly more.

There are postbus connections from Sion (see Access Towns earlier) to Arolla up to seven times daily, usually with a change in Les Haudères – the trip is quite scenic.

Le Chargeur

This hydroelectricity complex at 2141m lies at the base of the Lac des Dix dam wall. The **Hotel Grand Dixence** (☎ 027-281 13 22, **e** f.gessler@scopus.ch) has budget rooms and dorm beds.

There are up to four daily buses between Sion and Le Chargeur from around 20 June to early October. Outside this period the service stops. For roughly the same period a cable car runs up between Le Chargeur and the Lac des Dix station beside the dam wall (Sfr4/2 adults/children, no concessions).

GETTING TO/FROM THE WALK

For information on transport to/from Arolla and Le Chargeur, see Nearest Towns earlier.

THE WALK

See the Around Lac des Dix map, p239
Follow the road up from Arolla, short-cutting between the bends to reach the **Hôtel Kurhaus Arolla** (☎ 027-283 11 61) after 10 minutes. This historic mountain hotel, dating from the 1890s, has rooms from just Sfr43 per person. Take the signposted broad path above the Kurhaus, and head up into forest of lovely old larches and arolla pines. The route soon passes a right turn-off to the SAC's Cabane de Vignettes as it switchbacks up to meet a rough alp track. Follow this quickly up past a left turn-off to the Glacier de Piece to reach a small alp hut at **Tsijiore Nouve**.

A signpost directs you off right along a winding path leading through the uppermost scattered pines to the disused alp huts of **La Remointse d'Arolla** (2399m), 50 minutes to 1¼ hours from the Hôtel Kurhaus Arolla. This grassy terrace looks out toward the

mighty ice-encrusted Mont Collon (3637m) towering above the Glacier d'Arolla in the south-east .

Continue up Alpine pastures of the **Montagne d'Arolla** beside the perfectly formed lateral moraine left by the Glacier de Tsijiore Nouve, whose debris-strewn mass snakes down from the 3790m domed form of Pigne d'Arolla. The path ducks under ski tows before crossing a bridge over the small stream draining Les Fontanesses, the snowy basin up to your right. Cut on up west through grassed-over old moraines and boulder fields to a route junction, one to 1½ hours from La Remointse d'Arolla.

The *right* branch heads up into the broad open gully to follow a partly revegetated moraine ridge, before cutting up left into the rocky gap of the **Col de Riedmatten** (2919m) after 20 to 30 minutes. It then makes a steep 10-minute descent through a broken-rock gully.

The *left* branch sidles up slopes dotted with yellow groundsels, Alpine houseleeks and occasional purple gentians, making a few minor switchbacks to arrive at the **Pas de Chèvres** (2855m). On its west side, the pass drops away in 20m cliffs, and the only way down is via a fixed steel ladder. If you find this too unnerving, go back to the Col de Riedmatten route. Once down, follow red paint markings right for 300m through the glacial rubble to meet the path from the Col de Riedmatten, 25 to 30 minutes from the junction on the east side of the col.

Both the col and the pass offer sensational views across the vast **Glacier de Cheilon** (see the Cabane des Dix Side Trip at the end of the walk description), directly below. The north face of the 3869m Mont Blanc de Cheilon at the head of the valley is particularly impressive, and the enormous **Lac des Dix** stretches along the valley down to your right.

The path traverses north-west through coarse moraine rubble high above the glacier, whose lower portion resembles a giant gravel dump. As you gradually come out onto sparsely vegetated slopes, begin a winding descent across several eroded gullies into **La Giétret**, a steep wild-flower

meadow of field gentians, yellow-mauve Alpine asters and the rare edelweiss. The route crosses a suspension footbridge spanning a deep gorge of the Dixence, just where this stream enters Lac des Dix, to meet a narrow dirt road cut into the cliff side – the so-called **Pas du Chat** (2371m) – 1½ to two hours from the junction west of the Col de Riedmatten. Directly opposite, a feeder tunnel spills out over the rocks into the lake in a dramatically spectacular – if unnatural – waterfall.

Follow the road around the south-west corner of the lake, where the **Glacier de l'En Darrey** streams down from the 3703m Le Pleureur. The way now gently rises and dips along the lake's western shore through pastures sprinkled with yellow mountain saxifrage and grazed by Hérens cattle. Above high grassy ridges up to your left, hanging glaciers cling to the peaks of the Rosablanche range. Crags of the Aiguilles Rouges d'Arolla rise up on the other side of Lac des Dix, in which drowned alp huts are visible during periods of low water. After one to 1½ hours you come to **La Barma**, where a signposted path climbs away left to the 2804m Col des Roux (a short-cut route to the Cabane de Prafleuri – see the Prafleuri–Louvie Traverse walk later).

The road continues on through a series of tunnels (the longest with lights), passing the main path to the Col de Prafleuri just before it reaches the upper cable-car station at the **Barrage de la Grande Dixence**, 30 to 40 minutes on. From this massive dam wall, there are good views down along the Val d'Heremence and back up along the lake.

If you don't take the cable car down to the village of Le Chargeur, a well-trodden foot track descends below the dam wall in steep switchbacks to reach the village in 20 to 30 minutes.

Side Trip: Cabane des Dix
1–1¼ hours return, 2.5km return,
90m ascent
Cabane des Dix (☎/fax 027-281 15 23) at 2928m stands on a high knoll below the Glacier de la Luette icefall. From the junction on the west side of the col, an unmarked

Lac des Dix

With a storage capacity of up to 400 million cubic metres, Lac des Dix is easily Switzerland's largest artificial lake. For decades after its completion in 1962, the 285m-high dam wall remained the highest in the world (now the third highest). This colossal concrete structure is 700m long and almost 200m wide at the base. Along with the somewhat smaller Lac de Mauvoisin, Lac des Dix is the centrepiece of the enormous Grande Dixence hydroelectric scheme, which is fed by a vast system of tunnels and aqueducts that tap every larger waterway in the Pennine Alps.

route cuts south-west across a crevasse-free section of the Glacier de Cheilon to this SAC-run hut, with dorm beds for Sfr25. Although this is a popular and generally quite safe route, walkers should tread cautiously on the ice.

Prafleuri–Louvie Traverse

Duration	2–3 days
Distance	18km
Standard	medium-hard
Start	Le Chargeur
Finish	Fionnay

Summary This outstandingly scenic walk leads across several narrow passes through a postglacial landscape of raw moraine basins, meltwater tarns, glacial lakes and smaller receding glaciers. The walk largely overlaps with the 6th leg of the two-week Haute Route.

The route leads out of the upper Val d'Heremence from the huge Lac des Dix reservoir through these glaciated ranges into the upper Val de Bagnes. There are some breathtaking views of the high '3000er' peaks of the Pennine Alps, most particularly the Combin de Corbassière, but it's not all stark, bare terrain. The upper Val de Bagnes is a prime wildlife habitat, with large populations of chamois, ibex, marmots, snow hares and martens. The golden

Looking north across Switzerland's largest reservoir, the Lac des Dix.

eagle and snow grouse are found here, and the valley is a nesting site for the endangered chough (see the boxed text 'The Chough' later in this section).

The route is almost entirely above the tree line, and walkers can expect to encounter quite a bit of snow until at least mid-July. The path is rougher on the central part of the walk, although route markings are usually adequate.

Maps

The route is covered by SAW/FSTP's 1:50,000 *Arolla* No 283T (Sfr22.50) or the K+F 1:60,000 *Val d'Anniviers-Val d'Hérens-Montana* (Sfr24.80).

Regulations

West of the Col de Louvie, the walk transits a nature reserve (Zone Protégée Haut Val de Bagnes), which Swiss conservationists would like to become part of a larger national park. The flora and fauna are strictly protected, and camping and dogs are not allowed in the reserve.

NEAREST TOWNS
Le Chargeur

For information on accommodation and transport, see the Col de Riedmatten/Pas de Chèvre walk earlier.

Fionnay

This tiny village at 1491m is dominated by the Mauvoisin hydroelectricity plant.

The **Pension-Restaurant Grand Combin** (☎ 027-778 11 22, fax 027-778 16 22) has singles/doubles for Sfr50/100 and dorm beds for Sfr32 with breakfast. In the village of Loutier, about 1½ hours' walk on downvalley, is the **Hôtel La Vallée** (☎ 027-778 11 75, fax 027-778 16 04), with rooms and dorms at marginally higher prices.

There are just four daily postbuses to Fionnay from Le Châble (see Access Towns in the Lower Valais section later) from approximately 24 June to 24 September, but only two buses daily outside this period. The service from Loutier is more frequent.

GETTING TO/FROM THE WALK

From mid-late June until early October four daily buses run from Sion to Le Chargeur (a pleasant trip taking just over an hour); outside these times there is no service at all. The first section of Day 1 can be done by cable car, which during the same period runs from Le Chargeur to the upper Lac des Dix station at the western side of the dam wall (Sfr4/2 adults/children, no concessions). The last trip is around 6.25pm.

THE WALK

See the Around Lac des Dix map, p239
As the only huts on this essentially two-day walk are an hour or so from the start and finish, most walkers will combine either Day 1 or Day 3 with Day 2.

Day 1: Le Chargeur to Cabane de Prafleuri

1½–2¼ hours, 3.5km, 521m ascent
The broad path from Le Chargeur winds up south-west under the stupendously high dam wall to reach the upper cable-car station (2433m) after 30 to 45 minutes. From here you get a fine view along the enormous **Lac des Dix** reservoir stretching up the drowned valley to the 3869m Mont Blanc de Cheilon.

Walk a few minutes south beside Lac des Dix and take a narrow vehicle track leading up right. This climbs in several switchbacks past a road tunnel (a viable, but decidedly less scenic alternative route) to end near a ski hut. Here follow a broad, well-graded path around south-west and sidle high above the **Combe de Prafleuri**, a tiny side valley of the Dixence. The route rises gently opposite a waterfall to cross the small stream just before reaching a raw glacial hollow, one to 1½ hours from the dam wall. Quarrying here during construction of Lac des Dix has added to the desolation.

On an outcrop up to your left, just a few minutes away, stands the **Cabane de Prafleuri** (☎ 077-28 46 23) at 2662m. This recently extended SAC hut has dorm beds for Sfr26, and is staffed in July and August. From the hut a route crosses the Col des Roux to La Barma (see the Col de Riedmatten walk earlier).

Day 2: Cabane de Prafleuri to Cabane de Louvie

4–5 hours, 11km, 556m total ascent
Cross the stream and ascend north-west over grassy slopes above a small diversion weir then via a gully to an old road. Follow this around north-west just past a concrete building, before you break away right again across a gravel wash in the Prafleuri basin. The route turns westward as it cuts up along a rocky shelf overlooking several murky tarns to reach the **Col de Prafleuri** (2987m), one to 1¼ hours from the Cabane de Prafleuri. This gap in the ridge offers an excellent perspective on the 3336m Rosablanche, at the head of the Glacier de Prafleuri just to the south-west, and there are new views west toward Mont Fort (3328m).

The route now picks its way down west through boulders (where some minor handwork may be required) before heading on around meltwater ponds at the rounded snout on the eastern section of the **Grand Désert** glacier. At the last of these tarns (where markings are poor) skirt briefly left around the fractured rock, then double-back up right.

You now begin a spectacular high traverse along a ledge strewn with glacial debris, where tiny blue gentians shelter in the rock crevices. Winter snows lie long here, but orange poles and white-red-white paint splashes show the way. To the north an escarpment falls away into the lakeland basin of Grands Bandons. The route gradually

The Chough

In Switzerland, the chough *(Pyrrhocorax pyrrhocorax)*, an extremely rare and endangered European member of the crow (Corvid) family, is found almost exclusively in the upper Val de Bagnes. With its glistening all-black plumage, the chough can be readily distinguished from the Alpine jackdaw and black crow species by its red legs and long, curved, orange-red beak. The chough gets its English name from its clear 'chee-oof' call.

descends to a signposted junction near a small pool (2826m) at the edge of the Grand Désert glacier, one to 1¼ hours from the Col de Prafleuri. A path turns away north from here to Haute-Nendaz (passing the **Refuge St-Laurent** (☎ 027-288 50 05) – which has a dorm – after one hour), from where there are buses to Sion.

Ahead, there are two minor route variants. The best advice is to cut down north-west over boggy, recent moraines to cross the outlet of a meltwater tarn (around 2750m), then skirt around back up through the rubble. Most walking maps, however, show the route cutting directly south-west across the glacier – a more arduous and somewhat hazardous route that takes almost as long. Orange poles mark where you meet the path again on the far side. Climb through a rock-filled gully – earlier in the season snow makes this section easier – and into a steep chute to arrive at the **Col de Louvie** (2921m), 30 to 40 minutes from the junction at 2826m. The magnificent Combin de Corbassière (3715m), a hulking, glacier-shrouded summit, comes into sight a few paces on.

Head down over sparse Alpine slopes grazed by timid herds of long-horned ibex, hopping across small boulder fields to pass a minor right turn-off to the Col de la Chaux. The glorious views of the magnificent Corbassière massif continue as you make a high, sidling descent along the northern side of the new valley to reach a minor intersection, one to 1¼ hours from the Col de Louvie.

Turn left here (the way ahead sidles on to the Col Termin) and drop steeply along a vague ridge to **Plan da Gole**, a lawn-like flat by the stream. The path winds on down onto waterlogged meadows covered with monk's rhubarb and purple common monkshood to **Lac de Louvie**. Here, on the lake's picturesque northern shore, are several historic alp huts, including the **Ecurie de Louvie**, an early 19th-century cowshed with unique dry-stone arches and flagged roof. Also of interest are an old cheese cellar and a drinking trough carved from a single stone block. In summer algae turn the lake a cloudy green, but the water is quite clean and suitable for swimming or angling.

Skirt around the west shore past small springs to reach *Cabane de Louvie (☎ 027-778 17 40)*, 30 to 40 minutes from Plan da Gole. This new timber hut at 2250m looks out over the tranquil lake and (behind) across the upper Val de Bagnes to the Combin de Corbassière. It's staffed from mid-June to mid-September (otherwise closed), and offers dorm beds for Sfr25 (breakfast/dinner costs Sfr8/22 extra); showers are available.

Day 3: Cabane de Louvie to Fionnay
1¼–1½ hours, 3.5km

Walk down around a tiny weir, briefly following the meandering outlet stream (past an information board on flora and fauna of the surrounding nature reserve) before crossing on a footbridge. Begin a steep descent of tight switchbacks into the spruce forest, then sidle around south-east high above the Val de Bagnes and the massive fortress-like Lac de Mauvoisin dam wall at the head of the valley. The path finally cuts down through open slopes (past a left turn-off to Le Da) to reach a large concrete stabilisation pond, protected from avalanches by a mighty stone wall, at the edge of Fionnay (1491m). The post office is a few minutes up the road.

Lower Valais

After flowing through the cantonal capital of Sion, the Swiss Rhône enters the Lower Valais. At the Coude du Rhône near the ancient city of Martigny, the river makes an abrupt right-angle turn and continues northward between the Muverans and the Dents-du-Midi massifs to mouth in Lake Geneva. The so-called 'Drance valleys' – the Val de Bagnes, the Val d'Entremont and Val Ferret – and the Vallée du Trient intersect with the main Rhône valley at the Coude du Rhône.

The Lower Valais occupies a zone of climatic transition between the moister environs of Lake Geneva and the almost semi-arid conditions in the central part of the Rhône Valley. The age-old trade and travel route via the Col du Grand St-Bernard passes through the Lower Valais, and this French-speaking region is rather less isolated compared to the upper Rhône Valley. At least since Roman times this trans-Alpine pass at the head of the Val d'Entremont has been the most important crossing point between Italy and northern Europe.

The Mont Blanc massif extends well into Valaisan territory, and France, Italy and Switzerland actually converge on the 3820m summit of the Dolent. The highest and most intensely glaciated of all Alpine ranges, the mountains of the Mont Blanc massif provide stunning backdrops that dominate the views from many lookout points in the Lower Valais.

The Giétro Ice Avalanche

In the early 1870s, the entire lower section of the Glacier du Giétro broke away, crashing into the valley and impounding the Drance de Bagnes river where Lac de Mauvoisin now lies. This colossal ice dam was to take more than half a century to melt, and by 1918 locals had become alarmed at the height of the backwaters. Just as efforts were being made to drain the lake, however, the ice wall suddenly gave way, releasing a catastrophic wave that killed dozens of people as it swept down the Val de Bagnes.

VALAIS

ACCESS TOWNS
Martigny

Martigny (467m) lies at the Coude du Rhône, where the Swiss Rhône makes a sudden sweep around to the north before flowing into Lake Geneva. Virtually surrounded by some of the very highest summits in the Alps, this small city is well situated for hikes in the Dents-du-Midi, Mont Blanc and Grand Muveran massifs. A short day hike from Martigny follows the Chemin Vignoble through the nearby vineyards. The historic Roman Way (known locally as the Chemin de Rome), a long-distance pilgrim's route from Canterbury in England to Rome, passes through Martigny.

Martigny was the Roman centre of the Valais, and this small city retains more than a few vestiges of its Roman past. These include the large amphitheatre, where the Combat de Reines (traditional Valaisan cowfights) are held in spring and autumn, and the wide collection of Roman artefacts in the Gallo-Roman Museum. Also worth seeing are the 17th-century church and the 13th-century Château de la Bâtiaz on a hill just above town.

For more information contact the tourist office (☎ 027-721 22 20, fax 027-721 22 24, e info@martignytourism.ch, w www.martignytourism.ch), Place Centrale 9.

At *Camping Les Neuvilles* (☎ *027-722 45 44, fax 027-722 35 44, Rue de Levant 68)* tent sites cost Sfr7.50 plus Sfr6.40 per person (high season) and dorm beds for Sfr20 without breakfast. The *Pension Poste-Bourg* (☎ *027-722 25 17, Ave du Grand St-Bernard 81)* has singles/doubles for Sfr45/80.

The *Migros* supermarket is on Rue du Manoir. For sandwiches and fast food, try *Lord's Sandwich* on Place Plaisance. *Café-Restaurant Les Touristes*, also on Place Plaisance, has good Italian and Swiss food starting at Sfr13.

Martigny is the transport hub for the Lower Valais, and a major stop on the main Lausanne–Brig rail line. The *St-Bernard Express* trains run from Martigny to Orsières and Le Châble, and the *Mont Blanc Express* leaves at least every two hours to the French Alpine resort of Chamonix. Buses go from Martigny via Orsières and the Grand St-Bernard tunnel to Aosta in Italy.

Orsières

Orsières (901m) lies at the junction of the Val d'Entremont and the Val Ferret on the road over the Col du Grand St-Bernard into Italy. The belltower of the town church dates from the 15th century.

For information contact the Orsières tourist office (☎ 027-783 12 27, fax 027-783 35 27, e orsieres@saint-bernard.ch, w www.saint-bernard.ch).

The *Hôtel de Catogne* (☎ *027-783 12 30, fax 027-783 22 35)* has dorm beds for Sfr30 with breakfast and singles/doubles for Sfr50/80. The *Hôtel de l'Union* (☎ *027-783 11 38, e faulandj@yahoo.com)* has rooms from Sfr55/100 and dorm beds for Sfr22.50 (no breakfast).

There are roughly hourly train connections to Orsières from Martigny (with a change at Sembrancher) until just after 8pm. There are buses from Orsières via the Grand St-Bernard road tunnel to Aosta in Italy.

Le Châble-Verbier

Le Châble (820m), which is the administrative centre of Val Bagnes, lies in the lower Val de Bagnes below the ski resort of Verbier (1526m).

From Verbier popular walks go to the Lac des Vaux and the SAC's *Cabane Mont Fort* (☎ *027-778 13 84)*, although many walkers find the area excessively developed for winter sports. The Tour des Combins (a 10-day international circuit walk around the Grand Combin massif), also passes through Verbier.

For information contact the Verbier tourist office (☎ 027-775 38 88, e verbiertourism@verbier.ch, w www.verbier.ch).

In Verbier, the École d'Alpinisme La Fantastique, CH-1936 (☎ 027-771 41 41, fax 027-771 42 41) runs mountaineering courses as well as guided climbs and treks.

Le Châble's *Restaurant L'Escale* (☎ *027-776 27 07, fax 027-776 16 83)* and *Hotel La Ruinette* (☎ *027-776 13 52, e d.d.laruinette@dransnet.ch)* both have singles/doubles from Sfr45/90. Up in Verbier, the

Hôtel Rosablanche (☎ 027-771 55 55) has rooms for Sfr45/90.

The *St-Bernard Express* runs hourly from Martigny to Le Châble, and postbuses to Verbier meet arriving trains. A cable car also runs from Le Châble up to Verbier (Sfr7/10 one way/return).

Fenêtre d'Arpette

Duration	5–6¼ hours
Distance	14km
Standard	medium
Start	Col de la Forclaz
Finish	Champex
Nearest Town	Trient

Summary This walk (a leg of the eight- to 10-day Tour du Mont Blanc, or Mont Blanc Circuit) crosses the Fenêtre d'Arpette, a narrow gap that leads out of the spectacular upper Val du Trient into the beautiful Val d'Arpette.

At 2665m, the Fenêtre d'Arpette is a minor pass at the northern edge of the Mont Blanc massif. The valleys on either side offer contrasting high-Alpine scenery. The upper Val Trient is filled by the 7km Glacier du Trient whose broken ice spills down from hidden névés under the 3540m Aiguille du Tour in a jumbled mass of séracs. The Val d'Arpette is a wild little valley dominated by slopes of broken rock and talus, although the lower valley is a lovely area of highland pastures.

The Fenêtre d'Arpette is essentially a longish day walk, which can be done as an overnight route by staying at the Relais d'Arpette. The walk is best done between late June and late September, although old winter snows cover upper sections earlier in the season.

Maps

Recommended are either of two walking maps: the SAW/FSTP's 1:50,000 *Martigny* No 282T (Sfr22.50) or the local tourist authority's 1:40,000 *Au Pays du Grand St-Bernard* (Sfr20). A reasonable alternative is K+F's 1:60,000 *Grand St-Bernard–Dents-du-Midi–Les Diablerets* (Sfr24.80).

NEAREST TOWNS & FACILITIES
Trient

This small village (1279m) lies at the western foot – and it's a steep drop – of the Col de la Forclaz. It has a small tourist office (☎ 027-722 46 23, fax 027-722 19 29).

The *Relais du Mont Blanc (☎ 027-722 46 23, fax 027-723 29 91)* offers dorm beds for Sfr28 and rooms from Sfr46 per person. *Le Café Moret (☎ 027-722 27 07)* has similar prices.

Champex

Champex lies at 1472m above Orsières beside the Lac de Champex, an idyllic lake with a superb mountain backdrop that includes the snowcapped peaks of the Grand Combin. A cable car ascends above the lake to La Breya at 2374m, from where a four-to five-hour scenic semicircuit leads up past the Glacier d'Orny and the Glacier Saleina to Praz de Fort.

For information contact the tourist office (☎ 027-783 12 27, fax 027-783 35 27, e info @champex.ch, w www.champex.ch).

The tent sites at *Camping Les Rocailles (☎ 027-783 12 16, e pnttex@bluewin.ch)* are Sfr12 plus Sfr5.60 per person. The *Chalet Bon Abri (☎ 027-783 14 23, fax 027-783 31 76)* and *Auberge de la Forêt (☎ 027-783 12 78, e laforetchampex@dransnet.ch)* both offer dorm beds for Sfr35 and singles/doubles from Sfr50/100 (prices include breakfast).

Champex is reached by up to seven daily buses (until around 6pm) from Orsières.

Col de la Forclaz

At the start of the walk, the *Hôtel de la Forclaz (☎ 027-722 26 88, e forclaz@rooms .ch)* charges Sfr54/108 for singles/doubles, Sfr28 for dorm beds with breakfast and Sfr7 per person to camp.

GETTING TO/FROM THE WALK

Postbuses run from Martigny (see Access Towns at the start of the section) via the Col de la Forclaz to Trient up to five times daily; the last bus leaves Martigny at around 6.25pm. There are less frequent connections between Trient and Le Châtelard, on the

VALAIS

Mont Blanc Express rail line running between Martigny and Chamonix in France.

THE WALK

From opposite Hôtel de la Forclaz take the signposted alp track leading directly to the **Bisse du Trient**, and follow this small aqueduct into the spruce and pine forest high above the village of Trient. This broad walkway rises imperceptibly against the contour as it turns around into the upper Vallée du Trient to reach the **Buvette du Glacier** (1583m) after 40 to 50 minutes. This pleasant restaurant beside the rushing Trient (stream) sells light meals and refreshments. Just below the buvette, a prominent path goes off right to the Col de Balme on the Franco-Swiss frontier.

Head upvalley beside the stream through an open avalanche slope before beginning the long, winding climb left away from the stream. After leaving the forest for slopes of scattered larch trees, the views toward the

Glacier du Trient steadily develop. The heavily crevassed glacier tumbles down from a broad snowfield sandwiched between 3500m peaks, terminating in a typical snout with a milky stream emanating from an icy cavern. Traverse on up the mountainsides covered with alpenroses and other wild flowers, enjoying continual wonderful views of the glistening glacier ahead, to pass the ruins of a stone alp hut at **Vésevey** (2096m), one to 1¼ hours from the Buvette du Glacier.

Follow the well-trodden path leading up left (not the fainter trail leading right alongside the glacier) and begin the final ascent. The route steepens as it gains height, avoiding an area of coarse talus to arrive at the 2665m **Fenêtre d'Arpette**, 1¼ to 1½ hours on. The views from the pass itself are very satisfying, but by climbing a short way south along the rocky ridge you'll get a much better idea of the surrounding Alpine scenery, including part of the Plateau du Trient and the 3540m Aiguille du Tour. To

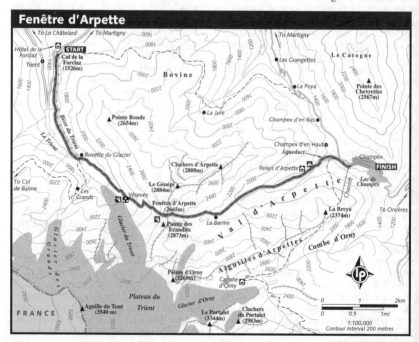

the north-west the mighty dam wall of the Lac d'Emosson can be identified.

Pick your way down over eroding rubble and snowdrifts into the upper Val d'Arpette, rock-hopping over a small bouldery section below the pass. The white-red-white marked path sidles on down through the sparse vegetation of the upper valley, whose southern sides are dominated by sweeping scree fields below frozen couloirs. Continue down into the beautiful larch forest along the north side of the tiny stream before crossing to a junction (where a path turns off right to La Breya). From here a rough alp track fringed by pink willowherb and birch shrub leads gently down through a lovely meadow to the **Relais d'Arpette** (☎ 027-783 12 21, fax 027-783 38 02), 1¾ to 2¼ hours from the pass. This pleasant mountain hotel at 1630m offers dorm beds from Sfr52 and rooms for Sfr70 per person (prices include full board); camping costs Sfr6 per person.

Crossing it several times on bridges, follow the stream downhill into the spruce and fir forest. From a small diversion weir the route commences a gentle descent alongside a canal (which feeds the artificial Lac de Champex) to emerge just above the lower station of La Breya chairlift immediately above the main road. The village of **Champex** (1472m) is clustered around the lake about 1km on to the right, or 25 to 30 minutes from Arpette.

Pas de Lovenex

Duration	5–7¼ hours
Distance	16km
Standard	easy-medium
Start	Miex/Le Flon
Finish	St-Gingolph

Summary This varied day or overnight walk leads through the rugged limestone ranges of the northern Chablais – one of Switzerland's lesser-known walking areas – fronting the French border on the southern side of Lake Geneva.

Unlike the rest of the Valais, the Chablais belongs to the pre-Alps rather than the Alps proper. Despite their modest height, the area's limestone ranges impress with craggy ridges and almost overhanging pinnacles. Small doline lakes, including the enchanting Lac de Tanay, are another interesting feature. Views from the upper slopes invariably include Lake Geneva, and the influence of this large water body produces a moist and relatively mild local climate. Consequently, the northern Chablais has a rich and diverse vegetation.

Maps

Recommended are either the regional tourist authority's 1:25,000 walking map *Region Chablais* (Sfr23), a larger sheet that also covers the Dents-du-Midi, or the Bouveret municipal council's small-format 1:25,000 *Sentieres pédestre du notre region* (Sfr4). The K+F 1:60,000 map *Grand St-Bernard–Dents-du-Midi–Les Diablerets* also covers the route.

Regulations

A sizable area surrounding Lac de Tanay lies within a nature conservation area – flora and fauna is protected and dogs must be kept on a leash.

NEAREST TOWNS
Miex/Le Flon

The scattered village of Miex/Le Flon (1080m) looks out across the Rhône valley toward the range of the Tour d'Aï. There is a *restaurant* here but nowhere to stay. From Vouvry, there are up to seven postbuses to Miex/Le Flon each day. Various public transport options are available to Vouvry, either by Lake Geneva ferry via Bouveret, or by train and/or postbus from Monthey, St Maurice or Aigle on the main Rhône valley rail line. Ferry connections tend to be less convenient.

Tanay

The walk passes through Tanay (also spelled Taney or Tannay), a tiny village at 1415m on the western shore of the idyllic Lac de Tanay under impressive limestone peaks.

Camping Municipal (022-755 24 65), on the lake's north-west shore, has tent sites for Sfr5 plus Sfr4.50 per person. The

Buvette Nicole Quille (☎ *024-481 14 80*), in a lovely old timber farmhouse, has dorm beds from around Sfr16 (without breakfast) and rooms from around Sfr40 per person, and serves meals and refreshments. *Café-Restaurant du Grammont* (☎ *024-481 11 83*) and *Petit-Auberge des Jumelles* (☎ *024-481 10 40*) have similar prices.

St-Gingolph

This attractive village lies on the south-eastern shore of Lake Geneva. Romantic bridged laneways connect both sides of St-Gingolph, which is divided into French and (the noticeably neater) Swiss halves by the small La Morge stream. The Musée des traditions et de barques du Léman (entry Sfr5) deals with the lake's maritime history.

The Swiss tourist office (☎ 024-481 84 31, e office@st-gingolph.ch, w www.st-gingolph.ch) is in the train station.

St-Gingolph is the rail terminus of the line from Monthey, although there are more postbuses to Aigle and St Maurice.

GETTING TO/FROM THE WALK

For information on transport to/from Miex/Le Flon and St-Gingolph, see Nearest Towns earlier.

Private vehicles can be left in the free car park at the start of the walk.

THE WALK

From the postbus terminus in the car park at the upper edge of Miex/Le Flon (1080m), turn off right and follow a narrow lane a few paces before cutting up left along a broad foot track. The route ascends increasingly steeply beside the dirt road (authorised vehicles only) through forest of beech mixed with spruce and maples, crossing the road before reaching a path turn-off to Prelagine below a high round pinnacle of the **Sechon**. Walk on up across the **Col de Tanay** (1440m), then stroll gently down past chalets above the picturesque, crystal-clear **Lac de Tanay** to arrive at **Tanay**, one to 1½ hours from Miex/Le Flon. The village and lake lie in a depression under abrupt limestone crags.

As is common in limestone areas, Lac de Tanay (1408m) drains subterraneously, and has no outlet.

Just across the bridge over the small inlet, turn left along an alp track leading directly past neat houses and take a left turn-off. This path recrosses the stream and heads up west through moist meadows of yellow gentians into the Vallon de Tanay, a tiny valley bordered on both sides by steep white ridges. The route makes a short steep climb out of the trees beside the cascading stream to rejoin the alp track. Turn around here for a last overview of the lake basin before heading on upvalley through karst fields and clusters of monk's rhubarb, an Alpine sorrel species. The alp track rises into the undulating grassy bowl of **Montagne de l'Au** (sometimes written 'Monton de Loz') to the **Chalet de l'Au**, an alp hut with cheese for sale.

After passing another alp hut at 1847m, the route goes over into a simple foot track and rises smoothly north-west past a peat bog to reach the **Pas de Lovenex** (1850m), 1¼ to 1¾ hours from Tanay. The pass overlooks the **Lac de Lovenex**, a shallow, reedy tarn in an undrained doline basin ringed by jagged limestone pinnacles. Skirt north-west through coarse talus slopes high above the lake for 20 to 25 minutes to reach the **Col de la Croix** (1755m). This final pass gives a good view of the rugged range of Le Dent d'Oche in France.

Drop down steeply west into a gully colonised by purple monkshood into the open pastures of **L'Haut de Morge**. The route cuts down sharply right – just a hare's breath from the Franco-Swiss border – to meet a road, which it follows quickly right to reach **L'Au de Morge** (1181), 50 minutes to 1¼ hours from the Col de la Croix. This alp dairy sells butter and cheese.

Follow the road downvalley toward Vevey and Montreux, which sprawl along Lake Geneva's narrow northern shoreline, and cross through a farm gate at the forest edge. The road winds down past a turn-off to the nearby French village of Novel through **Grand Pré** (898m), a small clearing under the sheer walls of **Rocher de la Croix**,

Pas de Lovenex

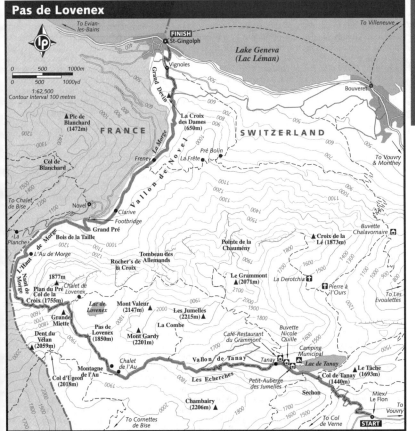

then on past holiday houses to **La Freney** (780m), where there is a small *café*.

Continue 2km down to a spring fountain marked by a cross known as **La Croix des Dames** (650m). A few paces on, turn down left and sidle 100m below the road, then take a (poorly marked) left turn-off. An old, heavily eroded path leads steeply down through shady beech forest with a holly understorey to emerge at a road in **Vignoles**. Follow the sealed road on down along the Rue du Freney into St-Gingolph, bearing down left to reach the village centre, 1½ to 2¼ hours from L'Au de Morge.

Other Walks

Rhonegletscher

Snaking down past the Galenstock in the uppermost part of Goms, the Rhonegletscher is the ultimate source of the Rhône, one of Europe's largest river systems. At the height of the ice ages the Rhonegletscher formed a colossal stream of ice that extended the whole way down through the Rhône Valley as far as Lake Geneva. Today the glacier is a comparatively meagre 9km in length, and – like glaciers the world over – has continued to creep steadily backward over the last century and a half.

The Gletscherpfad makes a very short return day walk introducing you to the interesting landscape left in the wake of recent glacial recession. Already small leafy plants are beginning to displace the primitive mosses and lichen that first colonised the moraines. The path begins near *Hotel Glacier du Rhône* (☎ 027-973 15 15, fax 027-973 29 13) in Gletsch, which at the time of its construction stood right next to the Rhonegletscher's snout.

From early until late September there are up to 10 daily postbuses from Oberwald to Gletsch. There are also several daily postbus connections to Gletsch from Oberwald, Andermatt and Meiringen (via the Grimselpass).

The standard 1:25,000 series *Ulrichen* map covers the Rhonegletscher route; otherwise use two SAW/FSTP 1:50,000 maps: *Nufenenpass* No 265T and *Sustenpass* No 255T.

Albrunpass

The 2409m Albrunpass (or Bocchetta Arbola) links Goms with northern Italy via the remote and fascinating Binntal, a side valley of the Rhône. Once the dangerous gorge at the lower Binntal had been negotiated, the way to the south was almost without natural hindrances, making this a favoured crossing point for trade, transport and military purposes from the early Middle Ages. In the 1840s English geologists found sulphate-based crystals in the Binntal, which exist nowhere else on earth. The first road into the Binntal was only completed in 1938, and before then the valley dwellers led a pious and spartan existence.

An easy-medium walk begins at the uppermost village of Binn (1400m), accessible by postbus from Fiesch, a station on the FOB railway. Binn's *Hotel Albrun* (☎ 027-971 45 82) has rooms at standard rates.

An old mule trail leads over an arched bridge and up via Fäld (a unique 17th-century hamlet), Brunnebiel, Freichi and the SAC's *Binntalhütte* (☎ 027-971 47 49) at 2269m, to reach the pass in around four hours. There is some superb Alpine scenery on both sides, and it's well worth continuing the hike into Italy. The descent leads via Alpe Dèvero to the village of Gòglio (1133m) in the Val Arbola; from here bus routes lead through the Valle Antigorio to Domodossola.

K+F's 1:60,000 *Aletsch-Goms-Brig* (Sfr24.80) covers the route.

Sirwoltseen & Gebidumpass

This popular walk grants you some truly wonderful views northward over the Spitzhorli as far as the Bernese Alps, eastward toward the ice-bound Monte Leone (3553m) and southward to the Pennine Alps.

It is a roughly six-hour walk of medium standard that is normally done from Engiloch (1813m), 4km south of the Simplonpass, and climbs over steep pastures past the Sirwolteseen, two lovely Alpine lakes, to the Bistinepass (2417m). The route skirts down around the upper Nanztal, then makes a high north-west traverse above the valley to the flat, open 2201m Gebidumpass. The Gebidumsee, a mountain tarn, is nearby. The descent to Visperterminen (1378m) can be made by chairlift from Giw (1976m), but the Kapellenweg route down through the forest past the Antoniuskapelle (chapel) is recommended.

From Visperterminen walkers can continue along the Rebenweg route, which leads down through vineyards – at around 1100m, the highest in Europe – to Visp in about two hours. Otherwise, there are roughly hourly postbuses to Visp.

Postbuses run every couple of hours from Brig over the Simplonpass, past the historic hospice (Alte Spittel), originally built in 1235 and extended by Stockalper as a summer residence and guesthouse for his mule drivers.

K+F's 1:40,000 map *Rund um Visp* (Sfr14.50) covers the route well.

Zwischbergenpass

One of the great high-Alpine passes on the continental divide, the 3268m Zwischbergenpass links the upper Saastal with the isolated southern Simplon region. The two- to three-day walk over the pass, which offers especially marvellous views of the peaks and glaciers above Saas Fee, is of medium-hard standard. There are several en-route places with dorms (and a few rooms).

The route climbs through the Almagellertal past the *Berghotel Almagelleralp* (☎ 027-957 32 06) to the SAC's *Almagellerhütte* (☎ 027-957 11 79) to the pass, then descends through the deep Zwischbergental past the *Restaurant Zwischetbergen* (☎ 027-979 13 79) at 1359m. From here walkers can either head north over the 1872m Furggu to Gstein (1228m), or continue downvalley to Gondo (855m). In October 2000 this village was largely destroyed by a landslide that killed over a dozen people.

From Gstein and Gondo there are regular postbuses north over the Simplonpass to Brig. The only walking map that shows the route on a single sheet is K+F's 1:60,000 *Visp-Zermatt-Saas Fee-Grächen* (Sfr24.80).

Matterhorn Hörnligrat

The Hörnligrat is the craggy north-east ridge that leads up like a knife-blade to the 4477m summit of the Matterhorn, giving the mountain its characteristic sharply angular appearance. Although considered unscaleable at the time, the Matterhorn was first climbed via the Hörnligrat route by a party led by the English mountaineer Whymper on 14 July 1865.

From Zum See (1766m), 2km upvalley from Zermatt, the route climbs to the upper cable-car station at Schwarzsee (2583m), where the **Hotel Schwarzsee** (☎ 027-967 22 63) has dorm beds for Sfr78 and singles/doubles from Sfr115/170 (prices include full board). An increasingly steep but well-travelled path ascends on via the lower Hörnligrat as far as the **Berghaus Matterhorn** (☎ 027-967 22 64). This SAC-affiliated hut (until recently known as the Hörnlihütte) stands at 3260m, and has dorm beds for Sfr66/73 SAC members/nonmembers and a few basic double rooms for Sfr198 (prices include full board). From here there are truly humbling views of the immense sheer rock walls that form the Matterhorn's east face – with a pair of binoculars you may even be able to follow the progress of the numerous climbing parties that tackle the Matterhorn every day. The summit is only accessible to experienced mountaineers (or very fit hikers accompanied by a locally accredited mountain guide – the all-inclusive ascent fee is Sfr935).

The return walking time from Zermatt to the Berghaus Matterhorn is about eight hours, which can be cut considerably by taking the Schwarzsee cable car (Sfr21 return fare). The best map is the 1:25,000 *Wanderkarte Zermatt* walking map (Sfr24.90).

Lötschberg Südrampe

The completion in 1913 of the Lötschberg railway with its 15km-long tunnel provided a transport link between Bern and the Upper Valais, and was a major engineering feat comparable to the construction of the Gotthard railway. The easy 5½-hour Lötschberg Südrampe (or 'southern terrace') accompanies the rail line as it makes a winding descent to the valley floor from Hohtenn (1078m) to Lalden (801m). The route leads along the steep northern side of the Rhône through some 20 smaller tunnels and 10 avalanche galleries, in places following small aqueducts that bring water to the thirsty fields below.

The walk offers some wonderful vistas southward as far as the Pennine Alps, and can be shortened by catching a train from the en-route stations at Ausserberg or Eggerberg. Being very exposed to the sun, the Lötschberg Südrampe remains snow-free for most of the year and can normally be done from early spring until late autumn – but summer walkers will need a good hat and sunscreen. K+F's 1:40,000 *Rund um Visp* (Sfr14.50) shows the route.

Bois de Finges/Pfynwald

A serene little wilderness in the otherwise hectic Rhône Valley, the Bois de Finges/Pfynwald lies just 2km east of Sierre. Its name originates from the Latin *ad fines*, meaning 'at the borders', and for over 1000 years the area has marked the division between the francophone and German-speaking regions of the Valais. The Bois de Finges/Pfynwald sits on old alluvial deposits onto which unstable mountainsides later collapsed to create this oddly scattered group of forested hillocks. Huge blocks of rock up to 50m in height still lie strewn around the area.

Here the Rhône flows at whim along its ancient river bed in meandering channels past the largest stands of black pine in lowland Switzerland. Shallow marshy lakes lie hidden within the forest, providing important wetlands in the dry landscape of the Central Valais. As a large obstacle impeding movement between the two parts of the valley, this 'no man's land' was left much to its own devices. Today the Bois de Finges/Pfynwald is protected as a nature reserve, but the area is still recovering from a major forest fire in May 1996.

A very easy circuit walk taking several hours can be made from the public car park near the camping ground at the western end of the reserve. The route leads through the quiet woods to the lakes of Rosensee and Pfafforetsee, then returns via the stud farm of Milljere. The free tourist maps probably best indicate the walking routes, but the 1:25,000 sheet *Sierre-Leuk*, published by local tourist authorities, shows the Bois de Finges/Pfynwald in more accurate topographical detail.

Val d'Anniviers

One of the Valais' major side valleys, the Val d'Anniviers, opens out directly south of the city of Sierre.

A six-hour panoramic walk leads from the village of Chandolin (1979m) southward high along the eastern side of the valley via Tignousa, the **Hôtel Weisshorn** (☎ 027-465 11 05), which has rooms and a dorm, and Lirec to Zinal (1675m). There are glorious views of the Alpine summits dominated by the mighty 4357m Dent Blanche at the valley head.

The walk can be shortened by an hour or so by taking the funicular up the village of St-Luc (on the road to Chandolin). From Sierre there are seven daily postbus connections to both Chandolin and Zinal (change in Vissoie); the last bus from Zinal leaves around 6.45pm. The best walking map is the local tourist authority's 1:25,000 *Val d'Anniviers* (Sfr20).

Glacier de Corbassière

Rising in the extensive névés that smother the Grand Combin massif, the Glacier de Corbassière is the fourth-largest glacier in Switzerland. This walk through a heavily glaciated, high-Alpine landscape gives spectacular vistas up this highway of ice to the mighty 4000m peaks of the Grand Combin. It is a two-day 12km route of medium-hard standard with a total ascent of 1400m.

From Fionnay climb south-west via Mardiuet and Plan Goli, before traversing alongside the broad icy belt of the Glacier de Corbassière to the *Cabane de Pannossière* (☎ 027-771 33 22), a modern SAC hut at 2645m. The route continues up east over the Col des Otanes (2880m), then descends via La Tseumette to Mauvoisin, below the massive dam wall of the Lac de Mauvoisin. The *Hôtel de Mauvoisin* (☎ 027-778 11 30) has singles/doubles for Sfr49/98.

There are several postbuses from Mauvoisin to Le Châble (via Fionnay) from approximately 24 June to 24 September.

The SAW/FSTP 1:50,000 *Arolla* No 283T (Sfr22.50) fully covers the route.

Col de Grand St-Bernard to Ferret

Used as a crossing point between the Val d'Aosta in Italy and the Lower Valais since prehistoric times, the 2469m Col de Grand St-Bernard is one of the great Alpine passes. The busy main transport route now bypasses the col via a long tunnel, but the less transited old road snakes its way right up to the pass height. From here a wonderfully scenic walk leads north-west via the minor passes of the Col de Chevaux (2714m) and the Col de Bastillon (2761m) to the Lac de Fenêtre, several lovely highland lakes at 2456m. The descent leads down to the hamlet of Ferret (1707m) in the upper Val Ferret. (This route is a section of the 10-day Tour des Combins circuit walk.)

This is a medium-standard route taking four to five hours. There are rooms and a dorm at the *hospice* (☎ 027-787 12 36, fax 027-787 11 07) on the Col de Grand St-Bernard. From late May to around 24 September there are five daily postbuses to the Col de Grand St-Bernard from Orsières; two of these services, at around 8.10am and 4.30pm, actually leave from Martigny and run all year. Postbuses run up to seven times daily from Ferret back to Orsières only between late May and about 24 September.

Best is the 1:40,000 *Au Pays du Grand St-Bernard* (Sfr20), published by local tourist authorities. A good alternative is K+F's 1:60,000 *Grand St-Bernard–Dents-du-Midi–Les Diablerets* (Sfr24.80).

Gorges du Trient

Originating at the Glacier du Trient, the Trient river flows down through a series of everdeeper gorges before meeting the Rhône 4km downvalley from Martigny. From point 1214m, on the road to Le Châtelard 1.5km north of Trient, a high-level route gently descends northeastward above the Gorges du Trient via the isolated hamlets of Litro, La Crêta, La Tailla and Gueuroz, before dropping down to the train station of La Verrerie in the Rhône Valley. The walking time is three to four hours.

The easiest access is by postbus from Martigny to Trient, from where you can either walk or take one of the several postbuses that continue (from late June to late September only) to Le Châtelard. Alternatively, take one of the roughly hourly trains from Martigny to Le Châtelard, then the postbus in the opposite direction. SAW/FSTP's 1:50,000 *Martigny* No 282T (Sfr22.50) or the local tourist authority's 1:25,000 *Vallée du Trient* (Sfr16) cover the walk.

Tour des Dents-du-Midi

This marvellous three- to four-day (preferably anticlockwise) circuit of medium standard leads around the spectacular Dents-du-Midi massif fronting the western side of the Rhône Valley, just north of where the river makes its abrupt northward turn. Highlights of the walk include the Col du Susanfe (2494m) and the lovely Lacs d'Antème in a superb cirque.

The best starting/finishing points are the village of **Mex** (1118m), accessible by postbus from St-Maurice, the scenic *Van d'en Haut* camping ground (☎ 027-761 11 26) just off-route at **Van d'en Haut** (1391m), accessible by postbus from Salvan (on the Martigny–Le Châtelard–Chamonix railway), or the resort of **Champéry** (1035m), accessible by hourly train from Aigle (on the main Rhône Valley railway line).

Five en-route places have dorms (most also rooms): *Auberge de Salanfe* (☎ 027-761 14 38) beside Lac de Salanfe, *Centre sportif* (☎ 024-471 34 94) at Des Jeurs, *Café Chindonne* (☎ 024-471 33 96) at Chindonne, *Cabane Anthemoz* (☎ 024-479 23 45) at the cirque of Antème, and the SAC's *Cabane de Susanfe* (☎ 025-79 16 46), on the west side of the Col du Susanfe.

The local tourist authority's 1:25,000 *Region Chablais* (Sfr23) is the recommended map. The SAW/FSTP's *St-Maurice* No 272T (Sfr22.50) is also good (but just cuts out Van d'En-Haut).

Ticino

The Italian-speaking southern canton of Ticino (Tessin in German) is quite different from any other part of Switzerland. On their southern side the Swiss Alps rise up abruptly from altitudes of scarcely 300m, with long and deep valleys, most notably the Valle Leventina, stretching northward far up into the mountains. In southern Ticino, Lago Maggiore and Lago di Lugano dominate the landscape. Created by massive ice-age glaciers, these large elongated lakes have fjord-like arms whose watery depths sink down below sea level. Ticino's major rivers, the Maggia, Verzasca and Ticino flow into Lago Maggiore. Lago di Lugano lies farther south beyond the minor watershed of Monte Ceneri in the small but interesting region known as the Sottoceneri.

Although well within the realm of the Alps, Ticino has a decidedly temperate climate. Conditions are surprisingly mild, with average winter temperatures in the valleys remaining above 0°C. Ticino's climate favours the cultivation of Mediterranean species such as figs and oranges, and has produced a rich native flora. Chestnuts thrive in the mountains, often forming beautiful forests (see the boxed text in the Sottoceneri section later).

Many of Ticino's hiking paths originated as routes used by itinerate Alpine shepherds, who for centuries drove their animals from pasture to pasture. This practice, known as *transumanza*, has now died out, but disused stone herders' cottages can still be seen throughout the Ticino Alps. Many of Ticino's Alpine valleys have experienced dramatic depopulation during the last 150 years, as industrialisation has attracted people away from the hardship and isolation of the mountains.

All this makes Ticino a true paradise for hikers – in fact many northern Swiss prefer to come here to walk. This chapter features 10 of Ticino's best hikes, and gives plenty of other walking suggestions.

Highlights

CLEM LINDENMAYER

A small church stands on a rocky outcrop high above the Valle Leventina.

- Resting in the charming rustic hamlet of Compietto on the Val di Carassino walk

- Taking a quick dip in the chilly Laghi di Formazzöö on the San Carlo to Bosco/Gurin walk

- Overnighting in old stone alp huts on the Barone Circuit

- Tracing undulating grassy ridges on the Tamaro–Lema Traverse

- Picking ripe bilberries on the highland heaths around Alpe Cardada

INFORMATION
Maps
The Kümmerly + Frey (K+F) 1:120,000 *Holiday Map Tessin/Ticino* (Sfr24.80) gives an excellent overview of the region, and shows important features for walkers. Sheet No 4 of the Federal Office of Topography's 1:200,000 series also covers Ticino.

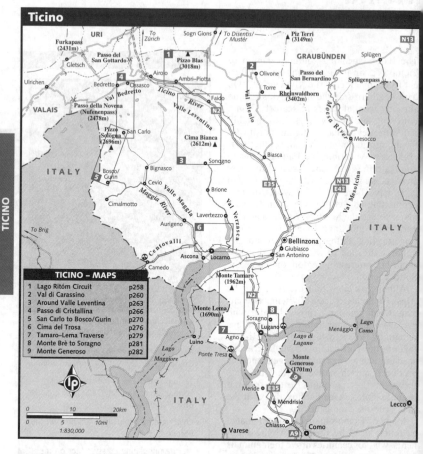

Ticino

TICINO – MAPS

0   10   20km
0   5   10mi
1:830,000

Books

The only English-language walking guide is *Walking in Ticino* by Kev Reynolds (Cicerone Press, UK£9.99). The guide provides a good coverage of walks throughout the entire Ticino region.

The German-language Kümmerly + Frey (K+F) *Rundwanderungen Tessin* (Sfr22.80) describes a number of good circuit walks throughout the region. Another German-language guide is *Strada Alta, Leventina, Bedrettotal* (Sfr27.80) by Hans Peter Nething, which covers walks in the northern part of Ticino.

Information Sources

The regional tourist office is Ticino Turismo (☎ 091-825 70 56, fax 091-825 36 14, e info@ticino-tourism.ch, w www.ticino-tourism.ch), Casella Postale 1441, CH-6501 Bellinzona. Information on the Valle Maggia is available from the tourist office in Maggia (☎ 091-753 18 85, e vallemaggia @etlm.ch, w www.vallemaggia.ch).

The Web site www.capanneti.ch lists mountain huts in Ticino (in Italian and German only). For information (in Italian only) on guided climbs, walks and courses contact Guide Alpine Ticino (☎ 091-968 11 19,

e info@guidealpine.ch, **w** www.guide
alpine.ch), Gradinata Pometta 3, 6900
Massagno.

GETTING AROUND

The *Arcobaleno* is a 'module' type pass that
gives unlimited travel on public transport in
any or all of the 22 zones (numbered 10 to
32) in Ticino and the Moesano region (Val
Mesolcina and Val Calanca) of Graubünden.
The minimum one-month pass costs from
Sfr33 (Sfr55 in 1st class) for two zones up to
Sfr158 (Sfr261) for all zones – the latter offers excellent value. The *Arcobaleno* gives a
50% reduction on the Monte Brè funicular.

A separate seven-day pass for the Lugano
region costs Sfr92 (Sfr82 with Swiss rail
passes) or Sfr70 (Sfr62) for three days'
travel with reductions on the other four. It
gives unlimited travel on regional public
transport plus the Monte Brè and San Salvatore funiculars. There is a 50% reduction on
all other mountain transport as well as on
most regional postbuses; a 25% reduction
applies for the Monte Generoso cog railway.

The three-day *Ticino Card* costs Sfr35
(Sfr75 for families) and gives unlimited
travel or reductions on public buses as well
as some postbuses and cableways around
Locarno and the Valle Maggia.

GATEWAY
Bellinzona
Situated in the centre of Ticino at the crossroads of several important trans-Alpine
routes, for centuries the town of Bellinzona
controlled the lucrative pass trade. Today, it
is dominated by its three medieval fortifications, the largest of which is the central
Castelgrande. The regional tourist office (see
Information earlier) is based in Bellinzona.

Hotel Tsui-Fok (☎/fax 091-825 13 32, Via
Nocca 20) has singles/doubles for Sfr45/70
(without breakfast). The *Hotel Garni Mod-
erno* (☎/fax 091-825 13 76, Viale Stazione
17b) and *Hotel San Giovanni* (☎/fax 091-
825 19 19, Via San Giovanni 7) both offer
rooms from around Sfr60/90.

For cafeteria meals try the *Migros (Piazza del Sole)* and the *Coop (Via H Guisan)*
supermarkets or the *Ristorante Inova* in the

Innovazione department store on Viale
Stazione. *Bar-Ristorante Piazzetta (Piazza
Collegiata 1)* serves Mediterranean-style
dishes from around Sfr18.

Bellinzona is Ticino's main transport
hub, and all trains on the Milan–Zürich line
(via Lugano) stop here. Trains also run half-
hourly to Locarno. There are postbuses
north-east (via the Passo del San Bernardino)
to Chur; reservations are essential (☎ 091-
825 77 55).

Northern Ticino

In its upper reaches, the Ticino River flows
through the Valle Leventina, whose typical
'trough' form reveals its glacial origins. This
broad and fertile valley forms the heart and
backbone of northern Ticino. Enclosed by
the mighty Gotthard massif to the north and
the arc of ranges extending from the Basodino to Pizzo Campo Tencia on its southern
side, northern Ticino (Alto Ticino to the locals) has an Alpine character less typical of
the canton as a whole. The only large side
branch of the Valle Leventina is the Val Blenio, which meets the main valley just above
the town of Biasca.

ACCESS TOWNS
Airolo
Airolo (1141m) is immediately south of
the Gotthard rail and motorway tunnels.
This attractive little town on the steep hillsides of the upper Valle Leventina serves
as a convenient base for walks in the surrounding mountains. Stepped stone
laneways lead from the train station to the
old town centre, built in solid Gotthard
stone.

Airolo's tourist office, Leventina Turismo, (☎ 091-869 15 33, fax 091-869 26 42)
is at the top of the town near the church.

Dorm beds at *Alloggio Girasole* (☎ 091-
869 19 27, **e** girasole@airolo.ch) are Sfr20
(without breakfast). The newly renovated
Hotel Alpina (☎ 091-869 19 66, fax 091-869
21 62), formerly Hotel Innovacanza, has
rooms for around Sfr60 per person. *Hotel
Forni* (☎ 091-869 12 70, **e** info@forni.ch)

offers better-standard singles/doubles from Sfr80/140.

Airolo is a minor transport hub on the trans-Gotthard railway, and many (but not all) trains running through the tunnel stop here. Postbuses travel north over the Passo del San Gottardo to Andermatt, west over the Passo della Novena (Nufenenpass) to Ulrichen in Goms, and down the Valle Leventina to towns where the trains no longer stop.

Olivone

Lying in the upper Val Blenio at the crossroads of the Greina and Lucomagno passes is Olivone (889m). The village's charming old Gotthard-style houses have painted exterior frescoes indicating contact with areas to the north. The museum is in an interesting stone and timber building dating from 1640. The San Marino church has an exterior square clock tower more typical of the Ticino style.

Walking routes go off in all directions, including marked trails to Campo (Blenio), the Val di Campo and the Bassa di Nara (to Faido), as well as the Val di Carassino (which is featured later in this chapter) and the Plaun la Greina (see the Graubünden chapter) walks.

Olivone has a tourist office (☎ 091-872 14 87, ℮ info@blenioturismo.ch, ⓦ www .vallediblenio.ch).

The *Ostello Marzano* (☎ *091-872 14 50)* has dorm beds (mainly for groups) for around Sfr25 with breakfast. *Hotel San Martino* (☎ *091-872 15 21, fax 091-872 26 62)* and *Osteria Centrale* (☎ *091-872 11 07)* have rooms from around Sfr45/90. *Hotel Olivone e Posta* (☎ *091-872 13 66)* has more luxurious rooms for Sfr119/140.

There are several daily postbus connections from Disentis (Graubünden) via the Passo del Lucomagno, but Olivone is most accessible from Biasca. In all seasons there are almost a dozen daily buses in either direction between Biasca and Olivone (around 40 minutes).

Only slower regional trains stop at Biasca, so it may be necessary to change at Arth-Goldau, Airolo or Bellinzona.

Lago Ritóm Circuit

Duration	3 days
Distance	24.5km
Standard	easy-medium
Start	Piora
Finish	Altanca
Nearest Towns	Airolo, Ambri-Piotta

Summary This varied walk circumnavigates Lago Ritóm, exploring the interesting valley basin that surrounds the lake. The route passes several scenically located mountain huts.

Lago Ritóm lies in a nature reserve that takes in a good part of the Gotthard massif's southern slopes. Above Piora (at around 1800m) the steep-sided Valle Leventina opens out into a gentler landscape of rolling grassy highlands that shelter a dozen or so deep blue Alpine lakes. Although the Lago Ritóm area fronts one of the busiest transport thoroughfares in the Alps, visitors remain oblivious to the bustling traffic far below.

The Ritóm area has rich vegetation, including forests of larch and mountain pines and over 500 species of flowering plants. Geologically it is diverse, with the crystalline formations of the Gotthard region converging with the gneiss rocks more typical of the Pennine Alps in the southern Valais. Originally a natural lake, Lago Ritóm was raised by almost 10m for the production of hydroelectricity. Fortunately, the water level is maintained at a fairly constant level, so the lake has kept its untouched appeal.

Maps

The recommended walking map is K+F's 1:50,000 *San Gottardo*, which is one of the few maps that take in the whole Gotthard region on a single sheet. Otherwise you'll need two SAW/ESS 1:50,000 sheets for this walk: *Disentis* No 256T and *Valle Leventina* No 266T (Sfr22.50 each).

NEAREST TOWN
Ambri-Piotta

This village in the northern Valle Leventina is nationally famous for its champion ice-hockey team.

Top: A walker approaches Capanna Tamaro on the slopes of Monte Rotondo, near the start of the Tamaro–Lema Traverse, Ticino Pre-Alps.
Bottom Left: The hills are alive with the sound of ... cowbells? **Bottom Right:** Alpine meadows show a striking diversity of wild flowers, including geraniums, buttercups and daisies.

Top Left: The village of Zernez, on the edge of the Swiss National Park. **Top Right:** The red scree of the Parpaner Rothorn meets the paler talus of the Parpaner Weisshorn near Arosa, Graubünden. **Bottom Left:** 'No fires' sign, Swiss NP. **Bottom Middle:** The fringed gentian is a less-common Alpine wild flower. **Bottom Right:** Birch tree in autumn colours, Engadine.

Warning

The Gotthard range is one of the Swiss Alps' strongest weather divisions, and it frequently has better weather than the northern side of the mountains. While these mostly south-facing slopes often get sun-drenched, they are also very exposed in poor weather, and conditions here can deteriorate rapidly.

Ristorante Vais (☎ 091-868 15 31) right by the postbus stop has singles/doubles for around Sfr40/80.

Trains do not stop anywhere in the Valle Leventina except Airolo, Faido and Biasca; places between these three centres – including Ambri-Piotta – are accessible only by the (roughly hourly) postbuses running between Airolo and Bellinzona.

GETTING TO/FROM THE WALK

The circuit begins from the upper station of the Piotta–Piora funicular (Funicolare Piora), Europe's steepest mountain railway. The return fare is Sfr22/11 adults/children (standard concessions apply).

Between 1 July and 1 October there is an extra postbus from Airolo right to the lower funicular station (Piotta Centrale FPR) at around 9.15am, returning at 4.30pm. Otherwise, the funicular is a 10-minute signposted walk from Piotta village.

The return to Ambri-Piotta can be made on the funicular (the last car leaves soon after 6pm), or you can walk back via the tiny village of Altanca. Postbus vans running between Lurengo and Ambri-Piotta pass through Altanca several times per day; the last bus to Piotta goes at around 7.15pm.

Motorists can leave vehicles at the lower funicular station or at the small car park below the Lago Ritóm dam wall. The most convenient motorway exit is at Airolo.

THE WALK
Day 1: Piora to Capanna Cadlimo

2¼–3 hours, 6.5km, 975m ascent
With a gradient of 88%, the funicular heaves you up some 850m from the valley-floor village of Piotta to the upper station of Piora in the cooler Alpine zone at 1793m, thus saving your strength for the higher slopes.

Follow the sealed road up to the right to the **Lago Ritóm** dam wall, climbing gently on left around the lakeside to **Alpe Ritóm**, where a signpost points you off left. A dirt track leads up through an open gully to the alp hut of **Alpe Tom** beside **Lago di Tom** (2021m) after one to 1¼ hours. This shallow lake with sandy shores lies in a broad basin enclosed by grassy hillsides.

Disregarding a walking route going eastward to Capanna Cadagno, take a foot track around to the (often dry) inlet stream, then cross and begin climbing away to the right. The path brings you up past the **Laghetti di Taneda**, two tarns perched on a small uneven terrace, before winding its way up more steeply over the continental watershed of the **Bassa del Lago Scuro**. Here **Lago Scuro** (2451m) comes into sight, a deep highland lake whose outwaters flow northward into the Rhine.

Make your way around the lake's western side over persistent snowdrifts to a high signposted cairn, then dip across a stream gully to join with a more prominent path. Blending into its rocky Alpine surroundings 200m up to your left is the SAC's *Capanna Cadlimo (☎ 091-869 18 33)*, 1¼ to 1¾ hours from Lago di Tom. At 2570m the grey-stone is the highest mountain hut in Ticino. The charge for a dorm bed is Sfr26.

Day 2: Capanna Cadlimo to Capanna Cadagno

2½–3¼ hours, 11.5km
Follow a sporadic line of neat round cairns down over the grassed-over moraine slopes of the **Motto dell'Isra** past **Lago dell'Isra**, a little lake surrounded by moist grassy flats where the Val Cadlimo narrows. Soon passing a right-hand turn-off going over the Bocchetta della Miniera to Cadagno, the way leads gently down through this pretty little valley along the often snowed-over left bank of the Reno di Medel, and comes to **Stabbio Nuovo** (2250m) after one to 1¼ hours. Here a small herders' shelter is built against a rock block beside a meadow grazed by horses.

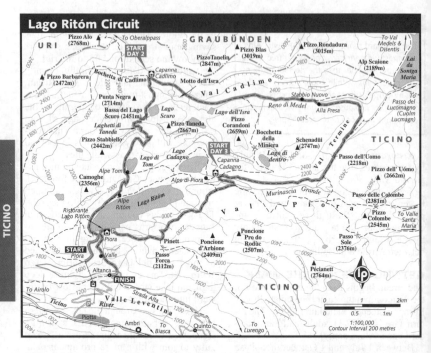

Lago Ritóm Circuit

Head a short way on and cross the stream at a small diversion weir called **Alla Presa** (2229m), following a rough vehicle track a few paces on to where another marked trail continues left. The route rises steadily away from the stream over open ridges granting clear views north-east toward the Lai da Sontga Maria hydroelectric reservoir, before beginning an easy descending traverse around into the **Val Termine** to meet an old dirt road running along the base of the valley. Here continue up 400m to recross the north-south watershed at the indistinct **Passo dell'Uomo** (2218m), 45 minutes to one hour from Stabbio Nuovo.

Walk 700m on down the road (just past a route going south-east toward Passo Colombe and Passo Sole), to where a signpost directs you down rightward over a concrete bridge. The track runs along the undulating northern slopes of the **Val Piora**, a wide expanse of treeless Alpine pastures into which the Murinascia Grande stream has

eroded a deep gully, falling slowly against the contour to reach **Capanna Cadagno** (☎ 091-868 13 23), after 50 minutes to one hour. This homey SAT-run hut (1987m) sits on a hillock overlooking Lago Cadagno, and serves excellent Italian dishes. Dorm beds are Sfr16/9 for adults/children (Sfr36/50 with full board); showers are available.

Day 3: Capanna Cadagno to Altanca (via Pinett)
2–2¾ hours, 6.5km, 92m ascent
A shorter alternative to this final leg is to continue down along the road through Alpe di Piora and on around the northern shore of Lago Ritóm.

Pick up the left-hand path (signposted 'Passo Forca'), which leaves the road not far down from two barns roofed with corrugated iron and immediately crosses a stone footbridge. After bearing right at a route junction shortly on, climb around to the south-west and sidle high above the blue waters of Lago

Ritóm on slopes looking out toward peaks of the main Gotthard range.

The route leads on through light forest interspersed with rhododendrons, heath and lovely patches of moor, before dropping down to **Pinett**, a small isolated Alpine pasture at around 2070m; a left branch goes off to Passo Forca. Continue down below a stone cottage and on past gnarled old larch trees, descending more steeply along the line of a fence to **Piora**, on the eastern side of the dam wall. Here *Ristorante Lago Ritóm* (☎ *091-868 13 24)* offers refreshments and pleasant singles/doubles for around Sfr45/90. Follow the dirt road beneath the curved dam wall to a small car park, 1½ to two hours from Capanna Cadagno. Your circle closes at this point, and the return to Piotta is made either by funicular, or on foot via Altanca as now described.

Steps connect with an ancient mule trail, whose original stone paving is still largely intact and provides an excellent walkway. It brings you down via the traditional old hamlet of **Valle** (1697m), spirals on through the forest, then skirts above a sloping field to rejoin the road. The tiny village of **Altanca** (1390m) is a short way down along the sealed road, 30 to 45 minutes from Piora. There are irregular mini-postbuses back to Piotta from here. Otherwise, a steep path leads below the small church, repeatedly crossing the winding road before coming out by the lower funicular station at Piotta after 50 minutes to one hour.

Val di Carassino

Duration	2 days
Distance	15.5km
Standard	medium
Start	Olivone
Finish	Dangio
Summary	This mostly leisurely overnight walk through the charming Val di Carassino, a tiny valley draining into the upper Val Blenio, can easily be done as a longer day hike.

The Val di Carassino runs north-west from the Rheinwaldhorn (3402m), which is the highest peak in Ticino, although the mountain's summit is shared with the neighbouring canton of Graubünden. Made interesting by its long and extremely narrow form, this lonely Alpine valley was formed by glaciers that once descended from the Adula range. Less commonly seen wild flowers, including the rare edelweiss, can now be seen growing on the valley's inaccessible and steep-sided slopes.

Maps
Recommended is the SAW/ESS 1:50,000 sheet *Valle Leventina* No 266T (Sfr22.50). K+F's 1:60,000 *Sopraceneri* (Sfr24.80) also covers the route.

NEAREST TOWN
Dangio
Dangio (801m) – not to be confused with Dongio farther downvalley – is dominated by the Cima Norma building, a former chocolate factory shut down in 1968 and now used by the military.

There is a scarcity of places to stay, although *Ostello Adula* (☎ *091-872 15 13)* has a dorm (mainly for groups with bookings). The small *Albergo Greina* (☎ *091-871 12 37)* in nearby Torre has singles/doubles for around Sfr40/80.

Postbuses running between Olivone and Biasca pass through Dangio.

GETTING TO/FROM THE WALK
The walk begins in Olivone (see Access Towns earlier in this chapter) and finishes at Dangio.

THE WALK
Day 1: Olivone to Capanna Adula (SAC)
4–5 hours, 11km, 1123m ascent
From the post office, follow the road to a signpost 50m after the Brenno bridge, then turn left up a stairway and walk on around past the village church to the trailhead. Another route here, the 'Sentiero Basso', leaves off down the valley. A short farm track brings you quickly onto a mule path, which climbs through scrubby woodland of birch and wild hazelnuts to cross a small stream.

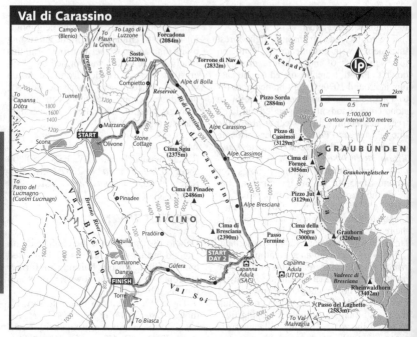

Val di Carassino

Now ascending more steeply, continue in switchbacks up the increasingly forested hillsides giving continual glimpses of the cascading Ri di Carassino.

Soon after passing an isolated stone cottage (1537m) on a high pasture overlooking Olivone, the path begins sidling along the undulating slopes, crossing the river on a footbridge just as it comes to **Compietto** (1570m), two to 2½ hours from Olivone. Occupying lawn-like river flats, this charming summer-only settlement of a dozen or so old stone houses and a little church dating from the 15th century is the perfect place to stop for a rest, a snack and a look.

Head on up the winding road to an artificial waterfall at the dam spillway, then proceed past the small reservoir into the farmhouse of **Alpe di Bolla** into **Val di Carassino**. These open Alpine meadows are sprinkled with rhododendron heaths, and the 3000m peaks of the Adula tower above to your left. The road leads entirely along the

eastern banks of the **Ri di Carassino**, which tumbles and meanders its way down through the narrow – in places less than 200m wide – floor of the upper valley past the farmlets of Alpe Carassino, Alpe Cassimoi and Alpe Bresciana to a track division at the head of the Val di Carassino, 1¾ to 2¼ hours from Compietto.

The way to the nearby *Capanna Adula (SAC)* (☎ *091-872 15 32)* moves up to the right past the small chapel at **Passo Termine** (approximately 2030m), then cuts down leftward over the ridge line to arrive at the hut after just 10 to 15 minutes. The resident warden/cook is only there in July and August, but the hut is always open. The Capanna Adula (SAC) is perched on a shelf at 2012m looking down through the Val Soi to the villages in the Val Blenio. The charge for a dorm bed is around Sfr25.

The longer left-hand trail climbs steeply up an indistinct grassy spur, before swinging rightward across a stream in a more

Mountains of Rivalry

The presence of two mountain huts so close together is indicative of the historic rivalry between the nationally organised SAC and Ticino's locally strong Alpine clubs. While on the northern side of the Alps almost all mountain huts belong to the Swiss Alpine Club (SAC), in Ticino the SAC – Club Alpino Svizzero (CAS) in Italian – owns only 10 of the region's 50-odd huts. Over 20 huts belong to the Federazione Alpinistica Ticinese (FAT), and another 16 are the property of various other smaller clubs.

Unlike the lofty summits of the Bernese Oberland, the Valais and the Engadine, Ticino's generally more modest mountains did not attract significant numbers of early Alpine tourists. Ticino's first (Leventina) section of the SAC was formed only in the late 1890s by German-Swiss staff of the newly opened Gotthard railway. Local Italian-speaking workers resented this elitist grouping, however, and in 1919 they founded their own mountain club, the Unione Ticinese Operai Escursionisti (UTOE). One of the UTOE's first projects was the construction in 1923 of a 'superior' Capanna Adula – a year before, and almost 400m higher than, the nearby SAC hut.

Internal feuding within the UTOE led to the creation of the breakaway Società Alpinistica Ticinese (SAT) in 1938, but 27 years later the UTOE and the SAT reconciled their differences to form the FAT. In recent decades most of Ticino's other smaller clubs have joined the FAT.

gentle ascent to reach *Capanna Adula (UTOE)* (☎ 091-872 16 75) after 30 to 45 minutes. This hut stands at 2393m in the shadow of the Rheinwaldhorn and is staffed from late June to mid-September (but otherwise left open). Nearby is an old lateral moraine of the Vadrecc di Bresciana, a rapidly receding glacier whose icy masses covered this site until relatively recently. Being over 350m higher than the SAC hut, the Capanna Adula (UTOE) enjoys more far-ranging views, which stretch out toward the mountains of the Gotthard region. Prices and conditions are fairly similar. Return to the main path via the ascent route.

Day 2: Capanna Adula (SAC) to Dangio

2–2½ hours, 4.5km

From near the hut's flagpole, descend rightward (north) a short way to join the main route coming from Passo Termine. The countless zigzags of a cut mule trail bring you down the initially very steep slopes above the Val Soi to meet a rough road at the scattered locality of **Soi** (1295m) after one to 1¼ hours.

Follow the road on beside the rubble-choked river through the hamlet of **Güfera**, and continue on to a left-hand turn-off, just after a more prominent path going to Aquila

and Olivone. A foot track leads down past houses in the forest to a chapel on the uphill side of **Dangio**, then via narrow laneways through the traditional stone village to reach the main street, one to 1¼ hours on.

Campolungo Circuit

Duration	4¼–6 hours
Distance	15km
Standard	easy-medium
Start	Rodi-Fiesso/Lago Tremorgio
Finish	Faido

Summary This (near) loop walk explores the area around the 2689m summit of Pizzo Campolungo on the southern side of the Valle Leventina, which forms one of Ticino's most interesting nature reserves.

Lago Tremorgio, a lake nestled in a rounded trough high above the Valle Leventina, is a curious natural feature of the Campolungo area. Its origins have been something of an enigma in the past. Its Italian name refers to its 'funnel' form, and at one time Lago Tremorgio was believed to be an ancient volcano, although it is more likely the impact crater of a large meteorite.

Exposed bands of white dolomite stand out sharply on the ridges high above Lago Tremorgio, and the Campolungo area is known for its rock crystals, including red and blue corundums (rubies and sapphires). Farther to the south the beautiful Alpine lake of Lago di Morghirolo is the source of the Val Piumogna, whose lower valley area is a forested wilderness. The Piumogna stream enters the Valle Leventina in a spectacular waterfall, which is visible from passing trains.

As this is such a lovely area it is worth stretching out the walk an extra day by staying at one of the three mountain huts you pass along the way. The best time to walk the circuit is between mid-June and mid-October.

Maps

The best map to use is either the SAW/ESS 1:50,000 sheet *Valle Leventina* No 266T (Sfr22.50) or Editions MPA Verlag's 1:50,000 *Valle Maggia-Val Verzasca* (Sfr27.90). K+F's 1:60,000 walking map, *Ticino Sopraceneri* (Sfr24.80), also covers the route adequately.

NEAREST TOWNS
Rodi-Fiesso

Down in the valley at Rodi-Fiesso, *Ristorante Guscetti* (☎ 091-867 12 32) offers singles/doubles from Sfr45/80.

Trains do not stop in Rodi-Fiesso, but postbuses running between Airolo and Faido pass through roughly hourly in either direction.

Dalpe

The walk passes through this small village, which sits at 1192m high above the Valle Leventina. Dalpe's parish church, built in 1661, has interesting frescoes.

Albergo delle Alpi (☎ 091-867 14 24) offers singles/doubles for around Sfr35/70.

There are about five buses back to Rodi-Fiesso (the last at about 5.30pm).

Faido

This village at the end of the walk is the location of Valle Leventina's regional tourist office, Leventina Turismo (☎ 091-866 16 16, e levtourism@leventinanet.ch).

Hotel Barondone (☎ 091-866 12 44) is a classic old-style place with singles/doubles for just Sfr30/45.

Airolo–Bellinzona postbuses pass through regularly. Slower regional trains stop at Faido train station.

GETTING TO/FROM THE WALK

The Campolungo Circuit starts at Lago Tremorgio, which is accessible by a 15-minute cable-car ride from Rodi-Fiesso. This private mountain lift (Sfr9) offers no fare concessions and only has two small four-person cabins, so queues can build up quickly. The last upward cable car goes at 5pm. Otherwise, Lago Tremorgio is a steep 2½-hour climb through the forest from Rodi-Fiesso. Private vehicles can be parked at Rodi-Fiesso's little-used train station or at the cable-car station.

The walk can be ended in Dalpe. Another alternative is to walk on from Dalpe to Piano Selva, where a private cable car (☎ 091-867 15 46) runs directly down to Faido on demand (Sfr8 one way).

THE WALK

See the Around Valle Leventina map, p263 The small cable car hauls you up almost 900m out of sticky Valle Leventina in around 15 minutes. Close to the upper cable-car station is *Capanna Tremorgio* (☎ 091-867 12 52), a restaurant-hut with dormitory accommodation (including hot showers) for around Sfr50 with half-board, and open from early June to the end of September.

From below Capanna Tremorgio a well-trodden path leads around the eastern side of **Lago Tremorgio**, which sits at 1830m in an interesting rounded cirque enclosed by steep-sided grassy peaks. The lake level is gradually sinking, evident by old water-line markings around its sides. The path climbs steadily out of the forest onto open slopes above the lake, reaching a signposted intersection at the tiny Alpine valley of **Alpe Campolungo** after 30 to 40 minutes. Turn left and head up for five to 10 minutes under the high-tension powerlines to **Passo**

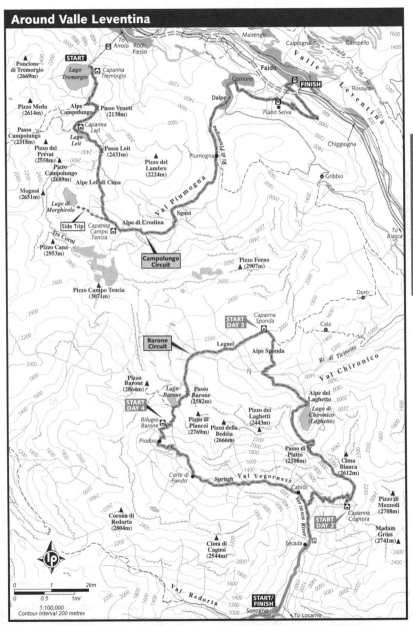

Around Valle Leventina

To Airolo Rodi Fiesso
START
Lago Tremorgio
Capanna Tremorgio
Mairengo
Calpiogna
Campello
V a l l e
Faido
Cornone
FINISH
Dalpe
Piano Selva
Rossura
Poncione di Tremorgio (2669m)
Pizzo Meda (2614m)
Alpe Campolungo
Passo Venett (2138m)
Capanna Leit
Lago Leit
Passo Leit (2431m)
Pizzo del Lambro (2224m)
Piumogna
L e v e n t i n a
Chiggiogna
Passo Campolungo (2318m)
Pizzo del Prévat (2558m)
Pizzo Campolungo (2689m)
Alpe Lei di Cima
Ri di Piumogna
Gribbio
Mognoi (2651m)
Lago di Morghirolo
Side Trip
Capanna Campo Tencia
Alpe di Croslina
Sgnoi
Val Piumogna
Tre Corni
Pizzo Cana (2953m)
Campolungo Circuit
Pizzo Forno (2907m)
To Biasca
Pizzo Campo Tencia (3071m)
Doro
START DAY 3
Capanna Sponda
Cala
Barone Circuit
Legnei
Alpe Sponda
Ri di Ticinetto
Val Chironico
Pizzo Barone (2864m)
Lago Barone
Passo Barone (2582m)
Pizzo dei Laghetti (2443m)
Alpe del Laghetto
Lago di Chironico (Laghetto)
START DAY 4
Rifugio Barone
Pizzo di Piancoi (2769m)
Pizzo della Bedéia (2666m)
Piodoo
Passo di Piatto (2108m)
Cima Bianca (2612m)
Corte di Fondo
Sprügh
Val Vegorness
Cabiói
Pizzo di Mezzodi (2708m)
Corona di Redorta (2804m)
Capanna Cognora
START DAY 2
Madam Gröss (2741m)
Cima di Cagnoi (2544m)
Secada
Val Redorta
START/FINISH
Sonogno
To Locarno

0   1   2km
0   0.5   1mi
1:100,000
Contour Interval 200 metres

TICINO

Venett, a small pass looking out toward Dalpe and Faido. Continue right, contouring along the slopes of eroding dolomite, then make your way around to the left over Alpine pastures to reach *Capanna Leit (☎ 091-868 19 20)*, at 2260m, after another 20 to 30 minutes. This SAT hut with self-catering facilities has dorm beds for Sfr14.

Walk a few minutes on, past a cross mounted on a prominent rock, to **Lago Leit**. This glacial lakelet is stocked with rainbow trout and is a popular fishing spot. Head left around the shoreline then follow red-white paint markings that lead up steeply through the rocks to a gap on the ridge, 30 to 45 minutes from Capanna Leit. This is **Passo Leit** (2431m), from where there are nice views across the heavily forested Val Piumogna down to your left.

Sidle over to the obvious col just over to the right. The glacier-clad mountain directly to the south is Pizzo Campo Tencia (3071m). The path descends gently through the grassy meadows of the **Alpe Lei di Cima**, before dropping down more steeply to reach the Ri di Piumogna. Cross the shallow stream on a row of stepping stones, then climb on quickly to a small tarn after one to 1½ hours. Here the path intersects with the trail leading up from the large *Capanna Campo Tencia (☎ 091-867 15 44)*. This SAC hut (2140m), a short way down to the left, charges Sfr22 for dorm beds (Sfr43 with full board), and is open mid-June to mid-October.

The 1½-hour return side trip to **Lago di Morghirolo** is a highlight of this walk and not to be missed. The right-hand path continues upvalley along the rocky ridge before climbing over low mounds of moraine rubble to grassy flats near the outlet stream. Lago di Morghirolo (2264m) lies at the very head of the valley and is surrounded by craggy peaks.

Pick up the foot track below the hut and descend across two side streams flowing down from the moraine slopes to the right. The path soon cuts down left to the valley floor and continues along the banks of the Ri di Piumogna to cross the small river on a footbridge after 15 to 20 minutes. Head up over the low rhododendron-covered ridges

of the **Alpe di Croslina**, then around left where stunted larch trees mark the upper forest line. Here the gradient steepens, and an old stone-laid trail brings you down to the attractive grassy clearing of **Sgnoi** (1650m) after 45 minutes to one hour.

Walk on down through the beautiful spruce and larch forest of the Val Piumogna. The path takes a course well away from the river, gently dropping against the contour for 30 to 40 minutes to meet a dirt road just above the hamlet of **Piumogna**. Follow the road down through birch woodland growing in a loose stony wash and continue a short way past a bridge to where a signposted foot track leaves off to the right. This goes down through more forest, before coming out onto a narrow cobbled lane which leads down into the quaint village of **Dalpe**, 30 to 40 minutes from Piumogna.

Walkers continuing on to the cable car at **Piano Selva** (30 to 40 minutes) or to **Faido** (one to 1½ hours) should turn right to Dalpe-Cornone, where trail markings from the Albergo delle Alpi lead down onto the Piano Selva road.

Passo di Cristallina

Duration	2 days
Distance	17km
Standard	medium
Start	Ossasco
Finish	San Carlo
Nearest Towns	Airolo, Campo

Summary This popular walk leads over the 2568m Passo di Cristallina, a high pass connecting the Val Bedretto – really just an extension of the Valle Leventina – with the Val Bavona, one of the upper branches of the Valle Maggia.

The Cristallina area is in Ticino's north-western corner. It has scenery more typical for the northern side of the Alps, with the only significant expanse of snowfields and glaciers within Ticino. Having been extensively developed for hydroelectricity, these are some of Switzerland's most industrially productive mountains (see the boxed text 'Hydroelectricity Reservoirs' later). The four or five small storage dams detract little from the magnificence of the high-Alpine scenery, however, and as engineering feats they definitely inspire admiration.

The Passo di Cristallina can be done as a day walk, although stretching the hike out to two days is a more leisurely option. Snow is likely to cover higher sections of the route early in the season, and on the northern approach to the pass a small permanent snowfield must be negotiated.

Maps

The map that best covers this walk is the SAW/ESS 1:50,000 sheet *Nufenenpass* No 265T (Sfr22.50). Other alternatives are Editions MPA Verlag's 1:50,000 *Valle Maggia-Val Verzasca* (Sfr27.90) or K+F's 1:60,000 *Ticino Sopraceneri* (Sfr24.80). K+F's 1:50,000 *San Gottardo* (Sfr24.80) is also of use, although it only just includes Capanna Basodino and completely cuts off San Carlo.

NEAREST TOWNS
San Carlo

See Access Towns in the Valle Maggia & Val Verzasca section later in this chapter.

Ossasco

Ossasco (1313m) is a tiny village in the Val Bedretto, some 10km west of Airolo by road (see Access Towns earlier in this chapter). Ossasco has no accommodation, but there is a restaurant.

Postbuses to Ossasco run from Airolo post office (near the train station) about a dozen times a day from late May to early October; outside this time services are far less frequent.

GETTING TO/FROM THE WALK

For information on transport to/from San Carlo, see Access Towns in the Valle Maggia & Val Verzasca section later in this chapter.

From Robièi walkers have the option of taking the cable car down to San Carlo, which cuts off the final section of Day 2. The cable car runs hourly from early June to mid-October. The one-way fare is Sfr16/8 adults/juniors; the last scheduled downward ride is at 5.20pm.

THE WALK
Day 1: Ossasco to Passo di Cristallina

3¼–4¼ hours, 8km, 1255m ascent

From the postbus stop on the uphill side of Ossasco, take the signposted trail which immediately leads over the stone footbridge and alongside the gushing Ri di Cristallina. Climb steeply through mixed conifer and broadleaf forest, ignoring several track turnoffs to reach **Leiunscia** (1539m) after 30 to 45 minutes. A large clearwater spring flows out of the ground here, and it's a nice spot for a quick rest.

The path heads on a few paces to meet a rough road, and crosses this a number of times, cutting off sharp bends as it ascends. Continue up through open larch forest and lovely Alpine meadows scattered with martagon lilies to arrive at **Alpe di Cristallina** after a further 40 to 50 minutes. This group of farm buildings lies just above the forest line at 1800m, and looks out northward toward the mountains of the Gotthard massif.

Pick up the trail above the long barn, and follow the white-red-white paint markings that lead across slopes covered with Alpine rhododendrons. The path makes its way up beside the cascading stream, passing the memorial plaque to Mario Leonardi (a warden of the Cristallina hut who was killed here by an avalanche in 1964), before entering the pleasant **Val Torta**, where the gradient eases. Head a short way on past a signposted intersection, where a side route over the Passo del Narèt heads off left, then continue up over grassy hills to reach the temporary *Capanna di Cristallina* (☎ 091-994 66 83, 869 23 30 or 079-643 49 46), 1¼ to 1¾ hours from Alpe di Cristallina.

This hut (2349m) is to be demolished once the new Capanna Cristallina is completed (around late summer 2002) higher up on the Passo di Cristallina. The temporary hut is open mid-June to early October and charges Sfr22 for dorm beds (Sfr28 with full board).

Walk into the head of the tiny upper valley, passing under the decidedly unscenic row of high-tension power lines. This is otherwise a typical glacial-recession landscape, with several small lakes among the

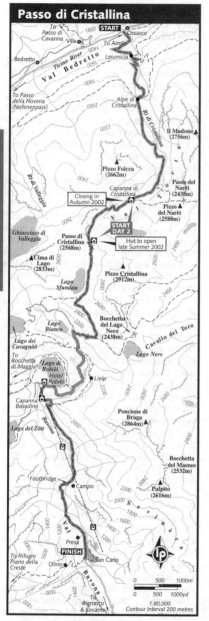

Passo di Cristallina

mounds of recent moraines. Follow the path up along the right side of the gully, which normally remains snow-covered long into the summer, to reach **Passo di Cristallina** after 40 to 50 minutes.

This 2568m pass is the highest point on this walk and offers direct views of the Ghiacciaio del Basodino, a broad névé to the south-west. To the west are the peaks of Cima di Lago, Poncione di Valleggia and Pizzo di San Giacomo, all slightly less than 3000m. A tiny lake lies in the rocky basin just below the pass. The new Capanna Cristallina is under construction here.

Day 2: Passo di Cristallina to San Carlo
3¼–4½ hours, 9km

Drop down first in short switchbacks, then cut left across the slope along a graded track that quickly brings Lago Sfundau into view. Lying in a deep trough, **Lago Sfundau** (or 'sunken lake') has no visible outlet and is generally ice-choked even during high summer. Although it is a natural lake, the peculiar waterfall that spurts out of the rock wall on its far side is an artificial feeder tunnel, not a natural stream.

Continue around high above the eastern shore of Lago Sfundau (with occasional fixed cables to provide extra confidence), then climb on away from the lake to reach a cliff face, 30 to 40 minutes from Passo di Cristallina. Immediately below in the valley is Lago Bianco, a natural lake, and just to the right the impressive arched dam wall of the 2310m-high Lago dei Cavagnöö; also visible to the south are two other hydroelectricity reservoirs, Lago di Robièi and Lago del Zött.

Following the standard white-red-white paint markings, make your way down across the open rocky slopes, passing the signposted path to Lago Nero after 20 minutes. This natural lake is an easy 15 to 20 minutes' walk away and makes a pleasant side trip. From the Lago Nero track intersection descend right for 15 to 20 minutes via a steep ridge to meet a sealed road leading around Lago Bianco.

Walk 400m down to a road bridge, from where a slower route (signposted 'Lielp')

Hydroelectricity Reservoirs

High elevations and precipitation levels in the Swiss Alps allow heads of water (the altitude difference between reservoir and power station) of sometimes 1000m or so. This makes Switzerland ideal for hydroelectricity, and around 60% of the country's power comes from its numerous storage dams, most of them in Alpine regions. Many walking routes pass hydro reservoirs, and it's hard not to admire the engineers' work as you look up to an impressive curved-concrete dam wall built across a deep mountain ravine. Switzerland has already reached 90% of its viable hydroelectric potential, however, and conservationists are determined to prevent the construction of any more dams.

follows the left side of the Bavona stream to *Capanna Basodino* (☎ *091-753 27 97*). This SAC hut (1856m) is open throughout the year and has dorm beds for Sfr20.

Otherwise continue 45 minutes to one hour down the road to the upper station of the Robièi cable car. *Hotel Robièi* (☎ *091-756 50 20*), open early June to early October, has singles/doubles from Sfr44/70 and dorm beds for around Sfr30 (including breakfast and showers). From here, either take the cable car down to San Carlo or drop down another five to 10 minutes to the Capanna Basodino.

The well-constructed path down to San Carlo leaves from below Capanna Basodino, descending steeply along the left side of the narrow **Bavona** stream under cliffs and cable-car wires. After passing through the hamlet of **Campo**, cross the stream on a footbridge, and continue down steeply through the forest past the historic chapel at **Presa**. The disproportionately large bell tower shows the year 1638, but the small church has frescoes of early 16th-century origin. You reach the road below the ground station of the Robièi cable car after 1½ to two hours. The nearest postbus stop is five to 10 minutes' walk on below the village of **San Carlo**.

Valle Maggia & Val Verzasca

Although the mountains of central-western Ticino have a lower average height than the main Alpine summits farther to the north, they rise from their valley floors with surprising abruptness. The Valle Maggia and the Val Verzasca are two long valleys that drain the rugged ranges of central-western Ticino. With a catchment area that includes various wild and beautiful side valleys, this region takes in over a third of the canton. The Maggia and Verzasca rivers flow southward from the mountains fringing the Valle Leventina to enter Lago Maggiore on either side of the city of Locarno.

Once much more densely settled, both valleys – but particularly the Val Verzasca – experienced a dramatic population drift from the mid-1800s, severely reducing their already marginal agricultural base. Left to nature, old mule tracks have become overgrown, abandoned alp huts have disappeared under tangled thickets and the advancing forest has reclaimed former pastures. Today, tracts of new wilderness separate the scattered villages. With low, easily crossed passes and few glaciers to block the way, this is arguably the most attractive region for walking in Ticino.

ACCESS TOWNS
Locarno
Situated on the north-eastern shoreline of Lago Maggiore at just 197m, Locarno is the lowest city in Switzerland. With its grand old Lombardic-style villas and balmy subtropical climate, Locarno has something of a 'Riviera' atmosphere. The city hosts the Locarno Film Festival in the first two weeks of August, and at this time hotels are completely booked out.

The local and regional tourist office is Lago Maggiore Turismo (☎ 091-751 03 33, e locarno@ticino.com, w www.maggiore .ch). Ochsner Sport (☎ 091-760 04 45), Via Ramogna 4, sells outdoor gear.

The local *youth hostel* (☎ *091-756 15 00, fax 091-756 15 01, Via Varenna 18)* has dorm beds for Sfr31 and singles/doubles from Sfr57/66. *Pensione Città Vecchia (☎/fax 091-751 45 54, ℯ cittavecchia@dat acomm.ch, Via Toretta 13)* has dorm beds from Sfr24 and several basic rooms for Sfr35/70. *Osteria Reginetta (☎/fax 091-752 35 53, ℯ reginetta.locarno@bluewin.ch, Via della Motta 8)* has nicer rooms from around Sfr50/100.

Albergo Montaldi/Stazione (☎ *091-743 02 22)*, across the road from the train station, has rooms in the rear annexe for Sfr47/88 and better-standard rooms from Sfr55/100.

The *youth hostel restaurant* offers lunch and dinner for around Sfr12. *De Gustibus* on Piazza Grande serves pizza slices (Sfr4), chips and other snacks.

At *Ristorante Inova* on Piazza Stazione you can eat for around Sfr10. *Ristorante Cittadella (☎ 091-751 58 85, Via Cittadella 18)* has fish specialities from around Sfr35.

Locarno is not on the main Gotthard rail line, but there are trains from Bellinzona almost half-hourly. The city is also linked with Brig in the Valais by the railway route via Domodossola in Italy (which is covered by Swiss rail passes).

San Carlo (Val Bavona)

Not to be confused with its namesake in the adjacent Valle di Peccia, San Carlo (938m) is the uppermost settlement in the wild Val Bavona. It is the only place in the valley with a permanent (ie, year-round) population. Another of Ticino's typical stone villages, San Carlo's church dates from 1595 and has interesting 17th-century frescoes. San Carlo makes an excellent base for walks into the Cristallina region (quickly accessible by the Robièi cable car) as well as the rugged mountains along Ticino's western frontier with Italy.

The only accommodation is *Ristorante Basòdino* (☎ *091-775 11 92)*, open June to October, with several simple singles/doubles for Sfr45/90.

Frequent public (FART) buses run between Locarno and Bignasco, where you must change to a mini-postbus for San Carlo. From early April to the end of October there are some four connections in either direction; the last bus leaves Bignasco at around 4.25pm and returns from San Carlo at about 5.15pm.

San Carlo to Bosco/Gurin

Duration	2 days
Distance	17km
Standard	hard
Start	San Carlo
Finish	Bosco/Gurin

Summary This high-level traverse introduces one of Ticino's wildest and most scenic corners – the spectacular mountains fronting the Swiss–Italian border between the Val Bavona and the Val di Campo, two side valleys of the Valle Maggia.

No other large valley in Ticino has the dramatically enclosed features of the Val Bavona, whose sheer and unstable sides gave way in a catastrophic rock landslide in 1594. Whole forests and villages were buried under millions of tonnes of rubble, and life in the valley never fully recovered. With the steady population drift over the last 150 years or so, mountain pastures and agricultural fields have fallen into disuse.

The relative remoteness of this region is a boon to serious walkers, who can explore a little-visited Alpine landscape of rugged peaks, crisp glacial lakes, highland heath, semi-abandoned shepherds' cottages and rough moraine slopes. Interesting too is the area's mixture of (Germanic) Walser and Italian elements, reflected in local place names and architecture.

This is essentially a two-day walk, the second day of which is relatively long and tiring. The route goes through extensive sections of steep, loose rock. Bear in mind that these mountains are rather prone to summer thunderstorms.

Maps

Most recommended is K+F's 1:60,000 *Ticino Sopraceneri* (Sfr24.80). Although MPA's 1:50,000 *Valle Maggia-Valle Verzasca*

(Sfr27.90) is actually a better map and a very good alternative, its coverage doesn't include much of the adjoining Italian territory to the west.

NEAREST TOWNS
Bosco/Gurin

The town of Bosco/Gurin (Italian/German) lies at the end of the Valle di Bosco, a small side valley of the Valle Maggia. Apart from being the highest permanently occupied village in Ticino, Bosco/Gurin (1503m) is the canton's only established German-speaking settlement. The Guriners are descendants of the Walsers, German-speaking colonists originally from Goms in the upper Valais who resettled from the adjacent (now Italian) Valle Formazza (Pomattal) in 1244. Bosco/Gurin's wood-based houses, such as the 18th-century Walserhaus, which contains the village museum, contrast with the heavy stone constructions commonly seen elsewhere in Ticino.

For information contact the tourist office (☎ 091-759 02 02, e info@bosco-gurin.ch, w www.bosco-gurin.ch).

Residenza Ostello Giovanibosco (☎ 091-759 02 02, e grossalp@bluewin.ch) offers dorm beds for Sfr30. The *Hotel Edelweiss* (☎ 091-754 19 00) has singles/doubles for Sfr50/100.

Walser Hotel (☎ 091-759 02 02, e hotel .walser@bosco-gurin.ch) offers rooms of a better standard from Sfr100/140; there is a pizzeria downstairs.

The Guriner Metro

As part of a major project designed to attract more winter tourists to this remote corner of Ticino, a new 4km-long 'metro' tunnel linking Bosco/Gurin with the Valle Formazza in Italy is currently under construction. New ski lifts have been installed around Grossalp and a large new hotel completed in the village. A shopping complex is also planned. Concern has been raised that the 40 million franc project is both economically unviable and environmentally intrusive – at best a risky venture.

Bosco/Gurin is accessible by public (FART) bus from Locarno – you change to a postbus at the village of Cevio in the main Valle Maggia. There are five daily buses between Cevio and Bosco/Gurin all year round; the last leaves Cevio around 6pm, and returns from Bosco/Gurin at about 6.45pm.

GETTING TO/FROM THE WALK

For information on transport to/from San Carlo, see Access Towns earlier.

THE WALK
Day 1: San Carlo to Rifugio Piano delle Creste

3–3½ hours, 4km, 1170m ascent

A signpost at the postbus stop (938m) by the road bridge just before San Carlo directs you into the beech forest past a small shrine dedicated to St Francis of Assisi. Begin the long winding ascent on a sometimes stepped path beside the deep ravine of the **Val d'Antabia**. Ignoring unmarked trails leading off to the left, climb steeply through mountainside clearings with lonely stone cottages, then traverse up leftward through the larch trees, crossing debris-choked side streams before you come to **Corte Grande** after 2¼ to 2¾ hours. This group of rustic shepherds' huts sits at 1914m on nettle-infested slopes looking out toward the adjacent crags of Pizzo Castello.

Make your way on up – rather more gently now – over the open rolling slopes of **Alpe d'Antabia**, then move down into the basin of a tiny mountain stream. The route heads quickly across the grassy flats, before following a short ridge up to arrive at *Rifugio Piano delle Creste* (☎ 091-775 14 14), 40 to 50 minutes on. These two self-caterers' huts at 2108m belong to the local mountain club, the Società Alpinistica Valmaggese (SAV), and stand in a beautiful upper-Alpine valley bordered by the high peaks on the Swiss–Italian frontier, including the 3272m Basòdino. The hut fee for dorm beds is around Sfr20. Drinks are on sale, but you'll have to bring all food with you; showers are available.

TICINO

San Carlo to Bosco/Gurin

Day 2: Rifugio Piano delle Creste to Bosco/Gurin

6–8 hours, 13km, 562m ascent

Now leaving the route that continues on over the Tamierpass into the Valle Formazza in Italy, head roughly southward through a shallow gully and up past the smaller lake of **Laghetti d'Antabia**. Bearing right at a junction not far on, ascend via a small ridge past the larger upper lake (2189m), whose deep-blue waters nestle into screeslides below Pizzo Solögna.

Follow the white-red-white markings on around to the right up the broken-rock slopes, finally cutting along an uneven grassy ledge – with fixed ropes for moral rather than physical support – to reach the obvious gap in the jagged ridge after one to 1¼ hours. Known to locals as the **Bocchetta dei Laghi Cròsa**, this point lies at around 2480m and enjoys a splendid view back into the upper Val d'Antabia.

Descend directly to a signposted route intersection at the small tarn visible from above, where the two picturesque Alpine lakes called the **Laghi della Cròsa** come into sight. Continue left through more rocky terrain, then sidle along a mostly grassy ridge leading down across the stony outlet of the upper lake (2153m). Walk a short distance around the lower lake's steep southern side, then pick up a cairned and paint-splashed route that cuts up over the hill top before dropping down to a derelict shelter at the Alpe della Cròsa. The path continues to descend very steeply through mountain heath to reach **Gradisc** (1703m), 45 minutes to one hour from the bocchetta. Here, several stone huts stand on this grassy little shelf fringed with raspberry thickets, perched high above the wild Val Calnegia.

Avoiding the main foot track going straight down into the valley, find the less pronounced trail that contours off to the right (southward) through the larch forest and abandoned Alpine pastures. Although prone to overgrowing, the route is easily followed across an avalanche chute to reach the scattering of rustic buildings at **Alpe Formazzöö** (1824m) after 35 to 45 minutes. Small herds of adroit chamois find a favoured habitat on these remote mountainsides.

Waymarkings near the upper hut guide you gently on over pretty moors and rhododendron fields, crossing several streamlets before climbing more steeply through tiered grassy slopes to the west. After 50 minutes to 1¼ to hours you get to the upper lake (2251m) of **Laghi di Formazzöö**. With talus rubble edging the lake's inner sides and green sunny lawns around the outer shore, some walkers prefer to camp out up here. The crisp clear waters of the lake make a challenging spot for a (quick) dip on a hot day.

Cross the lake outlet and make your way up steeply again through a broad expanse of the granite-slab rock overlooking the lower lake to reach a yellow signpost, where a high route intersects from the right. Watching carefully for bright paint splashes on broken blocks in this bare landscape, traverse up leftward for some distance, then double-back to the right over rough moraines past a tiny grassy gap (this is a false pass, which nevertheless offers a nice overview of Grossalp). The actual ridge crossing, **Bocchetta Formazzöö** (2670m), is a little farther up across a snowy gully below the 2863m Wandfluhhorn (Pizzo Biela), one to 1¼ hours from the upper Formazzöö lake.

Rock-hop southward onto the poor uppermost pastures, picking up walking pads that lead down along steep and muddy ridges to meet a well-trodden international path below the Hendar Furggu. Go left here, cutting down through pleasant undulating meadows to reach the alp cottages of **Bann** (2104m) after one to 1¼ hours.

Walkers who still have the time and energy can take an interesting longer route to Bosco/Gurin going off left up to the Uesser See (Lago Poma), one of three well-spaced tarns on an elongated high terrace. The main path to **Bosco/Gurin** descends steeply into light larch forest, edging leftward across a stream about midway to reach the upper village, 50 minutes to one hour down from Bann.

Alternative Finish via Capanna Grossalp

1¼-1½ hours, 3km

Take the right-hand turn-off from Bann, crossing countless trickling brooklets as you contour along the open slopes. Where you meet a dirt track, cut down left under winter ski tows to reach the dozen-odd stone buildings of **Grossalp** after 35 to 45 minutes. Here *Capanna Grossalp (☎ 091-754 16 80)*, a large FAT/UTOE-run hut at 1896m, overlooks the Valle di Bosco (whose lower half is indeed heavily forested). The Capanna (open early June to late October) has a *restaurant* and offers dorm beds for Sfr20 (including showers).

A new cableway from near here runs down to **Bosco/Gurin**. The 40- to 50-minute walk down short-cuts bends in the road as it follows the line of chairlifts through light forest, then swings left under the wires and descends alongside a stream to the edge of the village. The unusual elongated form of a 17-stage hay barn you pass here serves as protection from avalanches.

Barone Circuit

Duration	4 days
Distance	26.5km
Standard	hard
Start/Finish	Sonogno

Summary This excellent walk leads past two lovely highland lakes, over two mountain passes and through two wild little valleys in one of the most inaccessible parts of Ticino's central-western ranges.

The area around the 2864m Pizzo Barone is Alpine Ticino at its best. Ironically, the seemingly pristine nature of the Barone area is due to its over-exploitation in the first half of the 19th century, when the uncontrolled clearing of its once luxuriant forests turned these highland valleys into unproductive and dangerous ravines. Having been left to recover by itself, the vegetation has now largely regenerated. In recent years a small herd of ibex has taken up residence in these mountains. Today this

TICINO

is a surprising wilderness that attracts a modest but increasing number of hikers.

The circuit is probably best done in three days – many walkers will find the four day-sections described here too short – with a night spent at any two of the three en-route mountain huts. These are self-catering type huts (with no resident warden), and apart from drinks, you will have to carry supplies for the whole trip. An honesty system applies for the payment of hut fees – don't abuse it.

Maps

Any of the following walking maps covers the route: the SAW/ESS 1:50,000 sheet *Val Verzasca* No 266T (Sfr22.50), Editions MPA Verlag's 1:50,000 *Valle Maggia-Val Verzasca* (Sfr27.90), and K+F's 1:60,000 *Ticino Sopraceneri* (Sfr24.80).

NEAREST TOWNS
Sonogno

Situated at the head of the Val Verzasca, Sonogno (918m) lies well within range of central Ticino's higher peaks. Despite its remoteness, a steady stream of visitors is attracted by the village's charming stone houses and little laneways, as well as the outstanding walks into the surrounding mountains. There is a small local museum, while the Casa della Lana sells locally produced wool.

Ristorante Alpino (☎ 091-746 11 63) and *Osteria Sportiva* (☎ 091-746 11 48) have singles/doubles for around Sfr40/80. There is one small store selling basic *groceries*.

Postbuses run between Locarno and Sonogno some six times daily in either direction throughout the year. The trip, lasting

a bit over an hour, takes you right through the beautiful Valle Verzasca. The valley road is open to private traffic, and cars can be parked near the village entrance.

GETTING TO/FROM THE WALK
The circuit's starting and finishing point is Sonogno at the end of the Valle Verzasca. Motorists can leave their vehicles right by the trailhead, at the carpark 3.5km up from Sonogno.

THE WALK
See the Around Valle Leventina map, p263
Day 1: Sonogno to Capanna Cògnora
3–4 hours, 5km, 1020m ascent

Walk a few paces uphill from the Sonogno post office and turn right at the main street. This leads north-east into the Val Vegorness, quickly leaving the village for green hay fields littered with blocks that must have crashed down from the mountainsides above. Follow the road up along the narrow valley floor past clustered hamlets, crossing the Verzasca on a bridge 1km before you reach a signpost indicating the trailhead, 45 minutes to one hour from Sonogno. The remains of an old stone-wall dam used to float timber can still be seen on the river here.

The route heads up steeply beside a tumbling stream, which it crosses twice in quick succession before veering right to begin a long and winding ascent of the very steep slopes. Higher up the gradient eases, with attractive stands of larch trees followed by meadows of Alpine rhododendrons, and after two to three hours of solid climbing you arrive at the **Alpe di Cògnora**. On this tiny grassy terrace at 1938m stands the Società Escursionistica Verzaschese's *Capanna Cògnora* (☎ 091-745 28 87 *for information*), which looks west over the deep trough of the Val Vegorness toward the peaks of Cima di Cagnoi and Corona di Redorta. Grazing stock have not been driven up here for generations, and this neat stone hut, converted from a disused herders' shelter, offers dorm beds for around Sfr12.

The Return of the Forest

Despite its idyllic image, traditional Alpine grazing has been in steady decline for over 150 years, a trend most evident in western Ticino. Squeezed by the structural changes in modern agribusiness, many mountain farmers simply abandon their properties and move away. In Switzerland, the forest is reclaiming Alpine meadows – which may have been cleared centuries ago – at a rate of 50 sq km per year. The view of church steeples poking up out of regenerating forest may become common-place in some areas!

But the transition from managed Alpine pasture to natural mountain forest is less straightforward than is often assumed. Due to long-term livestock grazing, the tree line on many Alpine slopes is several hundred metres lower than its natural level. Once grazing ceases, the ungrazed grass is pushed flat by winter snow, hindering new growth in spring. The slippery grassy surface favours avalanches, which can tear out vegetation, opening up long avalanche chutes in the mountain sides. The process may take hundreds of years before natural stability is fully re-established.

Day 2: Capanna Cògnora to Capanna Sponda

3–4 hours, 7km, 178m ascent

From the hut swing up around to the left, following the well-cut foot track as it rises and dips along slanted shelves between bands of cliffs. There are some fixed cables and ladders for added security. After 50 minutes to one hour you'll come up to the flat grassy saddle of **Passo di Piatto** (2108m). Immediately below lies a basin filled by the clear bluish waters of Lago di Chironico (shown on most maps as Laghetto).

Drop a short way to the right, then follow the white-red-white paint markings back left through a short section of scree. The path contours on around the western rim of **Lago di Chironico** (1763m) above high bluffs, before heading down a small scrubby ridge to reach the north shore after 40 to 50 minutes. Remains of an old dam wall here bear witness to previous human exploitation, although the lake has long since returned to its former natural state. Its decidedly cool waters are enticing in hot weather, but swim well away from the still-functioning outlet tunnel.

Pick up the route at a broad flat rock, and continue quickly past a stone fishing cottage. Across the valley the compact little village of Cala stands out clearly on the isolated mountainside. The route now steers off leftward to make a descending traverse into the **Val Chironico**, coming out of the stunted forest at an avalanche slope covered by bilberry and raspberry bushes. Cut up through this rocky area toward the powerful waterfall surging from a small gorge, where a footbridge leads you over the Ticinetto stream. No roads penetrate this intact upper valley area, and it remains a surprising wilderness so close to the Valle Leventina.

At a signposted intersection not far down the left (northern) bank of the river, take the initially vague left-hand trail. This direct route leads past a semi-abandoned stone shelter, before climbing more steeply in zigzags, first through pleasant larch forest then over Alpine pastures. When you meet the more distinct path (coming from Cala) at two barns, proceed left for 500m to arrive at **Capanna Sponda** (☎ 091-745 23 52), a large, three-storey SAT club hut at 1997m, 1½ to two hours from Lago di Chironico – the lake is visible from the hut.

Day 3: Capanna Sponda to Rifugio Barone

2¾–3½ hours, 5km, 585m ascent

Find the continuation of the foot track below the capanna's flagpole and start sidling along the often boggy mountain-sides past lonely alp huts. The route crosses numerous streamlets coming down from the slab-rock faces higher up to reach a grassy basin at the very head of the valley. There is no bridge, but several side streams join here to form the Ticinetto and are easily jumped as you begin ascending southward over the moraine-scattered slopes.

Paint markings or the odd cairn show the way up across a large permanent snowfield, then on in steep zigzags through very loose rubble. At times it's pretty hard going. A short final climb up a rocky chute brings you to the **Passo Barone** (2582m), two to 2½ hours after leaving Capanna Sponda. In the rugged cirque immediately below is the kidney-shaped **Lago Barone** (2391m), whose deep, blue waters can stay icebound well into July.

A winding foot track now takes you back down into the watershed of the Verzasca, descending to the lakeshore over partially revegetated scree-slopes and lingering winter snowdrifts. Walk on around the grassed-over moraines at Lago Barone's southern edge to where the trail up to the 2864m Pizzo Barone departs. White-red-white route markings lead up in an S-bend through talus on the lake's south-eastern sides. Make your way down past where the subterranean lake outlet emerges, following this stream a short way before easing over to the right to reach ***Rifugio Barone*** (☎ 091-859 07 06) at 2172m after 40 to 50 minutes. This cosy hut (a converted old alp dairy) has sleeping space for just 15 people. In front the land falls away abruptly into the Val Vegorness, with the Corona di Redorta rising up behind.

Day 4: Rifugio Barone to Sonogno

2¾–3¾ hours, 9.5km, 1254m descent

The path picks its way through bluffs below the rifugio, dropping down in wide switch-backs past **Piodoo**, an alp hut protected from avalanches by a sizeable boulder. From here the ridge running between Pizzo Barone and the Corona di Redorta appears as a dramatic line of crags and rock turrets. Cliffs not far down from Piodoo force the route leftward to make a traversing descent that eventually brings you into the valley floor at **Corte di Fondo** (1487m) after one to 1¼ hours.

The remainder of the way through the upper Val Vegorness is easy and very pleasant. Cross over the Verzasca to a brick house, from where a broad mule track continues down along the right bank of the river through alternating patches of light forest and bilberry fields. A series of natural spill-ways flowing through granite pools offers intrepid bathers a cooling respite from summer heat soon before the path comes to another footbridge slightly upstream from **Cabiói**. Recross and proceed 400m past this clustered hamlet of stone buildings to arrive back at the trailhead up to the Capanna Cògnora after one to 1½ hours. Now retrace your steps as taken in Day 1, returning to Sonogno after a further 45 minutes' to one hour's walk.

Cima del Trosa

Duration	3¾–5 hours
Distance	10km
Standard	easy
Start	Cardada
Finish	Mergoscia
Nearest Town	Locarno

Summary This short high-level route leads over the rounded mountaintops immediately north of Lago Maggiore.

Passing centuries-old hamlets and villages occupied only in summer and still only accessible on foot or horseback, this walk has a rustic flavour that shows how easy it can be to get off the beaten track in Ticino. Like in other parts of Ticino, many of the mountain farm cottages *(rustici)* in the tiny Valle di Mergoscia have long been disused and are falling into ruin.

Although this is essentially a short walk, spending a night 'on the mountain' is a cheaper and more scenic alternative than staying down in Locarno. The walk can be done from the middle of spring right through to late autumn. Spring-fed drinking fountains along the route make carrying water unnecessary, except perhaps on the hottest of summer days, but you'll need protection from the elements – at least a hat and rain-jacket – regardless of when you do the Cima del Trosa.

Maps

The most detailed map for this walk is Orell Füssli's 1:25,000 *Locarno/Ascona* (Sfr25).

Any of the following walking maps will also do: K+F's 1:60,000 *Ticino Sottoceneri* or *Ticino Sopraceneri* (both Sfr24.80); Editions MPA Verlag's 1:50,000 *Valle Maggia-Val Verzasca* (Sfr27.90); and the SAW/ESS 1:50,000 sheet *Val Verzasca* No 266T (Sfr22.50).

NEAREST TOWNS
Cardada
The funicular/cable-car combination pulls you up from the muggy summer temperatures of Locarno into the crisp air of Cardada (1332m).

Albergo Cardada (☎ *091-751 55 91)*, being renovated at the time of writing, has better-standard rooms. A short stone-laid pathway leads up around through the subalpine forest to the lower station of the chairlift, where the small *Albergo Colmanicchio* (☎ *091-751 18 25)* has rooms from around Sfr40/80.

Mergoscia
This picturesque old village sits high above the Val Verzasca, looking out to the south across stone roofs and the Lago di Vogorno reservoir toward Monte Tamaro (identifiable by the telecommunications tower).

Osteria della Posta serves meals and refreshments, but there is nowhere to stay in Mergoscia. The 'Sentierone' walking route also continues from here up the Val Verzasca as far as Sonogno (see Other Walks at the end of this chapter).

There are about seven daily (FART) buses back to Locarno; the last one leaves around 7.20pm.

GETTING TO/FROM THE WALK
The walk begins from the upper cable-car station at Cardada at 1332m, high above Locarno (see Access Towns earlier). To get to Cardada first take the funicular from near Locarno train station, or walk up the Via al Sasso to the famous 15th-century Madonna del Sasso sanctuary. It's worth stopping to visit the interesting pilgrim church and museum here, before taking the cable car on up to Cardada. For the less energetic, a chairlift continues up to the top of 1671m Cimetta.

The combined one-way fare to Cardada is Sfr9/23 children/adults or Sfr15/30 to Cimetta (no concessions, but ask about special fares for families). The cable car and chairlift stop for maintenance in November.

THE WALK
Follow the dirt track on up to the right, climbing around the mainly open slopes past *Ristorante Capanna Cardada*, with its panoramic terrace. Make your way on to reach *Capanna Ostello Lo Stallone (☎ 091-743 61 46)* after 30 to 40 minutes. This large hut in the grassy hollow of **Alpe Cardada** (1488m) is usually open from mid-June to early October in summer, and offers accommodation in small dorms for around Sfr25 and rooms from Sfr40 with breakfast. Typical Ticino dishes and hot showers are available.

From the Alpe, the track cuts back left up over the bracken-covered mountainsides, crossing under winter ski-tows and the chairlift. It then swings up right, skirting the forest to arrive at the 1671m *Capanna Cimetta (☎ 091-743 04 33,* [e] *Capanna Cimetta@ticino.com)*, after 25 to 30 minutes. This mountain restaurant offers dorm beds from Sfr45 per person with full board. From just below the upper chairlift station, take the left-hand path leading quickly down to a tiny saddle (1610m) with a springwater fountain. Make a rising traverse of the south-western slopes of **Cima del Trosa**, doubling around right up to gain the ridge. A short side trail brings you to the large metal cross mounted on the windswept 1869m summit after a further 35 to 45 minutes. This lofty spot serves as a great lookout point giving excellent views stretching way across Lago Maggiore and including many surrounding peaks.

After signing the logbook, return to the main path. This soon begins winding down the north-eastern sides of the Cima del Trosa to a minor col at 1657m. From here a side trip up to **Madone** (2039m) can be done in 1½ to two hours; the straightforward route follows white-red-white paint markings along the ridge, with some harmless rock-scrambling higher up, from where

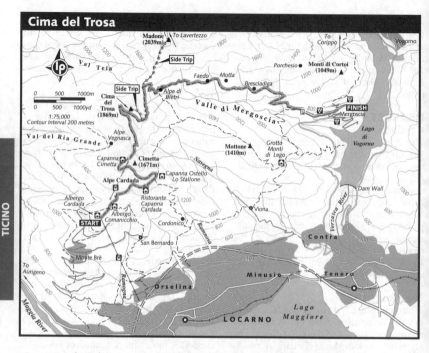

Cima del Trosa

you get another nice overview of the local scenery.

Descend in broad zigzags through brush and bilberry heath to the goat dairy of **Alpe di Bietri** (1499m), and continue on an old mule trail running along the northern slopes of the tiny Valle di Mergoscia. Dropping gently against the contour, the route passes dilapidated old houses and rustic hamlets built in local granite to reach the scattered village of **Bresciadiga** (1128m), 1¼ to 1¾ hours from the Cima del Trosa.

Bear right at a junction a short way on, where the path dips down into lush forest of chestnuts and beech, leading past small shrines before coming into a car park at the end of a road. Stroll 600m downhill to intersect with the main road, then follow the sealed road left up steep hillsides planted out with vineyards to arrive at the little square beside the large baroque church of **Mergoscia** at 731m, after a final one to 1¼ hours.

Sottoceneri

Known as the Sottoceneri (after the low, 554m watershed of Monte Ceneri, 10km south-west of Bellinzona), the most southerly part of Ticino forms a conical wedge that protrudes down to meet Italy's Lombardy Plain. This compact region lies in the southern pre-Alps, an area characterised by lower limestone ranges that nevertheless rise up surprisingly abruptly. Dominated by the contorted shape of Lago di Lugano, the Sottoceneri has a somewhat confusing geography with seemingly irregular borders. The fingers of the large lake spread out through the densely forested Alpine foothills, presenting a magnificent backdrop when viewed from all over the region. Although it makes up no more than 10% of the canton's area, the Sottoceneri offers some outstanding opportunities for walking.

Ticino's Chestnut Forests

The Romans introduced the sweet chestnut tree to the southern Alpine foothills over 2000 years ago, and today the tree forms whole forests in Ticino. In local dialects of Italian, the chestnut is called simply *arbur* – literally 'tree'. Countless generations of mountain people have been nourished – at times saved from starvation – by the carbohydrate-rich chestnuts. Traditionally the nuts were dried and ground into flour that was used to bake bread or boiled into a starchy porridge.

With the rise of cash-cropping (especially of maize and potatoes) after WWII, the importance of the chestnut declined dramatically, however, and the ancient forests have been handed back to nature. Absurdly, the Swiss eat enormous quantities of imported chestnuts – roasted over hot coals and sold at streetside stands during the colder months – while the fruit in their own southern forests is left to rot.

ACCESS TOWNS

Lugano

Ticino's largest city lies on a broad bay of Lago di Lugano surrounded by high hills. Among the pedestrian lanes of Lugano's old town are the 16th-century churches of Santa Maria degli Angioli and San Lorenzo. Lugano has several excellent museums and art galleries, including the Thyssen-Bornemisza in the Villa Favorita, Castagnola – one of the world's greatest private art collections (entry Sfr6/10 students/adults).

The tourist office (☎ 091-921 46 64, [e] info @lugano-tourism.ch, [w] www.luganotourism .ch) is at Riva Giocondo Albertolli 5.

There are about half a dozen camping grounds around the shore of Lago di Lugano, including *La Piodella* (☎ 091-994 77 88) with tent sites for Sfr14 plus Sfr8 per person (high season). The *youth hostel* (☎ 091-966 27 28, [e] lugano@youthhostel.ch, Via Canonale 13) has dorm beds for Sfr28/30.50 in the low/high season.

The *Hotel Montarina* (☎ 091-966 72 72, [e] asbest@tinet.ch, Via Montarina 1) offers

dorm beds from Sfr20 and singles/doubles from Sfr50/80. *Hotel Dischma* (☎ 091-994 21 31, [e] dischma@swissonline.ch, Vicolo Geretta 6) has rooms for Sfr65/110 and a restaurant with full meals from around Sfr20.

The *Migros* on Via Pretorio and the *EPA* department store on Via Nassa at Piazzetta San Carlo have cheap restaurants. *Ristorante Inova* offers buffet fare from around Sfr10.

Lugano is on the main Gotthard–Chiasso rail and road route.

Mendrisio

The town of Mendrisio lies at the southern tip of the Sottoceneri, an area known as the Mendrisiotto. Along with several superb old churches the old town hub has many buildings dating from the 15th to the 18th century.

For information contact the tourist office (☎ 091-646 57 61, fax 091-646 33 48, [e] etm @tintet.ch, [w] www.mendrisiotourism.ch).

Ristorante Grutli (☎ 091-646 18 60, Piazzetta L Fontana 3) has singles/doubles for Sfr40/80. *Osteria del Ponte* (☎ 091-646 32 96, Via Rinaldi 2) charges Sfr50/100.

Modern *Albergo Hotel Milano* (☎ 091-646 57 41, [e] info@hotel-milano.ch) on Piazzale Stazione has rooms from Sfr95 per person.

Trains running between Chiasso and Bellinzona stop at Mendrissio.

Tamaro–Lema Traverse

Duration	3¾–4½ hours
Distance	13km
Standard	easy-medium
Start	Alpe Foppa
Finish	Monte Lema
Nearest Towns	Rivera-Bironico, Miglieglia

Summary The Sottoceneri's classic ridge walk, this traverse route (using cableways at either end) leads south over the 1961m pyramid form of Monte Tamaro to Monte Lema, giving wonderful views of the Ticino Alps, the pre-Alps and Lago di Lugano.

The treeless upper ridge tops of the main range connecting Monte Tamaro and Monte

TICINO

Lema are exposed to the winds and southern sun. This has favoured a dry-climate vegetation of Alpine grasses and low heath. Grazed only by flocks of hardy sheep and goats, these bare rolling ranges are strangely reminiscent of the Scottish highlands.

The traverse stays above 1600m for almost the entire way, with fairly moderate climbs and descents. The going can get hot in summer, and as no running water is available it is important to carry plenty of liquids. The range's southerly aspect generally keeps it snow-free from mid-May until mid-November. This is nevertheless Alpine country, and the appropriate rainwear belongs in the pack.

Maps

Recommended is Orell Füssli's 1:25,000 *Valli di Lugano* (Sfr17). Good alternatives include Editions MPA Verlag's 1:50,000 map *Locarno-Lugano* No 5007 (Sfr27.90) or K+F's 1:60,000 map *Ticino Sottoceneri* (Sfr24.80). The standard 1:50,000 *Malcantone* sheet No 286 (Sfr13.50) also covers the walk.

NEAREST TOWNS & FACILITIES
Alpe Foppa

The gondola lift from Rivera-Bironico takes you up more than 1000m to the Corte di Sopra upper station at Alpe Foppa (1534m). The large *Ristorante Alpe Foppa (☎ 091-946 22 51)*, which is open early May to late October, offers refreshments and dormitory accommodation.

Rivera-Bironico

The sprawling village of Rivera-Bironico lies just south of Monte Ceneri.
Pensione Elvezia (☎ 091-946 46 27) and *Hotel Garni Posta (☎ 091-946 14 40)* have singles/doubles from around Sfr40/80.

Only the slower (at least hourly) regional trains running between Bellinzona and Lugano stop in Rivera-Bironico.

Miglieglia

Miglieglia is a lovely old Ticino village. It's worth having a wander through its old laneways or visiting the interesting Santo Stefano village church, which has 16th-century frescoes.
Hotel San Stefano (☎ 091-609 19 35), or Via alla Chiesa, has nice rooms from around Sfr45/85.

There are up to eight daily postbuses to Lugano (fewer on Saturday and Sunday); the last leaves around 5.30pm (6.30pm on Saturday).

GETTING TO/FROM THE WALK

The walk begins at Alpe Foppa, accessible by gondola lift (☎ 091-946 23 03). The lower gondola station is 10 minutes' walk north from Rivera-Bironico train station. The last ride up is at around 5pm. The gondola does not run after early November.

The walk finishes at Monte Lema, from where a gondola lift (☎ 091-609 11 68) takes you down to the village of Miglieglia. The one-way fare is around Sfr14 and the lift stops running around 5.30pm. The one-way fare on both cableways is around Sfr14 (no concessions).

Private vehicles are best left at the car park by the lower gondola-lift station in Rivera-Bironico.

THE WALK

Fill up your water bottle at the spring fountain at Alpe Foppa, as there's precious little water along the walking route.

Head up the open grassy hillsides above the gondola station on a rough vehicular track leading below winter ski-tows. Many people prefer to continue right up the more gently winding road, but the white-red-white marked path follows the initially very steep spur past the upper ski-tow station and the futuristic-looking telecommunications tower on Motto Rotondo (1928m) to *Capanna Tamaro (☎ 091-946 23 03)*. This UTOE-run hut stands at around 1928m and offers dorm beds for around Sfr30 with breakfast.

Sidle on around the mountainside along a well-cut mule track to a small gap, then follow the main ridge quickly up to reach **Monte Tamaro**, 1¼ to 1½ hours from Alpe Foppa. The outstanding, almost 360-degree panorama from the 1962m summit includes

Tamaro–Lema Traverse

reach **Passo Agario** (1574m), a low point hut in the range (where there is a customs hut), after 1¼ to 1½ hours. From here a path goes off right to the nearby Capanna Merigetto (☎ 091-039-332-510014 from outside Italy), a basic Club Alpino Italiano (CAI) mountain hut just across the border.

Traverse fields of bilberry bushes on the eastern slopes of **Monte Magno**, then make your way on to another minor saddle at **Zottone** (1567m). The path passes through a narrow and rocky section of the ridge top, rising on over the **Poncione di Breno** (1654m) before dipping down to the small col of **Forcola d'Arasio** (1481m). Head up the steep dirt road directly to arrive at the upper chairlift station just below **Monte Lema** after a final 1¼ to 1½ hours. Here *Ostello Vetta* (☎ *091-967 13 53*) offers dormitory accommodation for around Sfr25 (including light breakfast and showers).

The short side trip up to the 1621m summit is recommended for more great views, including the lower part of Lago Maggiore to the west, Lugano clustered on the lakeshore far below, and Chiasso farther away to the south-east. If you don't want to take the chairlift, a good foot track leads down below the cables in countless zigzags to reach Miglieglia in 40 to 50 minutes.

Monte Brè to Soragno

Duration	2¾–3¼ hours
Distance	11km
Standard	easy
Start	Monte Brè
Finish	Soragno
Nearest Towns	Lugano, Brè
Summary This is a short but scenic traverse through beech forests and meadows above Lago di Lugano.	

the three main cities of southern Ticino – Lugano, Locarno and Bellinzona – as well as Lago Maggiore and Lago di Lugano. On your right a picturesque string of isolated villages stretches from Indemini along the forested slopes of the Valle Vedasca into Italy.

Drop down southward beside an old fence to the small flattened saddle of **Bassa di Indemini** (1723m), before climbing on more steeply through stunted Alpine scrub to the top of **Monte Gradiccioli** (1936m). A smooth rolling descent brings you down over the grassy hillock of **Monte Pola** (1742m) to

The 925m Monte Brè (not to be confused with another Monte Brè above Locarno) rises up directly from the northern sides of Lago di Lugano. Although one of the lower summits in the Alpine foothills, Monte Brè offers superb views across the lake's shimmering blue waters. These porous limestone

TICINO

mountainsides nurture a rich vegetation that thrives in the mild climate produced by the close proximity of Lago di Lugano. Here, many plant species typical for the southern pre-Alps find their only habitat within Switzerland.

The walk can be done in any season apart from midwinter, when snow often covers the upper slopes. Midsummer weather can be hot, but drinking water is available and there are restaurants along the route. October and November are perhaps the best months for the walk, as the area's deciduous forests are then at their prettiest and grant better views through the thinning foliage.

Maps

Recommended maps are as for the Tamaro–Lema Traverse, covered earlier.

NEAREST TOWNS
Brè

The walk passes through Brè (800m), a lovely little village with narrow stone-paved alleys and a parish church dating from 1591. *Albergo Brè (☎ 091-971 47 61)* has nice singles/doubles from around Sfr50/100.

The No 12 bus runs from Lugano to Brè – a less attractive alternative to taking the funicular, it shortens the walk by 15 to 20 minutes.

Soragno

The walk finishes at the small village of Soragno (416m). There is nowhere to stay here, but there are buses back to Lugano at least hourly until around 8.15pm.

GETTING TO/FROM THE WALK

The walk starts at the upper station of the Monte Brè funicular (**W** www.montebre .ch). To reach the lower funicular station, catch the No 9 bus from Lugano station to Piazza Manzoni, then take the No 9 bus to the Cassarate/Monte Brè stop. Except for several weeks in January when it closes for maintenance, the funicular runs half-hourly until 6.15pm all year round. The one-way fare is Sfr13 (Half Fare Card and Swiss Pass both valid).

THE WALK

The funicular leaves the stifling summe heat around Lago di Lugano, pulling you u steeply past well-to-do residences on th cooler mountain slopes to the low summit c **Monte Brè** (925m) in less than 15 minutes The panoramic terrace looks out acros Lago di Lugano to Monte San Salvatore an Monte San Giorgio.

A stepped walkway leads you gently u through the light forest before droppin down to **Brè**. Make your way up past th village museum, then head left across th open grassy fields. The route first follows flagged path (signposted 'Sentiero Alp Bolla') which crosses a winding road sev eral times as it climbs into the woods, the continues along an old vehicle track fringe by blackberry bushes to reach **Carbone** (1033m) after one to 1¼ hours. There is water tank here for thirsty walkers.

Ascend steadily on through the beec forest (ignoring a right-hand trail branchin off to Monte Boglia), then make a stee climb up to the right. The well-cut foo track sidles north-eastward around th slope, with glimpses through the beec trees down to Lugano. The track finall comes out at a path junction at the edge o a small clearing. Walk on across thes pretty pastures to arrive at **Alpe Bolla**, 40 t 50 minutes from Carbonera. Here th *Grotto Alpe Bolla (☎ 091-943 25 70)* sits a 1129m, and gives a pleasant view north west toward the Val Capriasca and th round hump of Monte Gradiccioli. Th Grotto is open from early May to late Oc tober, and has a small dorm where walker can sleep for around Sfr25 (includin breakfast).

Retrace your steps to the signpost an descend diagonally through the forest to th *Osteria Alpe Pietragrossa*, a simple restaur ant in a small clearing at 809m. At this poin double-back around to the right and con tinue to **Colorino** (696m) from where a left hand path spirals on down to meet gravelled road. Head 600m left, then tur off right onto a narrow old cobbled lane be tween low stone walls, continuing dow right via a stepped pathway that leads unde

Monte Brè to Soragno

Alps. Although at 1701m the mountain's height is modest compared with the Alpine summits, Monte Generoso provides a superb natural lookout with vistas stretching north across the lake and south to the plains of Italy's Po River basin. Once threatened by limestone mining for the cement industry, the forested lower slopes are now part of the Monte Generoso nature reserve. Monte Generoso is the only place in Switzerland where the wild peony *(Paeonia officinalis)* blooms.

Given suitable weather and snow-free conditions, the walk can be done from mid-May up until late October. The midsummer sun can be quite penetrating, so carry fluids or stop at one of the restaurants en route.

Maps

Recommended is K+F's 1:25,000 *Mendrisiotto Basso Ceresio* (Sfr17), or the 1:25,000 *Monte Generoso* (Sfr13) published by Ferrovia Monte Generoso (available at its ticket office). K+F's 1:60,000 *Ticino Sottoceneri* (Sfr24.80) is another alternative, and shows a much larger part of southern Ticino.

NEAREST TOWN & FACILITIES
Capolago

Capolago lies near the southern tip of Lago di Lugano. *Albergo Svizzero (☎ 091-648 19 75)* has good-standard singles/doubles for Sfr65/120, while in nearby Riva-San Vitale *Osteria San Giorgio (☎ 091-648 11 80)* has cheaper rooms from Sfr40/80.

Capolago can be reached by ferry during the tourist season, or by train via Lugano. Only regional trains stop in Capolago, so a ferry may work out faster. Throughout the summer season, ferries run roughly hourly between Lugano and Capolago from around 9.30am until 3.30pm.

Monte Generoso

Hotel Vetta (☎ 091-649 77 22, e *info@mon tegeneroso.ch)* on the summit of Monte Generoso has singles/doubles for Sfr50/100 and dorm beds for around Sfr30.

GETTING TO/FROM THE WALK

The walk begins from the summit of Monte Generoso, reached from Capolago on the

road bridge to come out at a street just above **Soragno**. The final section follows the sealed road down through the village to reach the main road after one to 1¼ hours. The local bus stop is a short way along to the right.

Monte Generoso

Duration	5¼–6½ hours
Distance	12km
Standard	easy
Start	Monte Generoso
Finish	Mendrisio
Nearest Town	Capolago

Summary This is a long but leisurely downhill walk from the lookout summit of Monte Generoso passing by rustic Ticino hamlets.

Towering above the eastern shores of Lago di Lugano, the isolated form of Monte Generoso is the most southerly bastion of the historic old cog railway operated by Ferrovia Monte Generoso (W www.montegeneroso .ch). Trains run every one to 1½ hours between 1 April and 30 October (no service in November); the last uphill departure is at 5pm. The one-way fare is Sfr33, but the Half Fare Card and the Lugano regional pass (see Getting Around at the beginning of this chapter) give major discounts.

The walk finishes at Mendrisio (see Access Towns at the beginning of the Sottoceneri section).

Motorists can leave vehicles at the station car park in Capolago free of charge.

THE WALK

The cog railway heaves you up to the terminus at 1601m. Since it's downhill for the rest of the walk, taking the signposted foot track up the last 100m ascent to the 1701m top of **Monte Generoso** is a must. In clear weather the magnificent views stretch across the central Alps from Mont Blanc to Piz Bernina in the north. To the south the land sweeps down to the Lombardy plains of northern Italy, and with a good pair of binoculars you should even be able to make out the steeple of the Milan cathedral!

Back at the hotel/restaurant, follow the broad path over the open slopes alongside the rail lines and turn off left when you get to **Quota** at 1452m. Sidle on downward around the heath-scattered slopes, passing between the rustic cottages of **Alpe Génor** (1275m) and below the farmhouse of Nadigh. The white-red-white marked trail follows a grassy, rocky spur before dropping down to the left to reach the tiny village of **Roncapiano** at 970m after one to 1¼ hours. Upvalley is the larger village of Scudellate (904m), which clings to the sides of Monte Generoso near the Italian border.

Walk down the narrow road past quaint stone houses to the church at the bottom of Roncapiano, where the road ends. A broad foot track (signposted 'Bellavista') now winds around the steep hillsides, falling gently against the contour through beech forest mixed with wild hazelnuts and gnarled old chestnut trees. When you come to a hillside paddock, climb away to the

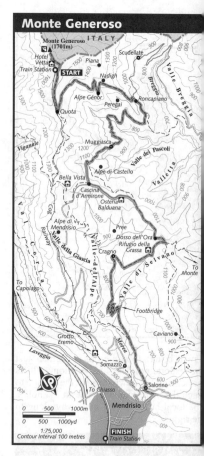

Monte Generoso

right along the edge of the trees to meet a road just uphill from the idyllic little village of **Muggiasca**, 50 minutes to one hour on.

Continue up along the sealed road through hay fields and birch forest to intersect with another road at **Cascina d'Armirone** (1152m). Head on southward along the ridge top past *Osteria Balduana*, a scenic restaurant with a garden terrace. When you reach **Dosso dell'Ora**, go 200m rightward along a narrow lane then take a signposted path down left to the *Rifugio della Grassa*, another simple mountain restaurant. The route makes a sidling descent around the slopes to rrive at the isolated village of **Cragno** (at 45m) after 1½ to two hours.

Turn left at the first road bend a few aces below Cragno, following a disused ehicle track down in repeated switchbacks under a thick cover of forest to cross a large ide stream on a footbridge. Bear left at a ork a short way on and cut alongside green astures to meet a dirt road running through he valley. Proceed 600m south to where a cobblestone mule trail descends past vineyards to reach **Salorino** (465m), one to 1¼ ours on from Cragno. The houses of this ypical southern-Ticino village have red-tile oofs and big wooden courtyard gates.

There are (infrequent) postbuses from Salorino, but the final section leads over the ridge then immediately down Via Genroso, coming out at the cathedral in the old art of **Mendrisio**. Walk on along the Via Borella to arrive at the train station after 30 o 40 minutes.

Other Walks

Gotthard Lakes Circuit

Apart from forming a clear north-south division, the Gotthard region is a geographical centre separating the western and eastern Alps. This easy-medium five-hour day walk leads through an interesting highland plateau scattered with lovely Alpine lakes and moorland. The route begins at the cluster of historic buildings (including a chapel and museums) surrounding the hospice, or *Albergo San Gottardo* (☎ 091-869 12 35, e hotel@gotthard-hospiz.ch), which offers rooms and dorm accommodation.

From 500m north of the Passo del San Gottardo (2191m), the route follows a road up to halfway around Lago di Lucendro (reservoir). It then climbs north on a path leading past Laghi della Valletta and Laghi d'Orsirora to Lago d'Orsino before descending back to the Lago di Lucendro dam wall.

From late June until late September postbuses run three times daily between Airolo and Andermatt via the Passo del San Gottardo.

K+F's 1:50,000 *San Gottardo* (Sfr24.80) is the recommended map.

Strada Alta

The 45km-long Strada Alta runs between Airolo and Biasca along the old track used by the muleteers on the Passo del San Gottardo route. This 'high road' followed a course far up the northeastern sides of the Valle Leventina in order to avoid the gorges, flooding and rockfalls that often made travel in the valley floor a dangerous prospect.

Gently rising and dipping at a relatively constant level of 1000m to 1400m, today this ancient panoramic roadway makes an ideal walking route. The Strada Alta leads through highland forests, subalpine pastures and some of northern Ticino's most picturesque mountainside villages where traditional Alpine farming methods are still widely practised. The walk is in the easy-medium range, and can be done in two, or better still, three, day sections.

The Strada Alta is very popular with walkers, and most of the villages you pass through on the way have good accommodation options. Recommended is *Osteria La Baita* (☎ 091-866 10 84, e b.bkingman@datacomm.ch) in Calpiogna, which has singles/doubles for Sfr38/76 and dorm beds for Sfr29.

The SAW/ESS 1:50,000 map *Valle Leventina* No 266T (Sfr22.50) covers the whole of the route.

Sentierone

The Sentierone follows the old mule trail up through the Val Verzasca. It leads past the ruins of hamlets, old stone fences and disused farm land that was gradually reclaimed by the forest as much of the valley's population migrated to the industrial centres from the mid-1800s. The 6½-hour walk starts at Mergoscia and ends at Sonogno.

The Val Verzasca's sunny southerly aspect tends to keep it snow-free in winter, so this walk can generally be done all year round. This is an easy route with the gentlest of inclines, and in warm weather the Verzasca River is perfect for swimming.

The SAW/ESS 1:50,000 sheet *Val Verzasca* No 276T (Sfr22.50) covers the route.

Val Bavona

At the town of Bignasco the Valle Maggia forks into two upper branches. The western branch is the Val Bavona, Ticino's deepest and most impressive glacial valley. Its sheer walls support numerous towering peaks, and huge boulders lie along the valley floor, sheltering stone goat sheds and farm cottages from avalanches. Remote and wildly beautiful, the Val Bavona has a summer-only population, and in winter the valley is virtually abandoned. From Bignasco a thoroughly enjoyable walking route leads up the Val Bavona through quaint hamlets as far as the village of San Carlo. The going is easy with a relatively low gradient, but unfortunately the route follows the (often busy) valley road itself in many places. The recommended walking map is Editions MPA Verlag's 1:50,000 *Valle Maggia-Val Verzasca* (Sfr27.90).

Alzasca-Sascola Traverse

This excellent medium-hard two-day walk leads from the village of Vergeletto (905m) in the remote Val di Vergeletto to Cevio (418m) in the upper Valle Maggia. The route leads north up through the narrow Val da la Camana across the Bocchetta di Doia before dropping down to a beautiful lake at Alpe Alzasca; the SAC's nearby *Capanna Alzasca* (☎ 091-753 25 15) at 1734m has dorm beds for Sfr22. The walk continues up north-west over the ridge to another lovely lake at Alpe Sascola, from where a winding path leads to a descent via the rustic hamlet of Rotonda to Cevio.

In Vergeletto, *Ristorante Fondovalle* (☎ 091-797 16 66) and *Hotel Villa Olandese* (☎ 091-797 14 33) offer rooms; *Ostello della Gioventù* (☎ 091-797 17 96) has rooms from around Sfr40 per person.

In Cevio, *Ristorante Posta* (☎ 091-754 18 96) charges Sfr45/90 for simple singles/doubles and *Osteria Castello* (☎ 091-754 16 45) has similar rooms for Sfr40/76.

Vergeletto is reached by postbus from Locarno (with a change in Russo); there are four daily connections (until around 6pm).

Use MPA's 1:50,000 *Valle Maggia-Val Verzasca* (Sfr27.90) or K+F's 1:60,000 *Ticino Sopraceneri* (Sfr24.80).

Gazzirola & Camoghè

The two neighbouring mountains of Gazzirola (2116m) and Camoghè (2227m) stand near the southern end of the chain of mountains that stretches from the Passo della Spluga along the Swiss–Italian border as far as Monte Brè. Making easily accessible and very scenic lookout points, these are the Sottoceneri's only peaks above 2000m and therefore the highest in the region.

A nice eight-hour route leaves from the village of Corticiasca (1016m), climbing to the rounded 1816m top of Monte Bar. The path continues east along the open ridge to the summit of Gazzirola, then turns north-west and traverses over the Camoghè before descending steeply into the Val di Caneggio and following the valley to the village of Isone (743m).

Capana Monte Bar (☎ 091-966 33 22), a SAC hut at 1600m on the southern slopes of Monte Bar, has dorm beds. To reach Corticiasc take a postbus from Lugano to Tesserete, the change to a postbus running via Maglio di Coll (but not via Bidogno) to Bogno; there are man daily connections. Isone has accommodation and regular postbuses to the train station a Rivera-Bironico. Orell Füssli's 1:25,000 *Valli Lugano* (Sfr17) covers the walk.

Monte San Salvatore

Monte San Salvatore lies in Lugano's backyard and is accessible by a funicular (closed from early November to mid- to late March) from the lakeside suburb of Paradiso. From the top this 912m-high mountain, the fjord-like arms Lago di Lugano reach out into Italian territory A popular four-hour route leads southward pas the village of Carona to Alpe Vicania (659m thence descending through hillside vineyards t the fishing village of Morcote on Lago Lugano. There are ferries and buses from Mor cote back to Lugano. K+F's 1:60,000 *Ticin Sottoceneri* (Sfr24.80) covers the route.

Monte San Giorgio

Monte San Giorgio forms a broad and heavil forested peninsula that projects northward be tween two arms of Lago di Lugano. Having bee little changed by human intervention, much the Monte San Giorgio area lies within a natur reserve. These ranges sit on a base of ancier volcanic rocks with more recent overlying sedi mentary deposits containing rich saurian fossils The small local museum in the village of Merid (not to be confused with Melide) houses a co lection of 200-million-year-old fossilised di nosaur bones found near Serpiano.

A short and easy day walk starts out from Meride (578m), and climbs up through the for est via Cassina to the 1097m lookout summit o Monte San Giorgio, from where there are glori ous views across Lago di Lugano. After drop ping to the restaurant at Alpe di Brusino, yo can descend on foot directly to the small lake side resort of Brusino-Arsizio, or detour to th nearby chairlift for a faster mechanical descent

Meride can be reached by postbus from Men drisio. From Brusino-Arsizio, at the end of th walk, there are buses to the train station a Capolago and ferries across the lake to Lugano The best walking map is K+F's 1:25,000 *Men drisiotto Basso Ceresio* (Sfr17).

Graubünden

Switzerland's largest and easternmost canton, Graubünden (also known to English speakers as Grisons) makes up almost one-fifth of the country's area. This is a rugged and thinly settled region (of which around 70% lies above 1800m) dissected by countless remote mountain valleys that take in some of the wildest and most intact landscapes found anywhere in the Alps. The complex folding and uplifting of the Bündner Alps has brought quite varied rock types to the surface, including limestones, crystalline slates, gneiss and dolomite, giving the landscape a correspondingly varied topography.

Regional isolation is reflected in Graubünden's diverse ethnic mix. Although mainly German-speaking, the canton also has significant Italian and Romansch-speaking minorities. In many parts of Graubünden, Germanic Walser dialects are still spoken, having been introduced from the Goms region of the upper Valais by the first settlers in medieval times.

Spread over three of Europe's major drainage systems, Graubünden's waters flow into the North, Black and Mediterranean seas, giving this pivotal Alpine canton an unusually complex geography. The northern three-quarters of Graubünden is part of the Rhine basin, with its twin upper branches, the Vorderrhein and Hinterrhein. The valley of the Engadine, in the canton's south-east, is drained by the En (or Inn) and lies within the catchment area of the Danube. The Val Müstair, an appendage of the Engadine, and Graubünden's three most southerly valleys, the Valle Mesolcina, the Val Bregaglia and the Val Poschiavo, all flow southward into Italy's Po river system.

With its important passes such as the Bernina, Maloja, Splügen, San Bernardino and Lucomagno, Graubünden has a history which has been dominated by trans-Alpine trade routes. Many of the mountain valleys earned their living by servicing the pass trade, and the control of these vital communication and transport links brought political

Highlights

A church perched high above the En (Inn) River at Scuol in the Lower Engadine.

- Watching chamois and ibex grazing on Alpine meadows in the Swiss National Park

- Standing under the towering eroded cliffs of the Ruin' Aulta gorge along the Vorderrhein (Rein Anteriur)

- Walking through the remote, wild grasslands of the Plaun la Greina

- Trekking through spectacular dolomite ranges on the Rhätikon Höhenweg

and economic power. Today, many walking routes in Graubünden follow old mule paths that not so long ago were the only means of carrying cargo across the Alps.

INFORMATION
Maps

Kümmerly + Frey's (K+F) 1:120,000 *Holiday Map Graubünden* (Sfr24.80) gives an excellent overview of the region, and

GRAUBÜNDEN

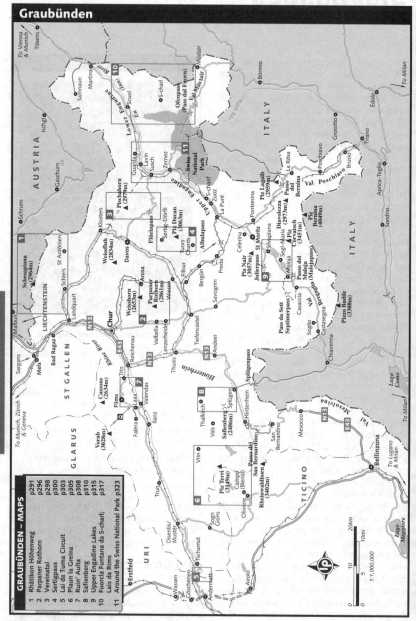

shows trails, huts and other important features for walkers. Sheet Nos 2 and 4 of the BL/OFT's (four-sheet) 1:200,000 series cover Graubünden.

Books
Kev Reynolds's *Walks in the Engadine, Switzerland* (Cicerone Press, UK£8.99) covers routes in the Upper and Lower Engadine (including the Swiss National Park), the Val Bregaglia and Bernina regions.

In German, *Wanderfuhrer Graubünden* (Sfr28) by HP Gansner is the most thorough general walking guide to the region. The SAC's *Alpinwandern Graubünden* (Sfr46) by Peter Donatsch and Paul Meinherz details dozens of mountain walks. K+F's German-language *Rundwanderungen Graubünden* (Sfr22.80) has a regional walking guide describing circuit (loop) walks throughout Graubünden. *Kulturwege in Graubünden* features walks to places of particular historic or cultural interest.

Information Sources
Online information can be found at W www .touristinfo-graubuenden.ch or W www .graubuenden.ch Unfortunately, both Web sites have little in English.

Pro Raetia (W www.pro-raetia.ch), an organisation dedicated to the preservation and promotion of Graubünden's cultural and natural heritage, publishes numerous (mostly German-language) titles, including regional walking guides and the bimonthly *Terra Grischun*.

GETTING AROUND
The *Graubünden Regionalpass* is good for travel on all Rhaetian Railways (☎ 081-254 91 00, W www.rhb.ch) trains, postbuses and mountain cableways, including the Palm Express. The minimum version, giving three days of free travel and seven days at 50% off, costs Sfr140 in 2nd class and Sfr210 in 1st class. The maximum version, giving 11 days of free travel, costs Sfr290/ 250. Holders of the Half Fare Card get a small discount.

The *Ferienkarte Engadin Bassa/Val Mustair* is valid on postbuses in the Lower Engadine between Brail and Samnaun (including S-charl). It costs Sfr65 (Sfr50 for children and with the Half Fare Card) for seven days' unlimited travel during a two-week period, or Sfr45 (Sfr35) for three days within a week.

The *Ferienkarte Surselva* covers the whole Vorderrhein (Rein Anteriur) region from Flims Dorf and Versam-Safien train station to Disentis and Cuolm Lucmagn (Lukmanierpass). It costs Sfr57 (Sfr42 for children and with the Half Fare Card) and gives seven days free postbus travel within two weeks. The *Ferienkarte Region Thusis* is identical in price and conditions, and covers the Hinterrhein (Rein Posteriur) region between Tumegl/Tomils and Passo San Bernardino, including the Val Avers.

GATEWAY
Chur
The cantonal capital of Chur (600m) is the only place of any real size in Graubünden. The oldest city north of the Alps, Chur's origins date back to pre-Roman times. The old town has many historically interesting buildings and a very good museum of natural history. A local two-day hike goes up to the 2805m summit of the Haldensteiner Calanda, the highest peak of the Calanda range immediately north-west of Chur, using the SAC's *Calandahütte* (☎ *081-285 15 37*).

The tourist office (☎ 081-252 18 18, fax 081-252 90 76, e info@churtourismus.ch, W www.churtourismus.ch), Grabenstrasse 5, can provide information. Norbert Joos Bergsport (☎ 081-253 74 14, e joos @spin. ch, W www.bergsport.ch), Comercialstrasse 24 and Sporthütte Obertor (☎ 081-252 23 39), Obere Gasse 47, stock a good range of outdoor gear.

Camping Obere Au (☎ *081-284 22 83,* e *info@camping-chur.ch)* has pleasant Rhine-side tent sites from Sfr6.20 plus Sfr6.20 per person. The *Hotel Schweizerhaus* (☎ *081-252 10 96,* e *hotel@schweiz erhaus-chur .ch, Kasernenstrasse 10)* offers dormitory beds for Sfr35 and singles/doubles from Sfr40/80. *Hotel Pizzeria Collina delle Rose* (☎/fax *081-252 23 88,* e *rosenhue gel@freesurf.ch, Malixerstrasse 32),* five

GRAUBÜNDEN

minutes' walk uphill from town, has rooms from Sfr50/100.

The *Coop* supermarket and restaurant is on Alexanderstrasse; *Migros* is on Gürtelstrasse. Grabenstrasse has a couple of *pizzerias*, or try the upmarket restaurant at *Hotel Stern* (☎ 081-252 35 55, Reichsgasse 11).

Chur is accessible by regular direct trains from Zürich. The city is one of Switzerland's most important transport hubs, with Rhaetian Railways trains to Arosa, Disentis, and St Moritz/Engadine (via the lower Hinterrhein and Filisur). Numerous postbus routes operate out of Chur's imaginative hangar-design bus terminal above the train station.

Northern & Central Bündner Alps

Occupying the north-eastern half of Graubünden's Rhine basin, this region takes in the canton's heartland. Its once overwhelmingly Romansch-speaking inhabitants have gradually been assimilated by the German-Swiss language and culture, and today Romansch survives only in remoter valleys of the Central Bündner Alps.

The Northern Bündner Alps form a hub around the cantonal capital of Chur, extending from the Landwasser/Albula River across the Schanfigg and Prättigau valleys to the Rhätikon range on the Swiss–Austrian border. This area includes the majestic peaks around Arosa and the Weissfluh near Davos. The Northern Bündner Alps are the most developed and accessible mountains of Graubünden, but nevertheless have some great areas for walking.

The Central Bündner Alps present a mighty barrier separating the Engadine from the rest of Graubünden. This range stretches eastward from the Sursés (Oberhalbstein) Valley as far as the Swiss–Austrian border. Forming the main continental divide, it includes major peaks such as Piz d'Err (3378m), Piz Kesch (3418m), Piz Vadret (3229m), Piz Buin (3312m) and the Silvrettahorn (3244m). The Central Bündner Alps are accessible by several important pass

routes, with roads and/or railways crossing the Julierpass (Pass da Güglia), Albulapass (Pass d'Alvra) and the Flüelapass. These rugged ranges of Central Graubünden are especially well blessed with wild mountain valleys and sparkling glacial lakes.

ACCESS TOWNS
Klosters

This town lies at 1206m in the upper valley of the Prättigau. Originally a monastic settlement, Klosters (ie 'cloisters') has developed into a winter sports resort favoured by British royals. Of historical interest are its 13th-century church with stained-glass windows and the Nutli-Hüschi museum (entry Sfr2) in a 16th-century Walser house. A simple and rewarding walk from Klosters leads over the Landquart/Landwasser watershed via the hamlet of Drussetscha and around the lakeshore of the Davoser See to Davos.

Information is available from the tourist office (☎ 081-410 20 20, fax 081-410 20 10, ℮ info@klosters.ch, ⓦ www.klosters.ch), Alte Bahnhofstrasse 6. The local mountaineering school is the Bergsteigerschule Silvretta (☎/fax 081-422-36 36).

Klosters' *youth hostel* (☎ 081-422 13 16, ℮ klosters@youthhostel.ch, Talstrasse 73) charges Sfr26.50 for dorm beds. The *Hotel Malein* (☎ 081-422 10 88, Landstrasse 120) has rooms from Sfr42 per person. The *Kurhaus Klosters* (☎ 081-422 44 41, ℮ kurhaus@spin.ch, Landstrasse 22) has rooms from Sfr55.

The *Coop* supermarket is 50m to the right of the train station, and Bahnhofstrasse has some cheap eateries. For a treat, make a resrvation at *Walserstube* in Hotel Walserhof (☎ 081-410 29 29).

Klosters is on the Rhaetian Railway's Landquart–Klosters–Filisur line, and trains run hourly.

Davos

Davos sits at 1560m in the upper valley of the Landwasser River. The town is divided into two western and eastern parts – Davos Platz and Davos Dorf. Davos is internationally renowned as a centre for winter sports, conferences and scientific research. The

Top Left: Erosion has created bizarre formations in the Ruin' Aulta gorge on the Vorderrhein River, Graubünden. **Top Right:** The Inn Valley divides the mountains of the Lower Engadine.
Middle Right: Sgraffito design on a traditional Engadine house. **Bottom Left:** Alp hut, Swiss National Park. **Bottom Right:** A clustered bloom of short-leaved gentians.

Top Left: A traditional farmhouse below the towering peaks of the Churfirsten.
Top Right: A fearless scarecrow guards its pumpkin barrow, Appenzell.
Middle Right: A handcrafted cafe sign welcomes weary travellers in St Gallen.
Bottom: An alp hut stands on the Wichlenmatt wild-flower meadows, east of the Richetlipass.

CLEM LINDENMAYER

MARTIN MOOS

MARTIN MOOS

CLEM LINDENMAYER

Alpinum Schatzalp, at the upper station of the Schatzalp funicular railway, has an extensive Alpine garden nurturing 800 plants from mountain regions all over the world.

Further information is available from the tourist office (☎ 081-415 21 21, fax 081-415 21 00, e davos@davos.ch, w www.davos .ch), Promenade 67.

Camping Farich (☎ 081-416 10 43, e tcs *.camp.hotze@bluewind.ch)*, open mid-May to late September, has tent sites for Sfr5/6 plus Sfr4.80/6.60 per person in low/high season. The *Friends of Nature hostel* (☎/fax 081-413 63 10)*, at nearby Clavadel-eralp (1960m), has rooms from Sfr57 per person. *Hotel Montana* (☎ 081-416 34 44, *Bahnhofstrasse 2)*, by Davos Dorf station, has singles/doubles from Sfr45/70. The *Sportzentrum* (☎ 081-415 36 36, fax 081-415 36 37, Talstrasse 41)* offers beds in small dorms for Sfr58 and rooms from Sfr60/100 with full board.

There are supermarkets and cafes close to Davos Platz and Davos Dorf stations. *Hotel Dischma* (Promenade 128)* has a range of affordable places to eat, or for fine dining try *Hotel Davoserhof* (☎ 081-415 66 66)*.

Davos is on the Rhaetian Railway's Landquart–Klosters–Filisur line, and trains run hourly. Passengers arriving via Chur may have to change at Landquart; from the Upper Engadine change at Filisur. Postbuses run from Davos over the scenic Flüelapass to the Lower Engadine. There are postbuses from Davos to Susch (via the Flüelapass) between early June and late October.

Bergün

Bergün sits at 1367m in the upper reaches of the Albula (Alvra) River. The ornate houses of this still largely Romansch-speaking village are built in the solid stone Bündner style. From Bergün the two to 2½-hour Bahnlehrpfad leads upvalley beside the historic railway line completed in 1903, which spirals up via several tight tunnels to the tiny village of Preda (1792m). A more difficult local route goes up via the *Camona d'Ela*, a basic SAC hut, across the 2724m Pass d'Ela to Tinizong in the adjacent valley of Sursés (Oberhalbstein). The

Sertigpass walk described later can also finish at Bergün.

For further information contact the tourist office (☎ 081-407 11 52, fax 081-407 14 04, e info@berguen.ch, w www.berguen.ch).

Albula-Campingplatz (☎ 079-629 30 37, 081-407 11 52)* offers tent sites from Sfr2 plus Sfr6.30 per person. The *Hotel Piz Ela* (☎ 081-407 23 23, fax 081-407 23 21)* and the *Hotel Sonnenheim* (☎ 081-401 11 29, e sonnenheim@datacomm.ch)* has singles/doubles from around Sfr45/90. In nearby Preda, the *Pension Sonnenhof* (☎ 081-407 13 98, fax 081-407 16 01)* offers slightly cheaper rooms.

Bergün is a stop on the Rhaetian Railway's Chur–Filisur–Samedan–St Moritz line, and there are at least hourly trains in either direction.

Rhätikon Höhenweg

Duration	4 days
Distance	37km
Standard	medium-hard
Start	St Antönien
Finish	Malbun (Liechtenstein)
Summary	The classic Rhätikon Höhenweg is a 'high route' tracing the crest of Graubünden's Rhätikon range along the Swiss–Austrian–Liechtenstein border. The rugged limestone peaks along the frontier offer marvellous, continually changing vistas.

With their heavily folded and upturned rock strata the magnificent limestone crags are sometimes called the 'Rhaetian Dolomites', and a resemblance to the mountains of South Tirol is unmistakable. Alpine rock climbers value the hard grip of the dolomite rock, yet the Rhätikon's highest peak, the 2964m Schesaplana, is quite accessible to non-mountaineers – as indicated by the summit crowds.

The Rhätikon Höhenweg is generally well-marked, but walkers need good fitness and perhaps some experience in Alpine walking. Keep a careful watch on the weather, particularly for the high-level walking on Days 2 and 3.

GRAUBÜNDEN

Maps

Recommended is the local tourist authorities' 1:40,000 *Wanderkarte Rhätikon Prättigau*, excellent value at Sfr5. A reasonable alternative is K+F's 1:60,000 *Prättigau-Albula* (Sfr24.80). The standard 1:50,000 series *Montafon* No 238 (green cover) – which at the time of research still had not been published as a special SAW/FSTP 'T' walking map – covers almost the entire walk. The initial (roughly 2km) section from St Antönien is on the adjoining SAW/FSTP *Prättigau* No 248T (orange cover, Sfr22.50).

NEAREST TOWNS
St Antönien

St Antönien (pronounced zangt an-TER-nien) at 1420m is the highest village in the Rhätikon. Originally colonised by Walser families in the 14th century, the St Antöniental is a classic example of a scattered Walser settlement. Until the construction of grids on the surrounding slopes, this highland valley was particularly prone to avalanches, and over the centuries scores of people (and hundreds of farm buildings) in the St Antöniental were claimed by the 'white death'.

For information, St Antönien has a small tourist office (☎/fax 081-332 32 33, 🆆 www .st-antoenien.ch).

Hotel Rhätia (☎ *081-332 13 61, fax 081-332 33 10*) has singles/doubles from Sfr70/ 140 and dorm beds for Sfr37 with breakfast. *Pension Gasthaus Bellawiese* (☎ *081-332 15 36*, 🅴 *bellawiese@spin.ch*), in nearby Ascharina, offers rooms from Sfr57/104 and has similar dorm prices. *Berggasthaus Älpenrosli* (☎ *081-332 12 18*) and *Berghaus Sulzfluh-Partnun* (☎ *081-332 12 13*), in Partnun at the head of the valley, also have rooms and dorms.

St Antönien is 35 minutes' ride by postbus from Küblis train station; there are up to 10 buses daily; reservation is essential for the last bus from Küblis at 7.30pm (☎ 079-642 27 48 before 12pm). Walkers arriving from Zürich or Chur should change at Landquart.

Malbun

The walk finishes at Malbun (1600m), a modern ski resort (originally settled by Walsers in 1280) in the principality of Liechtenstein. Although politically independent, Liechtenstein has close ties with Switzerland – the Swiss franc is legal tender, and the telephone, postal and transport systems are integrated. The Web site 🆆 www .searchlink.li/tourist has general information about Liechtenstein.

For information, try Malbun's tourist office (☎ 423-263 65 77, fax 423-263 73 44, 🅴 malbuninfo@lie-net.li).

Alpenhotel Malbun (☎ *+423-263 11 81*) has singles/doubles from Sfr45/90. *Hotel Turna* (☎ *+423-265 50 40*, 🅴 *lampert1 @bluewin*) has better rooms from Sfr70/110. Both hotels have inexpensive restaurants, and there is a supermarket.

Postbuses run (until 7pm) from Malbun to Vaduz, from where there are postbus connections to Buchs and Sargans (see Access Towns in the Sarganserland & Glarner Alps section of the North-Eastern Switzerland chapter).

GETTING TO/FROM THE WALK

The walk starts in St Antönien and ends in Malbun (see Nearest Towns earlier). For walkers who want to bail out in the middle, a cable car from the Douglasshütte on the Lünersee in Austria connects with a postbus service via the (Walser) village of Brand to Bludenz.

THE WALK
Day 1: St Antönien to Garschinahütte

2¼–3 hours, 6km, 801m ascent

Walk 50m up the turn-off behind the St Antönien post office (1420m), then shortcut to the right over steep pastures back to the road. Continue up past a sharp curve, before taking an old alp track going off rightward across open slopes that overlook the village to a small telecommunications tower. From here an unsignposted path winds up through regenerating coniferous forest to reach the scattered wooden houses of **Älpli** (1801m) after 40 to 50 minutes. The small Restaurant Älpli, a short way off-route down left, offers basic refreshments.

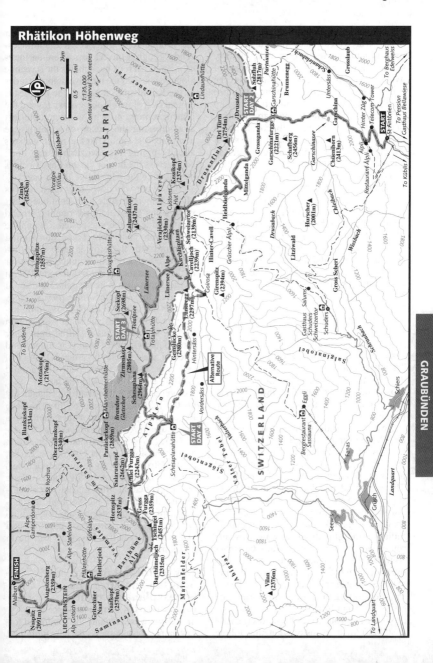

Rhätikon Höhenweg

To Berghaus Edelweiss

2km

1mi

1:135,000

Contour Interval 200 meters

AUSTRIA

SWITZERLAND

GRAUBÜNDEN

Follow the road uphill past a hairpin bend, before you break away north-eastward onto mountainsides strewn with bilberry heath below a veritable standing army of avalanche grids guarding St Antönien. The route makes a steadily climbing traverse over rolling Alpine meadows, then cuts up left beside a brooklet to the **Garschinasee**, one to 1¼ hours on. Partially covered with reeds and water lilies, this small lake sits at 2180m in a shallow depression of the grassy terrace known as Garschina.

The path leads on over a gentle crest (where the 2817m Sulzfluh first comes into view ahead) crossing tiny streams as it rises and dips along the closely cropped slopes to arrive at the **Garschinafurgge** (2221m) after 40 to 50 minutes. The SAC's *Garschinahütte* (☎ *079-418 22 80, 081-416 35 22*), staffed from mid-June to mid-October, stands at 2236m just east of this saddle. The hut has dorm beds for Sfr22 (Sfr48 with full board). With the spectacular backdrop of the Sulzfluh's abrupt sides, it's easy to see why these mountains have been likened to the Dolomites of Italy.

Day 2: Garschinahütte to Totalphütte
3½–4½ hours, 13km, 421m ascent
This is the first section of the thrilling high-level route via Austria to the Schesaplanahütte.

Head across broken-rubble slopes toward the Drusatorpass, swinging around to the north-west at a branching just before the pass. In the distant west the snowcapped peaks of the Glarner Alps can be made out. The well-trodden path edges below fields of scree and coarse talus separated by broad grassy spurs coming off the impressive grey-white ridge known as the Drusenfluh. Sidle on alongside the sheer walls past side routes going down left toward Grüscher Älpli before beginning a short, steep climb over rock (aided by the odd fixed cable) to reach **Schweizertor** after 1¾ to 2¼ hours. This narrow gap at 2139m forms the Swiss–Austrian frontier.

Walk across the boggy basin to a (usually unstaffed) Austrian customs hut, then follow

the grassy ridge leading westward up over the **Verajöchle**, a minor col at 2330m. Descend through a tiny valley, where an interesting pinkish rock band marks the screeline along the base of the massive dolomite sides of the Kirchlispitzen range. The path leads around over slopes looking down toward the Lünersee, merging with another route just after crossing the stream on a footbridge after one to 1¼ hours. At this point, walkers already pining for Switzerland can duck back across the border via the Cavelljoch as described in the Alternative Route later.

Make your way down over the meadows of the **Lünersee Alpe**, and continue westward along the wide track running around the lakeside to the signposted Totalphütte turn-off on your left. If you don't mind strolling with the crowds, the 30 to 40-minute return side trip around the reservoir to the restaurant/cable-car station at 1979m on the dam wall is quite pleasant. Here you'll also find the *Douglasshütte (for bookings outside Austria ☎ +43-(0)5559-206)*, belonging to the Österreichischer Alpenverein (ÖAV). This large hut is staffed from early June to mid-October (open year-round), and offers singles/doubles for around OS240/480 (€17.50/35) and dorm beds for around OS160 (€11.50) without breakfast.

A yellow-red marked path cuts diagonally up the hillside, climbing on first in steep loops through unstable slopes then via a rock ridge to reach the *Totalphütte (☎ +43-663-053128)* after 45 minutes to one hour. This three-storey timber ÖAV hut at 2318m (staffed from early June to mid-October) looks out north across the 'dead alp' – a bare basin left behind after glacial recession – toward the crags of the Seekopf and Zirmenkopf, and has dorm beds for around OS160 (€11.50). Breakfast costs around OS90 (€6.50) extra. Payments can be in Swiss francs.

Day 3: Totalphütte to Schesaplanahütte (via Schesaplana Summit)
3½–4¾ hours, 4.5km, 646m ascent
Sink down westward into the **Totalp** and follow paint splashes across the bare moraines,

then head up steeply again through more loose rock past a route going off left to the Gemslücke to reach a tiny shelf at 2660m. Bearing right at the path division here, ascend through a gap in the cliffs onto a high rounded spur providing a relatively easy way up to the top of **Schesaplana**, 1¾ to 2¼ hours from the Totalphütte. The 2964m summit is crowned with an enormous metal cross and gives a truly superb panorama stretching in all directions; in fine weather it's standing-room only!

Go back along the spur a short way, before dropping down the Schesaplana's eroding western slopes to the broad rock backbone marking the international border. Standing out to the north-west at the far edge of the Brandner Gletscher is the Mannheimerhütte. Walk gently down alongside this sweeping icy expanse to a low point in the main ridge, from where white-blue-white markings lead off left.

The route now makes an exhilarating descending traverse along the abrupt southern side of the Alpstein range, then begins picking its way down very steeply through the crags to cross a small ravine. Although there are no really exposed places, some care is required where you have to downclimb (assisted by the usual steel cables). The final section follows a grassy ridge directly down to arrive at the *Schesaplanahütte* (☎ 081-325 11 63), 1¾ to 2½ hours from the Schesaplana summit. This SAC hut occupies a picturesque spot at 1908m, right at the foot of the Alpstein; it's staffed from mid-June until mid-September (otherwise unlocked). From here various walking routes lead downvalley to Seewis, Grüsch and Schiers.

Alternative Route: Garschinahütte to Schesaplanahütte (via Cavelljoch)

4½–5½ hours, 16km
This more straightforward route variant to the Schesaplanahütte can easily be done in a single day, but – although a lovely walk – it lacks some of the spectacular high-Alpine scenery of Days 2 and 3.

Make your way to the route intersection above the Lünersee Alpe as in Day 2, then follow blue and yellow paint stripes southward up through flowery meadows to the 2239m **Cavelljoch** (spelt 'Gafalljoch' in Austria). Sidle effortlessly around slopes on the Swiss side of the border, coming to a signpost on a grassy mountainside after 30 to 40 minutes.

Descend directly westward (or walk around via the small alp restaurant on the saddle at **Golrosa** (2128m) not far down to the left), then begin traversing the slopes above isolated farmlets in the attractive upper valley of the Valserbach. The worn path keeps roughly to the 2000m contour line, rising and dipping past clumps of stunted conifers and large fields of scree that fan out below the massive rock walls of the Alpstein. The last section edges downward across Alpine pastures to the distant tinkling of cowbells, arriving at the *Schesaplanahütte* (see Day 3), 1¼ to 1¾ hours from Golrosa.

Day 4: Schesaplanahütte to Malbun

4¼–5¾ hours, 13.5km, 451m ascent
Head north-west around the slopes, soon passing a high-Alpine route diverging to the right. The foot track eases gently up against the contour under talus slides, then on more steeply past where a sizable spring emerges. Here it's worth a quick climb off right to the **Chlei Furgga** (2243m, sometimes signposted as 'Kleine Furke') for a look down into the wild screes of Im Salaruel, before you continue sidling westward above the tiny grassy bowl to reach the **Gross Furgga**, a larger gap at 2359m, after 1½ to two hours. From here you get a clear view back along the Alpstein range as far as the Sulzfluh.

Drop down into Austria and traverse leftward along the high grassy platforms formed by the rock strata at the head of a serene Alpine valley, passing just below the **Barthümeljoch** after 30 to 40 minutes. The path picks an easy route across slab terraces as it swings around north-westward below the 2570m 'borderstone' peak of the Naafkopf, before crossing over the main ridgeline into Liechtenstein. The large *Pfälzerhütte* (☎ +423-263 36 79) is just a short way down on the **Bettlerjoch** (2108m), 45 minutes to one hour on from the Barthümeljoch.

One of the two huts within the principality run by the Liechtensteiner Alpenverein (LAV), the Pfälzerhütte is only staffed from mid-June until early October, but a section of the hut is always left open for walkers. The hut overnighting fees are: Sfr15 for a bunk and Sfr15 for a mattress; breakfast costs around Sfr8.

Follow the hut's narrow service road down over a spur to a signposted track going off right just before you come to the stone farmstead of **Alp Gritsch**. The often muddy path sidles northward along dairy pastures high above the Saminatal, before making a short, steep ascent to a ridgetop overlooking Malbun. Descend past a group of wooden avalanche-prevention stands into the grassy basin, then move over right under winter ski lifts to meet a gravelled roadway. The route continues briefly left, before dropping down along a final section of path that brings you out to the main road through Malbun after 1½ to two hours. The postbus stop and tourist office are five minutes' walk downhill.

Parpaner Rothorn

Duration	5–7 hours
Distance	18km
Standard	medium
Start	Arosa (Hörnlibahn, Innerarosa)
Finish	Lenzerheide

Summary This popular day walk leads past lovely Alpine lakes under some of the rawest crags in the Swiss Alps, culminating at the highest summit in the Plessur massif.

The Parpaner Rothorn owes its striking 'red horn' formation to the brittle, copper-bearing rock typical of the Plessur massif. From the early medieval period the ore was mined high up on these bare mountainsides and carried down to Arosa for smelting. In places, the remains of old shafts and mining huts are still visible.

After the disastrous Plurs landslide of 1618 wiped out the entire Vertemati-Franchi family, owners of the mine, the workings gradually fell into disuse.

Although there are few real difficulties, this is a serious high-Alpine walk with an ascent of over 1000m. The route is likely to be out of condition before late June or after late October.

Maps

Most recommended is the local tourist authorities' 1:25,000 *Lenzerheide-Valbena Wander- und Bike-Karte* (Sfr15). Another good option is K+F's 1:40,000 *Region Lenzerheide* (Sfr12.80). Otherwise, two SAW/FSTP 1:50,000 maps are required: *Prättigau No 248T* and *Bergün No 258T* (Sfr22.50 each).

NEAREST TOWNS
Arosa

Arosa (1800m) lies in the upper Schanfigg, a side valley of the Swiss Rhine above Chur, at the edge of a large grassy bowl that in winter offers some of Graubünden's best ski slopes. Despite its rather crass high-rise developments, Arosa is also popular as a base for walkers.

For more information contact the tourist office (☎ 081-378 70 20, fax 081-378 70 21, e arosa@arosa.ch, w www.arosa.ch).

Camping Arosa (☎ *081-377 17 45, fax 081-377 30 05)* has sites from Sfr4.50 plus Sfr7.30 per person. The *youth hostel* (☎ *081-377 13 97,* e *arosa@youthhostel.ch)* on Seewaldweg has dorm beds for Sfr27. The *Pension Suveran* (☎ *081-377 19 69, fax 081-377 19 75)* offers singles/doubles for Sfr47/84 and the *Hotel Daheim* (☎ *081-377 13 25)* charges Sfr50/100.

Near the train station is a *Denner* supermarket, and the *Coop* is by the tourist office. Between the tourist office and Oberseeplatz is *Café-Restaurant Oasis*, where tasty meals cost around Sfr10. Opposite is alcohol-free *Orelli's Restaurant*, offering good vegetarian dishes.

Arosa is accessible by hourly trains on the Rhaetian Railway's scenic narrow-gauge line from Chur (Sfr11.80).

Lenzerheide-Valbella

Lenzerheide-Valbella lies at 1470m on the Igl Lai (Heidsee), a lovely lake in a broad, semi-forested upper valley at the western foot of the Parpaner Rothorn. There is a tourist office (☎ 081-385 11 20, fax 081-385 11 21, e info@lenzerheide.ch, w www.lenzerheide.ch).

Nearby Valbella's *youth hostel (☎ 081-384 12 08,* e *valbella@youthhostel.ch)* has dorm beds for Sfr24. Otherwise, the cheapest place to stay is the *Hotel Postli (☎ 081-384 11 60, fax 081-384 52 12),* which has singles/doubles for Sfr60/110.

Postbuses running between Chur and Tiefencastel pass through Lenzerheide-Valbella hourly in either direction.

GETTING TO/FROM THE WALK

The walk begins at the lower station of the Hörnli Express gondola lift. From Arosa train station there are free public buses at least half-hourly to the Hörnli Express.

The walk can be shortened by taking the cable car (Rothornbahn, ☎ 081-385 03 30) down from Parpaner Rothorn to Lenzerheide, but the one-way fare is a horrendous Sfr14.50/29 for children/adults and the roughly three-hour walk down is very pleasant. The cable car runs at least half-hourly on weekends from early June, then daily between late June and late October; the last downward ride is at 4.50pm.

A one-day *Wanderbillett* covering cable-car, train and postbus travel (Lenzerheide–Rothorn–Arosa–Chur–Lenzerheide) is available from tourist offices for Sfr47.60 (Sfr24 with Half Fare Card).

THE WALK

From the Hörnli Express bus stop (1811m), a path (signposted 'Erzhornsattel') leads south-west below the cableway up to an alp track. Continue left gently out of the tree line on slopes overlooking Arosa to reach the **Schwellisee** (1933m) after just 15 to 20 minutes. Ringed by pastures grazed by sheep, this turquoise lake is a pleasant if very popular spot.

Cross the small outlet (Plessur) and continue up a foot track around the lake's eastern side above the meadows of the **Arosa Alp** past the isolated cluster of old arolla pines known as **Arven** (2060m). Several springs – to which locals once attributed magical powers – emerge just above here. The path recrosses the gravelly stream to meet routes going off to the Restaurant Alpenblick and Innerarosa. There is a large wooden *emergency shelter* (day use only) a few minutes down from this junction.

A short, steeper climb brings you up over a grassy crest above the **Älplisee** (2156m), 30 to 45 minutes from the Schwellisee. This still Alpine lake fills a deep gully directly under the Schaftällihorn (2546m) and Älpliseehorn (2725m), whose rugged crags drop away into sweeping scree slides. There are also some last clear views north toward the Weisshorn and the green, rolling Churer Alpen.

Head on above the Älplisee and make a long sidling ascent through the Alpine pastures of **Schafälpli**, an area inhabited by hordes of whistling marmots. The path continues up through the sparse slopes of **Gredigs Älpli** high above the tiny **Tötseeli**, an often snow-filled tarn in the very head of the valley, to arrive at **Gredigs Fürggli** (2617m), one to 1½ hours from the Älplisee. This gap in the ridge gives views stretching north-east to the limestone peaks of the Rhätikon and north-west toward the snow-capped Glarner Alps. Below in the valley of Lenzerheide lies the idyllic Igl Lai (Heidsee).

The Älplisee lies above Arosa, between grassy pastures and sweeping scree slopes .

GRAUBÜNDEN

CLEM LINDENMAYER

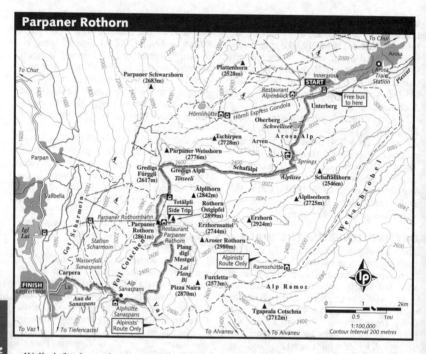

Parpaner Rothorn

Walk left along the narrow dirt road through a long wooden avalanche gallery (the curious 'box tunnel' visible on your ascent) to a winter chairlift. A geological path (with signs in German explaining local mineral phenomena) leads on up the redrock ridge barren but for sparse grasses, lichen and white Alpine marguerites to the upper cable-car station on the summit of the **Parpaner Rothorn** (2861m), 45 minutes to one hour from Gredigs Fürggli. Here the *Restaurant Parpaner Rothorn* has a small terrace overlooking these raw ranges, but is rather pricey. A marked path continues east along the ridge to the slightly higher summit of the Rothorn Ostgipfel at 2899m (40 minutes return).

A broad trail winds down steeply southward to a turnoff at a minor dip in the ridge. Here, cut down left (east) into the **Plang digl Mestgel**, a grassy bowl under the Aroser Rothorn (2980m). Continue along an old lateral moraine covered with bilberry

heath past the tiny, shallow **Lai Plang Bi**. The route leads on smoothly down through the alpenrose meadows and cow pastures of **Val**, crossing the deeply eroded Aua da Sanaspans just before reaching the farmlet of **Alp Sanaspans** (2045m), 1½ to two hours from the Parpaner Rothorn. Not far down is the *Alphütte Sanaspans* (open early July to late September), where refreshments are served to outside tables and alp-made cheeses are on sale.

A few paces down turn off right and recross the stream on a footbridge above several springs gushing out of the mossy embankment. The path now descends in steep switchbacks through forest of spruce, larch and mountain pine past the **Wasserfall Sanaspans** (1840m), a spouting 20m cascade, to a meet a narrow gravelled forest road. Follow this briefly right, then cut down left under power transmission cables before coming out onto the park-like meadow of **Carpera** (1545m) at the upper edge of Lenzerheide. Voa Trotsch (street) leads down past holiday houses to the main road through Lenzerheide, one to 1½ hours from Alp Sanaspans. The postbus terminal is a few minutes along to the right.

Vereinatal

Duration	2 days
Distance	19km
Standard	medium
Start	Wägerhus
Finish	Monbiel
Nearest Towns	Davos, Klosters

Summary This walk from near the Flüelapass crosses the Jöriflüelafurgga into the enchanting highland valley of the Vereinatal in the headwaters of the Landquart River, which drains the Prättigau district. After an initial steep ascent, it is a downhill walk.

Not even the Walsers – who were so often the first colonists in Graubünden's remote mountain valleys – settled in the upper Vereinatal. Having kept its wild nature up until the present day, the upper Vereinatal is inhabited by many colonies of marmots and chamois, while its lower reaches are forested with beautiful stands of arolla, mountain and dwarf pines. One of the highlights of the hike are the Jöriseen, a handful of milky-green lakes lying scattered around a sparsely vegetated moraine basin at the foot of the Flüela Wisshorn, whose southern slopes are covered by extensive glaciers. In more severe winters the Jöriseen freeze completely solid, and often take until the middle of summer to thaw out completely.

Maps

The recommended walking map is the local tourist authority's 1:50,000 *Wanderkarte Klosters-Prättigau* (Sfr14). Excellent alternatives include the Davos tourist authority's 1:25,000 *Davos Wanderkarte* (Sfr29.50), or the SAW/FSTP's *Prättigau No 248T* (Sfr22.50), although both of these maps show the route rather close to the edge of the sheet. Either of K+F's 1:60,000 walking maps *Prättigau-Albula* or *Engadina*

Bassa/Unterengadin (Sfr24.80 each) can also be used.

NEAREST FACILITIES
Flüelapass
Passhotel Flüela-Hospiz (☎ 081-416 17 47) on the Flüelapass height (2383m) 1.5km up from Wägerhus has rooms and dormitories.

GETTING TO/FROM THE WALK

The walk begins at Wägerhus (also called 'Abzweigung Jöri'), a bus stop and car park at 2207m on the Flüelapass road about 1.5km north of the pass itself. Postbuses running between Davos Platz (see Access Towns earlier) and Susch in the lower Engadine pass by Wägerhus six times daily from late June to mid-October. Outside this period there is no bus service at all.

The walk can be shortened by taking the private minibus from Berghaus Vereina to Klosters (see Access Towns earlier). Reservations are essential – for fares call the Berghaus Vereina or Gotschna-Sport (☎ 081-422 11 97, [e] sportshop@gotschnasport.ch). The minibus runs around five times daily while the Berghaus Vereina is open; the last bus leaves for Klosters at around 5.30pm.

The walk ends at the tiny village of Monbiel, from where the local public bus takes you down to Klosters Platz (passing the turn-off to the youth hostel on the way). Buses run roughly hourly year-round; the last bus leaves Monbiel at around 7.45pm.

THE WALK
Day 1: Wägerhus to Berghaus Vereina
3½–4½ hours, 9km, 518m ascent

Take the signposted foot track from the lone cottage near the postbus stop at **Wägerhus**

Vereinatal

To Klosters **FINISH**
Monbiel
Pardenn ● Restaurant Alp Garfiun
Landquart River
Chüenisch Boden
Alp Novai
To Seetalhütte
Bridge
Lauizughorn (2469m) ▲
Chänzeli
Stutzegg
Wisshorn (2832m) ▲
Stutzalp
START DAY 2
Berghaus Vereina
Pischahorn (2979m) ▲
Pischa
Säss Frömdvereina
Süserbach
Gorihorn (2986m) ▲
Rosställispitz (2929m) ▲
Jöriflüelafurgga (2725m)
Muttelhorn (2826m) ▲
To Davos & Klosters
Jöriseen
Jöriflesspass (2561m) ▲
Karlimatten
Winterlücke
Jöriglestcher
Wägerhus **START**
Sentisch Horn (2827m) ▲
Flüela Wisshorn (3085m) ▲
To Davos & Klosters
Flüelapass (2383m)
Passhotel Flüela-Hospiz
To Susch
Schottensee
Susasca
Chant Sura

0   1   2km
0 0.5   1mi
1:135,000
Contour Interval 200 metres

dropping down through meadows scattered with yellow-dotted gentians to the shore of the northernmost lake of the **Jöriseen**. Unlike the others it is fed by a clearwater spring, and early in the season ice floating on the aqua-blue water gives the lake an Arctic feel. Continue through grassed-over moraine hillocks across a metal footbridge over the milky-green outlet stream of the largest lake, climbing on to reach a signposted intersection at 2519m after 40 to 50 minutes.

Directly to the south stands the 3085m Flüela Wisshorn, on whose northern slopes the icy mass of the Jörigletscher descends into the Jörisee basin. Drop down steeply into the Jörital, picking your way through regenerated glacial debris to meet the **Jöribach**. The path now leads down in staggered stages through the tiny upper valley along the eastern side of the stream, which alternately cascades in little gorges and meanders gently beside green river flats.

After crossing the **Süserbach** on a footbridge near **Säss Frömdvereina**, make your way on through slopes of lovely Alpine heath and thickets of dwarf birch. The path crosses another large sidestream at the gushing **Vernelabach** just before you arrive at the ***Berghaus Vereina*** (☎ 081-422 12 16), 1¼ to 1¾ hours from the Jöriseen turn-off. This homy mountain hotel (open from the start of July to around 20 October) is powered by a tiny hydroelectric generator, and sits on a rock outcrop below the 2979m Pischahorn. The Berghaus offers rooms from around Sfr45 per person and dorm beds for around Sfr25.

Day 2: Berghaus Vereina to Monbiel
2½–3½ hours, 10km
The private road through the wild and glaciated valley of the Vereinatal is closed to all traffic other than vehicles servicing the Berghaus Vereina, and therefore makes an easy walkway. Follow it smoothly down across the Vereinabach and on through attractive riverside meadows below a long waterfall coming off the Pischahorn. After re-crossing the river at a small chasm, the dirt road winds down more steeply through

(2207m) and climb steadily away from the busy Flüelapass road over stony pastures browsed by listless cows. The broad and well-graded path passes a side route going off to the Winterlücke, winding its way on up through fields of coarse broken rock before circling around a small gully to arrive at the **Jöriflüelafurgga** after 1½ to two hours. This gap in the range at 2725m gives the first excellent view down to the Jöriseen.

Head a short way left below the craggy ridge secured by fixed cables. Follow red-white-red markings down over rocky slopes covered by occasional snowdrifts, before slopes of arolla and dwarf pines to reach a path turn-off (signposted 'Fussweg') at **Chänzeli** (1570m), 1¼ to 1¾ hours from the hotel.

Leave the road and descend steeply into the spruce forest, crossing sidestreams as you come out onto open pastures above the river. Head over the grassy flats and then along a levee embankment to once again cross the Vereinabach on a narrow road bridge near the farmhouse at **Alp Novai** (1360m), where an interesting long and narrow avalanche chute cuts straight down through the forest on the adjacent slope. The route runs along a rough farm road down the left bank of the stream past its confluence with the somewhat larger Verstanclabach, then continues close to the fast-flowing river (now called the Landquart) through the occasional forest clearings of **Masura**.

When you come to **Chüenisch Boden** at 1276m, turn off right onto a signposted foot track leading across the Landquart on a footbridge, before climbing quickly up to arrive at the bus stop at the village of **Monbiel** (1291m) after a final 1¼ to 1¾ hours. If you miss the last bus, Klosters-Platz (1206m) is about 30 minutes' walk down the road.

Sertigpass

Duration	4–5 hours (6–8 hours to Bergün)
Distance	15km (23km to Bergün)
Standard	medium
Start	Sertig-Dörfli
Finish	Tuors Chants or Bergün
Nearest Town	Davos

Summary One of the most scenically rewarding walks in the Central Bündner Alps, this gentle pass crossing takes you across the 2739m Sertigpass (known in Romansch as the Pass da Sett), which marks the language division between German-speaking Davos and the predominantly Romansch Albula region.

The area on the southern side of the Sertigpass is a nature reserve, in which the gorgeous Lai da Ravaisch lie nestled into grassy moraine mounds, ringed by 3000m summits of grey dolomite. The absence of training runners since recent rerouting of the Swiss Alpine Marathon – which now crosses the nearby Scalettapass (see Other Walks) – has made the Sertigpass a much less hectic route.

Maps
The best map covering the route in one sheet is SAW/FSTP's 1:50,000 *Bergün* No 258T (Sfr22.50). K+F's 1:60,000 *Prättigau-Albula* (Sfr24.80) is a fair alternative.

NEAREST TOWN
Sertig-Dörfli
First settled by medieval Walsers, the tiny village of Sertig-Dörfli (1860m), lies in the upper Sertigtal, a lovely basin of highland meadows bordered by old wooden fences and surrounded by heath-covered slopes culminating in craggy peaks.

At the hamlet of Sand, about 500m upvalley from the village, is the **Walserhuus Sertig** (☎ *081-410 60 30*, e *walserhuus@swissonline.ch*), open mid-June to mid-October, which offers dorm beds for Sfr25 and rooms for Sfr60 per person.

GETTING TO/FROM THE WALK
The walk begins at the Walserhuus Sertig in Sand. A year-round daily bus service runs almost hourly from Davos Platz (see Access Towns earlier) to the Walserhuus Sertig; it's a scenic 25-minute drive.

The walk ends at the tiny village of Tuors Chants in the upper Val Tuors. Some walkers prefer to continue on foot to Bergün (see Access Towns earlier), while others are obliged to hike the extra two hours in any case because the postbus from Tuors Chants to Bergün only runs for a seven-week period over summer. There are three minibuses daily from the start of July and to around 20 August – outside this period the service stops completely. The last bus leaves Tuors Chants at around 5pm; reservations are essential (☎ 081-407 11 840). Passes are not valid and special fares apply (Sfr8).

THE WALK
From the Walserhuus follow the unsealed road 700m past wooden farmhouses to

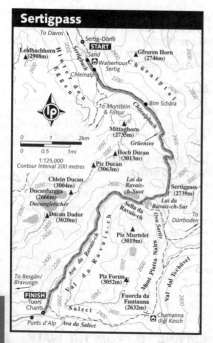

Sertigpass

To Davos
Sertig-Dörfli
START
Leidbachhorn (2908m)
Sand
Walserhuus Sertig
Gfroren Horn (2746m)
Chleinalp
Hinteren Eggen
Sertigbach
Chüealptal
To Monstein & Filisur
Bim Schära
Chüealpbach
Mittaghorn (2735m)
Grüensee
Hoch Ducan (3013m)
Piz Ducan (3063m)
Chlein Ducan (3004m)
Lai da Ravais-ch-Suot
Sertigpass (2739m)
Ducanfurgga (2666m)
Lai da Ravais-ch-Sur
To Dürrboden
Ducangletscher
Sella da Ravais-ch
Ducan Dador (3020m)
Ava da Ravais-ch
Ona Sartiv
Piz Murtelet (3019m)
Munt Platta Naira
Val dal Tschüvel
To Bergün/ Bravuogn
Val da Ravais-ch
Piz Forun (3052m)
FINISH Tuors Chants
Fuorcla da Funtauna (2632m)
Salect
Chamanna digl Kesch
Purits d'Alp
Ava da Salect

0 1 2km
0 0.5 1mi
1:125,000
Contour Interval 200 metres

GRAUBÜNDEN

where it crosses the Sertigbach on a narrow bridge and heads toward the Ducantal, a side valley that ends in a waterfall spilling over a high rock terrace. Here proceed left along an alp track leading up into the valley of the Chüealptal past scree fields below the 2735m Mittaghorn to reach the long milking shed of **Bim Schära** at 2101m after 40 to 50 minutes.

Make your way on into the upper valley, crossing the Chüealpbach on a little footbridge just below the **Grüensee** (2197m). A white-red-white marked path now ascends away from the stream past the greenish lakelet to traverse slopes of alpenroses, before picking its way up through snowdrifts and fields of coarse rock sprinkled with hardy Alpine buttercups. Adjacent are the hanging glaciers below the 3077m Chüealphorn. A final climb past a shallow ice-choked tarn brings you up to the **Sertigpass** at 2739m, 1½ to two hours from Bim Schära. Directly to the south the majestic 3417m summit of Piz Kesch, the highest

peak in the Central Bündner Alps, rises up above the broad icy band of the Vadret da Porchabella.

Drop down rightward from the pass over grassy mountainsides grazed by tinkling cows to the **Lai da Ravais-ch-Sur** (2562m). The path crosses ancient moraine hillocks before coming to a signposted trail intersection, where the way to the Chamanna digl Kesch (see the Scalettapass in Other Walks at the end of the chapter) departs left. Continue west toward the towering greyrock walls of Piz Ducan (3063m) high above the southern shore of the beautiful **Lai da Ravais-ch-Suot** (2505m), a much larger and deeper glacial lake. The route heads on down into the Val da Ravais-ch, a wild Alpine valley whose eastern sides are protected by a nature reserve.

Follow the well-graded path as it descends gently through open slopes abundant with herb fields and colonies of marmots, crossing the Ava da Ravais-ch stream a number of times on footbridges. In the distance more lofty summits around Piz Ela (3339m) can be made out beyond the mouth of the Val da Ravais-ch. The route finally leads down past haymaking fields into the scattered village of **Tuors Chants** at 1822m, 1¾ to 2¼ hours from the Sertigpass. Here three small valleys merge to form the Val Tuors. There is a restaurant but nowhere to stay in Tuors Chants.

Alternative Finish: Tuors Chants to Bergün

2–2¾ hours, 8km

Walk 500m down the road, then turn off left past a cluster of houses. After crossing the Ava da Tuors pick up a foot track that rises and dips along the southern side of the river to meet the road again near the hamlet of **Tuors Davant** (1704m). The route follows the road across another bridge near a heavily eroding chasm, then breaks away left again on a path leading past the cloudy tarn of **Igls Lajets** to the clearing of **Resgia da Latsch**.

Recross the stream and take a vehicle track winding up through forests of spruce and mountain pines. The final section follows the road or short-cut trails on down under the rail lines to arrive at **Bergün** (1367m). The train station is on to the right down along the main street past the old Bündner-style buildings of the town centre.

Vorderrhein & Hinterrhein

Above the small town of Reichenau (10km west of Chur) the valley of the Swiss Rhine divides into two upper branches. These unequal twins are the Vorderrhein (Rein Anteriur in Romansch) and the Hinterrhein (Rein Posteriur), a region taking in the whole south-western corner of Graubünden.

Rising in the Lai da Tuma, a lovely lake near the Oberalppass, the Vorderrhein is normally regarded as the true source of the Rhine. Known as the Surselva, the Vorderrhein's 60km-long valley forms the largest Romansch-speaking region in Graubünden. Surselva means 'above the forest' in Romansch, a reference to the dense forests that once grew around the confluence of the Vorderrhein and Hinterrhein.

On its northern side the Surselva is cut off by the Alps of Central Switzerland, the Glarnerland and the St Galler Oberland, whose unbroken line of high peaks rise abruptly to over 3000m. To the south half a dozen or so long side valleys – whose rivers have Romansch names such as Rein da Maighels and Rein da Sumvitg, indicating that they are Rhine tributaries – stretch south toward the mountains on the Graubünden–Ticino cantonal border.

During the ice ages, a massive glacier smothered the whole of the Surselva under a colossal river of ice that extended right down the Rhine valley as far as Lake Constance. The Vorderrhein glacier has long since disappeared, but its effect on the landscape is obvious. Today the Surselva is a broad valley intermittently broken by gorges, including the rugged 15km-long Ruin' Aulta along the lower section of the river.

The source of the Hinterrhein is not a lovely Alpine lake, but the extensive glaciers of the 3402m Rheinwaldhorn, and the river is even more dissected by gorges than the Vorderrhein. The deep Viamala and Rofla gorges divide the Hinterrhein valley into three stages: the largely Romansch-speaking Domleschg and Schons (Schams), and the uppermost area known as the Rheinwald, whose inhabitants speak German. The Rheinwald has two important trans-Alpine passes, the Splügenpass and the Passo del San Bernardino, and the valley gradually oriented itself more to the transport of goods than to dairy farming.

From medieval times Walsers migrated from Goms across the Oberalppass into the Vorderrhein and Hinterrhein, settling many upper-valley areas such as the Safiental and Rheinwald. The mix of Romansch and Germanic cultures gives this region a particularly fascinating flavour. Although rather less well known abroad than other parts of Graubünden, the Vorderrhein and Hinterrhein are a wonderland for the adventurous hiker prepared to get off the beaten track.

ACCESS TOWNS
Thusis
The town of Thusis lies at 720m and divides the Domleschg and Schons regions of the once overwhelmingly Romansch-speaking lower Hinterrhein (or Rein Posteriur). Thusis is famous for the nearby Viamala ('Bad Road'), where the Rein Posteriur flows through a deep and narrow gorge. The amazing walk through the Viamala follows short sections of the old mule path originally constructed in medieval times as part of the San Bernardino trade route. Another very popular local hike, the Burgenweg, leads down past the numerous historic castles of the Domleschg via the villages of Scharans, Almens and Tumegl/Tomils as far as Rothenbrunnen. A new four-day walking route, the Via Splüga, follows the historic trade route over the Splügenpass to Chiavenna in Italy's Valle San Giacomo.

For information contact the regional tourist office (☎ 081-651 11 34, fax 081-651 25 63, e wthusis@spin.ch, w www.thusis-viamala.ch), Neudorfstrasse 70.

The local ***Campingplatz Viamala*** *(☎ 081-651 24 72, fax 081-651 24 72)* has tent sites for Sfr4.50 plus Sfr4.50 per person. The *Hotel Restaurant Albula* (☎ 081-651 11 32, Hauptstrasse 27) offers singles/doubles for Sfr48/96. The *Hotel Weiss Kreuz* (☎ 081-650 08 50, e hotel.weisskreuz@spin.ch, Neudorfstrasse 81) offers rooms from Sfr53/90.

Thusis is on the Rhaetian Railway's Chur–Samedan–St Moritz line, with at least hourly through-connections from Zürich; from Davos it's often quicker travelling via Filisur. There are frequent postbuses between Thusis and Splügen/Rheinwald, from where connecting bus routes lead over the San Bernardino and Splügen passes.

Disentis/Mustér

Although quite a small place, Disentis is the centre of the predominantly Romansch-speaking Surselva region. The town's Romansch name, Mustér, is a reference to the enormous St Martin's Benedictine monastery on the site, founded in 750 AD, which is open to visitors (tours most days). The Senda Sursilvana walking route passes through Disentis, which makes a good base for numerous other walks in the surrounding mountains, including the Plaun la Greina and the Fuorcla da Cavardiras.

For information contact the tourist office (☎ 081-920 40 30, fax 081-920 40 39, e info @sedrundisentis.ch, w www.sedrundisentis.ch), Via Alpsu 62. The local mountaineering school is Aventuras Alpinas Surselva (☎ 081-936 45 25, e bergsport @surselva.ch).

Camping Fontanivas (☎ 081-947 44 22), 2.5km out along the Lucomagno road (postbus stop) has tent sites for Sfr7 plus Sfr5.40 per person. The *Pensiun Schuoler* (☎ 081-947 52 46) 15 minutes' walk east of the train station, has singles/doubles for around Sfr50/90. The more central *Hotel Alpsu* (081-947 51 17, e hotelalpsu@bluewin.ch) has better-standard singles/doubles from Sfr64/104.

Disentis can be reached on the Rhaetian Railway's direct line from Chur (trains at least once hourly), from Andermatt via the Oberalppass and on postbuses from Ticino

via the Passo del Lucomagno (Cuolm Lucmagn in Romansch). The *Glacier Express* tourist trains running between Zermatt and St Moritz also pass through Disentis.

Lai da Tuma Circuit

Duration	3¼–4½ hours
Distance	8.5km
Standard	easy-medium
Start/Finish	Oberalppass
Nearest Town	Disentis

Summary This is a high-level route (entirely above the treeline) along the crest of the Pizolstock range in an Alpine nature reserve near the Oberalppass on the Graubünden–Uri cantonal border.

The crystal-clear lake known to Romansch speakers as Lai da Tuma (or Thomasee in German) is considered the ultimate source of the Rhine. Here Graubünden meets the Gotthard region – the central mountain hub of the Swiss Alps. Walkers often sight golden eagles soaring about the surrounding granite summits since these magnificent Alpine raptors were successfully reintroduced into the area during the early 1990s.

This is a circuit walk that returns to Oberalppass. Setting out from an altitude of over 2000m, walkers have a relatively modest ascent of less than 700m to negotiate. The top of the range around the Pazolastock is very exposed to the elements, however, so keep an eye on the weather.

Maps

Recommended is the SAW/FSTP 1:50,000 walking map *Disentis/Mustér No 256T* (Sfr22.50). Two good alternatives are the 1:50,000 *Wanderkarte Disentis* (Sfr16) or K+F's 1:50,000 *San Gottardo*.

NEAREST FACILITIES
Oberalppass

With its famous old abbey, the beautiful elongated Oberalpsee (a lake popular with anglers) and surrounding granite peaks, the Oberalppass (2044m) is a very pleasant spot spoilt only slightly by the presence of a military barracks. Here, the ***Hotel Rhein-quelle*** *(☎/fax 081-949 11 12, 079-325 04 35)* and the ***Gasthaus Piz Calmot*** *(☎ 081-949 12 13, 041-887 15 34)* offers singles/doubles for around Sfr45/90.

GETTING TO/FROM THE WALK

The walk begins and ends at the Oberalp-pass, the highest point on the narrow-gauge Furka-Oberalp-Bahn (FOB) mountain railway (which links Disentis with Brig in the Valais). There are almost hourly train connections in both directions (some with a change in Andermatt) from late May to mid-October, with less frequent services outside these times. The scenic train known as the *Glacier Express* also passes the Oberalppass. If you're coming by train from Zürich (or anywhere else in northern Switzerland) it's quicker travelling to Oberalppass via Göschenen and Andermatt; from Ticino take a postbus from Airolo to Andermatt.

Private vehicles can be left at the car park on the Oberalppass.

THE WALK

From the tiny train station by the lake, walk 200m up to the ***Restaurant Alpsu***. Take the dirt road opposite, then cut up left over the open slopes above a cross mounted on a rock outcrop. The often steep path climbs alongside a grassy and rocky spur past lovely highland moors in the tiny upper valley of **Puozas** and makeshift stone bunkers built by wartime soldiers, coming to a signpost on the exposed ridgetop at 2571m after one to 1½ hours. A side route from here goes down to the village of Andermatt, now visible to the west in the valley of the Reuss. Behind Andermatt, the 3500m summits of the Winterberg massif and Galenstock rise up on the Uri–Valais cantonal border.

The white-red-white marked route continues up the ridge past two rustic military buildings just under the 2739m **Pazolastock** (Piz Nurschalas), traversing the crest of the craggy range with just enough rockhopping to make the going fun and unstrenuous. At point 2743 follow the **Fil Tuma** south-eastward, and sidle steadily down along the grassy right-hand side of the ridge to arrive

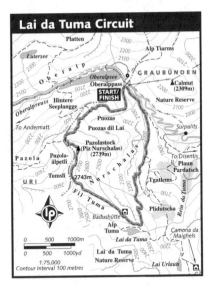

at the ***Badushütte*** *(☎ 01-301 48 56)* after one to 1¼ hours.

This cosy SAC hut at 2505m is built against a low cliff face looking out toward the 2928m Badus (Six Madun). The charge for a dorm bed is Sfr20 for non-members. Simple meals and refreshments are served in season (from June to September), but the hut is always kept unlocked.

The path descends quickly to a signposted trail leading off down to the shore of **Lai da Tuma** (2345m), 15 to 20 minutes from the hut. This lovely lake lies in a hollow formed by the grinding action of an extinct hanging glacier. In hot weather its snow-fed waters are good for a speedy splash, and the lush natural lawns around the inlet are ideal for that midday picnic. Cotton grass, a species typical in waterlogged soils, thrives here. On the ungrazed slopes of the Alp Tuma just above here you can find plants that are rare on cow-trodden pastures.

While the lake outlet, the Rein da Tuma, burbles out of sight to the north-east, the walk continues northward from the signpost above Lai da Tuma. Wind your way down the initially rocky hillside toward the multiple hairpin bends of the busy pass road, then turn left where you come onto the trail leading down from the Val Maighels. The path now sidles along slopes studded with sporadic alpenrose bushes, gradually moving around to meet the small stream flowing down from the pass. Follow the often boggy banks gently up to arrive back at the Oberalppass, one to 1½ hours from the Lai da Tuma.

Plaun la Greina

Duration	2 days
Distance	27km
Standard	medium
Start	Vrin
Finish	Olivone
Nearest Towns	Campo (Blenio)

Summary This wonderful walk transits one of Switzerland's few remaining untouched landscapes, the Plaun la Greina, a more than 2200m-high expanse of Alpine plains surrounded by craggy ranges.

The gentle Passo della Greina, at the southern edge of the Greina, forms the continental watershed dividing the Rhine basin from the catchment area of the Po River. It was long a trade route for cargo-carrying mule teams, although traffic never reached the levels of other Bündner passes. The Greina is also at a geological crossroads, and the green or pitch-black shale rocks typical of the Graubünden are interspersed with crystalline silicates of the Gotthard region.

Only lightly grazed by sheep during summer, this roughly 10 sq km area of grassland is resplendent with wild flowers and provides a perfect habitat for marmots and chamois. Little brooks fringed by cotton grass meander through Alpine meadows and moors dotted with peaty tarns – at times the Greina is strangely reminiscent of the Scandinavian Arctic.

Maps

The SAW/ESS 1:50,000 *Valle Leventina* No 266T (Sfr22.50) covers almost the entire route; two adjoining SAW/ESS sheets, *Safiental* No 257T and *Disentis/Mustér* No

---

Saving the Greina

During the 1980s, Swiss conservationists fought a protracted – and ultimately successful – battle against the construction of a hydroelectric scheme that would have submerged the entire Plaun la Greina under a large reservoir. Local communities, which had supported the project, were compensated for the loss of income. Today the Greina has been declared a 'landscape of national significance' and is protected as a nature reserve.

256T are recommended but not really necessary. One of the few walking maps that covers the walk in a single sheet is K+F's 1:60,000 *Surselva* (Sfr24.80).

NEAREST TOWNS
Vrin

The small farming village of Vrin (1448m) lies near the head of the strongly Romansch-speaking Val Lumnezia (Lugnez in German), the largest side valley of the Surselva. Little touched by tourism, Vrin is known for its traditional architecture, including old dark-stained wooden houses, a superb baroque-style Santa Maria church built in 1689 and a charnel house containing human skulls.

The Val Lumnezia tourist office (☎ 081-931 18 58, fax 081-931 34 13, e info@vallumnezia.ch, w www.vallumnezia.ch) is in Vella, lower down the valley.

The only place to stay in Vrin itself is the *Hotel Piz Terri* (☎ 081-931 12 55), which has a dorm (mostly for groups) and singles/doubles for Sfr45/90.

Vrin can be reached by postbus from Ilanz, on the Rhaetian Railway's Chur-Disentis line; there are up to 10 daily buses, and the last departure is around 6.40pm (8.40pm on Friday).

Campo (Blenio)

The walk passes the tiny village of Campo (Blenio), in the Val Blenio, a large northern side valley of the Val Leventina in Ticino, one hour before reaching Olivone.

The ***Ristorante Broggi*** (☎ *091-872 11 41*) and the ***Trattoria Genziana*** (☎ *091-872 11 93)*, 500m down the road from the village, have rooms for around Sfr40/80.

From Campo (Blenio) there are two or three daily postbus vans to Olivone; for groups of more than five people, it is essential to make a reservation (☎ *091-862 31 72*, e ABLE@Ticino.com).

GETTING TO/FROM THE WALK

The walk starts in Vrin and ends at Olivone (see Access Towns in the Northern Ticino section of the Ticino chapter), but it can be

shortened slightly by taking a postbus from Campo (Blenio).

THE WALK
Day 1: Vrin to Camona da Terri
3–4 hours, 11 km, 451m ascent

From Vrin post office follow the winding road upvalley through haymaking fields past the settlement of **Cons** to **Sogn Giusep**, where the ***Ustria Tgamanada*** (☎ *081-931 17 43)* has singles/doubles from Sfr50/90 and dorm beds with cooking facilities for around Sfr25. The road continues to the hamlet of **Puzzatsch** (1667m), one to 1¼ hours from

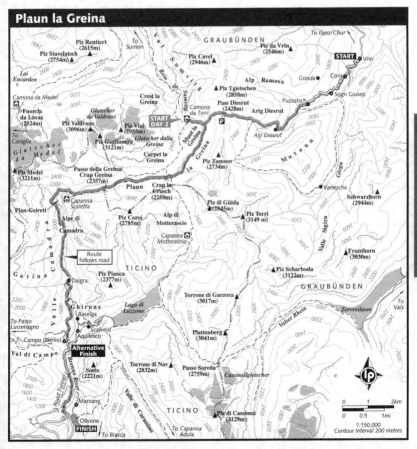

GRAUBÜNDEN

Vrin, where occasional summer concerts are held in the chapel, which dates from 1744.

Walk through the tiny village and across a bridge, then a short way on take the signposted track that continues ahead. The whited-red-white marked route cuts steadily up the grassy slopes above the stream to the herders' huts at **Alp Diesrut** (1899m), with views toward the adjacent 3149m Piz Terri and 2734m Piz Zamuor. Climb briefly around to the right, then sidle up westward along the mountainside to cross the now small stream. A signpost here indicates a side trail going off to the Fil Blengias and Vanescha.

The path begins ascending more steeply beside the stream, then moves away to the left to arrive at the **Pass Diesrut** (2428m), 1½ to two hours from Puzzatsch. The pass, whose Romansch name means 'broken back', is the lowest point between Piz Zamuor and Piz Tgietschen. Pass Diesrut is also the highest point on the walk and grants a view of the icy summits of Piz Vial and Piz Valdraus immediately adjacent.

Head down just right of another small stream, quickly descending past a side track that goes off leftward to reach the valley floor. Here the broad grasslands of the **Plaun la Greina** stretch out to the south-west, drained by the **Rein da Sumvitg**, which meanders in numerous tiny channels before flowing away through a series of gushing gorges. The route now crosses the footbridge over the river, then follows markings up around the northern edge of the **Muot la Greina** ridge. After a short difficult section with a fixed rope, drop down again to reach *Camona da Terri* (☎ 081-943 12 05, ⓦ *www .terrihuette.ch)* at 2170m after 30 to 40 minutes. This SAC hut looks out northward to the 3614m Tödi marking the Graubünden–Uri cantonal border, and has dorm beds for Sfr26.

Day 2: Camona da Terri to Olivone

4¾–6 hours, 16km, 187m ascent

Backtrack to the Rein da Sumvitg, then re-cross the footbridge and turn right (south) onto a good path running alongside the lovely river flats. Gradually rise away to

the right over regenerated moraine slopes and cross a large glacial stream to pass above the gentle **Crap la Crusch** at 2259m after 50 minutes to one hour. A prominent signposted foot track goes south from the Crap la Crusch to Olivone via the *Capanna Motterascio (☎ 091-872 16 22)*, an SAC hut roughly 30 minutes' walk off-route beyond the Crap la Crusch. However, the nicer route continues ahead across the Plaun la Greina.

Make your way west across the narrowing upper valley toward the mighty 3211m Piz Medel. Continue on through an interesting rocky landscape, where upturned pale limestone strata contrast with brittle black shales. The route leads on past a small private club hut sheltered from avalanches within a broad rock rib to cross – some way above – the **Passo della Greina** (Crap Greina), 40 to 50 minutes on. This watershed at 2357m marks the north-south continental divide and the Graubünden–Ticino cantonal border.

The path traverses over loose broken shale and occasional small snowdrifts along the left side of the new valley, which has formed along the line of more quickly eroding strata of upended limestone. Where the main route crosses the stream, take the path that continues 400m on down to reach the *Capanna Scaletta (☎ 091-872 10 67, 872 26 28)* after 20 to 25 minutes. This A-frame SAT-owned hut rests on a round outcrop at 2205m, below which the land falls away abruptly into the Valle Camadra. Dorm beds cost around Sfr20. Directly across the upper valley are the sheer walls of Piz Medel.

Jump the stream at the main path above the hut to meet a flagged donkey track winding its way down the rocky, grassy mountainside. A fine view opens out southward to Campo and the interesting Sosto (2221m) with a steeply tilting pasture just below its pyramid-shaped summit. Farther down, the route is blocked by heavily eroded slopes dropping away into a gully of accumulated snow dumped by winter avalanches. Here, pick your way around rightward through the unstable rubble to reach the end of a dirt road at **Pian-Geirett** after 25 to 30 minutes.

Walk past a utility cableway servicing Capanna Scaletta and begin a snaking descent through the **Valle Camadra**, with occasional (poorly marked) short cuts at tight curves in the road fringed by wild raspberry bushes. Where the sealed road commences at **Daigra** (1408m), take a signposted path leading left between the hamlet's half-dozen dwellings. After briefly rejoining the main road, the trail continues rightward along a pleasant forested track through the locality of **Ghirone**. Near a bridge over the Brenno, bear right past rustic old barns in fields adjacent to the church of Baselga to arrive at **Campo** (Blenio) at 1216m 1¾ to 2¼ hours on.

Even if you have the option of taking an (infrequent) minibus from Campo, it's worthwhile continuing on foot to Olivone. Just after the bridge follow a short right-hand path above the *Ristorante Genziana* back to the road. Continue along the outer side of a concrete avalanche barrier to where the road enters a long tunnel, then head left along the old valley road cut into cliffs above a gorge. Although small landslides have long made this narrow carriageway quite impassable for vehicles, the walking is easy. The way leads down past a water tunnel spouting into the stream, then loops around hillsides overlooking **Olivone** to join the main road just down from the post office, 50 minutes to one hour after leaving Campo. For information on Olivone (889m), see Access Towns in the Northern Ticino section of the Ticino chapter.

Ruin' Aulta

Duration	3¼–3¾ hours
Distance	12km
Standard	easy-medium
Start	Trin
Finish	Staziun Valendas-Sagogn
Nearest Towns	Chur, Disentis

Summary This walk leads through the deeply eroding Ruin' Aulta, a fascinating gorge where natural erosion has produced weird pillars and columns that stand out in the chalky white cliffs. In places, the continually eroding path calls for some sure-footedness.

The local Romansch-speaking people – who have inhabited the valley for the last 1500 years – call the gorge the Ruin' Aulta, or 'high ruin', while to the German Swiss the area is more familiar as the Vorderrheinschlucht. Until the construction of the railway through the gorge itself, no transport route went via this rugged section of the upper Swiss Rhine. The Ruin' Aulta is still impassable for motor vehicles, and hence is an important natural sanctuary for wildlife.

Maps
Recommended is the SAW/FSTP 1:50,000 *Sardona* No 247T. K+F's 1:60,000 *Surselva* (Sfr24.80) also covers the walk. The local tourist authority's otherwise excellent 1:25,000 *Wanderkarte Flims Laax Falera* (around Sfr15), excludes a short initial section of the route.

NEAREST TOWN
Trin
Trin is a small village on the Tamins–Flims–Laax road.

The *Ustarias Ringel* (☎ 081-635 11 09, 079-475 06 07) has singles/doubles from

The 'Swiss Grand Canyon'

The Ruin' Aulta resulted from the largest mountain landslide that has ever occurred in Europe, known as the Flimser Bergsturz. As the last ice age drew to an end around 14,000 years ago, the enormous glacier filling the Surselva valley retreated back to the headwaters of the Rein Anteriur (Vorderrhein). Without this icy buttress to support them, the mountains on the northern side of the valley (about where the skiing village of Flims now stands) suddenly collapsed, blocking a 15km stretch of the river under some 15 billion cubic metres of rock and pulverised earth.

Backwaters built up behind this natural dam to create a large lake, which eventually broke through the mass of rubble, causing further devastation downstream. Over the following millennia the Rein Anteriur continued cutting its way through the deposits of debris to form this chalky 400m-deep gorge.

GRAUBÜNDEN

around Sfr45/90 and dorm beds for around Sfr30.

Postbuses run at least hourly from Chur (just under 30 minutes). There are also less frequent postbus connections via Laax from Falera, on the Rhaetian Railway's Chur–Disentis line.

GETTING TO/FROM THE WALK

The walk ends at the Valendas-Sagogn train station on the Chur–Disentis line (see Gateway at the start of the chapter).

THE WALK

On the main road at the uphill side of Trin (876m) take the signposted footpath leading down through the lower village of **Trin-Digg**. A lonely country lane (the Senda Sursilvana marked with yellow diamonds) continues south-west through rolling pastures and pockets of beech forest on a long, broad terrace overlooking the valley of the Surselva. The impressive rock formation ahead to the right is the Crap da Flem, whose massive cliffs rise up abruptly behind the Alpine resort of Flims, giving the mountain an awesome fortress-like appearance.

After the roadway swings around northward, follow route markings down left across the **Flem** stream and continue up a farm track to pass the houses of **Pintrun** (832m). Walk on up the dirt road over a slight crest (where the Senda Sursilvana departs on the right to Conn, then descend on to **Ransun**, a lookout point at 805m above the Rein Anteriur (Vorderrhein). A white-red-white marked path now drops down quite steeply into the gorge, crossing the river on the pedestrian section of the railway bridge, 1¼ to 1½ hours from Trin.

A worthwhile 15-minute side trip to the tip of the peninsula known as **Chli Isla** can be made 200m after the rail bridge, where various rough trails lead rightward down through 'wild' camp sites. Immediately opposite, the spectacular chalky white cliffs of the Ruin'

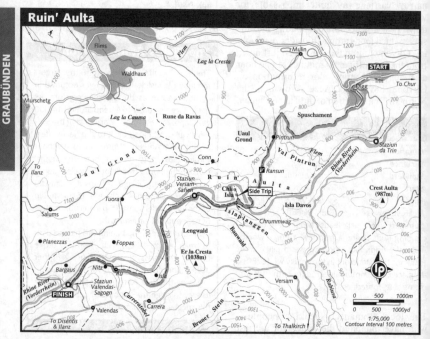

Ruin' Aulta

Aulta tower above the river. After climbing over a small, steep ridge past the turn-off to Versam village, the main path drops down to the **Chrumwag** tunnel and makes its way upstream between the train tracks and the Rein Anteriur. In places the swift-flowing river forms white-water rapids, and on summer days the odd inflatable raft may float past.

Where the stream makes another sweeping curve, cut straight ahead through more damp forest, rising slightly to cross over the rail tracks at the **Staziun Versam-Safien** (635m), 25 to 30 minutes on. The train station (for the village of Versam sitting high up on a glacial terrace at the mouth of the Safiental) looks across to another impressive cliff face of the Ruin' Aulta. Except in midsummer this part of the valley receives little direct sunlight.

Continue on above the rail lines, in places following embankments that protect the railway from landslides. Here the route leads through an eroded landscape of caverns, chasms and columns formed in the unstable pulverised earth. Climb on leftward and skirt above the farmlet of **Isla** (692m), from where the ski villages of Laax and Falera stand out on the slopes across the valley, then descend gently through the forest to reach the picturesque hamlet of **Au** after one to 1¼ hours. Cross the gushing Carreratobel via the rail bridge, and once again make your way upstream between the train tracks and the river. After passing final sections of chalk cliffs the path arrives at the **Staziun Valendas-Sagogn** (669m) after a further 15 to 20 minutes.

Safienberg

Duration	4½–5¼ hours
Distance	15km
Standard	medium
Start	Thalkirch
Finish	Splügen

Summary This walk crosses the Safienberg on a historic mule trail connecting the hamlet of Thalkirch in the upper Safiental, a remote side valley of the Surselva, with the village of Splügen.

Despite its German name, the 2486m Safienberg is really a pass. During the early 14th century, the first Walser settlers migrated north across the Safienberg into this quiet highland valley from the Rheinwald. In the lower reaches of the Safiental the Rabiusa stream runs through a deep gorge, cutting off the valley. Apart from the Safienberg itself, the Glaspass (east to Thusis) and the Tomülpass (west to Vals) were the best routes in and out of the valley. The Safiental therefore remained isolated from the Surselva until the early part of the 20th century, when the valley was penetrated by a proper road from Versam. Today the Safiental still lies well off the beaten track, and has kept much of its rural Alpine charm, with old timber houses and the traditional 'woven' wooden fences.

The walk involves an ascent of around 800m. Despite the odd bit of loose rock or boggy ground, this old route is in good condition and can easily be undertaken by all walkers with a reasonable level of fitness. The Safienberg is also quite popular with mountain bikers.

Maps

Best is K+F's 1:60,000 walking map *Surselva* (Sfr24.80). Otherwise, two SAW/FSTP 1:50,000 sheets cover the route: *Safiental* No 257T and *San Bernardino* No 267T (Sfr22.50 each).

NEAREST TOWNS
Thalkirch

Thalkirch (also called Malönja) at 1686m is the uppermost hamlet in the Safiental.

The rudimentary *youth hostel* in Thalkirch (☎ *081-647 11 07* e *thalkirch@youthhostel.ch*) is in an old farmhouse nearby. Check in at the next house up from the post office. It's a self-catering arrangement with no washing facilities, but at Sfr10 per night it's very cheap and has much rustic charm. There is no shop in Thalkirch, so hostellers should bring provisions with them.

Thalkirch is accessible by postbus from Versam-Safien railway station on the Chur–Disentis line, and from Chur there are seven daily train/bus connections. (Walkers arriving directly from the Valais or Ticino travel via Disentis.) The 1¼-hour ride through the wild valley of the Safiental is interesting and scenic. Earlier postbuses go the whole way to the Turrahus.

Splügen

Originally a Walser settlement, Splügen (1457m) is the gateway to the Splügenpass and the Passo del San Bernardino, two of the most historically important passes in the Central Alps. For centuries Splügen lived well by transporting (and taxing) goods on these trans-Alpine trade routes. Splügen's early 18th-century buildings, such as the Posthotel Bodenhaus and the Schorsch-Haus (now a museum), bear witness to the town's prosperous role as a major stopping post. A short half-day walk from Splügen leads westward along the southern banks of the river to the village of Hinterrhein at the head of the Rheinwald valley.

For more information contact the tourist office (☎ 081-650 90 30, e splugen@via malaferien.ch, w www.splugen.ch).

Camping Auf dem Sand (☎ *081-664 14 76, fax 081-664 14 60*) has tent sites from Sfr6 plus Sfr6.40 per night. The *Wadens-wilerhaus* (☎ *081-664 13 34, 079-357 75 35*) charges Sfr41 in the dorm including full board. The *Posthotel Bodenhaus* (☎ *081-650 90 90, fax 081-650 90 99*) has singles/doubles from Sfr50/100.

Postbuses run between Thusis and Splügen approximately every 1½ hours in either direction. The less frequent postbuses between Thusis and Bellinzona in Ticino (via the Passo del San Bernardino) also call in at Splügen. Reservation is necessary for some services (☎ 081-256 31 66).

GETTING TO/FROM THE WALK

For information on transport to/from Thalkirch and Splügen, see Nearest Towns. Until midday, postbuses from Thalkirch continue upvalley to Turrahus.

THE WALK

From Thalkirch post office (1686m) opposite the quaint old stone-roofed church, follow the sealed road 1.5km upvalley past old wooden Walser-style houses and barns to the *Berggasthaus Turrahus* (☎ *081-647 12 03*)

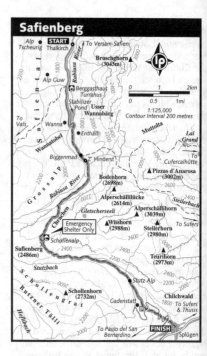

at 1694m. The Berggasthaus offers rooms and some relatively expensive dormitory accommodation.

Disregarding a signposted path that branches off right up via the Tomülpass into the Valsertal, proceed past a stabilisation pond and cross the **Rabiusa** on a bridge. The road leads on over riverside meadows scattered with small farms (from where another walking route goes up left toward the Alperschällilücke) to pass the hamlet of **Z'Hinderst**. Contrasting with the gentle grassy slopes to your right, the 3000m crags of the Pizzas d'Anarosa poke up from behind lower rock buttresses on the eastern side of the valley.

Continue along an old mule track past cascading rivulets, and begin climbing away to the left through a rocky gravel wash. The often steep trail brings you up beside an eroding stream, briefly follows a rounded ridge, then makes a final ascent in switchbacks past a small shelter to reach the

Safienberg (2486m), 2½ to three hours up from the Turrahus. This broad opening in the rocky ridge overlooks the upper Safiental, which – unlike the heavily forested lower valley area – is characterised by broad mountain pastures. To the south-east you can make out the glaciated peaks of the Suretta group beyond Splügen.

Start descending the initially boggy grass slopes along a line of paint markings, then sidle down over to the left to cross the **Stutzbach** on a fixed-log footbridge, with the bare-rock outline of the Alperschällihorn (3039m) rising up from steep talus slopes to your left. The path drops gradually against the contour above the true right bank of the stream, passing the stone alp hut of **Stutz Alp** (2018m) not long before coming to a car park at the end of the road at **Gadenstatt**.

Follow the sealed road past a right-hand turn-off to Medels, then take well-signposted shortcuts down the steeply rolling hillsides above **Splügen** (1460m) between the many hairpin bends in the road to enter the old town via an arched walkway 30 to 40 minutes on. Cobbled lanes lead either left over the bridge to the tourist office or rightward down to the post office/bus stop.

Engadine

The Engadine extends roughly 90km along the valley of the En (Inn) River, from the Passo del Maloja as far as the Austrian border. Enclosed by mountain ranges that hinder the inflow of moist air masses, the Engadine has a dry climate typical for a high inner-Alpine valley, with warm, sunny summers and severe winters – similar to the Goms region of the Upper Valais. The Engadine can be divided into two fairly distinct upper and lower sections.

The 40km section of the Upper Engadine (Engadin' Ota in Romansch) stretches north-east from the Passo del Maloja to Zernez. Here the valley floor is surprisingly broad with a very low gradient, and the upper half of the valley is filled by a chain of large highland lakes over 1800m above sea level. Rather than meeting the head of

another valley at the Passo del Maloja, the Upper Engadine falls away abruptly southwest into the Val Bregaglia (Bergell), which is one of the Upper Engadine's two Italian-speaking appendages – the other is the Val Poschiavo (Puschlav). The Bernina massif borders the Upper Engadine on its southern side. The highest summit of this spectacular glacier-clad range, the 4049m Piz Bernina, is Graubünden's only 'four-thousander'.

The Lower Engadine (Engadina Bassa in Romansch) is somewhat different geographically from the Upper Engadine. Here the valley is rather lower and much narrower, repeatedly forcing the En (Inn) to flow through ravines and gorges. The Engadine's generally dry climate is particularly pronounced, and annual precipitation in the Scuol area scarcely exceeds 700 mm. The ranges surrounding the Lower Engadine are also comparatively low, with beautiful forests of larch and mountain fir fringing the valley and interesting areas of Alpine plateaus higher up.

No other part of Switzerland has such fine walking in such a wild and undisturbed setting as the Lower Engadine. Relatively undeveloped and inaccessible, this region, with its large southern appendage, the Val Müstair, forms one of the last real strongholds of Switzerland's waning Romansch-speaking population, whose local dialect – called Ladin – is universally spoken throughout the region.

ACCESS TOWNS
St Moritz

St Moritz (San Murezzan in Romansch) is spread out along the lakeshore of the Lej da San Murezzan at around 1800m. Despite its elitist image, the resort makes a good base for walks in the Upper Engadine. The Engadine Museum (entry Sfr5) deals with local history. The Segantini Museum (entry Sfr10) has the world's finest collection of works by Giovanni Segantini (1858-99), a famous landscape painter from the Upper Engadine. A very scenic day walk directly from St Moritz goes up over the Pass Suvretta before descending via the Val Bever to the village of Bever in the main Engadine valley.

GRAUBÜNDEN

The tourist office (☎ 081-837 33 33, fax 081-837 33 77, e information@stmoritz.ch, w www.stmoritz.ch), Via Maistra 12, has further information.

In St Moritz Bad, on the west side of the lake, are the *Olympiaschanze* (☎ 081-833 40 90, fax 081-834 40 96) camping ground and the large *youth hostel* (☎ 081-833 39 69, e st.moritz@youthhostel.ch), which has dorm beds from Sfr40.50 with full board. The *Hotel Reine Victoria* (☎ 081-833 40 32, e tivigest@bluewin.ch) has singles/doubles from Sfr45/90 (rising to Sfr60/120 in July and August).

The cheapest restaurants are between Dorf and Bad. The *Coop* supermarket is in Via dal Bagn; next door is rustic *La Fontana*, with mostly Italian meals from Sfr12.

There are roughly hourly trains from Chur directly to St Moritz (via Filisur). There are also regular trains via the Passo del Bernina to Tirano in Italy (with further connections to Milan). The *Palm Express* postbus service runs between Lugano and St Moritz twice daily; reservation is obligatory (☎ 081-837 67 64).

Pontresina

The stretched-out village of Pontresina (1805m) occupies a sunny and sheltered position in the Val Bernina, the highest side valley of the Upper Engadine. Pontresina's Santa Maria chapel has medieval frescoes; also of interest is the pentagonal Moorish tower. The Alpine Museum (entry Sfr5/1 adults/children) deals with the history and ecology of the surrounding mountains.

A classic local day walk involves taking the funicular up to Muottas Muragl (2453m) and then hiking via the SAC's *Segantini-hütte* (☎ 079-681 35 37) at 2731m to Alp Languard (2270m), from where the descent continues either on foot or by chairlift to Pontresina.

Guided day walks in the Swiss National Park (free for people staying in Pontresina) are operated by the tourist office (☎ 081-838 83 00, fax 081-838 83 10, e info@pontresina.com, w www.pontresina .com). The local mountaineering school, the Berg-steigerschule Pontresina (☎ 081-838 83 83,

w www.bergsteiger-pontresina.ch), is one of the absolute best in Switzerland.

Plauns (☎ 081-842 62 85, e a.bruel @bluewin.ch) is the local camping ground. The 117-bed *youth hostel* (☎ 081-842 72 23, e pontresina@youthhostel.ch) charges Sfr41.50 with full board. *Pensione Valtel-lina* (☎ 081-842 64 06) has singles/doubles for Sfr56/108.

The *Coop* supermarket is near the post office. Inexpensive eating options are limited, but *Bahnhof* (☎ 081-838 80 00), by the station, has meals from Sfr15 and there's a *pizzeria* at the Sportpavillon.

Pontresina is on the rail line from St Moritz, which continues over the Passo del Bernina to Tirano in Italy. There are also roughly half-hourly postbuses between Pontresina and St Moritz.

Maloja

The village of Maloja (1809m) lies just north of the Passo del Maloja. This peculiar pass plummets directly into the Italian-speaking Val Bregaglia on its western side, but drops imperceptibly to the east. There are interesting glacier mills, formed by water pressurised by ice, within easy walking distance. Maloja provides an excellent base for numerous other popular walks, including routes into the Val Bregaglia, along the Upper Engadine lakes, and over the historic Pass da Sett (Septimerpass) or the Passo de Muretto leading into Italy.

For information contact the tourist office (☎ 081-824 31 88, fax 081-824 36 37, e info @maloja.ch, w www.maloja.ch).

Maloja's *Camping Plan Curtinac* (☎ 081-824 31 81, fax 081-824 31 73) has tent sites from Sfr6 plus Sfr4.50 per person, and the *youth hostel* (☎ 081-833 39 69, e maloja@youthhostel.ch) charges Sfr24 for dorm beds. The *Hotel Longhin* (☎ 081-824 31 31, e hotel.longhin@bluewin.ch) and the *Hotel Schweizerhaus* (☎ 081-838 28 28, e schweizerhaus.maloja@bluewin.ch) have singles/doubles from around Sfr50/100.

There is a *supermarket* opposite the post office, and *Hotel Longhin* has a restaurant.

Depending on the season, there are up to 20 daily postbuses in either direction between

St Moritz and Maloja. The *Palm Express* bus service between Lugano and St Moritz passes through Maloja twice daily in the summer season; reservation is compulsory (☎ 081-837 67 60).

Poschiavo

Beyond the Passo del Bernina (Bernina Pass) lies the isolated Val Poschiavo, one of several Italian-speaking valleys in Graubünden. The only place of any size in the valley is the attractive town of Poschiavo itself.

The valley tourist office (☎ 081-844 05 71, fax 081-844 10 27, e info@valposchiavo.ch, w www.valposchiavo.ch) is in Poschiavo.

The *Caffè Semadeni Garni* (☎ 081-844 07 70, fax 081-844 33 46) offers singles/doubles for Sfr45/90. The *Hotel Crameri* (☎ 081-844 16 24, fax 081-844 18 90) has rooms from Sfr50/100. There is good alternative accommodation elsewhere in the Val Poschiavo.

Poschiavo is on the Rhaetian Railways line between St Moritz and the Italian border town of Tirano. Postbuses run between the Passo del Bernina and Poschiavo via Sfazù (for the Val da Camp walk under Other Walks at the end of the chapter) and other localities high above the valley.

Scuol

Scuol (Schuls in German) lies at 1243m in the lower part of the Lower Engadine and is the administrative hub of the region as well as its main tourist centre. Although many of the town residents still speak Romansch, past fires and recent development have left a modern town centre with less of the charm of other places in the Lower Engadine.

The town museum is in the Chagronda ('big house'). The nearby Tarasp castle, built on a rocky hillock that looks over most of the valley, is also worth visiting (entry Sfr7).

The tourist office (☎ 081-861 22 22, fax 081-861 22 23, e info@scuol.ch, w www.scuol.ch) is 10 minutes' walk down from the train station.

The local camping ground is *Gurlaina* (☎ 081-864 15 01, fax 081-864 07 60). The

Hotel Grusaida (Alpenrose) (☎ 081-864 14 74, fax 081-864 18 77) and the *Hotel Quellenhof* (☎ 081-864 12 15, fax 081-864 02 34) have singles/doubles from Sfr55/110.

The *Coop* supermarket and restaurant is on the main street, and *Schü-San* Chinese takeaway, in the Bogn bathing centre, offers meals from Sfr9.

The new Vereina tunnel from Klosters has made Scuol easily accessible from northern Switzerland. People arriving from Zürich will have to change trains in Landquart; there are connections hourly.

Santa Maria & Müstair

Santa Maria (1275m) is a typical Romansch village in the Val Müstair, with old houses adorned with geometric and floral *sgrafitto* designs fronting the narrow main street. Several kilometres downvalley near the Italian border is the larger village of Müstair, famous for its 8th-century monastery.

There are tourist offices in both Santa Maria (☎ 081-858 57 27, fax 081-858 62 97, e tourismusstamaria@bluewin.ch) and Müstair (☎ 081-858 50 00, fax 081-081 858 50 26, e info@muestair.ch, w www.valmuestair.ch).

There are tent sites available at the camping grounds *Santa Maria* (☎ 081-858 71 33, fax 081-858 50 79) in Santa Maria and *Clenga* (☎ 081-858 54 10, fax 081-858 54 10) in Müstair.

For hard-top accommodation, Santa Maria's *youth hostel* (☎ 081-858 50 52, 858 54 96) offers dorm beds for Sfr24. *Pensiun Crusch-Alba* (☎ 081-858 51 06, fax 081-858 61 49) offers singles/doubles from Sfr49/94. *Hotel Chasa Randulina* (☎ 081-858 51 24, fax 081-858 50 09) charges slightly more, while in nearby Müstair, *Chalavaina* (☎ 081-858 54 68) has rooms from Sfr38/75.

From Zernez, up to a dozen postbuses run daily via the Pass dal Fuorn (Ofenpass) to Santa Maria and Müstair. From early July until mid-October there are also bus connections from Santa Maria across the scenic passes of Pass Umbrail and Passo di Stelvio (Stilfserjoch) into Italy.

Upper Engadine Lakes

Duration	2¾–3½ hours
Distance	14km
Standard	easy
Start	Maloja
Finish	Silvaplana
Nearest Towns	Segl-Maria, St Moritz

Summary This walk takes you along the south-eastern shore of the two largest of the Upper Engadine lakes through beautiful forests of larch, arolla pine and mountain pine, and offers a continually changing perspective of Alpine and waterside scenery.

One of the region's special features, the four highland lakes of the Upper Engadine lie strung together like a pearl necklace along the valley floor below towering craggy ranges. In Romansch, the two largest are called the Lej da Segl and the Lej da Silvaplauna, or, in the now almost as widely spoken German, the Silvaplanersee and the Silsersee. In the broad valley of the Upper Engadine it's easy to forget you're standing at around 1800m above sea level – not much less than most higher summits in the Alpine foothills! Some 10,000 years ago a single larger lake covered the Upper Engadine, but alluvial debris washed out of the side valleys gradually separated this larger lake into several water bodies.

In winter the lakes of the Upper Engadine freeze over solidly, forming a 1m-thick layer of ice easily strong enough to support the thousands of participants in the world-famous Engadine Ski Marathon from Maloja to Zuoz.

The walk can generally be done at any time of the year except winter. The nicest time is October, when the larch trees are their best autumn gold, but late in the season uncleared snow or black ice on the trail may make the walk unsafe.

Maps

The recommended walking map is the SAW/ESS 1:50,000 *Julierpass* No 268T (Sfr22.50). Also suitable is K+F's 1:60,000 *Oberengadin* (Sfr24.80).

NEAREST TOWN
Segl-Maria

About midway, the walk passes through Segl-Maria (Sils-Maria in German), a tranquil village at 1809m between the Lej da Segl and the Lej da Silvaplauna.

Segl-Maria has a tourist office (☎ 081-838 50 50, fax 081-838 50 59, ℮ info@sils.ch) and a small mountaineering school, La Marga (☎ 081-828 88 15). The German philosopher Friedrich Nietzsche spent his summers in the Nietzsche Haus (entry Sfr4) between 1881 and 1888.

The *Baukantine Kuhn (☎ 081-826 52 62, fax 081-826 59 30)*, on the south bank of the river toward the Lej da Silvaplauna, has dorm beds from Sfr15. The *Pension Schulze (☎ 081-826 52 13)* has singles/doubles from Sfr60/120.

GETTING TO/FROM THE WALK

For information on transport to/from Maloja, see Access Towns earlier. Regular buses running between St Moritz and Maloja stop in Segl-Maria and the village of Silvaplana, at the end of the walk.

THE WALK

From the northern edge of Maloja, turn off the main road onto a minor road heading north-east. This goes across a grassy plain past a little church to meet a dirt track at the shore of the **Lej da Segl**; there is a small car park here. The well-marked route leads around the lakeside following short sections of path (or the dirt road itself) through beautiful larch forest with an alpenrose understorey. The views across the water are dominated by the 3164m summit of Piz Lagrev as you move out of the trees onto open grassland to reach **Isola** (1812m) after 45 minutes to one hour. These dozen or so rustic buildings stand at the edge of a flat alluvial fan formed by the Aua da Fedoz.

Cross this stream on a wooden footbridge, and continue on into the forest above cliffs that fall directly into the Lej da Segl. The path passes the tiny islands of Chaviolas in front of the picturesque Chastè peninsula, gradually descending back to the shoreline before it comes to a side trail

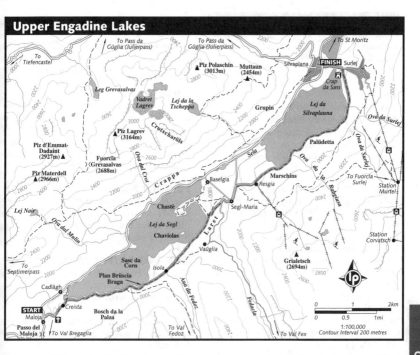

Upper Engadine Lakes

(signposted 'Laret/Segl'). Here leave off to the right away from the lake past several minor divergences to intersect with a broad road, following the sealed road down to arrive in **Segl-Maria**, 45 minutes to one hour on. This is another of the Upper Engadine's captivating old villages with Romansch-style stone houses.

Continue down the main street past the Nietzsche Haus, a museum in philosopher Friedrich Nietzsche's former residence, to where a signpost points you off right. The route follows a small road over grassy fields past the lower station of the Furtschellas cable car to the south-western edge of the **Lej da Silvaplauna**. Turn right and make your way along a broad walkway/bridle trail that traces the shoreline through more attractive open coniferous forest, with frequent clear views across the lake toward Piz Güglia (Julier) and ranges farther downvalley.

After merging into a road, the route cuts over meadows fringed by gravel beaches

and past a distant thundering waterfall of the Ova da Surlej stream to meet a road near the pseudo-medieval castle of **Crap da Sass**. Here, sediments washed down by two opposing streams have gradually separated the Lej da Silvaplauna from the smaller Lej da Champfer. A short walk on across the bridge brings you up into the tourist town of **Silva-plana**, 1¼ to 1½ hours on from Segl-Maria.

The Maloja Wind

In summer, countless windsurfers take advantage of the unfailingly consistent 'Maloja Wind', one of the most unusual airstreams in the Alps. Quite contrary to the rules of wind dynamics in mountainous regions, the Maloja Wind blows continuously in the 'wrong' direction, namely *down* through the Engadine valley, sparing the Upper Engadine from oppressively hot summer weather.

Fuorcla Funtana da S-charl

Duration	3–3½ hours
Distance	14km
Standard	easy
Start	Pass dal Fuorn (Ofenpass)
Finish	S-charl
Nearest Towns	Zernez, Scuol

Summary The (mostly downhill) route over the 2393m Fuorcla Funtana da S-charl links the Pass dal Fuorn with the beautiful Val S-charl, the longest side valley of the Lower Engadine.

The Val S-charl is a romantically wild area with the highest stands of mountain pines found in Europe. These forests were once heavily exploited to process the silver and zinc mined in the surrounding mountains. Smelting works were built at the Pass dal Fuorn (*fuorn* means 'furnace' in Romansch) and in the village of S-charl. Relics of the area's mining and smelting past include old shafts, slag heaps and kilns. While historically very interesting, they are lasting reminders of the devastating ecological damage caused by this long-abandoned industry.

Maps

The recommended walking map is the SAW/FSTP 1:50,000 *Ofenpass (Pass dal Fuorn)* No 259T (Sfr22.50). K+F's 1:60,000 *Unterengadin* (Sfr24.80) is a larger-format walking map covering the Lower Engadine.

NEAREST TOWN & FACILITIES
S-charl

S-charl (pronounced es-KARL), at 1810m and just east of the Swiss National Park boundary, is a typical example of a small Engadine mountain village. In its heyday around 1570, when it was the centre of local mining and smelting activities, S-charl had some 70 houses. Today its buildings number just 13, and the village is almost deserted during winter. The village museum (Sfr3/5 children/adults) deals with S-charl's fascinating history. S-charl is in the municipal area of Scuol (see Access Towns at the start of the Engadine

section), whose tourist office can provide information.

The **Gasthaus Mayor** (☎ 081-864 14 12 *fax 081-864 99 83*) has rooms from Sfr60 per person. The **Usaria e Pensiun Crusch Alba** (☎ 081-864 14 05, e cruschalba@sunwel .ch) charges from Sfr75 per person.

Postbuses run between S-charl and Scuol up to five times daily from early June until around 20 October; outside of this time there is no public transport. The last postbus leaves S-charl shortly before 5pm; reservation is advisable (☎ 081-864 16 83).

Pass dal Fuorn

The **Hotel Süsom Givè** (☎ 081-858 51 82 *fax 081-858 61 71*), on the Pass dal Fuorn offers dorm beds for Sfr27 and rooms for Sfr58 per person.

GETTING TO/FROM THE WALK

The walk begins at Süsom Givè on the 2149m Pass dal Fuorn. Up to a dozen postbuses daily from Zernez to Müstair stop at Süsom Givè.

For information on transport to/from the end of the walk at S-charl, see Nearest Town & Facilities.

THE WALK

The path departs from directly opposite the hotel, first climbing slightly before contouring eastward through the forest above the pass road to meet an alp track in the attractive Alpine meadow called the **Plaun de l'Aua** (2190m). To the south-east the magnificent wave-like form of the 3899m Ortler stands out as a solitary summit in perpetual snowfields. At the signpost a short way on (where the Senda Surova walking route through the Val Müstair continues right, follow white-red-white markings off left. The trail ascends the rolling slopes in steep switchbacks to another dirt road, and follows this over a small plain past winter ski-lifts to reach the **Fuorcla Funtana da S-charl** (2393m), 1½ to 1¾ hours from the Pass dal Fuorn.

Descend into the grassy basin below the pass, making your way left around a marshy flat past a large thumb-shaped boulder. After

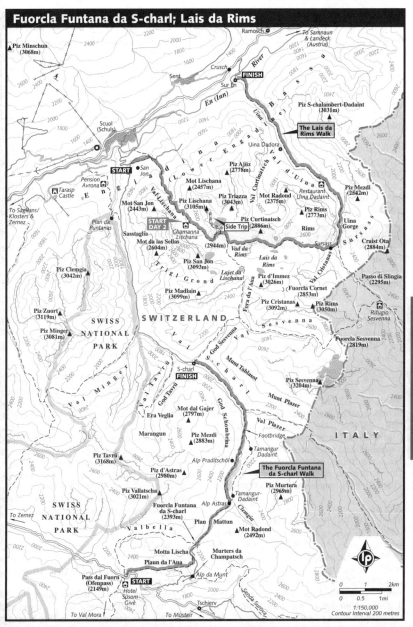

Fuorcla Funtana da S-charl; Lais da Rims

Piz Minschun (3068m)

Ramosch

To Samnaun & Landeck (Austria)

River

Crusch

Sent

FINISH

Sur En

En (Inn)

Scuol (Schuls)

Uina Dadora

Piz S-chalambert-Dadaint (3031m)

The Lais da Rims Walk

Tarasp Castle

Pension Avrona

START

San Jon

To Saglians/ Klosters & Zernez

Plan da Puntanas

Mot San Jon (2443m)

Val Lischana

Piz Ajüz (2778m)

Mot Lischana (2457m)

Piz Lischana (3105m)

Piz Triazza (3043m)

Piz Curtinatsch (2886m)

Mot Radond (2375m)

Restaurant Uina Dadaint

Piz Rims (2773m)

Piz Mezdi (2542m)

Uina Gorge

START DAY 2

Chamanna Lischana

Side Trip

Rims 2600

Sursass

Craist Ota (2884m)

Sasstaglia

Mot da las Sellas (2604m)

(2944m)

Vad da Rims

Lais da Rims

Piz San Jon (3093m)

Lajet da Lischana

Piz d'Immez (3026m)

Fuorcla Cornet (2853m)

Passo di Slingia (2295m)

Piz Clemgia (3042m)

Piz Madlain (3099m)

Fora da l'Aua

Piz Cristanas (3092m)

Piz Rims (3050m)

Rifugio Sesvenna

Piz Zuort (3119m)

SWISS

SWITZERLAND

Val Cristanas

Sesvenna

Piz Minger (3081m)

NATIONAL PARK

Fuorcla Sesvenna (2819m)

Val Sassa

God Sesvenna

Munt Tablasot

Piz Sesvenna (3204m)

Val Tavrü

God Tavrü

S-charl

FINISH

Val S-charl

Munt Plazer

Piz Minger

Mot dal Gajer (2797m)

Val Plazer

Footbridge

ITALY

Era Veglia

Marangun

Piz Mezdi (2883m)

Alp Praditschöl

Tamangur Dadaint

Piz Tavrü (3168m)

Piz d'Astras (2980m)

The Fuorcla Funtana da S-charl Walk

Piz Murtera (2969m)

Piz Vallatscha (3021m)

Tamangur-Dadaint

Alp Astras

SWISS

Fuorcla Funtana da S-charl (2393m)

Plan Mattun

Clemgia

Mot Radond (2492m)

To Zernez

NATIONAL PARK

Valbella

Murters da Champatsch

Motta Lischa

Plaun da l'Aua

Pass dal Fuorn (Ofenpass) (2149m)

START

Hotel Süsom Givè

Alp da Munt

Senda Suruta

To Val Mora

To Müstair

Tschierv

0   1   2km

0   0.5   1mi

1:150,000
Contour Interval 200 metres

GRAUBÜNDEN

dropping down via a steep ridge above a streamlet the path comes onto a dirt road (with restricted vehicle access) at **Alp Astras** (2135m). This neat farmhouse sits under the eroding ranges near the junction of two pretty upper valleys. Walk on gently down above the meandering river past ruined homesteads on the adjacent eastern banks and through forests of nice old mountain pines. The route crosses the Clemgia on a small wooden bridge and leads on down through the beautiful Val S-charl past little riverside flats with picnic tables to arrive in **S-charl** after 1½ to 1¾ hours.

For those with the time, it's worthwhile extending the walk down through the Val S-charl to Scuol (2½ hours).

Lais da Rims

Duration	2 days
Distance	22.5km
Standard	hard
Start	Scuol/San Jon
Finish	Sur En

Summary The high-Alpine lakeland area known (in Romansch) as the Lais da Rims forms one of the Engadine's least-touched wildernesses, receiving relatively few visitors due to its remoteness and inhospitable nature.

The Lais da Rims lie scattered and hidden across a stark plateau at between 2500m and 2800m. Having been intensely glaciated in the recent past, this sparsely vegetated area resembles a moonscape. The lakes are drained by the Uina stream, which flows through an amazing narrow gorge about 1km in length and up to 400m deep.

Maps

The SAW/FSTP's 1:50,000 *Tarasp* No 249T fully covers the walk, but the adjoining *Ofenpass* No 259T is also useful (Sfr22.50 each). The Lower Engadine tourist authority's 1:50,000 *Wanderkarte Scuol* (Sfr16) is the most detailed walking map covering the Lais da Rims area. K+F's 1:60,000 *Unterengadin* (Sfr24.80) takes in the entire Lower Engadine.

This walk is physically demanding and crosses exposed high-Alpine country. Parts of the route may be snow-covered in places well into July or after late September. Of course you'll need sturdy footwear for the rocky terrain, as well as fine and stable weather

NEAREST TOWN
Sur En

The walk ends at this tiny village, which has a small *camping ground* (☎ 081-866 35 44). *Chasa Lischana* (☎ 081-866 34 19, fax 081-866 32 05) has rooms from Sfr40 per person and dorm beds from around Sfr20. The *Gasthof Val d'Uina* (☎ 081-866 31 37, fax 081-866 32 16) has better rooms from Sfr90 per person. Information is available from the Scuol tourist office (see Access Towns at the beginning of the Engadine section).

There are five daily postbuses to Scuol (via the charming Romansch village of Sent); the last departure is around 5pm. Otherwise walk 15 minutes across the quaint roofed wooden bridge over the En to nearby Crusch on the main road, where regular postbuses running between Scuol and Martina stop.

GETTING TO/FROM THE WALK

This walk starts from the bus stop at San Jon, a short way above Scuol (see Access Towns earlier) on the road to S-charl (see Nearest Towns under the Fuorcla Funtana da S-charl earlier). From early June until around 20 October, postbuses from Scuol pass San Jon up to five times daily. The last postbus leaves Scuol train station around 3.30pm; reservations are advisable (☎ 081-864 16 83). Otherwise it's a pleasant walk of about one hour. There is free parking at San Jon.

THE WALK

See the Fuorcla Funtana da S-charl; Lais da Rims map, p317

Day 1: San Jon to Chamanna Lischana

2¾–3½ hours, 5.5km, 1039m ascent

From the San Jon bus stop, walk a few paces along the unsurfaced turn-off before heading up right along an alp track. This leads past the stud farm of San Jon at 1466m, then continues eastward through a broad clearing to merge with another walking route in the trees. The path now begins a steep and tiring ascent in endless zigzags beside a small stream, leaving the forest as it leads into small, enclosed upper Val Lischana to arrive at the *Chamanna Lischana (☎ 081-864 95 44)*.

This small SAC hut at 2500m is staffed in July, August and September (otherwise left open). The charge for a dorm bed is around Sfr25. The hut occupies a scenic position atop a prominent rock outcrop, and looks directly down toward Scuol in the main Engadine valley.

Day 2: Chamanna Lischana to Sur En

5–6¾ hours, 17km, 444m ascent
Ascend over grassed moraines and coarse talus slides below Piz Lischana to near the end of the valley. The path cuts up leftward between rock walls to climb rather more steeply via a scree-filled gully leading up to point 2944m on a broad, barren ridgetop (see Piz Lischana Side Trip at the end of the route description), 1¼ to 1¾ hours from the Chamanna Lischana. Ahead of you lies a raw high-Alpine plateau, on which the numerous larger and smaller lakes known as the Lais da Rims lie scattered and hidden in the lunar landscape.

Walk a short distance along the ridge to a signpost at a track junction, where a trail continues ahead to the Lajet da Lischana. This starkly beautiful lake at 2857m can just be made out to the south in the direction of the 3905m Ortler (the unmistakable snowcapped peak in Italian South Tirol). Here, head east and follow occasional red-white-red markings down through the bare terrain, slowly picking your way over mounds of glaciated rubble to pass above an attractive lake after 30 to 45 minutes. The route leads on left, rising slightly past a lone tarn before descending steadily above a rocky stream bed to Sursass (2157m), a grassy area in the valley floor, after a further 50 minutes to 1¼ hours.

Cross two little wooden bridges, then cut left across the meadows past a large boulder block to meet a foot track coming over the Passo di Slingia (2295m). The *Rifugio Sesvenna (☎ 0039-473-830234)*, a large mountain hut belonging to the Alpenverein Sudtirol (AVS) is 30 to 40 minutes' walk away, 1.5km inside Italian territory across the Passo di Slingia; it charges around IL15,000 (€7.75) for dorm beds.) Walk a short way on to where the valley narrows into the impressive **Uina gorge**. Here, the path has been blasted into high cliffs; there are several short tunnels, and safety rails or steel cables secure the more dangerous sections.

Below the gorge the route enters the **Val d'Uina** proper, and goes over onto an unsealed road (with vehicle access only by special permit). Make your way down through this lovely upper valley forested mainly with larch, soon passing the *Restaurant Uina Dadaint (☎ 081-866 31 37)*, a large yellow building at 1772m, open mid-June to early October. The restaurant has dorm beds for around Sfr25. The road descends gently on to the hamlet of **Uina Dadora** (1499m), which until the late 19th century was a thriving mountain village with several dozen inhabitants. You continually cross and recross the stream before arriving at the tiny village of **Sur En** (1124m), 2½ to three hours from Sursass.

Side Trip: Piz Lischana

1½–2 hours, 4km, 161m ascent
From point 2944m experienced walkers can hike up to the 3105m summit of Piz Lischana, the highest summit in this massif. Follow a rough but well-trodden route northward along the spur. In early to midsummer snow may be encountered on Piz Lischana's southern slopes The summit gives a great panorama of the Silvretta, Ötztaler, Ortler and Bernina massifs.

Swiss National Park

Straddling the Val dal Spöl on the west side of the Pass dal Fuorn (Ofenpass), the Swiss National Park marks a division between the Upper and Lower Engadine.

Although it was once Switzerland's most environmentally degraded area, today the park is arguably the only true wilderness in the country (see the boxed text 'Establishment of the Swiss National Park'). Extensive forests of mainly mountain pine cover the slopes of these ranges, and the park has the largest herds of chamois, ibex, and red deer in the country. Many Swiss are optimistic that some time in the future populations of bears – perhaps even wolves – will be re-established in the park. Having learned that humans present no danger, the animals feel less disturbed by the throngs of summer walkers and can be viewed at surprisingly close range – during the autumn hunting season, game actually takes refuge in the park!

Regulations

There is no entry fee to the Swiss National Park, but fines of up to Sfr500 may be imposed for violations of the park regulations. To minimise the environmental impact of large numbers of visitors, it is important that you carefully observe the following rules.

In particular, walkers must not leave the official paths – access to some areas of the park is therefore not possible – and should use the designated rest areas at popular scenic spots.

The following activities are also strictly prohibited: fishing and hunting; camping (including bivouacking without a tent); lighting fires; picking flowers, berries or mushrooms; feeding or otherwise disturbing fauna; riding bicycles (except on public roads); and bringing dogs into the park. Natural material – anything from wild flowers to discarded horns to rocks – must not be taken out of the park.

Walkers should also note that during the tourist season the paths and huts in the park become quite crowded – call ahead to reserve your bed. The National Park House in Zernez (Chasa dal Parc Naziunal; ☎ 081-856 13 78, fax 081-856 17 40, ⓔ info@national park.ch, ⓦ www.nationalpark.ch) is the headquarters and information centre for the park, and has worthwhile exhibits on natural phenomena.

ACCESS TOWN
Zernez

Zernez (1471m) is situated at the upper end of the Lower Engadine near its junction with the Val da Spöl. The fire of 1871 destroyed most of the old town and today Zernez has a largely modern, though pleasant, streetscape. Significant architectural survivors are the castle of Wildenberg and

Establishment of the Swiss National Park

At the beginning of the 20th century the rugged mountain ranges that now form the Swiss National Park (Parc Naziunal Svizzer in Romansch) were an ecological disaster area. Centuries of mining, uncontrolled clearing of the Alpine forests, local smelting of silver, zinc and lime, overgrazing and the ruthless hunting of wild animals had devastated the local environment. Many believed the ecology would never recover.

Some people, however, saw a rare opportunity in the area. Switzerland's emerging conservation movement successfully pushed for the creation of an initial nature reserve in 1909, which in 1914 was considerably enlarged to become the Swiss National Park. With minor additions since then, including the 3.6 sq km Macun area, the Swiss National Park now totals 172 sq km.

Since the park's establishment the recovery of the area has been remarkable, although it will be at least 100 years before a natural equilibrium is fully achieved. Ecologists worry that the park is still too small to be a truly viable ecosystem. Swiss conservationists, led by Pro Natura, are working toward its gradual enlargement to roughly 500 sq km, with an outer buffer reserve with limited land use (including biologically sustainable agriculture, fishing and hunting) and an inner core under total protection. Unfortunately, vehement local opposition is likely to block significant expansion of the park for decades to come.

the early Baroque church on the town's eastern edge.

The tourist office (☎ 081-856 13 00, fax 081-856 11 55, e info@zernez.ch, w www .zernez.ch) has further information.

Camping Cul *(☎/fax 081-856 14 62)* has tent sites for Sfr5 plus Sfr6.50 per person. The ***Hotel Bär-Post*** *(☎ 851 55 00, fax 081-851 55 99,* e *baer-post@bluewin.ch)* offers dorm beds for Sfr30 with breakfast. The ***Pensiun Parc Naziunal*** *(☎/fax 081-856 12 32)* has singles/doubles from Sfr42/84. The ***Hotel Adler*** ☎ *081-856 12 33,* e *adler @engadin.ch)* charges only slightly more. There is a ***Friends of Nature hostel*** *(☎ 081-852 31 42)* at Ova Spin, 7km along the Pass dal Fuorn (Ofenpass) road, with dorm beds for Sfr15 (without breakfast).

The ***Coop*** supermarket is opposite the tourist office.

Zernez is on the Samedan–Scuol train line. The fastest train connections from northern Switzerland run via the Vereina rail tunnel. Walkers arriving from Zürich and Chur will have to change trains at Landquart and Sagliains. In summer there are around a dozen daily postbuses from Zernez via the Pass dal Fuorn (Ofenpass) to the Val Müstair.

Lakes of Macun

Duration	6½–8½ hours
Distance	16km
Standard	medium-hard
Start	Lavin
Finish	Zernez

Summary This highly rewarding – if rather strenuous – day walk leads up from the main valley of the Engadine into the magical lakeland landscape of the Macun basin.

Set in an impressive cirque enclosed by numerous craggy peaks rising to over 3000m, this 3.6 sq km area sprinkled with almost two dozen Alpine lakes and tarns was added – as an isolated enclave – to the Swiss National Park on 1 August 2000. The Macun lies at around 2600m, and only the hardiest wild flowers and snow grasses can survive in the area's harsh high-Alpine climatic conditions.

This long day walk has a total ascent/descent of around 1400m. The highest part of the route leads along an exposed ridge at nearly 3000m, and the Macun area may remain snow-bound into June.

Maps

The recommended walking map is the Lower Engadine tourist authority's 1:50,000 *Wanderkarte Scuol* (Sfr16). K+F's 1:45,000 *Parc Naziunal Svizzer* (Sfr14) or K+F's 1:60,000 *Engadina Bassa/Unterengadin* (Sfr24.80) are other options. Otherwise, two SAW/FSTP 1:50,000 sheets are needed: *Ofenpass (Pass dal Fuorn)* No 259T and *Tarasp* No 249 (Sfr22.50 each).

NEAREST TOWN
Lavin

Lavin (1432m), situated directly south of Piz Buin above the En (Inn) River, is the start of the walk. Although largely destroyed by an 1869 fire, today Lavin is one of the most picturesque villages of the Engadine. Lavin's church has 16th-century frescoes and the ruins of Gonda, a village abandoned in the late medieval period, are just 15 minutes' walk away.

Lavin has a tourist office (☎/fax 081-862 20 40). The ***Hotel Crusch Alba*** *(☎ 081-862 26 53, fax 081-862 28 04)* has singles/doubles from 53/102. The ***Hotel Piz Linard*** *(☎ 081-862 26 26, fax 081-862 26 42)* is slightly more upmarket.

There are hourly train connections from Zürich via Landquart and Sagliains, just west of Lavin at the southern end of the new Vereina rail tunnel. Between late June and mid-October postbuses also run six times daily in either direction between Davos and Zernez (over the Flüelapass) via the nearby village of Susch, on the Engadine rail line 3.5km upvalley from Lavin.

GETTING TO/FROM THE WALK

For information on transport to/from Lavin see Nearest Town; for information on Zernez, see Access Towns at the start of the section.

THE WALK

See the Around the Swiss National Park map, p323

From the village square just below Lavin's train station (1412m), walk 250m down the main street to a barrel-like fountain, then proceed down left to cross the En (Inn) River on a roofed wooden bridge. Continue up to the right along the gravelled road for 1.25km past a tight bend, before leaving off left on a smaller forestry track that heads eastward under buzzing high-tension power lines to **Plan Surücha** (1577m).

A broad path rises on gently up the forested slopes, turning gradually southward to cross the **Aua da Zeznina** on a small wooden bridge a short way before reaching the stone cottage at **Alp Zeznina Daidant** (1958m), 1½ to two hours from Lavin. These pleasant Alpine meadows look out northward to the 3000m snowcapped peaks around Piz Buin, on whose southern slopes the side valleys of Val Sagliains, the Val Lavinuoz and the Val Tuoi drop steeply into the Engadine.

Make your way into the **Val Zeznina** past a trail going off left to Murtèra, then climb in numerous steep switchbacks through Alpine pastures strewn with alpenroses. The steep ascent continues via a gully filled with loose old moraines, but the gradient eventually eases as you rise up to a rustic shelter built against cliffs beside a tarn. Cross over the streamlet and continue along its rocky western banks to enter the national park. After passing a larger lake, the upper valley opens out into the undulating basin of **Macun**, 1¼ to 1¾ hours from Alp Zeznina Daidant.

The Macun is enclosed on three sides by a craggy mountain cirque. Numerous lakes and tarns lie hidden among the grassed-over moraine mounds, the highest of which is known in Romansch as the **Lai da la Mezza Glüna** (2631m). To the north, the glacier-clad mountains crowned by the 3312m Piz Buin make a spectacular backdrop to this exceptionally scenic place.

Cross the stream and follow the white-red-white markings southward up sparsely vegetated ridges of glacial debris. As it gets higher the route climbs over steeper slopes of coarse, loose rock, with occasional sections of scrambling that bring you up to the **Fuorcletta da Barcli**, a gap in the range at 2850m. From here traverse west along the rocky ridgetop to reach a minor peak at 2945m after 50 minutes to 1¼ hours.

This point makes a superb lookout. To the south-west the panorama stretches up the Engadine valley from Zernez immediately below as far as the glistening white outline of 4049m Piz Bernina, and to the south-east across the park's wild valleys to the 3899m Ortler in South Tirol, Italy. There is also a fine view back down into the Macun basin.

Trace a prominent spur running south-west directly from the summit, then drop away rightward out of the national park. The route leads down through rows of avalanche grids on the open slopes of **Munt Baselgia** to meet an alp track at **Plan Sech** (2268m). Apart from occasional short-cuts at some of the curves keep to this (gradually improving) road, making a long serpentine descent into the mixed coniferous forest via **La Rosta** and **God Baselgia**. The final stretch leads out onto grassy fields just above the town, then down past the church to arrive at the main road in **Zernez** at 1471m after 2½ to three hours. The train station is a further 10 to 15 minutes' walk on to the left.

Val Cluozza

Duration	5–7 hours
Distance	13.5km
Standard	medium
Start	Vallun Chafuol
Finish	Zernez
Nearest Town	Scuol

Summary This lovely day (or better overnight) walk leads over the scenic Murter pass and down through the romantically wild Val Cluozza in the heart of the Swiss National Park.

The beautiful 22 sq km Val Cluozza was the first area set aside in the reserve that became the national park. Cloaked in forest of mountain pine and larch fringing scree slides that descend from (naturally) eroding dolomite ranges, the valley represents 100 years of regeneration since the

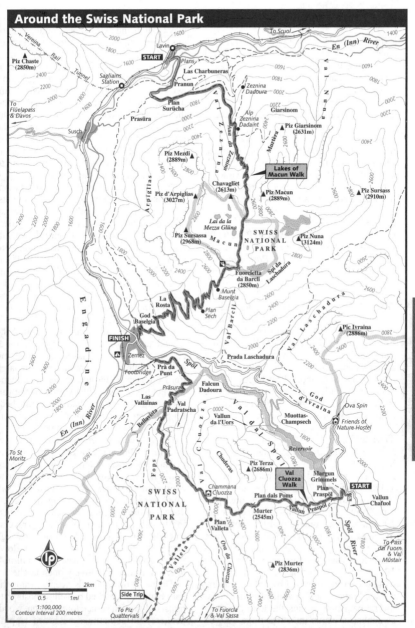

Around the Swiss National Park

To Scuol

En (Inn) River

Vereina Rail

Piz Chaste (2850m)

Lavin

START

Tunnel

Sagliains Station

Plans

Las Charbuneras

Pranun

To Flüelapass & Davos

Susch

Plan Surücha

Prasüra

Zeznina Dadoura

Alp Zeznina Dadaint

Giarsinom

Val da Zeznina

Val Nuna

Piz Mezdi (2889m)

Chavagliet (2613m)

Muritera

Piz Giarsinom (2631m)

Lakes of Macun Walk

Piz d'Arpiglias (3027m)

Piz Macun (2889m)

Piz Sursass (2910m)

Arpiglias

Lai da la Mezza Glüna

Macun

Piz Sursassa (2968m)

SWISS NATIONAL PARK

Piz Nuna (3124m)

Fuorcletta da Barcli (2850m)

Spi da Laschadura

La Rosta

Munt Baselgia

God Baselgia

Plan Sech

Val Barcli

Val Laschadura

Pic Ivraina (2886m)

FINISH

Engadine

Zernez

Prada Laschadura

Footbridge

Prà da Punt

Spöl

Präsura

Falcun Dadoura

Las Vallainas

Val Padratscha

Vallun da l'Uors

Val dal Spöl

God d'Ivraina

Ova Spin

Bellavista

Muottas-Champsech

Friends of Nature Hostel

Fops

Chuderas

Reservoir

En (Inn) River

To St Moritz

Val Cluozza

Piz Terza (2686m)

Val Cluozza Walk

Margun Grimmels

Plan Praspöl

START

SWISS NATIONAL PARK

Chammana Cluozza

Plan dals Poms

Yallun Praspöl

Vallun Chafuol

Spöl River

Murter (2545m)

Plan Valleta

Valletta

Piz Murter (2836m)

To Pass dal Fuorn & Val Müstair

Ova da Cluozza

Side Trip

To Piz Quattervals

To Fuorcla & Val Sassa

0   1   2km
0   0.5   1mi
1:100,000
Contour Interval 200 metres

GRAUBÜNDEN

Warning

There is no safe drinking water available on the sweaty first section of the hike, so carry something to drink. The walk involves ascents totalling around 1200m. The route crosses exposed terrain above the treeline, so watch for approaching bad weather.

park's establishment – when it was a barren wasteland completely stripped of trees. The lower Val Cluozza (whose Romansch name loosely translates as 'hole valley') forms a dramatically deep gorge, which the walk avoids in a high traverse.

Maps

Recommended is the SAW/FSTP 1:50,000 *Ofenpass (Pass dal Fuorn)* No 259T (Sfr22.50). K+F's 1:45,000 *Parc Naziunal Svizzer* (Sfr14) or 1:60,000 *Engadina Bassa/ Unterengadin* (Sfr24.80) also cover the walk.

GETTING TO/FROM THE WALK

The walk begins at Vallun Chafuol on the Pass dal Fuorn (Ofenpass) road. Postbuses from Zernez to Müstair pass Vallun Chafuol (the fourth bus stop from Zernez) up to a dozen times daily. At Vallun Chafuol there is parking space for about 30 vehicles.

For information on transport to/from the end of the walk at Zernez, see Access Towns at the start of the section.

THE WALK

See the Around the Swiss National Park map, p323

From the north end of the parking area at Vallun Chafuol (1766m), follow the broad path down through the coniferous forest past a right turnoff to Margun Grimmels. After 10 minutes the route crosses a footbridge over a narrow gorge of the **Spöl River**, where it flows through gravelly channels into a small reservoir downstream. Climb five to 10 minutes to **Plan Praspöl** (1690m), a small natural clearing browsed by red deer. Here, a route branches off upvalley to Punt Periv.

The path now begins the long ascent in switchbacks via an indistinct ridge. As you

rise higher the mountain pine gradually gives way to larch and dwarf pine. Continue out of the treeline to the level grassy shoulder of **Plan dals Poms**, then cut up open rolling slopes frequented by complacent herds of chamois and ibex to reach **Murter** (2545m), two to 2¾ hours from Plan Praspöl. From this flat saddle you enjoy views down into the moraine-choked headwater valleys of the Val Cluozza and across the raw tops of the ranges to the west. The summits of Piz Laschadurella (3046m), Piz Sampuoir (3023m) and Piz Murters (3013m) rise up to the east, back across the valley of the Spöl. To conserve the fragile Alpine vegetation, stay inside the area marked by yellow posts.

First drop down south-west over grassy Alpine meadows, then make a winding descent north-west above the beautiful wild valley. The path dips down into forest to intersect with a mountain trail going off left to the Fuorcla Val Sassa and Piz Quattervals (see the Side Trip at the end of the walk description) just before arriving at the historic **Chamanna Cluozza** (☎ 081-856 16 89, 081-856 12 35) after 50 minutes to 1¼ hours.

Originally – and often still – called the Blockhaus Cluozza, this thoroughly modernised mountain hut dates from 1910 and stands unintrusively among graceful larch trees on a small terrace above the stream. The hut has a room with exhibits on the valley's natural history. There are dorm beds for Sfr25 and rooms from Sfr35 per person. Breakfast costs Sfr10 and dinner Sfr18.

Head on down to cross a footbridge over the small **Ova da Cluozza**, where recent avalanches have flattened out the vegetation. The route switchbacks and sidles up to a tiny grassy shelf. This natural lookout gives a nice view back along the valley. Take a refreshing sip from the nearby drinking trough fed by a small spring. Traverse smoothly on along the slopes of **Fops** high above the Ova da Cluozza, which flows through a deep canyon, past a (left) turnoff to Bellavista among lovely open larches.

The path now descends steeply near to the park boundary (marked by yellow posts) into moist old-growth spruce forest, where woodpeckers can sometimes be heard tapping away at the dead trunks. After passing a plaque dedicated to the conservationist Paul Sarasin, who led the movement to create the Swiss National Park, the path merges with a rough vehicle track.

At this point cut down right through terraced hayfields, passing under buzzing power cables to meet a narrow lane. This leads directly onto the river flats of **Prà da Punt** to recross the Spöl on a quaint roofed bridge at the main Pass dal Fuorn road, two to 2½ hours from the Chamanna Cluozza. Turn left and follow the road 15 to 20 minutes on past the National Park House into the centre of Zernez.

Side Trip: Ascent of Piz Quattervals

6½–8½ hours return, 12km return, 1283m ascent

The challenging side trip to the 3165m summit of Piz Quattervals – the highest peak (entirely) inside the national park – is exclusively for experienced Alpine walkers who set off early and in fine weather.

From the Chamanna Cluozza, follow the path south to Plan Valletta (1835m). Here a white-blue-white marked Alpine route leads off right (west) across the Ova da Cluozza (stream) and up into the Val Valletta. Where the markings end (at around 2100m), pick your way on through the raw, broken rock to the valley head. In early summer the final ascent is best made directly up the snowy slopes on the mountain's northern side. By late summer, however, when loose scree makes that route arduous, climbing via the north-west spur is preferable. The summit gives stunning panoramas of the Engadine peaks.

Other Walks

Dreibundstein

Medieval Graubünden was united under the loose alliance of the Rhaetian Dreibund, or 'three leagues'. On the 2160m Dreibundstein, a ridge top 7km south-west of Chur, a borderstone marks the point where the three leagues converged. The Dreibundstein also serves as a natural lookout with views of the surrounding mountains.

A four- to five-hour walk starts at Brambrüsch (1595m), directly accessible by cable car from Chur. The *Friends of Nature hostel (☎ 081-284 42 67)* has dorm beds for Sfr15. The route climbs up over the 2174m Furggabüel to the Dreibündstein, then continues via Alp dil Plaun to the village of Feldis/Veulden (1469m), from where a cable car descends to Rhäzüns on the main Chur–Filisur rail line.

Use the SAW/FSTP 1:50,000 *Sardona* No 247T (Sfr22.50).

Weissfluh

The 2834m Weissfluh stands immediately northwest of Davos. The range has been intensively developed for winter sports, and some walkers find the numerous ski lifts, cable cars and mountain railways a bit much. An easy and scenic three to 3½-hour route goes north from the upper station of the Schatzalp–Strelapass gondola lift via the Wasserscheid (pass) to the Weissfluhjoch (2686m), where the internationally famous Eidgenössisches Institut für Schnee- und Lawinenforschung (Federal Institute for Snow and Avalanche Research) is based. From here a side trip can be made on foot or by cable car to the summit of the Weissfluh. The walk continues past the Totalpsee Parsennhütte, then follows the Panoramaweg to Gotschnagrat, from where another cable car takes you down to Klosters. The best available walking map is the local tourist authority's 1:25,000 *Wanderkarte Davos* (Sfr29.50).

Scalettapass

Of Graubünden's many trans-Alpine routes the Scalettapass had the most fearsome reputation, and in winter avalanches could wipe out whole teams of mule-drivers. Although this historic crossing is rather less dangerous today, it is no less wild. The Swiss Alpine Marathon (**W** www .swissalpine.ch), a gruelling 78km circuit from Davos held in late July, crosses the Scalettapass, and in early summer walkers are sure to encounter athletes training for the event.

The route begins at Dürrboden (2007m), reached from Davos by infrequent postbuses. This summer hamlet has 300-year-old stables that once housed pack animals. The *Restaurant Dürrboden (☎ 081-416 34 14)* offers dorm beds for around Sfr25. The descent can be made through the Val Susauna to Cinuoschel/Brail, a station on the Rhaetian Railway's Engadine line. A popular alternative is to follow the marathon route west via the SAC's *Chamanna digl Kesch (☎ 081-407 11 34)* to Tuors Chants.

Two SAW/FSTP 1:50,000 maps cover the route: *Bergün* No 258T and (for the Val Susauna only) *Ofenpass* No 259T (Sfr22.50 each).

Pass da Sett/Septimerpass

The 2310m Pass da Sett (or Septimerpass in German) was once an important trans-Alpine trade route, but after the opening of the Gotthard railway in 1882 the old mule trail soon fell into disuse. The restoration of the route was completed for Switzerland's 700th anniversary in 1991, and today the Pass da Sett is one of Switzerland's most popular historic walkways. The start of this long day hike is the village of Bivio (1769m), at the foot of the main range of the Alps in the predominantly Romansch-speaking Sursés (Oberhalbstein) Valley. The name Bivio refers to the 'two ways' that lead via the Julierpass into the Engadine, and over the Pass da Sett into the Italian-speaking Val Bregaglia.

The route leads south from Bivio, rising at an agreeable rate through the pastures of the Val Tgavretga to the Pass da Sett, before making a shorter, steeper descent into the Val Maroz and on to the village of Casaccia (1485m). Unfortunately, high-tension transmission cables accompany walkers the whole way, detracting from the otherwise marvellous scenery.

A popular (and recommended) route variant goes east from the Pass da Sett over the Pass Lunghin to Maloja or Segl-Maria. This alterative not only avoids those unsightly cables, but allows a side trip up to Piz Lunghin, whose 2780m summit forms the watershed between three of Europe's major river systems (which flow into the North, Black and Mediterranean seas).

Postbuses run approximately hourly between Chur and Bivio; some services involve a change in Tiefencastel. There are postbus connections between Bivio and St Moritz via the Julierpass.

SAW/FSTP's 1:50,000 *Julierpass* No 268T (Sfr22.50) or the local tourist authority's 1:50,000 *Wanderkarte Bivio* (Sfr12) cover the walk.

Monstein to Filisur

Between Monstein and Filisur the railway runs along a deep and narrow gorge of the Landwasser River, and the completion of the line in 1909 was quite an achievement of engineering. Ducking through several long tunnels on the way, the railway has scarcely affected the natural attractiveness of the area, while the road takes an altogether different route high up the slopes on the opposite side of the valley. From Monstein train station (1346m) an easy and well-graded path rises and dips along the steep, forested southern slopes of the Landwasser. After passing through the hamlet of Jenisberg (1504m) the route descends to meet the railway at Wiesen station (1197m), then crosses the 90m-high Wiesener Viadukt bridge and continues on to Filisur (999m).

This is an easy day hike with an average walking time of 3½ hours. The SAW/FSTP 1:50,000 *Bergün* No 258T (Sfr22.50) shows the route.

Zervreilasee to Vals

Known for its hot springs since prehistoric times (and, more recently, for its bottled mineral water), the Valsertal was settled by Walsers in the 13th century. In the 1950s a dam was built in the upper Valsertal, flooding the historic summer village of Zervreila to create the Zervreilasee lake. The sharp pointed summit of the 2898m Zervreilahorn is the landmark peak of the upper valley. From the postbus stop at the Zervreilasee dam (1868m), a 4½- to 5½-hour high-level route leads up to the Guraletschsee, a lovely Alpine lake at 2409m. The descent is made via the Ampervreilsee and Selvasee lakes to Peil/Bodenhus, then along the road to Vals, the main village in the upper valley. The best walking map is the SAW/FSTP *Safiental* No 257T (Sfr22.50).

Hohenrätien & Carschenna

This easy circuit walk from Thusis takes you up to the fascinating ruins of Hohenrätien, on a terrace high above the Viamala gorge at 946m. In prehistoric times a pagan temple existed here, but after the arrival of Christianity the site developed into a fortified settlement with a church. The castle complex stands on the old transit route of the San Bernardino and Splügen passes and presumably later served as a control and toll post. With the construction of an alternative road on the Hinterrhein's left bank in the late 15th century, the Hohenrätien fell into ruin. The site has been extensively restored since the early 1970s.

Another feature of interest can be found 1.5km uphill near Crap Carschenna (1180m), where ancient rock markings are chiselled into smooth, glacier-polished slabs. The surprisingly intact patterns of concentric circles are believed to date back to Neolithic times, but their significance and exact origin is unknown. Visitors are requested not to stand on the rock slabs.

The descent leads through the forest to Campi, and thence via Sils back to Thusis. The average walking time is four hours. Use either the local tourist authority's 1:25,000 *Wanderkarte Thusis-Viamala-Heinzenberg* (Sfr16), the SAW/FSTP 1:50,000 *Safiental* No 257T (Sfr22.50), or K+F's 1:60,000 *Surselva* (Sfr24.80)

Sentiero Alpino Calanca

The Valle Mesolcina (Misox in German) and Val Calanca lie south of the 2065m Passo San Bernardino, one of the great trans-Alpine passes, in the Italian-speaking south-western corner of Graubünden. Separating these two southward-tilting valleys is the Calanca range. A superb medium-hard three-day (45km) route, the Sentiero Alpino Calanca (Calanca Höhenweg in German), leads from the village of San Bernardino (1608m), just below the pass, along the crest of the Calanca 'range to Santa Maria (966m), from where there are postbuses via Grono to Bellinzona. There are two self-caterers' huts en-route: the small *Rifugio Pian Grand*, where dorm beds cost Sfr12, and the *Capanna Buffalora* (☎ 091-828 14 67, ℮ *buffalora@bluewin.ch*) with dorm beds for Sfr20. K+F's 1:60,000 *Hinterrheintäler* (Sfr24.80) covers the route on one sheet. Otherwise use the SAW/FSTP's 1:50,000 *San Bernardino* No 267T (Sfr22.50) with the BL/OFT's standard 1:50,000 *Roveredo* No 277 (Sfr13.50).

Val Rosegg & Fuorcla Surlej

Graubünden's mountains seldom attain the lofty heights of the Alps in the Valais or the Bernese Oberland. The exception is the Bernina massif, a superb range of glacier-smothered mountains in the Upper Engadine that touches 4000m.

This long day (or overnight) walk leads south-west from Pontresina through lovely larch forests of the 5km-long Val Rosegg to the *Hotel Roseggletscher* (☎ 081-842 64 45), open June to mid-October, which offers upmarket rooms but has dorm accommodation for Sfr35. The route then climbs diagonally up the slopes to the 2755m Fuorcla Surlej, where the *Berghaus Fuorcla Surlej* (☎ 081-842 63 03), open early July to late September, also has dorm beds. From this high, narrow pass the views across to the Bernina massif include the classic knife-edge form of the Biancograt, one of the finest snow ridges in the Alps. The descent can be made by cable car from the 2699m middle station at Murtel (Sfr14) or on foot via the tarn of Lej da la Fuorca.

A worthwhile side trip goes to the *Chamanna Coaz* (☎ 081-842 62 78), an SAC hut at 2610m. The best walking map is the SAW/FSTP 1:50,000 *Julierpass* No 268T (Sfr22.50).

Val Bregaglia Sentiero Panoramico

The Val Bregaglia (Bergell in German) is an Italian-speaking valley on the western side of the Passo del Maloja (Malojapass). The Sentiero Panoramico leads through mixed forest and mountain pastures on the northern slopes of the Val Bregaglia. This five-hour 'panoramica route' from Casaccia (1458m) passes through the hamlets of Braga, Rotticio, Durbegia and Parlongh to end at the village of Soglio (1097m), from where there are postbuses back toward St Moritz.

Casaccia's *Hotel Stampa* (☎ 081-844 31 62, fax 081-824 34 74) has singles/doubles from Sfr50/100. In Soglio, the *Pensione Garni Chesa Mürias* (☎ 081-822 17 37, fax 081-822 15 00) has rooms from Sfr55/110.

Two walking maps covering the route are the SAW/FSTP *Julierpass* No 268T (Sfr22.50) and K+F's 1:60,000 *Oberengadin* (Sfr24.80).

Val da Camp/Poschiavo

Lying beyond the Passo di Bernina (Bernina Pass), the Val Poschiavo (Puschlav in German) is – like the Val Bregaglia – another of Graubünden's Italian-speaking valleys and one of Switzerland's remotest corners. The Val da Camp (or Val Campo), a small and quite enchanting side valley of the Val Poschiavo, has unusually rich flora with a decidedly south-eastern Alpine character.

From the hamlet of Sfazù, a narrow road and walking route lead up through lovely forests and pastures past the SAC's *Rifugio Saoseo* (☎ 081-844 07 66) to Alp Camp (2070m), where the *Ostello Crameri* (☎ 081-844 04 82, ℮ *riservazione @valdicampo.ch*) also has dorm beds for Sfr30. A minibus service runs between Sfazù and Alp Camp (Sfr11/15 one-way/return – no passes, no adult concessions; booking is essential (☎ 081-844 10 42, 079-405 91 28). Lago di Saoseo, an emerald-green lake formed when a section of the nearby Cima di Saoseo collapsed into the valley, is less than one hour upvalley from Alp Camp. You can then continue up past the larger lake of Lagh da Val Viola over the 2432m Pass da Val Viola to the *Rifugio Viola* (☎ 0039-342-985136, ℮ *fraquell@valtline.it)*, a mountain hut just inside Italian territory (five to six hours from Sfazù) with dorm beds (IL15,000, €7.75) and meals (from IL10,000, €5.15).

The best walking map is the new 1:40,000 *Val Poschiavo* (about Sfr15). K+F's 1:60,000 *Unterengadin* (Sfr24.80) is a reasonable alternative.

Val Mora & Val Vau

Although they lie directly behind a low range just to the south of the Val Müstair, the two tiny valleys of the Val Mora and Val Vau are relatively little visited by walkers and make gentle and very pleasant walking country. A five to six-hour walk through the Val Mora leads from Süsom Givè, at the Pass dal Fuorn. The route passes Jufplaun before crossing over the gentle pass of Döss Radond (2234m) and descending via the narrow Val Vau to Santa Maria. A longer but worthwhile route variant goes up from Döss Radond past the Lai da Rims, a majestic Alpine lake at 2420m, then drops back down to the Val Vau.

The SAW/FSTP's 1:50,000 *Ofenpass* No 259T (Sfr22.50) best covers the route.

GRAUBÜNDEN

North-Eastern Switzerland

Stretching southward from the rolling green Alpine foothills of the Swiss Mittelland and Lake Constance, the mountains of North-Eastern Switzerland – in the cantons of Glarus (the 'Glarnerland'), St Gallen and the two half-cantons of Appenzell (the 'Appenzellerland') – offer some of the most varied and interesting walking in the country. The Walensee (Lake Walen), a large Alpine lake in a long and deep glacial trough, divides the Alpstein and Churfirsten to its north from the Sarganserland and Glarner Alps region on the lake's southern side.

INFORMATION
Maps
Sheet No 2 of the BL/OFT's (four-sheet) 1:200,000 series covers North-Eastern Switzerland.

Information Sources
St Gallen's tourist office (☎ 071-227 37 37, fax 071-227 37 67, ℮ info@stgallen-i.ch), Bahnhofplatz 1a, is responsible for information on North-Eastern Switzerland. The regional Web site for North-Eastern Switzerland (W www.ostschweiz-i.ch) has links to tourist sites in all of the region's cantons.

For information on the Appenzellerland, contact either the tourist office in Appenzell (☎ 071-788 96 41, ℮ infotourismus@ai.ch) or the Stein tourist office(☎ 071-368 50 50, ℮ infotourismus@ar.ch) or try their joint Web site (W www.MyAppenzellerland.ch). The Web site W www.glarusnet.ch covers the Glarnerland.

GETTING AROUND
The *Appenzellerland-Toggenburg* regional pass costs Sfr78 (Sfr63 for holders of Swiss railpasses) for three days within a seven-day period, or Sfr98 (Sfr63) for five days over 15 days. On the selected days it gives unlimited travel on all public transport within the entire region stretching from Lake Constance (Bodensee) to the Walensee. Outside

Highlights

The peaks of the Churfirsten fall away in high escarpments on their southern sides.

- Looking out across the waters of the Fälensee under the Alpstein massif's towering peaks on the Zwinglipass walk

- Contemplating the tranquil beauty of the Fischersee on the Murgseefurggel walk

- Retracing (less painfully) the steps of General Suvorov on the crossing of the scenic Panixerpass

- Looking up in awe at the majestic Churfirsten peaks above the Walensee

the selected days of travel full-price fares must be paid.

The new *Ostwind* integrated regional transport network (see St Gallen under Gateway later) covers almost as large an area as the regional pass.

The *Ferienkarte Region Linth-Schwyz-Glarus* gives three days free postbus travel within a one-week period and costs Sfr25 (Sfr16 for children and with Half Fare Card).

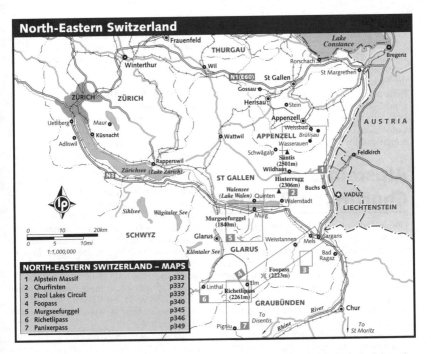

North-Eastern Switzerland

It covers the region from the eastern Zürich-see (Lake Zürich) and western Walensee south to the Klöntalersee and Brunni (in Schwyz Canton).

The *Heidiland Wanderpass* costs from Sfr55 for three consecutive days or Sfr95 for six days in one month, and gives free travel on all lake ferries (Walensee), mountain lifts and postbuses in the Sarganserland region, between Filzbach and Bad-Ragaz.

GATEWAY
St Gallen

St Gallen (also called St Gall in English) is North-Eastern Switzerland's only city and the region's transport hub. St Gallen's old town is worth exploring. The superb 18th-century cathedral has enormous twin towers and interesting ceiling frescoes. The Historical Museum (entry Sfr6/2 adults/students) gives a good introduction to the city.

For more information contact the tourist office (☎ 071-227 37 37, fax 071-227 37 67,

info@stgallen-i.ch), Bahnhofplatz 1a. Two good local outlets for outdoor gear are Transa (☎ 071-222 36 66, outdoor .stgallen@transa.ch), St Leonhardstrasse 20, and Ochsner Sport (☎ 071-310 09 88), Im West Center, Winkeln.

Places to Stay & Eat In nearby Wittenbach, *Camping Leebrücke* (☎ *071-298 49 69*) has tent sites for Sfr6 plus Sfr5.60 per person. The *youth hostel* (☎ *071-245 47 77,* *st.gallen@youthhostel.ch, Juchstrasse 25*) has dorm beds from Sfr24. The *Hotel Weisses Kreuz* (☎*/fax 071-223 28 43, Engelgasse 9*) has singles/doubles from Sfr45/80. The *Hotel Elite Garni* (☎ *071-222 12 36, fax 071-222 21 77, Metzgergasse 9–11*) offers rooms from Sfr60/100.

Restaurants in the *Migros* supermarket on St Leonhardstrasse, the *Manor department store* on Marktgasse and the *EPA* department store at Bohl 6 all have budget self-service food. The popular *Wirtschaft Zur*

NORTH-EASTERN SWITZERLAND

Alten Post on Gallusstrasse serves Swiss cuisine for around Sfr25 per main course.

Getting There & Away St Gallen is the terminus of the SBB's main rail line through the Swiss Mittelland to Geneva via Zürich, Bern and Lausanne. St Gallen's new *Ostwind* S-Bahn, a regional rail network with integrated fares, links the city with Lake Constance (Bodensee), the Alpstein (Säntis) region and the Rhine Valley.

Alpstein & Churfirsten Region

Dominated by the 2503m summit of the Säntis, the compact group of limestone ranges known as the Alpstein are the northernmost mountains of the Swiss Alps and form a very spectacular and interesting region. These impressive rock peaks jut up so abruptly from the more gently contoured hills of the Appenzellerland and Toggenburg that their relatively low height is not obvious.

Separated only by the valley of Obertoggenburg, the nearby Churfirsten are no less majestic. From the north this unique range appears as a serrated row of individual mountains divided by deep grassy saddles, yet when viewed from the Walensee the Churfirsten present a seemingly impenetrable barrier.

The Alpstein and Churfirsten are geologically very similar, being composed of hard limestone originating from the ancient Tethys ocean. These mountains are also of relatively recent origin, having been gradually uplifted and buckled from around 10 million years ago by tectonic forces into their remarkable form. The Alpstein and Churfirsten have perhaps the best conditions for Alpine rock climbing in Switzerland, although humble walkers still greatly outnumber the alpinists.

Books

The only regional walking guides available are in German. Kümmerly + Frey's (K+F) *Rundwanderungen Schweiz* (Sfr22.80), and *20 Bergwanderungen Region Ostschweiz* (Sfr29.90) by Bruno Rauch & Rudolf Bahler (Werdverlag), includes easy to medium walks in the Alpstein region, Glarner Alps, St Galler Oberland and Liechtenstein.

ACCESS TOWNS
Appenzell

Although very touristy, Appenzell, which is the capital of the (Catholic) half-canton of Appenzell-Innerrhoden, makes a nice temporary walking base. The streets and lanes of this very small town are lined with quaint old Appenzeller houses, many with elaborately painted facades. Also worth a visit are the baroque St Mauritius church, which has beautiful stained glass, and the 16th-century town hall. A nice half-day hike from Appenzell climbs south-west along the sandstone ridges via Scheidegg to the 1652m lookout summit of Kronberg, from where a cable car descends to the train station at Jakobsbad.

For information, contact the tourist office (☎ 071-788 96 41, fax 071-788 96 50, e info tourismus@ai.ch, w www.ai.ch/tourismus), Hauptgasse 4.

Accommodation is expensive. *Camping Eischen* (☎ *071-787 50 30,* e *info@eischen.ch)* has tent sites from Sfr9 plus Sfr6.10 per person. The *Hotel Stossplatz* (☎ *071-787 15 07,* e *stossplatz@mhs.ch, Riedstrasse 13)* has rooms for Sfr70/120. The *Gasthaus Hof* (☎ *071-787 22 10,* e *info@gasthaus-hof.ch, Engelgasse 4)* and the *Hotel Traube* (☎ *071-787 14 07,* e *info@hotel-traube.ch, Marktgasse 7)* both charge from Sfr85/130.

Appenzell is most easily accessible by roughly hourly trains (the narrow-gauge Appenzeller Bahn) from St Gallen via either Herisau or Gais.

Wildhaus

Wildhaus (1090m) is the main tourist centre of the upper Toggenburg (or Thur Valley). Originally a Walser settlement, this scenic village lies scattered along the Nesslau–Buchs road between the Alpstein massif and the Churfirsten. Urich Zwingli, the 16th-century religious reformer, came from Wildhaus, and his birthplace, the Zwinglihaus, is one of the oldest wooden buildings in Switzerland. The 87km Toggenburger Höhenweg walking route runs from Wil through the Toggenburg to Wildhaus, and the Rheintal-Höhenweg, a 115km walk along the Rhine Valley from Rorschach (on Lake Constance) to Sargans, passes through Wildhaus.

Wildhaus has the regional tourist office (☎ 071-999 99 11, e info@toggenburg.org, w www.toggenburg.org).

800m along the road toward Buchs, *Camping Schafbergblick* (☎ *071-999 19 34*) has tent sites for Sfr3 plus Sfr4 per person. The *Hotel Rösliwies* (☎*/fax 071-999 11 92*) offers rooms for Sfr40 per person.

The *Zwinglizentrum* (☎ *071-998 68 68,* w *www.zwinglizentrum.ch)*, a large Friends of Nature hotel on Steinrutistrasse, has rooms from Sfr80 per person with full board.

Postbuses running between Buchs (train connections to Sargans/Zürich, Altstätten/St Gallen and Chur) and Nesslau (train connections to Wil/Zürich) pass through Wildhaus approximately every hour until shortly after 9pm.

Säntis

Duration	4¼–5½ hours
Distance	9km
Standard	medium-hard
Start	Wasserauen
Finish	Säntis summit
Nearest Town	Schwägalp

Summary This walk takes you up through a tiny valley between the ranges of the Alpstein to the top of the Säntis, which was the main access route before the construction of the cable car from Schwägalp.

The 2503m Säntis is a northern outpost of the Alps and the highest peak in the Alpstein. In good conditions the summit – with its prominent telecommunications tower – is clearly visible from Zürich and southern Germany. For more than 100 years there has been a meteorological station on the Säntis, and the original weatherperson's house still sits on the summit.

This is an energetic day walk requiring a good level of fitness as it makes an often steep ascent totalling over 1600m. Those wanting something less strenuous can do the walk in the opposite direction in rather less time, but the constant descent can be hard on the knees. The going is easier in late summer and autumn, when less snow will be encountered.

Maps

Best for this walk is either St Gallische Wanderwege's 1:25,000 sheet *Wanderkarte Obertoggenburg-Appenzell* (Sfr27), or the SAW/FSTP's 1:50,000 *Appenzell* No 227T (Sfr22.50). Other good options are K+F's 1:40,000 *Säntis-Alpstein* (Sfr12) or 1:60,000 *St Gallen-Toggenburg Appenzellerland* (Sfr24.80), which covers a much broader swathe of North-Eastern Switzerland, including the Churfirsten area to the south.

NEAREST TOWNS
Wasserauen

This tiny village is at the railway terminus from Appenzell (see Access Towns earlier). *Hotel Bahnhof* (☎ *071-799 11 07,* e *hotel bahnhof@swissweb.ch)* has a good restaurant and singles/doubles for Sfr60/120.

There are roughly hourly train connections (Appenzeller Bahnen) from St Gallen via Herisau and Appenzell; if you're arriving by train from Graubünden, you'll travel via Sargans and Altstätten.

Schwägalp

Schwägalp (1352m) lies at the western foot of the Säntis around the lower cable-car station. *Hotel Schwägalp* (☎ *071-365 66 01,* e *kontakt@saentisbahn.ch)* by the lower cable-car station has dorm beds for Sfr39 and singles/doubles for Sfr90/155. The *Hotel Passhöhe* (☎ *071-364 12 43)* charges Sfr75/120 for its better-standard rooms. Guests staying at either hotel are eligible for a 50% discount on the Säntis cable car.

From Schwägalp there are some 10 postbuses per day to Urnäsch (with train connections to Herisau/St Gallen/Zürich) and up to seven buses daily to Nesslau (train connections to Wil/Zürich). In summer the last bus to Urnäsch leaves at around 6.20pm and to Nesslau at around 6.30pm. Reservations (made at least 30 minutes in advance) are necessary for some postbus services (☎ 071-994 18 47).

GETTING TO/FROM THE WALK

For information on transport to Wasserauen see Nearest Towns earlier. The walk ends on the 2503m summit of the Säntis. Cable cars (W www.saentisbahn.ch) run at least half-hourly from the Säntis down to Schwägalp from 7.30am until 6.30pm between late May and around 23 October (until 7pm in July

and August). The one-way downward fare is Sfr19 (or Sfr9.50 for children and holders of the Half Fare Card and most railpasses).

THE WALK

See the Alpstein Massif map

From Wasserauen railway station (868m), follow the sealed road through the narrow valley alongside the Schwendlibach stream, passing many typical Appenzell-style shingled houses and a small electricity station at Rössenaueli. Where the stream flows through the **Schwendlibachschlucht** (gorge), the road heads up through patches of light

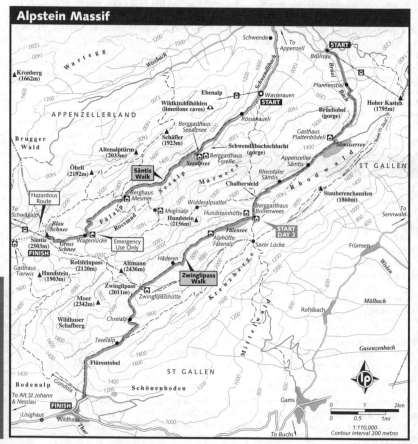

Alpstein Massif

forest to reach the **Seealpsee** (1141m) after 50 minutes to one hour. With the Säntis as a backdrop, this appealing lake nestles between craggy ranges of the Alpstein and makes a delightful spot for a rest and a snack. In hot weather the Seealpsee is suitable for bathing.

By the lakeshore are the ***Berggasthaus Seealpsee*** (☎ *071-799 11 40)* and the ***Berggasthaus Forelle*** (☎ *071-799 11 88)*. Both are open from early May to late October and offer singles/doubles for around Sfr50/90 and dorm beds for around Sfr19/27 children/adults.

Take the dirt farm road around the northern shore of the Seealpsee, continuing gently uphill across the **Seealp**. Past landslides off the peaks above have left these lovely meadows strewn with heavy boulders that now shelter small alp huts from avalanches and further rock fall. Where the vehicle track finishes near the Seealp's southeastern corner, a white-red-white marked path begins climbing in short spirals through a tiny steep gully fringed by abrupt bluffs. Shortly after passing a spring, where the small stream emerges from moraines, you come to **Unter Mesmer** (1613m), 1¼ to 1½ hours from the lake. Here the ***Berghaus Mesmer*** (☎ *071-799 12 55)*, open late May to mid-October, offers dorm bunks for Sfr24 (but no showers).

Continue up into the **Fälalp**, an enclosed upper basin of recent glacial origin where snow often lasts well into the season. The cut path sidles along cliffs to the right of a talus-choked sink with the red and white colours of the Säntis' telecommunications tower looming ahead, before making its way up an elongated rocky, grassy mound. A steep climb left brings you through loose slopes below a cross erected atop a rock needle on the Rossmad ridge, to reach the **Wagenlücke** (2072m) after 1¼ to 1½ hours. There is a small stone shelter here for emergency use.

Head westward to the left of the ridge, rising steadily against the contour, to bare rock slopes above the Gross Schnee, one of only two small (and gradually receding) glaciers within the Alpstein massif. The route now makes a final zigzagging ascent through the rock (with sections of fixed cable to ease the nerves) to arrive at a platform immediately below the **Säntis**, after one to 1½ hours.

As has been obvious for most of the way up, the mountaintop is crowded with the weather station, telecommunications tower, restaurant and cable-car buildings. On an average summer day this summit is teeming with cable-car visitors, but walkers can take pride that such artificial means will only be used for the descent. In clear conditions the panoramic views are stupendous in all directions, stretching southward across the nearby peaks of the Churfirsten to the Alps, west to Zürichsee, eastward to the mountains of Vorarlberg as well as north toward Lake Constance.

The only accommodation on the summit is the ***Berggasthaus Säntis*** (☎ *071-799 11 60)*, with singles/doubles for Sfr55/110 and dorm beds for Sfr35; there are only basic washing facilities.

The two-hour walk down to Schwägalp is extremely steep in places and requires considerable balance and surefootedness. The path passes the ***Gasthaus Tierwies*** (☎ *071-364 12 35)*, open late June to late October, with dorm beds for Sfr29 with breakfast. Schwägalp's Alpine dairy museum, the **Alpschaukäserei** (☎ *071-365 65 40)*, gives practical demonstrations of Appenzell and Toggenburg cheese-making methods and culture.

Zwinglipass

Duration	2 days
Distance	17.5km
Standard	medium
Start	Brülisau
Finish	Wildhaus
Nearest Town	Appenzell

Summary This walk through a picturesque corner of the Alpstein massif crosses a broad pass leading into the Toggenburg region at the northern foot of the Churfirsten.

Leading past the idyllic (if rather different) mountain lakes of the Sämtisersee and

Karst

Karst is a greyish type of limestone rock. In many places throughout the Swiss Alps, jagged slab-like formations known as karst fields (*Karrenfelder* in German) are found. These form when rainwater, which contains carbonic acid, seeps through the limestone, slowly dissolving it, and have been likened to petrified glaciers. A particularly interesting phenomenon encountered in ranges composed of karst are so-called doline depressions. These form when a large subterranean cavern produced by water seepage collapses into itself, leaving a broad hollow where water may accumulate to create a lake. The Alpstein massif, and the ranges around the Thunersee and Brienzersee (Lake Thun and Lake Brienz), the Swiss Jura and the Fribourg and Vaud Pre-Alps generally have the best examples of karst formations.

Fälensee, the route climbs through interesting karst fields (see the boxed text 'Karst' later). On the heights of the 2011m Zwinglipass this porous rock has formed interesting sinkholes. The Zwinglipass is lower than the nearby Säntis route, and the walk can normally be undertaken from around early June until early November.

Maps

For recommended walking maps, see the Säntis walk earlier.

NEAREST TOWN
Brülisau

This is a tiny village at the foot of the Alpstein. *Gasthaus Rössli* (☎ 071-799 11 04) has singles/doubles for Sfr60/110. Brülisau is best reached by train connections from St Gallen (via Herisau) or Appenzell (see Access Towns earlier) to Weissbad (on the Appenzell–Wasserauen line), from where there are at least hourly postbuses to Brülisau until just after 5.30pm.

GETTING TO/FROM THE WALK

For information on transport to/from Wildhaus, see Access Towns earlier.

A popular alternative to Day 1 involves taking the Hoher Kasten cable car from Brülisau (922m), then walking south-west from the upper station (1795m) along the ridge via the 1860m Stauberenchanzlen and the saddle of Saxer Lücke (1649m) to the Fälensee. This route offers some wonderful views of the Rhine Valley.

THE WALK

See the Alpstein Massif map, p332

Day 1: Brülisau to Berggasthaus Bollenwees

2¼–2¾ hours, 7.5km, 548m ascent

From the lower Hoher Kasten cable-car station follow the signposted sealed road southeast, quickly crossing underneath the wires, past scattered wooden-shingled houses in the green fields to **Pfannenstiel** (940m). The quiet dirt road leads into the forested Brüeltobel gorge, rising up over a watershed to reach the quaint old *Gasthaus Plattenbödeli* (☎ 071-799 11 52, e info@plattenboedli.ch) after one to 1¼ hours. This simple mountain hotel at 1279m has dorm beds for Sfr27 and singles/doubles for Sfr47/94 (prices include breakfast and showers).

About 50m on take a path (signposted 'Waldabstieg') down left to the **Sämtisersee**, making your way around the shoreline to meet the road again on flowery paddocks at the lake's upper side. Sandwiched between steep forested slopes, the Sämtisersee is one of the most attractive natural spots in the Alpstein massif, and in summer its shallow waters are generally warm enough for bathing.

Bear right at a fork at **Appenzeller Sämtis**, and head on toward the main peaks of the Alpstein through a charming little valley in which the stream flows through a terraced trench. The old dirt track peters out at the farmlet of **Rheintaler Sämtis** (1295m), and a foot track marked with red and white paint splashes continues up to the grassy flats of **Chalberweid** below impressive rock spikes of the Marwees ridge. Ignoring trails going off right to the Bogartenlücke and the Widderalpsattel ahead, ascend southward via a steep gully onto a tiny saddle from where the stark, elongated form of the **Fälensee** comes into view, 1¼ to 1½ hours from the Gasthaus Plattenbödeli.

A short way ahead at 1470m stands the scenic *Berggasthaus Bollenwees* (☎ *071-799 11 70)*. This large mountain hotel looks out across the deep-blue lake Fälensee, a typical karst lake, which drains away subterraneously to fill an enclosed glacial trough below towering craggy ranges. The Berggasthaus is open from early May to late October, and has singles/doubles for Sfr58/116 and dorm beds for Sfr28; showers are available.

Day 2: Berggasthaus Bollenwees to Wildhaus

3¼–4¼ hours, 10km, 966m ascent

Head around the Fälensee's northern edge, sidling across broad scree fields that slide right into the water to reach the rustic *Alphütte Fälenalp* at the lake's far end. Here, walkers can sleep in the hay barn during the summer months for around Sfr6.

Braving avalanches and rock fall, in season the alp huts of this romantic isolated pasture have milk for sale. Above you, spectacular needles protrude from the almost overhanging rock walls of the Hundstein (2156m). Continue on past marmot colonies in the tiny upper valley, before beginning quite a steep climb along a vague grassy ridge leading up to the three stone shelters of **Häderen** at 1738m, one to 1¼ hours from the Bollenwees.

The route now rises more gently through long fields of karst, with good views ahead to the rounded 2436m Altmann, the Alpstein's second-highest summit. After passing through a dry-stone fence marking the Appenzell–St Gallen cantonal border, cross over the **Zwinglipass** (2011m), a rocky, grassy plateau full of depressions and sinkholes, then descend briefly leftward to arrive at the *Zwinglipasshütte* (☎ *071-988 28 02)*, 40 to 50 minutes on. This self-catering hut owned by the SAC is staffed only on summer weekends (but is always open), and sits at 1985m on a lookout terrace opposite the majestic peaks of the Churfirsten.

Drop down the grassy mountainside, moving over to the left past **Chreialp**

(1817m), a group of herder's huts standing below sheer cliffs opposite a prominent rock needle. The well-formed path now makes a much steeper descent in numerous switchbacks to reach the dairy of **Teselalp** (1433m) at the end of a farm track in a pleasant upper valley, after 50 minutes to 1¼ hours.

Follow the dirt road for 1.25km to where a signposted foot track departs at the left. Make your way 400m down via the small dry chasm known as **Flürentobel**, before branching away to the right through little clearings in the spruce forest to meet another road near a gondola lift. Continue down, short-cutting the odd curve in the road to arrive at **Wildhaus**, 50 to 60 minutes from Teselalp. The village centre (1090m) is a short way down to the right along the main road.

Churfirsten

Duration	3¾–5 hours
Distance	13km
Standard	easy-medium
Start	Knoblisbühl Höhenklinik
Finish	Walenstadt

Summary This traverse route explores the high slopes between the Walensee and the main Churfirsten range, offering classic views of both.

The Churfirsten form one of the most striking ranges found anywhere in the Alps. Seen from the south this amazing row of horn-like peaks rises up as an abrupt barrier separating the Walensee from the Toggenburg region. The rock strata of the Churfirsten read like a textbook covering that last 100 million years of geological history. Its oldest sedimentary rocks were laid down in the 'Helvetic basin' that once existed in the area of today's Glarner Alps, and fossils of ancient marine life can be found on the summits.

Much of the route is out of the trees on open slopes with a southerly exposure, so during the middle of the day the going may get a bit hot. The southern side of the Churfirsten is generally snow-free by mid-May, making this a good walk to do in spring.

Warning

During summer and autumn military shooting exercises are conducted in the Schrina area. Access is guaranteed, but walkers may have to wait up to an hour before the sentry guides you through the firing range. For times and dates, call the Swiss Army's regional information office in Sargans-Mels (☎ 081-725 11 95, W www .vbs.admin.ch/internet/Heer/e/index.htm).

Maps

The best coverage is provided by the St Gallische Wanderwege 1:25,000 *Wanderkarte Sarganserland Walensee* (Sfr27); the 1:50,000 *Wanderkarte St Galler Oberland-Toggenburg* No 5015 (Sfr27) is also very good. Other options are the SAW/FSTP's 1:50,000 *Walenstadt* No 237T (Sfr22.50) and K+F's 1:60,000 *St Gallen-Toggenburg Appenzellerland* (Sfr24.80).

NEAREST TOWN
Walenstadt

This attractive small town is at the foot of the Churfirsten where the Seez flows into the Walensee. Of particular interest in the well-preserved historical centre are the old town hall and the church dating from the 8th century. Parts of the old town walls remain.

For information, contact the tourist office (☎/fax 081-735 22 22, e at@alpintravel.ch, W www.walenstadt.ch), Bahnhofstrasse 19.

Lakeside tent sites are available at *See-Camping Walenstadt* (☎ 081-735 12 12). *Hotel Krone* (☎ 081-735 11 70) charges Sfr35/70 per single/double. Rooms at *Hotel Lowen* (☎ 081-735 11 80) are Sfr40/76.

Walenstadt is on the main Zürich–Chur rail line, serviced at least hourly by expresses. From the small harbour you can catch one of the ferry boats that ply the Walensee, stopping at many villages around the lakeshore.

GETTING TO/FROM THE WALK

Postbuses run from Walenstadt train station to Knoblisbühl up to seven times per day, the last leaving at around 5.30pm. One of the morning buses continues up to Hochrugg if there are enough passengers.

THE WALK

From where the postbus lets you off at the **Knoblisbühl Höhenklinik** (approximately 960m), follow the sealed road uphill through the forest, short-cutting occasional curves. The road climbs out onto the open hillsides scattered with holiday houses and farmhouses before coming to the *Bergrestaurant Schrina* (☎ 081-735 16 30) at Hochrugg (1290m) after one to 1¼ hours. This large restaurant (open July and August) offers rather basic rooms for around Sfr35 and – when not taken over by the military – dorm beds for around Sfr25.

A short walk from here is the Paxmal, an interesting mosaic monument dedicated to peace, which was completed by artist Karl Bickel in 1949 after 25 years of work.

Continue a farther 1km up the road to where a signposted path departs on your right. Follow this over the grassy pastures of **Rutz**, then spiral up along a steep cowtrodden track to a piped spring spilling into a water trough. Head on eastward over the **Schrina** ridge, passing the stone cottage and barn at **Obersäss** (1727m) after 50 minutes to 1¼ hours. Far below lie the sparkling-blue waters of the Walensee, while ahead and directly above you the majestic rock walls of the Churfirsten present a dramatic outline.

Make your way along a broad, undulating balcony fringed by scree slides at the base of the Churfirsten. The trail rises gently over **Palis**, at 1641m on a minor spur running off the main range, then gradually drops against the contour through light coniferous forest to meet an alp track at the *Restaurant Tschingla* (☎ 081-735 21 61) at 1527m, 50 minutes to one hour on from Obersäss. The restaurant is open from early June to late September, and has a few singles/doubles for Sfr45/90 and dorm beds for around Sfr25.

The narrow dirt road sidles steadily around the slopes down past the picturesque isolated farmhouses of **Hinter Büls** and **Vorder Büls** to a stone cottage at **Brunnen** (1319m) after one to 1¼ hours. Descend into the beech forest to intersect with the better-transited road to Lüsis, which brings you down in increasingly long serpentine bends to a right-hand foot track.

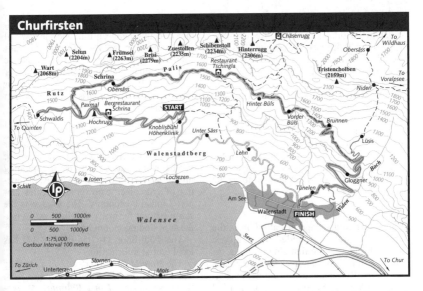

This path, marked with yellow diamonds, drops down beside meadows and tiny vineyards on the upper slopes of Walenstadt. Laneways lead past the high-steepled church to the soldiers' memorial fountain in the old centre of Walenstadt, one to 1¼ hours on. The train station is 10 minutes' walk southward along the main street.

Sarganserland & Glarner Alps

The small canton of Glarus essentially consists of the drainage basin of the Linthal. This long and deep Alpine valley stretches southward from the western end of the Walensee right up to the Glarner Alps. The Sarganserland includes the fascinating Murgtal, the Weisstannental and Pizol areas.

Together, the Sarganserland and Glarner Alps lie sandwiched between the Walensee and the line of high snowcapped peaks running west-to-east along the cantonal border with Graubünden, from the mighty summits of the Tödi and Clariden to the 2806m Calanda. At Sargans, on its eastern edge, the Sarganserland is bordered by the broad valley of the Rhine, while to the west the Glarner Alps converge with the slab-rock ranges of Schwyz and Uri Cantons. Although it's often overlooked by walkers from abroad, this region offers some particularly fine mountain scenery and numerous classic hikes.

ACCESS TOWNS
Sargans-Mels
These twin towns lie at around 500m on the flat watershed between the Swiss Rhine and the smaller Seez, the river draining the Weisstannental. Sargans was largely reconstructed after a disastrous inferno in 1811, and includes the onion-domed St Oswald church and the classic Gallatihaus; however, the prominent fortified castle overlooking the old town dates from the 13th century. Neighbouring Mels is somewhat smaller than Sargans, and has many charming old buildings clustered around the Dorfplatz. Of historical interest in Mels are the early 18th-century St Peter's parish church and the Capuchin monastery completed in 1654.

For information, contact the tourist office (☎ 081-723 53 30, W www.sargans.ch),

Stadtchenstrasse 1, or the regional Sarganserland ('Heidiland') tourist office (☎ 081-720 08 20, ℮ info@heidiland.net, ⓦ www.heidiland.net), Zurcherstrasse 11.

In Sargans, *Hotel Post* (☎ 081-720 47 47, ℮ info@hotelpost-sargans.ch) has singles/doubles from around Sfr45/90. In Mels, the *Gasthaus zum Löwen* (☎ 081-723 12 06) has rooms from around Sfr40/80.

An important transport hub, Sargans is on the main Zürich–Chur rail line. You can also reach Sargans by train from Lake Constance via St Margrethen. Postbuses run from Sargans to Weisstannen and to Vaduz in Liechtenstein.

Elm

This interesting village lies at 977m in the upper Sernftal surrounded by majestic peaks. Elm has some fine old buildings, including the 18th-century Suworowhaus, where the Russian general (known to English speakers as Suvorov) stayed in 1799 (see the boxed text 'Suvorov's Panixerpass Crossing' later). For centuries Elm has been famous for the Martinsloch, an amazing natural hole in the Tschingelhorn ridge. In a natural spectacle that occurs only twice each year – on 12 or 13 March and on 1 or 2 October – the sun shines through the Martinsloch onto the steeple of the 15th-century village church. Plaques on the pulpit of the church are dedicated to the tragedy of 1881, when 114 Elmers lost their lives when a nearby mountainside suddenly collapsed.

For information, contact the tourist office (☎ 055-642 60 67, ℮ info@elm.ch, ⓦ www.elm.ch).

The *Zeltplatz Wisli* (contact the tourist office) offers tent sites for Sfr5 plus Sfr5 per person. The *Gasthaus Segnes* (☎ 055-642 11 72) has singles/doubles from around Sfr45/90. *Hotel Elmer* (☎ 055-642 60 80, ℮ info@hotelelmer.ch) offers rooms from Sfr50 per person. The *Pension und Cafe zum Bergführer* (☎ 055-642 21 06), 15 minutes' walk upvalley, charges Sfr58 per person. The large *Hotel Sardona* (☎ 055-642 68 69, ℮ sardona@bluewin.ch) has rooms of various standards from Sfr52/104 per single/double.

Buses run hourly until around 9pm in either direction between Elm and the town of Schwanden, on the Ziegelbrücke–Glarus–Linthal rail line. A number of buses continue from Elm on to Steinibach, 3km upvalley, or (on demand) up to Obererbs (Matt) – near the start of the Richetlipass walk (see later in the chapter).

Linthal

This village deep in the glorious Glarner Alps owes its origins to the Linth, whose swift-flowing waters turned its first spinning mill in the early 1830s. Even today, production of hydroelectric power and textiles support Linthal's economy. The village is the starting point for many excellent walks into the surrounding mountains.

The Tödi-Shop (☎ 055-643 39 17) has local tourist information.

The *Hotel Adler* (☎ 055-643 15 15) offers dorm beds from Sfr25 and nice rooms from Sfr45 per person. *Hotel Bahnhof* (☎ 055-643 15 22) has rooms from Sfr35/70. The *Hotel Raben* (☎ 055-643 31 22) charges Sfr42/84.

Trains run hourly in each direction between Linthal and Ziegelbrücke (via Schwanden and Glarus), on the main Zürich–Chur rail line.

Pizol Lakes Circuit

Duration	3–4 hours
Distance	10km
Standard	easy-medium
Start	Pizolhütte upper chairlift station
Finish	Gaffia chairlift station
Nearest Town	Sargans-Mels, Furt

Summary This lovely lake-to-lake loop leads over the interesting Pizol range between the Weisstannental and the Rhine Valley.

This high-level route, also called the Five Lakes Hike (5-Seen-Wanderung), is one of the best panorama routes in the Swiss Alps. Hopping across small gaps in the ridge tops the circuit offers continually changing scenery. Although it follows a generally very good path, the walk is entirely above the tree line. Before at least mid-July winter snows may still cover parts of the route.

Maps

The best walking map is the St Gallische Wanderwege 1:25,000 *Pizolgebiet* No 2509 (Sfr27).

NEAREST TOWN
Furt

Furt is a tiny car-free ski resort at 1552m about halfway up the mountain. The *Berghotel Furt* (☎ 081-723 21 66, e *hotel.furt @spin.ch*) has singles/doubles from Sfr89/178 and dorm beds for Sfr82 (prices include full board). The *Berghotel Alpina* (☎ 081-723 20 86, e *alpina@spin.ch*) and *Berghotel Graue Hörner* (☎ 081-723 16 66) have comparable rates.

GETTING TO/FROM THE WALK

The walk begins near the Pizolhütte, reached by gondola/chairlift combination from Wangs, on the southern side of Sargans-Mels (see Access Towns earlier). Between early July and late October postbuses run hourly in either direction in a Sargans–Wangs–Vilters–Sargans circuit, giving roughly half-hourly departures to Wangs.

The Pizolbahnen (W www.pizol.com) from Wangs runs a gondola lift up to Furt, then a two-stage chairlift continues to the upper station. It's a 40-minute ride over forest, extensive pastures and karst fields totalling around 1700m ascent. At Sfr34 return, the cableway fare is rather expensive, but the *Heidiland Wanderpass* (see Getting Around at the start of the chapter), Half Fare Card and Swiss Pass are valid.

THE WALK

From the upper chairlift station walk a few paces up to a signpost ('Bergstation') on the ridge top at 2210m (but sometimes given as 2227m). From here there are excellent views north along the flat, fertile Rhine Valley as far as Lake Constance and south to the Bündner Alps. Just 350m left (east) on the broad grassy ridge by the attractive **Wangser See** (tarn) is the *Pizolhütte* (☎ 081-723 14 56,

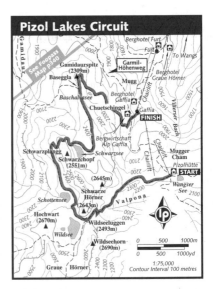

e *pizolhuette@bluewin.ch*). This (private) stone hut at 2227m is open from July to October, when a good range of dishes is served and dorm beds cost Sfr55 with full board.

Follow the path westward around into an old revegetated moraine basin, then begin a sidling ascent through a talus gully to reach the rubbly gap of the **Wildseeluggen** at 2493m after 45 minutes to one hour. From here you get a spectacular view across the blue-green waters of the **Wildsee** in a deep glacial trough formed by the receding Pizolgletscher, crowned by the 2844m Pizol, and ringed by the peaks known as the Graue Hörner ('Grey Horns').

Traverse briefly rightward along the slope high above the lake (watch out for rock fall here) to another rocky gap, where the **Schottensee** (2335m) and several smaller surrounding tarns come into view. The route winds on down through the debris, skirting the lake's eastern shore into undulating lawns frequented by small herds of ibex.

Sidle up north-west on steeply sloping meadows that fall away west into the Weisstannental, beyond which rows of ranges stretch back to the horizon. Alpine jackdaws often circle around the crags up to your

NORTH-EASTERN SWITZERLAND

right. A few switchbacks bring you up to the grassy ridge top of **Schwarzplangg** at 2505m, 45 minutes to one hour from the Wildseeluggen. This natural lookout offers more fine panoramas, including a first clear view of the Churfirsten range to the north-west. Directly below you is the Schwarzsee.

The path again descends in short spirals to cross the outlet of the **Schwarzsee** (2368m), another classic Alpine lake filling a small cirque below a prominent pinnacle, then cuts up onto another wide ridge top. Continue north past scores of high cairns erected by passing walkers (giving this place an eerie 'graveyard' atmosphere) to reach the grassy dip of **Baseggla**, 45 minutes to one hour from Schwarzplangg.

Drop south-east over pastures grazed by sheep to the **Baschalvasee** (2174m), a small pale-green tarn on a shelf high above the town of Sargans. Climb briefly on over a minor crest, where the Pizolhütte comes back into sight, then make a sidling descent south-east through rocky bluffs into the Alpine pastures of Chuetschingel. The route winds down left to cross the Wildbach on a footbridge by the *Alp Gaffia Bergwirtschaft*, a typical alp restaurant, to arrive back at the Gaffia chairlift station (1823m), 45 minutes to one hour from Baseggla. The *Berghotel Gaffia* (☎ *081-723 13 46,* e *info@ga ffia.ch*), about 300m down from the Gaffia chairlift station, offers dorm beds from Sfr30.

From here the walk can be extended by taking the three-hour Garmil-Höhenweg route down to Furt.

Foopass

Duration	2 days
Distance	34km
Standard	medium
Start	Sargans
Finish	Elm
Nearest Town	Weisstannen

Summary This walk leads across the 2223m Foopass out of the Sarganserland's Weisstannental into the Sernftal of Glarus Canton. It forms the first leg of the long Alpine Pass Route.

The upper valley area of the Weisstannental was first settled by Walsers from the Rheinwald and Safiental in Graubünden during the 14th century. For the descendants of these migrants the Foopass was the principle link with the outside world. Today the Weisstannental remains one of Switzerland's most unspoilt larger Alpine valleys, and is a very pleasant walking route along its entire length from Mels-Sargans up to the Foopass. The much shorter descent west from the Foopass to the village of Elm takes you through the wild and lonely valley of the Raminertal.

Maps

If you're starting the walk from Weisstannen, acceptable maps are the 1:50,000 *Glarnerland* (Sfr24), published by Verlag Baeschlin or the SAW/FSTP's 1:50,000 map *Sardona* No 247T (Sfr22.50). K+F's 1:60,000 walking map, *Glarnerland Walensee* (Sfr24.80), covers the walk from Sargans, and includes all of the Sarganserland and Glarner Alps.

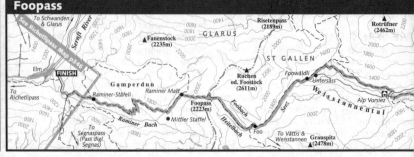

Foopass

NEAREST TOWN
Weisstannen

The walk passes through this pretty little village at the end of Day 1. Built in the traditional wooden architecture of the St Galler Oberland, of particular interest in Weisstannen is the small St John the Baptist parish church erected in 1665.

There are two places to stay: the *Hotel Gemse* (☎ *081-723 17 05*) and *Hotel Alpenhof* (☎ *081-723 17 63*); both offer singles/doubles for Sfr45/90 and dorm beds for Sfr30 with breakfast.

There are seven postbuses daily (five on Sunday) from Sargans train station; the last bus is at around 6.45pm.

GETTING TO/FROM THE WALK

For information on transport to/from Sargans and Elm, see Access Towns at the start of this section. The walk can be shortened to one day by taking the bus from Sargans to the village of Weisstannen.

THE WALK
Day 1: Sargans to Weisstannen

3½–4½ hours, 14km, 504m ascent

From Sargans train station, follow a signposted walkway 1.25km north-west beside the railway lines. On your right the sheer walls of the 1829m Gonzen rise up directly from the valley floor. Where you meet a busy road, head down the steps and continue through the underpass below the rail/motorway bridge. The road makes an S-bend as it brings you on to reach **Mels** after 30 to 40 minutes.

From Mels' town square (Dorfplatz), turn right along the road and cross the gushing Seez stream. Pick up a short-cut foot track (marked only by an arrow painted on a wall) just after the bridge and climb up directly back to the road. The route continues a short way up the sealed road past a small chapel at **St Martin** after 25 to 30 minutes. This attractive hamlet sits at 574m among vineyards looking north-east across Sargans to the mountains of Liechtenstein.

Not far uphill leave off left along an old flagged mule path leading up into the trees. This ascends steadily, briefly meeting the road again in several places, before coming to a signposted intersection inside the forest at **Tschess** (1020m), 45 minutes to one hour up from St Martin. The trail up to the right goes to Vermol and the Chapfensee (1030m), a nearby lake within a very pleasant nature reserve.

Take the left-hand branch and follow an alp track slightly downhill across sunny pastures, bearing right at another fork when you get to **Hundbüel** after 15 to 20 minutes. High peaks of the Pizol region stand on the other side of the valley, while back toward Mels the Seez flows through a deep gorge. The path now rises and dips as it gradually drops against the contour past small clearings and isolated alp huts, repeatedly crossing refreshing streamlets cascading down from the heavily wooded slopes above to the scattered farms of **Höhi**. From here a sealed road winds quickly down to arrive at **Schwendi** at 908m after a further 50 minutes to one hour. Here, the *Gasthaus Mühle*

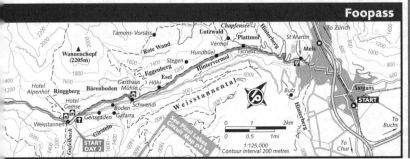

Foopass

(☎ 081-723 15 01) has singles/doubles for Sfr45/90.

Either head directly up the main valley road or take the gravelled farm track up right from near the Gasthaus. This soon leads onto a higher walking route that gently traverses field and forest – with frequent resting benches for enjoying the views of the valley and adjacent mountains – before descending again to cross the Seez on a small bridge just before you reach **Weisstannen** at 1004m after 45 minutes to one hour (or 30 to 40 minutes via the valley road).

Day 2: Weisstannen to Elm
6–8 hours, 20km, 1219m ascent

At the upper end of the village, cross the Gutelbach bridge and follow the road as it enters the upper Seez valley, passing waterfalls spilling into the sheer-sided valley before coming to another road bridge after 2km. At this point take the path leading along the southern side of the stream, which is dry in places because the water is diverted by an aqueduct. Where the trail comes back to the road, turn right and recross the stream to reach *Alp Vorsiez* (☎ 081-723 17 48) at 1175m, one to 1¼ hours up from Weisstannen. This mountain dairy (open late May to mid-October) sells milk and cheese, and walkers can sleep in the large dorm for around Sfr25 with breakfast.

Head left along a farm track running beside a line of telephone poles, which gradually becomes a marked trail as it makes its way through patches of spruce forest and moist meadows often grazed by deer. The route continues beside the Seez to cross the smaller Siezbach side stream on a wooden footbridge, rising briefly to a dirt road before it descends gently to arrive at the farmstead at **Untersäss** (1361m) after 45 minutes to one hour.

Walk along the old alp road to an attractive stand of trees known as the **Foowäldli**, which forms both the upper limit of vehicle access and the tree line. From here the path does a spiralling ascent through glacial and avalanche rubble, passing natural lookouts offering nice views back down into the Weisstannental. The gradient eases where

A traditional wooden-shingled farmhouse in the Weisstannental.

CLEM LINDENMAYER

you enter an elongated section of the small valley covered with stunted birch scrub. It steepens again as you head up beside the tumbling stream to reach the alp huts of **Foo** at 1875m, 1¼ to 1¾ hours from Untersäss. Spectacular rock walls surround this high upper basin, whose rich pastures are ablaze with a wide variety of wild flowers in early summer.

Drop quickly down across the Foobach, and (ignoring a left-hand side trail here, which goes up to Mätteli) follow white-red-white route markings that gradually veer around to the right into the tiny Alpine valley drained by the Heitelbach. Climbing at a steady pace, the path leads over rolling grassy slopes inhabited by colonies of marmots to arrive at the 2223m **Foopass** after 50 minutes to one hour. The Foopass lies on the St Gallen–Glarus cantonal border, and offers a wonderful vista ahead toward numerous peaks of the Glarner Alps such as the Kärpf and the Hausstock.

The path makes a descent in steep zigzags to the stone farmhouse of **Raminer Matt** at 1897m in the lonely upper valley. From here, walkers get their first real look toward the arc of craggy ranges stretching south-west from the nearby Surenstock (Piz Sardona) as far as the glacial snows of the Vorab. Make your way on along the farm track to reach the alp huts of **Mittler Staffel** at 1757m, 45 minutes to one hour from the Foopass.

Continue right across the bridge, where the first scattered conifers mark the upper limit of the forest. The road snakes down beside sloping meadows far above the deep gorge of the Raminer Bach past spectacular waterfalls plummeting off Piz Segnas on the opposite side of the valley before intersecting with a larger road at **Raminer-Stäfeli** (1248m) after one to 1¼ hours.

The route descends in tight curves, passing Elm's small camping ground hidden in the forest just before departing left along a trail down beside the stream. A wooden footbridge leads over to the left bank about halfway before the much larger Sernft River is crossed a short way before arriving in **Elm** at 977m, 30 to 40 minutes on.

For the next (second) leg of the Alpine Pass Route, see the Richetlipass walk (Elm to Linthal) later in this chapter.

Murgseefurggel

Duration	2 days
Distance	23.5km
Standard	medium
Start	Filzbach
Finish	Murg
Nearest Town	Walenstadt

Summary This wonderful semicircuit leads over gentle mountain passes linking several valley heads on the southern side of the Walensee, then descends through the beautiful nature reserve of the Murgtal.

Mouthing on the Walensee (Lake Walen) near the village of Murg (448m), about halfway along the southern shoreline, the 10km-long Murgtal has a climate milder than anywhere else in Switzerland north of the Alps. This 'Föhn valley' rises up steadily to terminate at the 1825m Oberer Murgsee, a lovely mountain lake nestling below the ranges of the Gufelstock. The Murgtal's roughly north-south alignment and steep gradient duct warm southerly winds (known in German as the Föhn) down through the valley (see the boxed text 'Föhn Winds' in the Facts about Switzerland chapter). This effect, together with the gently warming influence of the nearby Walensee, allows sweet chestnut trees and other species more usually associated with Mediterranean climes to thrive in the valley's lower reaches.

Maps
Best are any of the following 1:50,000 walking maps: Verlag Baeschlin's *Glarnerland* (Sfr24); the SAW/FSTP *Walenstadt* No 237T (Sfr22.50); or the St Gallische Wanderwege *Wanderkarte St Galler Oberland-Toggenburg* No 5015 (Sfr27). Another option is K+F's 1:60,000 *Glarnerland Walensee* (24.80).

NEAREST TOWNS
For information on Walenstadt, see Nearest Towns under the Churfirsten walk earlier.

Filzbach
Filzbach is the highest village on the slopes of the Kerenzerberg overlooking the Walensee. Above the village is one of Switzerland's best summer bobsled runs.

For information, contact the tourist office (☎ 055-614 16 12, [e] info@kerenzerberg.ch, [w] www.kerenzerberg.ch).

The local *youth hostel (☎ 055-614 13 42, [e] filzbach@youthhostel.ch)* offers dorm beds for Sfr28. The *Hotel Mürtschenstock (☎ 055-614 13 59)* offers rooms from Sfr45 per person. The more upmarket *Hotel Rössli (☎ 055-614 18 32)* charges Sfr80/155 a single/double.

Postbuses running between Näfels-Möllis (on the Linthal line) and Mühlehorn (on the shore of the Walensee) pass through Filzbach and Murg. From Zürich the train/postbus connections to Filzbach are much better via Näfels-Möllis than via Mühlehorn.

Murg
The village (448m) has a tourist office (☎ 081-738 11 13, [e] vv@murg.ch, [w] www .murg.ch).

Camping Murg am See (☎ 081-738 15 30) has lakeside tent sites from Sfr4 plus Sfr6.20 per person. *Gasthaus Rössli (☎ 081-738 11 97)* has singles/doubles for Sfr80.

Taking a ferry across the lake from Murg to the village of Quinten, the only lowland settlement in Switzerland not accessible by road, is thoroughly recommended.

GETTING TO/FROM THE WALK

The walk starts at the upper station of the Habergschwänd chairlift above Filzbach, which in summer costs Sfr9/7 one way for adults/children and runs until 5pm.

For a fee, private vehicles can be left at the car park adjacent to the lower Filzbach–Habergschwänd chairlift station.

THE WALK
Day 1: Habergschwänd to Berggasthaus Murgsee

3½–4½ hours, 10.5km, 703m ascent

The chairlift from Filzbach carries you up over an all-seasons toboggan run to **Habergschwänd** (1282m), at the start of the bob-sled run on the Kerenzerberg terrace high above the Walensee. Here, at the *Berggasthaus Habergschwänd* (☎ 055-614 12 17), open June to mid-October, you can sleep in the hay for Sfr25 or in the dorm for Sfr35 (prices with breakfast).

Follow the gravelled road gently eastward down around the lightly forested hillside to **Vorder Tal**, where the *Restaurant Talalpsee*, in a converted alp hut at 1111m, serves light meals and refreshments from early July to late October. An alp track now leads south along the eastern side of the **Talsee**, a shallow lake that sits like a puddle below chalky white crags whose sheer walls show numerous large natural cavities. Continue past barns in the grassy pastures of **Hinter Tal** to where the road finishes at a utility cableway, 50 minutes to one hour from Habergschwänd.

Climb up to the right in steep zigzags along a well-cut old mule trail to get to the top of the ridge (1498m), from where a lookout ramp gives a nice view back into the head of the enclosed upper valley. Sidle on along the regenerating talus slopes under the almost overhanging rock sides of the Mürtschenstock, with the **Spaneggsee** (1425m), another small attractive lake with no direct outlet, in the undrained basin below. The path cuts up left past the alp huts of **Hummel** at 1560m, before steepening slightly as it ascends via the tiny valley of the Chüetal to reach the **Mürtschenfurggel**, a dip in the ridge at 1840m, after 1½ to two hours.

Drop down leftward through a shallow, grassy gully to the farmhouse and barn at **Ober Mürtschen** (1732m), a pretty, flat bowl covered by waterlogged moors and surrounded by lovely stands of scattered pines. Walk 250m down left, then cross the small clearwater Mürtschenbach on a halved-log bridge. White-red-white markings guide you up beside a gurgling brook to the **Murgseefurggel** (1985m), a little saddle on the Glarus–St Gallen cantonal border which overlooks the picturesque **Oberer Murgsee**. Originally dammed by local iron-ore miners in the 1800s, today the tranquil shallow waters of the Oberer Murgsee draw a steady stream of anglers.

Descend diagonally leftward over the snow grass slopes above a farmhouse, then follow an alp track on around the lakeshore. The route crosses a small concrete levee a short way before arriving at the *Berggasthaus Murgsee* (☎ 079 635 19 38), 1¼ to 1½ hours on from the Mürtschenfurggel. Also known as the Fischerhütte or Murgseehütte, this cosy little angler's hut at 1825m is open mid-May to late October. It offers dorm beds for Sfr37 (with breakfast) and better-than-average meals, but washing facilities are basic.

A 40-minute return walk can be made up to the 2013m pass to the south known as **Widersteinerfurggel**. Walk on around the lakeshore, then climb up through Alpine pastures to the right of a minor ridge. In clear conditions the view stretches along the Üblital as far as the Vorabfirn (Glatscher dil Vorab in Romansch), the large snowfield directly to the south.

Day 2: Berggasthaus Murgsee to Murg

3¼–4 hours, 13km

The beautiful walk through the Murgtal is fairly straightforward, following a (restricted access) road virtually the whole way down to Murg.

Take the old vehicle track on down around the northern shore of the **Mittel-Murgsee**, recrossing the Murgbach just above where the stream tumbles over cliffs in a spectacular waterfall and flows on into

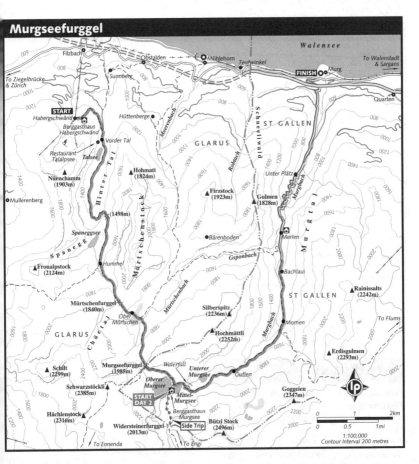

Murgseefurggel

the **Unterer-Murgsee**. The road leads on down over slopes scattered with alpenrose bushes to the grassy flats of **Guflen** (1600m), then continues in a steady sidling descent through beautiful mixed coniferous forest. Shortly after passing a signposted route going up right toward Flumserberg you come to **Mornen** at 1335m, after 1¼ to 1½ hours. The alp huts on these pastures look out westward to the peaks of the Silberspitz.

Make your way down more gently now past **Bachlaui** to the farmlet of **Merlen** at 1089m, a short distance below where the Mürtschental joins the main valley. The incline steepens sharply again after the road crosses the river and begins winding down through an area of rubble left by an ancient landslide toward the serrated outline of the Churfirsten on the far side of the Walensee. Short-cut trails at many of the hairpin bends bring you quickly down to reach **Unter Plätz** (713m), 1¼ to 1½ hours from Mornen.

Proceed left past a fork, following the now more prominent main road down through long clearings and small stands of sweet chestnut trees. Take the last few road curves leading down to arrive in **Murg** after a final

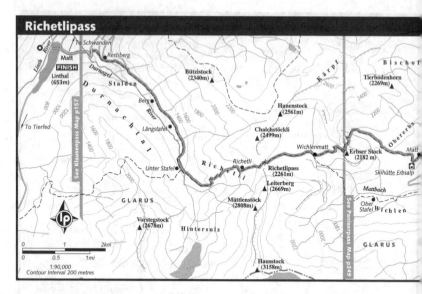

45 minutes to one hour. This tiny industrial town is on a little peninsula (actually an alluvial fan formed by the Murgbach), which juts out into the Walensee.

Richetlipass

Duration	6½–8 hours
Distance	21km
Standard	medium
Start	Elm
Finish	Linthal

Summary This delightful pass crossing (the second leg of the Alpine Pass Route) connects the Glarnerland's two main upper valleys, the Sernftal and the Linthtal.

On the eastern side of the Richetlipass is the Wichlenmatt, one of the loveliest areas of highland wild-flower meadows in the Swiss Alps. On the west side of the pass is the Durnachtal, a small side valley of the Linth with a stubbornly wild nature. The Durnagel stream washes large quantities of loose rock down through the Durnachtal from the slopes of the nearby Hausstock, and in the past the rich pastures of the Linthtal were continually

threatened by these masses of alluvial rubble. Today concrete obstructions have been built along the course of the Durnagel as part of an ambitious project to tame the stream.

The walk involves a climb of over 1250m vertical, with an even longer descent totalling more than 1600m. There is nowhere to stay en route.

Maps

Recommended are Verlag Baeschlin's 1:50,000 *Glarnerland* (Sfr24) or K+F's 1:60,000 *Glarnerland Walensee* (Sfr24.80). Two SAW/FSTP maps, *Sardona* No 247T and *Klausenpass* No 246T, make good alternatives (Sfr22.50 each).

GETTING TO/FROM THE WALK

For information on transport to/from Elm and Linthal, see Access Towns at the beginning of this section.

Walkers can save a couple of hours by taking the bus on from Elm to Obererbs (Matt). From mid-June to mid-October there are buses at approximately 9am, 10am, 11am and 1pm; it is highly advisable to book in advance (☎ 055-642 17 17, or on weekends ☎ 055-642 17 18).

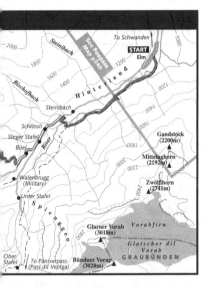

THE WALK

At the fork 300m up the street from the Elm post office, turn left along a country lane. The route soon crosses the Sernft River and rises over rolling meadows before taking a right-hand path alongside the sharply sloping banks of the river to meet a gravelled farm track. Head on until you come to a sealed roadway and continue down over the bridge, then make a short, steep climb back to the main road not far up from Steinibach. Walk upvalley along the road for 1.25km to a stone drinking fountain near a turn-off at **Büel** (1261m).

Turn right and follow this narrow road up 800m, then take a steep short-cut path off (right) through forest and high pastures to reach the hamlet of **Matt** (1698m), two to 2¾ hours from Elm. At the end of the road here is the *Skihütte Erbsalp* (☎ *055-642 14 66 or 079-407 03 41*), open early July to late October, which offers dorm beds for Sfr12 (excluding breakfast). Head on up through the alps of **Obererbs**, almost to the source of a small mountain stream, before swinging around south-west. The route ascends in short switchbacks to a gap in the ridge at 2161m just west of the Erbser Stock

(2182m), then makes an almost direct descent to the alp hut of **Wichlenmatt**, 1¼ to 1¾ hours from Matt.

The final stretch traces the meandering brook for a distance, picking its way through areas of gravel and loose earth as it steepens into an ascent of short zigzags. Even in high summer, snow covering the upper slopes may slow you down, but the 2261m **Richetlipass** is usually reached in 35 to 45 minutes. This neat dip between the Chalchstöckli and the Leiterberg offers excellent vistas westward to the unmistakable hub of the Ortstock (2716m) at the northern end of the Jegerstöck.

At first the path spirals down the steep slopes from the pass, then continues along a small spur past **Richetli** (1916m), where a shepherd's hut is sheltered by a large boulder. Veer right here to link up with an old moraine ridge, then follow this down until it ends at a line of cliffs. At this point, drop down leftward through a rocky gully before cutting back to the right across the open hillsides to where a wooden bridge brings you over the swiftly flowing glacial waters of the Durnagel stream. Just a few paces downstream is the farmhouse of **Unter Stafel** at 1386m, around 1¼ to 1¾ hours from the pass.

The route recrosses the river a short way on, staying on the road as it gradually falls against the contour past the remote farms of Längstafel (1314m) and **Berg** (1231m), perched high above the Durnachtal. Visible along the river's course are dozens of concrete constructions built to contain the great volumes of debris washed down from the loose mountainsides upvalley. Directly ahead is the familiar tiered form of the Ortstock, while just to its right the summits of the Bächlistock and Bös Fulen have now come into sight.

Farther down, the road becomes sealed, passing the grassy hillsides of **Restiberg** as it begins a steeper descent in numerous hairpin bends through the forest. In midsummer aromatic wild strawberries and raspberries growing beside the way are an irresistible reason to pause for a spell. The route crosses the Durnagel a final time, and heads 1km west before coming out on the main valley road at **Matt**, near the small local museum. Follow the 'Bahnhof' signposts leading down through the village and across the Linth River to reach the train station in **Linthal**, 1½ to two hours after leaving Unter Stafel.

For the next (third) leg of the Alpine Pass Route, see the Klausenpass (Linthal to Altdorf) walk in the Central Switzerland chapter.

Panixerpass

Duration	6½–8 hours
Distance	22km
Standard	medium-hard
Start	Elm
Finish	Pigniu/Panix
Nearest Town	Andiast

Summary This ancient route linking the Sernftal and Graubünden's Romansch-speaking Surselva region leads (in places along the original mule trail) through an interesting Alpine landscape.

For centuries the 2407m Panixerpass (Pass dil Veptga in Romansch) was the only viable pass route from the Glarnerland into Graubünden. Medieval herders drove their animals via the Panixerpass to market in Lugano, and carried back rice and salt. After more than 200 years, the Panixerpass still conjures up the image of General Suvorov's disastrous crossing in 1799 (see the boxed text 'Suvorov's Panixerpass Crossing' later).

Although there are relatively few strenuous sections, the Panixerpass makes a long day walk (with an overnight option) that involves a total ascent of almost 1500m.

Maps

Any of the following 1:50,000 walking maps can be used: Verlag Baeschlin's *Glarnerland* (Sfr24), or the SAW/FSTP *Sardona* No 247T (Sfr22.50). K+F's 1:60,000 *Surselva* (Sfr24.80) is a good alternative, but the locally available 1:25,000 *Wanderkarte Sernftal* leaves off the last section of the route.

NEAREST TOWNS
Pigniu/Panix

This tiny Romansch-speaking village (called Panix in German) lies at 1301m in the tiny Val da Pigniu of Graubünden's Surselva region. The *Ustaria Alpina* (☎ 081-941 19 90) serves meals and refreshments, but only offers dorm accommodation for larger pre-booked groups.

In summer there are four daily postbuses to Rueun (15 minutes), on the Rhaetian Railway's Disentis–Chur line. The last postbus leaves Pigniu at around 6pm; reservation at least one hour in advance is essential for some services (☎ 079-216 49 83).

Andiast

Andiast (W www.andiast.ch) lies at 1185m where Val da Pigniu joins the main Surselva valley. *Hotel Postigliun* (☎ 081-941 10 33, e info@postigliun-andiast.ch) has rooms from Sfr44 per person and will shuttle guests to/from Pigniu for Sfr5 per person (minimum charge Sfr20).

There are around seven daily postbuses via Rueun to Ilanz (25 minutes), on the Rhaetian Railway's Disentis–Chur line; the last postbus leaves Andiast at around 6.40pm (around 8.40pm on Friday).

GETTING TO/FROM THE WALK

Buses from Schwanden to Elm continue up to the Sportbahnen cable-car station, 1.5km upvalley from Elm, and some services go on as far as Steinibach, 3km beyond Elm.

For information on transport to/from the walk's end, see Pigniu/Panix under Nearest Towns earlier.

THE WALK

The walk starts as for the Richetlipass walk earlier. At the fork 300m from the Elm post office, turn left along a lane. The route crosses the Sernft River and rises over meadows before taking a right-hand path beside the river to meet a gravel track. Continue over meadows on the stream's eastern side via the alp hut of **Jetzberg** (1188m). The route climbs gradually around southward into a narrow valley to a tiny diversion weir. Walkers who take the bus to Steinibach

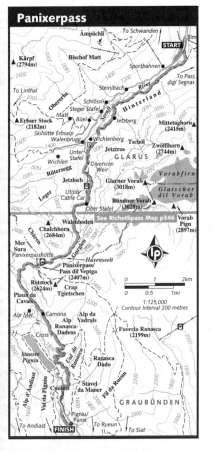

Panixerpass

1673m between the wings of a massive avalanche wall near where the main stream spills over a 60m-high waterfall.

Cut up across rocky alps above the basin of Walenboden past a spring emerging from the base of the Chalchhorn (2684m). Continue over snowdrifts through the raw, narrow chasm of **Gurglen**, then skirt around the tiny, shallow tarn of **Haxenseeli**. The route ascends moraine slopes across a splashing streamlet and past a small stone alp hut to arrive at the **Panixerpass**, 1¾ to 2½ hours from Ober Stafel. The broad pass area offers fine views north-west to the 3158m Hausstock above the much-receded Glatscher da Mer, and back north-east to the Vorab summits.

Here, the ***Panixerpasshütte***, a simple, unstaffed timber hut (owned jointly by Glarus and Graubünden Cantons), has sleeping space for 16 people. The hut fees are: day use Sfr4, dorm beds Sfr6 and wood for the stove Sfr3. There are no blankets, so walkers who intend staying here should carry a sleeping bag. Bookings are not possible (for more information contact Elm tourist office).

Steel poles and white-red-white markings lead gently down westward into pleasant Alpine tundra beside a tiny meandering stream. The path makes a steep switchbacking descent through sparse meadows plentifully dotted with low-growing Alpine marguerites and yellow mountain saxifrage to cross the stream on a bridge (made from old railway tracks). Head down beside the wide, coarse-pebble stream over the **Plaun da Cavals**, a rich undulating pasture scattered with thorny thistles. Recross the stream at a narrow little gorge with interesting 'mill pots' created by the churning water, and sidle up past an alp hut (shown as 'Camona' on most maps) built against the cliffs, where in summer milk and cheese are on sale.

A broad track cut into overhanging precipices now makes an exhilarating traverse far above the Stausee Pigniu to reach a wooden cross on a minor crest (2031m) at **Alp Ranasca-Dadens**, 1¼ to 1½ hours from the pass. Here, Pigniu comes into view, perched on a shelf high above the Surselva before the backdrop of the 3121m Piz Aul almost directly south. Opposite, a roaring

can simply head on up the sealed road past Büel to the large car park beside the military firing range at Unter Stafel, then follow a narrow, rough road up the west side of the dry stream to the weir.

Head up under a small utility cableway along the east side of the Jetzloch (gorge) opposite smooth, grey slabs. The path crosses several side streams cascading down from névés on the twin Glarner (3018m) and Bündner (3028m) Vorab peaks, whose 1000m rock walls are intersected by tiny grassy terraces, to reach **Ober Stafel**, 2¼ to three hours from Elm. This alp hut stands at

Suvorov's Panixerpass Crossing

After costly victories against Napoleonic forces in northern Italy, in September 1799 the Russian General Italinsky Suvorov (also spelled Suworoff or Suworow) marched his exhausted army of 22,000 troops across the St Gotthard Pass into Switzerland. In Altdorf, however, Suvorov found that the French had blocked his retreat by seizing all ships on Lake Lucerne, forcing the general to make a frantic detour across the Chinzig Chulm into the Muotatal, thence over the Pragelpass and finally south across the snow-bound Panixerpass. Caught in a terrible blizzard on 6 October as they descended the icy path 600m above the Alp da Pigniu (now covered by the Stausee Pigniu reservoir), hundreds of Suvorov's soldiers and pack animals fell to their deaths. When they reached Pigniu, the desperate Russians tore down buildings for firewood and slaughtered livestock – the village never fully recovered. Five days later as they crossed into Austria only 14,000 of Suvorov's troops had survived their Swiss ordeal.

glacial torrent plummets over several high terraces into the reservoir.

Head on down over lovely Alpine pastures scattered with juniper and purplish bearded bellflowers to cross a rough alp track. Skirt on down rightward around the tree line, then begin a winding descent past another left turn-off (1790m) to cross a steel bridge over the **Ual da Ranasca** chasm. An old vehicle track leads on down (right) through spruce forest past a small water-diversion station to join the rough road (running upvalley to the dam wall, painted with a mural depicting Suvorov's crossing), 50 minutes to 1¼ hours from Alp Ranasca-Dadens.

From this point, walkers heading to Andiast should turn up (right) to Cuolms, then take the path (labeled 'Senda Sursilvana') that cuts around south along the opposite side of the Val da Pigniu (around 1¼ hours). Otherwise, follow the road down (left) to arrive in **Pigniu** after a final 15 to 20 minutes.

Other Walks

Rossmatter Tal

Enclosed by the glaciated peaks of the Glärnish to the east and the rugged Silberen to the west, the Rossmatter Tal is one of the nicest and most scenic valleys of the Glarner Alps. From Hinter Klöntal near the western shore of the Klöntaler See, an excellent route leads south up through the Rossmatter Tal via the locality of Chäseren, where **Restaurant Käsernalp** (☎ 055-640 11 77) offers rooms and dorm beds, to Drackloch on the cantonal border with Schwyz. From Drackloch either return to Hinter Klöntal along the high-traverse route via Alpeli (six to seven hours return) or continue up through an interesting slab-rock landscape to the Brunalpelihöchi, a pass at 2207m, to the SAC's **Glattalphütte** (☎ 041-830 19 39) – two days. Use either Baeschlin Verlag's 1:50,000 *Glarnerland* (Sfr24), or K+F's 1:60,000 *Glarnerland-Walensee* (Sfr24.80).

Glarner Alps

This relatively straightforward two-day high-Alpine route traverses the eastern slopes of the Clariden and the Tödi, two of the highest peaks of the Glarner Alps. The walk gives some quite breathtakingly spectacular vistas of the mountains and glaciers around the headwaters of the Linth River.

From Argseeli, at around 1330m on the Klausenpass road (postbus from Linthal), either take the small private cable car (☎ 055-643 33 73) or walk up to Vorder Orthalden (1869m). From here a path goes over the Fisetenpass (2036m), and sidles around via Friteren high above the Linthtal to the **Claridenhütte** (☎ 055-643 31 21), an SAC-run hut at 2453m. The route continues up through the Beggilücke (2537m) then down across the Oberstafelbach, before climbing Bifertengrätli to the SAC's **Fridolinhütte** (☎ 055-643 34 34) at 2111m. From here a scenic side trip can be made to the **Grünhornhütte** (☎ 055-643 34 34), an historic SAC hut built in 1863. The descent goes via Hinterer Sand, then along an alp track to Tierfed and down the left bank of the Linth to the village of Linthal.

The recommended walking map is the SAW/FSTP's *Klausenpass* No 246T (Sfr22.50).

Kistenpass

The 2714m Kistenpass is another outstanding high-Alpine crossing that leads over the Glarner Alps into the Surselva region of Graubünden. The walk passes through a superbly wild and rugged landscape formed by intense glaciation, but is unsuited to inexperienced walkers.

From Linthal the route heads upvalley to Tierfed (805m) then makes a long, strenuous climb to the *Muttseehütte* (☎ *055-643 31 67)*, an SAC hut at 2501m (staffed mid-June to late October). A faster and easier route variant involves taking the cable car from Tierfed to Ober-Baumgarten (1860m), then walking through the 3km tunnel – headlamp essential – to the Limmernsee reservoir, from where a good path leads up to the Muttseehütte. The cable car (operated by Kraftwerke Linth-Limmern, ☎ 055-643 31 67) runs four times daily until around 4.15pm.

The route continues up over moraine slopes then traverses high above the Limmernsee past the *Kistenpasshütte* (☎ *079-480 41 18)*. The descent leads via the basin of Cavorgia da Breil and Alp Quader to the Romansch-speaking village of. Breil/Brigels; from here there are postbuses to Tavanasa (on the Chur–Disentis line) until around 6.25pm.

The SAW/FSTP's 1:50,000 *Klausenpass* No 246T (Sfr22.50) covers the route.

Language

Language Areas
- Romansch
- German
- French
- Italian

Basel • • Zürich
• Lucerne
✪ Bern • Chur
Lausanne • • St Moritz
• Bellinzona
Geneva •

Switzerland has four official languages – German, French, Italian and Romansch. Easily the most important of these, both in its population and regional coverage, is German.

Swiss German

The term Swiss German (or *Schwyzerdütsch)* describes the group of Alemannic dialects spoken throughout the German-speaking regions of Switzerland. Unlike the status of regional dialects in neighbouring Austria and Germany, in Switzerland dialects are used for verbal communication, even in quite formal situations.

Swiss German is perhaps best described as a sub-language, with a somewhat different grammar and vocabulary to standard (or 'High') German. There are also some very important regional variations between the half-dozen or so main Swiss German dialects. Hardly anyone writes in Swiss German and, apart from witty advertising slogans or 'folksy' poetry, everything from cook books to the house rules in Swiss mountain huts is written in High German.

To outsiders familiar with High German, Schwyzerdütsch can sound like a ridiculous parody, due to the many dialects. The Bernese talk in slow melodic tones quite reminiscent of the soft mooing of their cows, while the strong guttural dialect spoken around Zürich has been unkindly likened to the sound made by someone with a severe throat infection. In everyday usage there is a preference for foreign (especially French) words over their High German counterparts. The usual word for 'bicycle' is *vélo* (not *Fahrrad)*, an icecream is a *Glace* (not a *Sahneneis)*, and a station platform is usually called a *Perron* (rather than a *Bahnsteig)*. English words have increasingly come into vogue as well.

German Swiss have no trouble understanding High German, though at times you may come across people who slip back into dialect because their High German has become a bit rusty. If you don't understand, just say *Bitte, sprechen Sie Hochdeutsch* (Please speak High German). Unless you plan to stay a few years (or are writing a master's thesis in linguistics), there's really no point trying to learn Schwyzerdütsch. You can impress your walking companions, however, by using the Swiss German greetings, *Grüezi* (formal) or *Hoi* (informal – use for children), when you meet others along the way.

High German

Pronunciation

Unlike English or French, German has no real silent letters. You pronounce the **k** at the start of the word *Knie* (knee), the **p** at the start of *Psychologie* (psychology), and the **e** at the end of *ich habe* (I have). One distinctive feature of German is that all nouns are written with a capital letter.

Vowels

As in English, vowels can be pronounced long, like the 'o' in 'pope', or short, like the 'o' in 'pop'. As a rule, German vowels are long before one consonant and short before two consonants: the **o** is long in the word *Dom* (cathedral), but short in the word *doch* (after all).

a	short, as the 'u' in 'cut'; long, as in 'father'
au	as the 'ow' in 'cow'
ä	short, as the 'a' in 'act'; long, as the 'ai' in 'hair'
äu	as the 'oy' in 'boy'
e	short, as in 'bet', long, as in 'prey'
ei	as the 'ai' in 'aisle'
eu	as the 'oy' in 'boy'
i	short, as in 'it'; long, as in 'marine'
ie	as the 'i' in 'marine'
o	short, as in 'pot'; long, as in 'note'
ö	like the 'er' in 'fern'
u	short, as the 'u' in 'pull'; long, as the 'oo' in 'cool'
ü	similar to the 'u' in 'pull' but with stretched lips

Consonants

Most German consonants sound similar to their English counterparts. One important difference is that **b**, **d** and **g** sound like 'p', 't' and 'k', respectively, when they occur at the end of a word.

b	usually as the English 'b', but as 'p' at end of a word
ch	like the 'ch' in Scottish *loch*
d	usually as the English 'd', but like 't' at the end of a word
g	usually as the English 'g', but as 'k' at the end of a word, or 'ch' in the Scottish *loch* at the end of a word when after **i**
j	as the 'y' in 'yet'
qu	like 'k' plus 'v'
r	can be trilled or guttural, depending on the region
s	usually as the 's' in 'sun', but like the 'z' in 'zoo' when followed by a vowel
sch	as the 'sh' in 'ship'
sp, st	the **s** sounds like the 'sh' in 'ship' when at the start of a word
tion	the **t** sounds like the 'ts' in 'hits'
v	as the 'f' in 'fan'
w	as the 'v' in 'van'
z	as the 'ts' in 'hits'

Greetings & Civilities

Hello.	*Guten Tag.*
Hello. (in southern Germany)	*Grüss Gott.*
Goodbye.	*Auf Wiedersehen.*
Bye bye.	*Tschau.* (informal)
Yes.	*Ja.*
No.	*Nein.*
Please.	*Bitte.*
Thank you.	*Danke.*
That's fine/ You're welcome.	*Bitte sehr.*
Sorry/Excuse me/ Forgive me.	*Entschuldigung.*
Just a minute!	*Ein Moment!*
What's your name?	*Wie heissen Sie?*
My name is ...	*Ich heisse ...*
Where are you from?	*Woher kommen Sie?*
I'm from ...	*Ich komme aus ...*
How old are you?	*Wie alt sind Sie?*
I'm ... years old	*Ich bin ... Jahre alt.*

Language Difficulties

Do you speak English?	*Sprechen Sie Englisch?*
Does anyone here speak English?	*Spricht hier jemand Englisch?*
I understand.	*Ich verstehe.*
I don't understand.	*Ich verstehe nicht.*
Please write that down.	*Können Sie es bitte aufschreiben?*

Getting Around

Where is the ...?	*Wo ist ...?*
bus stop	*die Bushaltestelle*
train station	*der Bahnhof (Bf)*
tram stop	*die Strassenbahn-haltestelle*

When does the next ... arrive/leave?	*Wann fährt (das/der) nächste ... an/ab?*
boat	*das Boot*
(city) bus	*der Bus*
train	*der Zug*

I'd like a ...	*Ich möchte eine ...*
one-way ticket	*Einzelkarte*
return ticket	*Rückfahrkarte*

1st class	*erste Klasse*
2nd class	*zweite Klasse*

Accommodation

camping ground	Campingplatz
guesthouse	Pension/Gästehaus
hotel	Hotel
youth hostel	Jugendherberge

Where is a cheap hotel?	Wo ist ein billiges Hotel?
What is the address?	Was ist die Adresse?
Do you have any rooms available?	Haben Sie noch freie Zimmer?

I'd like ...	Ich möchte ...
a single room	ein Einzelzimmer
a double room	ein Doppelzimmer
a room with a bathroom	ein Zimmer mit Bad
to share a dorm	einen Schlafsaal teilen
a bed	ein Bett

How much is it per night/per person?	Wieviel kostet es pro Nacht/pro Person?
Can I see it?	Kann ich es sehen?
Where is the bathroom?	Wo ist das Bad?

Around Town

I'm looking for ...	Ich suche ...
a bank	eine Bank
the city centre	die Innenstadt
the ... embassy	die ... Botschaft
my hotel	mein Hotel
the market	den Markt
the police	die Polizei
the post office	das Postamt
a public toilet	eine öffentliche Toilette
a public telephone	eine öffentliches Telefon
the tourist office	das Verkehrsamt

Can you show me (on the map)?	Können Sie mir (auf der Karte) zeigen?
near/far	nahe/weit
Go straight ahead.	Gehen Sie geradeaus.
Turn left.	Biegen Sie links ab.
Turn right.	Biegen Sie rechts ab.

Signs – German

Eingang	Entrance
Ausgang	Exit
Offen	Open
Geschlossen	Closed
Zimmer Frei	Rooms Available
Voll/Besetzt	No Vacancies
Auskunft	Information
Verboten	Prohibited
Polizei	Police
Polizeiwache	Police Station
Toiletten (WC)	Toilets
Herren	Men
Damen	Women

Shopping

How much is it?	Wie viel kostet es?
I'd like to buy ...	Ich möchte ... kaufen.
I'd like a film for this camera.	Ich möchte einen Film für diese Kamera.
Could you lower the price?	Könnten Sie den Preis reduzieren?

bookshop	Buchhandlung
camera shop	Fotogeschäft
chemist/pharmacy	Apotheke
department store	Kaufhaus
laundry	Wäscherei
market	Markt
newsagency	Zeitungshändler
supermarket	Supermarkt

Food

bakery	Bäckerei
delicatessen	Feinkostladen
grocery	Lebensmittelladen
restaurant	Restaurant/Gaststätte
breakfast	Frühstück
lunch	Mittagessen
dinner	Abendessen

I'd like the set lunch.	Ich hätte gern das Tagesmenü.
Can I see the menu, please?	Kan ich bitte die Spiesekarte haben?
I'm a vegetarian.	Ich bin Vegetarierin/ Vegetarier. (f/m)

Health

I'm ...	Ich bin ...
diabetic	Diabetikerin (f)
	Diabetiker (m)
epileptic	Epileptikerin (f)
	Epileptiker (m)
asthmatic	Asthmatikerin (f)
	Asthmatiker (m)

I'm allergic to ...	Ich bin allergisch gegen ...
antibiotics	Antibiotika
penicillin	Penizillin

antiseptic	Antiseptikum
aspirin	Aspirin
condoms	Kondome
constipation	Verstopfung
contraceptive	Verhütungsmittel
diarrhoea	Durchfall
medicine	Medizin
nausea	Übelkeit
sunblock cream	Sonnenschutzmittel
tampons	Tampons

Time & Dates

today	heute
tomorrow	morgen
in the morning	morgens
in the afternoon	nachmittags
in the evening	abends

Monday	Montag
Tuesday	Dienstag
Wednesday	Mittwoch
Thursday	Donnerstag
Friday	Freitag
Saturday	Samstag
Sunday	Sonntag

Numbers

0	null
1	eins
2	zwei

(zwo on the phone or public announcements)

3	drei
4	vier
5	fünf
6	sechs
7	sieben
8	acht
9	neun
10	zehn
11	elf
12	zwölf
13	dreizehn
14	vierzehn
15	fünfzehn
16	sechzehn
17	siebzehn
18	achtzehn
19	neunzehn
20	zwanzig
21	einundzwanzig
30	dreissig
40	vierzig
50	fünfzig
60	sechzig
70	siebzig
80	achtzig
90	neunzig
100	hundert
1000	tausend

one million	eine Million

ON THE WALK

Is this the trail/ road to ...?	Ist das der Weg/ die Strasse nach ...?
Which trail goes to ...?	Welcher Weg führt nach ...?
Is the trail steep/ wide/narrow?	Ist der Weg steil/ breit/eng?
How many kilometres to ...?	Wieviele Kilometer sind es bis ...?
Where are you going?	Wohin gehst du?
Do you know this area well?	Kennst du dich hier gut aus?
Is the trail safe?	Ist der Weg sicher?
Where can I hire a guide/tent?	Wo kann ich hier einen bergführer/ein Zelt mieten?
Is there a camp site nearby?	Gibt es dort in der Nähe einen Zeltplatz?
Can we camp here?	Dürfen wir unser Zelt hier aufbauen?
I'm lost.	Ich habe mich verlaufen.
Do I need a guide?	Brauche ich einen Bergführer?

What's that animal called?	Wie heisst dieses Tier?
What's that plant called?	Wie heisst diese Pflanze?

Weather

It's cloudy.	Ist bewölkt.
It's cold.	Ist kalt.
It's frosty.	Es friert.
It's hot.	Ist heiss.
It's raining.	Es regnet.
It's snowing.	Es schneit.
What will the weather be like tomorrow?	Wie wird das Wetter morgen sein?

Useful Words

alp hut	Alphütte
alp track	Alpweg
alpine garden	Alpengarten
alpine rhododendron	Alpenrose
arolla pine	Arve/Zirbe
avalanche	Lawine
backpack	Rucksack
beech	Buche
bilberry	Heidelbeere
bridge	Brücke
buttercup	Hahnenfuss
cable car	Luftseilbahn
cairn	Steinmännchen
camping ground	Zeltplatz
chairlift	Sessellift
chamois	Gämse
chestnut tree	Kastanienbaum
cirque	Kar/Felszirkus
contour	Höhenlinie
cornice	Wächte
crampons	Steigeisen
crossing	Übergang
direction	Richtung
dormitory	Massenlager/ Touristenlager
east	Ost
edelweiss	Edelweiss
fog	Nebel
forest	Wald
gap	Furgge/Scharte
gentian	Enzian
glacier	Gletscher

Emergencies – German

Help!	Hilfe!
Call a doctor!	Holen Sie einen Arzt!
Call an ambulance!	Rufen Sie einen Krankenwagen!
Call the police!	Rufen Sie die Polizei!
Go away!	Gehen Sie weg!
I've been robbed.	Ich bin bestohlen werden.
I've been raped.	Ich bin vergewaltigt werden.
I'm lost.	Ich habe mich verirrt.

gondola lift	Gondelbahn
gorge/ravine	Schlucht
hanging glacier	Hängegletscher
hill	Hügel
hut	Hütte
ibex	Steinbock
ice axe	Eispickel
lake	See
larch	Lärche
lynx	Luchs
map	Landkarte
maple	Ahorn
marmot	Murmeltier
moraine	Moräne
mountain	Berg
mountain guide	Bergführer
mule path	Saumpfad
north	Nord
outlet	Auslauf
pasqueflower/ anemone	Anemone
path/trail	Pfad/Wanderweg
peak/summit	Gipfel
Pre-Alps	Voralpen
red spruce	Rottanne/Fichte
reservoir	Stausee
ridge	Grat
river	Fluss
rock fall	Steinschlag
saddle	Joch/Sattel
scree/talus	Geröll
signpost	Wegweiser
silver fir	Weisstanne
slope	Hang

snow	Schnee
snowfield	Firn
snow free	aper
south	Süd
spring/fountain	Quelle/Brunnen
stream	Bach
the (Swiss) Alps	die (Schweizer) Alpen
thunderstorm	Gewitter
torrent	Tobel/Wildbach
tourist office	Verkehrsbüro
tower	Turm
valley	Tal
walking map	Wanderkarte
waterfall	Wasserfall
west	West

Swiss French

Although in past centuries strong so-called 'provincial' dialects existed in the French-speaking regions of Switzerland, today a more or less standard form of French is spoken throughout the country. Some important departures from standard French still persist, however. For example, the Swiss French term for 'postbox' is *case postale* rather than *boîte postale*, a female waiter is addressed as *sommelière* instead of *serveuse*, and a *gymnase* is a place you go to gain an education, not to work off excess body fat. Suisse Romand, as the language is called in Switzerland, is also identifiable to other French speakers by its slower pace and slight accent.

Pronunciation

Most letters in French are pronounced more or less the same as their English equivalents. A few which may cause confusion are:

j   as the 's' in 'leisure', eg, *jour* (day)

c   before **e** and **i**, as the 's' in 'sit'; before **a**, **o** and **u** it's pronounced as English 'k'. When undescored with a cedilla (ç) it's always pronounced as the 's' in 'sit'.

French has a number of sounds that are difficult for Anglophones to produce. These include:

- The distinction between the 'u' sound (as in *tu*) and 'oo' sound (as in *tout*). For both sounds, the lips are rounded and projected forward, but for the 'u' the tongue is towards the front of the mouth, its tip against the lower front teeth, whereas for the 'oo' the tongue is towards the back of the mouth, its tip behind the gums of the lower front teeth.

- The nasal vowels. With nasal vowels the breath escapes partly through the nose and partly through the mouth. There are no nasal vowels in English; in French there are three, as in *bon vin blanc* (good white wine). These sounds occur where a syllable ends in a single **n** or **m**; the **n** or **m** is silent but indicates the nasalisation of the preceding vowel.

- The **r**. The standard **r** of Parisian French is produced by moving the bulk of the tongue backwards to constrict the air flow in the pharynx while the tip of the tongue rests behind the lower front teeth. It's similar to the noise made by some people before spitting, but with much less friction.

Greetings & Civilities

Hello.	Bonjour.
Goodbye.	Au revoir.
Yes.	Oui.
No.	Non.
Please.	S'il vous plaît.
Thank you.	Merci.
You're welcome.	Je vous en prie.
Excuse me.	Excusez-moi.
Sorry. (Excuse me/ Forgive me.)	Pardon.
What's your name?	Comment appelez-vous?
My name is ...	Je m'appelle ...
Where are you from?	Vous venez d'où?
I'm from ...	Je viens de/d' ...
How old are you?	Quel age avez-vous?
I'm ... years old.	J'ai ... ans.

Language Difficulties

Do you speak English?	Parlez-vous anglais?
Does anyone here speak English?	Est-ce qu'il y a quelqu'un qui parle anglais?
I understand.	Je comprends.

I don't understand. *Je ne comprends pas.*
Just a minute. *Attendez une minute.*
Please write that *Est-ce-que vous pouvez*
  down. *l'écrire?*

Getting Around

Where is the bus/ *Où est l'arrêt d'auto-*
  tram stop? *bus/de tramway?*

What time does *À quelle heure part/*
the ... leave/arrive? *arrive le ...?*
  boat *bateau*
  bus (city) *bus*
  train *train*

I would like ... *Je voudrais ...*
  a one-way ticket *un billet aller simple*
  a return ticket *un billet aller retour*

1st class *première classe*
2nd class *deuxième classe*

Accommodation

Where can I find a *Où est-ce que je peux*
  cheap hotel? *trouver un hôtel bon*
    marché?
What's the address? *Quelle est l'adresse?*
Do you have any *Est-ce que vous avez*
  rooms available? *des chambres libres?*

I'd like ... *Je voudrais ...*
  a single room *une chambre à un lit*
  a double room *une chambre double*
  a room with a *une chambre avec*
    shower and toilet *douche et WC*
  to stay in a dorm *coucher dans un*
    dortoir
  a bed *un lit*

How much is it per *Quel est le prix par*
  night/per person? *nuit/par personne?*
Can I see it? *Est-ce que je peux la*
    voir?
Where is the *Où est la salle de bain/*
  bathroom/shower? *douche?*

Around Town

I'm looking for ... *Je cherche ...*
  a bank *une banque*
  the city centre *le centre-ville*
  the ... embassy *l'ambassade de ...*
  my hotel *mon hôtel*

Signs – French

Entrée	**Entrance**
Sortie	**Exit**
Ouvert	**Open**
Fermé	**Closed**
Chambre Libres	**Rooms Available**
Complet	**Full/No Vacancies**
Interdit de Fumer	**No Smoking**
Renseignements	**Information**
Interdit	**Prohibited**
Police	**Police**
(Comissariat de)	**Police Station**
Police	
Toilettes/ WC	**Toilets**
Hommes	**Men**
Femmes	**Women**

the market *le marché*
the police *la police*
the post office *le bureau de poste*
a public toilet *des toilettes*
the railway station *la gare*
a public *une cabine*
  telephone *téléphonique*
the tourist office *l'office de tourisme/*
    le syndicat
    d'initiative

Can you show it to *Est-ce que vous pouvez*
  me (on the map)? *me le montrer (sur*
    la carte)?

near/far *proche/loin*
Go straight ahead. *Continuez tout droit.*
Turn left. *Tournez á gauche.*
Turn right. *Tournez á droite.*

Shopping

How much is it? *C'est combien?*
I'd like to buy ... *Je voudrais ...*
Do you accept *Est-ce que je peux*
  credit cards? *payer avec carte de*
    crédit?
Could you lower *Vous pouvez baisser le*
  the price? *prix?*

bookshop *librarie*
camera shop *boutique de*
    photographe

chemist/pharmacy	*pharmacie*
laundry	*blanchisserie*
market	*marché*
newsagency	*papeterie*
supermarket	*supermarché*

Food

bakery	*boulangerie*
cake shop	*pâtisserie*
cheese shop	*fromagerie*
delicatessen	*charcuterie*
grocery	*épicerie*
restaurant	*restaurant*
breakfast	*petit déjeuner*
lunch	*déjeuner*
dinner	*dîner*

I'd like the set menu.	*Je prends le menu.*
Is service included in the bill?	*Le service est compris?*
Can I see the menu, please?	*Est-ce que je peux voir la carte, s'il vous plaît?*
I'm a vegetarian.	*Je suis végétarien/ végétarienne.* (m/f)

Health

I'm ...	*Je suis ...*
anaemic	*anémique*
asthmatic	*asthmatique*
constipated	*constipé(e)*
diabetic	*diabétique*
epileptic	*épileptique*

| I'm allergic to antibiotics/ penicillin. | *Je suis allergique aux antibiotiques/à la pénicilline.* |

antiseptic	*antiseptique*
aspirin	*aspirine*
condoms	*préservatifs*
contraceptive	*contraceptif*
diarrhoea	*diarrhée*
medicine	*médicament*
nausea	*nausée*
sanitary napkins	*serviettes hygiéniques*
sunblock cream	*crème solaire*
tampons	*tampons hygiéniques*

Time & Dates

today	*aujourd'hui*
tomorrow	*demain*
yesterday	*hier*
in the morning	*le matin*
in the afternoon	*l'après-midi*
in the evening	*le soir*

Monday	*lundi*
Tuesday	*mardi*
Wednesday	*mercredi*
Thursday	*jeudi*
Friday	*vendredi*
Saturday	*samedi*
Sunday	*dimanche*

Numbers

0	*zéro*
1	*un*
2	*deux*
3	*trois*
4	*quatre*
5	*cinq*
6	*six*
7	*sept*
8	*huit*
9	*neuf*
10	*dix*
11	*onze*
12	*douze*
13	*treize*
14	*quatorze*
15	*quinze*
16	*seize*
17	*dix-sept*
18	*dix-huit*
19	*dix-neuf*
20	*vingt*
21	*vingt-et-un*
22	*vingt-deux*
30	*trente*
40	*quarante*
50	*cinquante*
60	*soixante*
70	*soixante-dix*
80	*quatre-vingts*
90	*quatre-vingt-dix*
100	*cent*
1000	*mille*
one million	*un million*

Emergencies – French

Help!	Au secours!
Call a doctor!	Appelez un médecin!
Call an ambulance!	Appelez une ambulance!
Call the police!	Appelez la police!
I've been raped!	On m'a violée!
I've been robbed.	On m'a volé.
I'm lost.	Je me suis égaré/ égarée. (m/f)
Leave me alone!	Laissez-moi la paix!

ON THE WALK

Is this the trail/ track to ...?	C'est la chemin pour aller à ...?
Which trail goes to ...?	Je prends quel chemin pour aller à ...?
Is the trail steep/ wide/narrow?	Est'ce que ce chemin est raide/large/ étroit?
How many kilometres to ...?	Combien de kilomètres à ...?
Where are you going?	Où allez-vous?
Do you know this area well?	Vous connaissez bien cette région?
Is the trail safe?	Est-ce que le chemin est sauf?
Where can I hire a guide/tent?	Où puis-je louer un guide/une tente?
Is there a camp site nearby?	Y a-t-il un camping tout près?
Can we camp here?	Pouvons-nous camper ici?
Can we stay here tonight?	Nous sommes permis à rester ici ce soir?
I'm lost.	Je suis perdu(e).
Do I need a guide?	Est-ce qu'il faut un guide?
What's that animal called?	Qu'est-ce que c'est cet animal?
What's that plant called?	Qu'est-ce que c'est cette plante?

Weather

It's cloudy.	Le temps est couvert.
It's cold.	Il fait froid.
It's frosty.	Il gèle.
It's hot.	Il fait chaud.
It's raining.	Il pleut.
It's snowing.	Il neige.

Useful Words

alp hut	chalet (de alpage)
alp track	chemin de alpage
alpine garden	jardin alpin
alpine rhododendron	rhododendron des Alpes
arolla pine	arolle/pin Mediterranéen
avalanche	avalanche
backpack	sac à dos
beech	hêtre/foyard
bilberry	myrtille
bridge	pont
buttercup	renoncule
cable car	téléphérique
cairn	cairn
camping ground	camping
chairlift	télésiège
chamois	chamois
cirque	cirque
contour	contour
cornice	corniche
crampons	crampons
crossing	passage
direction	direction
dormitory	dortoir
east	est
edelweiss	étoile des Alpes
fog	brouillard
forest	forêt/bois
gap	brèche
gentian	gentiane
glacier	glacier
gondola lift	télécabine
gorge/ravine	gorge
hanging glacier	glacier suspendu
hill	colline
hut	cabane
ibex	bouquetin
ice axe	piolet
lake	lac
larch	mélèze
lynx	lynx
map	carte
maple	érable
marmot	marmotte
moraine	moraine

mountain guide	*guide de montagne*
mule path	*chemin muletier*
north	*nord*
outlet	*issue*
pasqueflower/ anemone	*anémone*
path/trail	*sentier/chemin*
peak/summit	*sommet/cime*
Pre-Alps	*Préalpes*
red spruce	*épicéa/sapin rouge*
reservoir	*réservoir*
ridge	*crête*
river	*rive*
rock fall	*chute de pierres*
saddle	*col/selle*
scree/talus	*éboulis*
signpost	*poteau indicateur*
silver fir	*sapin blanc*
slope	*pente*
snow	*neige*
snowfield	*névé*
snow free	*dénudé*
south	*sud*
spring/fountain	*source/fontaine*
stream	*ruisseau*
sweet chestnut tree	*marronnier*
the (Swiss) Alps	*les Alpes (suisses)*
thunderstorm	*orage*
torrent	*torrent*
tourist office	*office du tourisme*
tower	*tour*
valley	*vallée*
walking map	*carte pédestre*
waterfall	*chute*
west	*ouest*

Swiss Italian

The differences between standard Italian and the Ticinese dialects are relatively small. In northern Ticino certain Romansch-sounding expressions are often used, such as *Bun di* instead of *Buongiorno* (Hello) or *Buona noc* (pronounced 'nockh') instead of *Buona notte* (Goodnight).

Pronunciation

Italian is not difficult to pronounce once you learn a few easy rules. Some of the more clipped vowels and stress on double letters require a little practice. Stress usually falls on the second last syllable. When a word has an accent the stress falls on that syllable.

Vowels

Vowels are generally more clipped than in English.

a	as the second 'a' in 'camera'
e	as the 'ay' in 'day', but without the 'i' sound
i	as in 'marine'
o	as in 'dot'
u	as the 'oo' in 'too'

Consonants

The pronunciation of many Italian consonants is similar to that of English. The following sounds depend on certain rules:

c	as in 'cot' before **a**, **o** and **u**; as the 'ch' in 'choose' before **e** and **i**
ch	a hard 'k' sound, as in 'kit'
g	as in 'get' before **a**, **o**, **u** and **h**; as in 'gin' before **e** and **i**
gh	a hard 'g' sound, as in 'get'
gli	as the 'lli' in 'million'
gn	as the 'ny' in 'canyon'
h	always silent
r	a rolled 'r' sound
sc	as the 'sh' in 'sheep' before **e** and **i**; as in 'school' before **h**, **a**, **o** and **u**
z	as the 'ts' in 'lights' or the 'ds' in 'beds'

Greetings & Civilities

Hello.	*Buongiorno.* (polite) *Ciao.* (informal)
Goodbye.	*Arrivederci.* (polite) *Ciao.* (informal)
Yes.	*Sì.*
No.	*No.*
Please.	*Per favore/Per piacere.*
Thank you.	*Grazie.*
You're welcome.	*Prego.*
Excuse me/Sorry.	*Mi scusi/Mi perdoni.*
What's your name?	*Come si chiama?*
My name is ...	*Mi chiamo ...*
Where are you from?	*Da dove viene?*
I'm from ...	*Vengo da/Sono di ...*
How old are you?	*Quanti anni ha?*
I'm ... years old.	*Ho ... anni.*

Language Difficulties

Do you speak English?	*Parla inglese?*
Does anyone here speak English?	*C'è qualcuno che parla inglese?*
I understand.	*Capisco.*
I don't understand.	*Non capisco.*
Just a minute!	*Un momento!*
Could you please write that down?	*Può sciverlo, per favore?*

Getting Around

What time does the ... leave/arrive?	*A che ora parte/ arriva ...?*
boat	*la barca*
bus	*l'autobus*
train	*il treno*
first	*la prima/il primo* (f/m)
last	*l'ultima/l'ultimo* (f/m)
I'd like a ... ticket.	*Vorrei un biglietto ...*
one-way	*di solo andata*
return	*di andata e ritorno*
1st class	*prima classe*
2nd class	*seconda classe*

Accommodation

camping ground	*campeggio*
guesthouse	*pensione*
hotel	*albergo*
youth hostel	*ostello per la gioventù*
Where is a cheap hotel?	*Dov'è un albergo che costa poco?*
What is the address?	*Cos'è l'indirizzo?*
Do you have any rooms available?	*Ha camere libere?*
I'd like ...	*Vorrei ...*
a single room	*una camera singola*
a double room	*una camera per due*
a room with a bathroom	*una camera con bagno*
to share a dorm	*un letto in dormitorio*
a bed	*un letto*

Signs – Italian

Ingresso/Entrata	**Entrance**
Uscita	**Exit**
Aperto	**Open**
Chiuso	**Closed**
Camere Libere	**Rooms Available**
Completo	**Full/No Vacancies**
Vietato Fumare	**No Smoking**
Informazioni	**Information**
Proibito/Vietato	**Prohibited**
Polizia/Carabinieri	**Police**
Questura	**Police Station**
Gabinetti/Bagni	**Toilets**
Uomini	**Men**
Donne	**Women**

How much is it per night/per person?	*Quanto costa per la notte/ciascuno?*
May I see it?	*Posso vederla?*
Where is the bathroom?	*Dov'è il bagno?*

Around Town

I'm looking for ...	*Sto cercando ...*
a bank	*un banco*
the church	*la chiesa*
the city centre	*il centro (città)*
the ... embassy	*l'ambasciata di ...*
my hotel	*il mio albergo*
the market	*il mercato*
the museum	*il museo*
the post office	*la posta*
a public toilet	*un gabinetto/bagno pubblico*
the telephone centre	*il centro telefonico/ SIP*
the tourist office	*l'ufficio di turismo/ d'informazione*
Where is ...?	*Dov'è ...?*
I want to go to ...	*Voglio andare a ...*
Can you show me (on the map)?	*Me lo può mostrare (sulla carta/pianta)?*
near/far	*vicino/lontano*
Go straight ahead.	*Si va sempre diritto.*
Turn left ...	*Gira a sinistra ...*
Turn right ...	*Gira a destra ...*

Shopping

How much is it?	*Quanto costa?*
I'd like to buy ...	*Vorrei comprare ...*
Do you accept credit cards?	*Accetta la carta di credito?*
Could you lower the price?	*Può farmi lo sconto?*
camera shop	*negozio di fotografo*
chemist/pharmacy	*famacia*
laundry	*lavanderia*
market	*mercato*
newsagency	*edicola/cartolaio*
supermarket	*supermercato*

Food

breakfast	*prima colazione*
lunch	*pranzo/colazione*
dinner	*cena*
I'd like the set lunch.	*Vorrei il menu turistico.*
Is service included in the bill?	*È compreso il servizio?*
I'm a vegetarian.	*Sono vegetariana/ vegetariano.* (f/m)

Health

I'm ...	*Sono ...*
diabetic	*diabetica/o* (f/m)
epileptic	*epilettica/o* (f/m)
asthmatic	*asmatica/o* (f/m)
I'm allergic ...	*Sono allergica/ allergico ...* (f/m)
to antibiotics	*agli antibiotici*
to penicillin	*alla penicillina*
antiseptic	*antisettico*
aspirin	*aspirina*
condoms	*preservativi*
contraceptive	*anticoncezionale*
diarrhoea	*diarrea*
medicine	*medicina*
nausea	*nausea*
sunblock cream	*crema solare/latte solare*
tampons	*tamponi*

Time & Dates

today	*oggi*
tomorrow	*domani*
yesterday	*ieri*
in the morning	*di mattina*
in the afternoon	*di pomeriggio*
in the evening	*di sera*
Monday	*lunedì*
Tuesday	*martedì*
Wednesday	*mercoledì*
Thursday	*giovedì*
Friday	*venerdì*
Saturday	*sabato*
Sunday	*domenica*

Numbers

0	*zero*
1	*uno*
2	*due*
3	*tre*
4	*quattro*
5	*cinque*
6	*sei*
7	*sette*
8	*otto*
9	*nove*
10	*dieci*
11	*undici*
12	*dodici*
13	*tredici*
14	*quattordici*
15	*quindici*
16	*sedici*
17	*diciassette*
18	*diciotto*
19	*diciannove*
20	*venti*
21	*ventuno*
22	*ventidue*
30	*trenta*
40	*quaranta*
50	*cinquanta*
60	*sessanta*
70	*settanta*
80	*ottanta*
90	*novanta*
100	*cento*
1000	*mille*
one million	*un milione*

Emergencies – Italian

Help!	*Aiuto!*
Call a doctor!	*Chiama un dottore/ un medico!*
Call the police!	*Chiama la polizia!*
I've been raped!	*Sono stata/o violentata/o! (f/m)*
I've been robbed.	*Mi hanno derubata/o. (f/m)*
I'm lost.	*Mi sono persa/ perso. (f/m)*
Leave me alone!	*Vai via! (inf)/Mi lasci in pace!*

ON THE WALK

Is this the trail/ road to ...?	*Questo è il sentiero giusto per ...?*
Which trail goes to ...?	*Quale sentiero va a ...?*
Is the trail steep/ wide/narrow?	*Questo sentiero è ripido/largo/stretto?*
How many kilometres to ...?	*Quanti chilometri a ...?*
Where are you going?	*Dove va?*
Do you know this area well?	*Conosce bene questa zona?*
Is the trail safe?	*Questo sentiero non è pericoloso?*
Where can I hire a guide/tent?	*Dove posso noleggiare una guida/tenda?*
Is there a camp site nearby?	*C'è un campeggio qui vicino?*
Can we camp here?	*Si può campeggiare qui?*
I'm lost.	*Mi sono persa/o. (f/m)*
Do I need a guide?	*Si ha bisogno di una guida?*
What's that animal called?	*Come si chiama quest'animale?*
What's that plant called?	*Come si chiama questa pianta?*

Weather

It's ...	*È ...*
cloudy	*nuvoloso*
cold	*freddo*
frosty	*gelido*
hot	*caldo*
It's raining.	*Piove.*
It's snowing.	*Nevica.*
What will the weather be like tomorrow?	*Come sarà il tempo domani?*

Useful Words

alp hut	*chalet alpino*
alp track	*sentiero alpino*
alpine garden	*giardino alpino*
alpine rhododendron	*rododendro delle Alpi*
arolla pine	*pino mediterraneo*
avalanche	*valanga*
backpack	*zaino*
beech	*faggio*
bilberry	*mirtillo*
bridge	*ponte*
buttercup	*ranuncolo*
cable car	*funicolare*
cairn	*tumolo (di pietre)*
camping ground	*campeggio*
chairlift	*seggiovia*
chamois	*camoscio*
contour	*contorno*
cornice	*cornicione*
crampons	*ramponi*
crossing	*passaggio*
direction	*direzione*
dormitory	*dormitorio*
east	*este*
edelweiss	*stella alpina*
fog	*nebbia*
forest	*foresta*
gap	*spazio vuoto*
gentian	*genziana*
glacier	*ghiacciaio*
gondola lift	*gondola*
gorge/ravine	*gola/burrone*
hanging glacier	*ghiacciaio sospeso*
hill	*collina*
hut	*baita*
ibex	*stambecco*
ice axe	*piccozza da alpinisti*
lake	*lago*
larch	*larice*
lynx	*lince*
map	*carta*
maple	*acero*
marmot	*marmotta*

moraine	*morena*
moutain guide	*guida di montagne*
mule path	*sentiero di mula*
north	*nord*
outlet	*scarico*
pasqueflower/ anemone	*anemone*
path/trail	*sentiero*
peak/summit	*cima/sommitá*
red spruce	*abete rosso*
reservoir	*bacino idrico*
ridge	*cresta/crinole*
river	*fiume*
rock fall	*caduta di pietre*
saddle	*sella*
scree/talus	*ghiaione*
signpost	*palo indicatore*
silver fir	*abete bianco*
slope	*pendio*
snow	*neve*
snowfield	*nevaio*
snow free	*denudato*
south	*sud*
spring/fountain	*sorgente/fontana*
stream	*ruscello*
sweet chestunut tree	*castagno*
Swiss Alps	*Alpi svizzeri*
thunderstorm	*oragio*
torrent	*torrente*
tourist office	*officio del turismo*
tower	*torre*
valley	*valle*
walking map	*carta pedestre*
waterfall	*cascata*
west	*ovest*

Romansch

Although the language is only spoken by around 1% of the population, hikers are likely to hear people speaking Romansch during their visit to Switzerland. This is because the Romansch-speaking regions, which lie entirely within Graubünden Canton, have some of the nicest and most spectacular walks in the country.

Originating from the common Latin spoken by the Roman settlers, Romansch was widely spoken throughout the medieval kingdom of Rhaetia, which once covered most of today's Graubünden. Due to the steady encroachment of German, the relative number of Romansch speakers has fallen dramatically over the last 100 years or so. One major problem facing the survival of the language is that Romansch is divided into five main dialect groups, and unlike other minority languages in Switzerland, it has neither a cultural, educational nor commercial centre. One step towards saving the language has been the development of a standard Romansch language, Rumantsch Grischun, which incorporates elements of each regional form. Even in areas of Graubünden where German has been spoken for centuries, local place names still show an unmistakable link with the Romansch past. Below is a short list of useful words to get you started.

Useful Words

alp hut	*tegia d'alp*
(alpine) pasture	*murtera/pra*
backpack	*loulscha/satgados*
bridge	*punt*
camping ground	*campadi*
castle/fort	*chastè*
church	*baseglia*
east	*ost/orient*
farmhouse	*chassa da pur*
fence	*saiv*
field	*chomp/fuus*
forest	*guaud*
glacier	*glatscher*
gorge	*chavorgia*
Graubünden	*Grischun*
lake	*lai*
map	*charta topografica*
mountain	*montagna/munt*
mountain guide	*guid da muntogna*
mountain hut	*chamoua*
north	*nord*
path/track	*senda/via*
peak/summit	*piz/culm*
pig	*pors*
post office	*uffizi postal*
Rhaetian Railways	*Viafer retica*
ridge	*cresta*
river	*flum*
rock	*crap*

LANGUAGE

sheep	*uina*
shore/bank	*riva*
signpost	*mussavia*
slope	*spunda/costa*
snow	*naiv*
snowfield	*vadret*
south	*sid*
spring/fountain	*fontauna*
stream/brook	*dutg*
Swiss National Park	*Parc Naziunal Svizzer*
Switzerland	*Svizra*
tourist office	*biro da traffic*
train station	*staziun da viafer*
valley	*val/vallada*
village	*vischnanca/vitg*
Walser route	*senda Gualser*
waterfall	*cas da aua*
west	*vest/occident*

Animals

alpine jackdaw	*curnagl*
badger	*tais*
bird	*utschè*
chamois	*chamutsch*
cow	*vatga*
fish	*pesch*
goat	*chaura/zila*
ibex	*capricorn*
marmot	*muntanella*
marten	*fiergna*
snow grouse	*urblauna*
snow hare	*lieur alva*
stoat	*mustaila*

Plants

arolla	*schember*
chestunut tree	*chastagner*
edelweiss	*stailalva*
larch	*laresch*
mountain pine	*tuletu*
mushroom	*bulieu*
red spruce	*pign*
silver fir	*aviez*
tree	*planta/pumer*

Glossary

The language of origin of non-English terms is noted in brackets: French (Fr), High German (Ger), Italian (It), Romansch (Rom) and Swiss German (Sch). Words that appear in italics within definitions have their own entries.

alp – Alpine pasture

alp huts – summer dwellings of Alpine herders

alp track – rough access road through an *alp*

alpenrose – Alpine rhododendron

Alpine foothills – see *pre-Alps*

Alpine Pass Route – classic 16-*leg* route from Sargans to Montreux

Alpine zone – the area above the *timberline*

Appenzellerland – collective name for the two half-cantons of Appenzell

avalanche gallery – protective construction built over a mountain road or railway in places prone to winter avalanches

avalanche slope – slope cleared of larger vegetation by frequent winter avalanches

avalanche grids – steel or wood structures on treeless Alpine slopes built to restrain winter snows and so prevent avalanches

Bach – (Ger) stream; often in compound nouns, eg, Milibach

balcony – a level or gently sloping terrace high above a valley

belvedere – (It, 'beautiful view') scenic high point (often a *balcony* or terrace)

Berggasthaus or **Berghaus** – (Ger) mountain inn

Bergsturz – (Ger) catastrophic mountain landslide

Bernese – pertaining to Bern Canton

bisse – (Fr) mountain aqueduct in the Valais

BL/OFT – (Ger/Fr) Bundesamt für Landestopographie/Office Fédéral de Topographie (Swiss national mapping authority)

BLS – Bern–Lötschberg–Simplon, a private railway (to be taken over by the SBB/CFF from 2004) which runs from Bern to Domodossola (in Italy) via the Lötschberg and Simplon tunnels

Bündner – pertaining to Graubünden

Bündner Oberland – older term for Graubünden's Surselva region

buvette – (Fr) a simple mountain restaurant that may also offer basic (especially dormitory) accommodation

BVZ – Brig–Visp–Zermatt private railway in the upper Valais

cabane – (Fr) *mountain hut*

cableway – a general term encompassing chairlifts, gondola lifts, cable cars and private utility lifts

CAI – Club Alpino Italiano, Italy's main mountain club

cairn – piles of stones, often used to mark a route or path junction

camona – (Rom) *mountain hut*

canton – the self-governing regions within the Swiss Confederation

capanna – (It) *mountain hut*

car-free resort – a resort town where private motorised traffic is banned

chamanna – (Rom) *mountain hut*

circuit – a walk that ends back at its starting point

cirque – a rounded high precipice formed by the action of ice in the high-*Alpine zone*

cog railway – a steep railway with a rack between the tracks into which a cogwheel grips as the train climbs or descends

col – a mountain pass

contour – to move along a slope without climbing or descending appreciably

crevasse – an often dangerously deep crack in the ice of a glacier

doline – a landform typically found in *karst* ranges where a subterranean cavern formed by water seepage collapses to create a basin; if this impedes further seepage a doline lake may form

dolomite – a hard limestone of calcium-magnesium composition

dorm – short for dormitory; a room with sleeping space for many people

dormitorio – (It) dormitory

dortoir – (Fr) dormitory
downclimb – to descend using your hands

FAT – Federazione Alpinistica Ticinese, an umbrella organisation of Ticino's non-SAC mountain clubs
fixed cable – steel cable mounted along a potentially dangerous section of mountain path to give walkers added confidence
flagged path – stone-laid path, usually originally built as a mule track
full board – accommodation that includes both evening meal and breakfast in the price (compare *half board*)
Föhn – (Rom) warm southerly wind
FOB – Furka-Oberalp-Bahn, a private railway running between Brig and Disentis via Andermatt

garni – accommodation that includes breakfast in the price
ghiacciaio – (It) glacier
glacier pots – formations produced by water action below glaciers
glacier mills – see *glacier pots*
Glarnerland – Glarus Canton
Gletscher – (Ger) glacier
gondola lift – continuously running cable onto which four- or six-person compartments are hitched
Gotthard region – the Swiss Alps' central massif around the Passo del San Gottardo
GPS – Global Positioning System; an electronic means of accurately fixing location using microwave satellite signals
grotto – (It) rustic Ticino-style restaurant

half board – accommodation that includes breakfast in the price (compare *full board*)
hamlet – group of farm buildings or *alp huts*
haute route – (Fr, 'high route') a high-level mountain route; also the classic Chamonix to Zermatt skiing and walking route through the Valais
hayfield – a meadow mown for hay rather than used for grazing
Helvetian – pertaining to Switzerland
high-Alpine – the upper mountains
Höhenweg – (Ger) *haute route*

Hütte – (Ger) hut, usually used in compounds, eg, Zwinglihütte

icefall – steep broken-up section of a glacier

Jura – a low chain of mountains forming Switzerland's north-western border with France

K+F – Kümmerly + Frey, Switzerland's largest commercial publisher of maps and guidebooks
karst – the charactersitic scenery of a limestone area

lago – (It) lake
lai – (Rom) lake
lajet – (Rom) lake
LAV – Liechtensteiner Alpenverein, the principality's mountaineering club
leg – an individual section (which may take more than one day) of a longer walk

massif – high mountain range
mattress room – sleeping quarters (standard in mountain huts) in which mattresses are lined up in long rows
MOB – Montreux-Oberalp-Bahn, a private railway running between Montreux and Spiez
moraine – debris carried and deposited by glacial movement
mountain hut – hut with accommodation (compare *alp hut*)
MTB – mountain bike
mule path/track – old *flagged paths* originally built as routes for cargo-carrying mule trains

Nagelfluh – (Ger) a cement-like rock consisting of very coarse alluvial sediments
névé – permanent, high-Alpine *snowfield*
north face – a mountain's sheer, north-facing rock walls

OAV – Osterreichischer Alpenverein, Austria's main mountaineering club
Oberland – (Ger) a term used to describe the regional 'uplands' of various cantons, eg, Bernese Oberland

pas – (Fr) mountain pass
passo – (It) mountain pass
pizzo – (It) peak, summit
pre-Alpine – pertaining to the *pre-Alps*
pre-Alps – the foothills fringing the northern and southern sides of the Alps
préalpes – (Fr) *pre-Alps*
postbus – regional public bus network run by Swiss Post
Pro Natura – Switzerland's leading conservation organisation

rack railway – see *cog railway*
Rhaetian Railways – the largest private railway in Switzerland, which owns and runs virtually all lines in Graubünden Canton
rösti – (Ger) fried potato pattie
route – refers to the main walking route in the walk descriptions
ri – (It) river
rustico/rustici – (It; singular/plural) rustic Ticino-style cottage(s) built of stone

SAC – Swiss Alpine Club
SAT – Società Alpinistica Ticinese, a mountain club in Ticino
SAW/FSTP – (Ger/Fr, 'Swiss Hiking Federation') Schweizerische Arbeitsgemeinschaft für Wanderwege/Fédération Suisse de Tourism Pédestre
SBB/CFF – (Ger/Fr, 'Swiss Federal Railways') Schweizer Bundesbahnen/Chemin de fer fédéral
Scheidegg – (Sch) watershed
scree – slopes of accumulated frost-shattered rock; often unstable and loose
Sennerei – (Ger) an Alpine cheesery
sérac – prominent block of ice typically seen on steep icefalls
sidle – to move along a slope horizontally
skirt – to move along the edge of (eg, a forest)

slab – smooth, flat expanse of rock, formed by glacial or water erosion
snowfield – a large permanent accumulation of snow
Suone – (Sch) see *bisse*
Swiss Mittelland – the 'midlands', a low plateau between the Alps and the Jura; often divided into cantonal regions such as the Bernese Mittelland or the Fribourg Mittelland
switchbacks – route that follows a zigzag course up or down a steep incline

Tal – (Ger) valley; often in compound place names, eg, Mattertal ('Matter valley')
talus – similar to *scree* but generally coarser
tarn – tiny Alpine lake
terrace – see *balcony*
tiers – staged levels of a range formed either by rock strata or glacial action
timberline – the uppermost (natural) level at which forest can grow in a given area (roughly 2000m)
trans-Alpine – crossing the main north-south Alpine watershed
traverse – see *sidle*
tree line – see *timberline*

UTOE – Unione Ticinese Operai Escursionisti, an indepedent (ie, non-SAC) mountain club in Ticino

val – (It/Rom) valley
Valaisan – pertaining to the Valais
valle – (It) valley
vehicle track – a rough road
Voralpen – (Ger) *pre-Alps*

Walsers – medieval settlers from Goms who settled numerous highland valleys in the central Alps

LONELY PLANET

Guides by Region

Lonely Planet is known worldwide for publishing practical, reliable and no-nonsense travel information in our guides and on our Web site. The Lonely Planet list covers just about every accessible part of the world. Currently there are 16 series: Travel guides, Shoestring guides, Condensed guides, Phrasebooks, Read This First, Healthy Travel, Walking guides, Cycling guides, Watching Wildlife guides, Pisces Diving & Snorkeling guides, City Maps, Road Atlases, Out to Eat, World Food, Journeys travel literature and Pictorials.

AFRICA Africa on a shoestring • Cairo • Cairo City Map • Cape Town • Cape Town City Map • East Africa • Egypt • Egyptian Arabic phrasebook • Ethiopia, Eritrea & Djibouti • Ethiopian Amharic phrasebook • The Gambia & Senegal • Healthy Travel Africa • Kenya • Malawi • Morocco • Moroccan Arabic phrasebook • Mozambique • Read This First: Africa • South Africa, Lesotho & Swaziland • Southern Africa • Southern Africa Road Atlas • Swahili phrasebook • Tanzania, Zanzibar & Pemba • Trekking in East Africa • Tunisia • Watching Wildlife East Africa • Watching Wildlife Southern Africa • West Africa • World Food Morocco • Zimbabwe, Botswana & Namibia
Travel Literature: Mali Blues: Traveling to an African Beat • The Rainbird: A Central African Journey • Songs to an African Sunset: A Zimbabwean Story

AUSTRALIA & THE PACIFIC Auckland • Australia • Australian phrasebook • Australia Road Atlas • Cycling Australia • Cycling New Zealand • Fiji • Fijian phrasebook • Healthy Travel Australia, NZ & the Pacific • Islands of Australia's Great Barrier Reef • Melbourne • Melbourne City Map • Micronesia • New Caledonia • New South Wales • New Zealand • Northern Territory • Outback Australia • Out to Eat – Melbourne • Out to Eat – Sydney • Papua New Guinea • Pidgin phrasebook • Queensland • Rarotonga & the Cook Islands • Samoa • Solomon Islands • South Australia • South Pacific • South Pacific phrasebook • Sydney • Sydney City Map • Sydney Condensed • Tahiti & French Polynesia • Tasmania • Tonga • Tramping in New Zealand • Vanuatu • Victoria • Walking in Australia • Watching Wildlife Australia • Western Australia
Travel Literature: Islands in the Clouds: Travels in the Highlands of New Guinea • Kiwi Tracks: A New Zealand Journey • Sean & David's Long Drive

CENTRAL AMERICA & THE CARIBBEAN Bahamas, Turks & Caicos • Baja California • Belize, Guatemala & Yucatán • Bermuda • Central America on a shoestring • Costa Rica • Costa Rica Spanish phrasebook • Cuba • Dominican Republic & Haiti • Eastern Caribbean • Guatemala • Havana • Healthy Travel Central & South America • Jamaica • Mexico • Mexico City • Panama • Puerto Rico • Read This First: Central & South America • World Food Mexico • Yucatán
Travel Literature: Green Dreams: Travels in Central America

EUROPE Amsterdam • Amsterdam City Map • Amsterdam Condensed • Andalucía • Austria • Baltic States phrasebook • Barcelona • Barcelona City Map • Belgium & Luxembourg • Berlin • Berlin City Map • Britain • British phrasebook • Brussels, Bruges & Antwerp • Brussels City Map • Budapest • Budapest City Map • Canary Islands • Central Europe • Central Europe phrasebook • Copenhagen • Corfu & the Ionians • Corsica • Crete • Crete Condensed • Croatia • Cycling Britain • Cycling France • Cyprus • Czech & Slovak Republics • Denmark • Dublin • Dublin City Map • Eastern Europe • Eastern Europe phrasebook • Edinburgh • England • Estonia, Latvia & Lithuania • Europe on a shoestring • Europe phrasebook • Finland • Florence • France • Frankfurt Condensed • French phrasebook • Georgia, Armenia & Azerbaijan • Germany • German phrasebook • Greece • Greek Islands • Greek phrasebook • Hungary • Iceland, Greenland & the Faroe Islands • Ireland • Italian phrasebook • Italy • Krakow • Lisbon • The Loire • London • London City Map • London Condensed • Madrid • Malta • Mediterranean Europe • Mediterranean Europe phrasebook • Moscow • Munich • Netherlands • Normandy • Norway • Out to Eat – London • Paris • Paris City Map • Paris Condensed • Poland • Polish phrasebook • Portugal • Portuguese phrasebook • Prague • Prague City Map • Provence & the Côte d'Azur • Read This First: Europe • Rhodes & the Dodecanese • Romania & Moldova • Rome • Rome City Map • Russia, Ukraine & Belarus • Russian phrasebook • Scandinavian & Baltic Europe • Scandinavian phrasebook • Scotland • Sicily • Slovenia • South-West France • Spain • Spanish phrasebook • St Petersburg • St Petersburg City Map • Sweden • Switzerland • Tuscany • Ukrainian phrasebook • Venice • Vienna • Walking in Britain • Walking in France • Walking in Ireland • Walking in Italy • Walking in Spain • Walking in Switzerland • Western Europe • World Food France • World Food Ireland • World Food Italy • World Food Spain
Travel Literature: After Yugoslavia • Love and War in the Apennines • The Olive Grove: Travels in Greece • On the Shores of the Mediterranean • Round Ireland in Low Gear • A Small Place in Italy

LONELY PLANET

Mail Order

Lonely Planet products are distributed worldwide.They are also available by mail order from Lonely Planet, so if you have difficulty finding a title please write to us. North and South American residents should write to 150 Linden St, Oakland, CA 94607, USA; European and African residents should write to 10a Spring Place, London NW5 3BH, UK; and residents of other countries to Locked Bag 1, Footscray, Victoria 3011, Australia.

INDIAN SUBCONTINENT & THE INDIAN OCEAN Bangladesh • Bengali phrasebook • Bhutan • Delhi • Goa • Healthy Travel Asia & India • Hindi & Urdu phrasebook • India • Indian Himalaya • Karakoram Highway • Kerala • Madagascar • Maldives • Mauritius, Réunion & Seychelles • Mumbai (Bombay) • Nepal • Nepali phrasebook • Pakistan • Rajasthan • Read This First: Asia & India • South India • Sri Lanka • Sri Lanka phrasebook • Tibet • Tibetan phrasebook • Trekking in the Indian Himalaya • Trekking in the Karakoram & Hindukush • Trekking in the Nepal Himalaya
Travel Literature: The Age of Kali: Indian Travels and Encounters • Hello Goodnight: A Life of Goa • In Rajasthan • Maverick in Madagascar • A Season in Heaven: True Tales from the Road to Kathmandu • Shopping for Buddhas • A Short Walk in the Hindu Kush • Slowly Down the Ganges

MIDDLE EAST & CENTRAL ASIA Bahrain, Kuwait & Qatar • Central Asia • Central Asia phrasebook • Dubai • Farsi (Persian) phrasebook • Hebrew phrasebook • Iran • Israel & the Palestinian Territories • Istanbul • Istanbul City Map • Istanbul to Cairo • Istanbul to Kathmandu • Jerusalem • Jerusalem City Map • Jordan • Lebanon • Middle East • Oman & the United Arab Emirates • Syria • Turkey • Turkish phrasebook • World Food Turkey • Yemen
Travel Literature: Black on Black: Iran Revisited • The Gates of Damascus • Kingdom of the Film Stars: Journey into Jordan

NORTH AMERICA Alaska • Boston • Boston City Map • Boston Condensed • British Columbia • California & Nevada • California Condensed • Canada • Chicago • Chicago City Map • Florida • Great Lakes • Hawaii • Hiking in Alaska • Hiking in the USA • Las Vegas • Los Angeles • Los Angeles City Map • Louisiana & the Deep South • Miami • Miami City Map • Montreal • New England • New Orleans • New York City • New York City City Map • New York City Condensed • New York, New Jersey & Pennsylvania • Oahu • Out to Eat – San Francisco • Pacific Northwest • Rocky Mountains • San Francisco • San Francisco City Map • Seattle • Southwest • Texas • Toronto • USA • USA phrasebook • Vancouver • Virginia & the Capital Region • Washington, DC • Washington, DC City Map • World Food New Orleans
Travel Literature: Caught Inside: A Surfer's Year on the California Coast • Drive Thru America

NORTH-EAST ASIA Beijing • Beijing City Map • Cantonese phrasebook • China • Hiking in Japan • Hong Kong • Hong Kong City Map • Hong Kong Condensed • Hong Kong, Macau & Guangzhou • Japan • Japanese phrasebook • Korea • Korean phrasebook • Kyoto • Mandarin phrasebook • Mongolia • Mongolian phrasebook • Seoul • Shanghai • South-West China • Taiwan • Tokyo • World Food Hong Kong
Travel Literature: In Xanadu: A Quest • Lost Japan

SOUTH AMERICA Argentina, Uruguay & Paraguay • Bolivia • Brazil • Brazilian phrasebook • Buenos Aires • Chile & Easter Island • Colombia • Ecuador & the Galapagos Islands • Healthy Travel Central & South America • Latin American Spanish phrasebook • Peru • Quechua phrasebook • Read This First: Central & South America • Rio de Janeiro • Rio de Janeiro City Map • Santiago de Chile • South America on a shoestring • Trekking in the Patagonian Andes • Venezuela
Travel Literature: Full Circle: A South American Journey

SOUTH-EAST ASIA Bali & Lombok • Bangkok • Bangkok City Map • Burmese phrasebook • Cambodia • Hanoi • Healthy Travel Asia & India • Hill Tribes phrasebook • Ho Chi Minh City • Indonesia • Indonesian phrasebook • Indonesia's Eastern Islands • Java • Lao phrasebook • Laos • Malay phrasebook • Malaysia, Singapore & Brunei • Myanmar (Burma) • Philippines • Pilipino (Tagalog) phrasebook • Read This First: Asia & India • Singapore • Singapore City Map • South-East Asia on a shoestring • South-East Asia phrasebook • Thailand • Thailand's Islands & Beaches • Thailand, Vietnam, Laos & Cambodia Road Atlas • Thai phrasebook • Vietnam • Vietnamese phrasebook • World Food Thailand • World Food Vietnam

ALSO AVAILABLE: Antarctica • The Arctic • The Blue Man: Tales of Travel, Love and Coffee • Brief Encounters: Stories of Love, Sex & Travel • Chasing Rickshaws • The Last Grain Race • Lonely Planet ... On the Edge: Adventurous Escapades from Around the World • Lonely Planet Unpacked • Not the Only Planet: Science Fiction Travel Stories • Sacred India • Travel Photography: A Guide to Taking Better Pictures • Travel with Children

LONELY PLANET

You already know that Lonely Planet produces more than this one guidebook, but you might not be aware of the other products we have on this region. Here is a selection of titles that you may want to check out as well:

Switzerland
ISBN 0 86442 723 9
US$17.99 • UK£11.99

German phrasebook
ISBN 0 86442 451 5
US$5.95 • UK£3.99

Walking in Italy
ISBN 0 86442 542 2
US$17.95 • UK£11.99

Walking in France
ISBN 0 86442 601 1
US$19.99 • UK£12.99

French phrasebook
ISBN 0 86442 450 7
US$5.95 • UK£3.99

Western Europe
ISBN 1 86450 163 4
US$27.99 • UK£15.99

Central Europe
ISBN 1 86450 204 5
US$24.99 • UK£14.99

Europe phrasebook
ISBN 1 86450 224 X
US$8.99 • UK£4.99

Europe on a shoestring
ISBN 1 86450 150 2
US$24.99 • UK£14.99

Read this First: Europe
ISBN 1 86450 136 7
US$14.99 • UK£8.99

Cycling France
ISBN 1 86450 036 0
US$19.99 • UK£12.99

Available wherever books are sold

Index

Text
For a list of walks, see the Table of Walks (pp4-7)

Bold indicates maps.

Boxed Text

MAP LEGEND

BOUNDARIES

·—··—··—··	International
— — — —	Regional
— — — —	Disputed

HYDROGRAPHY

	Coastline
	River, Creek
	Lake
	Intermittent Lake
	Salt Lake
·—·—·—·	Canal
◎ →→	Spring, Rapids
→))	Waterfalls
⊥ ⊥ ⊥ ⊥	Swamp

ROUTES & TRANSPORT

	Freeway
	Highway
	Major Road
	Minor Road
= = = = =	Unsealed Highway
= = = = =	Unsealed Major Road
- · - · - ·	Unsealed Minor Road
— — — —	Track
	Lane
⇒= = = =	Tunnel
—+—O—+—	Train Route & Station
—+—+—+—	Chairlift/Ski Lift
	Described Walk
▬ ▬ ▬ ▬	Alternative Route
● ● ● ● ● ●	Side Trip
— — — — —	Walking Track
· · · · · · · · ·	Route

AREA FEATURES

	Park (Regional Maps)	
	Park (Walk Maps)	
	Cemetery	
	Glacier	
	Neighbouring Country	
	Urban Area	

MAP SYMBOLS

☉	**CAPITAL**	National Capital	✈	Airport
◉	**CAPITAL**	Regional Capital	⊟	Bus Stop
●	**CITY**	City	⊕	Border Crossing
●	**Town**	Town	▣	Cable Car
●	Village	Village	⌂	Cave
			✚ ✝	Church
⬛		Camping Area		Cliff or Escarpment
⬒		Hut	500	Contour
▣		Lookout	—*—	Fence or Boundary
▼		Place to Eat	⊕	Gardens
⬛		Place to Stay	⋈	Gate
●		Point of Interest	✚	Hospital
⬛		Shelter	❶	Information
			⊠	Mine
▲		Mountain or Hill		
⬛		National Park		
▣		Parking		
)(		Pass/Saddle		
☯		Picnic Area		
✪		Police Station		
⬛		Post Office		
⚑		Ski Area		
+100m		Spot Height		
🏛		Stately Home		
⊙		Toilet		
❶		Tourist Information		
◒		Transport		
△		Trigonometric Point		

Note: not all symbols displayed above appear in this book

LONELY PLANET OFFICES

Australia
Locked Bag 1, Footscray, Victoria 3011
☎ 03 8379 8000 fax 03 8379 8111
ⓔ talk2us@lonelyplanet.com.au

USA
150 Linden St, Oakland, CA 94607
☎ 510 893 8555 or ☎ 800 275 8555 (toll free)
fax 510 893 8572
ⓔ info@lonelyplanet.com

UK
10a Spring Place, London NW5 3BH
☎ 020 7428 4800 fax 020 7428 4828
ⓔ go@lonelyplanet.co.uk

France
1 rue du Dahomey, 75011 Paris
☎ 01 55 25 33 00 fax 01 55 25 33 01
ⓔ bip@lonelyplanet.fr
ⓦ www.lonelyplanet.fr

World Wide Web: ⓦ www.lonelyplanet.com *or* AOL keyword: lp
Lonely Planet Images: ⓔ lpi@lonelyplanet.com.au